American Map®

Business Travel Atlas

United States • Canada • Mexico

Contents

Business Travel Atlas

TRANSPORTATION

CONTROLLED ACCESS HIGHWAYS

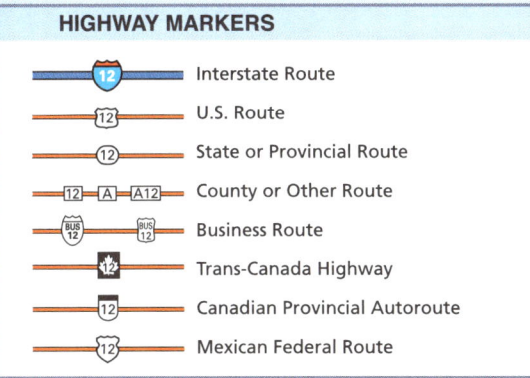

- Freeway
- Tollway; Toll Booth
- Under Construction
- Interchange and Exit Number
- Ramps
  Downtown maps only
- Rest Area; Service Area
  Yellow with facilities; city maps only

OTHER HIGHWAYS

- Primary Highway
- Secondary Highway
- Multilane Divided Highway
  Primary and secondary highways only; city maps only
- Multilane Divided Highway
  State and province maps only
- Other Paved Road
  State and province maps only
- Other Paved Road
  City maps only
- Unpaved Road
  State and province maps only; check conditions locally
- Unpaved Road
  City maps only; check conditions locally

HIGHWAY MARKERS

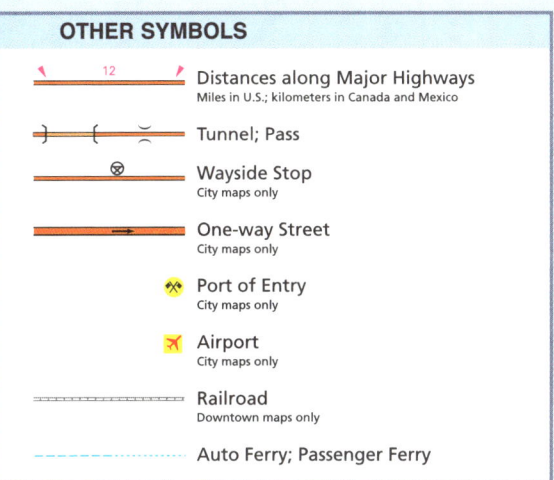

- Interstate Route
- U.S. Route
- State or Provincial Route
- County or Other Route
- Business Route
- Trans-Canada Highway
- Canadian Provincial Autoroute
- Mexican Federal Route

OTHER SYMBOLS

- Distances along Major Highways
  Miles in U.S.; kilometers in Canada and Mexico
- Tunnel; Pass
- Wayside Stop
  City maps only
- One-way Street
  City maps only
- Port of Entry
  City maps only
- Airport
  City maps only
- Railroad
  Downtown maps only
- Auto Ferry; Passenger Ferry

RECREATION AND FEATURES OF INTEREST

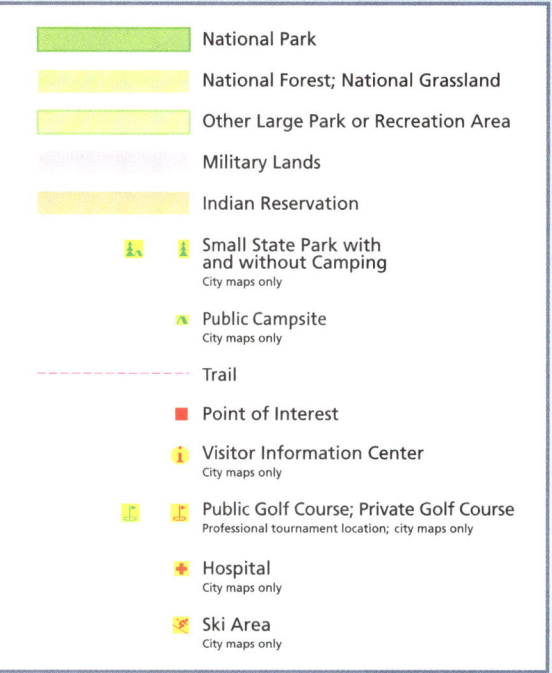

- National Park
- National Forest; National Grassland
- Other Large Park or Recreation Area
- Military Lands
- Indian Reservation
- Small State Park with and without Camping
  City maps only
- Public Campsite
  City maps only
- Trail
- Point of Interest
- Visitor Information Center
  City maps only
- Public Golf Course; Private Golf Course
  Professional tournament location; city maps only
- Hospital
  City maps only
- Ski Area
  City maps only

CITIES AND TOWNS

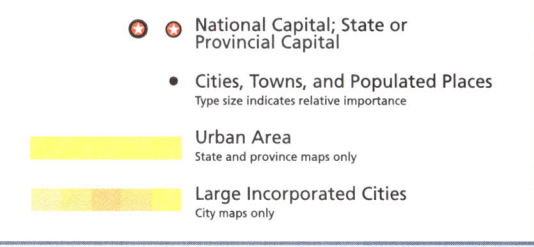

- National Capital; State or Provincial Capital
- Cities, Towns, and Populated Places
  Type size indicates relative importance
- Urban Area
  State and province maps only
- Large Incorporated Cities
  City maps only

OTHER MAP FEATURES

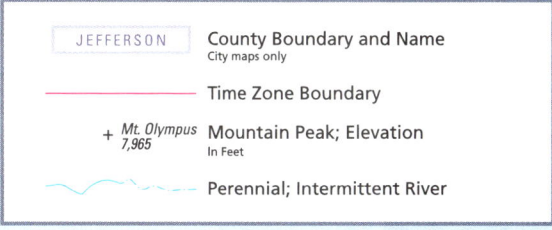

- JEFFERSON — County Boundary and Name
  City maps only
- Time Zone Boundary
- Mt. Olympus 7,965 — Mountain Peak; Elevation
  In Feet
- Perennial; Intermittent River

1 inch represents 195 miles
or 314 kilometers
(1:12,350,000)

© MapQuest, Inc.

Mileage Chart

BORDER CROSSING

CANADA

U.S. citizens entering Canada from the U.S. are required to present passports or proof of U.S. citizenship accompanied by photo identification. U.S. citizens entering from a third country must have a valid passport. Visas are not required for U.S. citizens entering from the U.S. for stays of up to 180 days. Naturalized citizens should travel with their naturalization certificates. Alien permanent residents of the U.S. must present their Alien Registration Cards. Individuals under the age of 18 and travelling alone should carry a letter from a parent or legal guardian authorizing their travel in Canada.

U.S. driver's licenses are valid in Canada, and U.S. citizens do not need to obtain an international driver's license. Proof of auto insurance, however, is required.

For additional information, consult http://travel.state.gov/tips_canada.html before you travel.

UNITED STATES (FROM CANADA)

Canadian citizens entering the U.S. are required to demonstrate proof of their citizenship, normally with a photo identification accompanied by a valid birth certificate or citizenship card. Passports or visas are not required for visits lasting less than six months; for visits exceeding six months, they are mandatory. Individuals under the age of 18 and travelling alone should carry notarized documentation, signed by both parents, authorizing their travel.

Canadian driver's licenses are valid in the U.S. for one year, and automobiles may enter free of payment or duty fees. Drivers need only provide customs officials with proof of vehicle registration, ownership, and insurance.

Distances in chart are in miles. To convert miles to kilometers, multiply the distance in miles by 1.609. Example: New York, NY to Boston, MA = 215 miles or 346 kilometers (215 x 1.609)	ALBANY, NY	ALBUQUERQUE, NM	AMARILLO, TX	ATLANTA, GA	BALTIMORE, MD	BILLINGS, MT	BIRMINGHAM, AL	BISMARCK, ND	BOISE, ID	BOSTON, MA	BUFFALO, NY	CHARLESTON, SC	CHARLESTON, WV	CHARLOTTE, NC	CHEYENNE, WY	CHICAGO, IL	CINCINNATI, OH	CLEVELAND, OH	COLUMBUS, OH	DALLAS, TX	DENVER, CO	DES MOINES, IA	DETROIT, MI	EL PASO, TX	HARTFORD, CT	HOUSTON, TX	INDIANAPOLIS, IN	JACKSON, MS	JACKSONVILLE, FL	KANSAS CITY, MO	LAS VEGAS, NV
ALBANY, NY		2095	1811	1010	333	2083	1093	1675	2526	172	292	913	634	771	1789	832	730	484	621	1680	1833	1155	571	2326	111	1768	795	1331	1094	1282	2586
ALBUQUERQUE, NM	2095		286	1490	1902	991	1274	1333	966	2240	1808	1793	1568	1649	538	1352	1409	1619	1476	754	438	1091	1608	263	2139	994	1298	1157	1837	894	578
AMARILLO, TX	1811	286		1206	1618	988	991	1398	1266	1957	1524	1510	1285	1365	534	1069	1126	1335	1192	470	434	808	1324	438	1855	711	1014	874	1517	610	864
ATLANTA, GA	1010	1490	1206		679	1889	150	1559	2218	1100	910	317	503	238	1482	717	476	726	577	792	1403	967	735	1437	998	800	531	386	344	801	2067
BALTIMORE, MD	333	1902	1618	679		1959	795	1551	2401	422	370	583	352	441	1665	708	521	377	420	1399	1690	1031	532	2045	321	1470	600	1032	763	1087	2445
BILLINGS, MT	2083	991	988	1889	1959		1839	413	626	2254	1796	2157	1755	2012	455	1246	1552	1597	1608	1433	554	1007	1534	1255	2153	1673	1432	1836	2237	1088	965
BIRMINGHAM, AL	1093	1274	991	150	795	1839		1509	2170	1215	909	466	578	389	1434	667	475	725	576	647	1356	919	734	1292	1114	678	481	241	494	753	1852
BISMARCK, ND	1675	1333	1398	1559	1551	413	1509		1039	1846	1388	1749	1347	1604	594	838	1144	1189	1200	1342	693	675	1126	1597	1745	1582	1024	1548	1906	801	1378
BOISE, ID	2526	966	1266	2218	2401	626	2170	1039		2697	2239	2520	2182	2375	737	1708	1969	2040	2036	1711	833	1369	1977	1206	2595	1952	1852	2115	2566	1376	760
BOSTON, MA	172	2240	1957	1100	422	2254	1215	1846	2697		462	1003	741	861	1961	1003	862	654	760	1819	2004	1326	741	2465	102	1890	940	1453	1184	1427	2757
BUFFALO, NY	292	1808	1524	910	370	1796	909	1388	2239	462		899	431	695	1502	545	442	197	333	1393	1546	868	277	2039	401	1513	508	1134	1080	995	2299
CHARLESTON, SC	913	1793	1510	317	583	2157	466	1749	2520	1003	899		468	204	1783	907	622	724	637	1109	1705	1204	879	1754	901	1110	721	703	238	1102	2371
CHARLESTON, WV	634	1568	1285	503	352	1755	578	1347	2182	741	431	468		265	1445	506	209	255	168	1072	1367	802	410	1718	639	1192	320	816	649	764	2122
CHARLOTTE, NC	771	1649	1365	238	441	2012	389	1604	2375	861	695	204	265		1637	761	476	520	433	1031	1559	1057	675	1677	760	1041	575	625	385	956	2225
CHEYENNE, WY	1789	538	534	1482	1665	455	1434	594	737	1961	1502	1783	1445	1637		972	1233	1304	1300	979	100	633	1241	801	1859	1220	1115	1382	1829	640	843
CHICAGO, IL	832	1352	1069	717	708	1246	667	838	1708	1003	545	907	506	761	972		302	346	359	936	1015	337	283	1543	901	1108	184	750	1065	532	1768
CINCINNATI, OH	730	1409	1126	476	521	1552	475	1144	1969	862	442	622	209	476	1233	302		253	105	958	1200	599	261	1605	760	1079	116	700	803	597	1955
CLEVELAND, OH	484	1619	1335	726	377	1597	725	1189	2040	654	197	724	255	520	1304	346	253		144	1208	1347	669	171	1854	570	1328	319	950	904	806	2100
COLUMBUS, OH	621	1476	1192	577	420	1608	576	1200	2036	760	333	637	168	433	1300	359	105	144		1059	1266	665	192	1706	659	1179	176	801	818	663	2021
DALLAS, TX	1680	754	470	792	1399	1433	647	1342	1711	1819	1393	1109	1072	1031	979	936	958	1208	1059		887	752	1218	647	1717	241	913	406	1049	554	1331
DENVER, CO	1833	438	434	1403	1690	554	1356	693	833	2004	1546	1705	1367	1559	100	1015	1200	1347	1266	887		676	1284	701	1903	1127	1088	1290	1751	603	756
DES MOINES, IA	1155	1091	808	967	1031	1007	919	675	1369	1326	868	1204	802	1057	633	337	599	669	665	752	676		606	1283	1225	992	481	931	1315	194	1429
DETROIT, MI	571	1608	1324	735	532	1534	734	1126	1977	741	277	879	410	675	1241	283	261	171	192	1218	1284	606		1799	679	1338	318	960	1060	795	2037
EL PASO, TX	2326	263	438	1437	2045	1255	1292	1597	1206	2465	2039	1754	1718	1677	801	1543	1605	1854	1706	647	701	1283	1799		2364	758	1489	1051	1642	1085	717
HARTFORD, CT	111	2139	1855	998	321	2153	1114	1745	2595	102	401	901	639	760	1859	901	760	570	659	1717	1903	1225	679	2364		1788	839	1351	1082	1326	2655
HOUSTON, TX	1768	994	711	800	1470	1673	678	1582	1952	1890	1513	1110	1192	1041	1220	1108	1079	1328	1179	241	1127	992	1338	758	1788		1033	445	884	795	1474
INDIANAPOLIS, IN	795	1298	1014	531	600	1432	481	1024	1852	940	508	721	320	575	1115	184	116	319	176	913	1088	481	318	1489	839	1033		675	879	485	1843
JACKSON, MS	1331	1157	874	386	1032	1836	241	1548	2115	1453	1134	703	816	625	1382	750	700	950	801	406	1290	931	960	1051	1351	445	675		598	747	1735
JACKSONVILLE, FL	1094	1837	1517	344	763	2237	494	1906	2566	1184	1080	238	649	385	1829	1065	803	904	818	1049	1751	1315	1060	1642	1082	884	879	598		1148	2415
KANSAS CITY, MO	1282	894	610	801	1087	1088	753	801	1376	1427	995	1102	764	956	640	532	597	806	663	554	603	194	795	1085	1326	795	485	747	1148		1358
LAS VEGAS, NV	2586	578	864	2067	2445	965	1852	1378	760	2757	2299	2371	2122	2225	843	1768	1955	2100	2021	1331	756	1429	2037	717	2655	1474	1843	1735	2415	1358	
LITTLE ROCK, AR	1354	900	617	528	1072	1530	381	1183	1808	1493	1066	900	745	754	1076	662	632	882	733	327	984	567	891	974	1391	447	587	269	873	382	1478
LOS ANGELES, CA	2859	806	1092	2237	2705	1239	2092	1702	1033	3046	2572	2554	2374	2453	1116	2042	2215	2374	2281	1446	1029	1703	2310	801	2944	1558	2104	1851	2441	1632	274
LOUISVILLE, KY	832	1320	1036	419	602	1547	369	1139	1933	964	545	610	251	464	1197	299	106	356	207	852	1118	595	366	1499	862	972	112	594	766	516	1874
MEMPHIS, TN	1214	1033	750	389	933	1625	241	1337	1954	1353	927	760	606	614	1217	539	493	742	594	466	1116	720	752	1112	1251	586	464	211	733	536	1611
MIAMI, FL	1439	2155	1834	661	1109	2554	812	2224	2883	1529	1425	583	994	730	2147	1382	1141	1250	1163	1367	2069	1632	1401	1959	1427	1201	1196	915	345	1466	2733
MILWAUKEE, WI	929	1426	1142	813	805	1175	763	767	1748	1100	642	1003	601	857	1012	89	398	443	454	1010	1055	378	380	1617	999	1193	279	835	1160	573	1808
MINNEAPOLIS, MN	1245	1339	1055	1129	1121	839	1079	431	1465	1417	958	1319	918	1173	881	409	714	760	771	999	924	246	697	1530	1315	1240	596	1151	1477	441	1677
MOBILE, AL	1344	1344	1106	332	1013	2019	258	1765	2302	1433	1165	642	837	572	1570	923	731	981	832	639	1478	1115	991	1231	1332	473	737	187	410	930	1922
MONTPELIER, VT	167	2226	1943	1193	516	2219	1308	1811	2661	178	423	1096	834	954	1925	967	861	615	752	1811	1969	1291	690	2458	195	1983	927	1546	1277	1413	2722
MONTREAL, QC	230	2172	1888	1241	564	2093	1289	1685	2535	313	397	1145	822	1003	1799	841	815	588	725	1772	1843	1165	564	2363	338	1892	872	1514	1325	1359	2596
NASHVILLE, TN	1003	1248	965	242	716	1648	194	1315	1976	1136	716	543	395	397	1240	474	281	531	382	681	1162	725	541	1328	1034	801	287	423	589	559	1826
NEW ORLEANS, LA	1440	1276	993	473	1142	1955	351	1734	2234	1563	1254	783	926	713	1502	935	820	1070	921	525	1409	1117	1079	1118	1461	360	826	185	556	932	1854
NEW YORK, NY	151	2015	1731	869	192	2049	985	1641	2491	215	400	773	515	631	1755	797	636	466	535	1589	1799	1121	622	2235	115	1660	715	1223	953	1202	2552
NORFOLK, VA	570	1970	1686	558	239	2141	708	1733	2584	660	573	437	415	319	1847	890	624	559	604	1350	1782	1213	714	1996	558	1360	735	944	617	1179	2537
OKLAHOMA CITY, OK	1549	546	262	944	1354	1227	729	1136	1506	1694	1262	1248	1022	1102	773	807	863	1073	930	209	681	546	1062	737	1593	449	752	612	1291	348	1124
OMAHA, NE	1292	973	726	989	1168	904	941	616	1234	1463	1005	1290	952	1144	497	474	736	806	802	669	541	136	743	1236	1362	910	618	935	1336	188	1294
ORLANDO, FL	1235	1934	1613	440	904	2333	591	2003	2662	1324	1221	379	790	525	1926	1161	920	1045	958	1146	1847	1411	1180	1738	1223	980	975	694	141	1245	2512
PHILADELPHIA, PA	223	1954	1671	782	104	2019	897	1611	2462	321	414	685	454	543	1725	768	576	437	474	1501	1744	1091	592	2147	219	1572	655	1135	866	1141	2500
PHOENIX, AZ	2561	466	753	1868	2366	1199	1723	1662	993	2706	2274	2184	2035	2107	1004	1819	1876	2085	1942	1077	904	1558	2074	432	2605	1188	1764	1482	2072	1360	285
PITTSBURGH, PA	485	1670	1386	676	246	1719	763	1311	2161	592	217	642	217	438	1425	467	292	136	190	1246	1460	791	292	1893	491	1366	370	988	822	857	2215
PORTLAND, ME	270	2338	2054	1197	520	2352	1313	1944	2795	107	560	1101	839	959	2059	1101	960	751	858	1917	2102	1424	838	2563	199	1988	1038	1550	1281	1525	2855
PORTLAND, OR	2954	1395	1695	2647	2830	889	2599	1301	432	3126	2667	2948	2610	2802	1166	2137	2398	2469	2464	2140	1261	1798	2405	1767	3024	2381	2280	2544	2994	1805	1188
RALEIGH, NC	639	1782	1499	396	309	2110	547	1702	2495	729	642	279	313	158	1758	861	522	568	482	1189	1680	1157	724	1834	627	1198	639	783	460	1077	2360
RAPID CITY, SD	1750	841	837	1511	1626	379	1463	320	930	1921	1463	1824	1422	1678	305	913	1219	1264	1275	1077	404	629	1201	1105	1820	1318	1101	1458	1859	710	1035
RENO, NV	2747	1020	1306	2440	2623	960	2392	1372	430	2919	2460	2741	2403	2595	959	1930	2191	2262	2257	1933	1054	1591	2198	1315	2817	2072	2073	2337	2787	1598	442
RICHMOND, VA	482	1876	1593	527	152	2053	678	1645	2496	572	485	428	322	289	1760	802	530	471	517	1309	1688	1126	627	1955	471	1330	641	914	609	1085	2444
ST. LOUIS, MO	1036	1051	767	549	841	1341	501	1053	1628	1181	749	850	512	704	892	294	350	560	417	635	855	436	549	1242	1080	863	239	505	896	252	1610
SALT LAKE CITY, UT	2224	624	964	1916	2100	548	1868	960	342	2395	1936	2218	1880	2072	436	1406	1667	1738	1734	1410	531	1067	1675	864	2293	1650	1549	1813	2264	1074	417
SAN ANTONIO, TX	1953	818	513	1000	1671	1500	878	1599	1761	2092	1665	1310	1344	1241	1046	1270	1231	1481	1332	271	946	1009	1490	556	1990	200	1186	644	1084	812	1272
SAN DIEGO, CA	2919	825	1111	2166	2724	1302	2021	1765	1096	3065	2632	2483	2393	2405	1179	2105	2234	2437	2300	1375	1092	1766	2373	730	2963	1487	2122	1780	2370	1695	337
SAN FRANCISCO, CA	2964	1111	1397	2618	2840	1176	2472	1749	646	3135	2677	2934	2620	2759	1176	2146	2407	2478	2474	1827	1271	1807	2415	1181	3034	1938	2290	2232	2822	1814	575
SEATTLE, WA	2899	1463	1763	2705	2775	816	2657	1229	500	3070	2612	2973	2571	2827	1234	2062	2368	2413	2424	2208	1329	1822	2350	1944	2969	2449	2249	2612	3052	1872	1256
TAMPA, FL	1290	1949	1628	455	960	2348	606	2018	2677	1380	1276	434	845	581	1941	1176	935	1101	1036	1161	1862	1426	1194	1753	1278	995	990	709	196	1259	2526
TORONTO, ON	400	1841	1557	958	565	1762	958	1354	2204	570	106	1006	537	802	1468	510	484	303	440	1441	1512	834	233	2032	509	1561	541	1183	1187	1028	2265
VANCOUVER, BC	3032	1597	1897	2838	2908	949	2791	1362	633	3204	2745	3106	2705	2960	1368	2196	2501	2547	2558	2342	1463	1956	2483	2087	3102	2583	2383	2746	3186	2007	1390
WASHINGTON, DC	369	1896	1612	636	38	1953	758	1545	2395	458	384	539	346	397	1659	701	517	370	416	1362	1686	1025	526	2008	357	1433	596	996	720	1083	2441
WICHITA, KS	1471	707	423	989	1276	1067	838	934	1346	1616	1184	1291	953	1145	613	728	7856	995	852	367	521	390	984	898	1515	608	674	771	1337	192	1276

	LITTLE ROCK, AR	LOS ANGELES, CA	LOUISVILLE, KY	MEMPHIS, TN	MIAMI, FL	MILWAUKEE, WI	MINNEAPOLIS, MN	MOBILE, AL	MONTPELIER, VT	MONTREAL, QC	NASHVILLE, TN	NEW ORLEANS, LA	NEW YORK, NY	NORFOLK, VA	OKLAHOMA CITY, OK	OMAHA, NE	ORLANDO, FL	PHILADELPHIA, PA	PHOENIX, AZ	PITTSBURGH, PA	PORTLAND, ME	PORTLAND, OR	RALEIGH, NC	RAPID CITY, SD	RENO, NV	RICHMOND, VA	ST. LOUIS, MO	SALT LAKE CITY, UT	SAN ANTONIO, TX	SAN DIEGO, CA	SAN FRANCISCO, CA	SEATTLE, WA	TAMPA, FL	TORONTO, ON	VANCOUVER, BC	WASHINGTON, DC	WICHITA, KS
	1354	2859	832	1214	1439	929	1245	1344	167	230	1003	1440	151	151	1549	1292	1235	223	2561	485	270	2954	639	1750	2747	482	1036	2224	1953	2919	2964	2899	1290	400	3032	369	1471
	900	806	1320	1033	2155	1426	1339	1344	2226	2172	1248	1276	2015	2015	546	973	1934	1954	466	1670	2338	1395	1782	841	1020	1876	1051	624	818	825	1111	1463	1949	1841	1597	1896	707
	617	1092	1036	750	1834	1142	1055	1106	1943	1888	965	993	1731	1731	262	726	1613	1671	753	1386	2054	1695	1499	837	1306	1593	767	964	513	1111	1397	1763	1628	1557	1897	1612	423
	528	2237	419	389	661	813	1129	332	1193	1241	242	473	869	869	944	989	440	782	1868	676	1197	2647	396	1511	2440	527	549	1916	1000	2166	2618	2705	455	958	2838	636	989
	1072	2705	602	933	1109	805	1121	1013	516	564	716	1142	192	192	1354	1168	904	104	2366	246	520	2830	309	1626	2623	152	841	2100	1671	2724	2840	2775	960	565	2908	38	1276
	1530	1239	1547	1625	2554	1175	839	2019	2219	2093	1648	1955	2049	2049	1227	904	2333	2019	1199	1719	2352	889	2110	379	960	2053	1341	548	1500	1302	1176	816	2348	1762	949	1953	1067
	381	2092	369	241	812	763	1079	258	1308	1289	194	351	985	985	729	941	591	897	1723	763	1313	2599	547	1463	2392	678	501	1868	878	2021	2472	2657	606	958	2791	758	838
	1183	1702	1139	1337	2224	767	431	1765	1811	1685	1315	1734	1641	1641	1136	616	2003	1611	1662	1311	1944	1301	1702	320	1372	1645	1053	960	1599	1765	1749	1229	2018	1354	1362	1545	934
	1808	1033	1933	1954	2883	1748	1465	2302	2661	2535	1976	2234	2491	2491	1506	1234	2662	2462	993	2161	2795	432	2495	930	430	2496	1628	342	1761	1096	646	500	2677	2204	633	2395	1346
	1493	3046	964	1353	1529	1100	1417	1433	178	313	1136	1563	215	215	1694	1463	1324	321	2706	592	107	3126	729	1921	2919	572	1181	2395	2092	3065	3135	3070	1380	570	3204	458	1616
	1066	2572	545	927	1425	642	958	1165	423	397	716	1254	400	400	1262	1005	1221	414	2274	217	560	2667	642	1463	2460	485	749	1936	1665	2632	2677	2612	1276	106	2745	384	1184
	900	2554	610	760	583	1003	1319	642	1096	1145	543	783	773	773	1248	1290	379	685	2184	642	1101	2948	279	1824	2741	428	850	2218	1310	2483	2934	2973	434	1006	3106	539	1291
	745	2374	251	606	994	601	918	837	834	822	395	926	515	515	1022	952	790	454	2035	217	839	2610	313	1422	2403	322	512	1880	1344	2393	2620	2571	845	537	2705	346	953
	754	2453	464	614	730	857	1173	572	954	1003	397	713	631	631	1102	1144	525	543	2107	438	959	2802	158	1678	2595	289	704	2072	1241	2405	2759	2827	581	802	2960	397	1145
	1076	1116	1197	1217	2147	1012	881	1570	1925	1799	1240	1502	1755	1755	773	497	1926	1725	1004	1425	2059	1166	1758	305	959	1760	892	436	1046	1179	1176	1234	1941	1468	1368	1659	613
	662	2042	299	539	1382	89	409	923	967	841	474	935	797	797	807	474	1161	768	1819	467	1101	2137	861	913	1930	802	294	1406	1270	2105	2146	2062	1176	510	2196	701	728
	632	2215	106	493	1141	398	714	731	861	815	281	820	636	636	863	736	920	576	1876	292	960	2398	522	1219	2191	530	350	1667	1231	2234	2407	2368	935	484	2501	517	785
	882	2374	356	742	1250	443	760	981	615	588	531	1070	466	466	1073	806	1045	437	2085	136	751	2469	568	1264	2262	471	560	1738	1481	2437	2478	2413	1101	303	2547	370	995
	733	2281	207	594	1163	454	771	832	752	725	382	921	535	535	930	802	958	474	1942	190	858	2464	482	1275	2257	517	417	1734	1332	2300	2474	2424	1036	440	2558	416	852
	327	1446	852	466	1367	1010	999	639	1811	1772	681	525	1589	1589	209	669	1146	1501	1077	1246	1917	2140	1189	1077	1933	1309	635	1410	271	1375	1827	2208	1161	1441	2342	1362	367
	984	1029	1118	1116	2069	1055	924	1478	1969	1843	1162	1409	1799	1799	681	541	1847	1744	904	1460	2102	1261	1680	404	1054	1688	855	531	946	1092	1271	1329	1862	1512	1463	1686	521
	567	1703	595	720	1632	378	246	1115	1291	1165	725	1117	1121	1121	546	136	1411	1091	1558	791	1424	1798	1157	629	1591	1126	436	1067	1009	1766	1807	1822	1426	834	1956	1025	390
	891	2310	366	752	1401	380	697	991	690	564	541	1079	622	622	1062	743	1180	592	2074	292	838	2405	724	1201	2198	627	549	1675	1490	2373	2415	2350	1194	233	2483	526	984
	974	801	1499	1112	1959	1617	1530	1231	2458	2363	1328	1118	2235	2235	737	1236	1738	2147	432	1893	2563	1767	1834	1105	1315	1955	1242	864	556	730	1181	1944	1753	2032	2087	2008	898
	1391	2944	862	1251	1427	999	1315	1332	195	338	1034	1461	115	115	1593	1362	1223	219	2605	491	199	3024	627	1820	2817	471	1080	2293	1990	2963	3034	2969	1278	509	3102	357	1515
	447	1558	972	586	1201	1193	1240	473	1983	1892	801	360	1660	1660	449	910	980	1572	1188	1366	1988	2381	1198	1318	2072	1330	863	1650	200	1487	1938	2449	995	1561	2583	1433	608
	587	2104	112	464	1196	279	596	737	927	872	287	826	715	715	752	618	975	655	1764	370	1038	2280	639	1101	2073	641	239	1549	1186	2122	2290	2249	990	541	2383	596	674
	269	1851	594	211	915	835	1151	187	1546	1514	423	185	1223	1223	612	935	694	1135	1482	988	1550	2544	783	1458	2337	914	505	1813	644	1780	2232	2612	709	1183	2746	996	771
	873	2441	766	733	345	1160	1477	410	1277	1325	589	556	953	953	1291	1336	141	866	2072	822	1281	2994	460	1859	2787	609	896	2264	1084	2370	2822	3052	196	1187	3186	720	1337
	382	1632	516	536	1466	573	441	930	1413	1359	559	932	1202	1202	348	188	1245	1141	1360	857	1525	1805	1077	710	1598	1085	252	1074	812	1695	1814	1872	1259	1028	2007	1083	192
	1478	274	1874	1611	2733	1808	1677	1922	2722	2596	1826	1854	2552	2552	1124	1294	2512	2500	285	2215	2855	1188	2360	1035	442	2444	1610	417	1272	337	575	1256	2526	2265	1390	2441	1276
		1706	526	140	1190	747	814	457	1485	1446	355	455	1262	1262	355	570	969	1175	1367	920	1590	2237	889	1093	2030	983	416	1507	600	1703	2012	2305	984	1115	2439	1036	464
	1706		2126	1839	2759	2082	1951	2031	2995	2869	2054	1917	2820	2820	1352	1567	2538	2760	369	2476	3144	971	2588	1309	519	2682	1856	691	1356	124	385	1148	2553	2538	1291	2702	1513
	526	2126		386	1084	394	711	625	963	920	175	714	739	739	774	704	863	678	1786	394	1062	2362	564	1215	2155	572	264	1631	1125	2144	2372	2364	878	589	2497	596	705
	140	1839	386		1051	624	940	395	1345	1306	215	396	1123	1123	487	724	830	1035	1500	780	1451	2382	749	1247	2175	843	294	1652	739	1841	2144	2440	845	975	2574	896	597
	1190	2759	1084	1051		1478	1794	727	1622	1671	907	874	1299	1299	1609	1654	232	1211	2390	1167	1627	3312	805	2176	3105	954	1214	2581	1401	2688	3140	3370	274	1532	3504	1065	1655
	747	2082	394	624	1478		337	1019	1064	939	569	1020	894	894	880	514	1257	865	1892	564	1198	2063	956	842	1970	899	367	1446	1343	2145	2186	1991	1272	607	2124	799	769
	814	1951	711	940	1794	337		1335	1381	1255	886	1337	1211	1211	793	383	1573	1181	1805	881	1515	1727	1273	606	1839	1216	621	1315	1257	2014	2055	1654	1588	924	1788	1115	637
	457	2031	625	395	727	1019	1335		1526	1575	450	146	1203	1203	799	1119	506	1115	1662	1019	1531	2731	730	1641	2545	861	688	2000	673	1960	2411	2799	521	1214	2933	970	958
	1485	2995	963	1345	1622	1064	1381	1526		138	1134	1656	310	310	1680	1428	1417	414	2693	685	196	3090	822	1886	2883	665	1167	2359	2084	3051	3099	3034	1473	457	3168	551	1602
	1446	2869	920	1306	1671	939	1255	1575	138		1094	1632	383	383	1625	1300	1466	454	2637	607	282	2963	871	1758	2756	714	1112	2232	2043	2931	2972	2907	1522	330	3041	600	1547
	355	2054	175	215	907	569	886	450	1134	1094		539	906	906	703	747	686	818	1715	569	1234	2405	532	1269	2198	626	307	1675	954	2056	2360	2463	701	764	2597	679	748
	455	1917	714	396	874	1020	1337	146	1656	1632	539		1332	1332	731	1121	653	1245	1548	1108	1660	2663	871	1643	2431	1002	690	1932	560	1846	2298	2731	668	1302	2865	1106	890
	1262	2820	739	1123	1299	894	1211	1203	310	383	906	1332		430	1469	1258	1094	91	2481	367	313	2920	499	1716	2713	342	956	2189	1861	2839	2929	2864	1150	507	2998	228	1391
	1076	2776	666	937	962	987	1303	891	753	801	720	1032	430		1424	1350	758	342	2436	428	757	3012	179	1808	2805	91	927	2282	1560	2725	3022	2957	814	747	3090	196	1368
	355	1352	774	487	1609	880	793	799	1680	1625	703	731	1469	1424		463	1388	1408	1012	1124	1792	1934	1237	871	1727	1331	505	1204	466	1370	1657	2002	1403	1295	2136	1350	161
	570	1567	704	724	1654	514	383	1119	1428	1300	747	1121	1258	1350	463		1433	1228	1440	928	1561	1662	1265	525	1455	1263	440	932	927	1630	1672	1719	1448	971	1853	1162	307
	969	2538	863	830	232	1257	1573	506	1417	1466	686	653	1094	758	1388	1433		1006	2169	963	1422	3091	601	1955	2884	750	993	2360	1180	2467	2918	3149	82	1327	3283	860	1434
	1175	2760	678	1035	1211	865	1181	1115	414	454	818	1245	91	342	1408	1228	1006		2420	306	419	2890	411	1686	2683	254	895	2160	1774	2779	2900	2835	1062	522	2968	140	1330
	1367	369	1786	1500	2390	1892	1805	1662	2693	2637	1715	1548	2481	2436	1012	1440	2169	2420		2136	2804	1335	2249	1308	883	2343	1517	651	987	358	750	1513	2184	2307	1655	2362	1173
	920	2476	394	780	1167	564	881	1019	685	607	569	1108	367	428	1124	928	963	306	2136		690	2590	497	1386	2383	341	611	1859	1519	2494	2599	2534	1019	321	2668	240	1046
	1590	3144	1062	1451	1627	1198	1515	1531	196	282	1234	1660	313	757	1792	1561	1422	419	2804	690		3223	827	2019	3016	670	1279	2493	2189	3162	3233	3168	1478	668	3301	556	1714
	2237	971	2362	2382	3312	2063	1727	2731	3090	2963	2405	2663	2920	3012	1934	1662	3091	2890	1335	2590	3223		2923	1268	578	2925	2057	771	2322	1093	638	170	3106	2633	313	2824	1775
	889	2588	564	749	805	956	1273	730	822	871	532	871	499	179	1237	1265	601	411	2249	497	827	2923		1777	2716	157	825	2193	1398	2563	2894	2926	656	820	3060	265	1266
	1093	1309	1215	1247	2176	842	606	1641	1886	1758	1269	1643	1716	1808	871	525	1955	1686	1308	1386	2019	1268	1777		1151	1720	963	628	1335	1372	1368	1195	1970	1429	1328	1620	712
	2030	519	2155	2175	3105	1970	1839	2545	2883	2756	2198	2431	2713	2805	1727	1455	2884	2683	883	2383	3016	578	2716	1151		2718	1850	524	1870	642	217	755	2899	2426	898	2617	1568
	983	2682	572	843	954	899	1216	861	665	714	626	1002	342	91	1331	1263	750	254	2343	341	670	2925	157	1720	2718		834	2194	1530	2684	2934	2869	805	660	3003	108	1274
	416	1856	264	294	1214	367	621	688	1167	1112	307	690	956	927	505	440	993	895	1517	611	1279	2057	825	963	1850	834		1326	968	1875	2066	2125	1008	782	2259	837	441
	1507	691	1631	1652	2581	1446	1315	2000	2359	2232	1675	1932	2189	2282	1204	932	2360	2160	651	1859	2493	771	2193	628	524	2194	1326		1419	754	740	839	2375	1902	973	2094	1044
	600	1356	1125	739	1401	1343	1257	673	2084	2043	954	560	1861	1560	466	927	1180	1774	987	1519	2189	2322	1398	1335	1870	1530	968	1419		1285	1737	2275	1195	1714	2410	1635	624
	1703	124	2144	1841	2688	2145	2014	1960	3051	2931	2056	1846	2839	2725	1370	1630	2467	2779	358	2494	3162	1093	2563	1372	642	2684	1875	754	1285		508	1271	2481	2601	1414	2720	1531
	2012	385	2372	2144	3140	2186	2055	2411	3099	2972	2360	2298	2929	3022	1657	1672	2918	2900	750	2599	3233	638	2894	1368	217	2934	2066	740	1737	508		816	2933	2643	958	2834	1784
	2305	1148	2364	2440	3370	1991	1654	2799	3034	2907	2463	2731	2864	2957	2002	1719	3149	2835	1513	2534	3168	170	2926	1195	755	2869	2125	839	2275	1271	816		3164	2577	140	2769	1843
	984	2553	878	845	274	1272	1588	521	1473	1522	701	668	1150	814	1403	1448	82	1062	2184	1019	1478	3106	656	1970	2899	805	1008	2375	1195	2481	2933	3164		1383	3297	916	1448
	1115	2538	589	975	1532	607	924	1214	457	330	764	1302	507	747	1295	971	1327	522	2307	321	668	2633	820	1429	2426	660	782	1902	1714	2601	2643	2577	1383		2711	563	1217
	2439	1291	2497	2574	3504	2124	1788	2933	3168	3041	2597	2865	2998	3090	2136	1853	3283	2968	1655	2668	3301	313	3060	1328	898	3003	2259	973	2410	1414	958	140	3297	2711		2902	1977
	1036	2702	596	896	1065	799	1115	970	551	600	679	1106	228	196	1350	1162	860	140	2362	240	556	2824	265	1620	2617	108	837	2094	1635	2720	2834	2769	916	563	2902		1272
	464	1513	705	597	1655	769	637	958	1602	1547	748	890	1391	1368	161	307	1434	1330	1173	1046	1714	1775	1266	712	1568	1274	441	1044	624	1531	1784	1843	1448	1217	1977	1272	

BORDER CROSSING

MEXICO

U.S. citizens entering Mexico are required to present passports or proof of U.S. citizenship accompanied by photo identification. Visas are not required for stays of up to 180 days. Naturalized citizens should travel with their naturalization certificates, and alien permanent residents must present their Alien Registration Cards. Individuals under the age of 18 traveling alone, with one parent, or with other adults must carry notarized parental authorization or valid custodial documents.

In addition, all U.S. citizens visiting for up to 180 days must procure a tourist card, obtainable from Mexican consulates, tourism offices, and border crossing points, which must be surrendered upon departure. However, tourist cards are not needed for visits shorter than 72 hours to cities along the Mexico/U.S. border.

U.S. driver's licenses are valid in Mexico.

Visitors who wish to drive beyond the Baja California Peninsula or the Border Zone (extending approximately 25 km into Mexico) must obtain a temporary import permit for their vehicles. Permits may be obtained from a Mexican Customs Office at border crossing points as long as the original and two copies of the following documents bearing the driver's name are provided: passport/proof of U.S. citizenship, tourist card, vehicle registration, driver's license, and a major international credit card for use in paying the prevailing fee. Permits are valid for 180 days, and they must be surrendered upon final departure from Mexico.

All visitors driving in Mexico should be aware that U.S. auto insurance policies are not valid and that buying short-term tourist insurance is virtually mandatory. Many U.S. insurance companies sell Mexican auto insurance. American Automobile Association (for members only) and Sanborn's Mexico Insurance (800.638.9423) are popular companies with offices at most U.S. border crossings.

N

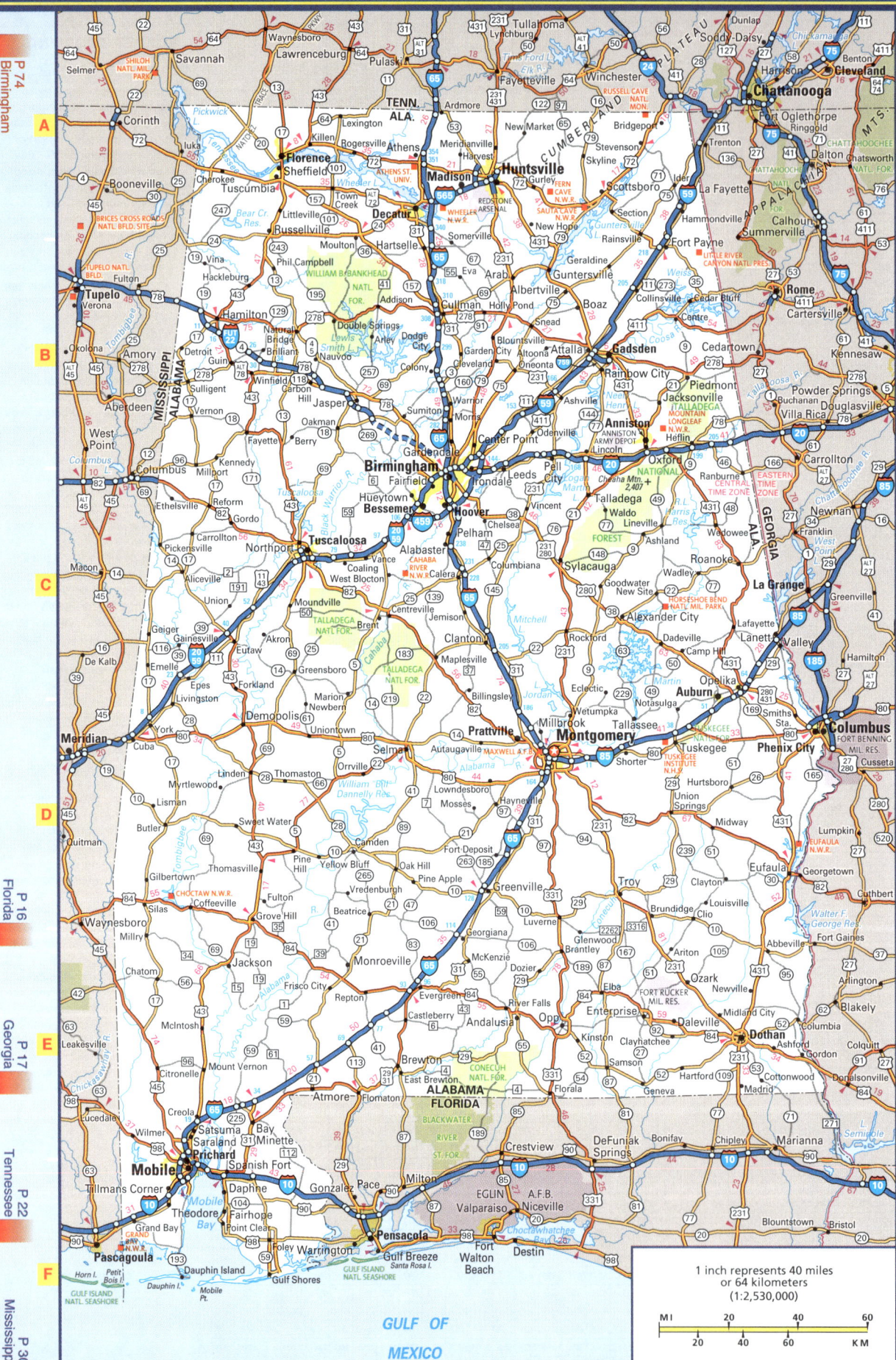

1 inch represents 40 miles
or 64 kilometers
(1:2,530,000)

© MapQuest, Inc.

P 74 Birmingham

P 16 Florida

P 17 Georgia

P 22 Tennessee

P 30 Mississippi

N

1 inch represents 229 miles
or 368 kilometers
(1:14,500,000)

© MapQuest, Inc.

Distances in the U.S. shown in miles
Distances in Canada shown in kilometers

1 inch represents 56 miles
or 91 kilometers
(1:3,570,000)

© MapQuest, Inc.

P 58 British Columbia

P 92 Honolulu

P 121 Phoenix
P 135 Tucson
P 11 California
P 12 Colorado
P 34 Nevada
P 37 New Mexico
P 50 Utah
P 68 Mexico

1 inch represents 52 miles
or 84 kilometers
(1:3,300,000)

© MapQuest, Inc.

Distances in the U.S. shown in miles
Distances in Mexico shown in kilometers

PARTIAL INDEX TO CITIES AND TOWNS

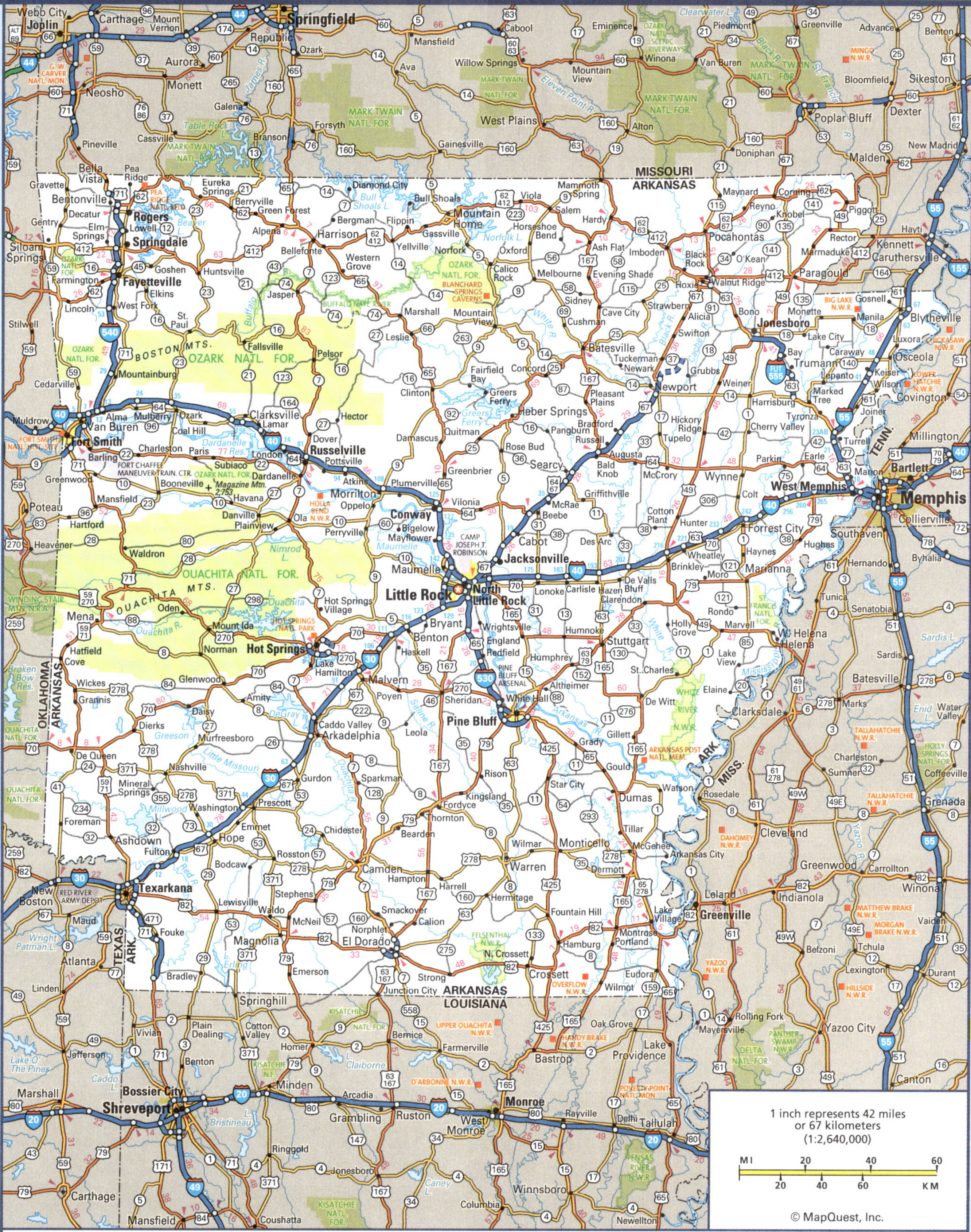

Map legend: 1 inch represents 42 miles or 67 kilometers (1:2,640,000)

© MapQuest, Inc.

N

PARTIAL INDEX TO CITIES AND TOWNS

Acton	H-6
Alturas	A-3
Amboy	H-5
Anaheim	J-4
Antioch	E-2
Apple Valley	H-4
Arcata	B-1
Avenal	G-2
Baker	G-5
Bakersfield	G-3
Barstow	H-4
Berkeley	E-2
Blythe	J-6
Brawley	K-5
Bridgeport	D-4
Carlsbad	J-4
Cathedral City	J-5
Ceres	F-2
Chico	D-2
Chula Vista	K-4
Clovis	F-2
Colfax	E-2
Concord	E-2
Corcoran	G-2
Corning	C-2
Coronado	K-4
Crescent City	A-1
Davis	E-2
Death Valley Springs	J-5
Desert Hot Springs	J-5
El Cajon	K-4
El Centro	K-5
Encinitas	J-4
Escondido	K-4
Eureka	B-1
Fort Bragg	C-1
Four Corners	H-4
Fremont	E-2
Fresno	F-2
Gilroy	F-2
Glendale	H-3
Grass Valley	E-2
Hanford	F-2
Hayward	E-2
Hemet	J-4
Hesperia	H-4
Huntington Beach	J-3
Imperial Beach	K-4
Inglewood	J-3
Irvine	J-4
Julian	K-5
King City	G-1
Klamath	A-1
Lakeside	K-4
Lancaster	H-4
Laytonville	C-1
Lemoore	F-2
Lindsay	G-3
Lodi	E-2
Lompoc	H-2
Lone Pine	F-4
Long Beach	J-3
Los Angeles	H-3
Madera	F-2
Manteca	F-2
Marina	G-1
Merced	F-2
Milpitas	E-2
Modesto	F-2
Monterey	G-1
Moreno Valley	J-4
Morro Bay	H-2
Napa	E-2
Needles	H-4
Nevada City	C-3
Newport Beach	J-4
Oakland	E-2
Oceanside	K-4
Ontario	J-4
Orick	A-1
Oxnard	H-3
Palm Springs	J-5
Palmdale	H-4
Paradise	D-2
Pasadena	H-3
Petaluma	E-2
Pismo Beach	H-2
Pomona	J-4
Porterville	G-3
Quincy	D-3
Ramona	K-4
Redding	C-2
Redwood City	E-2
Ridgecrest	G-4
Riverside	J-4
Roseville	D-3
Sacramento	E-2
Salinas	F-1
San Bernardino	J-4
San Diego	K-4
San Clemente	J-4
San Francisco	E-2
San Jose	E-2
San Juan	G-1
San Luis Obispo	G-2
San Mateo	E-2
San Rafael	E-2
Santa Ana	J-4
Santa Barbara	H-2
Santa Clarita	H-3
Santa Cruz	F-1
Santa Maria	H-2
Santa Monica	H-3
Santa Paula	H-3
Santa Rosa	D-2
Shoshone	G-5
Sierraville	D-3
Simi Valley	H-3
South Lake Tahoe	D-4
Stockton	E-2
Sunnyvale	E-2
Susanville	B-3
Taft	H-3
Tehachapi	H-4
Temecula	J-4
Thousand Oaks	H-3
Torrance	J-3
Tracy	F-2
Tulare	G-3
Turlock	F-2
Ukiah	D-1
Vacaville	E-2
Vallejo	E-2
Ventura	H-3
Victorville	H-4
Visalia	G-3
Wasco	G-3
Watsonville	F-1
Weed	B-2
Woodland	E-2
Yosemite Village	F-3
Yreka	A-2
Yuba City	D-2
Yucaipa	J-4

1 inch represents 50 miles or 80 kilometers (1:3,140,000)

© MapQuest, Inc.

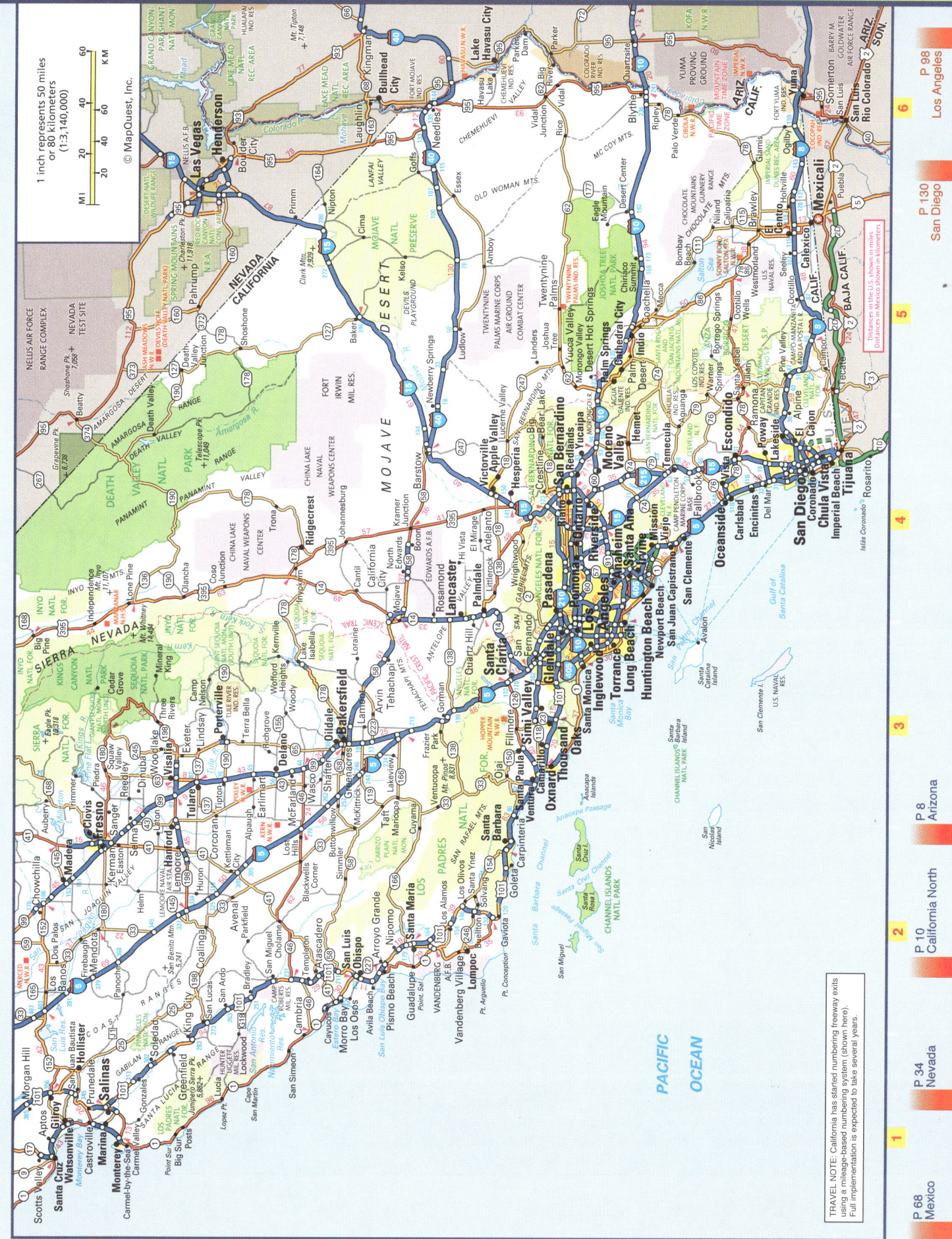

N

1 inch represents 50 miles
or 80 kilometers (1:3,140,000)

© MapQuest, Inc.

TRAVEL NOTE: California has started numbering freeway exits
using a mileage-based numbering system (shown here).
Full implementation is expected to take several years.

PACIFIC OCEAN

P 98 Los Angeles

P 130 San Diego

P 8 Arizona

P 10 California North

P 34 Nevada

P 68 Mexico

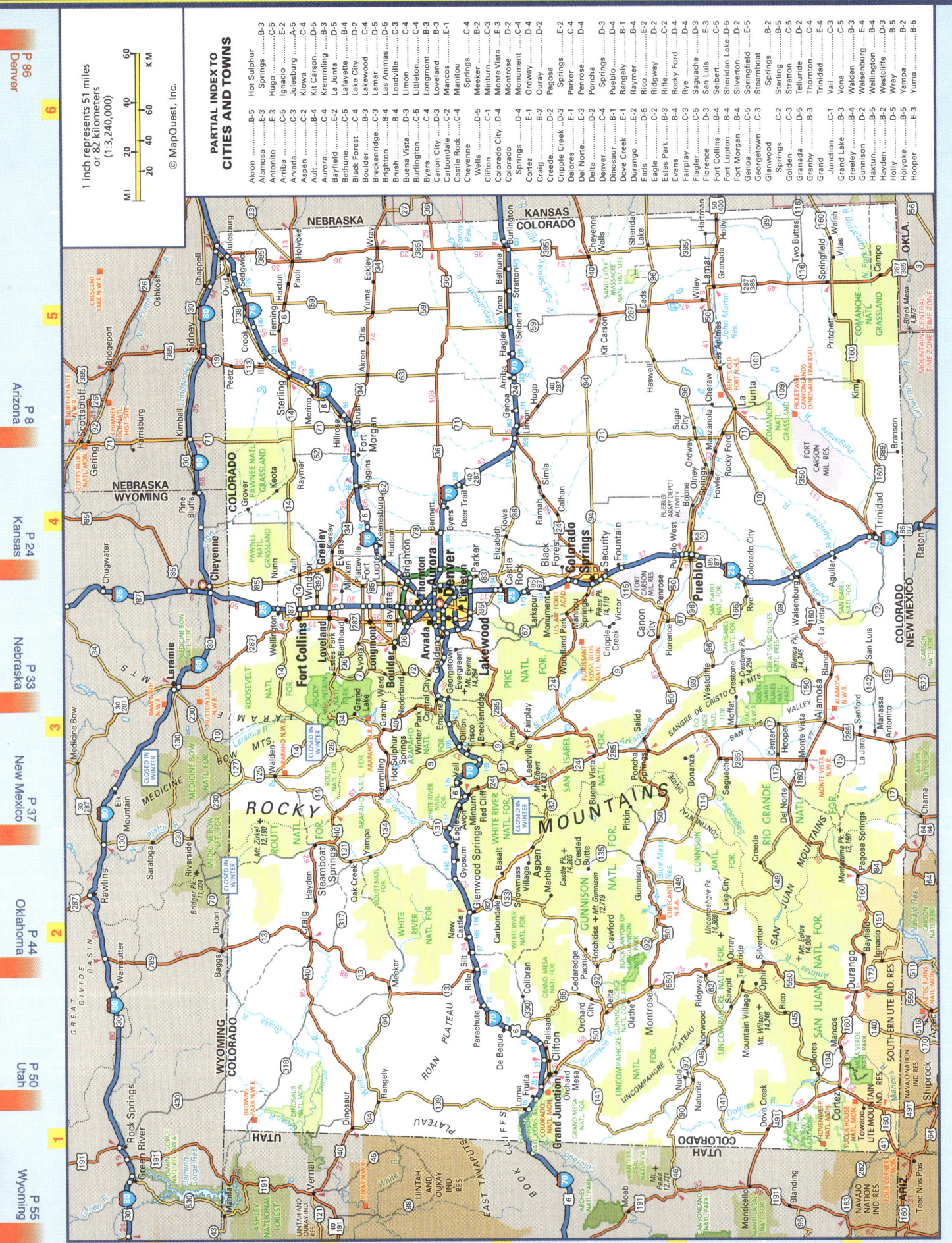

**1 inch represents 51 miles
or 82 kilometers
(1:3,240,000)**

© MapQuest, Inc.

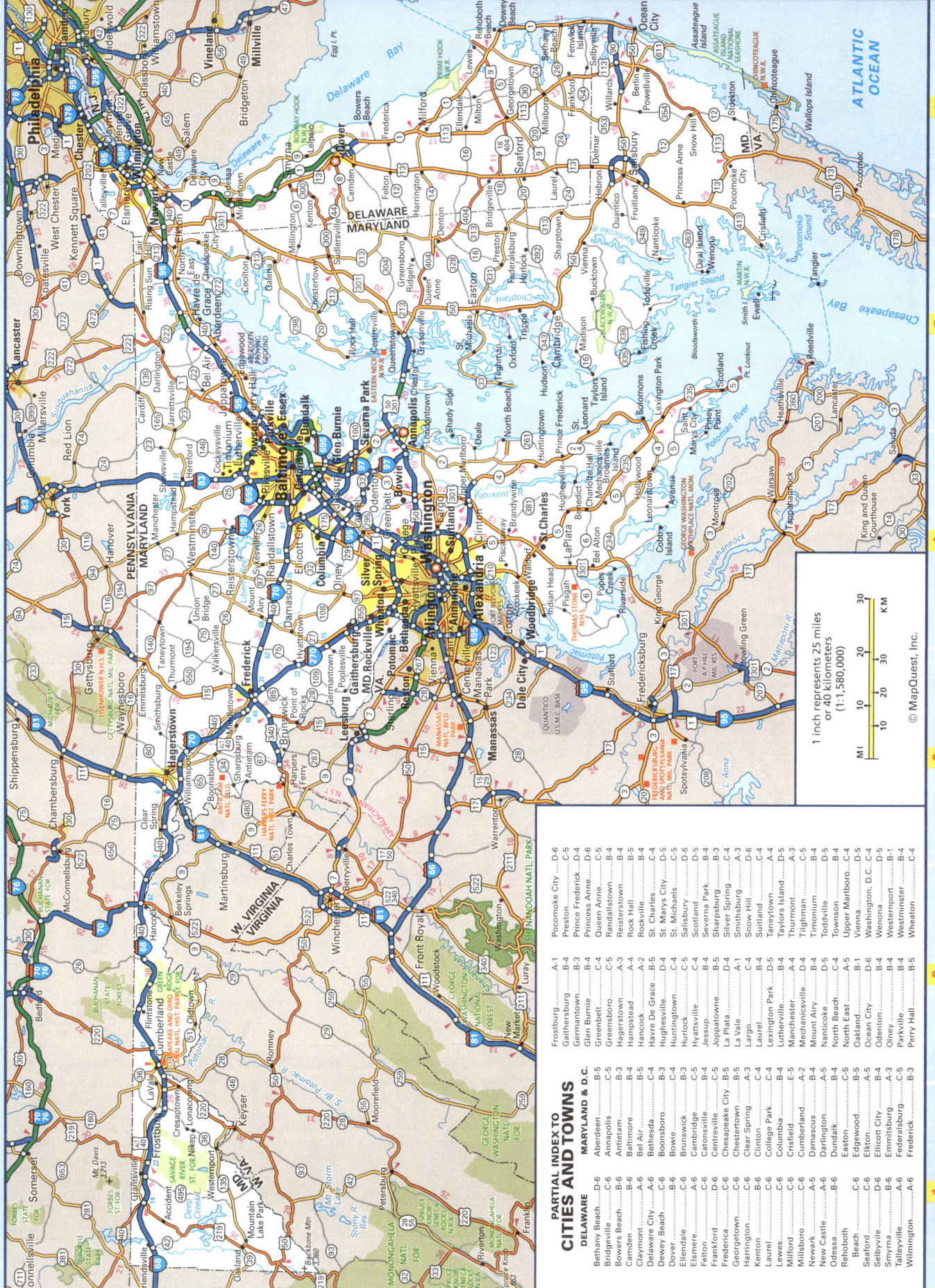

1 inch represents 25 miles
or 40 kilometers (1:1,580,000)

P 72 Baltimore
P 137 Washington, D.C.
P 36 New Jersey
P 46 Pennsylvania
P 52 Virginia
P 52 West Virginia

Map of Connecticut, Massachusetts & Rhode Island

Grid references A–F (left margin, top to bottom) and 1–5 (bottom margin, left to right).

Left margin labels: P 91 Hartford · New Hampshire · P 35 Vermont · P 35 · P 38 New York

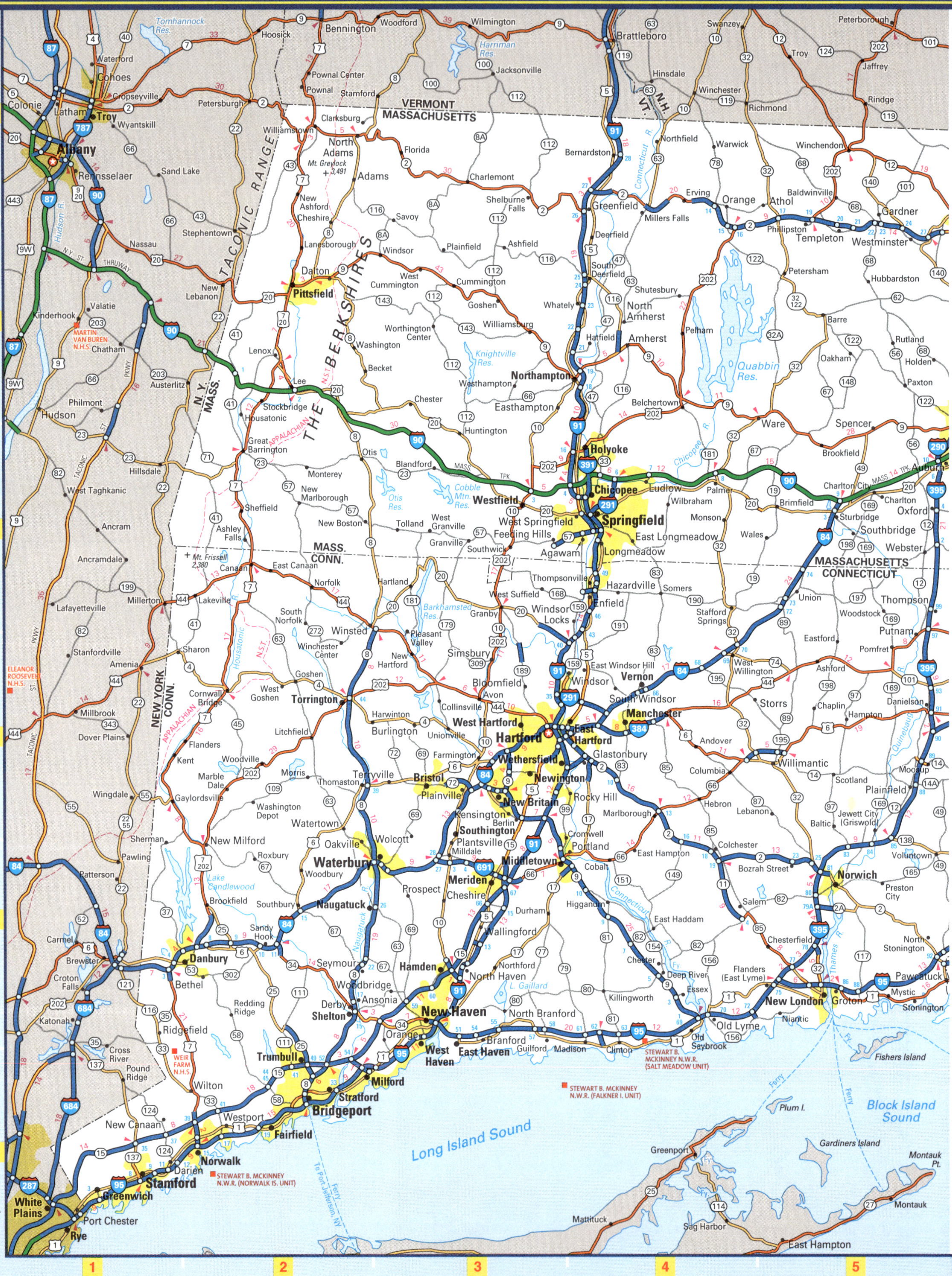

VERMONT
MASSACHUSETTS

MASSACHUSETTS
CONNECTICUT

N.Y. MASS.

MASS. CONN.

NEW YORK CONN.

THE BERKSHIRES

TACONIC RANGE

Selected place names:

Albany, Troy, Latham, Cohoes, Rensselaer, Watervliet, Colonie, Chatham, Hudson, Kinderhook, Philmont, Millerton, Amenia, Millbrook, Dover Plains, Wingdale, Pawling, Brewster, Carmel, Danbury, Bethel, Ridgefield, Katonah, Croton Falls, White Plains, Port Chester, Rye, Greenwich, Stamford, Darien, Norwalk, Westport, Fairfield, Bridgeport, Stratford, Milford, Trumbull, Shelton, Derby, Ansonia, New Haven, West Haven, East Haven, Branford, Guilford, Madison, Clinton, Westbrook, Old Saybrook, Old Lyme, Niantic, New London, Groton, Mystic, Stonington, Pawcatuck

Williamstown, North Adams, Adams, Cheshire, New Ashford, Lanesborough, Pittsfield, Dalton, Lenox, Lee, Stockbridge, Housatonic, Great Barrington, Sheffield, Ashley Falls, New Marlborough, Monterey, Becket, Washington, Otis, Blandford, Westfield, West Springfield, Feeding Hills, Agawam, Springfield, Chicopee, Holyoke, Ludlow, Wilbraham, Palmer, Monson, Northampton, Easthampton, Amherst, North Amherst, Hatfield, Whately, Deerfield, Greenfield, Bernardston, Northfield, Erving, Orange, Athol, Gardner, Templeton, Winchendon, Auburn, Sturbridge, Southbridge, Webster, Charlton, Oxford

Canaan, East Canaan, Norfolk, Winsted, Torrington, Litchfield, Thomaston, Terryville, Bristol, Plainville, Bristol, Southington, Plantsville, New Britain, Newington, Wethersfield, Hartford, West Hartford, East Hartford, Windsor, Windsor Locks, Enfield, Bloomfield, Avon, Simsbury, Farmington, Berlin, Kensington, Meriden, Wallingford, Cheshire, Waterbury, Naugatuck, Seymour, Woodbridge, Hamden, North Haven, Middletown, Portland, Cromwell, Rocky Hill, Glastonbury, Manchester, Vernon, South Windsor, Storrs, Willimantic, Columbia, Lebanon, Colchester, Norwich, New London

Block Island Sound, Long Island Sound, Fishers Island, Gardiners Island, Montauk Pt., Montauk, East Hampton, Sag Harbor, Greenport, Plum I.

Stewart B. McKinney N.W.R.

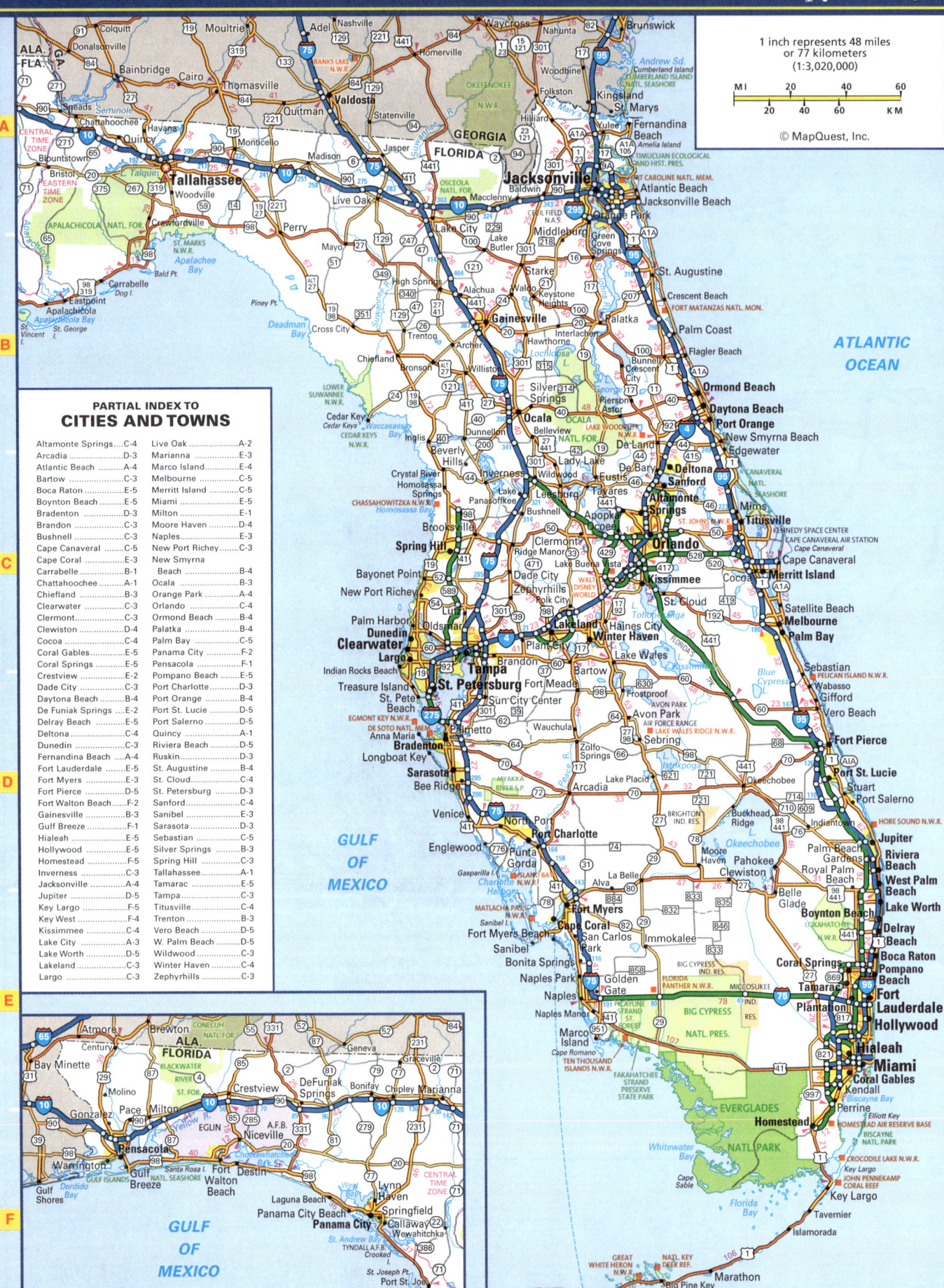

1 inch represents 41 miles
or 66 kilometers
(1:2,590,000)

© MapQuest, Inc.

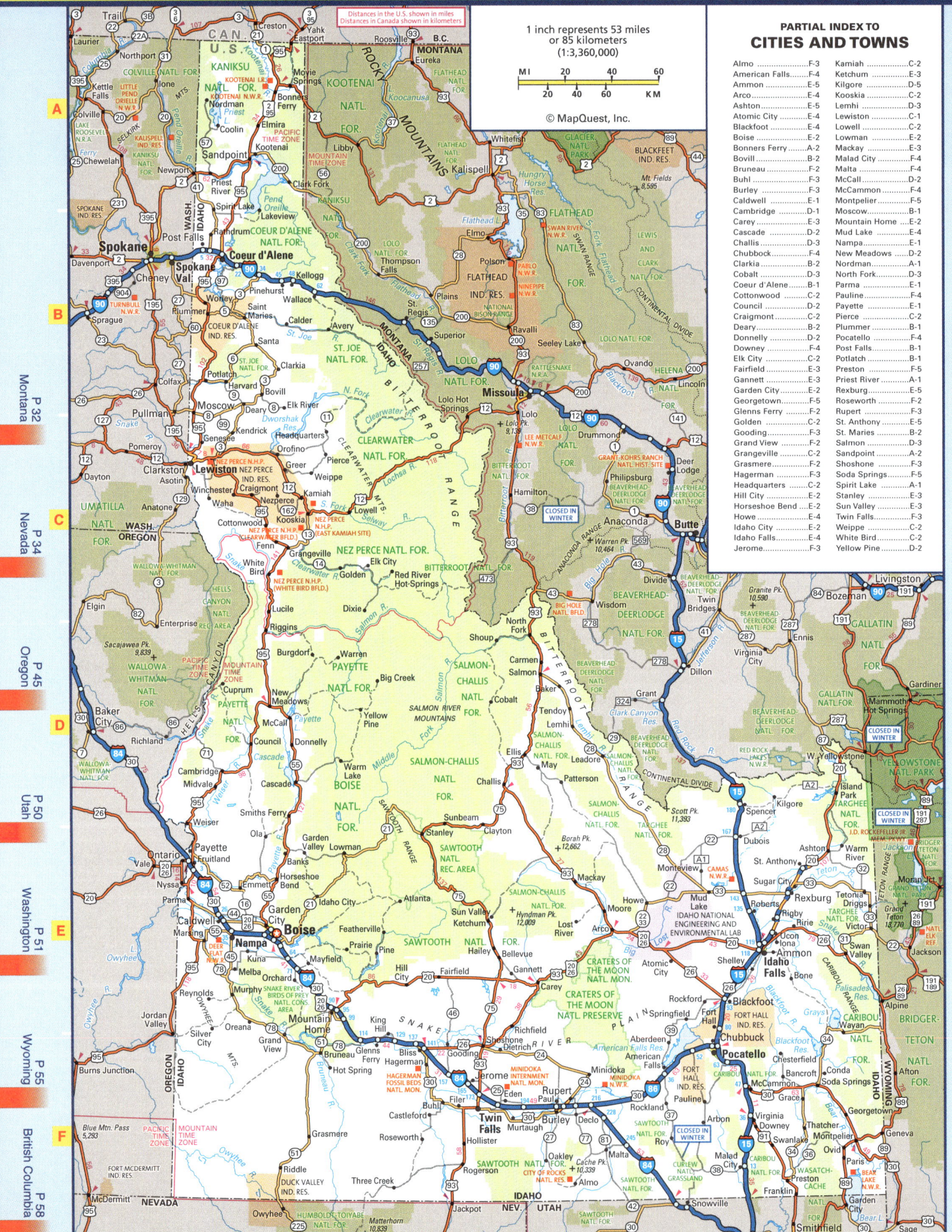

Distances in the U.S. shown in miles
Distances in Canada shown in kilometers

1 inch represents 53 miles
or 85 kilometers
(1:3,360,000)

© MapQuest, Inc.

P 32 Montana
P 34 Nevada
P 45 Oregon
P 50 Utah
P 51 Washington
P 55 Wyoming
P 58 British Columbia

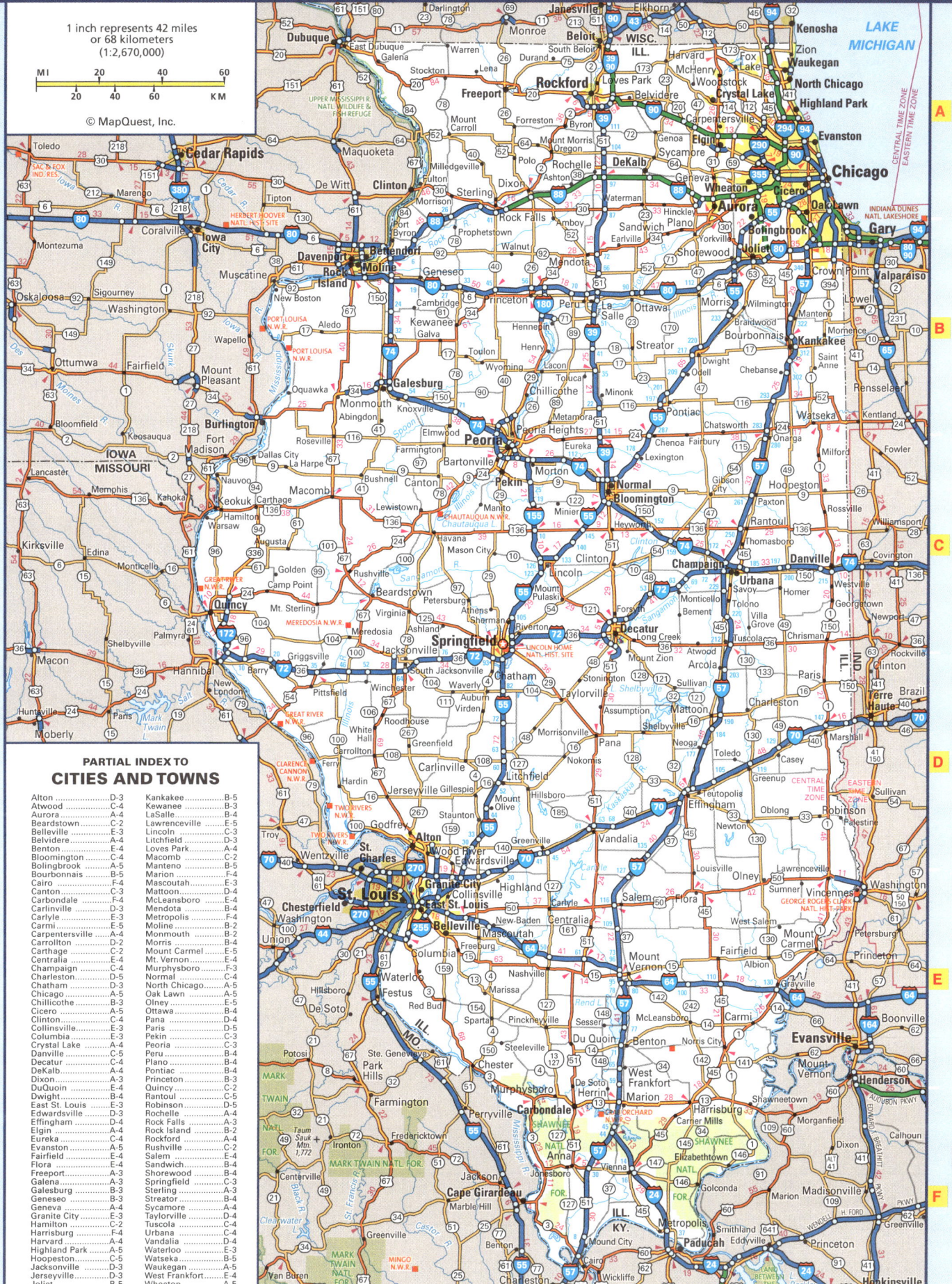

1 inch represents 42 miles
or 68 kilometers
(1:2,670,000)

© MapQuest, Inc.

P 78 N. Chicago
P 80 S. Chicago
P 20 Indiana
P 21 Iowa
P 22 Kentucky
P 31 Missouri
P 54 Wisconsin

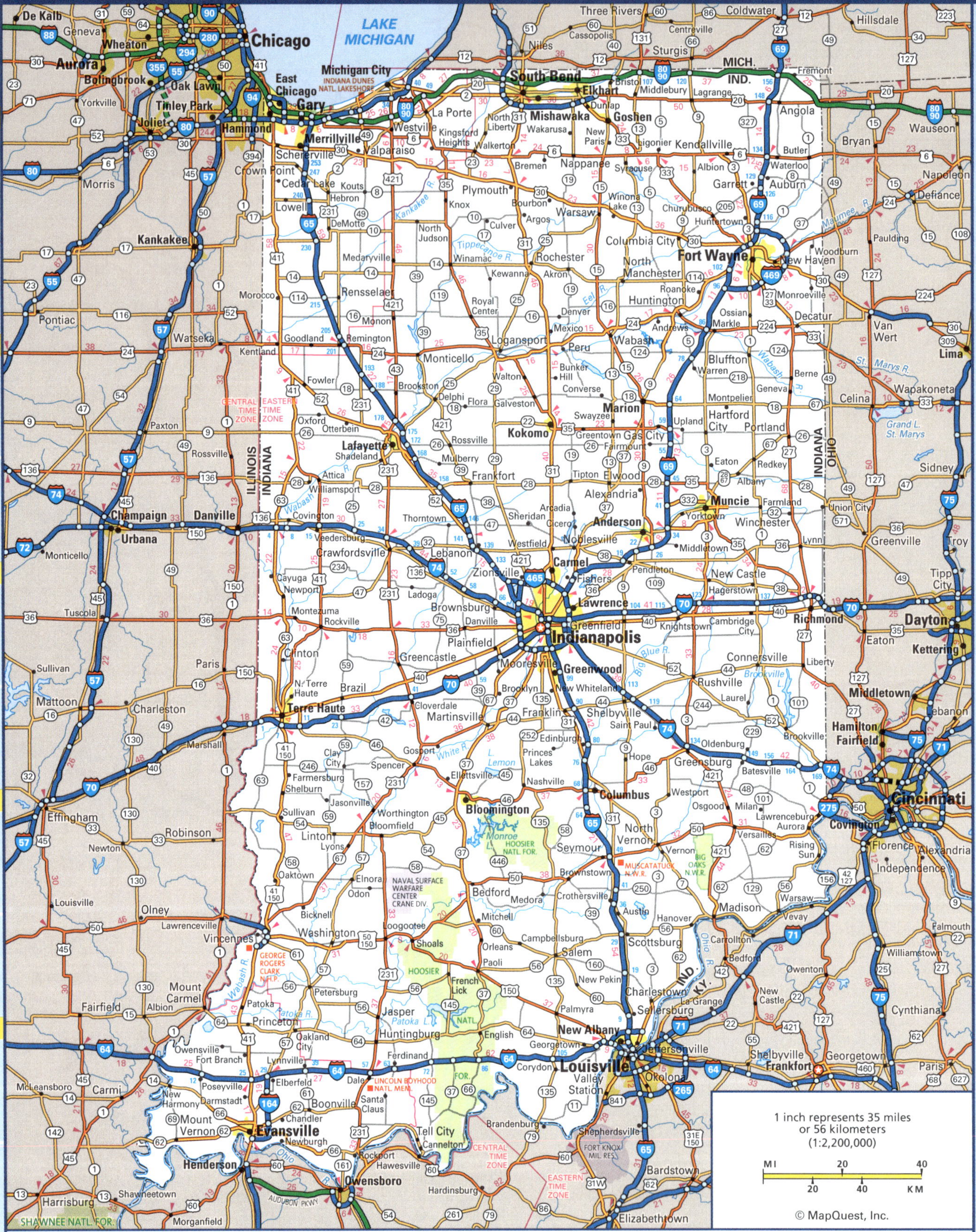

1 inch represents 35 miles or 56 kilometers (1:2,200,000)

© MapQuest, Inc.

P 79 Gary
P 94 Indianapolis
P 19 Illinois
P 22 Kentucky
P 28 Michigan
P 43 Ohio

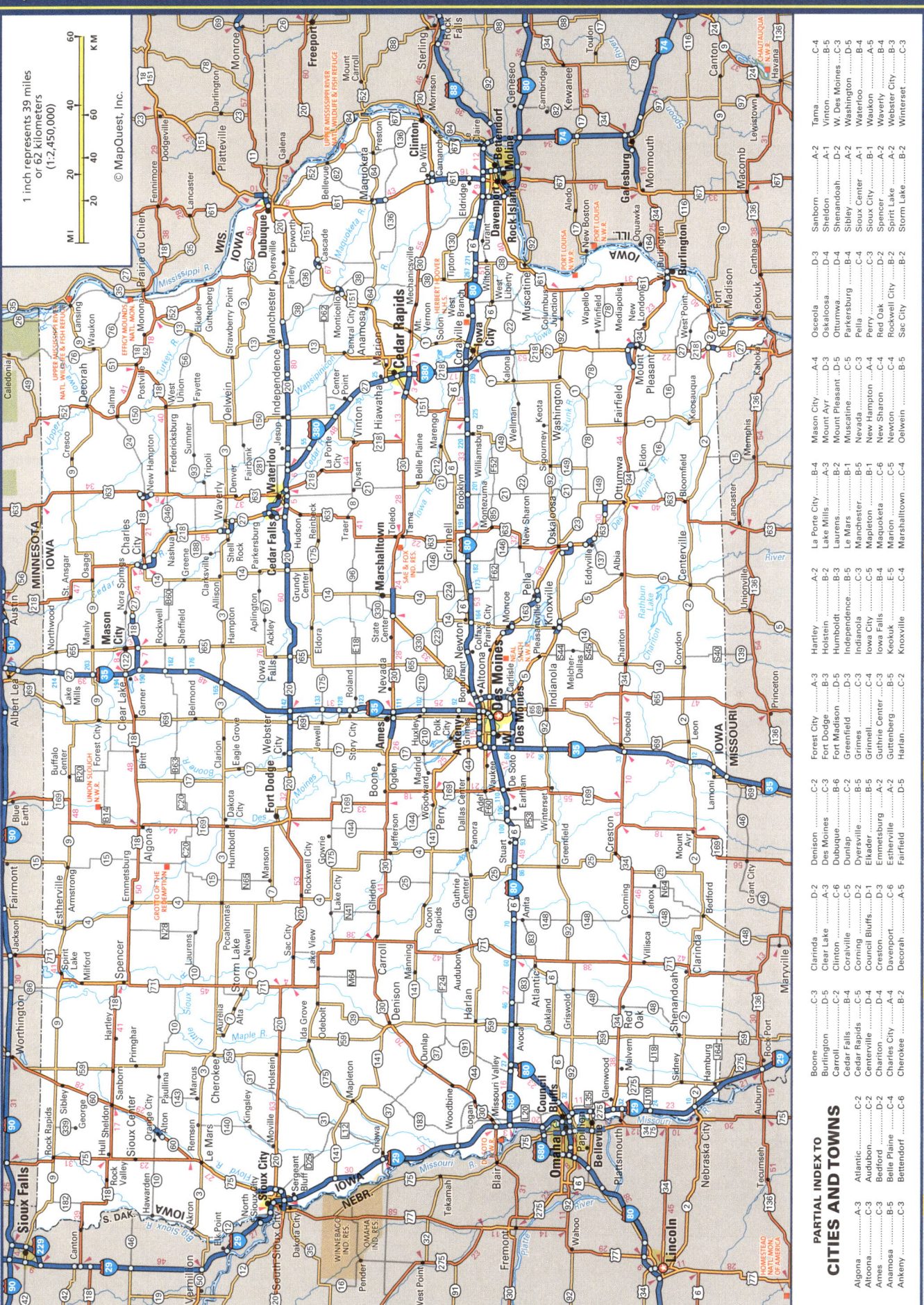

P 87 Des Moines
P 19 Illinois
P 27 Minnesota
P 31 Missouri
P 33 Nebraska
P 47 South Dakota
P 54 Wisconsin

P 104 Memphis
P 110 Nashville
P 6 Alabama
P 9 Arkansas
P 19 Illinois
P P 20 Indiana
P 30 Mississippi
P 31 Missouri

A B C D E F

PARTIAL INDEX TO CITIES AND TOWNS

KENTUCKY

Albany D-6	Glasgow D-6	Mt. Sterling B-8
Alexandria A-7	Greenville C-4	Mt. Vernon C-7
Ashland B-9	Hardin D-3	Mt. Washington ...B-6
Barbourville D-8	Hardinsburg C-5	Munfordville C-6
Bardstown C-6	Harlan D-8	Murray D-3
Beattyville C-8	Harrodsburg C-7	New Castle B-6
Booneville C-8	Hazard C-8	Nicholasville C-7
Bowling Green D-5	Hickman D-2	Owensboro C-4
Brandenburg B-5	Hindman C-9	Owenton B-7
Brooksville B-7	Hopkinsville D-4	Paducah D-3
Brownsville C-5	Hyden C-8	Paintsville C-9
Burkesville D-6	Independence A-7	Paris B-7
Cadiz D-4	Inez C-9	Pikeville C-9
Calhoun C-4	Jackson C-8	Pineville D-8
Campbellsville ...C-6	Jamestown D-6	Prestonburg C-9
Carrollton B-6	Lawrenceburg B-7	Princeton D-4
Catlettsburg B-9	Lebanon C-6	Providence C-4
Cave City D-6	Leitchfield C-5	Radcliff C-6
Clinton D-3	Lexington B-7	Richmond C-7
Columbia D-6	Liberty C-7	Russellville D-5
Corbin D-7	London C-7	Salyersville C-8
Covington A-7	Louisa B-9	Scottsville D-5
Cynthiana B-7	Louisville B-6	Shelbyville B-6
Danville C-7	Madisonville C-4	Somerset C-7
Dixon C-4	Marion C-3	Stanford C-7
Eddyville C-3	Mayfield D-3	Taylorsville B-6
Edmonton D-6	McKee C-8	Tompkinsville D-6
Elizabethtown ...C-6	Middlesboro D-8	Vanceburg B-8
Elkhorn City C-9	Monticello D-7	Versailles B-7
Falmouth B-7	Morehead B-8	Whitesburg C-8
Flemingsburg B-8	Morganfield C-4	Whitley City D-7
Frankfort B-7	Morgantown C-5	Wickliffe D-2
Franklin D-5	Mt. Olivet B-7	Williamsburg D-7
Fulton D-3		Williamstown B-7
Georgetown B-7		Winchester B-7

TENNESSEE

Adamsville F-3	Franklin E-5	New
Allardt D-7	Gatlinburg E-8	Johnsonville E-4
Ashland City D-4	Germantown F-2	New Market E-8
Athens E-7	Greeneville D-9	Newport E-8
Baileyton D-9	Harriman E-7	Oak Ridge E-7
Bartlett F-1	Harrogate D-8	Paris D-3
Benton E-7	Henderson E-3	Parsons E-3
Big Sandy E-3	Hendersonville ...E-4	Pigeon Forge E-8
Blaine D-8	Hohenwald E-4	Pikeville E-6
Brentwood E-5	Hornsby E-3	Portland D-5
Bristol D-9	Huntingdon E-3	Pulaski F-4
Brownsville E-2	Jackson E-3	Ripley E-2
Bulls Gap D-8	Jamestown D-7	Rockwood E-7
Calhoun E-7	Jefferson City ...D-8	Rogersville D-9
Camden E-3	Johnson City D-9	Rutledge D-8
Centerville E-4	Jonesborough D-9	Savannah F-3
Chattanooga F-6	Kingsport D-9	Selmer F-3
Clarksville D-4	Knoxville E-8	Sevierville E-8
Cleveland F-7	La Follette D-7	Shelbyville F-5
Collegedale F-7	Lake City E-7	Signal
Columbia E-4	Lawrenceburg F-4	Mountain F-6
Cookeville E-6	Lebanon E-5	Smyrna E-5
Covington E-2	Lenoir City E-7	Soddy-Daisy F-6
Crab Orchard E-7	Lexington E-3	Somerville F-2
Crossville E-7	Linden E-4	Sparta E-6
Dandridge E-8	Livingston D-6	Spencer E-6
Dayton E-7	Madisonville E-7	Springfield D-5
Dickson E-4	Manchester F-5	Sweetwater E-7
Dover D-4	Maryville E-8	Tazewell D-8
Dresden D-3	McKenzie E-3	Trenton E-3
Ducktown E-7	McMinnville E-6	Tullahoma F-5
Dunlap F-6	Memphis F-1	Union City D-2
Dyersburg E-2	Milan E-3	Waverly E-4
Elizabethton D-9	Milledgeville F-3	Waynesboro F-4
Elkton F-5	Monteagle F-6	Westmoreland D-5
Erin D-4	Monterey E-6	Whiteville F-2
Fayetteville F-5	Morristown D-8	Whitwell F-6
	Murfreesboro E-5	Winchester F-5
	Nashville E-5	Winfield D-7

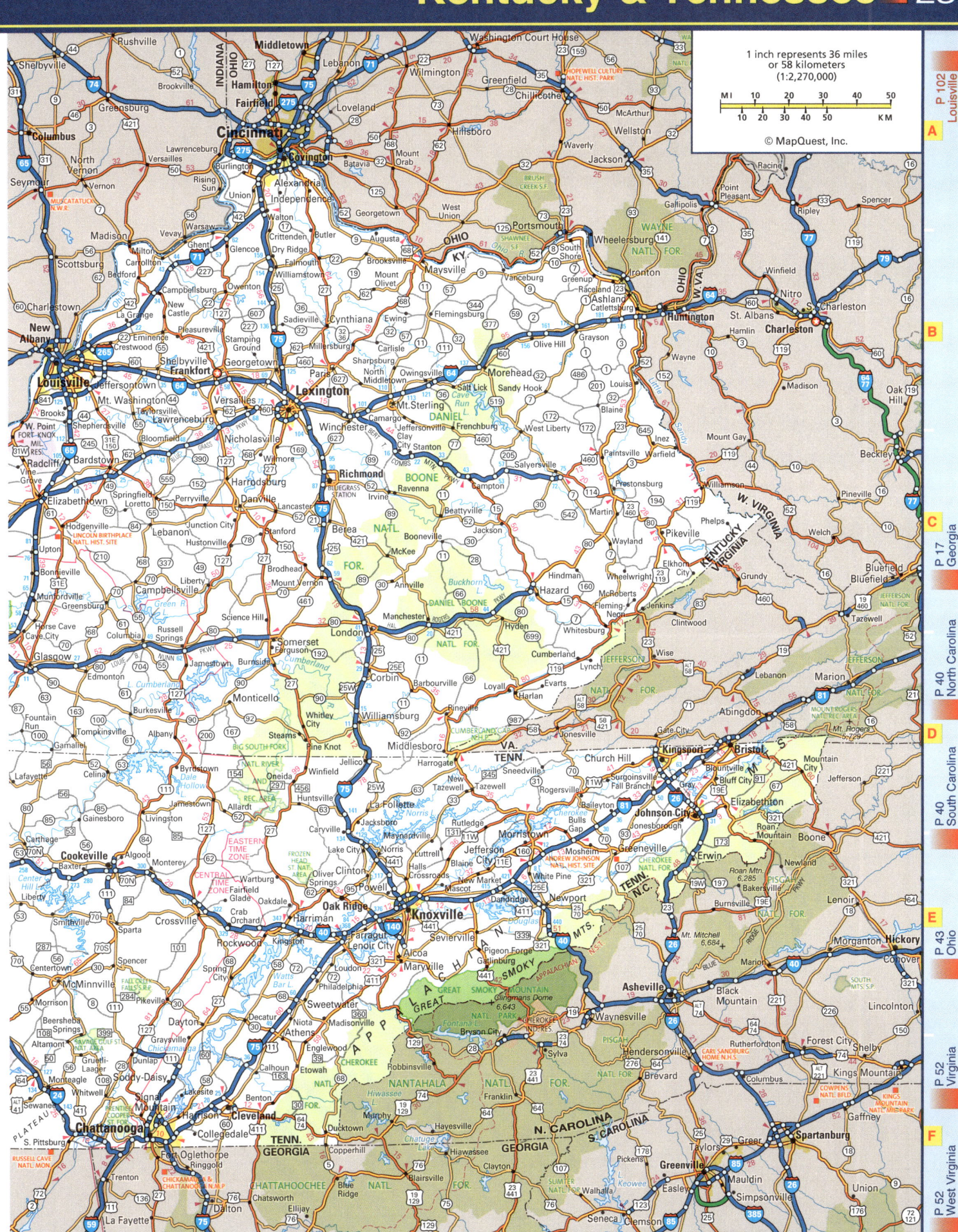

1 inch represents 36 miles
or 58 kilometers
(1:2,270,000)

© MapQuest, Inc.

P 96 Kansas City

P 12 Colorado

P 31 Missouri

P 33 Nebraska

P 44 Oklahoma

PARTIAL INDEX TO CITIES AND TOWNS

City	Grid	City	Grid
Abilene	B-4	Lyons	B-5
Alma	C-5	Manhattan	B-5
Arkansas City	D-5	LaCrosse	C-3
Atchison	B-6	Kinsley	B-3
Atwood	A-1	La Cygne	C-6
Augusta	D-5	Lansing	D-1
Baxter Springs	D-6	Lawrence	B-6
Belleville	A-4	Leavenworth	D-5
Beloit	B-4	Leoti	C-1
Bonner Springs	B-6	Lindsborg	D-1
Burlington	C-5	Newton	C-4
Caney	D-5	Norton	B-5
Chanute	D-5	Oakley	A-4
Clay Center	B-4	Olathe	C-6
Colby	C-6	Ottawa	D-2
Coffeyville	D-6	Osawatomie	C-6
Concordia	A-4	Parsons	D-6
Council Grove	B-5	Perry	B-6
Derby	D-4	Phillipsburg	D-5
Dodge City	D-2	Pittsburg	C-2
Douglass	D-4	Plainville	B-3
El Dorado	C-5	Pratt	A-2
Ellsworth	D-6	Russell	B-3
Emporia	B-4	Sabetha	B-6
Fort Scott	B-1	St. John	B-3
Galena	D-6	Salina	B-4
Garden City	A-4	Seneca	A-5
Goddard	B-5	Smith Center	A-3
Goodland	D-2	Stockton	D-6
Great Bend	D-2	Sublette	D-2
Greensburg	D-4	Syracuse	C-1
Halstead	C-5	Topeka	B-3
Hays	D-1	Tribune	D-3
Haysville	B-4	Ulysses	B-4
Hiawatha	C-5	Wakeeney	A-4
Hill City	C-6	Wamego	B-2
Hillsboro	D-6	Wellington	D-4
Hoisington	B-5	Wichita	D-5
Holton	C-3	Winfield	A-3
Hoxie	A-5	Yates Center	C-5
Hugoton	C-6		
Hutchinson	B-1		
Iola	D-5		
Jetmore	B-3		
Johnson City	A-6		
Junction City	B-2		
Kansas City	C-3		
McPherson	C-6		
Meade	B-6		
Medicine Lodge	D-3		
Minneola	C-1		
Mound City	C-6		
Ness City	C-4		

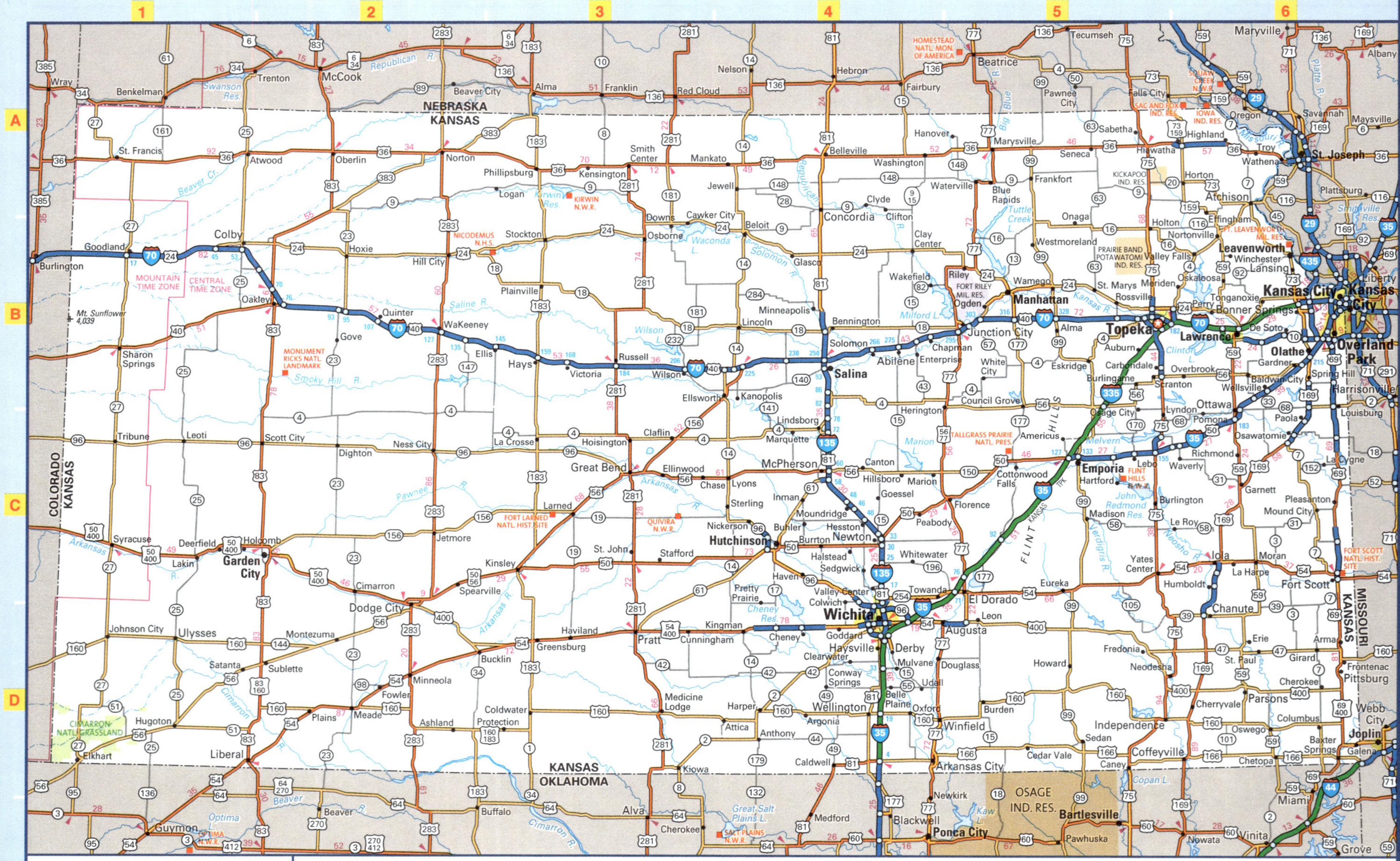

1 inch represents 43 miles or 70 kilometers (1:2,750,000)

MI 20 40 60
KM 20 40 60

© MapQuest, Inc.

N

PARTIAL INDEX TO CITIES AND TOWNS

Abbeville	D-5
Abita Springs	D-5
Alexandria	C-3
Arcadia	A-2
Baker	C-4
Bastrop	A-3
Baton Rouge	D-4
Bayou Cane	D-5
Bogalusa	C-5
Bossier City	A-1
Breaux Bridge	D-3
Bunkie	C-3
Carencro	D-3
Chalmette	D-5
Columbia	B-3
Crowley	D-3
Cut Off	E-4
De Ridder	C-2
Donaldsonville	D-4
Eunice	D-3
Franklin	D-3
Grambling	A-2
Gonzales	D-4
Hammond	D-4
Houma	E-4
Jeanerette	D-3
Jennings	D-3
Jonesville	B-3
Lacombe	D-5
Lafayette	D-3
Lake Charles	D-2
Lake Providence	A-4
Larose	E-4
Leesville	C-2
Mandeville	D-5
Mansfield	B-1
Marksville	C-3
Marrero	D-5
Metairie	D-5
Minden	A-2
Monroe	A-3
Morgan City	E-4
Moss Bluff	D-2
Natchitoches	B-2
New Iberia	D-3
New Roads	C-3
Oak Grove	A-3
Oakdale	C-2
Opelousas	C-3
Pineville	C-3
Plaquemine	D-4
Port Allen	D-4
Rayne	D-3
Raceland	D-4
Ruston	A-2
Shreveport	A-1
Slidell	D-5
Springhill	A-2
Sulphur	D-2
Thibodaux	D-4
Ville Platte	D-3
Westlake	D-2
Winnfield	B-2
Winnsboro	B-3
Zachary	C-4

1 inch represents 43 miles or 68 kilometers (1:2,700,000)

© MapQuest, Inc.

GULF OF MEXICO

P 73 Baton Rouge
P 111 New Orleans
P 9 Arkansas
P 30 Mississippi
P 48 Texas

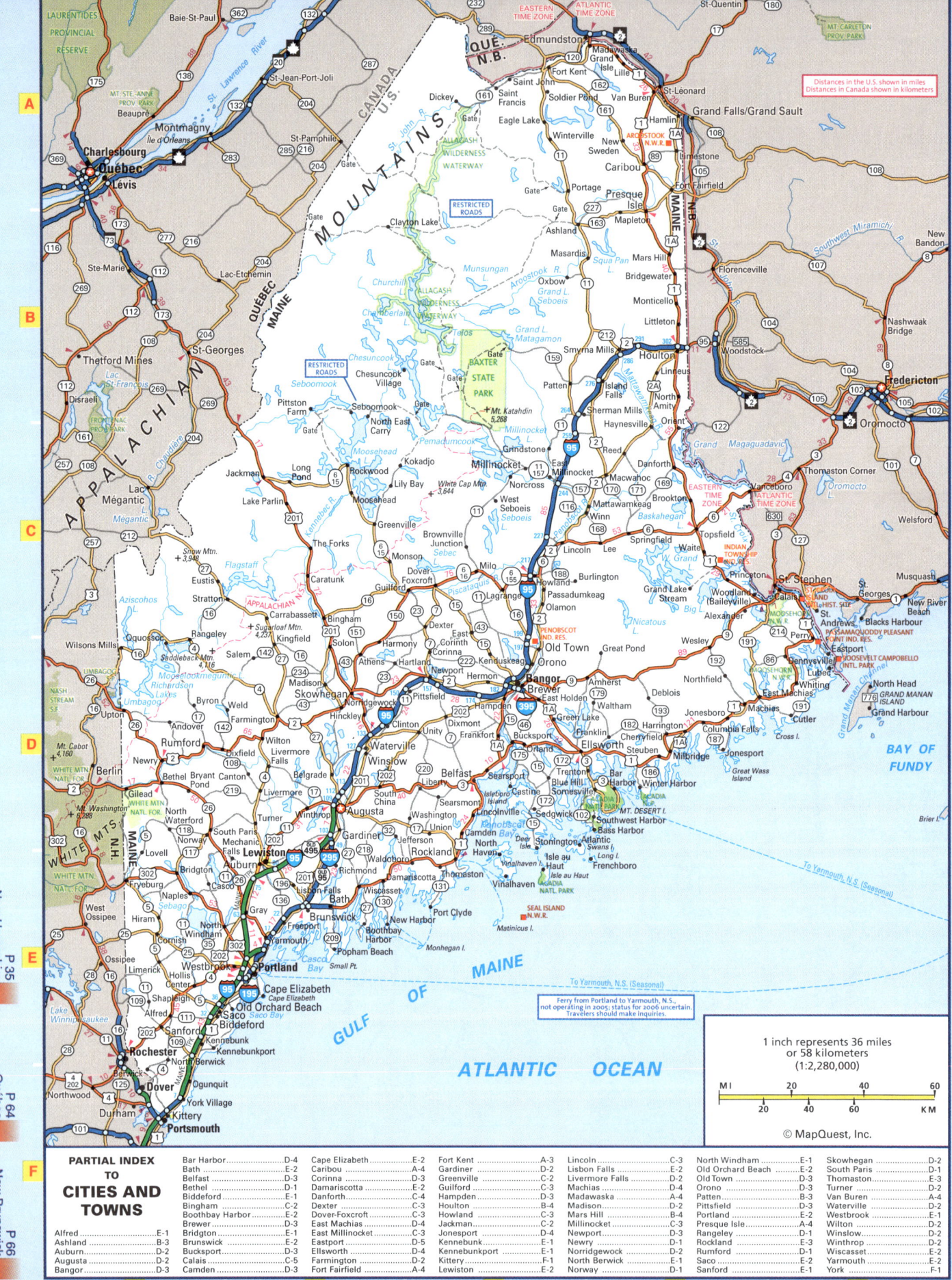

Distances in the U.S. shown in miles
Distances in Canada shown in kilometers

1 inch represents 36 miles
or 58 kilometers
(1:2,280,000)

© MapQuest, Inc.

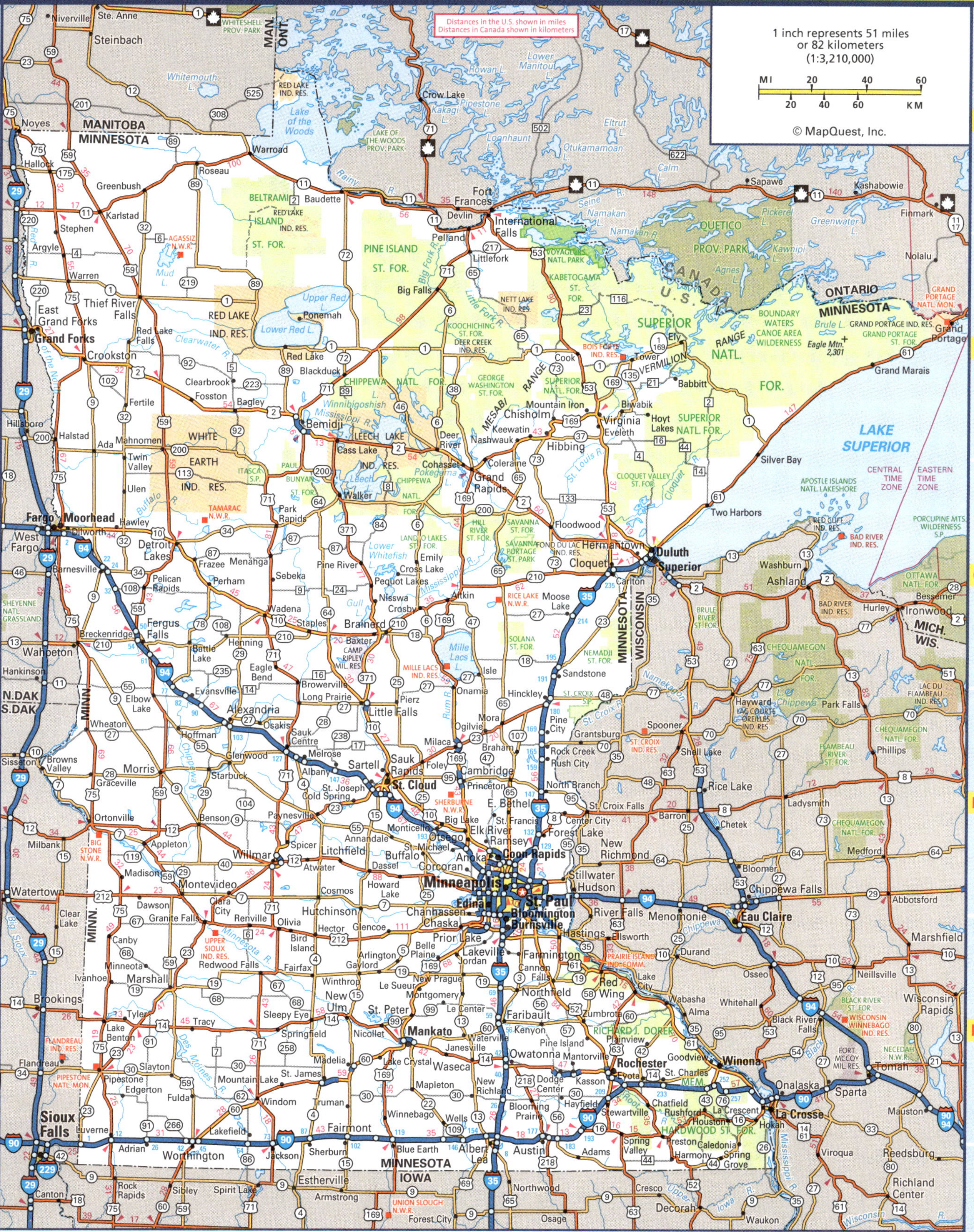

1 inch represents 51 miles
or 82 kilometers
(1:3,210,000)

MI 20 40 60
KM 20 40 60

© MapQuest, Inc.

Distances in the U.S. shown in miles
Distances in Canada shown in kilometers

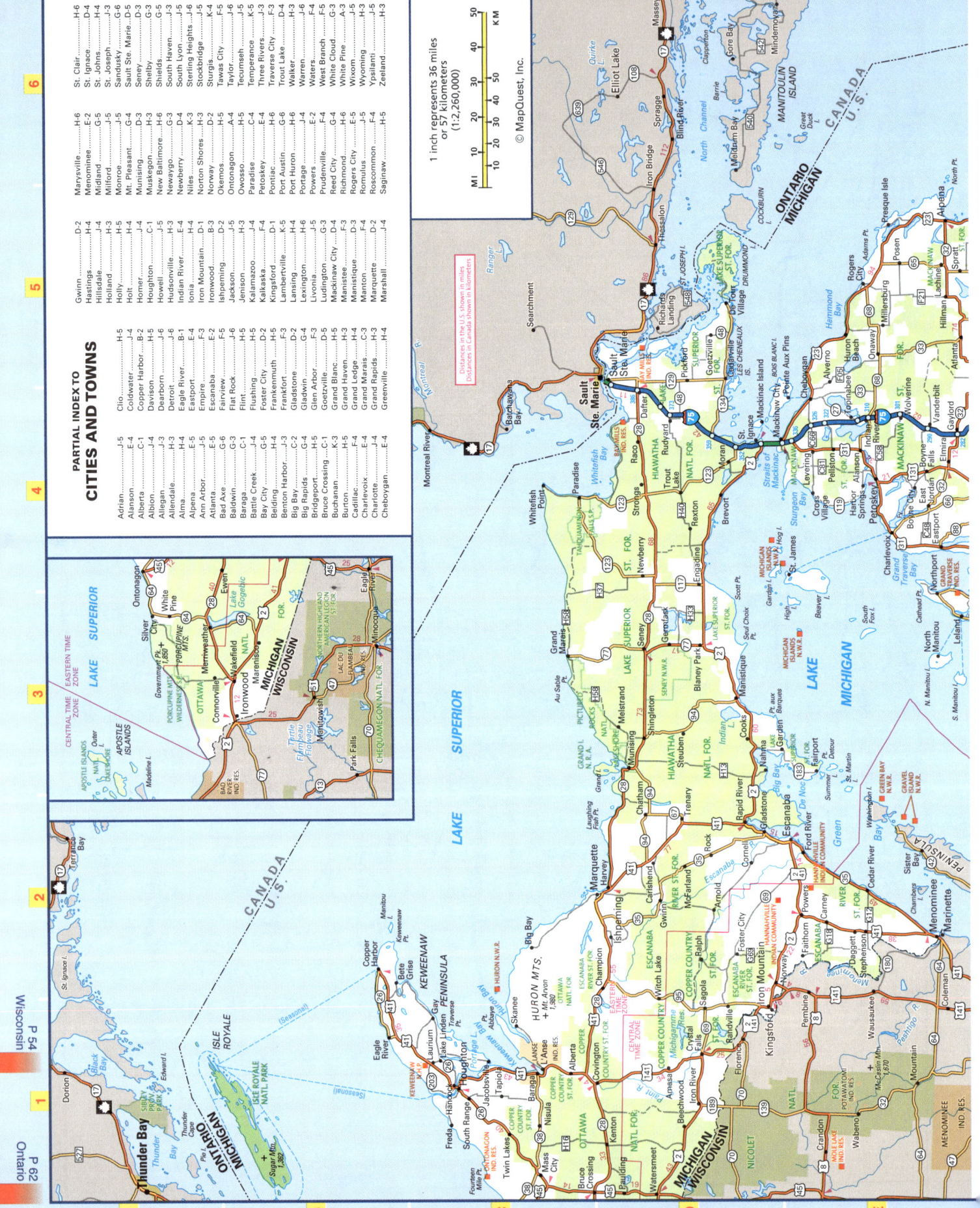

1 inch represents 36 miles
or 57 kilometers
(1:2,260,000)

© MapQuest, Inc.

Distances in the U.S. shown in miles
Distances in Canada shown in kilometers

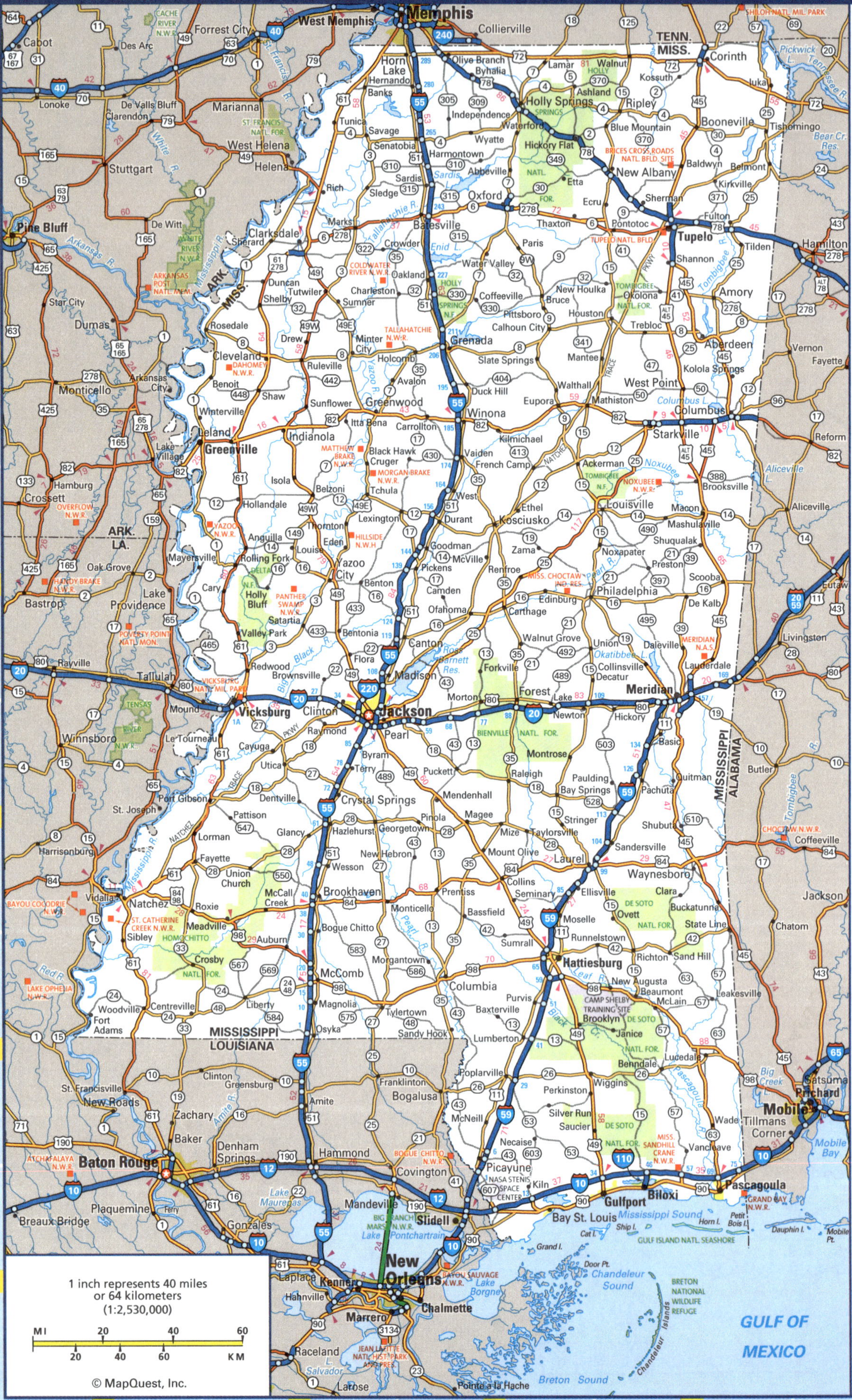

N

1 inch represents 40 miles
or 64 kilometers
(1:2,530,000)

© MapQuest, Inc.

GULF OF MEXICO

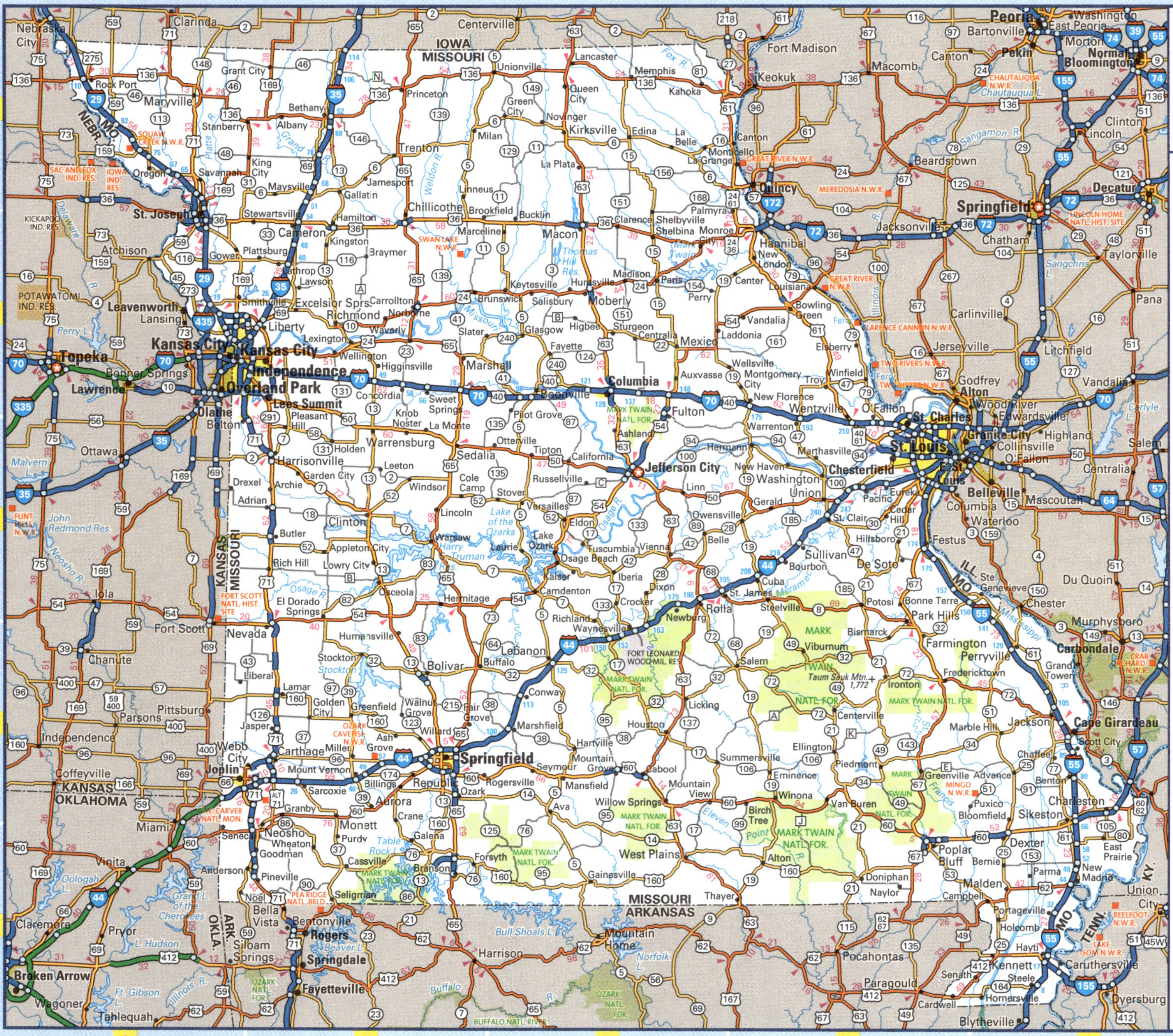

N

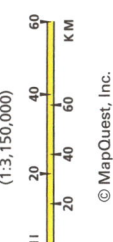

1 inch represents 50 miles
or 80 kilometers
(1:3,150,000)

© MapQuest, Inc.

MI 20 40 60
KM 20 40 60

PARTIAL INDEX TO CITIES AND TOWNS

Alton	A-3
Anderson	D-3
Appleton City	C-2
Ash Grove	D-2
Aurora	D-3
Belton	C-1
Bethany	B-3
Bolivar	D-3
Bonne Terre	E-5
Boonville	C-3
Bowling Green	A-1
Branson	D-3
Brunswick	B-3
Cabool	D-2
Camdenton	C-3
Canton	A-3
Cape Girardeau	D-5
Carrollton	B-4
Carthage	D-2
Caruthersville	E-5
Cassville	E-2
Charleston	D-4
Chesterfield	B-2
Chillicothe	B-4
Clinton	C-2
Columbia	C-3
Cuba	C-4
DeSoto	B-2
Dexter	E-4
Doniphan	D-2
Edina	A-3
Eldon	C-3
Eldorado Springs	D-2
Ellington	B-4
Elsberry	A-2
Eminence	D-4
Excelsior Springs	B-2
Farmington	C-4
Festus	B-3
Flat River	E-2
Forsyth	D-3
Fredericktown	C-4
Fulton	B-3
Gainesville	D-5
Gallatin	A-2
Greenfield	D-2
Greenville	D-4
Hamilton	B-4
Hannibal	A-2
Harrisonville	C-2
Hermitage	D-2
Houston	B-2
Independence	B-2
Ironton	C-2
Jackson	D-5
Jefferson City	C-3
Joplin	D-1
Kansas City	B-1
Kennett	E-5
Keytesville	A-3
King City	A-2
Kirksville	A-3
LaBelle	A-3
LaGrange	A-3
Lake Ozark	C-3
Lancaster	A-3
LaPlata	A-3
Lebanon	C-2
Liberty	B-2
Licking	D-3
Louisiana	B-4
Macon	B-3
Madison	B-3
Malden	E-5
Marshall	B-3
Marshfield	D-3
Maryville	A-1
Memphis	A-3
Mexico	B-3
Moberly	B-3
Monett	D-2
Monroe City	D-5
Montgomery City	B-4
Mountain Grove	D-3
Nevada	D-2
Neosho	E-2
O'Fallon	B-2
Owensville	C-4
Ozark	D-3
Paris	B-3
Perryville	D-5
Piedmont	D-4
Poplar Bluff	E-4
Potosi	C-4
Princeton	A-2
Republic	D-2
Richland	C-3
Richmond	B-2
Rock Port	A-1
Rolla	C-4
St. Charles	B-2
St. James	C-4
St. Joseph	B-1
St. Louis	B-2
Salem	C-4
Savannah	A-2
Sedalia	C-3
Shelbina	A-3
Sikeston	D-5
Springfield	D-2
Stanberry	A-2
Sullivan	C-4
Summersville	D-3
Trenton	A-2
Union	B-2
Unionville	A-2
Vandalia	B-3
Versailles	C-3
Viburnum	C-4
Vienna	C-3
Warrensburg	C-2
Warrenton	B-2
Warsaw	C-3
Washington	B-2
Waynesville	C-3
Webb City	D-1
Wentzville	B-2
West Plains	D-3
Willow Springs	D-3
Winona	D-4

P 96 Kansas City
P 128 St. Louis
P 9 Arkansas
P 19 Illinois
P 21 Iowa
P 22 Tennessee
P 24 Kansas
P 33 Nebraska
P 44 Oklahoma

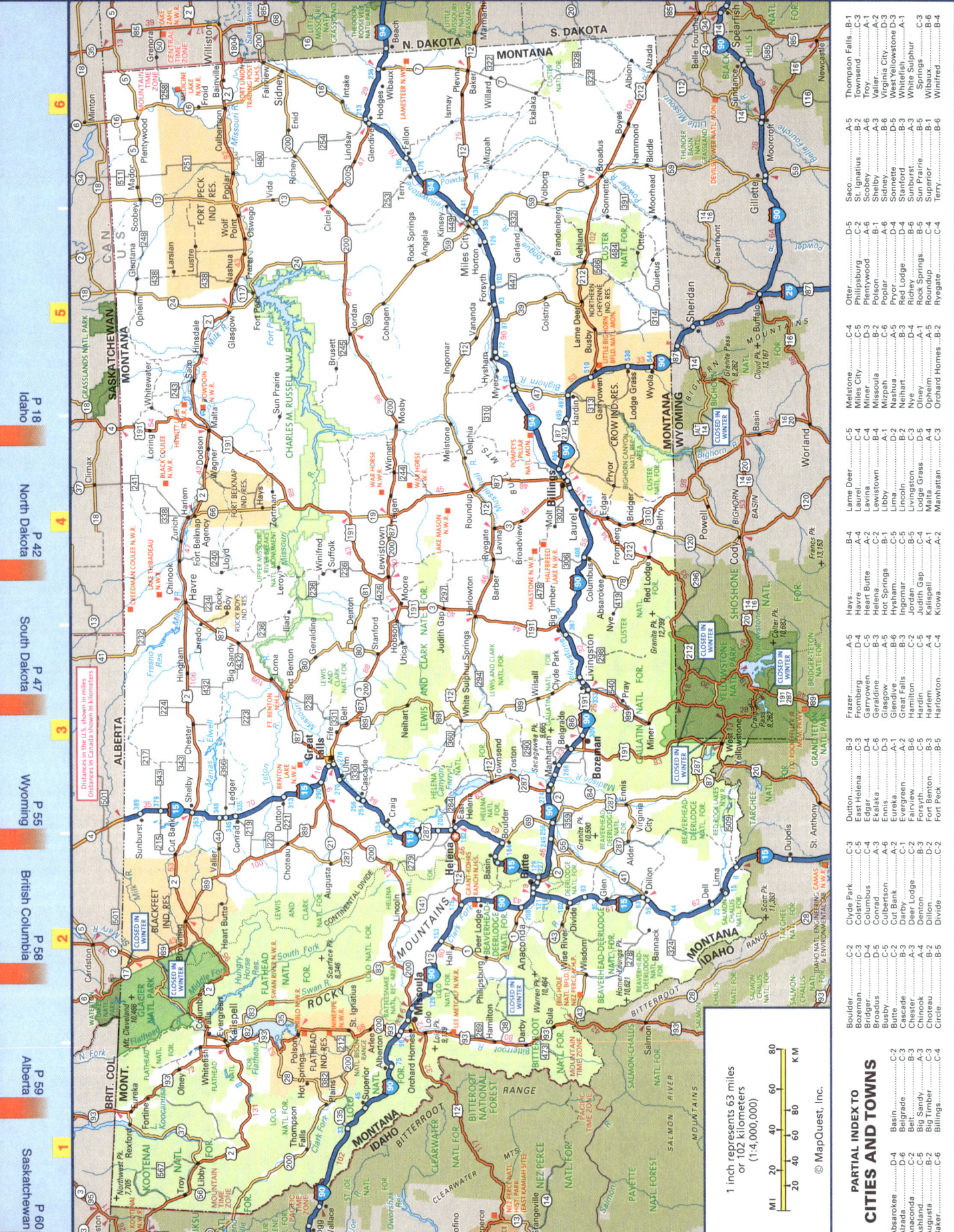

1 inch represents 63 miles or 102 kilometers (1:4,000,000)

© MapQuest, Inc.

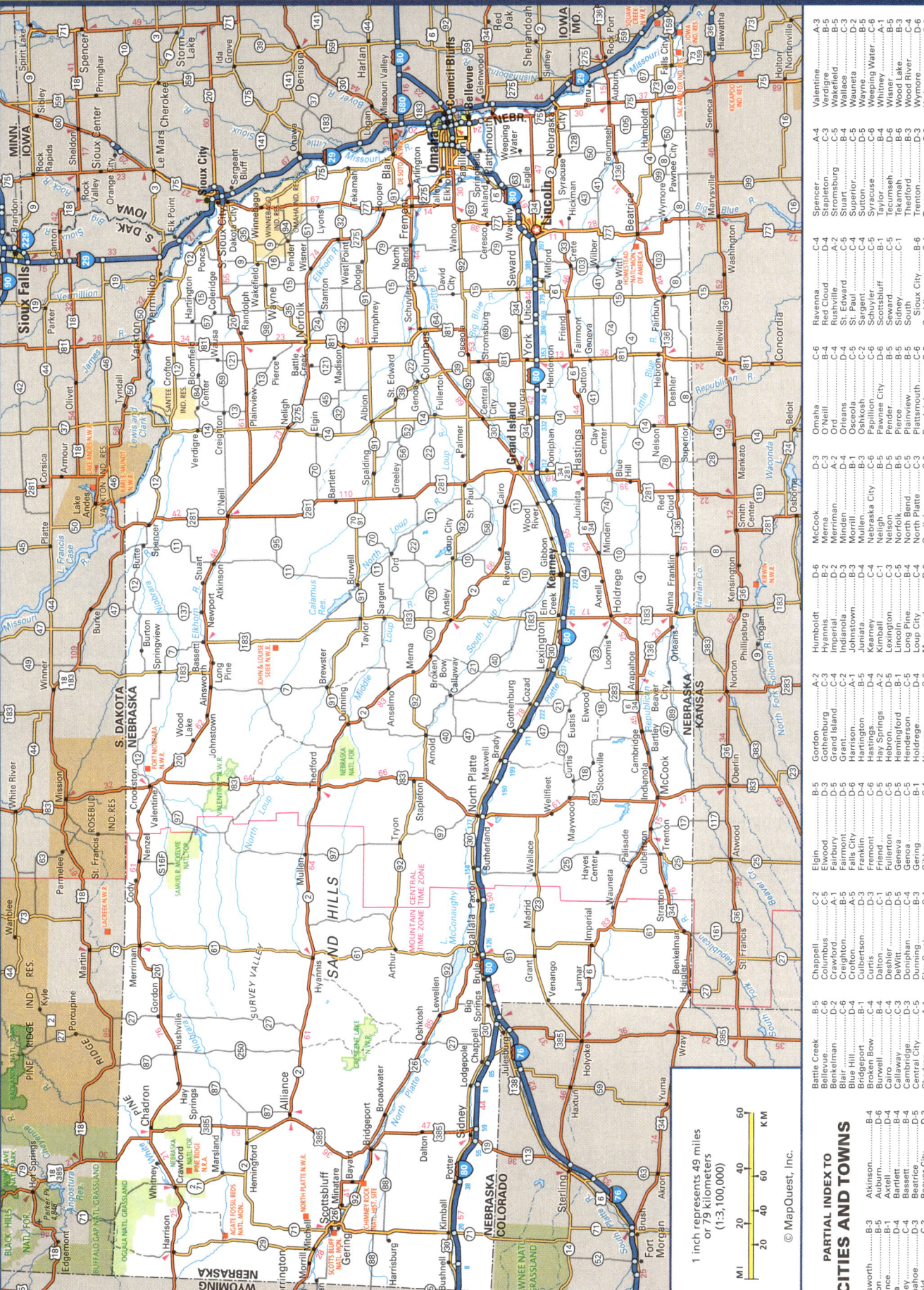

P 117 Omaha

P 12 Colorado

P 21 Iowa

P 24 Kansas

P 31 Missouri

P 47 South Dakota

P 55 Wyoming

1 inch represents 49 miles
or 79 kilometers
(1:3,100,000)

© MapQuest, Inc.

1 inch represents 52 miles
or 84 kilometers
(1:3,300,000)

© MapQuest, Inc.

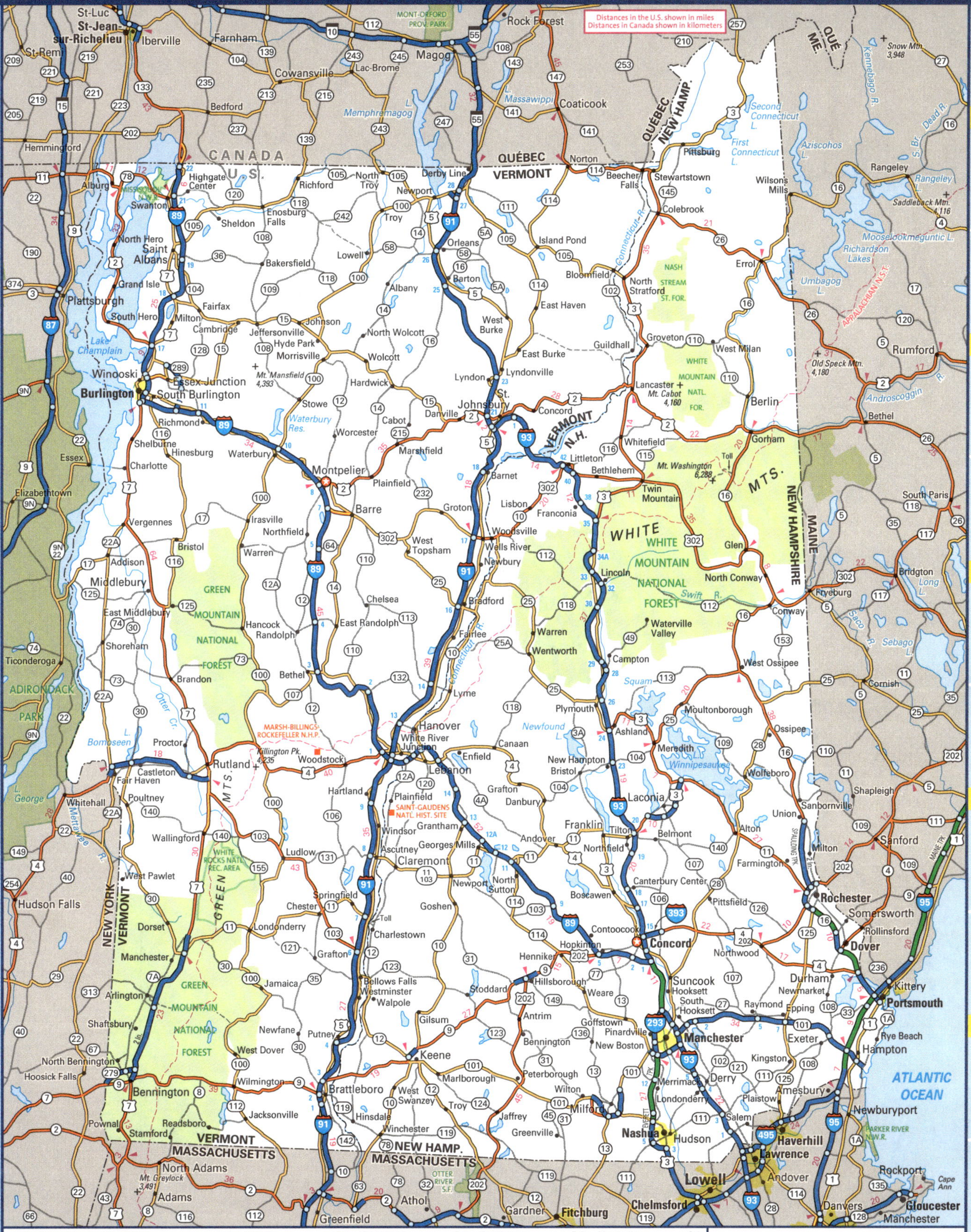

Distances in the U.S. shown in miles
Distances in Canada shown in kilometers

St-Luc
St-Jean-sur-Richelieu
St-Rem
Iberville
Farnham
Rock Forest
Snow Mtn. 3,948

QUÉBEC

VERMONT

Second Connecticut

First Connecticut

Pittsburg

Wilson's Mills
Rangeley

Saddleback Mtn. 4,116

Colebrook

Errol

Mooselookmeguntic L.

Richardson Lakes

Umbagog

CANADA
U.S.

QUÉBEC

Norton
Beecher Falls
Stewartstown

North Stratford

Groveton
West Milan

Berlin
Androscoggin R.
Bethel

Old Speck Mtn. 4,180

South Paris

Burlington
Winooski
Essex Junction
South Burlington

WHITE MOUNTAIN NATL. FOR.

Lancaster
Mt. Cabot 4,160

Whitefield
Littleton
Bethlehem

Mt. Washington 6,288

WHITE MOUNTAIN NATIONAL FOREST

MTS.

NEW HAMPSHIRE

Fryeburg
Bridgton
Sebago L.

Montpelier
Barre

Lincoln

North Conway
Conway

Cornish

GREEN MOUNTAIN NATIONAL FOREST

Middlebury
Warren

Waterville Valley
Campton
West Ossippee

Wolfeboro
Shapleigh

Rutland
Woodstock

Hanover
White River Junction
Lebanon

Plymouth
Ashland
Meredith

Lake Winnipesaukee

Sanbornville
Sanford

New Hampton
Bristol
Laconia

Rochester
Somersworth
Dover

NEW YORK
VERMONT

Franklin
Tilton

Concord

Portsmouth
Kittery

Bennington
Manchester

ATLANTIC OCEAN

Nashua
Hudson

Lowell
Chelmsford

VERMONT
MASSACHUSETTS

NEW HAMP.
MASSACHUSETTS

Greenfield
Athol
Gardner
Fitchburg

---

1 inch represents 23 miles
or 36 kilometers
(1:1,430,000)

MI   10   20   30
KM   10   20   30

© MapQuest, Inc.

P 14 Massachusetts
P 26 Maine
P 38 New York
P 64 Québec

N

PARTIAL INDEX TO CITIES AND TOWNS

Absecon E-3
Asbury Park C-4
Atlantic City E-3
Avalon F-3
Bay Point E-2
Beach Haven E-4
Beachwood D-4
Belmar C-4
Berlin D-2
Bernardsville B-3
Blackwood D-2
Boonton B-3
Bridgeton E-2
Brigantine E-3
Browns Mills D-3
Buena E-2
Burlington D-2
Butler A-3
Camden D-2
Cape May F-2
Chatham B-3
Cherry Hill D-2
Clifton B-4
Cranford B-4
Dover B-3
East Brunswick C-3
East Orange B-4
Eatontown C-4
Edison C-3
Elizabeth B-4
Englewood B-4
Fairfield B-3
Freehold C-4
Glassboro D-2
Gloucester City D-2
Green Bank E-3
Hackensack B-4
Hackettstown B-2
Hainesville A-2
Hammonton E-2
Highlands C-4
Hightstown C-3
Hopatcong B-3
Jamesburg C-3
Jersey City B-4
Keansburg C-4
Lakewood D-4
Linden B-4
Lindenwold D-2
Livingston B-4
Long Branch C-4
Madison B-3
Manalapan C-3
Manasquan D-4
Manville C-3
Margate City E-3
Marlboro C-4
Matawan C-4
Middlesex B-3
Millville E-2
Moorestown D-2
Morristown B-3
Mount Holly D-2
New Brunswick C-3
Newark B-4
Newton A-3
Oakland A-4
Ocean City F-3
Paramus B-4
Passaic B-4
Paterson B-4
Paulsboro D-2
Perth Amboy C-4
Phillipsburg B-2
Plainfield B-3
Pleasantville E-3
Point Pleasant D-4
Princeton C-3
Red Bank C-4
Ridgewood A-4
Salem E-1
Sayreville C-4
Seaside Heights D-4
Ship Bottom E-4
Silverton D-4
Somers Point E-3
Somerville B-3
South River C-3
Sparta A-3
Stone Harbor F-3
Toms River D-4
Trenton C-3
Union B-4
Union City B-4
Vernon A-3
Villas F-2
Vineland E-2
Warren Grove D-3
Washington B-2
Wayne B-4
West Milford A-3
Wildwood F-3
Williamstown E-2
Willingboro D-2
Woodbury D-2

1 inch represents 18 miles
or 29 kilometers
(1:1,160,000)

© MapQuest, Inc.

ATLANTIC OCEAN

UTAH • COLORADO • NEW MEXICO • ARIZONA • TEXAS • OKLAHOMA

Scale
1 inch represents 53 miles or 86 kilometers
(1:3,380,000)

MI 20 40 60
KM 20 40 60

© MapQuest, Inc.

Distances in the U.S. shown in miles
Distances in Mexico shown in kilometers

ABQ 123

CITIES AND TOWNS

N

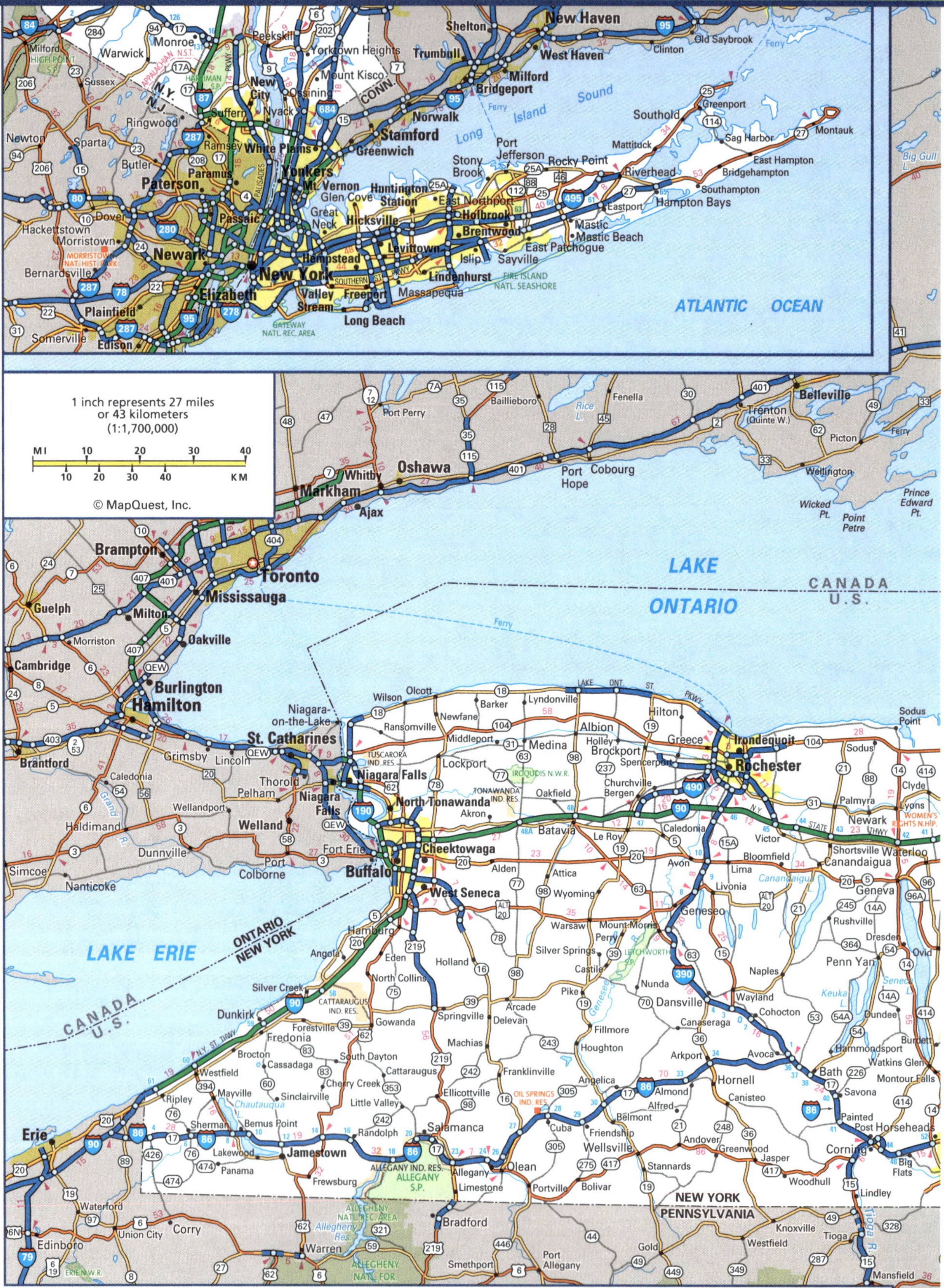

1 inch represents 27 miles
or 43 kilometers
(1:1,700,000)

© MapQuest, Inc.

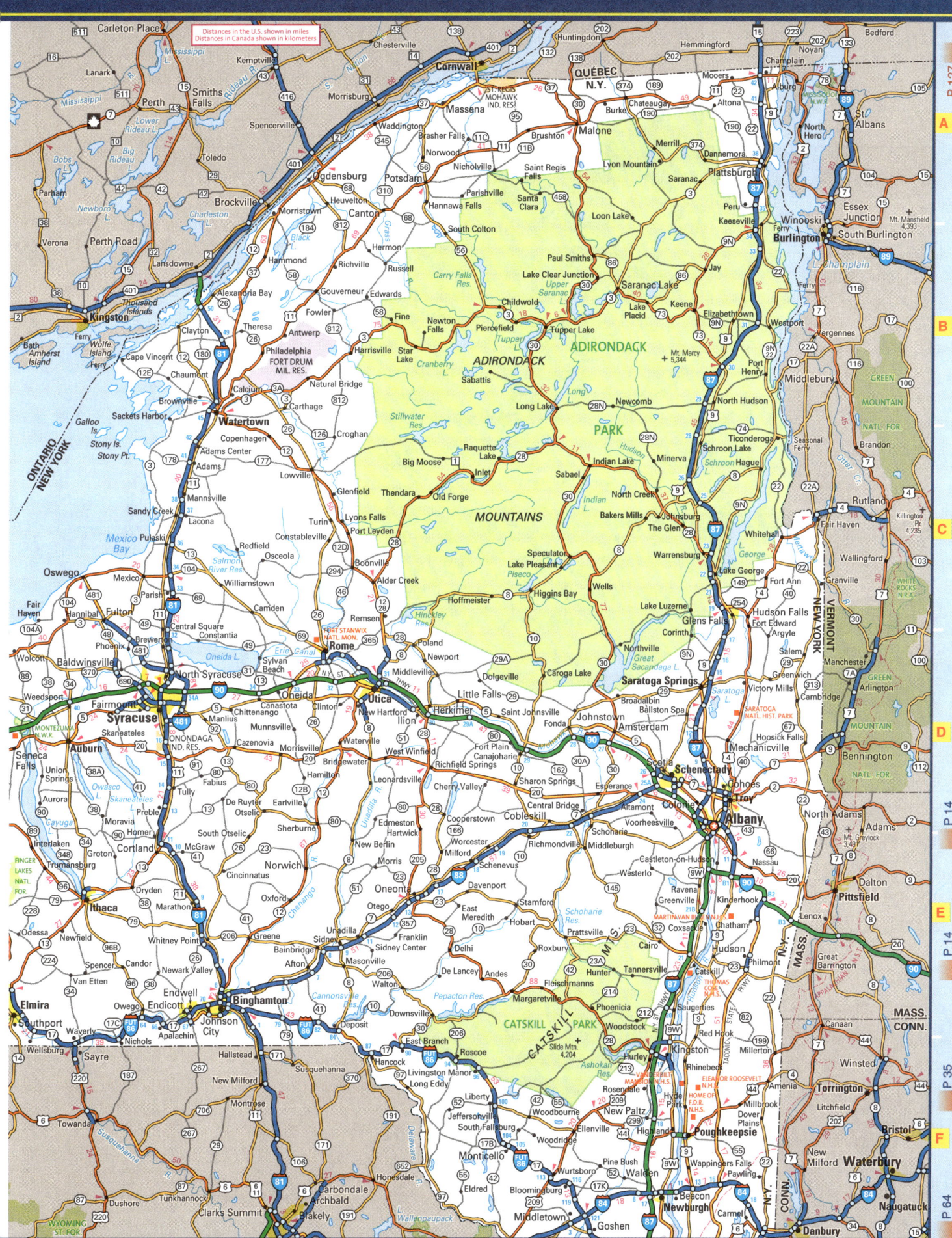

N

1 inch represents 36 miles
or 58 kilometers
(1:2,270,000)

MI 10   20   30   40   50
KM 10 20 30 40 50

© MapQuest, Inc.

P 73 Charleston

P 77 Charlotte

P 138 Winston-Salem

P 17 Georgia

P 22 Tennessee

P 52 Virginia

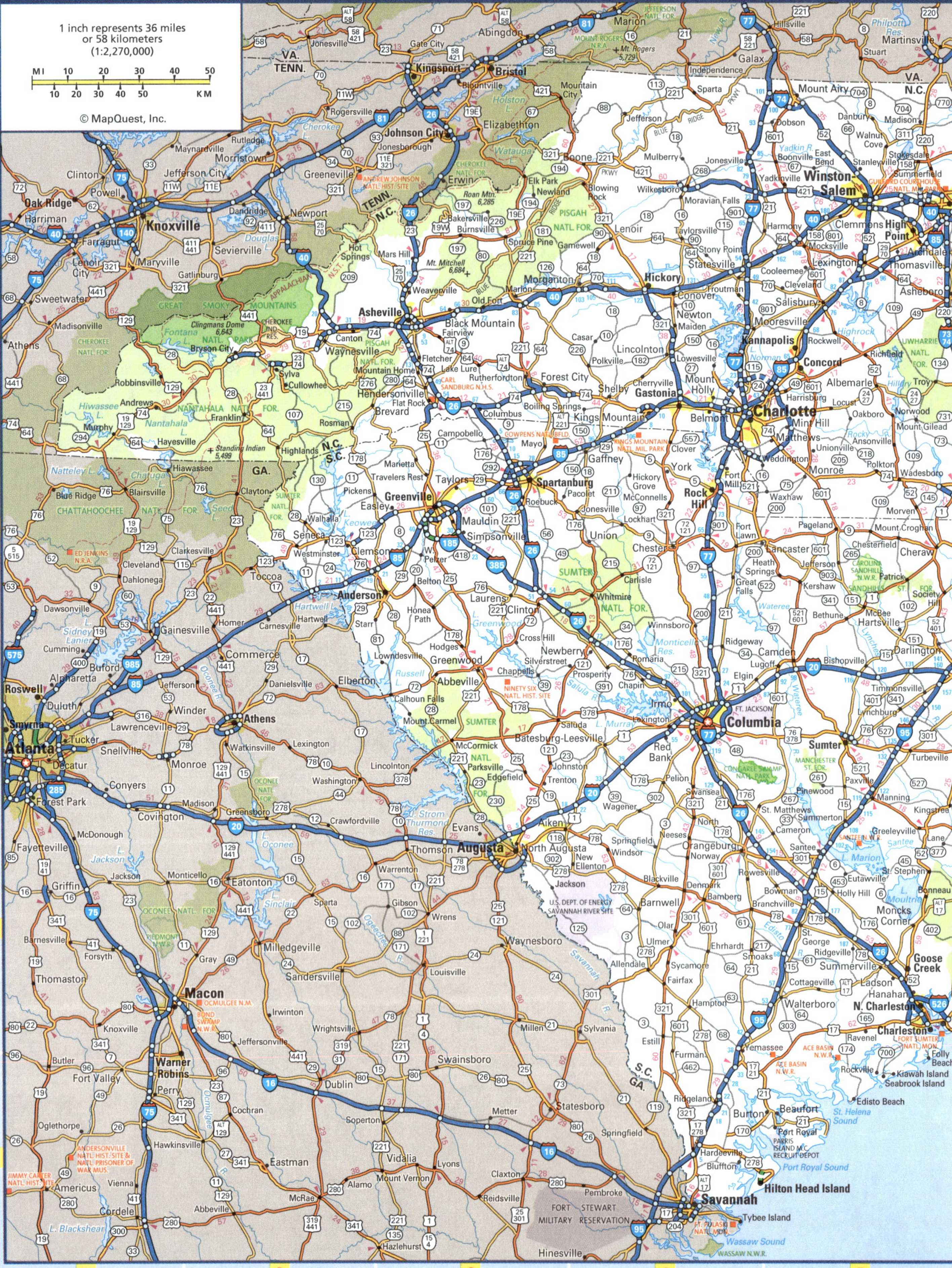

A

B

C

D

E

F

1   2   3   4   5

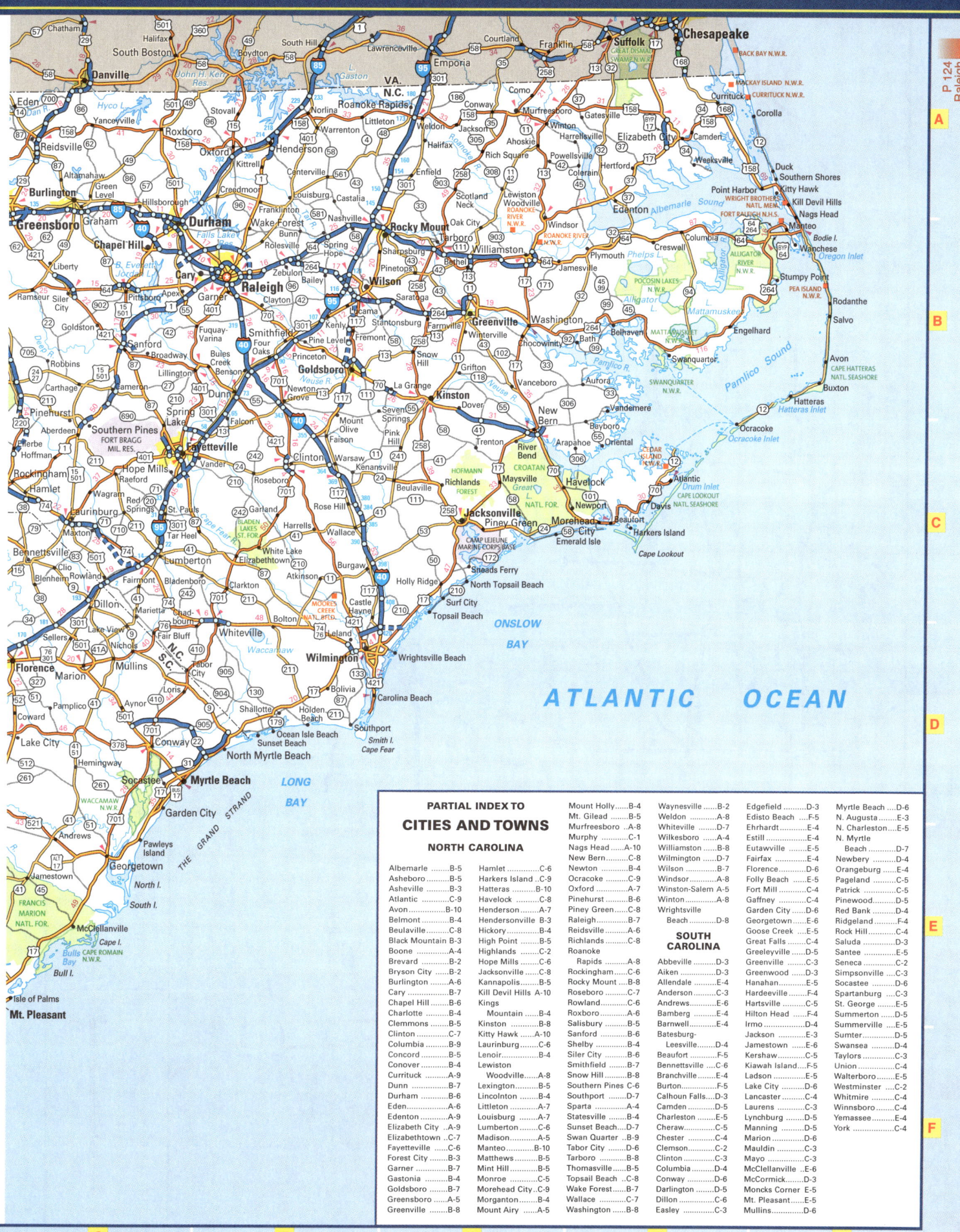

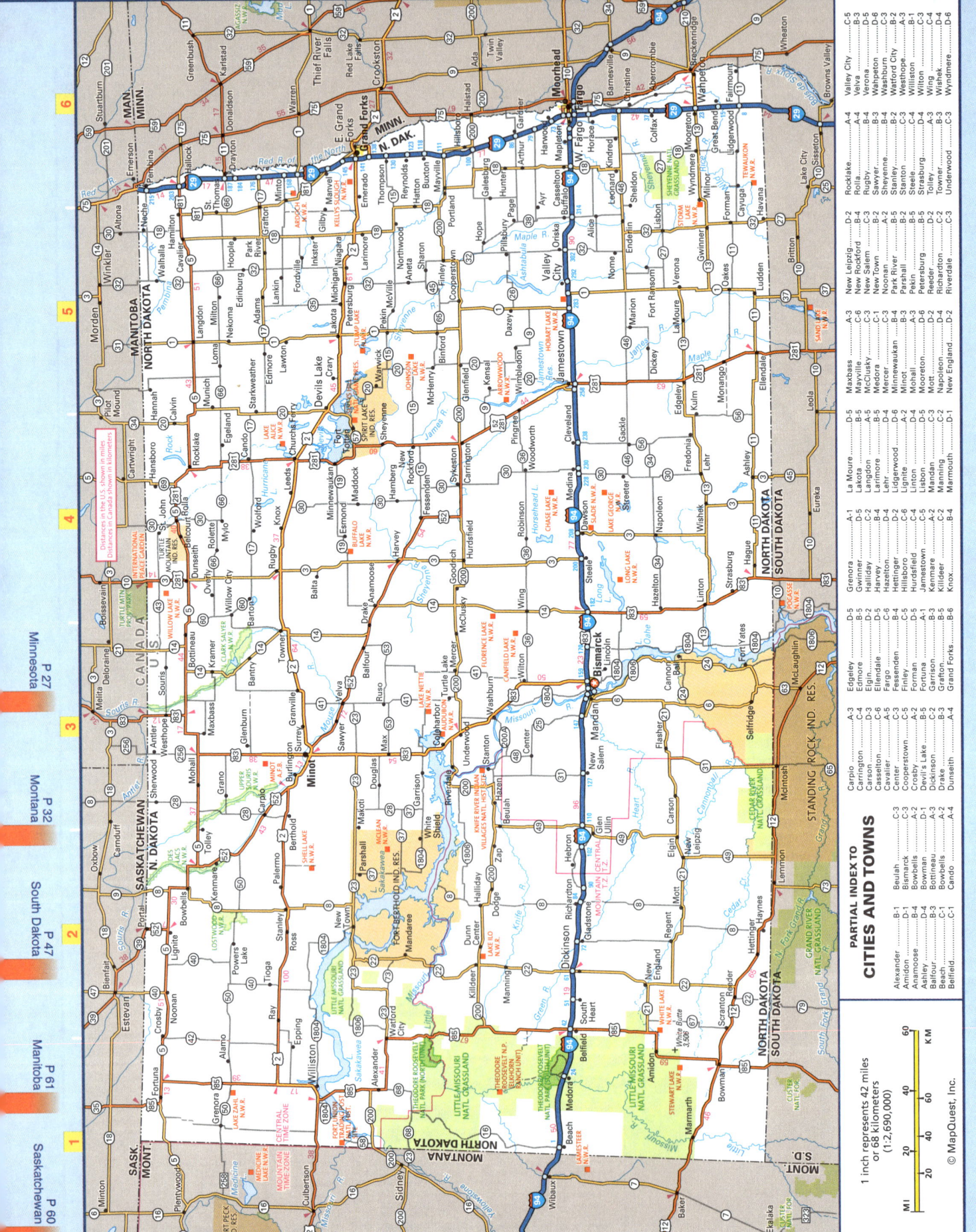

PARTIAL INDEX TO CITIES AND TOWNS

Alexander	B-1	Beulah	B-1	Grenora	D-5	Valley City	C-5
Amidon	D-1	Bismarck	D-1	Gwinner	B-5	Velva	B-3
Anamoose	A-4	Bowbells	A-2	Halliday	B-5	Verona	D-6
Ashley	A-3	Bowdon	A-4	Harvey	C-1	Washburn	B-2
Beach	C-1	Bottineau	B-3	Hettinger	C-5	Washburn	B-1
Belfield	C-1	Bowbells	C-1	Hillsboro	C-5	Watford City	A-3
		Cando	C-1	Hurdsfield	C-4	Westhope	B-1

(cities and towns index, partial)

Carpio C-3
Carrington C-4
Carson C-4
Casselton C-6
Cavalier B-6
Center C-3
Cooperstown C-5
Devil's Lake B-4
Drake A-3
Dunseith A-4

Edgeley A-3
Edmore C-4
Elgin C-6
Ellendale C-6
Fargo A-5
Fessenden C-3
Finan C-5
Forman C-4
Fortuna A-1
Garrison A-2
Grafton B-5
Grand Forks A-4

Grenora D-5
Gwinner B-5
Halliday D-5
Harvey C-1
Hettinger C-5
Hillsboro C-5
Hurdsfield C-4
Jamestown B-3
Killdeer B-5
Kenmare A-2
Killdeer B-3
Knox B-6

La Moure A-1
Lakota D-5
Langdon B-4
Lehr D-4
Lidgerwood D-6
Lignite C-4
Linton D-4
Lisbon D-5
Mandan A-2
Manning C-2
Marmouth B-4

Maxbass A-3
Mayville B-5
McClusky C-3
Medora B-4
Mercer C-3
Minnewaukan B-4
Minot A-2
Mohall A-3
Mooreton D-6
Mott C-3
Napoleon C-2
New England D-2

New Leipzig D-2
New Rockford B-4
New Salem C-3
Noonan C-2
Oakes B-5
Parshall A-2
Pekin B-5
Petersburg C-4
Reeder D-2
Richardton C-3
Riverdale B-2

Rocklake A-4
Rolla A-4
Rugby B-3
Sawyer B-3
Sheyenne B-4
Stanley B-2
Stanton C-3
Steele C-4
Strasburg D-4
Tolley A-3
Towner B-3
Underwood C-3

Valley City C-5
Velva B-3
Verona D-6
Washburn B-2
Watford City A-3
Westhope B-1
Williston C-4
Wing C-4
Wishek B-3
Wyndmere D-6

1 inch represents 42 miles
or 68 kilometers
(1:2,690,000)

© MapQuest, Inc.

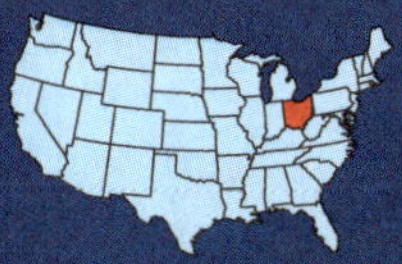

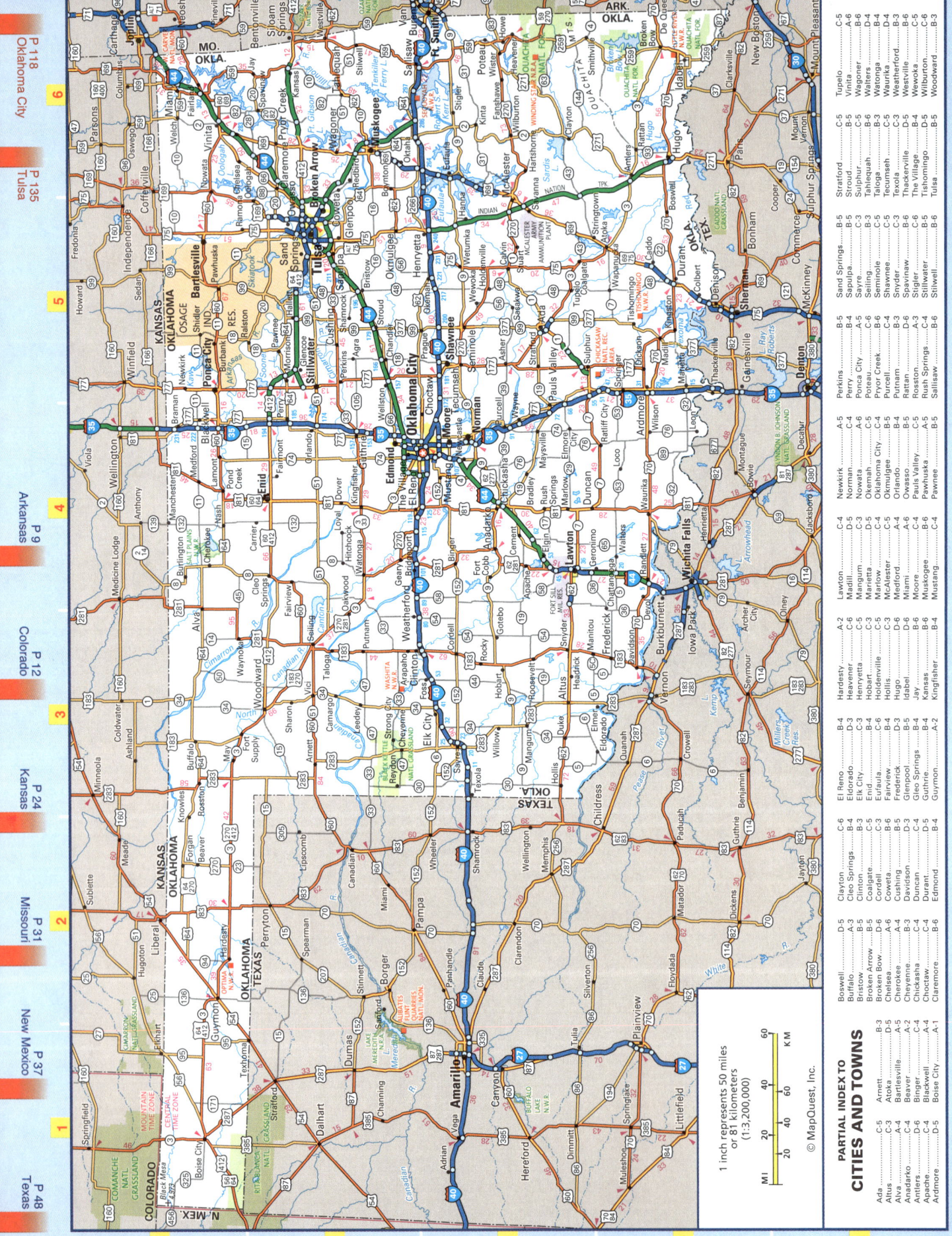

PARTIAL INDEX TO CITIES AND TOWNS

Ada	C-5	Arnett	B-3	Stratford	C-5
Altus	C-3	Atoka	D-5	Stroud	A-6
Alva	A-4	Bartlesville	A-5	Sulphur	D-4
Anadarko	C-4	Beaver	A-2	Tahlequah	B-6
Antlers	D-6	Binger	C-4	Tecumseh	C-5
Apache	C-4	Boise City	A-1	Texola	C-3

Sand Springs	B-5	Perkins	A-5	Thackerville	C-5
Sapulpa	B-4	Perry	B-5	The Village	D-5
Seiling	C-6	Poteau	C-6	Tishomingo	B-5
Seminole	C-5	Purcell	B-5	Tulsa	B-6
Shawnee	C-5	Putnam	A-3		
Snyder	C-3	Rattan	D-6		
Spavinaw	A-6	Roosevelt	C-4		
Stillwater	C-4	Rush Springs	A-5		
Stilwell	B-6	Sallisaw	B-5		

Newkirk	C-4	Lawton	A-2	Hardesty	B-4
Norman	D-5	Madill	C-6	Heavener	D-3
Nowata	A-5	Mangum	D-3	Hobart	C-3
Okemah	C-5	Marietta	C-3	Hollis	C-6
Oklahoma City	C-5	Marlow	A-6	Holdenville	C-6
Okmulgee	B-5	McAlester	B-5	Hugo	D-3
Orlando	B-4	Medford	D-6	Idabel	B-5
Owasso	A-6	Miami	D-6	Glenpool	D-3
Pauls Valley	B-5	Moore	C-4	Gleo Springs	C-4
Pawhuska	C-4	Muskogee	B-6	Guthrie	C-4
Pawnee	B-4	Mustang	B-4	Guymon	A-2

Clayton	D-5	Boswell	C-6	El Reno	C-4
Cleo Springs	A-3	Buffalo	B-4	Eldorado	D-3
Clinton	B-5	Bristow	B-3	Elk City	C-3
Coalgate	D-5	Broken Arrow	A-6	Enid	C-3
Cordell	C-4	Broken Bow	D-6	Eufaula	C-6
Coweta	A-6	Chelsea	D-5	Fairview	B-5
Cushing	A-4	Cherokee	A-5	Frederick	D-3
Davidson	D-6	Cheyenne	B-3	Glenpool	B-5
Chickasha	C-4	Duncan	C-4	Gleo Springs	C-4
Claremore	B-6	Edmond	B-4	Guthrie	B-4

© MapQuest, Inc.

1 inch represents 50 miles or 81 kilometers (1:3,200,000)

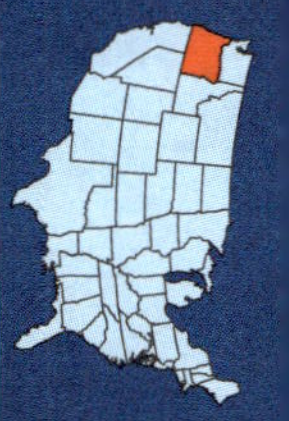

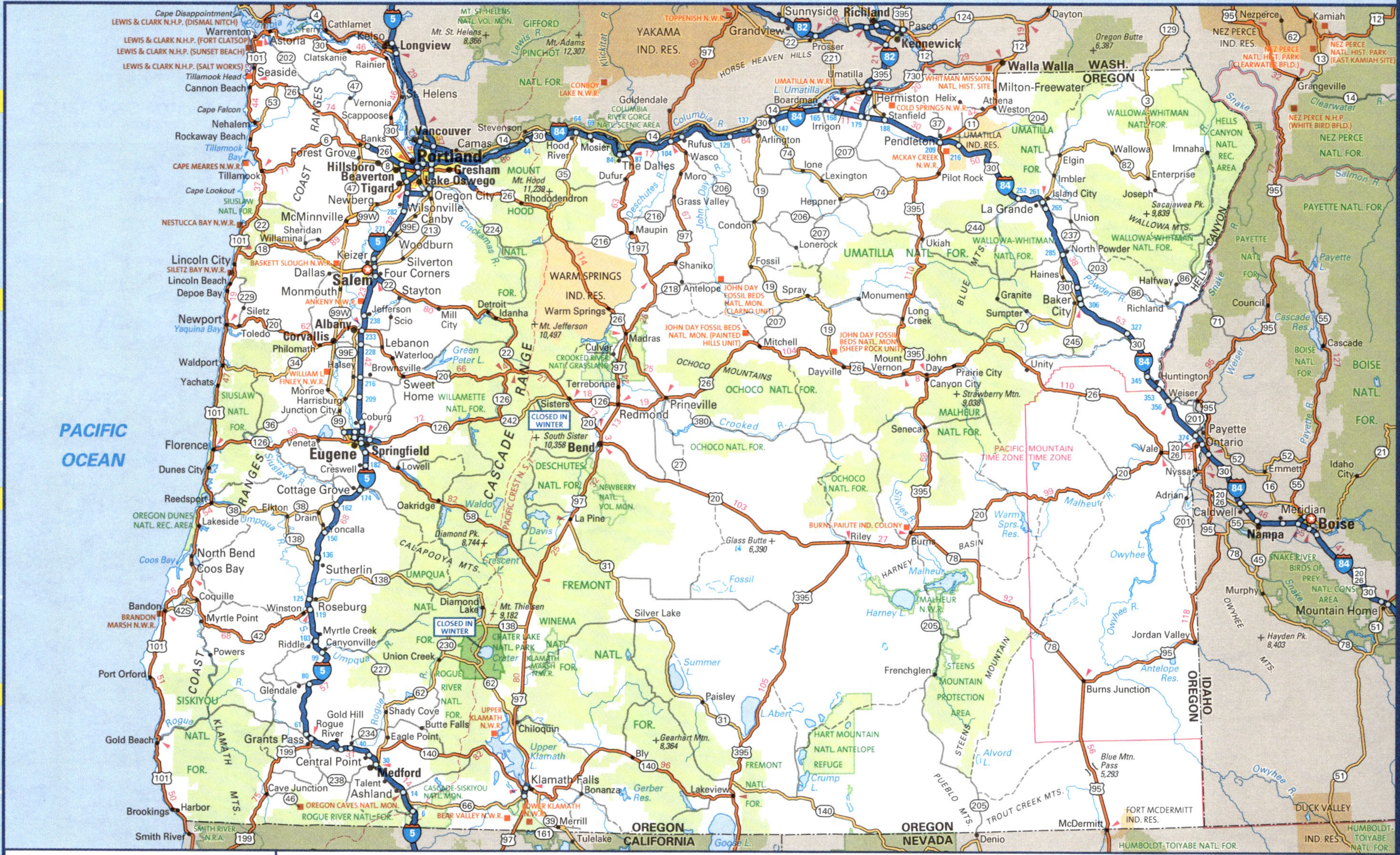

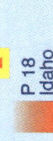
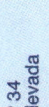

N

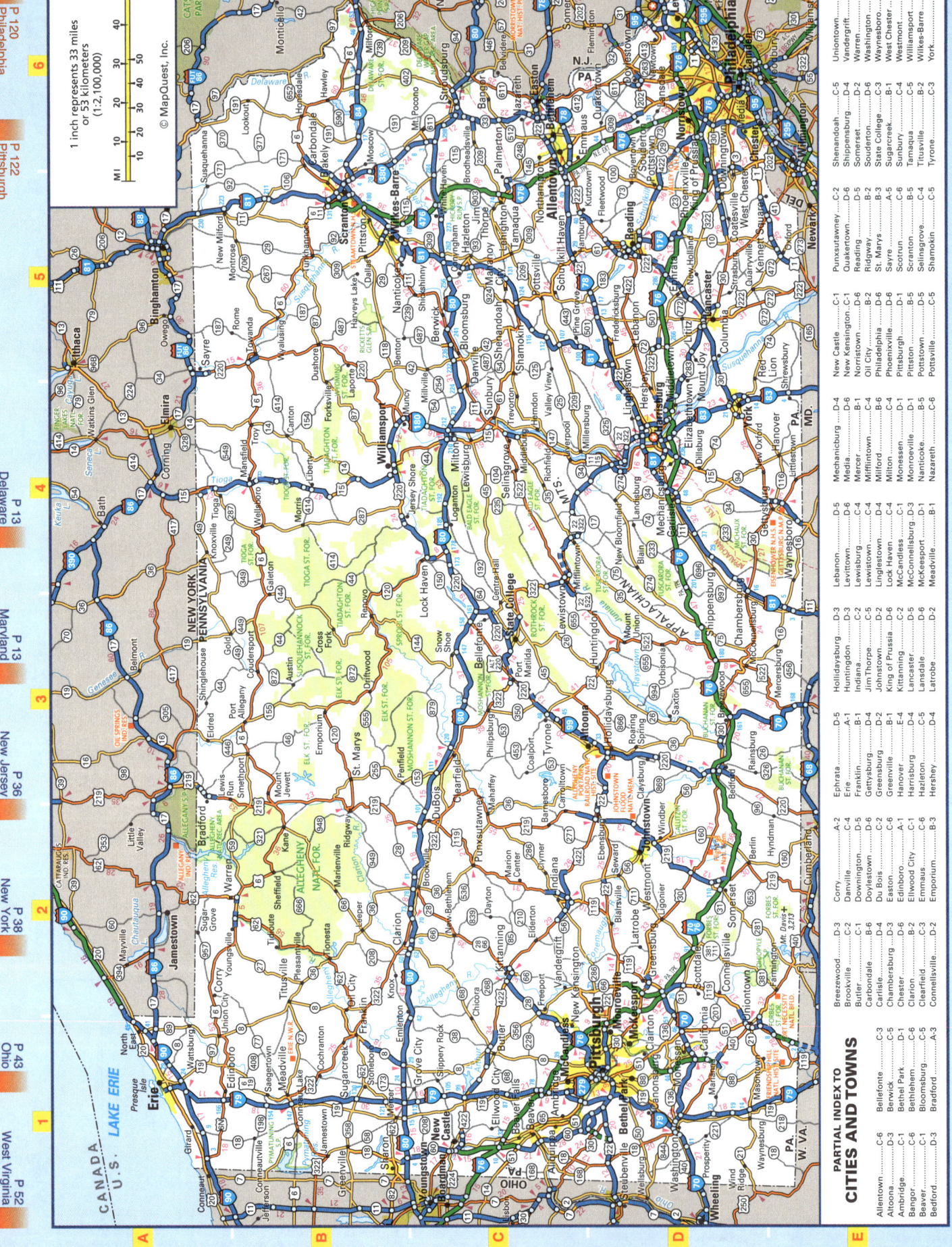

1 inch represents 33 miles
or 53 kilometers
(1:2,100,000)

© MapQuest, Inc.

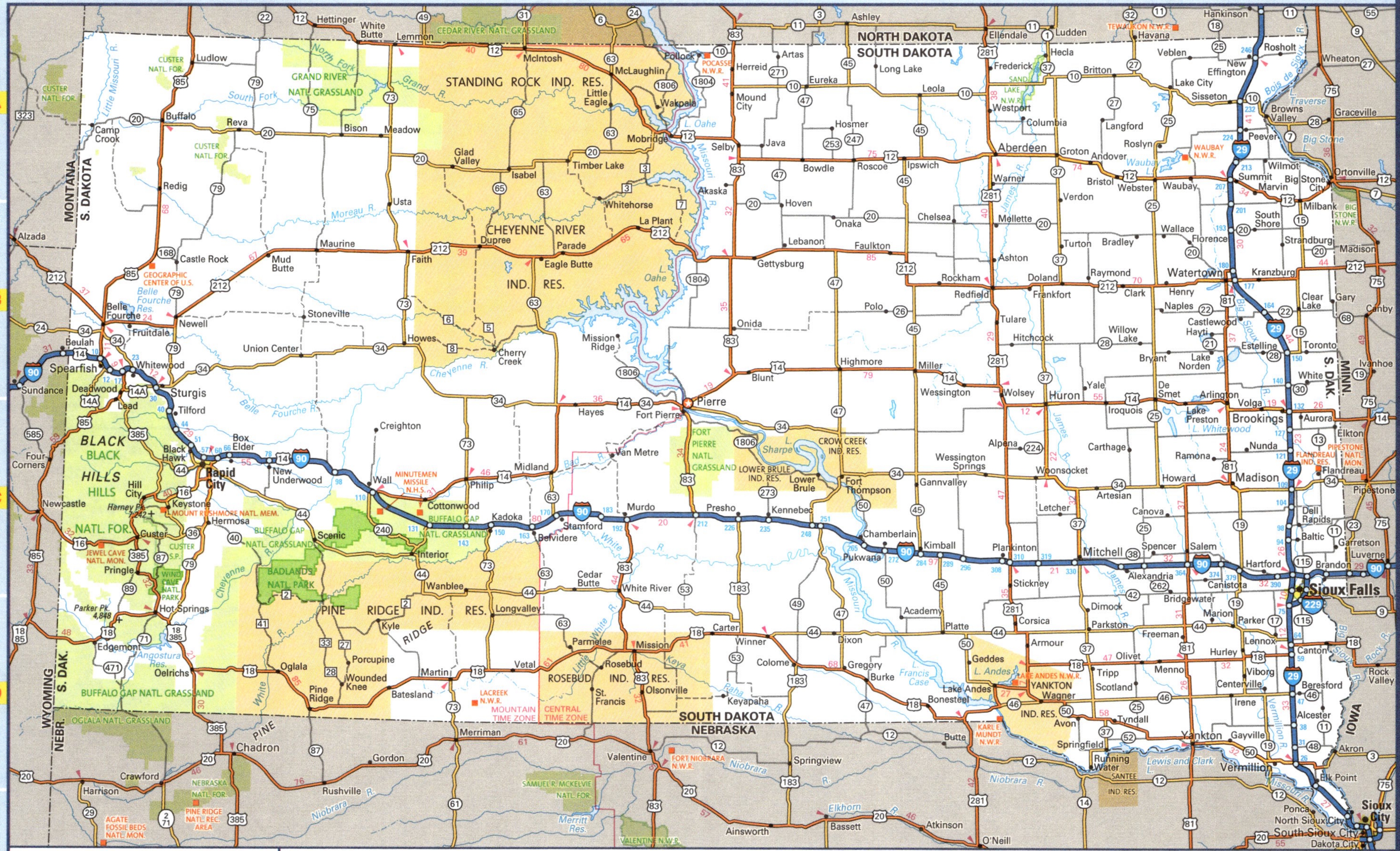

PARTIAL INDEX TO CITIES AND TOWNS

Aberdeen....A-5	Edgemont....D-4	Ipswich....D-4	Martin....A-4	Murdo....D-2	Rapid City....C-1
Alpena....C-5	Elk Point....D-6	Iroquois....A-5	Maurine....C-5	Oelrichs....B-2	Redig....D-1
Arlington....C-6	Elkton....C-6	Isabel....C-1	Meadow....A-3	Ogala....A-2	Redfield....B-5
Armour....D-5	Eureka....A-4	Kadoka....C-3	McIntosh....C-3	Onaka....B-3	St. Francis....C-3
Artesian....C-5	Faulkton....B-4	Keystone....C-1	McLaughlin....C-4	Parker....C-6	Selby....B-4
Avon....D-5	Fort Pierre....C-3	Kimball....C-4	Midland....C-4	Parkston....D-5	Sioux Falls....C-6
Batesland....D-2	Fort Thompson....C-4	La Plant....B-3	Miller....B-5	Pierre....B-4	Sisseton....A-6
Belle Fourche....C-1	Frederick....A-5	Lake Andes....D-5	Mission....D-3	Plankinton....C-5	Spearfish....C-1
Beresford....D-6	Freeman....D-6	Lead....C-1	Mitchell....C-5	Platte....D-5	Sturgis....C-1
	Gannville....C-4	Leola....A-4	Mobridge....C-5	Presho....C-4	Tripp....D-5
	Gettysburg....B-4	Longvalley....C-2	Mound City....C-6		Union Center....C-4
		Madison....C-2			
					Vermillion....D-6
					Wagner....D-5
					Wall....B-2
					Webster....A-6
					Wessington....B-5
					Wessington Springs....C-5
					White Butte....A-2
					White River....C-3
					Willow Lake....B-6
					Winner....D-4
					Wounded Knee....B-2
					Yankton....D-6

1 inch represents 42 miles
or 68 kilometers
(1:2,660,000)

© MapQuest, Inc.

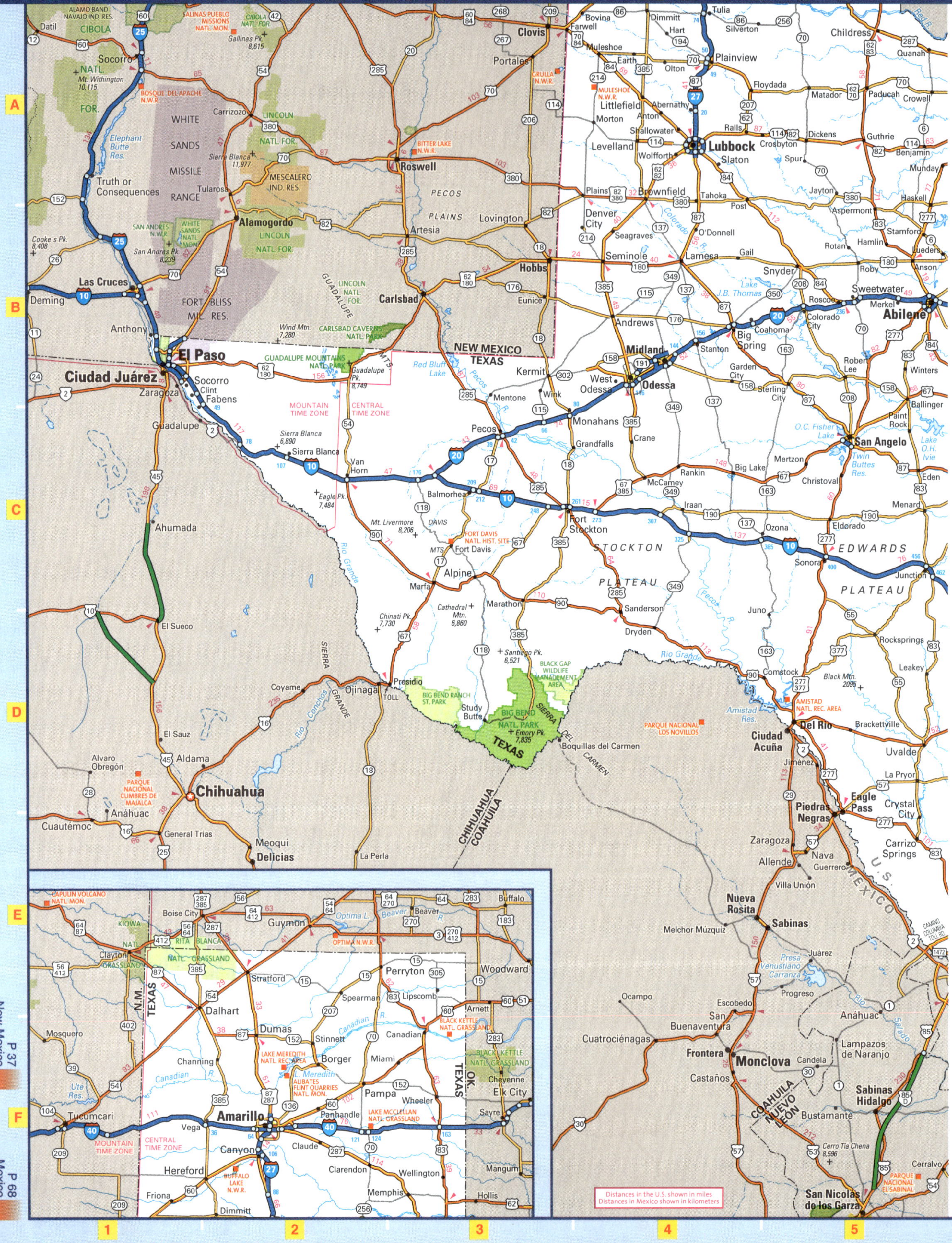

1 inch represents 63 miles
or 102 kilometers
(1:4,020,000)

MI   20   40   60   80

20   40   60   80
KM

© MapQuest, Inc.

P 70 Austin
P 88 Dallas
P 93 Houston
P 129 San Antonio
P 9 Arkansas
P 25 Louisiana
P 44 Oklahoma

1 inch represents 44 miles
or 71 kilometers
(1:2,810,000)

© MapQuest, Inc.

P 127 Salt Lake City

P 8 Arizona

P 12 Colorado

P 18 Idaho

P 34 Nevada

P 37 New Mexico

P 55 Wyoming

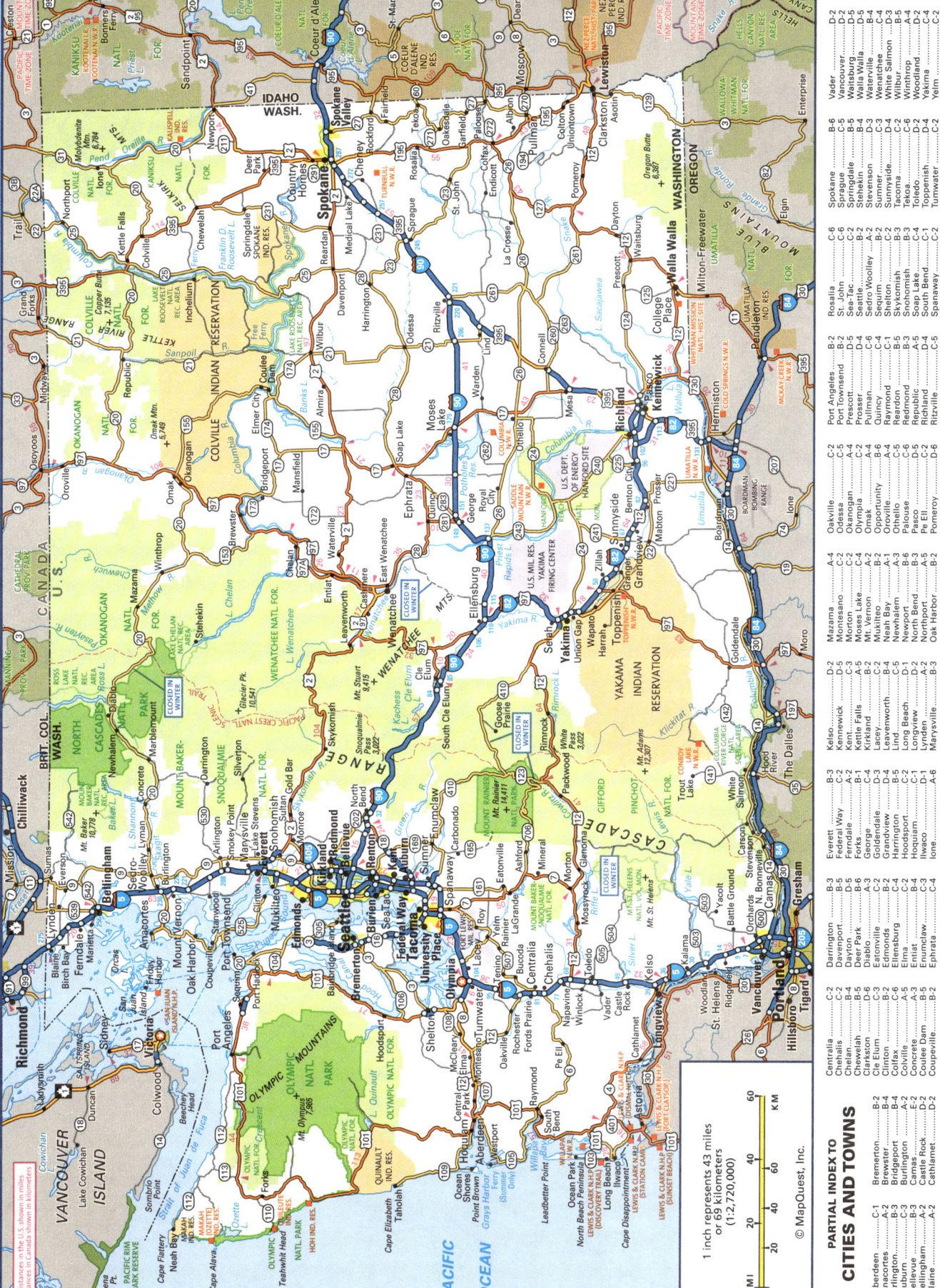

1 inch represents 43 miles or 69 kilometers (1:2,720,000)

© MapQuest, Inc.

1 inch represents 33 miles
or 53 kilometers
(1:2,100,000)

MI | 10 | 20 | 30 | 40 | 50
KM | 10 | 20 | 30 | 40 | 50

© MapQuest, Inc.

A

B

C

D

E

F

1   2   3   4   5

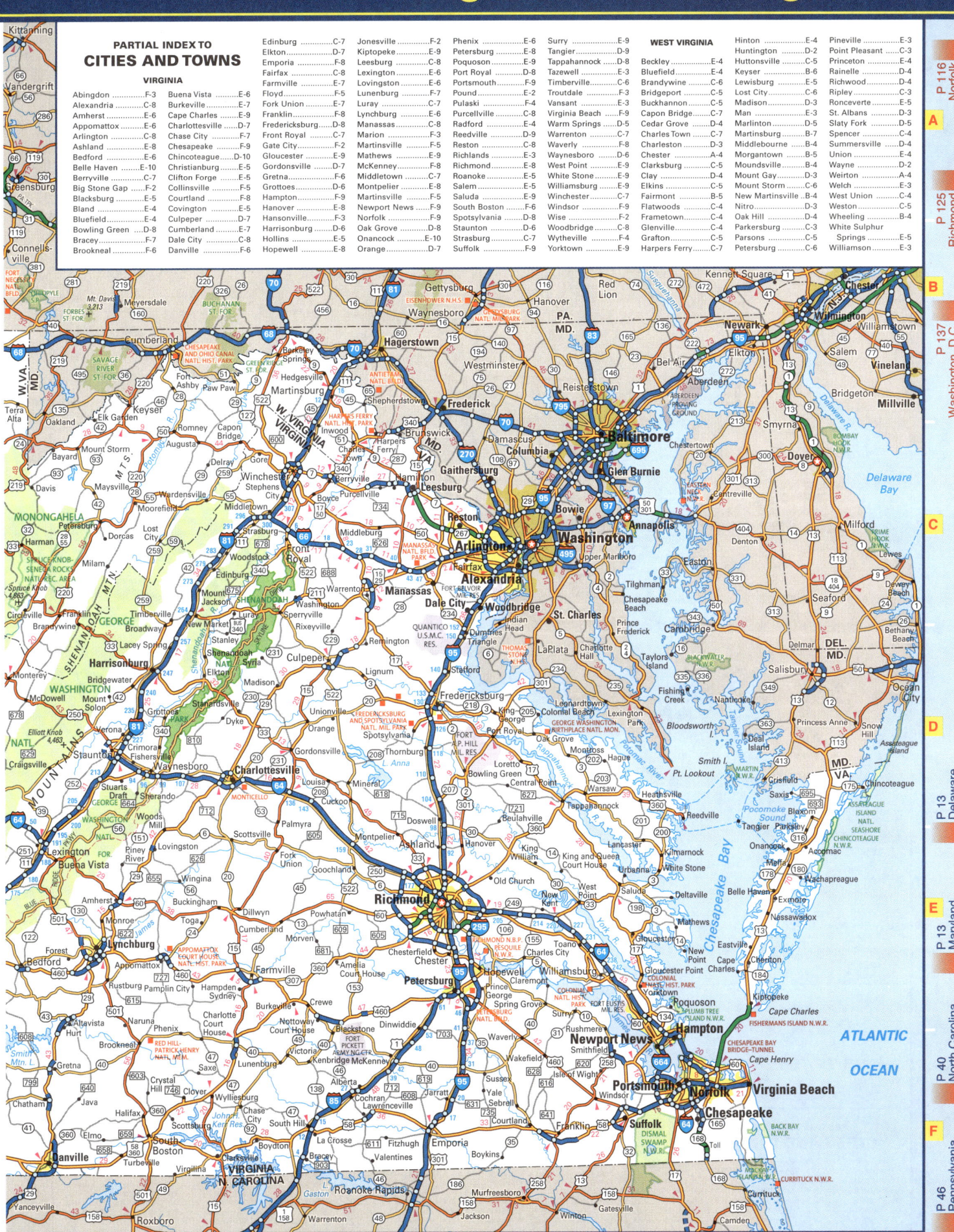

1 inch represents 43 miles
or 69 kilometers
(1:2,720,000)

© MapQuest, Inc.

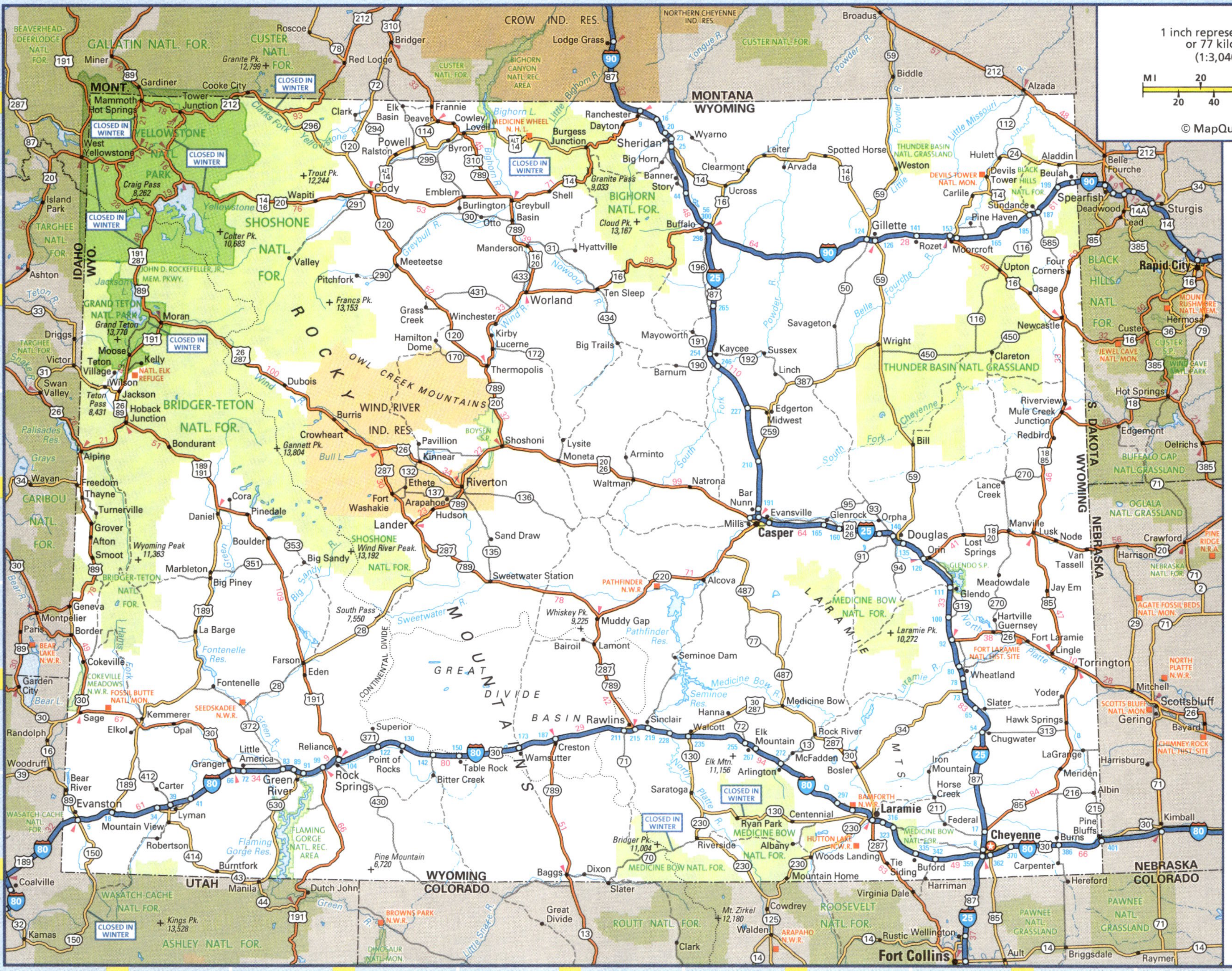

N

1 inch represents 48 miles
or 77 kilometers (1:3,040,000)

© MapQuest, Inc.

Colorado P 12
Idaho P 18
Montana P 32
Nebraska P 33
South Dakota P 47
Utah P 50

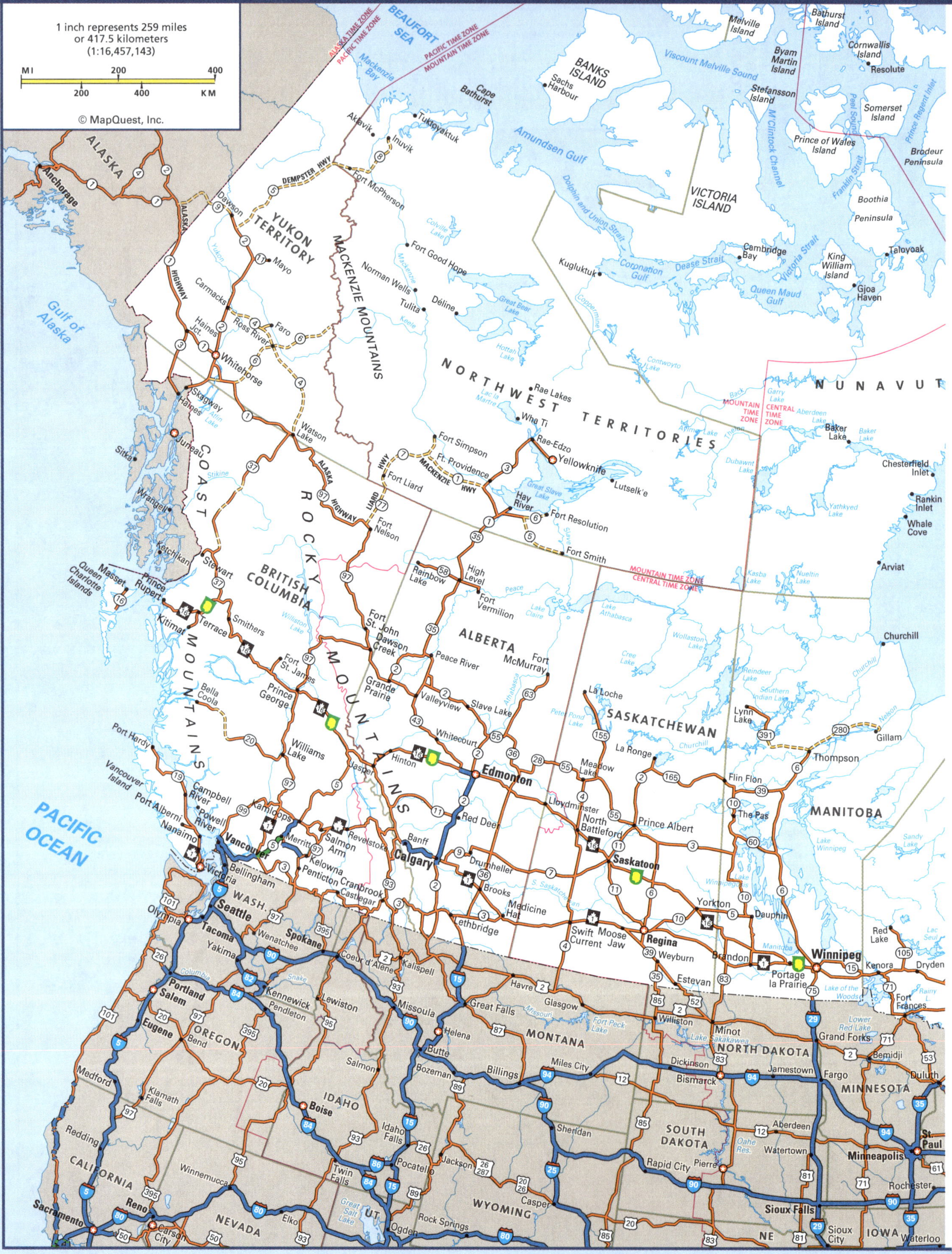

N

1 inch represents 259 miles
or 417.5 kilometers
(1:16,457,143)

MI   200   400
200   400   KM

© MapQuest, Inc.

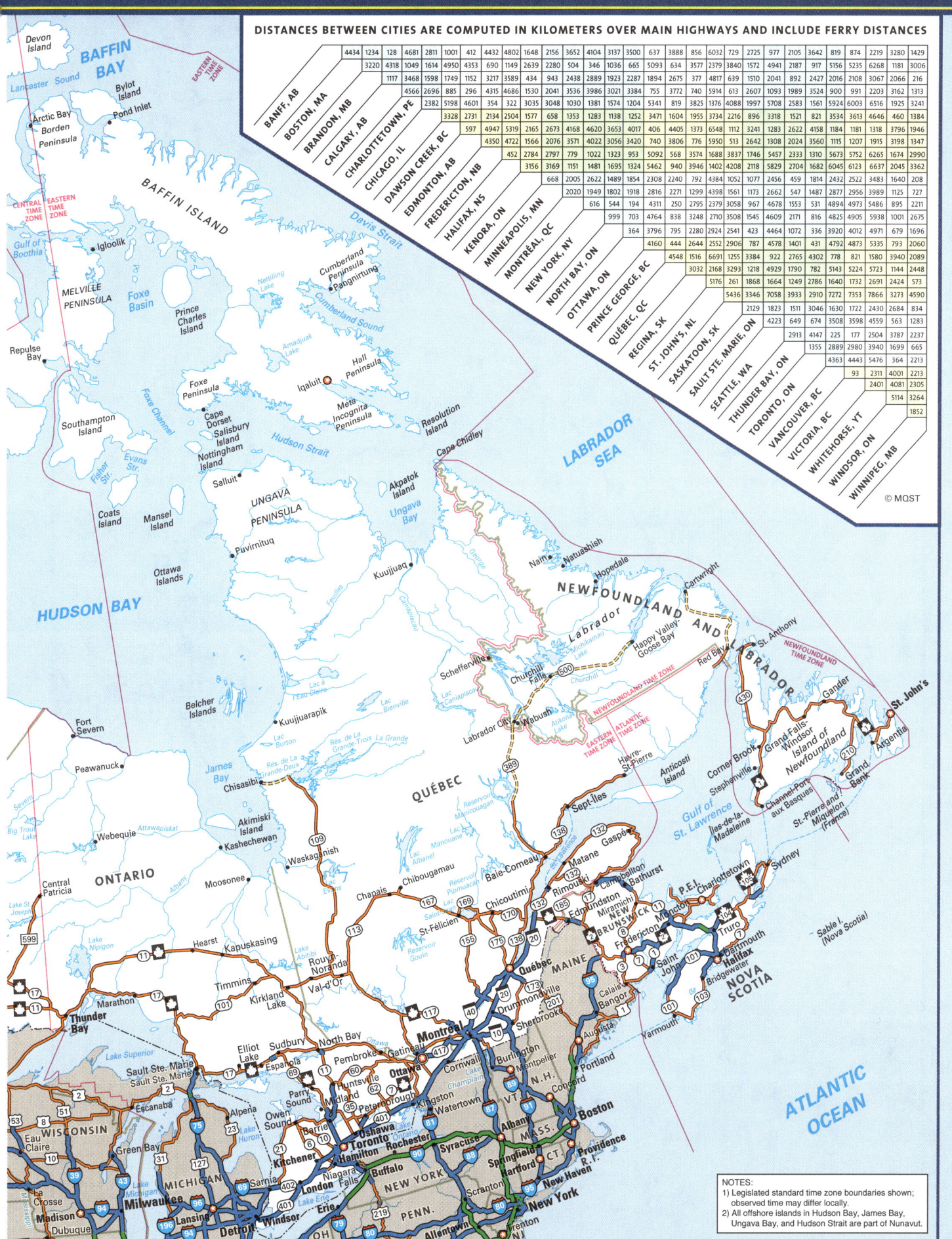

P 136 Vancouver

P 7 Alaska

P 18 Idaho

P 32 Montana

P 51 Washington

P 59 Alberta

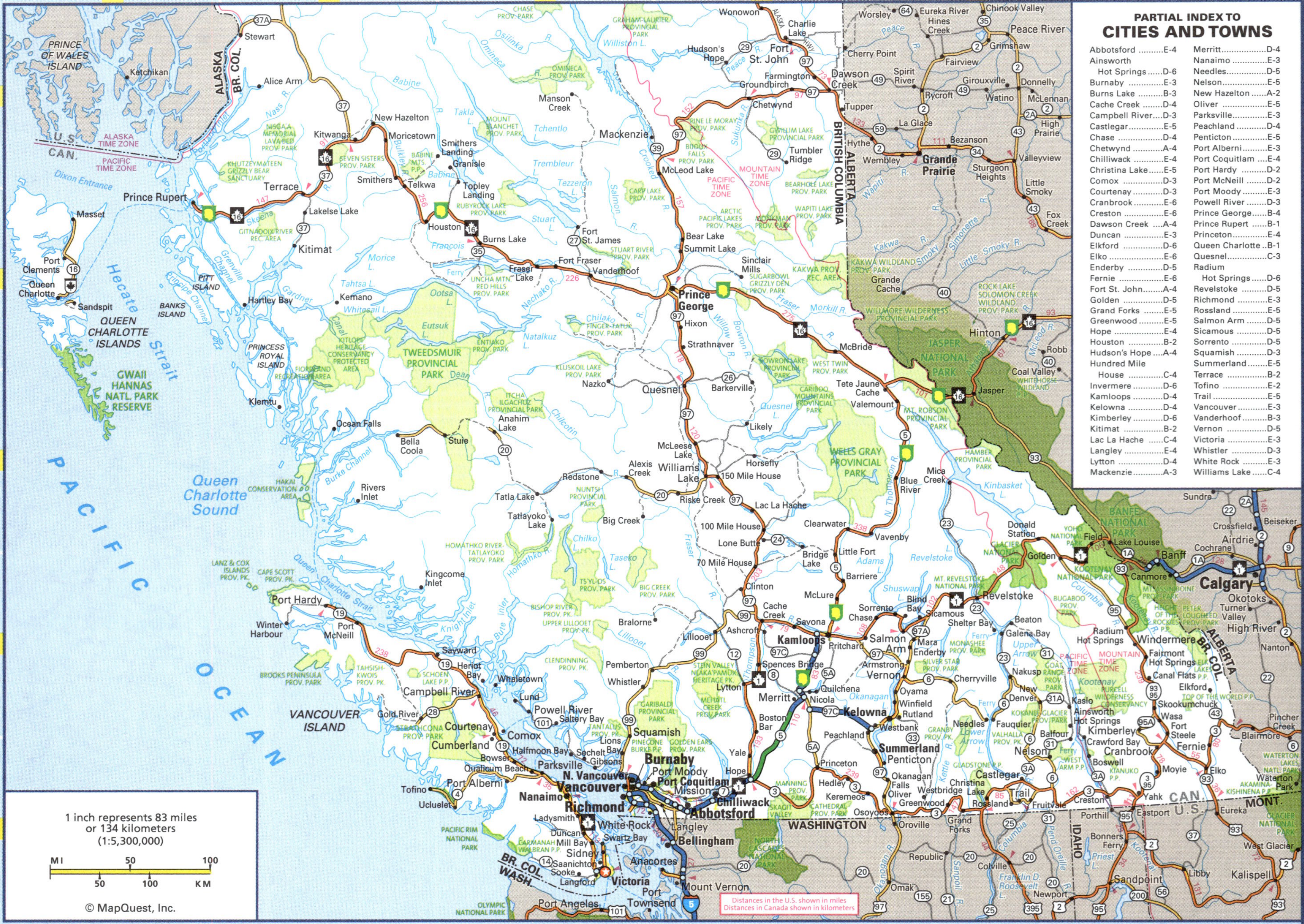

PARTIAL INDEX TO CITIES AND TOWNS

City/Town	Grid	City/Town	Grid	City/Town	Grid	City/Town	Grid
Abbotsford	D-4	Merritt	D-4	Hot Springs	D-6	Richmond	D-6
Ainsworth	E-3	Nanaimo	D-3	Invermere	E-4	Revelstoke	E-4
Hot Springs	E-5	Needles	E-5	Kamloops	D-4	Rossland	E-5
Burnaby	D-4	Nelson	E-5	Kelowna	D-5	Salmon Arm	D-5
Burns Lake	B-3	New Hazelton	A-2	Kimberley	E-5	Sicamous	D-5
Cache Creek	D-4	Oliver	E-5	Kitimat	A-2	Sorrento	D-5
Campbell River	D-3	Parksville	D-3	Lac La Hache	C-4	Squamish	D-3
Castlegar	E-5	Peachland	D-4	Langley	D-4	Summerland	E-5
Chase	D-4	Penticton	E-5	Lytton	D-4	Terrace	B-2
Chetwynd	C-4	Port Alberni	D-3	Mackenzie	B-4	Tofino	D-3
Chilliwack	D-4	Port Coquitlam	E-3			Trail	E-5
Christina Lake	E-5	Port Hardy	D-2			Vancouver	D-4
Comox	D-3	Port McNeill	D-2			Vanderhoof	B-3
Courtenay	D-3	Port Moody	E-3			Vernon	D-5
Cranbrook	E-5	Powell River	D-3			Whistler	D-3
Creston	E-5	Prince George	B-4			White Rock	E-3
Dawson Creek	B-4	Prince Rupert	A-2			Williams Lake	C-4
Duncan	D-4	Princeton	E-4				
Elkford	E-4	Queen Charlotte	B-1				
Elko	E-5	Quesnel	C-3				
Fernie	E-5						
Fort St. John	A-4						
Golden	E-4						
Grand Forks	E-5						
Greenwood	E-5						
Hope	D-4						
Hudson's Hope	A-4						
Hundred Mile	D-4						

1 inch represents 83 miles
or 134 kilometers
(1:5,300,000)

Distances in the U.S. shown in miles
Distances in Canada shown in kilometers

MI ... 50 ... 100

KM ... 50 ... 100

© MapQuest, Inc.

N

Worsley • Eureka River • Cherry Point • Hines Creek • Chinook Valley • Peace River • Grimshaw • Fairview • Spirit River • Rycroft • Girouxville • Watino • Donnelly • McLennan • Gift Lake • Wabasca • Desmarais • Fort McMurray • Wood Buffalo • La Loche

Dawson Creek • Demmitt • La Glace • Hythe • Beaverlodge • Wembley • Grande Prairie • Sturgeon Heights • Bezanson • Valleyview • Kathleen • Guy • High Prairie • Kinuso • Faust • Slave Lake • Smith • Breynat • Atmore • Lac La Biche • Iron River • Medley • Grand Centre • Cold Lake • Bonnyville

Tupper • Grande Cache • Grande Cache • Little Smoky • Fox Creek • Swan Hills • Ft. Assiniboine • Fort Assiniboine • Neerlandia • Fawcett • Athabasca • Boyle • Glendon • Mallaig • Ashmont • St. Paul • Elk Point • Brosseau • Onion Lake • Frenchman Butte

Grande Prairie • Whitecourt • Barrhead • Lac la Nonne • Clyde • Redwater • Warspite • Spedden • Marwayne

Willmore Wilderness Park • Rock Lake • Solomon Creek • Marlboro • Edson • Bickerdike • Niton Junction • Nojack • Entwistle • Wildwood • Carvel • Spruce Grove • Edmonton • Sherwood Park • Fort Saskatchewan • Vegreville • Innisfree • Vermilion • Kitscoty • Lloydminster • Lashburn

Hinton • Robb • Wabamun • Stony Plain • Devon • Leduc • New Sarepta • Bruce • Viking • Ryley • Tofield

Tête Jaune Cache • Red Pass • Jasper • Cadomin • Drayton Valley • Thorsby • Warburg • Camrose • Irma • Chauvin • Neilburg

Valemount • Albreda • Blue River • Lodgepole • Alder Flats • Winfield • Westerose • Wetaskiwin • New Norway • Daysland • Killam • Sedgewick • Hardisty • Wainwright • Macklin

Mica Creek • Nordegg • Saunders • Rimbey • Ponoka • Bashaw • Donalda • Forestburg • Hughenden • Provost • Denzil

Rocky Mountain House • Sylvan Lake • Lacombe • Stettler • Halkirk • Castor • Coronation • Consort • Compeer • Fusilier

Caroline • Penhold • Red Deer • Erskine • Big Valley • Veteran

Sundre • Innisfail • Pine Lake • Trochu • Hanna • Youngstown • Cereal • Alsask • Flaxcombe

Olds • Didsbury • Bowden • Three Hills • Carbon • Drumheller • Oyen • Empress

Crossfield • Beiseker • Airdrie • Irricana • Strathmore • Carseland • Bassano • Brooks • Buffalo

Banff • Exshaw • Morley • Cochrane • Calgary • Okotoks • Turner Valley • Black Diamond • High River • Nanton • Vulcan • Lomond • Scandia • Suffield • Redcliff • Medicine Hat

Canmore • Longview • Stavely • Champion • Vauxhall • Taber • Grassy Lake • Bow Island • Walsh • Irvine

Kananaskis • Claresholm • Granum • Monarch • Coaldale • Lethbridge • Stirling • Skiff • Etzikom • Manyberries

Blairmore • Fort Macleod • Magrath • Raymond • Foremost

Pincher Creek • Cardston • Milk River • Del Bonita • Sweetgrass

Waterton Lakes Natl. Park • Mountain View • Eureka • St. Mary

Scale

1 inch represents 63 miles or 102 kilometers (1:4,000,000)

MI 20 40 60 80
KM 20 40 60 80

© MapQuest, Inc.

P 73 Calgary
P 87 Edmonton
P 32 Montana
P 58 British Columbia
P 60 Saskatchewan

Saskatchewan

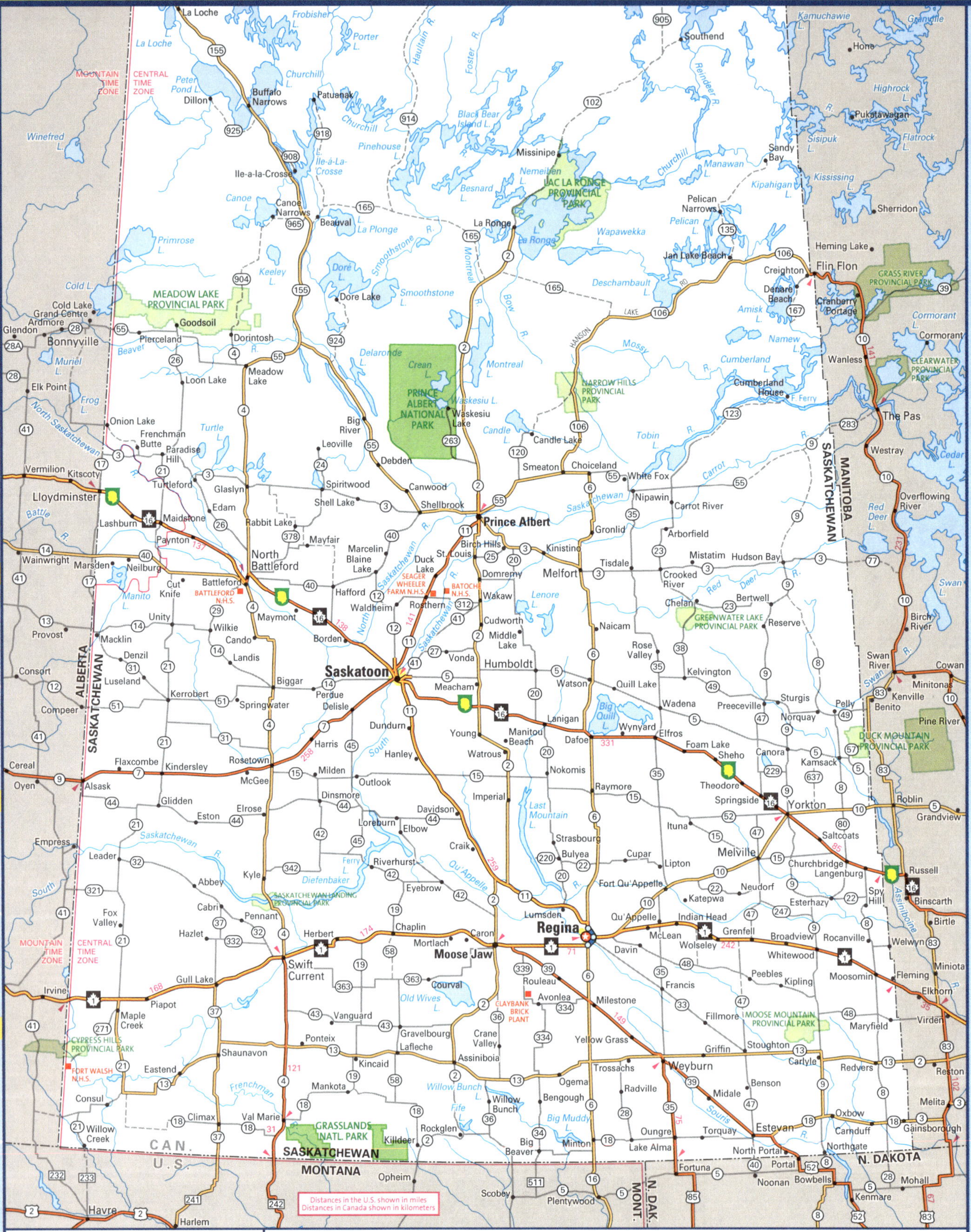
N
A
B
C
D
E
F
1
2
3
4
5
P 32 Montana
P 42 North Dakota
P 59 Alberta
P 61 Manitoba
ALBERTA
SASKATCHEWAN
MANITOBA
MONTANA
N. DAKOTA
N. DAK.
MONT.
CAN.
U.S.
MOUNTAIN TIME ZONE
CENTRAL TIME ZONE
La Loche
Buffalo Narrows
Ile-a-la-Crosse
La Ronge
Flin Flon
Meadow Lake
Lloydminster
North Battleford
Battleford
Prince Albert
Saskatoon
Humboldt
Melfort
Nipawin
Tisdale
Yorkton
Melville
Regina
Moose Jaw
Swift Current
Weyburn
Estevan
Kindersley
Rosetown
Maple Creek
Shaunavon
Assiniboia
Val Marie
Moosomin
The Pas
Havre
MEADOW LAKE PROVINCIAL PARK
PRINCE ALBERT NATIONAL PARK
LAC LA RONGE PROVINCIAL PARK
NARROW HILLS PROVINCIAL PARK
GREENWATER LAKE PROVINCIAL PARK
DUCK MOUNTAIN PROVINCIAL PARK
MOOSE MOUNTAIN PROVINCIAL PARK
CYPRESS HILLS PROVINCIAL PARK
GRASSLANDS NATL. PARK
SASKATCHEWAN LANDING PROVINCIAL PARK
Distances in the U.S. shown in miles
Distances in Canada shown in kilometers

1 inch represents 63 miles
or 102 kilometers
(1:4,000,000)

MI 20 40 60 80
20 40 60 80 KM

PARTIAL INDEX TO
CITIES AND TOWNS

PARTIAL INDEX TO
CITIES AND TOWNS

1 inch represents 63 miles
or 102 kilometers
(1:4,000,000)

© MapQuest, Inc.

Distances in the U.S. shown in miles
Distances in Canada shown in kilometers

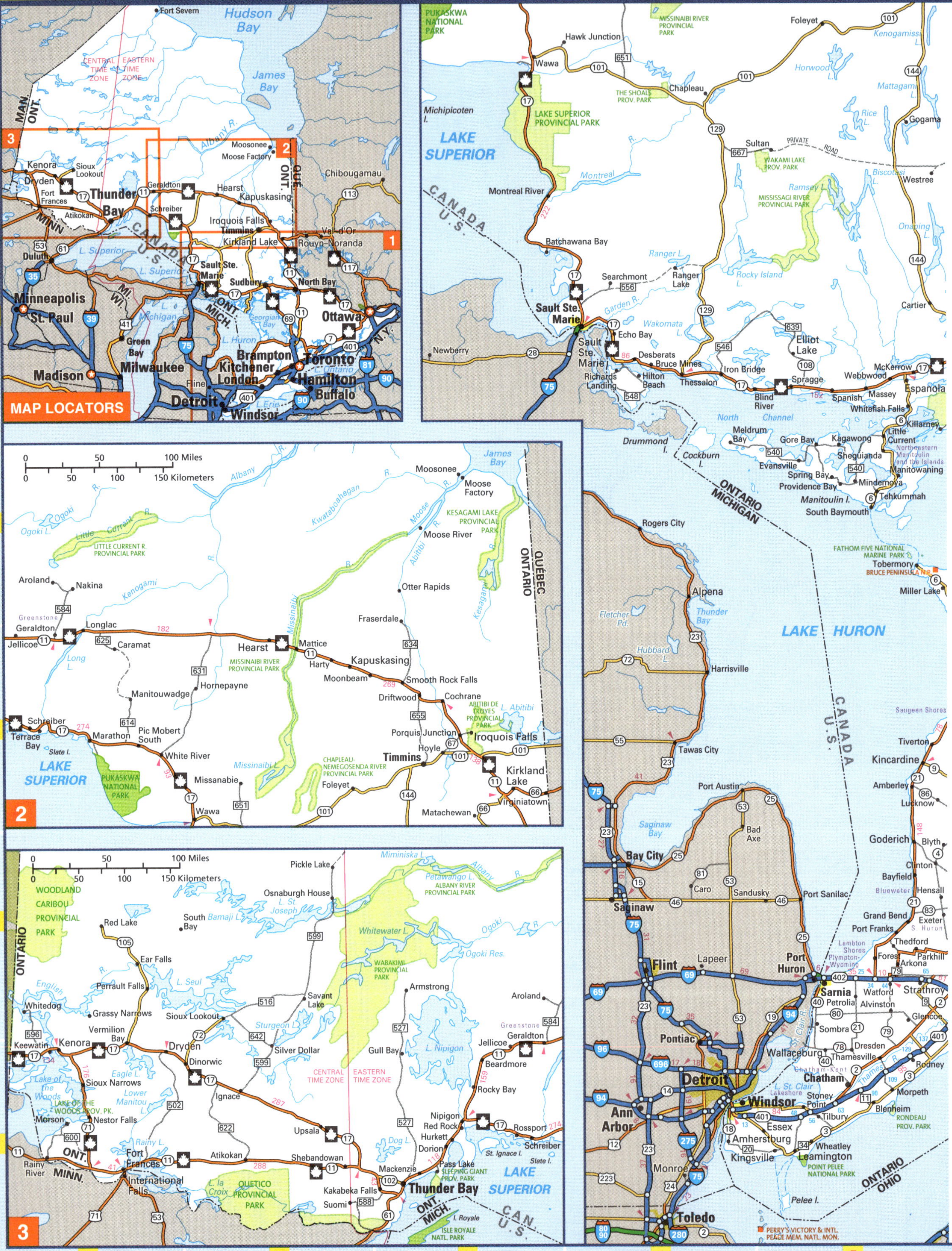

N

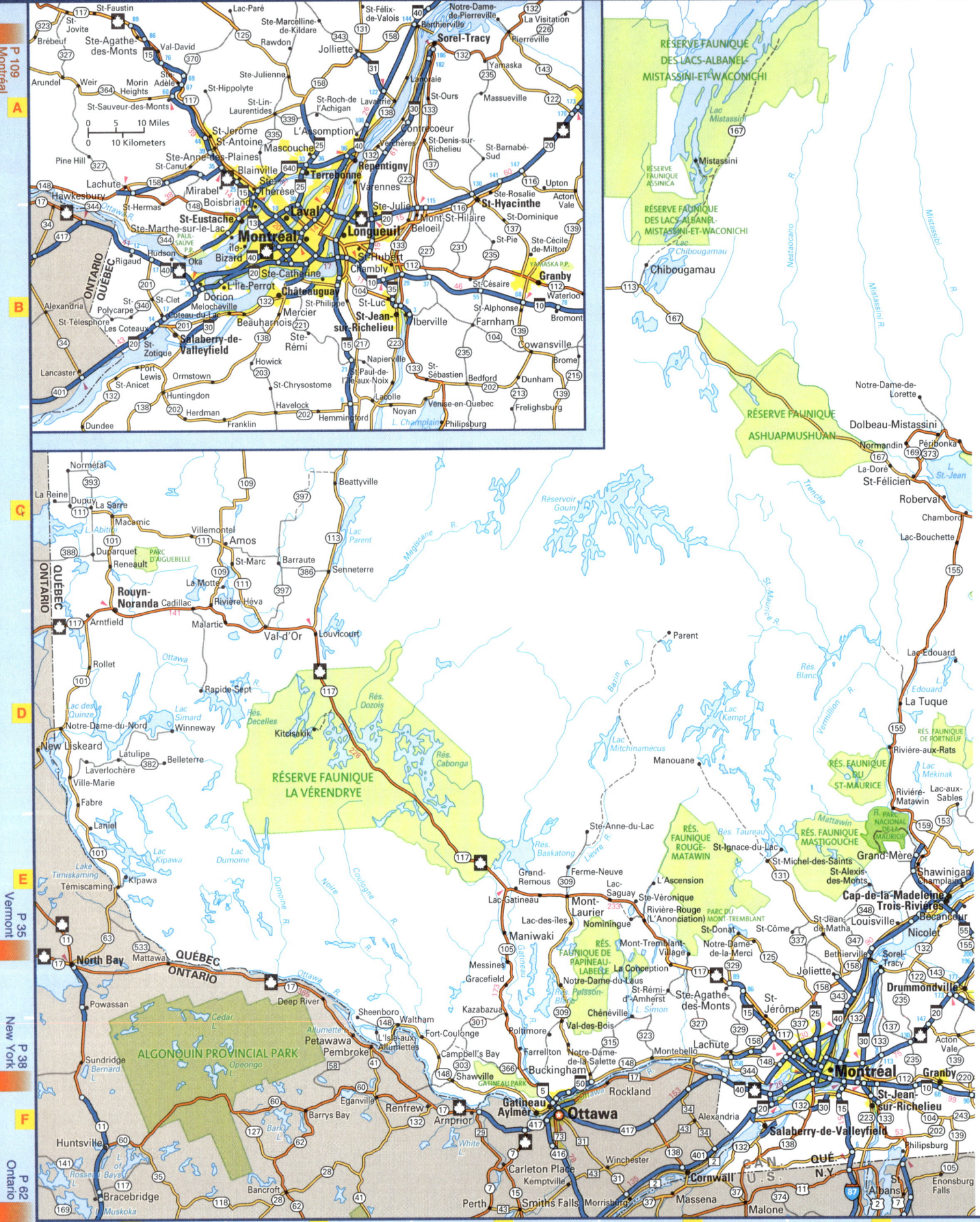

vers/to Labrador City

RÉS. FAUNIQUE DE PORT-CARTIER –SEPT-ÎLES

Longue-Pointe-de-Mingan
Magpie
Havre-St-Pierre
Rivière-aux-Graines
138
Sheldrake
RESERVE DE PARC NATIONAL DE L'ARCHIPEL-DE-MINGAN

Manicouagan

138
Clarke City
Moisie
Sept-Îles
Port-Cartier
Anticosti I.
Port-Menier

Rivière-Pentecôte

138
Les Islets-Caribou
389
Godbout
Pointe-des-Monts
Franquelin
Ste-Madeleine-de-la-Rivière-Madeleine
Petite-Vallée
Cloridorme
Gros-Morne
Mont-St-Pierre
132
Pointe-Jaune
Rivière-au-Renard
197
PARC NAT. DE FORILLON
Cap-aux-Os

Baie-Comeau
La Martre
Marsoui
Murdochville
198
Gaspé
Labrieville
Chute-aux-Outardes
Pointe-Lebel
Ste-Anne-des-Monts
132
Cap-Chat
GASPÉSIE
Douglastown
Barachois

Ragueneau
Les Méchins
RÉSERVE FAUNIQUE DES CHIC-CHOCS
299
Percé
385
138
Betsiamites
Matane
PARC DE LA GASPÉSIE
132
Grande-Rivière

Colombier
132
RÉSERVE FAUNIQUE DE MATANE
RÉSERVE FAUNIQUE DE DUNIÈRE
299
L'Anse-aux-Gascons
Chandler

Forestville
Baie-des-Sables
297
195
Sayabec
Amqui
RÉSERVE FAUNIQUE PORT-DANIEL
QUÉBEC N.B.

St-Ludger-de-Milot
Métis-sur-Mer
Mont-Joli
St-Angèle-de-Mérici
Causapscal
132
Nouvelle
Maria
New Richmond
Caplan
Bonaventure
New Carlisle
Miscou Centre
Ste-Monique
PARC DE LA POINTE-TAILLON
St-Henri-de-Taillon
St-David-de-Falardeau
Ste-Luce
Rimouski
Le Bic
234
St-Marcellin
Escuminac
Routhierville
Pointe-à-la-Croix
Carleton
132
New Carlisle
113
Chaleur Bay
Tracadie-Sheila

Alma
172
Chicoutimi (Saguenay)
Ste-Rose-du-Nord
172
232
St-Fabien
RÉSERVE FAUNIQUE DE RIMOUSKI
Matapédia
Campbellton
11
Caraquet
Shippegan

St-Bruno
170
PARC DU SAGUENAY
Jonquière
La Baie
St-Félix-d'Otis
Baie-Ste-Catherine
L'Isle-Verte
293
St-Cyprien
QUÉBEC N.B.
EASTERN TIME ZONE
160
Bathurst

Métabetchouan Lac-à-la-Croix
169
175
St-Jean
Rivière-Ste-Marguerite
Tadoussac
Trois-Pistoles
232
Lac-des-Aigles
ATLANTIC TIME ZONE

Boilleau
381
L'Anse-St-Jean
138
Cacouna
514
St-Hubert
180
Kedgwick
St-Quentin
MT. CARLETON PROV. PARK
Nepisiguit R.

RÉS. FAUNIQUE DES LAURENTIDES
St-Siméon
Rivière-du-Loup
291
295
185
499
488
Cabano
232
Notre-Dame-du-Lac
17

PARC DES GRANDS-JARDINS
St-André
St-Germain
20
289
Rivière Bleue
Dégelis
Edmundston
2
Madawaska
St-Léonard
Grand Falls
108
Plaster Rock
108

La Malbaie
362
Mont-Carmel
456
St-Marc-du-Lac-Long
Fort Kent
Van Buren
177
161
Caribou
1A

Les Éboulements
Baie-St-Paul
La Pocatière
444
St-Pacôme
11
Presque-Isle
163
109

St-Tite-des-Caps
138
St-Jean-Port-Joli
439
204
ALLAGASH
WILDERNESS WATERWAY
Ashland
851
Bristol
107

Beaupré
Île d'Orléans
Montmagny
285
204
St-Pamphile
1
Nashwaak Bridge

Rivière-à-Pierre
STATION ÉCOTOURISTIQUE DUCHESNAY
Stoneham
St-Michel
St-Vallier
Grand L. Seboeis
Fredericton

Charlesbourg
367
Québec
Lévis
St-Raphaël
281
St-Philémon
Allagash L.
Keswick Ridge
104

Pont-Rouge
40
Ste-Foy
Charny
73
Ste-Claire
277
Chamberlain L.
Woodstock

St-Nicolas
St-Apollinaire
Ste-Croix
Lac-Etchemin
St-Camille-de-Lellis
212
Houlton
St. Johns
Thomaston Corner

Donnacona
Deschaillons
265
Dosquet
275
Ste-Marie
St-Joseph-de-Beauce
204
159
95
1
122

Villeroy
20
St-Jacques-de-Leeds
112
271
269
Beauceville
BAXTER STATE PARK
Mt. Katahdin 5,268'
Patten
2A
Vanceboro
4

Plessisville
St-Georges
84
St-Zacharie
173
Seboomook
Chesuncook L.
1
Macwahoc
Thomaston Corner

Ste-Eulalie
955
Princeville
165
Thetford Mines
Colraine
108
St-Gédéon-de-Beauce
Millinocket
Pemadumcook L.
157
Topsfield
122

Victoriaville
Arthabasca
161
La Guadeloupe
Lambton
QUÉ. MÉ.
Moosehead L.
Lincoln
St-Stephen
St-Andrews

Notre-Dame-du-Bon-Conseil
Warwick
Beaulac
Stratford
St-Ludger
201
Jackman
Greenville
Big L.
Calais

Danville
Asbestos
PARC DE FRONTENAC
L. St François
Stornoway
204
Dover-Foxcroft
Schoodic
1
Ferry

55
88
Richmond
255
112
257
108
Gould
Scotstown
161
118
Macwahoc
Nicatous L.

116
143
Windsor Bromptonville
Lac Mégantic
Bangor
95
Brewer

222
243
E. Angus
212
Woburn
27
Flagstaff L.
201
Newport
2

Valcourt
Ste-Anne-de-la-Rochelle
143
Sherbrooke
253
St-Malo
Stratton
Bingham
7
15
1A

Magog
Lac Brome
147
141
Coaticook
MAINE N.H.
Kingfield
Rangeley
16
16

Mansonville
55
QUÉ. VT.
Eaton
Colebrook
Mooselookmeguntic L.
Skowhegan
201
202

Newport
100
105
114
3
26
Rumford
Farmington
27
Waterville
Belfast
1A

Distances in the U.S. shown in miles
Distances in Canada shown in kilometers

1 inch represents 47 miles
or 76 kilometers
(1:3,000,000)

MI 20 40 60
KM 20 40 60

© MapQuest, Inc.

P 26 Maine
P 35 New Hampshire
P 66 New Brunswick

A B C D E F
6 7 8 9 10

ATLANTIC OCEAN

A T L A N T I C O C E A N

1 inch represents 51 miles
or 83 kilometers
(1:3,250,000)

MI   20   40   60
20 40 60   KM

© MapQuest, Inc.

PARTIAL INDEX TO
CITIES AND TOWNS

N

OCÉANO PACÍFICO / PACIFIC OCEAN

Golfo de California

PARTIAL INDEX TO
CITIES AND TOWNS

P 8 Arizona
P 11 California
P 37 New Mexico

DISTANCES BETWEEN CITIES ARE COMPUTED IN KILOMETERS OVER MAIN HIGHWAYS

	973	2071	1913	2298	1120	1680	1231	897	2388	866	1450	1777	422	1404	488	611	834	1003	3272	1464	991	830
ACAPULCO	2118	1051	1446	584	940	421	272	1542	126	704	1928	473	579	586	263	168	568	2426	568	1405	838
AGUASCALIENTES		3290	3671	2128	3028	2051	2275	3736	2012	2726	321	1736	2416	1603	1958	1651	1355	1155	1374	1456	449	2417	1817
CANCÚN			385	1086	919	686	1283	579	1209	896	2810	1538	808	1651	1355	1155	1374	1456	449	2417	1817
CHIHUAHUA				1442	1304	1069	1667	795	1593	1242	3241	1923	1236	1983	1740	1540	1806	1202	834	2847	2247
CIUDAD JUÁREZ					1146	912	774	1666	608	1123	1725	682	288	797	636	438	243	2641	637	1331	731
CIUDAD VICTORIA						235	526	706	737	230	2430	1104	924	1425	921	710	1056	1596	914	2036	1469
CULIACÁN							599	941	525	319	2182	856	689	1067	673	475	821	1830	266	1788	1221
DURANGO								1233	211	523	1904	578	758	691	394	336	682	2121	958	1510	943
GUADALAJARA									1444	729	3137	1810	1387	2133	1627	1416	1762	884	1028	2742	2176
HERMOSILLO										715	1693	367	679	520	137	171	517	2333	877	1299	732
LEÓN											2408	1081	901	1195	898	687	1033	1822	892	2013	1447
MAZATLÁN												1326	2004	1282	1510	1707	1435	4025	2361	786	995
MÉRIDA													892	133	183	381	473	2700	689	932	365
MEXICO CITY														1035	708	509	528	2362	359	1609	1009
MONTERREY															355	496	586	3017	1125	930	346
PUEBLA																198	544	2517	906	1115	549
QUERÉTARO																	346	2305	706	1313	747
SAN LUIS POTOSÍ																		3005	925	1041	457
TAMPICO																			1905	3631	3064
TIJUANA																				2142	1346
TORREÓN																					690
TUXTLA GUTIÉRREZ																					
VERACRUZ																					

© MQST

Distances in the U.S. shown in miles
Distances in Mexico shown in kilometers

**GOLFO DE MÉXICO /
GULF OF MEXICO**

**MAR CARIBE /
CARIBBEAN SEA**

1 inch represents 191 miles
or 307 kilometers
(1:12,100,000)

© MapQuest, Inc.

Albuquerque map:

1 inch represents 3.9 miles or 6.3 kilometers (1:246,297)

© MapQuest, Inc.

CIBOLA NATIONAL FOREST

SANTA ANA PUEBLO

Bernalillo

SANDIA PUEBLO

Rio Rancho

Corrales

Alameda

Los Ranchos de Albuquerque

Paradise Hills

Albuquerque

KIRTLAND AIR FORCE BASE

MESA DEL SOL

ISLETA PUEBLO

Five Points

Armijo

Rio Grande

Old Town Albuquerque
Albuquerque Mus.
American Intl. Rattlesnake Mus.
iExplora!, Science Center &
Children's Mus. of Albuquerque
N. Mex. Mus. of Natural Hist. & Sci.
Old Town Plaza
San Felipe de Neri Church
Turquoise Museum

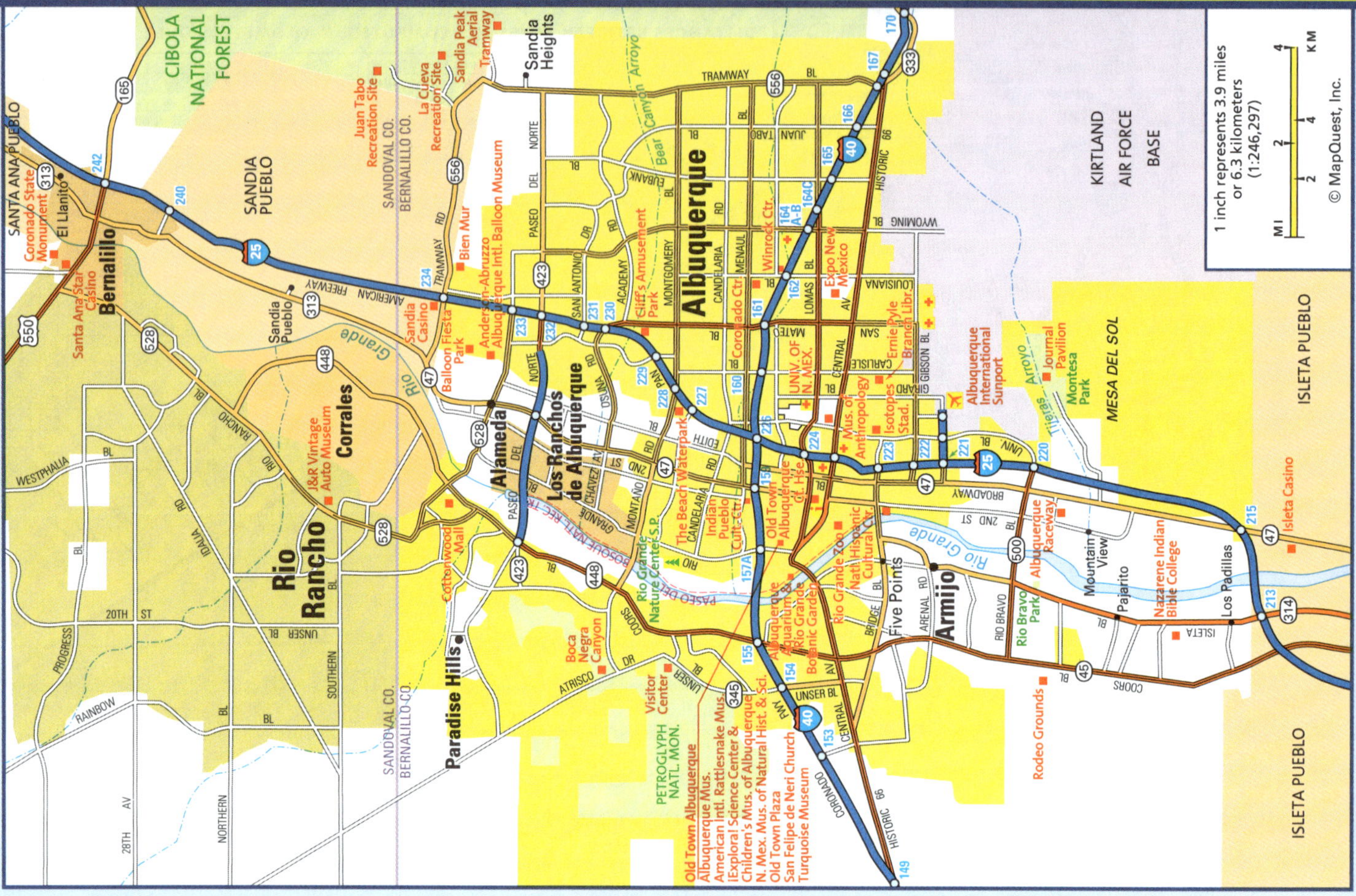

PETROGLYPH NATL. MON.

Austin map:

Austin

West Lake Hills

Austin-Bergstrom International Airport

McKinney Falls State Park

1 inch represents 2.3 miles or 3.7 kilometers (1:145,488)

© MapQuest, Inc.

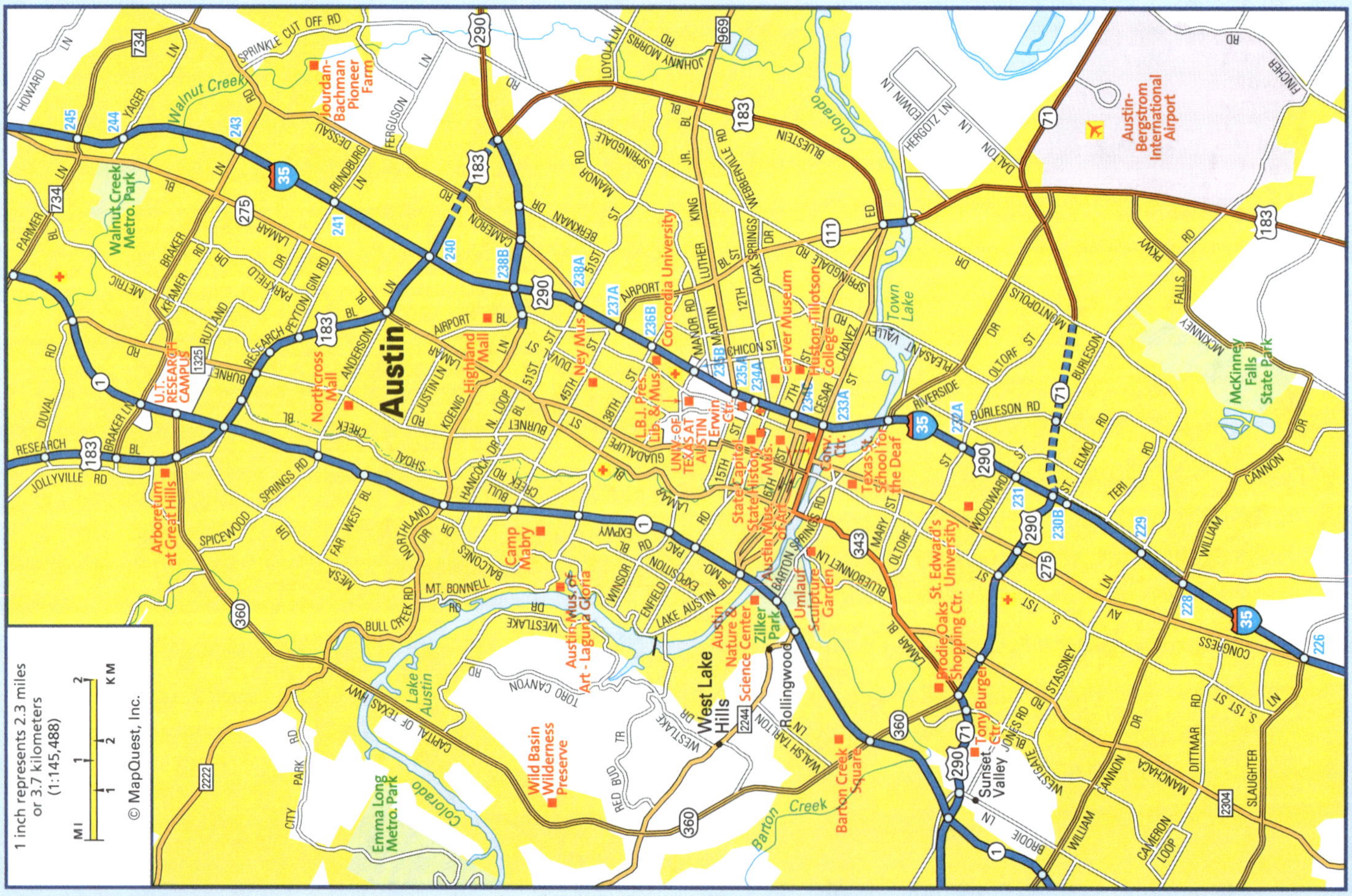

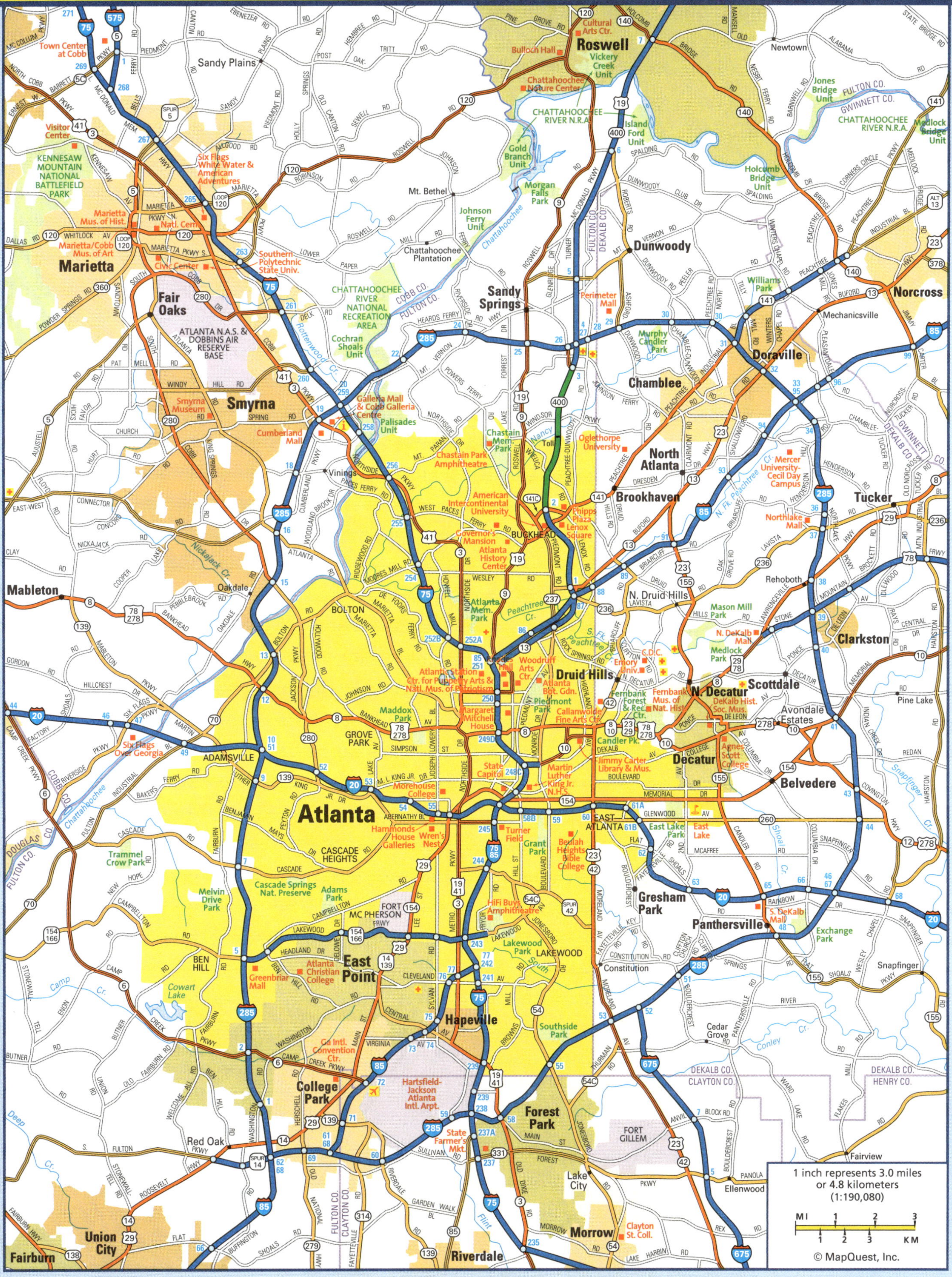

N

Baltimore

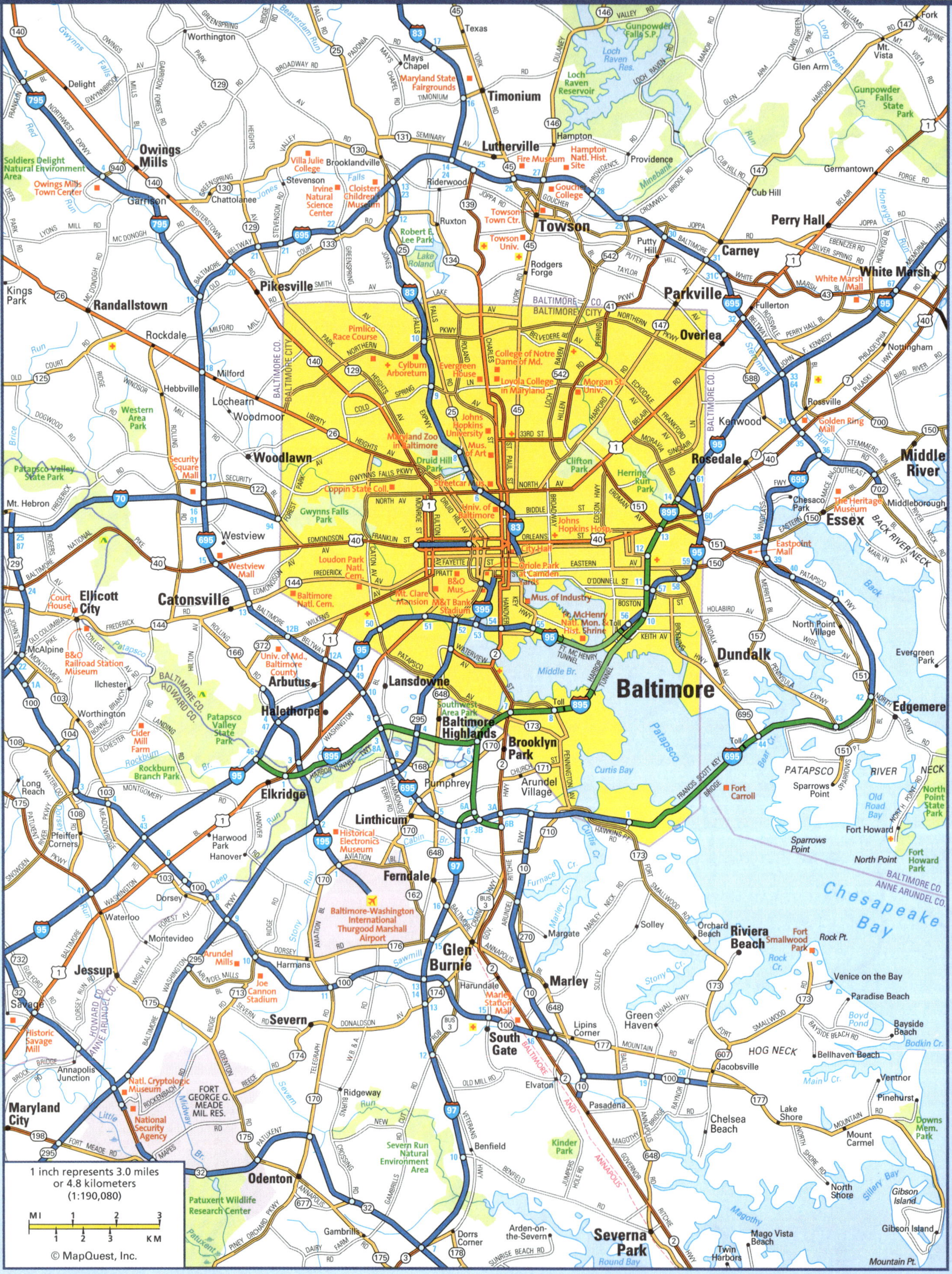

1 inch represents 3.0 miles
or 4.8 kilometers
(1:190,080)

© MapQuest, Inc.

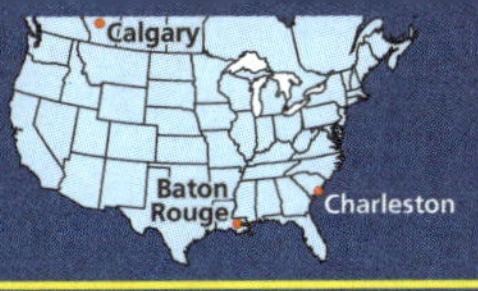

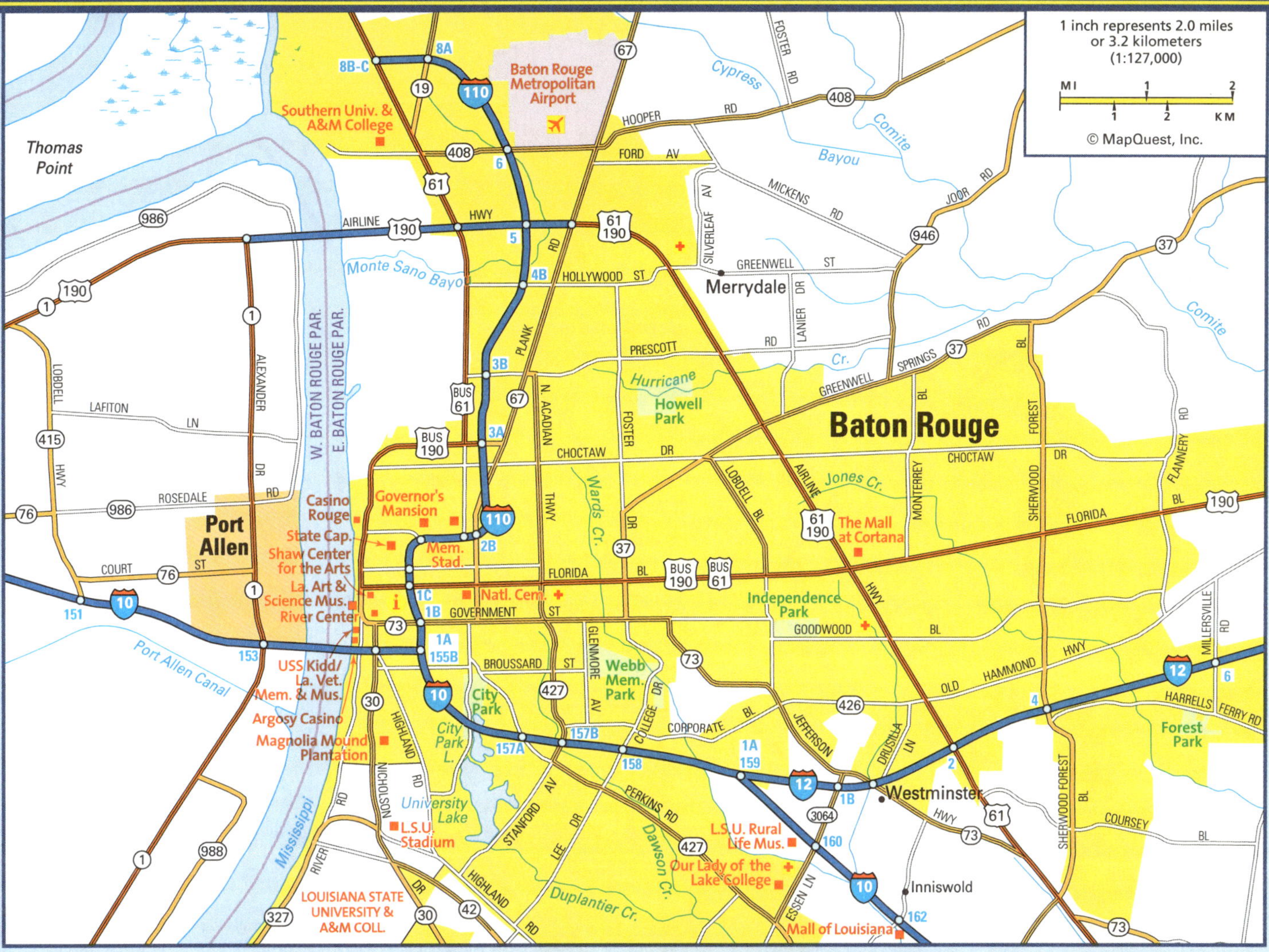

Calgary
Baton Rouge
Charleston
N

1 inch represents 2.0 miles or 3.2 kilometers (1:127,000)
MI
KM
© MapQuest, Inc.
Baton Rouge
Port Allen
Thomas Point
Merrydale
Westminster
Inniswold
Baton Rouge Metropolitan Airport
Southern Univ. & A&M College
Casino Rouge
Governor's Mansion
State Cap.
Shaw Center for the Arts
La. Art & Science Mus.
River Center
Mem. Stad.
Natl. Cem.
USS Kidd/ La. Vet. Mem. & Mus.
Argosy Casino
Magnolia Mound Plantation
L.S.U. Stadium
LOUISIANA STATE UNIVERSITY & A&M COLL.
University Lake
City Park
City Park L.
Webb Mem. Park
Howell Park
Independence Park
Forest Park
The Mall at Cortana
L.S.U. Rural Life Mus.
Our Lady of the Lake College
Mall of Louisiana
Mississippi
Port Allen Canal
Monte Sano Bayou
Cypress
Comite
Bayou
Hurricane Cr.
Jones Cr.
Wards Cr.
Dawson Cr.
Duplantier Cr.
W. BATON ROUGE PAR.
E. BATON ROUGE PAR.
AIRLINE HWY
HOOPER RD
FORD AV
MICKENS RD
GREENWELL ST
HOLLYWOOD ST
PRESCOTT RD
GREENWELL SPRINGS RD
CHOCTAW DR
FLORIDA BL
GOVERNMENT ST
BROUSSARD ST
GOODWOOD BL
OLD HAMMOND HWY
CORPORATE BL
PERKINS RD
COURSEY BL
HARRELLS FERRY RD
JOOR RD
FLANNERY RD
MILLERSVILLE RD
LOBDELL HWY
LAFITON LN
ROSEDALE RD
COURT ST
ALEXANDER DR
PLANK RD
N. ACADIAN THWY
FOSTER DR
GLENMORE AV
COLLEGE DR
JEFFERSON HWY
DRUSILLA LN
SHERWOOD FOREST BL
MONTERREY BL
STANFORD AV
LEE DR
HIGHLAND RD
NICHOLSON DR
RIVER RD
ESSEN LN
SILVERLEAF AV
LANIER DR
FOSTER RD

Calgary
1 inch represents 4.5 miles or 7.3 kilometers (1:285,405)
MI
KM
© MapQuest, Inc.
Calgary Intl. Airport
Nose Hill Park
Bowness Park
Canada Olympic Park
Market Mall
Univ. of Calgary
McMahon Stadium
S.A.I.T.
Deerfoot Mall
Aero Space Mus.
Sunridge Mall
TELUS Convention Centre
Glenbow Mus.
Naval Mus. of Alta.
Sci. Ctr.
Calgary Tower
Ft. Calgary
Zoo
Bow Habitat Station
Stampede Park & Saddledome
Mus. of the Regiments
River Park
Chinook Ctr.
Heritage Park
Sarcee Military Reserve
Glenmore Park
Glenmore Res.
SARCEE INDIAN RESERVE NO. 145
Edworthy Park
Bow
Elbow
COUNTRY BL
COUNTRY HILLS BLVD.
CROWCHILD TRAIL
SHAGANAPPI TR
STONEY TRAIL
DEERFOOT TRAIL
MEMORIAL DR
GLENMORE TRAIL
BARLOW TRAIL
MACLEOD TRAIL S.E.
OLD BANFF COACH RD
16TH AV
17TH AV S.E.
64TH AV N.E.
MC KNIGHT BL
ANDERSON RD
SOUTHLAND DR
114 AV S.E.

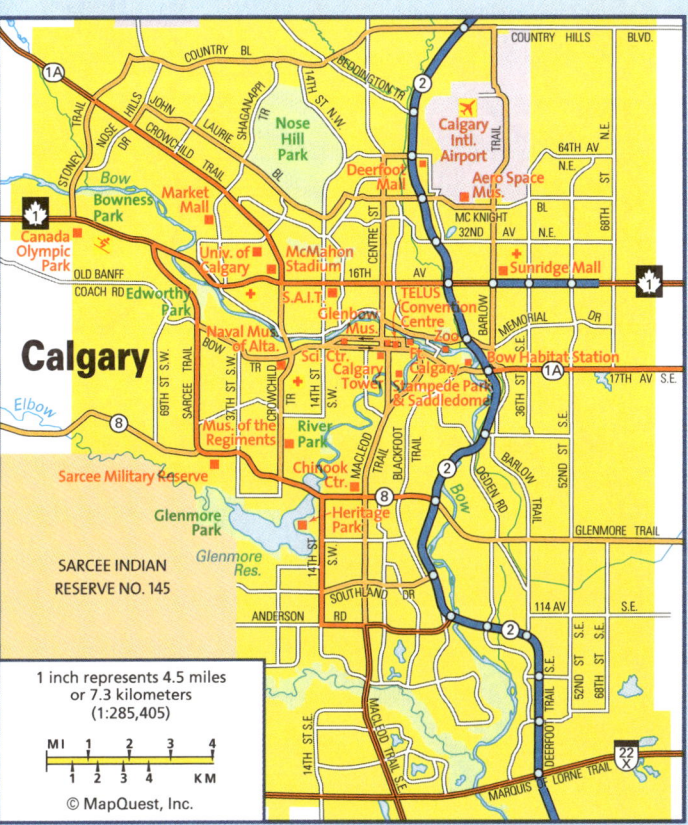

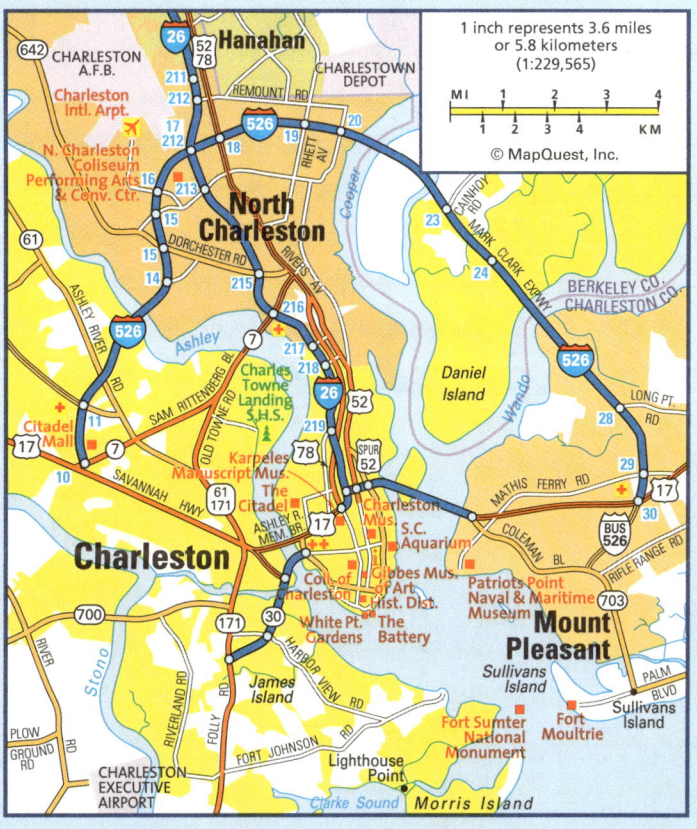

1 inch represents 3.6 miles or 5.8 kilometers (1:229,565)
MI
KM
© MapQuest, Inc.
North Charleston
Charleston
Hanahan
Mount Pleasant
CHARLESTON A.F.B.
Charleston Intl. Arpt.
N. Charleston Coliseum Performing Arts & Conv. Ctr.
CHARLESTOWN DEPOT
Charles Towne Landing S.H.S.
Citadel Mall
Karpeles Manuscript Mus.
The Citadel
Charleston Mus.
S.C. Aquarium
Gibbes Mus. of Art
Hist. Dist.
Coll. of Charleston
White Pt. Gardens
The Battery
Patriots Point Naval & Maritime Museum
Sullivans Island
Fort Sumter National Monument
Fort Moultrie
James Island
Daniel Island
Lighthouse Point
Morris Island
Clarke Sound
CHARLESTON EXECUTIVE AIRPORT
BERKELEY CO.
CHARLESTON CO.
Ashley
Cooper
Wando
Stono
ASHLEY RIVER RD
DORCHESTER RD
RIVERS AV
RHETT AV
REMOUNT RD
SAM RITTENBERG BL
OLD TOWNE RD
SAVANNAH HWY
MARK CLARK EXPWY
CAINHOY RD
LONG PT. RD
MATHIS FERRY RD
COLEMAN BL
RIFLE RANGE RD
PALM BLVD
HARBOR VIEW RD
FORT JOHNSON RD
FOLLY RD
RIVERLAND RD
RIVER RD
PLOW GROUND RD
ASHLEY R. MEM. BR.

P 25 Louisiana
P 40 South Carolina
P 59 Alberta

N

1 inch represents 3.4 miles
or 5.5 kilometers
(1:217,545)

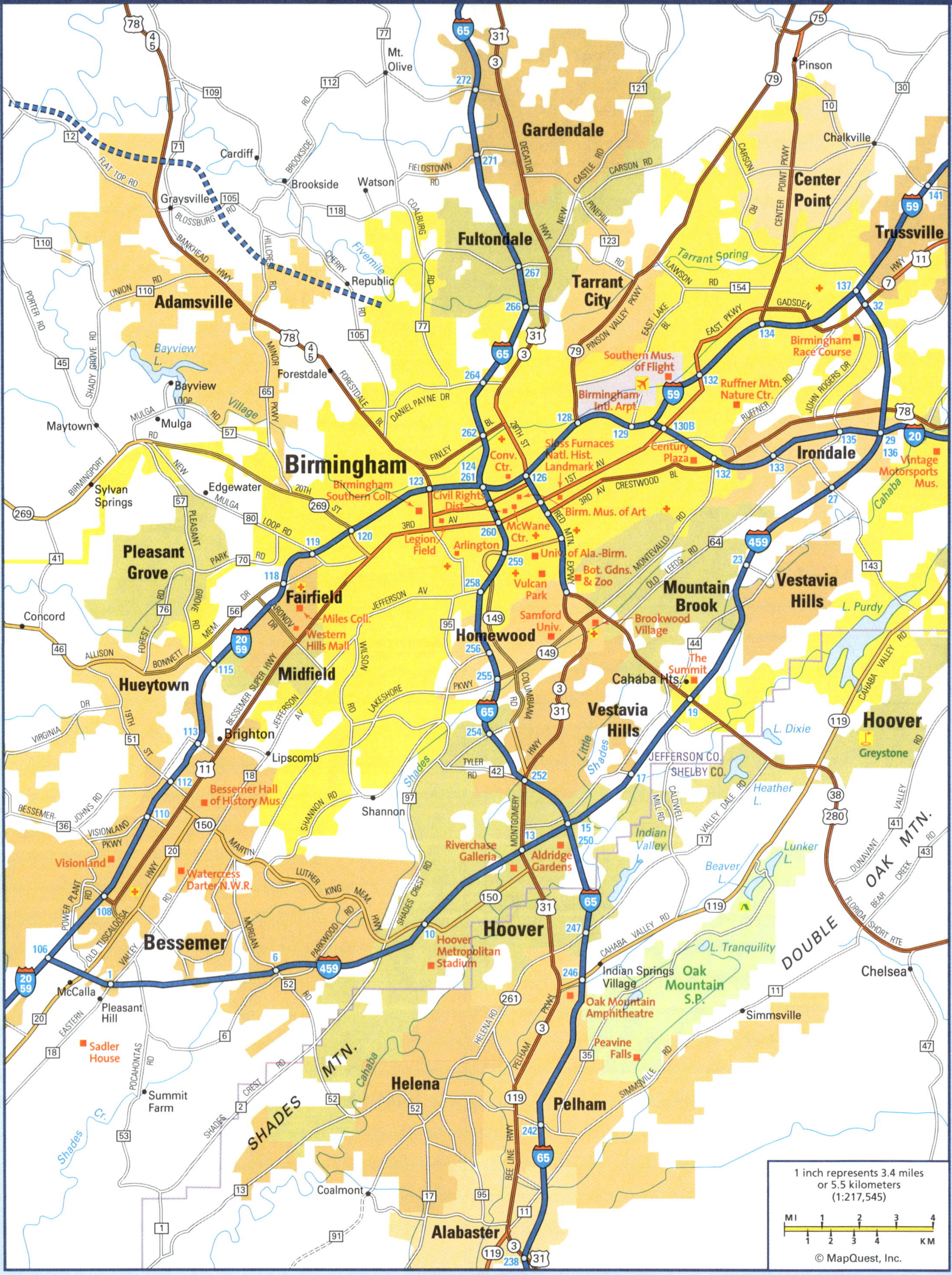

© MapQuest, Inc.

P 6
Alabama

78 45 Mt. Olive 65 31 75

Cardiff Brookside Watson 272 3 Pinson 79 10 30 141

Graysville 105 118 Republic 271 Gardendale 121 Chalkville

Flat Top Rd 71 Blossburg Rd Bankhead Hwy Coalburg Rd Fieldstown Rd Decatur Hwy Castle Rd Carson Rd Center Point Pkwy Center Point 59 11

Adamsville 110 78 45 105 Fultondale 267 123 Tarrant Spring Lawson Rd 154 Gadsden Trussville 7

110 Union Rd Minor Pkwy 77 266 Tarrant City Pinson Valley Pkwy East Lake East Pkwy 134 137 Birmingham Race Course 32

Porter Rd Forestdale Forestdale Bl 264 31 79 East Pkwy Ruffner Century 135 29 78 20

45 Bayview L. Daniel Payne Dr Southern Mus. of Flight 59 132 Ruffner Mtn. Nature Ctr. 133 136 Vintage Motorsports Mus.

Maytown Mulga Rd 57 Finley 262 Bl Birmingham Intl. Arpt. 128 129 130B Century Plaza Irondale 27

Sylvan Springs 269 Edgewater Mulga 80 Loop Rd Conv. Ctr. 26th St Sloss Furnaces Natl. Hist. Landmark 1st Crestwood Bl 132 Cahaba

Concord 41 Pleasant Grove 76 56 Fairfield 258 260 Birm. Mus. of Art 3rd AV Red Mtn. Expwy 64 459 23 Vestavia Hills 143

46 Allison Bonnett 115 Midfield Jefferson AV 95 259 Univ. of Ala.-Birm. Bot. Gdns. & Zoo Old Leeds Rd L. Purdy

Hueytown 113 Brighton Wilson Rd Vulcan Park Samford Univ. Mountain Brook The Summit 19 119 Hoover

Virginia 51 Lipscomb 18 Lakeshore 149 Homewood 256 149 Brookwood Village Greystone

Bessemer 36 Johns Rd 112 110 150 Bessemer Hall of History Mus. Shannon Rd 97 Shades 42 254 252 Cahaba Hts. Jefferson Co. Shelby Co. Heather L. 38 280

Visionland Pkwy Visionland 20 Watercress Darter N.W.R. Martin Luther King Mem. Hwy 255 65 31 Vestavia Hills Caldwell Mill Rd Indian Valley 41

108 Old Tuscaloosa Parkwood Shades Crest Rd Riverchase Galleria 13 15 250 17 Beaver L. Lunker L. Oak Mtn.

106 McCalla 1 6 459 10 Hoover Metropolitan Stadium Aldridge Gardens 247 65 Cahaba Valley Rd 119 L. Tranquility Double Chelsea

Pleasant Hill 52 Hoover 246 Indian Springs Village Oak Mountain S.P. 11

18 Sadler House Summit Farm Pocahontas Rd Shades Mtn. Cahaba 261 Helena Rd Pelham Pkwy 35 Oak Mountain Amphitheatre Peavine Falls Simmsville 47

53 Shades Cr. 2 Crest Rd 52 52 Helena 119 Pelham 242 11

13 Coalmont 17 95 65 11

1 91 238 31

Alabama Alabaster 119 3 31

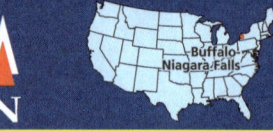

N

Niagara-on-the-Lake
Lewiston
Queenston
St. Davids
York RD
Model City
Dickersonville
Bond Lake Co. Park
Pekin
Lockport Locks
Niagara Co. Hist. Society
Lockport
South Lockport
Lockport Mall

Glenwood
Queenston Hts. N.H.S.
Earl W. Brydges Artpark
TUSCARORA INDIAN RESERVATION
Sanborn
Shawnee

Floral Clock
Devil's Hole S.P.
Butterfly Conservatory
Whirlpool S.P.
Niagara Univ
Power Reservoir
Niagara Power Project Vis. Ctr.
Reservoir S.P.
Colonial Village
Pendleton Center
Pendleton

Aquarium of Niagara
Casino Niagara
Skylon
Court House
Hyde Park
Niagara Falls
Niagara Falls International Airport
Bergholtz
St. Johnsburg
Summit Park Mall
Oppenheim County Park
Beach Ridge
Wendelville
Getzville
Swormville

American Falls
Horseshoe Falls
Goat I.
Seneca Niagara Casino
Buckhorn Island S.P.
Sandy Beach
North Tonawanda
Robinson

Marineland
Navy Island
Martin's Fantasy Island
GRAND ISLAND
Herschell Carrousel Factory Museum
Long Homestead
Ellicott Cr. Co. Park
Brighton Park
East Amherst
Great Baehre Swamp State Wetlands

Niagara Falls
Big Six Mile Creek Marina
Grandyle Village
Tonawanda
Sheridan Park
Boulevard Mall
Univ. at Buffalo, S.U.N.Y.

Snyder
Zooz
Stevensville
Beaver Island S.P.
Kenmore
Buffalo
Amherst
Eastern Hills Mall
Williamsville

Bowen
Port Colborne
Ridgeway Battlefield Museum
Fort Erie
Buffalo & Erie Co. Hist. Soc. Mus.
Delaware Park
Buffalo Zoological Gardens
Grover Cleveland Co. Park
Univ. at Buffalo, S.U.N.Y.
Buffalo Niagara Int'l Airport
Bowmansville
Depew
Walden Galleria
Cheektowaga

Sherkston
Fort Erie Hist. Mus.
Ridgeway
Buffalo State Coll. N.Y.
Fort Erie R.R. Mus.
Fort Erie Race Track
Albright-Knox Art Gallery
T. Roosevelt Inaugural N.H.S.
Buffalo Mus. of Science
Sloan
Reinstein Woods St. Unique Area

Peace Bridge Toll
La Salle Park
Historic Fort Erie
City Hall Observation Deck
Conv. Ctr.
U.S. Coast Guard Station
Naval & Military Park
HSBC Arena
Dunn Tire Park
West Seneca

Crystal Beach
Thunder Bay
Windmill Pt.
Tifft Farm Nature Preserve
South Park
Cazenovia Park

Abino Bay
Pt. Abino
LAKE ERIE
CANADA
UNITED STATES
Buffalo & Erie County Botanical Gardens
Our Lady of Victory Basilica
Lackawanna
Woodlawn
Blasdell
Woodlawn Beach State Park
Bay View
McKinley Mall
Webster Corners

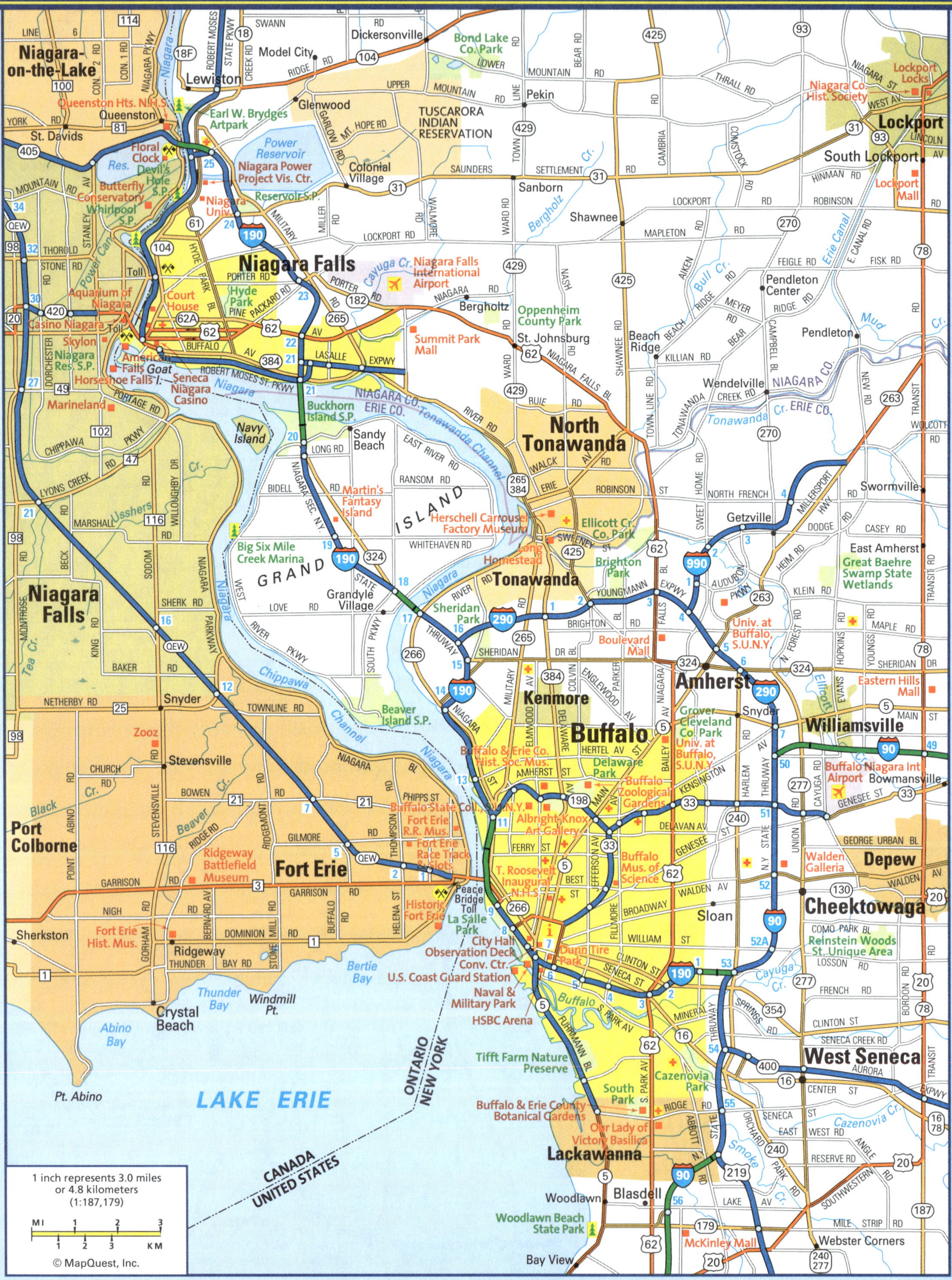

1 inch represents 3.0 miles
or 4.8 kilometers
(1:187,179)

MI
0 1 2 3
0 1 2 3
KM

© MapQuest, Inc.

P 38 New York
P 62 Ontario

ONTARIO
NEW YORK

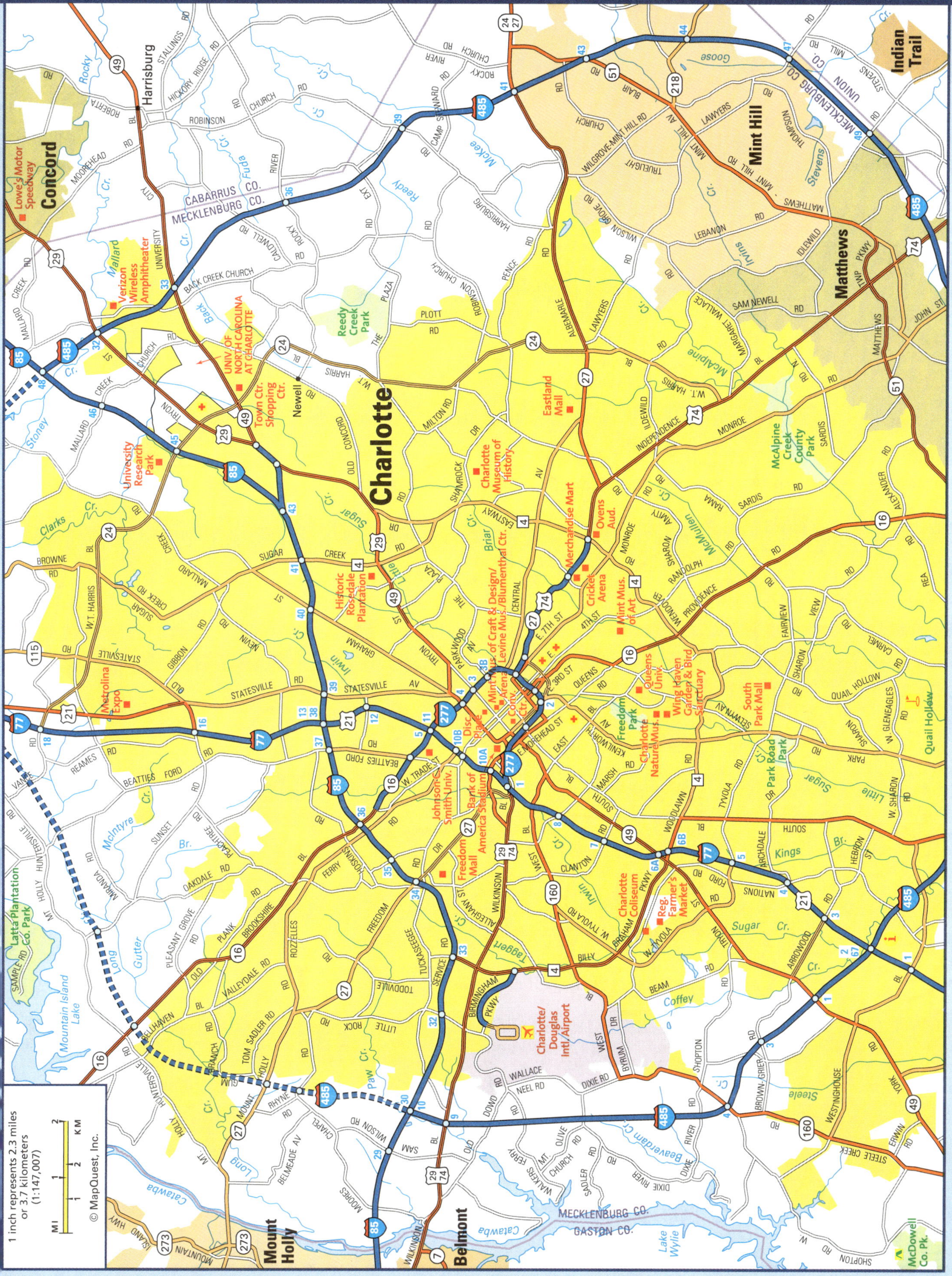

Charlotte

Concord

Harrisburg

CABARRUS CO.
MECKLENBURG CO.

Lowe's Motor Speedway

Verizon Wireless Amphitheater

Mallard Creek

University Research Park

UNIV. OF NORTH CAROLINA AT CHARLOTTE

Town Ctr. Shopping Ctr.

Newell

Indian Trail

Mint Hill

Matthews

MECKLENBURG CO.
UNION CO.

Goose

Eastland Mall

Charlotte Museum of History

Reedy Creek Park

McAlpine Creek County Park

Merchandise Mart

Owens Aud.

Cricket Arena

Mint Mus. of Art

Queens Univ.

Wing Haven Garden & Bird Sanctuary

South Park Mall

Park Road Park

Historic Rosedale Plantation

Metrolina Expo

Mint Mus. of Craft & Design/ Levine Mus./Blumenthal Ctr.

Disc. Place

Conv. Ctr.

Bank of America Stadium

Johnson C. Smith Univ.

Freedom Mall

Freedom Park

Charlotte Nature Mus.

Charlotte Coliseum

Reg. Farmer's Market

Charlotte/ Douglas Int. Airport

SAMPLE

Latta Plantation Co. Park

Mountain Island Lake

McIntyre

Mount Holly

Belmont

MECKLENBURG CO.
GASTON CO.

Lake Wylie

McDowell Co. Pk.

1 inch represents 2.3 miles or 3.7 kilometers (1:147,007)

© MapQuest, Inc.

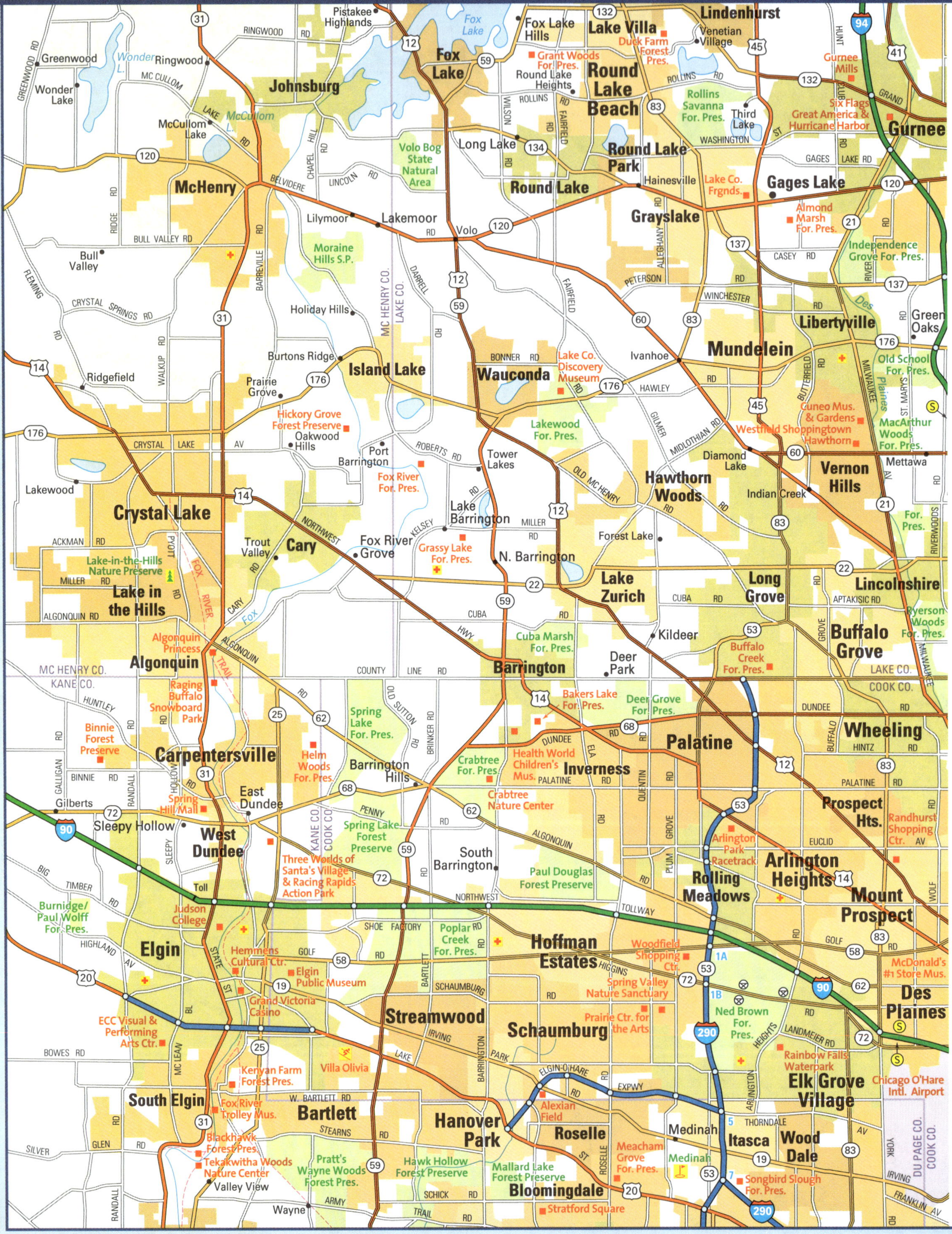

N

P 19
Illinois

Greenwood
Greenwood Rd
Wonder L.
Ringwood
Wonder Lake
McCullom Lake
McCullom Lake
Johnsburg
Pistakee Highlands
Fox Lake
Fox Lake Hills
Lindenhurst
Venetian Village
Grant Woods For. Pres.
Round Lake Heights
Lake Villa
Duck Farm Forest Pres.
Gurnee Mills
Round Lake Beach
Six Flags Great America & Hurricane Harbor
Gurnee
McHenry
Lilymoor
Lakemoor
Long Lake
Round Lake Park
Rollins Savanna For. Pres.
Third Lake
Gages Lake
Moraine Hills S.P.
Volo
Round Lake
Hainesville
Lake Co. Frgnds.
Almond Marsh For. Pres.
Bull Valley
Holiday Hills
Volo Bog State Natural Area
Grayslake
Independence Grove For. Pres.
Ridgefield
Burtons Ridge
Island Lake
Wauconda
Lake Co. Discovery Museum
Ivanhoe
Mundelein
Libertyville
Green Oaks
Prairie Grove
Hickory Grove Forest Preserve
Oakwood Hills
Port Barrington
Tower Lakes
Lakewood For. Pres.
Hawthorn Woods
Old School For. Pres.
MacArthur Woods For. Pres.
Lakewood
Fox River For. Pres.
Diamond Lake
Cuneo Mus. & Gardens
Westfield Shoppingtown Hawthorn
Mettawa
Crystal Lake
Trout Valley
Cary
Fox River Grove
Lake Barrington
N. Barrington
Grassy Lake For. Pres.
Forest Lake
Indian Creek
Vernon Hills
For. Pres.
Lake-in-the-Hills Nature Preserve
Lake in the Hills
Lake Zurich
Long Grove
Lincolnshire
Ryerson Woods For. Pres.
Algonquin Princess
Algonquin
Kildeer
Buffalo Grove
Raging Buffalo Snowboard Park
Cuba Marsh For. Pres.
Deer Park
Buffalo Creek For. Pres.
Binnie Forest Preserve
Barrington
Bakers Lake For. Pres.
Deer Grove For. Pres.
Wheeling
Gilberts
Sleepy Hollow
Carpentersville
Spring Lake For. Pres.
Helm Woods For. Pres.
Barrington Hills
Crabtree For. Pres.
Health World Children's Mus.
Inverness
Palatine
Prospect Hts.
Randhurst Shopping Ctr.
Burnidge/ Paul Wolff For. Pres.
East Dundee
Crabtree Nature Center
Arlington Park Racetrack
Arlington Heights
Mount Prospect
West Dundee
Spring Lake Forest Preserve
South Barrington
Rolling Meadows
Judson College
Three Worlds of Santa's Village & Racing Rapids Action Park
Paul Douglas Forest Preserve
Elgin
Hemmens Cultural Ctr.
Elgin Public Museum
Poplar Creek For. Pres.
Hoffman Estates
Woodfield Shopping Ctr.
Des Plaines
McDonald's #1 Store Mus.
ECC Visual & Performing Arts Ctr.
Grand Victoria Casino
Streamwood
Schaumburg
Spring Valley Nature Sanctuary
Prairie Ctr. for the Arts
Ned Brown For. Pres.
Rainbow Falls Waterpark
South Elgin
Kerwan Farm Forest Pres.
Villa Olivia
Hanover Park
Roselle
Medinah
Itasca
Wood Dale
Elk Grove Village
Chicago O'Hare Intl. Airport
Fox River Trolley Mus.
Bartlett
Alexian Field
Meacham Grove For. Pres.
Songbird Slough For. Pres.
Blackhawk Forest Pres.
Tekakwitha Woods Nature Center
Valley View
Pratt's Wayne Woods Forest Pres.
Hawk Hollow Forest Preserve
Mallard Lake Forest Preserve
Bloomingdale
Stratford Square
Wayne

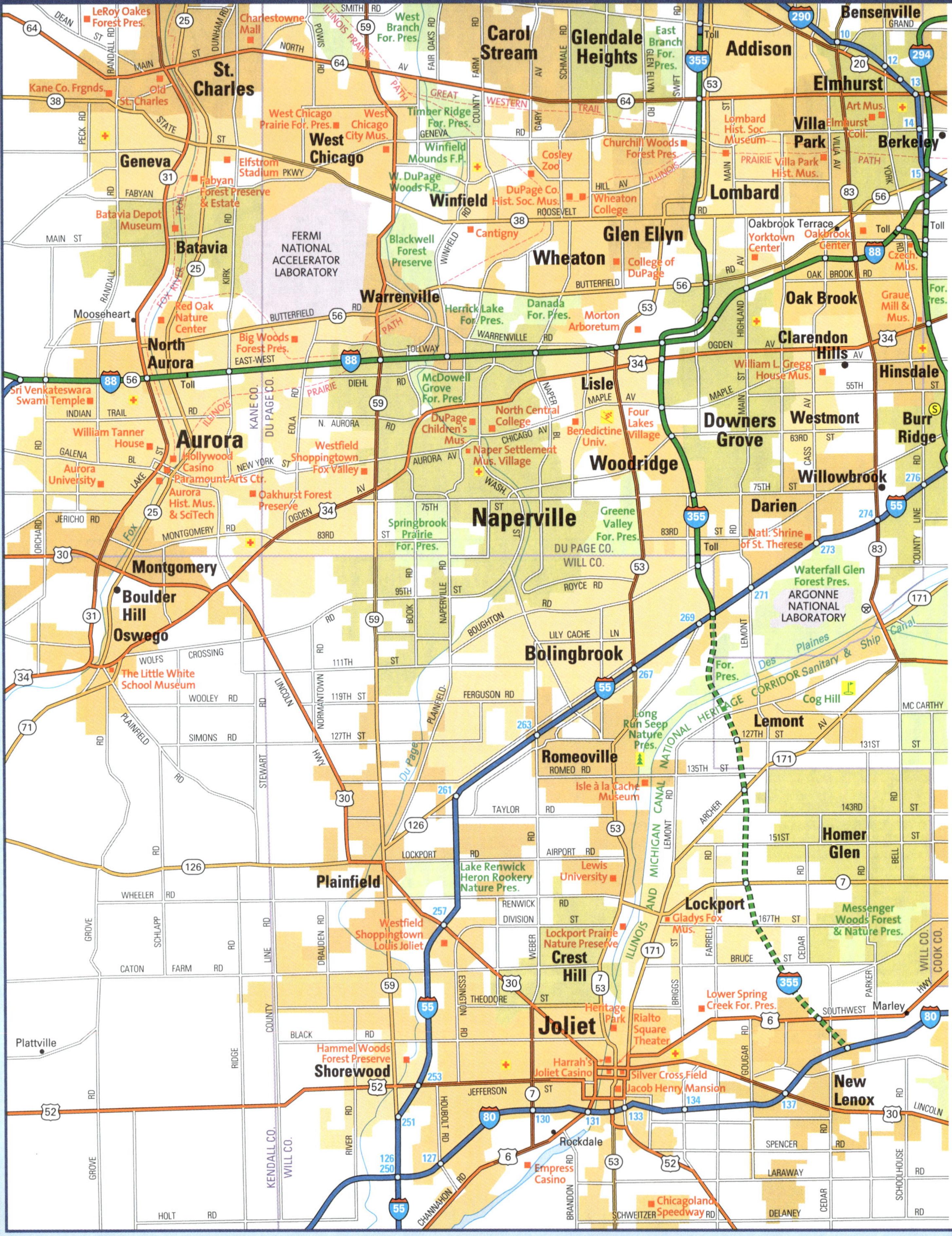

LAKE

MICHIGAN

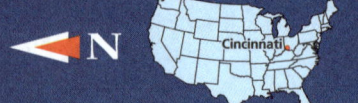

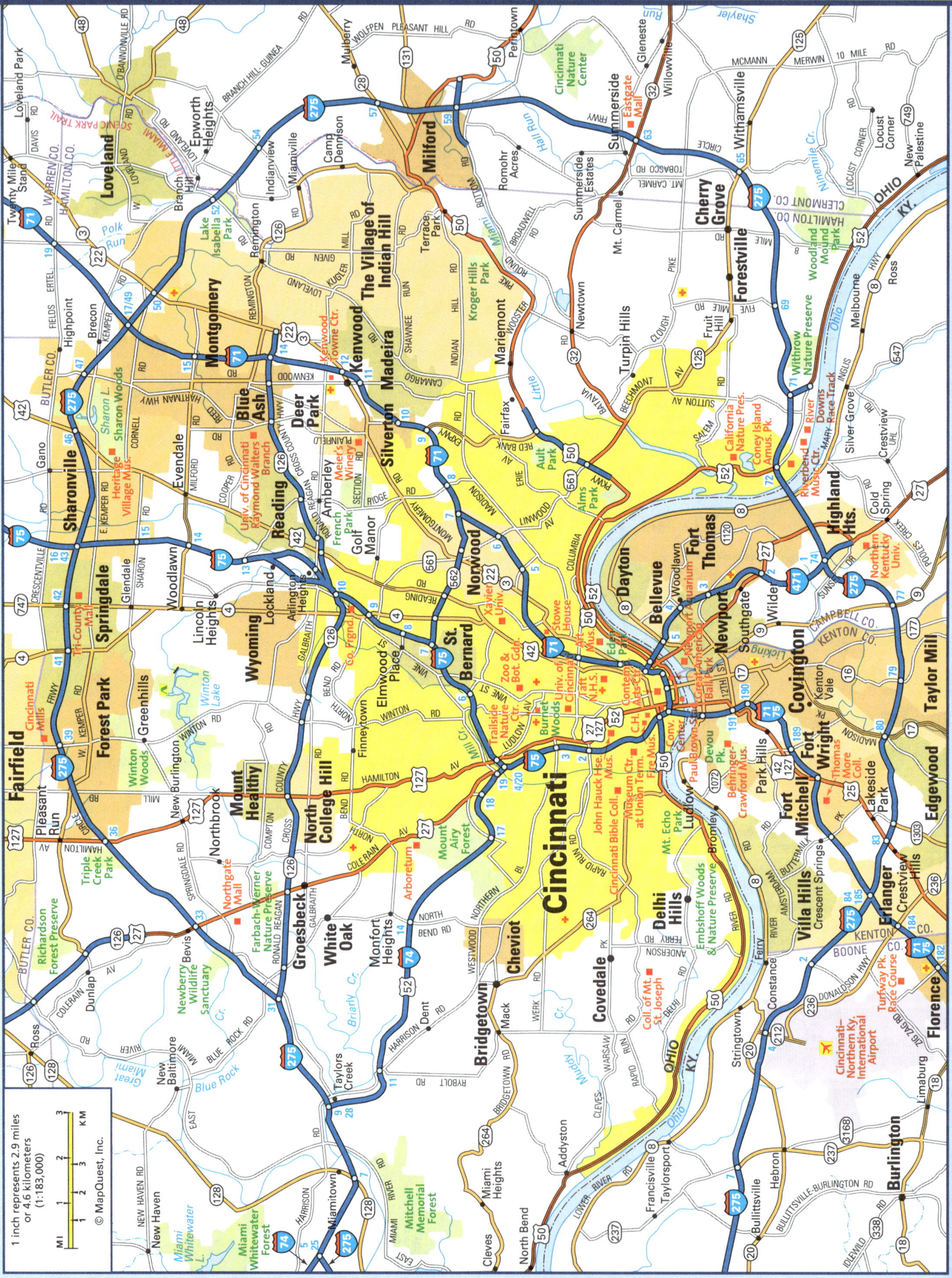

Cincinnati
Covington
Newport
Norwood
St. Bernard
Fairfield
Forest Park
Springdale
Sharonville
Montgomery
Blue Ash
Reading
Wyoming
Lockland
Loveland
Milford
Madeira
Kenwood
Mariemont
Silverton
Deer Park
The Village of Indian Hill
Cheviot
Bridgetown
Delhi Hills
Covedale
Groesbeck
White Oak
North College Hill
Mount Healthy
Forestville
Cherry Grove
Dayton
Bellevue
Fort Thomas
Highland Hts.
Fort Wright
Fort Mitchell
Erlanger
Villa Hills
Edgewood
Taylor Mill
Florence
Burlington
Cincinnati-Northern Ky. International Airport
1 inch represents 2.9 miles or 4.6 kilometers (1:183,000)
© MapQuest, Inc.

P 43 Ohio

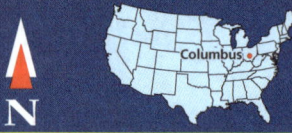

N

Columbus

Delaware Co. / **Franklin Co.**

Rathbone · HOME · RD · Lewis Center · Alum Creek Res. · WOODTOWN RD · 605

745 · 257 · O'Shaughnessy Res. · 315 · 23 · STATE · RD · BIG · AFRICA · RD · WORTHINGTON · RD · CENTER · VILLAGE · RD · Center Village

Shawnee Hills · ORANGE · RD · OLD · 71 · MAXTOWN · RD · SUNBURY · GORSUCH · RD · Harlem · FANCHER · RD

Columbus Zoo & Aquarium · Wyandot Lake · **Powell** · POWELL · RD · Highbanks Metro Park · 750 · Polaris Fashion Place · Polaris Amphitheater · Hoover Reservoir

Dublin · Tartan Fields · GLICK · Muirfield Village · Leatherlips Monument · JEWETT · RD · 315 · PARK · RD · 121 · **Westerville** · Hanby House · Otterbein Coll. · WALNUT · Hoover Dam Park

745 · Newmarket Mall · 20 · 257 · HARD · RD · SMOKEROW · RD · 22 · 23 · 26 · 119 · Sharon Woods Metro Park · 27 · 29 · Inniswood Metro Gardens · ROCKY

33 · 17 · Brookside Estates · 270 · 161 · DUBLIN-GRANVILLE · RD · **Worthington** · 710 · 117 · 161 · **Huber Ridge** · 30 · 161 · New Albany

SHIER RINGS · RD · POST · RD · Linworth · Ohio State University Airport · Antrim Park · Riverlea · State School for the Blind and Deaf · Minerva Park · 3 · GRANVILLE · RD · Blendon Woods Metro Park · 62

16 · Mall at Tuttle Crossing · 33 · BETHEL · RD · 315 · **Columbus** · 116 · Northland Mall · Easton Town Center · 32 · 33

HAYDEN RUN · RD · **Hilliard** · CEMETERY · HENDERSON · RD · COOKE · RD · 115 · FERRIS · RD · 33

Upper Arlington · 315 · INDIANOLA · 114 · OAKLAND PARK · AV · AGLER · RD · **Gahanna** · 62 · HAVENS · RD

13 · FISHINGER · RD · NORTH · BROADWAY · WEBER · RD · 113 · HUDSON · ST · 3 · 62 · 317 · HAVENS CORNERS · RD

San Margherita · KENNY · RD · TREMONT · Value City Arena · OHIO STATE UNIV. · Crew Stadium · Ohio Hist. Ctr. · Wexner Ctr. · 111 · STELZER · RD · 35 · Port Columbus International Airport · 37

10 · MCKINLEY · Marble Cliff · LANE · AV · Ohio Stad. · Ohio Expo Ctr. · 17TH · Ohio Dominican Univ. · 16

91 · Shrum Mound · **Grandview Heights** · 315 · 110A · 109 · 6 · 670 · DEFENSE SUPPLY CENTER · 39

8 · 93 · WILSON · RD · 95 · Nationwide Arena · 2 · 3 · 4A · MT. VERNON · AV · 16 · E. · BROAD · **Whitehall** · 270

70 · FISHER RD · 94 · Mus. of Art · COL Columbus · 40 · 62 · **Bexley** · MAIN · 317 · ST · 41

Valleyview · 96 · Franklin Univ. · Franklin Park · 40 · JAMES · **Reynoldsburg**

New Rome · 40 · 7 · BROAD · ST · 97 · 98 · State Capitol · German Village · 33 · 102 · Capital Univ. · LIVINGSTON · AV · 40

Alton · **Lincoln Village** · Westland Mall · SULLIVANT · AV · 99 · Cooper Stadium · 105 · 106 · 103 · 70 · 105A · Blacklick Woods Metro Park

HALL · RD · 62 · CLIME · RD · Lou Berliner Park · FREBIS · AV · 105B · 43 · 109 · Eastland Mall · 110 · 70

5 · Big Run Park · Briggsdale · FRANK · RD · 104 · 23 · AV · REFUGEE · RD · Brice · FAIRFIELD CO.

Galloway · 270 · ALKIRE · 2 · Big · Run · **Blacklick Estates**

Bolton Field Airport · Urbancrest · Columbus Motor Speedway · 46 · WINCHESTER · **Blacklick Estates**

Beulah Park Race Track · **Grove City** · 55 · 102 · WILLIAMS · Obetz · Three Rivers Park · 317

665 · 62 · 100 · STRINGTOWN · RD · 52 · 49 · 270 · GENDER · 33

Pleasant Corners · 71 · 99 · 104 · Shadeville · 317 · Groveport · 674

1 inch represents 2.7 miles or 4.4 kilometers (1:172,000)

MI · 1 · 2 · 3
KM · 1 · 2 · 3

© MapQuest, Inc.

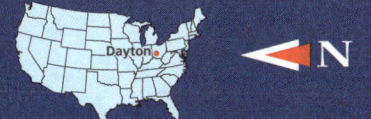

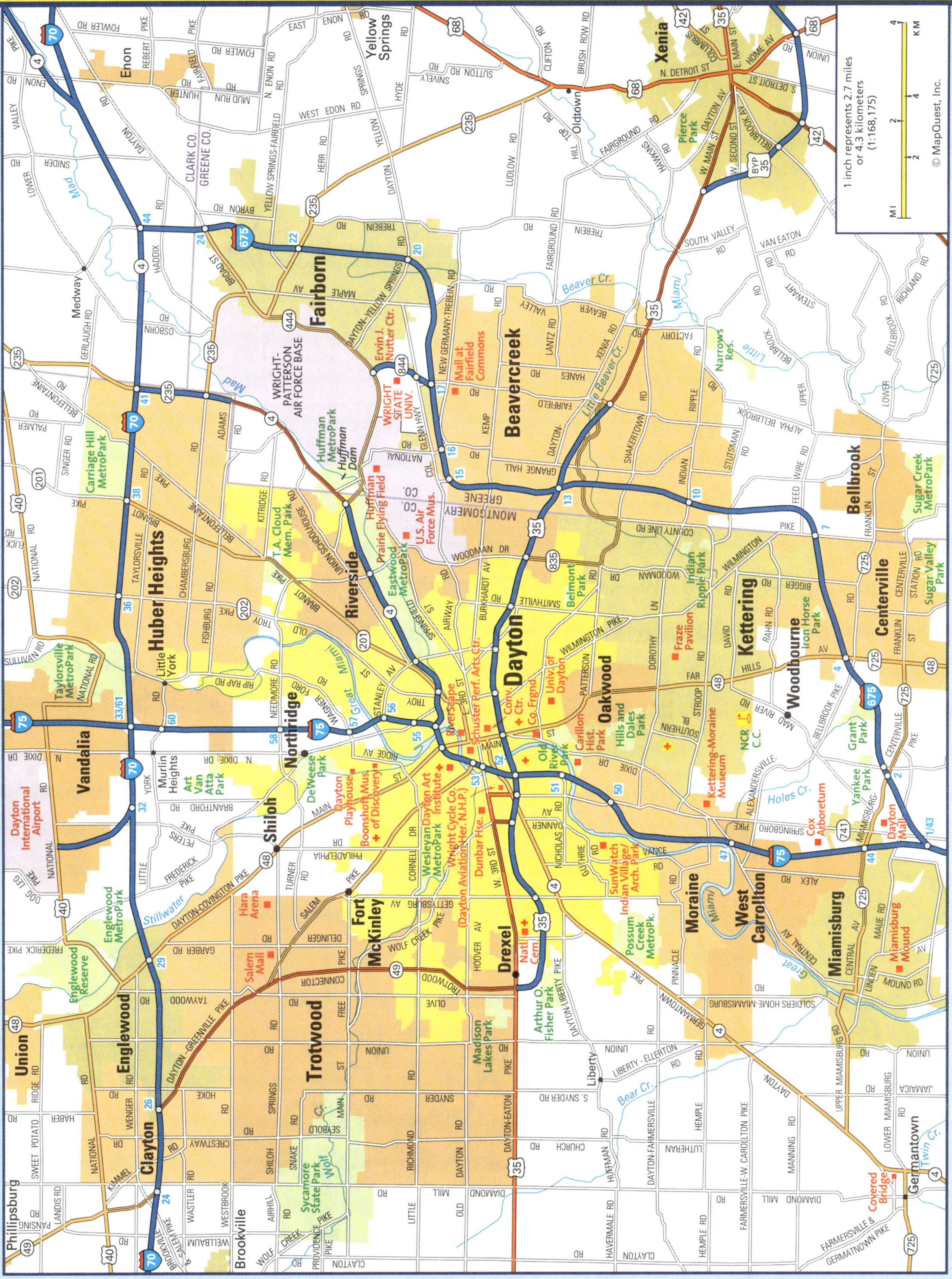
1 inch represents 2.7 miles or 4.3 kilometers (1:168,175)
© MapQuest, Inc.
Dayton
Kettering
Beavercreek
Fairborn
Xenia
Huber Heights
Vandalia
Riverside
Oakwood
Centerville
Miamisburg
West Carrollton
Moraine
Trotwood
Englewood
Clayton
Union
Northridge
Shiloh
Drexel
Fort McKinley
Bellbrook
Woodbourne
Germantown
Brookville
Phillipsburg
Yellow Springs
Enon
Medway
Oldtown
Liberty
Murlin Heights
Little York
WRIGHT-PATTERSON AIR FORCE BASE
WRIGHT STATE UNIV.
Dayton International Airport
U.S. Air Force Mus.
Univ. of Dayton
Mall at Fairfield Commons
Dayton Mall
Salem Mall
Hara Arena
Carillon Hist. Park
Fraze Pavilion
Cox Arboretum
Kettering-Moraine Museum
Dayton Art Institute
Dunbar Hse.
Wright Cycle Co. (Dayton Aviation Her. N.H.P.)
Boonshoft Mus. of Discovery
Dayton Playhouse
Schuster Perf. Arts Ctr.
Conv. Ctr.
RiverScape
Ervin J. Nutter Ctr.
Huffman Prairie Flying Field
Huffman MetroPark
Huffman Dam
Eastwood MetroPark
Carriage Hill MetroPark
Taylorsville MetroPark
Englewood MetroPark
Englewood Reserve
Sycamore State Park
Madison Lakes Park
Possum Creek MetroPk.
SunWatch Indian Village/ Arch. Park
Hills and Dales Park
Indian Ripple Park
Iron Horse Park
Sugar Creek MetroPark
Sugar Valley Park
Grant Park
Yankee Park
Miamisburg Mound
Covered Bridge
Narrows Res.
Pierce Park
Belmont Park
Arthur O. Fisher Park
Natl Cem.
Old River Park
NCR C.C.
Wesleyan MetroPark
DeWeese Park
Art Van Atta Park
T.A. Cloud Mem. Park
CLARK CO.
GREENE CO.
MONTGOMERY CO.
GREENE CO.
Mad
Great Miami
Little Miami
Stillwater
Beaver Cr.
Little Beaver Cr.
Holes Cr.
Bear Cr.
Twin Cr.
Wolf Cr.

P 43 Ohio

N

Denver

Lyons

UTE RD

Platteville

ROOSEVELT
NATIONAL
FOREST

Hygiene

McIntosh Lake

Longmont

St. Vrain Cr.

Calkins
Lake

Fort Vasquez
Mus.

Ione

Boulder Co.
Fairgrounds
Twin Peaks
Mall

Longmont
Museum

St. Vrain
S.P.

Niwot

Firestone

Frederick

Fort Lupton

Dacono

Hudson

Boulder

Erie

Colorado National
Speedway

Wattenberg

Lochbuie

Boulder Mus. of
Contemp. Art.
Pearl Street
Mall
Dushanbe Teahouse
Twenty Ninth Street (u.c., open mid 2006)
Univ of Colorado
Boulder Mus.
of History

Lafayette

WELD CO.
BROOMFIELD CO.
ADAMS CO.

Brighton

Chautauqua
Natl. Ctr. for
Atmospheric
Research

Louisville

Barr
Lake

Barr Lake
State Park

Walker
Ranch
Co. Park
Boulder
Mtn.
Park

Superior

Broomfield

Thornton

Henderson

Eldorado
Canyon S.P.
Eldorado
Springs

Flatiron Crossing
Shopping Center

Adams Co.
Reg. Park

BOULDER CO.
JEFFERSON CO.

JEFFERSON
CO.

ROCKY FLATS
ENVIRONMENTAL
TECHNOLOGY
SITE–D.O.E.

Marketplace at
Northglenn

Northglenn

Westminster

Rocky
Mountain
Arsenal
National
Wildlife Area

Denver
International
Airport

Butterfly Pavilion &
Insect Ctr.

Federal
Heights

Standley
Lake

Hyland
Hills
Water
World

Welby

Dupont

Westminster
Mall

Ralston
Res.

Two Ponds N.W.R.
Arvada Ctr. for the
Arts & Humanities

White
Ranch
Co. Park

Arvada

Mile High Greyhound
Park

Commerce City

Natl. Western Stock
Show Complex

Colorado
Railroad Museum

Regis Univ.

Astor
House
Hotel Mus.

Lakeside

Forney Trans. Mus.

Denver
Zoological
Gardens

Colorado
School of Mines
Coors
Brewing Co.
Natl. Renewable Energy Lab

Wheat Ridge

Mountain
View

City
Park

Denver Mus. of
Nature & Science

Windy Saddle
Park

Applewood

Edgewater

Invesco Field
at Mile High

Wings
Over the Rockies
Air & Space Mus.

Buffalo Bill
Memorial Mus.
& Grave

Colorado Mills

U.S. Mint

Bot.
Gdns.

Lowry Campus

Golden

Pleasant View

Heritage
Sq.

Federal
Center

Colo.
Christian
Univ.

Denver

Aurora Mall
Aurora Hist. Mus.

BUCKLEY
AIR NATL.
GUARD BASE

Genesee
Park

Hayden
Green
Mtn.
Park

U.S.G.S.

Denver
Art Mus.

Cherry Creek
Shopping Center

Glendale

Four Mile
Hist. Park

Aurora

El
Rancho

Matthews-Winters Park
Dinosaur Ridge
Red Rocks Park
Amphitheatre

Univ of
Denver

Buckingham Sq.
Shop. Ctr.

Lakewood

Englewood

Plains
Conservation
Ctr.

Kittredge

Idledale

Morrison

Bear Creek
Lake Park

Ft. Logan Natl. Cem.

Sheridan

Cherry Creek
State Park

Evergreen

Alderfer-
3 Sisters
Park

Indian
Hills

Bear Creek
Canyon Park

Mt. Falcon
Park

Bow
Mar

Cherry Hills
Village

Cherry Creek
State Park

Aurora Reservoir
Recreation Facility

Aurora
Res.

Greenwood Village

O'Fallon
Park

Tiny
Town

Mus. of Outdoor Arts
Fiddler's Green Amph.

Southwest
Plaza Mall

Columbine
Valley

Southglenn
Mall

Foxfield

Evergreen

Aspen
Park
Meyer Ranch
Park

Hudson Gardens
Aspen Grove
Mall

Littleton Hist. Mus.

Littleton

Littleton
Hist. Mus.

McLellan
Res.

Centennial

Conifer

Chatfield
State Park

Chatfield
Res.

Highlands
Ranch

Lone
Tree

Park Meadows
Shop. Ctr.

ARAPAHOE CO.
DOUGLAS CO.

Parker

Des Moines

Johnston, Grimes, Urbandale, Windsor Heights, Clive, West Des Moines, Norwalk, Altoona, Pleasant Hill

Northview Park, Merle Hay Mall, Walker Johnston Park, Living History Farms, Greenbelt Park, Valley West Mall, Jordan Creek Town Center, Holiday Pk., South Woods Park, Hist. Jordan House, Raccoon River Reg. Park, Brown's Woods Co. Park, Walnut Woods State Park, Dale Maffit Res.

Birdland Park, Drake Univ., Botanical Ctr., Union Park, McHenry Pk., Grand View College, Grandview Park, White Water Univ. Waterpark, St. Frgnds., Iowa State Fairgrounds, Sargent Park

Iowa Events Ctr., Hoyt Sherman Place, Terrace Hill, Ashworth Salisbury House, Des Moines Art Ctr., Waveland Pk., Sci. Ctr., Civic Center, Principal Park, State Capitol, Iowa Hist. Bldg., Doane Park, Grays

Des Moines Water Works Park, MacRae Park, Pioneer Park, Hubbell Tract, Yellow Banks Co. Park, Evergreen Av, Ewing Park, Yeader Ck. Lake Co. Park, Lake Easter

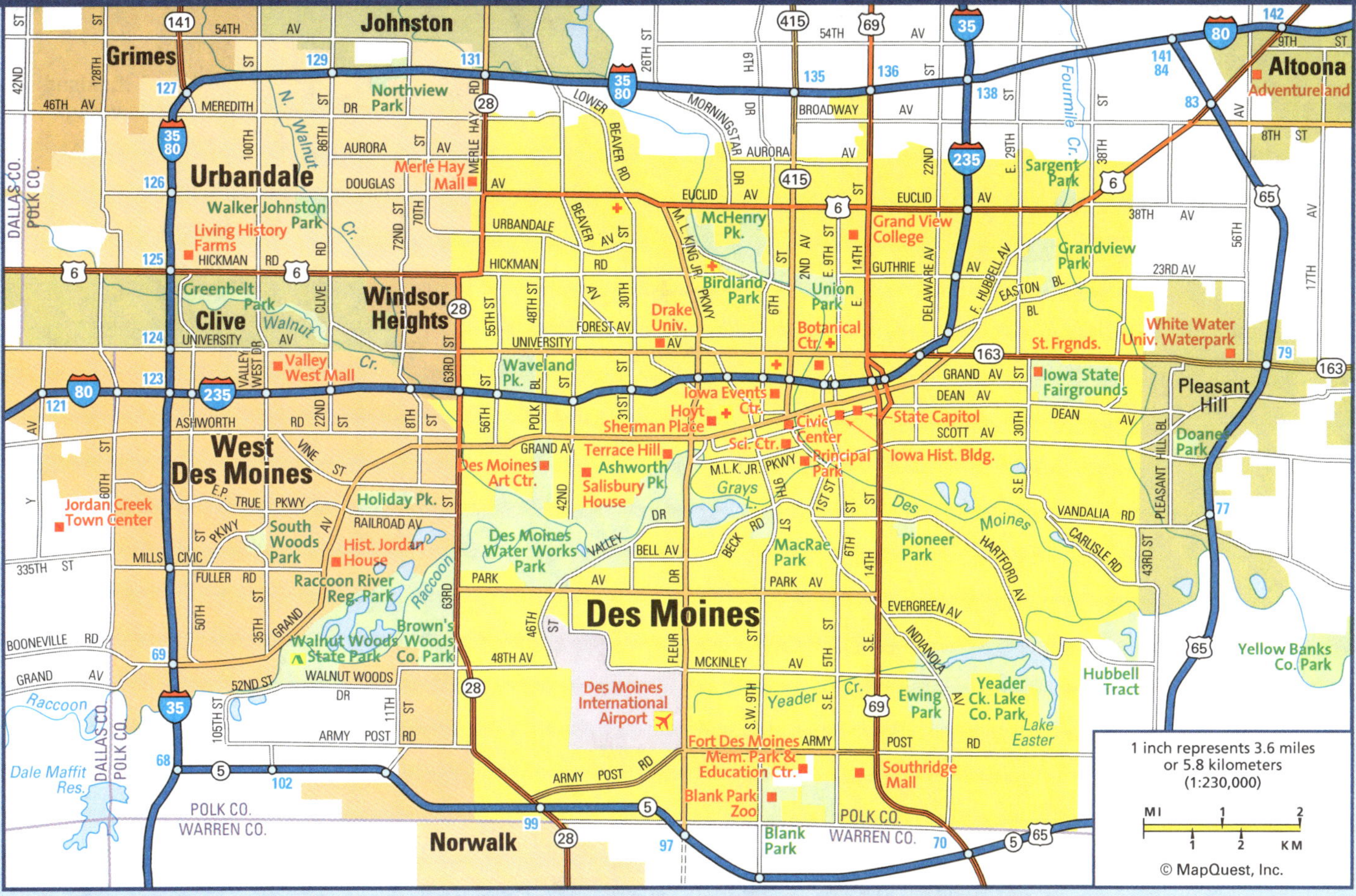

Des Moines International Airport, Fort Des Moines Mem. Park & Education Ctr., Blank Park Zoo, Southridge Mall, Blank Park

Polk Co., Warren Co., Dallas Co.

1 inch represents 3.6 miles or 5.8 kilometers (1:230,000)
© MapQuest, Inc.

Edmonton

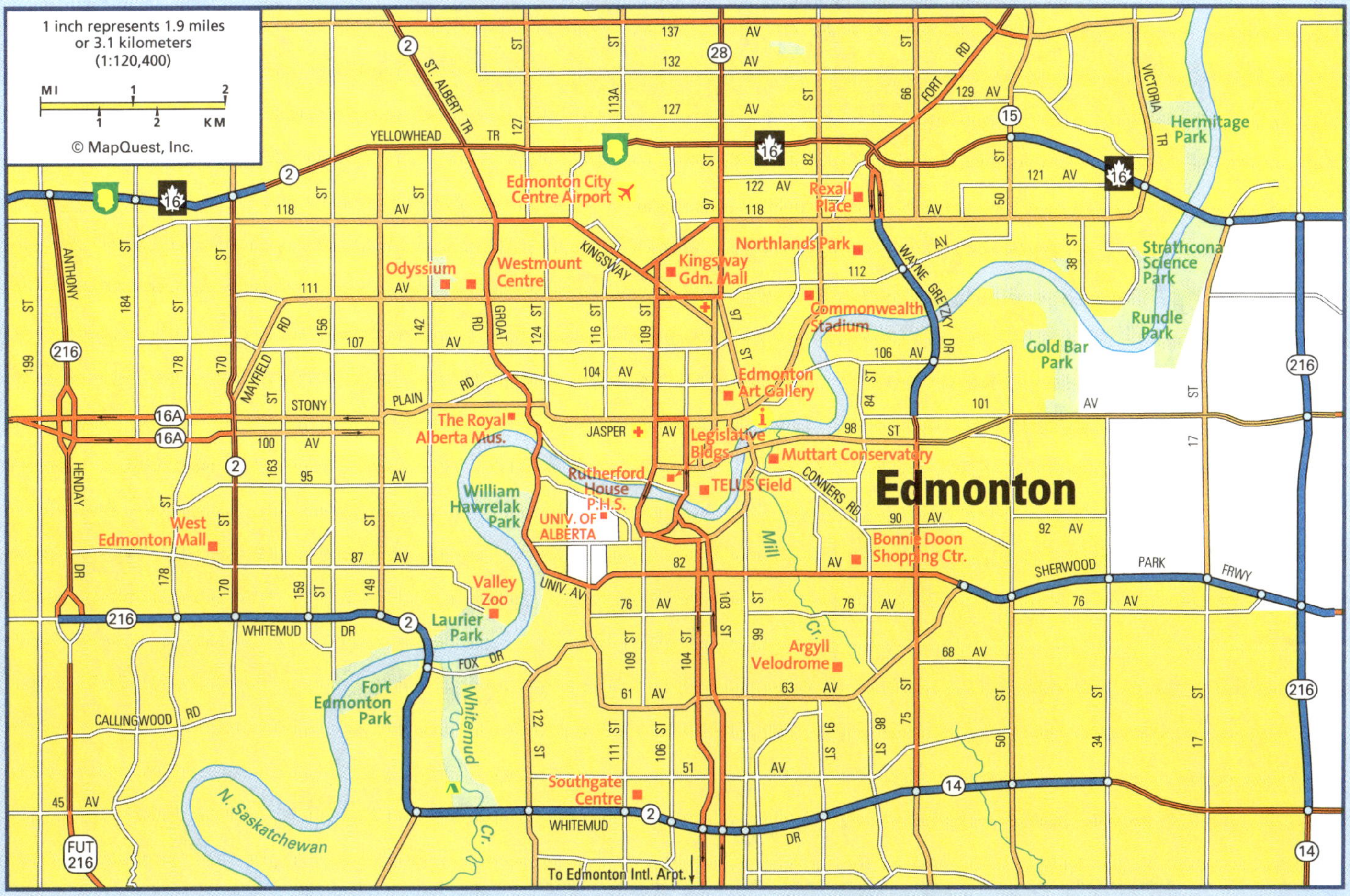

1 inch represents 1.9 miles or 3.1 kilometers (1:120,400)
© MapQuest, Inc.

Yellowhead, Edmonton City Centre Airport, Rexall Place, Hermitage Park, Odyssium, Westmount Centre, Kingsway Gdn. Mall, Northlands Park, Strathcona Science Park, Rundle Park, Gold Bar Park, Commonwealth Stadium, The Royal Alberta Mus., Edmonton Art Gallery, Legislative Bldgs., Muttart Conservatory, TELUS Field, Rutherford House, P.H.S., Univ. of Alberta, William Hawrelak Park, Valley Zoo, Laurier Park, Fort Edmonton Park, West Edmonton Mall, Bonnie Doon Shopping Ctr., Argyll Velodrome, Southgate Centre

Anthony Henday Dr., Calling wood Rd., Whitemud Dr., N. Saskatchewan, Whitemud Cr., Mill Cr., Conners Rd., Wayne Gretzky Dr., Victoria Tr., Fort Rd., Sherwood Park Frwy., Jasper Av, University Av

To Edmonton Intl. Arpt.

Copper
Canyon

Highland
Village

Bartonville

Double
Oak

Flower
Mound

Justin

Rhome

Texas
Motor
Speedway

Marshall Creek

Roanoke

Trophy
Club

Westlake

Grapevine

Grapevine
Rec. Area

Grapevine
Mills

Fairview

Newark

Keller

Southlake

Grapevine
Steam
Railroad

Briar

WISE CO.
DENTON CO.
TARRANT CO.

Haslet

Avondale

Lakeview

Bureau of Engraving
& Printing-Western
Currency Facility

Price St

Southlake Bl

Continental Bl

Dallas-
Ft. Worth
Intl.
Airport

Colleyville

Pelican
Bay

Azle

Eagle
Mountain
Lake

Fort Worth
Nature Center
and Refuge

Saginaw

Basswood

Blue Mound

N. Richland
Hills

Watauga

NRH2O Water Park

Bedford

Euless

Broadview
Park

Lakeside

Lake
Worth

Marine
Creek L.

Ft. Worth
Meacham
Intl. Arpt.

Fort
Worth

Haltom
City

Richland
Hills

Hurst

North East
Mall

American
Airlines C.R.
Smith Mus.

Lake
Worth

Lake Worth

Sansom
Park

River
Oaks

Stockyards Natl.
Hist. District
Ct Hse

Mosier Valley

River
Legacy
Living Sci. Ctr.

NAVAL AIR
STATION
FORT WORTH
JOINT RESERVE BASE
Westworth Vil.

Westover
Hills

Sundance Sq. &
Bass Perf. Hall

Six Flags
Hurricane Harbor

White
Settlement

Ridgmar
Mall

F.W. Cult.
Dist. & Will
Rogers Ctr.

Conv Ctr.

Arlington
Conv. Ctr.
Mus. of Art

Six Flags
Over Texas

Benbrook

Ft. Worth
Zoo

Colonial

Texas Christian
University

Forest
Park

Lancaster Av

Rosedale St

Texas
Wesleyan
Univ.

Univ of TX-
Arlington

Pantego

Ameriquest
Field in
Arlington

Six Flags
Mall

Pecan
Valley
Park

Hulen
Mall

Edgecliff Vil.

Forest
Hill

Dalworthington
Gardens

Lake
Arlington

The Parks at
Arlington Mall

Arlington

Dutch
Branch
Park

Benbrook
Lake

Kennedale

Mustang
Park

Everman

Crowley

Mansfield

Burleson

Retta

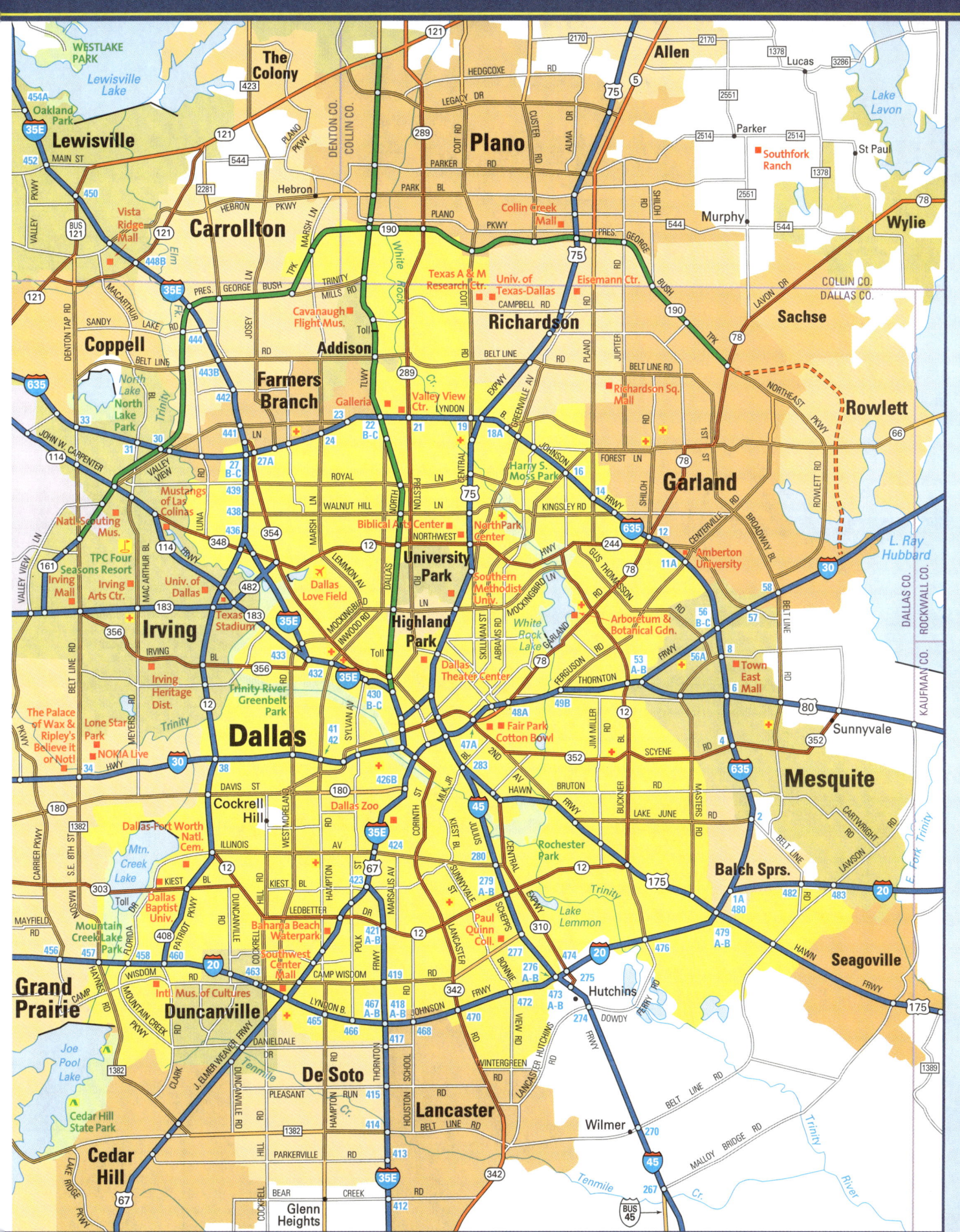

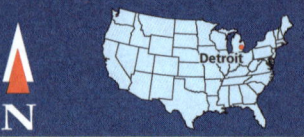

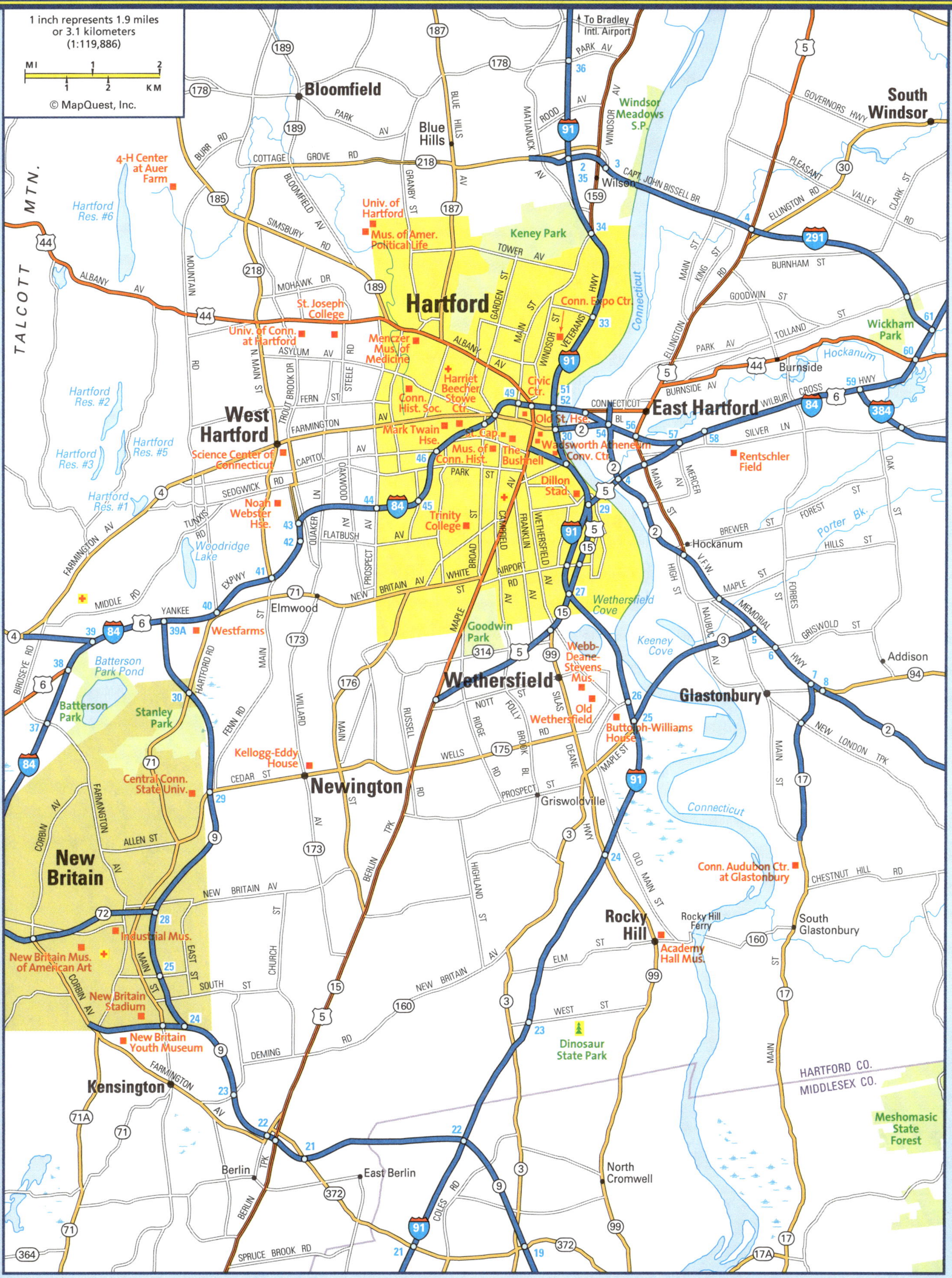

1 inch represents 1.9 miles
or 3.1 kilometers
(1:119,886)

MI

KM

© MapQuest, Inc.

N

Hartford

TALCOTT MTN.

Hartford Res. #6
Hartford Res. #2
Hartford Res. #3
Hartford Res. #5
Hartford Res. #1

4-H Center at Auer Farm

Bloomfield

Blue Hills

To Bradley Intl. Airport

Windsor Meadows S.P.

South Windsor

Univ. of Hartford
Mus. of Amer. Political Life

Keney Park

Wilson

Conn. Expo Ctr.

St. Joseph College

Hartford

Univ. of Conn. at Hartford

West Hartford

Menczer Mus. of Medicine

Harriet Beecher Stowe Ctr.

Conn. Hist. Soc.

Civic Ctr.

East Hartford

Rentschler Field

Science Center of Connecticut

Mark Twain Hse.

St. Cap.

Old St. Hse.

Wadsworth Atheneum Conv. Ctr.

Mus. of Conn. Hist.

The Bushnell

Noah Webster Hse.

Trinity College

Dillon Stad.

Hockanum

Wethersfield Cove

Elmwood

Westfarms

Goodwin Park

Webb-Deane-Stevens Mus.

Keeney Cove

Glastonbury

Addison

Wethersfield

Old Wethersfield

Buttolph-Williams House

Conn. Audubon Ctr. at Glastonbury

Kellogg-Eddy House

Newington

Griswoldville

Central Conn. State Univ.

New Britain

Industrial Mus.

New Britain Mus. of American Art

New Britain Stadium

Rocky Hill

Rocky Hill Ferry

Academy Hall Mus.

South Glastonbury

New Britain Youth Museum

Dinosaur State Park

Meshomasic State Forest

Kensington

Berlin

East Berlin

North Cromwell

HARTFORD CO.
MIDDLESEX CO.

Batterson Park Pond

Batterson Park

Stanley Park

Woodridge Lake

Connecticut

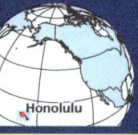

N

Honolulu

KO'OLAU RANGE

Wilson Tunnel

Kāne'ohe Forest Reserve

Pali Tunnels

Pali Lookout

Nu'uanu Pali St. Wayside
Pu'u'ulamihuli + 2,760

Kōnāhuanui + 3,105

Waimānalo Forest Reserve

WA'AHILA RIGE

MAU'UMAE RIGE

PALOLO

Wa'ahila Ridge S.R.A.

Kāne'ohe Forest Reserve

LAUKAHI ST

HALEKOA DR

Kapikipiki'ō Pt.

Doris Duke Foundation for Islamic Art (Shangri La)

Diamond Head State Monument
+ Diamond Head + 761

Diamond Head Lighthouse

Chaminade Univ. of Honolulu

Honolulu Zoo

Waikiki Shell

MONSARRAT AV

Kapi'olani Park

Waikiki Aquarium

UNIV. OF HAWAI'I AT MANOA

Imax Theatre

International Marketplace

WAIKĪKĪ

Waikiki Beach

U.S. Army Museum

Hawai'i Convention Center

FORT DE RUSSY MIL. RES.

Ala Moana Pk. (Magic Island)

Ala Moana Shopping Center

Aina Moana Park

PACIFIC OCEAN

Manoa Falls

Waihi

Paradise Park

Harold L. Lyon Arboretum

Tantalus + 2,013

Pu'u 'Ualaka'a St. Wayside

Round Top

The Contemporary Museum & Garden

Honolulu Acad. of Arts

Nat'l. Mem. Cem. of the Pacific

Queen Emma Summer Palace

Royal Mausoleum
St. Monastery

Foster Botanical Garden

Honolulu

Kamehameha Schools

Bishop Museum

Dole Cannery

Chinatown

Cathedral of Our Lady of Peace

Aloha Tower

Hawaii Maritime Ctr.

Victoria Ward Center

Mission Houses Mus.

Iolani Palace

St. Cap.

Blaisdell Ctr.

Kaka'ako Waterfront Park

Sand Island S.R.A.

Sand Island

Mokauea Island

Ke'ehi Lagoon Beach Park

Ke'ehi Lagoon

FORT SHAFTER MILITARY RESERVATION

TRIPLER ARMY MEDICAL CENTER

Moanalua Gardens

RED HILL NAV. RES.

Salt Lake

AIIAMANU MILITARY RESERVATION U.S. ARMY

Honolulu International Airport

HICKAM AIR FORCE BASE

Māmala Bay

USS Ariz. Mem. Visitor Ctr.

Pearl Harbor

Ford Island

KAMEHAMEHA HWY

U.S. NAVY RES.

Aloha Stadium

1 inch represents 1.3 miles or 2.1 kilometers (1:80,304)

© MapQuest, Inc.

KM

MI

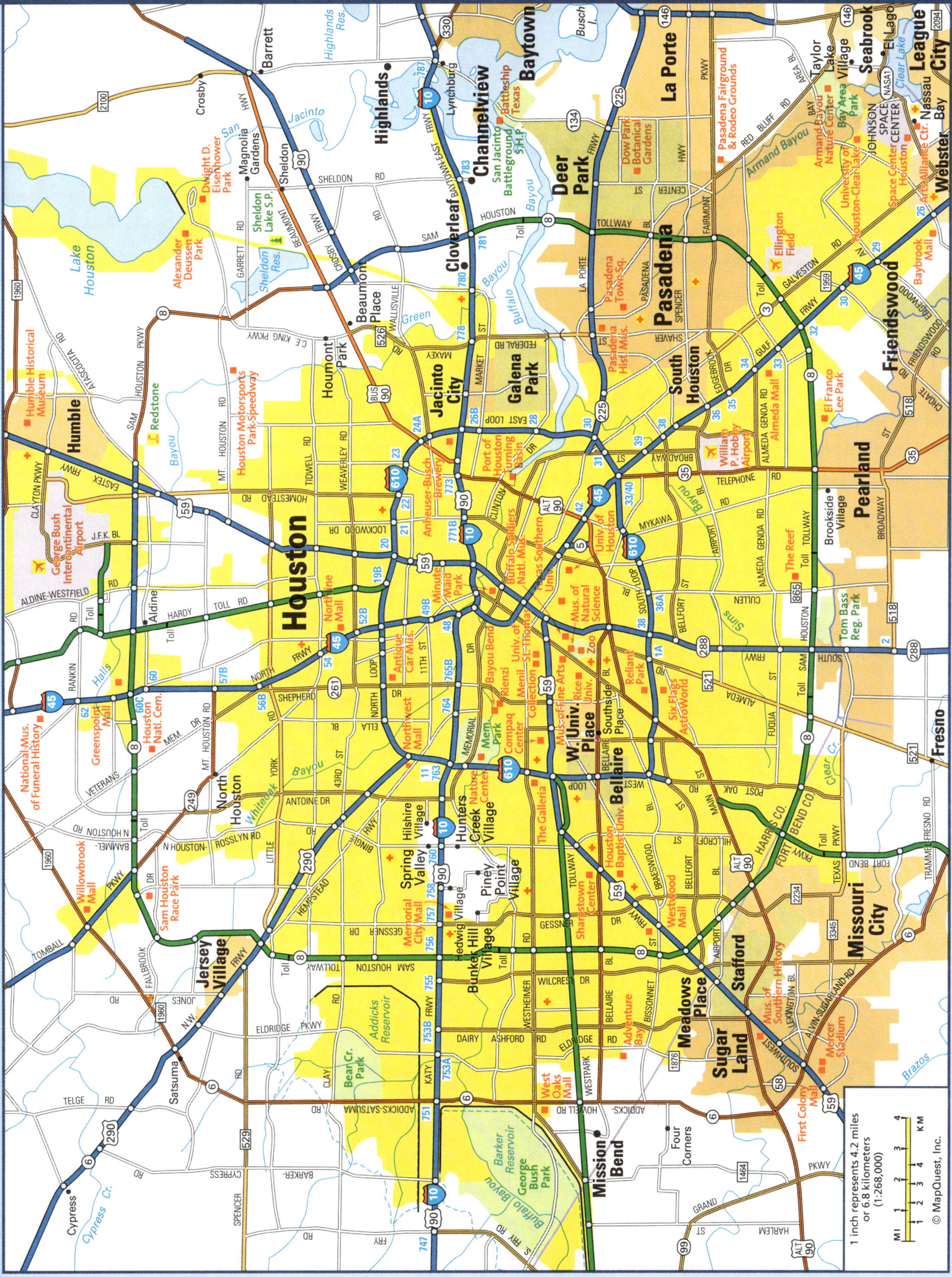

N

Eagle Village

Zionsville

Patrick Henry
Sullivan Mus.

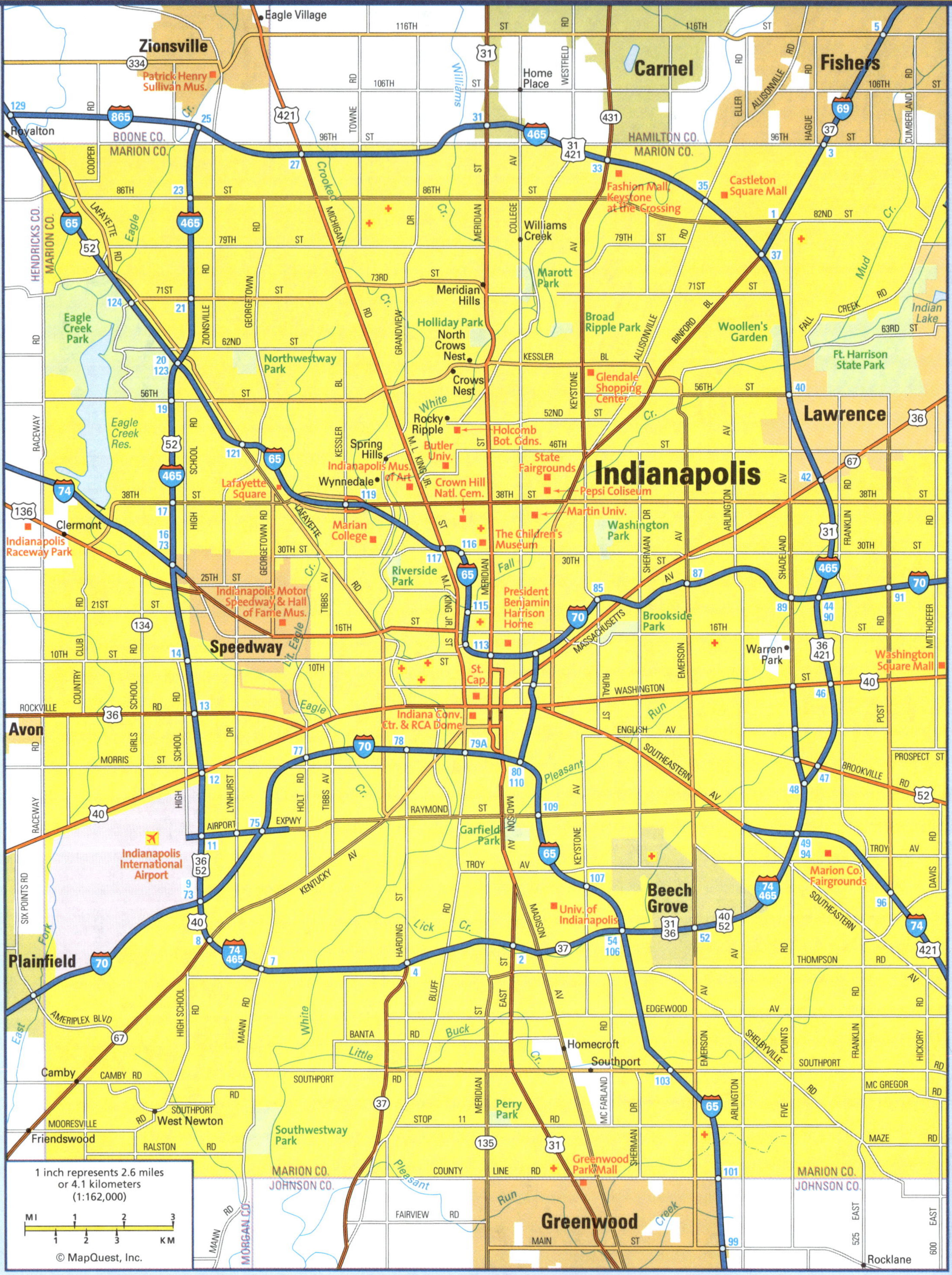

334

865

25

Royalton

129

BOONE CO.
MARION CO.

COOPER RD

LAFAYETTE RD

65

52

124

123
20

19

52

121

65

465

Eagle Creek
Res.

Eagle Creek
Park

RACEWAY

136

74

Clermont

Indianapolis
Raceway Park

134

16
73

17

Speedway

465

GEORGETOWN RD

ZIONSVILLE RD

GEORGETOWN RD

Lafayette
Square

Marian
College

Indianapolis Motor
Speedway & Hall
of Fame Mus.

14

13

ROCKVILLE

Avon

36

12

COUNTRY CLUB RD

GIRLS SCHOOL RD

40

MORRIS

11

Indianapolis
International
Airport

36
52

9
73

40

8

Plainfield

70

74
465

7

SIX POINTS RD

RACEWAY

East Fork

AMERIPLEX BLVD

67

Camby

Camby RD

Mooresville

West Newton

Friendswood

Southport RD

RALSTON RD

MANN RD

HIGH SCHOOL RD

White

Little

Southwestway
Park

MARION CO.
JOHNSON CO.

Pleasant

FAIRVIEW RD

27

421

116TH ST

106TH ST

96TH ST

86TH ST

79TH ST

73RD ST

62ND ST

56TH ST

MICHIGAN RD

TOWNE RD

Crooked Cr.

GRANDVIEW DR

KESSLER BL

Northwestway
Park

30TH ST

25TH ST

21ST ST

10TH ST

16TH ST

TIBBS AV

Lt. Eagle Cr.

HOLT RD

LYNHURST DR

AIRPORT EXPWY

TIBBS AV

KENTUCKY AV

Eagle Cr.

77

75

78

RAYMOND ST

HARDING ST

MANN RD

BLUFF RD

Banta RD

Buck Cr.

SOUTHPORT RD

Lick Cr.

4

Camby RD

COUNTY LINE RD

Pleasant Run

31

116TH ST

106TH ST

96TH ST

86TH ST

79TH ST

73RD ST

Williams Cr.

WESTFIELD

31

Home
Place

431

465
31
421

33

Fashion Mall
Keystone
at the Crossing

35

Meridian
Hills

Williams
Creek

Marott
Park

Holliday Park

North
Crows Nest

Crows
Nest

White Cr.

Rocky
Ripple

Holcomb
Bot. Gdns.

46TH

Spring
Hills

Butler
Univ.

Indianapolis Mus.
of Art

Wynnedale

119

Crown Hill
Natl. Cem.

38TH ST

State
Fairgrounds

Martin Univ.

116

The Children's
Museum

117

Riverside
Park

115

65

113

Fall Cr.

M.L. KING JR. ST

MERIDIAN ST

St.
Cap.

Indiana Conv.
Ctr. & RCA Dome

70

79A

80
110

109

Garfield
Park

TROY AV

107

Univ. of
Indianapolis

54
106

31
36

2

EAST ST

MADISON AV

KEYSTONE AV

Homecroft

Southport

Perry
Park

STOP 11 RD

135

31

Greenwood
Park Mall

99

COLLEGE AV

MERIDIAN ST

KESSLER BL

52ND

KEYSTONE AV

ALLISONVILLE RD

Broad
Ripple Park

Glendale
Shopping
Center

56TH

Washington
Park

85

70

MASSACHUSETTS AV

Brookside
Park

16TH

RURAL ST

SHERMAN DR

WASHINGTON ST

English Cr.

SOUTHEASTERN AV

48

Carmel

Indianapolis

Lawrence

HAMILTON CO.
MARION CO.

ELLER RD

ALLISONVILLE RD

HAGUE RD

82ND ST

71ST

63RD

BINFORD BL

Woollen's
Garden

Fall Cr.

Mud Cr.

Castleton
Square Mall

1

37

40

Ft. Harrison
State Park

Indian
Lake

Fishers

69

5

116TH

106TH

96TH

CUMBERLAND RD

42

ARLINGTON AV

SHADELAND AV

38TH

30TH

31

FRANKLIN RD

465

87

89

44
90

91

70

36
421

Warren
Park

46

Washington
Square Mall

POST RD

47

BROOKVILLE RD

52

PROSPECT ST

EMERSON AV

Marion Co.
Fairgrounds

49
94

TROY AV

96

74

421

THOMPSON RD

FRANKLIN RD

HICKORY RD

MC GREGOR RD

MAZE RD

EDGEWOOD AV

SHELBYVILLE RD

SOUTHPORT RD

103

65

Five Points RD

President
Benjamin
Harrison
Home

Beech
Grove

40
52

74
465

SOUTHEASTERN AV

DAVIS RD

EAST ST

MARION CO.
JOHNSON CO.

Greenwood

MAIN ST

525

101

600

Rocklane

HENDRICKS CO.
MARION CO.

**1 inch represents 2.6 miles
or 4.1 kilometers
(1:162,000)**

MI 0 1 2 3

KM 0 1 2 3

© MapQuest, Inc.

Indianapolis

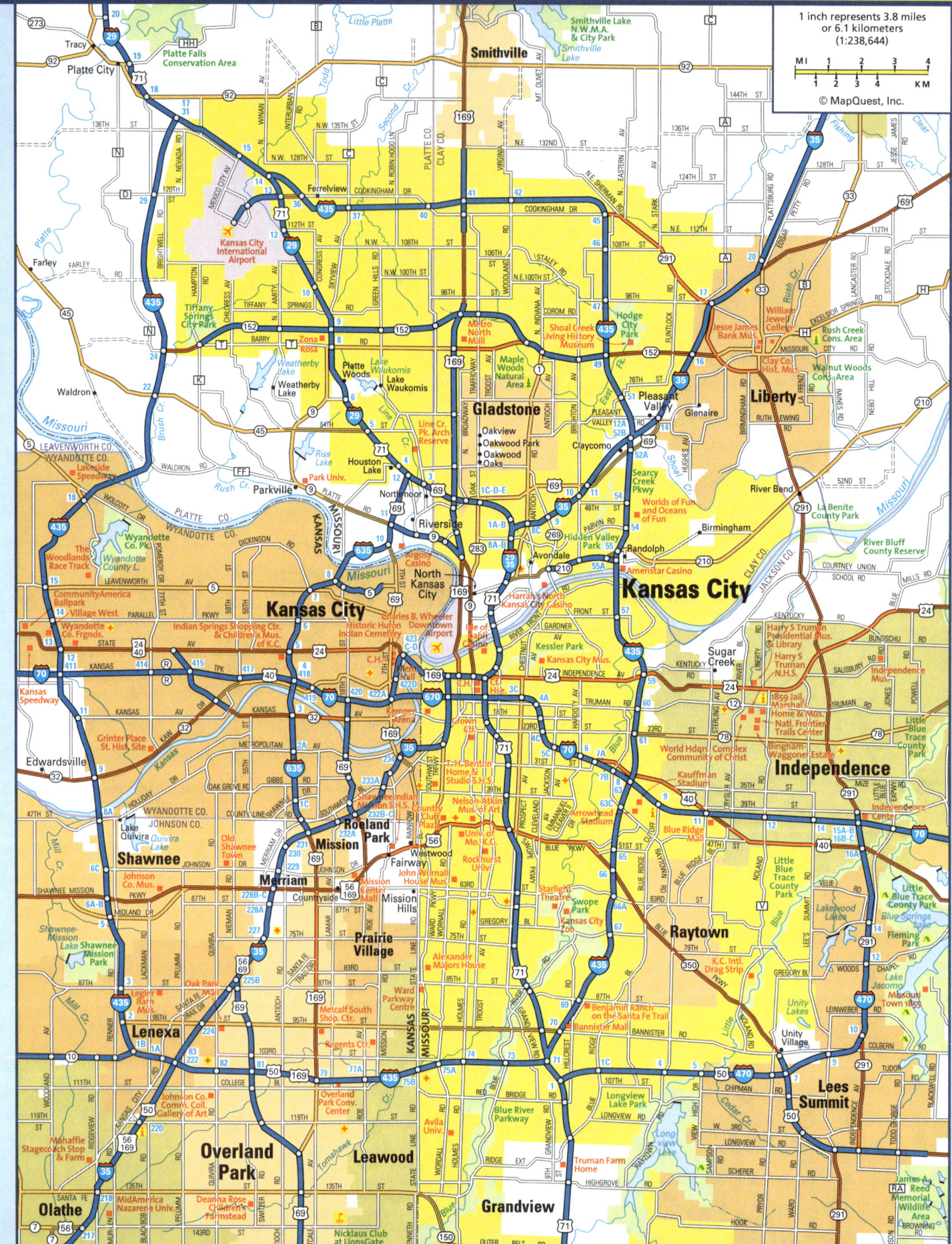

Los Angeles

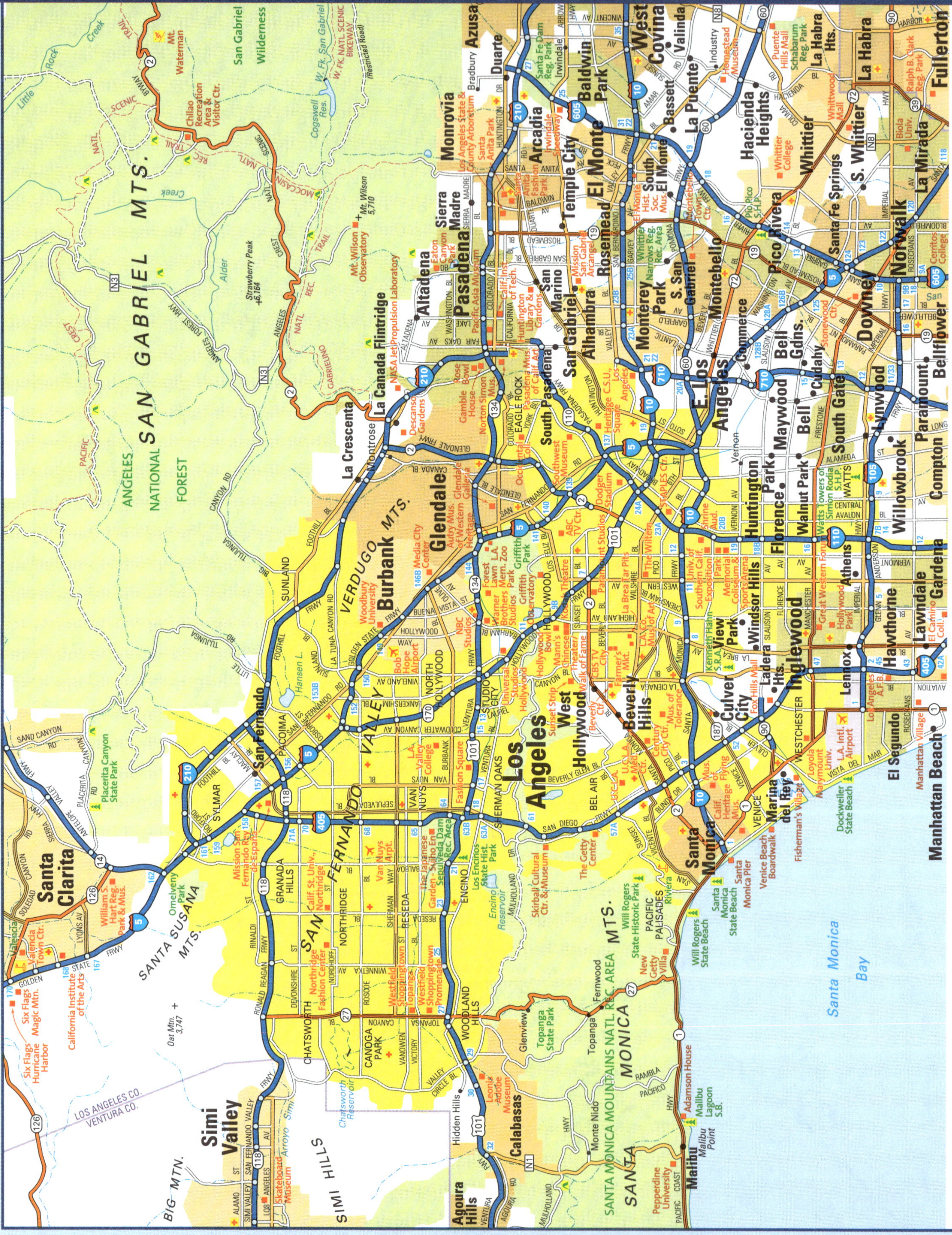

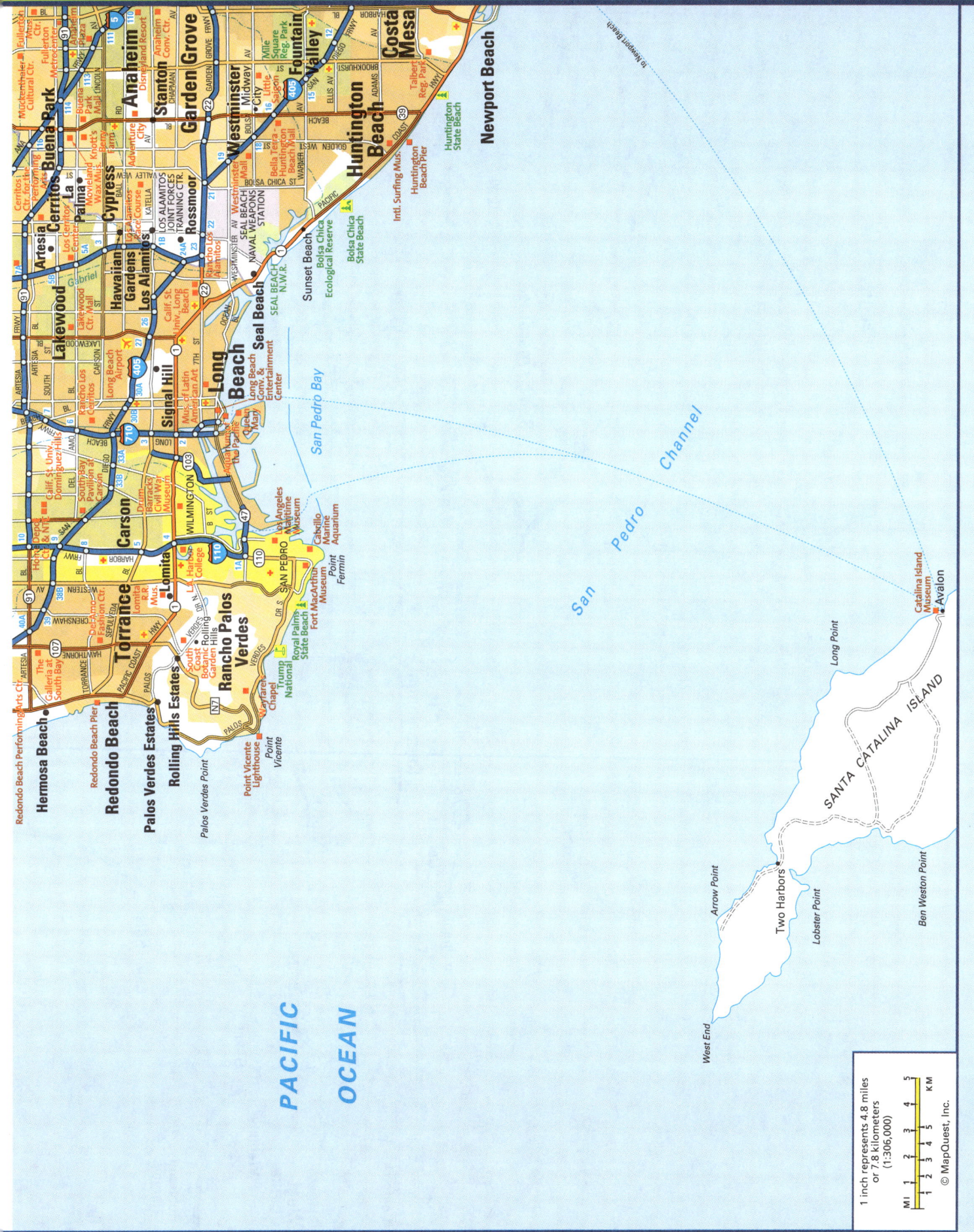

Luna Mtn. 5,969

SAN BERNARDINO NATIONAL FOREST

Arrowbear Lake

18

Running Springs

ROUNDUP WAY

330

HESPERIA

Cedar Glen

Lake Arrowhead

Skyforest

Crest Park

Rimforest Park

173

Blue Jay

189

Twin Peaks

The Arrowhead

Highland

Mentone

Crafton Hills College

Yucaipa

Calimesa

Norton Younglove Reserve

DAVIS

Univ. of Redlands

Kimberly CrestHouse

Redlands

10

63

SAN TIMOTEO CANYON

GILMAN SPRINGS

Silverwood Lake

138

173

Cedar Glen

Crestline

Lake Gregory Reg. Park

18

Devore

Univ. of Redlands

San Bernardino County Museum

79

81

Redlands Bowl

Loma Linda

Mojave River Forks Reg. Park

Mojave River Forks Res.

Silverwood Lake State Rec. Area

138

Calif. St. Univ. San Bernardino

50

San Bernardino

Muscoy

44B 44A

San Manuel Indian Res.

San Manuel Casino Highland

San Bernardino Intl. Airport

Pharaoh's Lost Kingdom

Carousel

Inland Center

10

Loma Linda Univ. Med. Ctr.

Grand Terrace

Colton

Moreno Valley

60

Moreno Valley Mall

March Field Museum

15

395

141

Summit

Cajon Summit 4,259

138

Summit

Cajon Junction

131

CAJON CANYON

15

Glen Helen Reg. Park

122

123

124

Hyundai Pavilion at Glen Helen

215

54B 54A

RIVERSIDE AV

SUMMIT AV

119

Rialto

Fontana

BASE LINE

Bloomington

66

10

64

Crestmore

Rubidoux

60

Riverside

Box Springs Mtn. Reg. Pk.

Box Springs Mtns. 3,047

215

27

29

Mission Inn

Riverside Plaza

Heritage House

Lytle Creek

Lytle Creek

CAJON BL

BARSTOW RD

131

138

CAJON CANYON

SMARTOUT CANYON

NATL. SCENIC TRAIL

Glen Helen Reg. Park

15

California Speedway

113

Rancho Cucamonga

Victoria Gardens Mall

Chaffey College

110

Ontario Mills

Cucamonga Guasti Reg. Park

108

106

15

Norco

Naval Warfare Assessment Sta.

La Sierra University

Jurupa Mts. Cultural Ctr.

Jensen-Alvarado Hist. Ranch & Mus.

Martha McLean- Anza Narrows Park

Orange Navel Tree

Hidden Valley Wildlife Area

Glen Avon

Mira Loma

Pedley

Louis Robidoux Nature Ctr.

Jurupa Hills Reg. Pk.

Sherman Indian Museum

Galleria at Tyler

Castle Park

Calif. Citrus S.H.P.

96

WRIGHTWOOD

Wrightwood

SAN BERNARDINO NATL. FOR.

Mt. San Antonio 10,064

Mt. Baldy

Cucamonga Wilderness

San Antonio Heights

Upland

Montclair

Ontario

Ontario Intl. Airport

Graber Olive House

Planes of Fame Air Museum

Chino

Prado Regional Park

71

Prado Basin

210

19TH

4TH ST

HOLT

Chino Hills

CHINO HILLS

SAN BERNARDINO CO.

LOS ANGELES CO.

Mountain High

Ski Sunrise Rec Area

2

Sheep Mountain Wilderness

Mt. Baldy Visitor Center

Mt. Baldy

MT. BALDY RD

Claremont

Claremont Colleges

Rancho Santa Ana Botanic Gdn.

Montclair Plaza

46

48B 46

66

83

Cal Poly Univ., Pomona

Pomona

Prado Flood Control Basin

Chino Hills State Park

142

Chino Hills

SAN BERNARDINO CO.

ORANGE CO.

Yorba Linda

ANGELES NATIONAL FOREST

Crystal Lake Recreation Area

The Pines Rec Area

PACIFIC CREST

2

NATL. SCENIC

BYWAY

HIGH DESERT

ANGELES CREST HWY

Snowcrest

39

Glendora

San Dimas Experimental Forest

San Gabriel

GLENDORA MTN. RD

San Dimas

San Dimas Canyon Reg. Pk.

Frank G. Bonelli Reg. Park

Raging Waters

L.A. Co. Fairgrounds

Univ. of La Verne

La Verne

57

Diamond Bar

Carbon Canyon Reg. Park

Richard Nixon Library and Birthplace

60

Historic George Key Ranch

Yorba Linda

Morris Res.

San Gabriel Reservoir

39

Azusa

Azusa Pacific University

Covina

Westfield Shoppingtown Eastland

210

10

Charter Oak

West Covina

Walnut

Cal St. Poly Univ., Pomona

57

Rowland Heights

60

57

Brea

Craig Reg. Pk.

Brea Mall

Fullerton

C.S.U. Fullerton

57

90

P 11
California

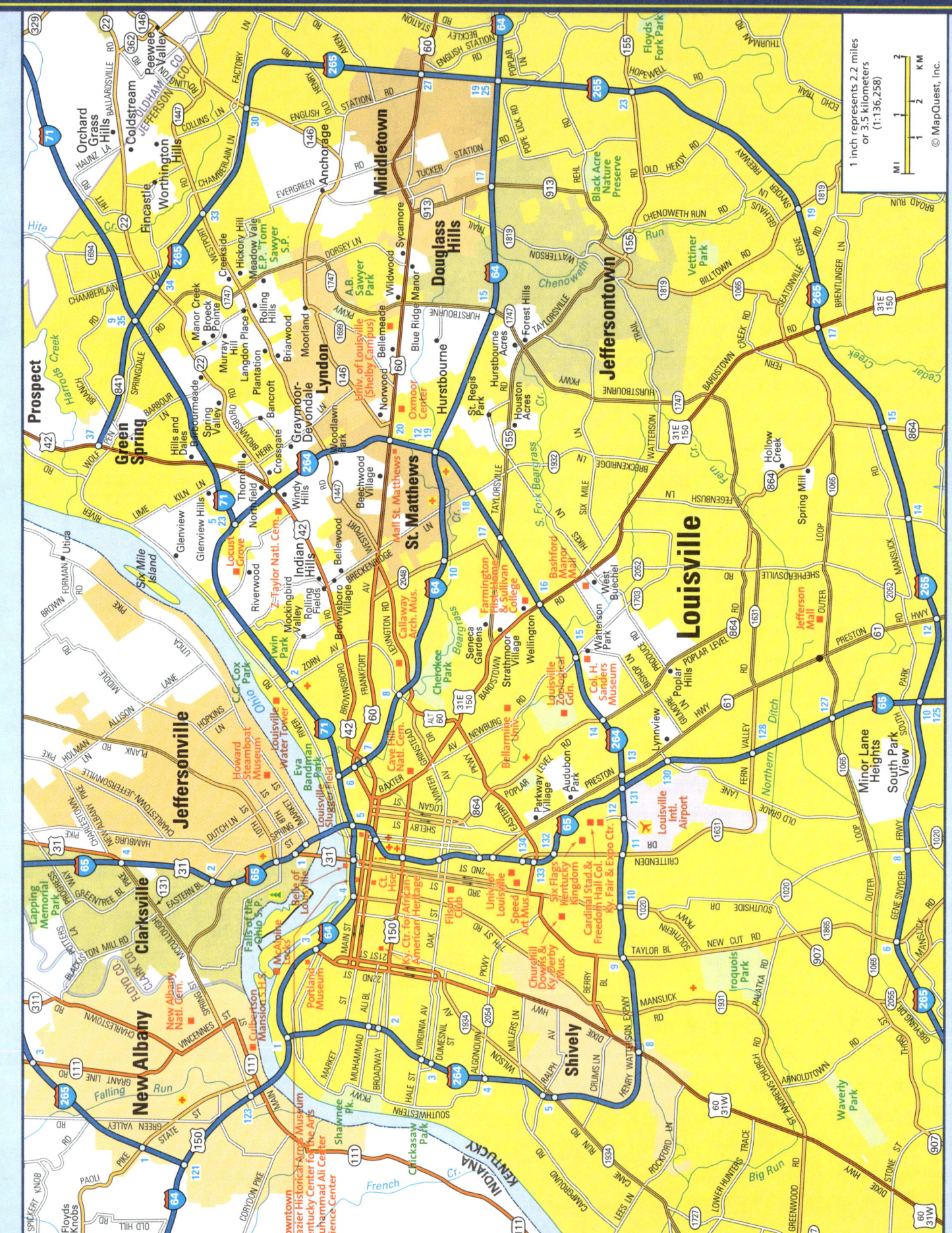

LAKE MICHIGAN

Milwaukee Bay

to Muskegon, Mich.

Bayside

Schlitz Audubon Nature Center
Fox Point

Cardinal Stritch University

Whitefish Bay

Bayshore Mall

Fox Point

River Hills

Glendale

Brown Deer

Kletzsch Park

Brown Deer Pk.

Havenwoods Environmental Awareness Ctr.

Teutonia

University of Wisconsin-Milwaukee

Lake Park

Kern Park

Charles Allis Art Mus.

Sprecher Brewery

Lincoln Park

Villa Terrace Decorative Arts Mus.

Juneau Park

Milwaukee Art Mus.

Black Holocaust Mus.

Allen-Bradley Clock Tower

South Shore Park

St. Francis

Sheridan Park

Warnimont Park

Poneade Icepoint

Cudahy

South Milwaukee

Oak Creek

Gen. Mitchell Intl. Airport

Milwaukee

Mitchell Pk. Conservatory

Pabst Mans.

Miller Brewing Co.

Washington Park

Lincoln Cr. Pkwy.

Milwaukee

Josephat's Basilica

Alverno College

Greenfield

Southridge Mall

Franklin

Milwaukee

Hank Aaron St. Trail

Lowell Damon Hse.

Miller Park

Pettit Natl. Ice Ctr.

State Fairgnd.

West Allis

McCarty Park

Jackson Park

Greendale

Brown Deer

Little Menomonee River Pkwy.

Mt. Mary College

The Annunciation Gr. Orthodox Ch.

Mayfair Mall

Wauwatosa

Hansen Park

Wis. Lutheran Coll.

Little Menomonee River Pkwy.

Dretzka Park

Harley Davidson Plant

Butler

Menomonee Co. Park

Menomonee Falls

Lannon

Sussex

Elm Grove

Brookfield Sq. Shop. Ctr.

Brookfield

Milwaukee Co. Zoological Gdns.

Greenfield Park

Greenfield

Root River Pkwy.

Hales Corners

Muskego

New Berlin

Minooka Co. Park

Pewaukee (village)

Pewaukee (city)

Pewaukee

Waukesha Co. Expo Center

Waukesha

Waukesha Co. Mus.

Carroll College

Ausblick

WAUKESHA CO.
MILWAUKEE CO.

1 inch represents 2.5 miles
or 3.9 kilometers
(1:155,167)

© MapQuest, Inc.

P 54
Wisconsin

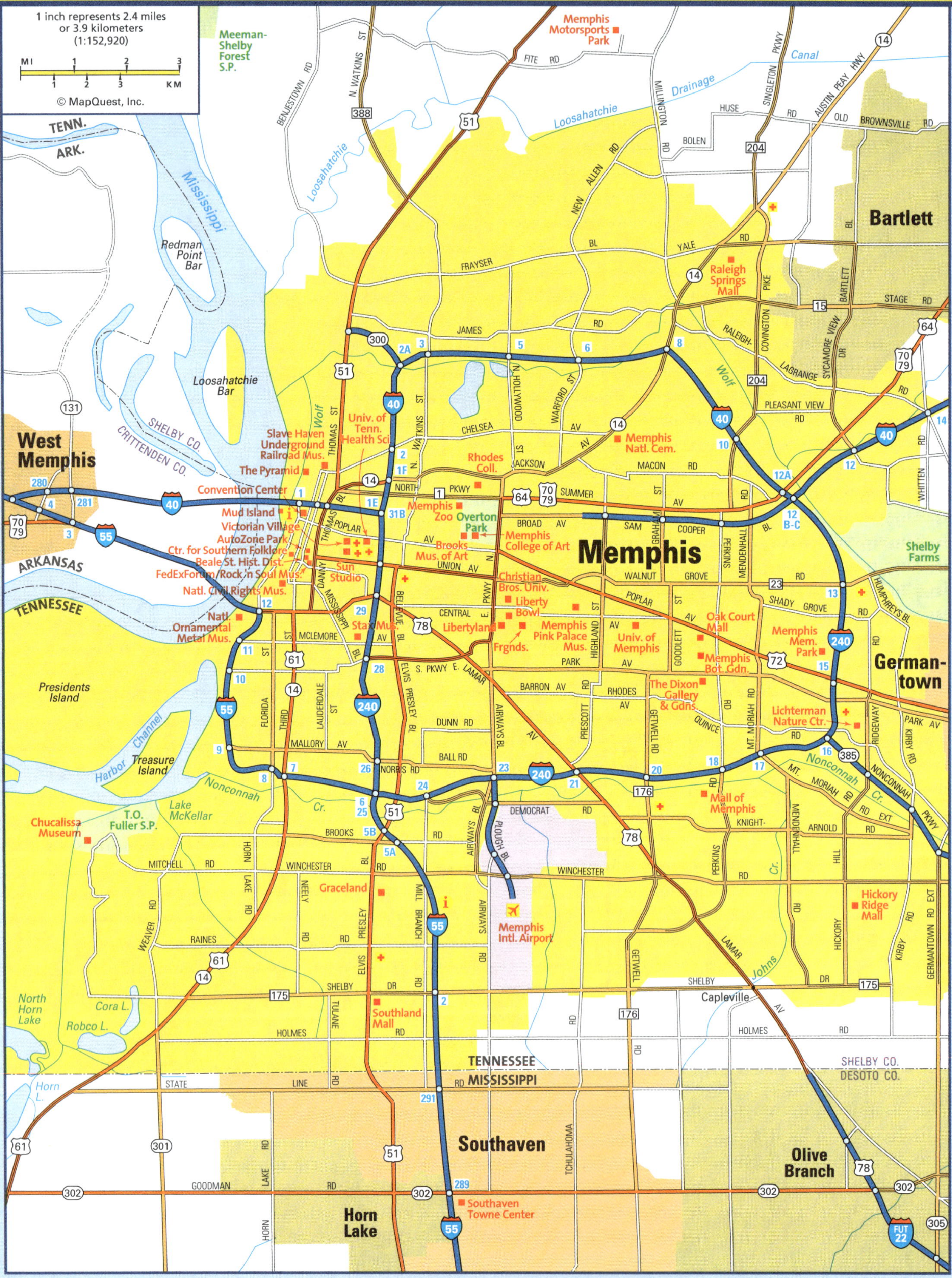

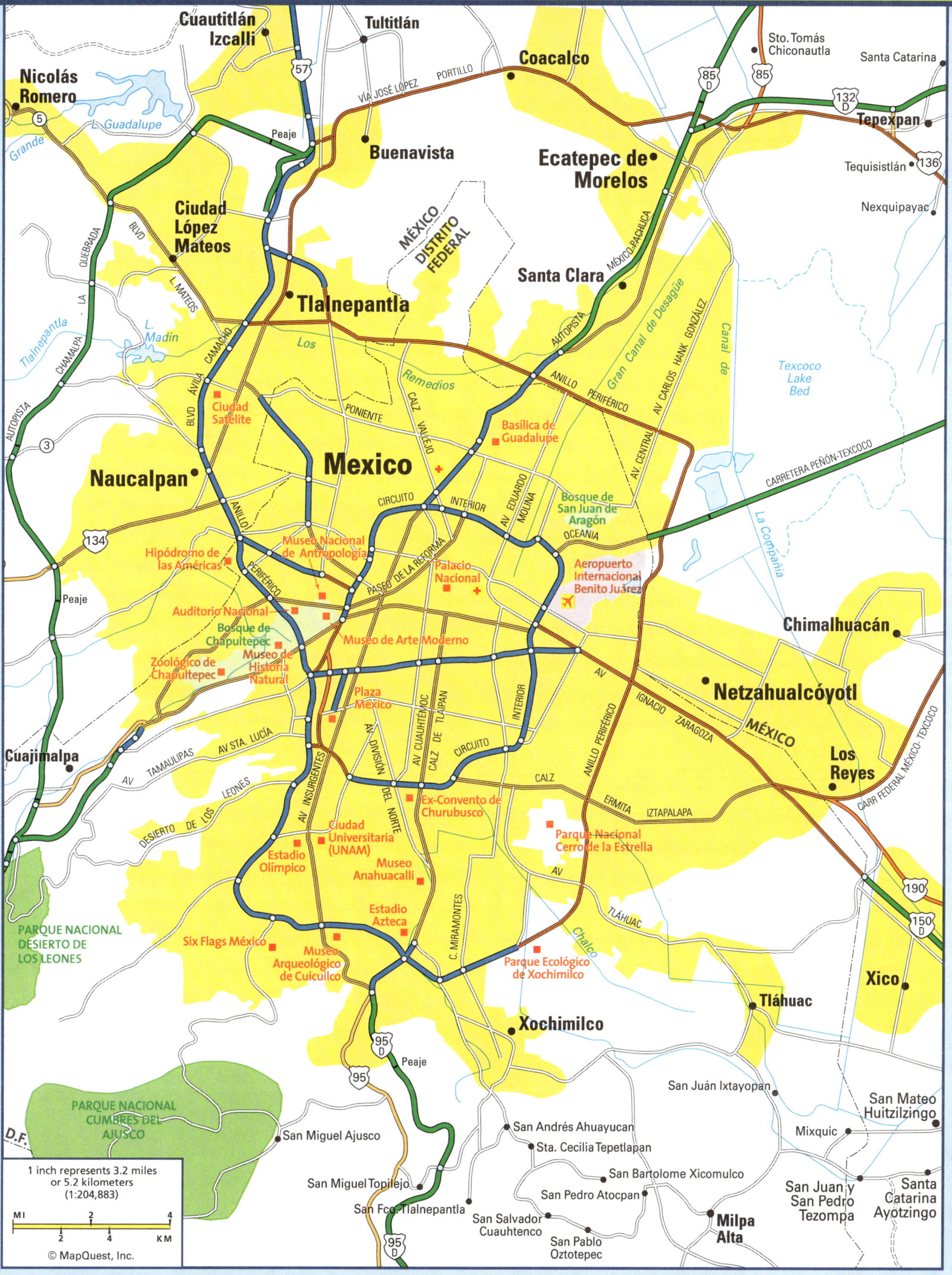

N

Cuautitlán Izcalli

Tultitlán

Coacalco

Sto. Tomás Chiconautla

Santa Catarina

Nicolás Romero

L. Guadalupe

Grande

VÍA JOSÉ LÓPEZ

PORTILLO

Tepexpan

Tequisistlán

Peaje

Buenavista

Ecatepec de Morelos

Nexquipayac

Ciudad López Mateos

MÉXICO DISTRITO FEDERAL

Santa Clara

MÉXICO-PACHUCA

L. Madín

Tlalnepantla

Los

AUTOPISTA

Gran Canal de Desagüe

Canal de

Texcoco Lake Bed

Ciudad Satélite

Remedios

CALZ VALLEJO

ANILLO PERIFÉRICO

AV CARLOS HANK GONZÁLEZ

PONIENTE

Basílica de Guadalupe

Canal de

La Compañía

CARRETERA PEÑÓN-TEXCOCO

Naucalpan

Mexico

AV CENTRAL

Bosque de San Juan de Aragón

Museo Nacional de Antropología

CIRCUITO

INTERIOR

AV EDUARDO MOLINA

OCEANIA

Chimalhuacán

Hipódromo de las Américas

PASEO DE LA REFORMA

Palacio Nacional

Aeropuerto Internacional Benito Juárez

Auditorio Nacional

Bosque de Chapultepec

Museo de Arte Moderno

Netzahualcóyotl

Zoológico de Chapultepec

Museo de Historia Natural

INTERIOR

AV

IGNACIO ZARAGOZA

MÉXICO

Los Reyes

Plaza Mexico

AV CUAUHTÉMOC

CALZ DE TLALPAN

CIRCUITO

ANILLO PERIFÉRICO

Cuajimalpa

AV STA. LUCÍA

TAMAULIPAS

DESIERTO DE LOS LEONES

AV INSURGENTES

AV DIVISIÓN DEL NORTE

CALZ

ERMITA

IZTAPALAPA

CARR FEDERAL MÉXICO TEXCOCO

Ex-Convento de Churubusco

Parque Nacional Cerro de la Estrella

Ciudad Universitaria (UNAM)

Estadio Olímpico

Museo Anahuacalli

AV

C. MIRAMONTES

TLÁHUAC

190

PARQUE NACIONAL DESIERTO DE LOS LEONES

Estadio Azteca

Six Flags México

Museo Arqueológico de Cuicuilco

Chalco

Parque Ecológico de Xochimilco

Xico

Tláhuac

95 D

Peaje

Xochimilco

150 D

PARQUE NACIONAL CUMBRES DEL AJUSCO

San Juán Ixtayopan

San Mateo Huitzilzingo

D.F.

95

San Miguel Ajusco

San Andrés Ahuayucan

Sta. Cecilia Tepetlapan

Mixquic

Santa Catarina Ayotzingo

San Miguel Topilejo

San Bartolome Xicomulco

San Juan y San Pedro Tezompa

San Fco. Tlalnepantla

San Pedro Atocpan

San Salvador Cuauhtenco

Milpa Alta

95 D

San Pablo Oztotepec

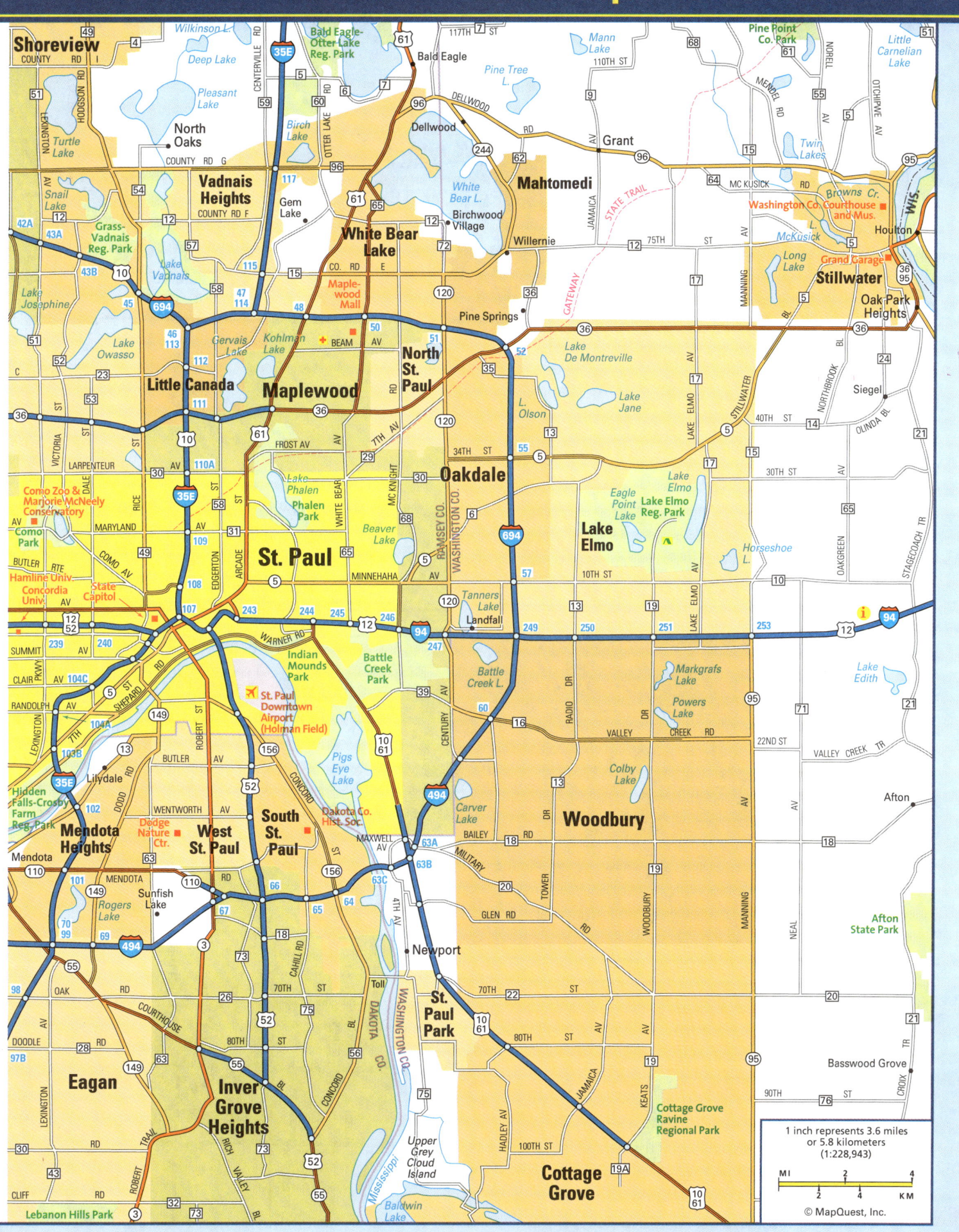

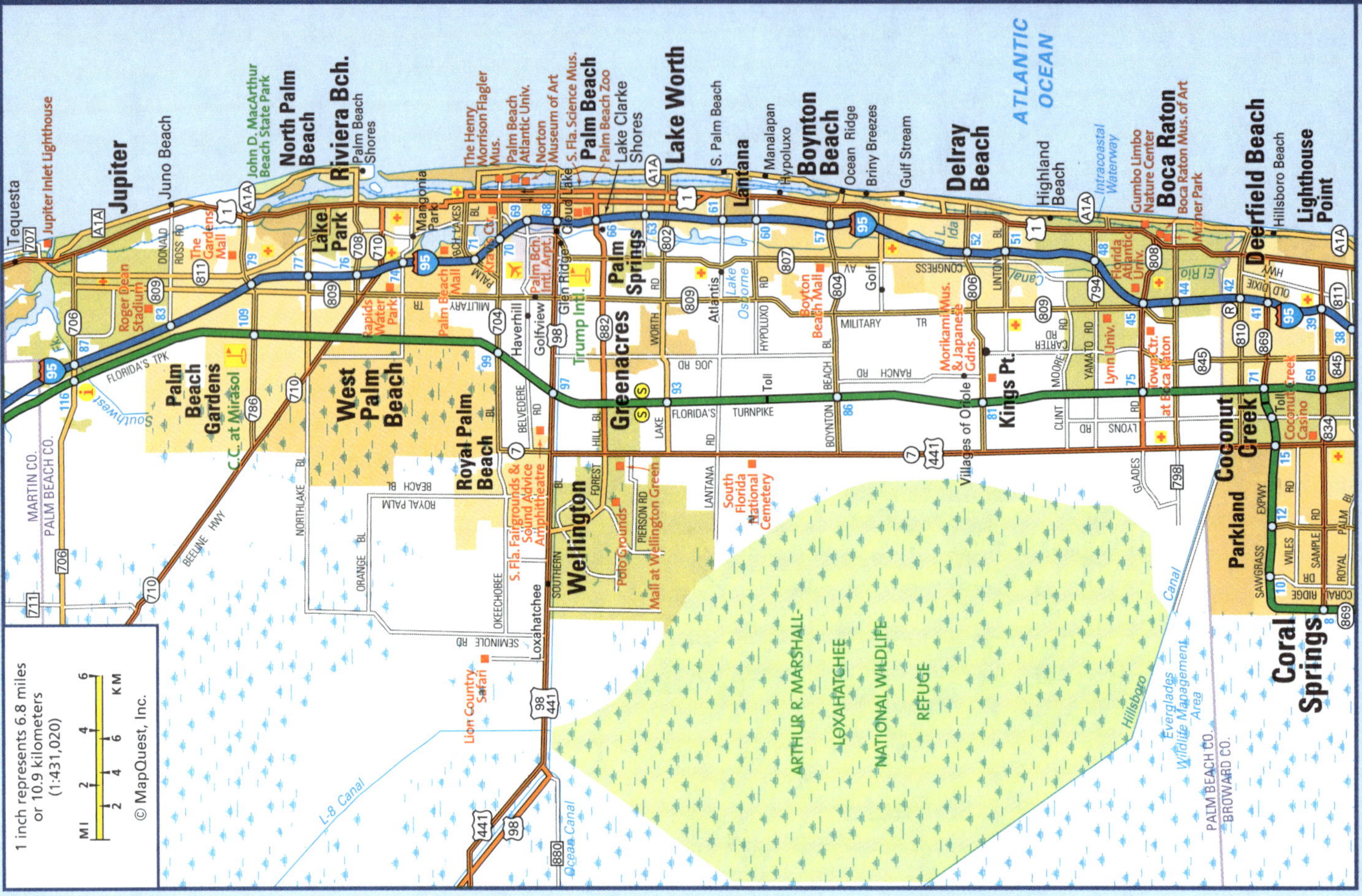

1 inch represents 4.5 miles
or 7.3 kilometers
(1:285,100)

© MapQuest, Inc.

MI
KM

Lake Borgne

Lake Pontchartrain

Goose Point

Point aux Herbes

ST. TAMMANY PARISH

ORLEANS PARISH

ST. BERNARD PARISH

PLAQUEMINES PAR.

Delacroix

Verret

Lake Lery

Kenilworth
Toca
St. Bernard
Poydras
Violet
Caernarvon
English Turn
Braithwaite
Scarsdale
Dalcour
Bertrandville

St. Bernard State Park

Faoe Ferry

Mississippi

New Orleans

Chalmette
Meraux
Arabi

NASA MICHOUD ASSEMBLY FACILITY

Six Flags New Orleans

Audubon La. Nature Ctr.

The Plaza

Bayou Sauvage N.W.R.

Fort Macomb

Point

Intracoastal

Southern Univ. at New Orleans

Bally's Casino

Jackson Barracks

Naval Supp. Activity

Jean Lafitte N.H.P. (Chalmette Bttld.)

Oakwood Shop. Ctr.

Our Lady of Holy Cross College

Terrytown

Gretna

Belle Chasse

Boomtown Casino Westbank

NAVAL AIR STATION JOINT RESERVE BASE

Crown Point

Oakville

JEFFERSON PARISH

ST. CHARLES PARISH

Kiefer UNO Lakefront Arena

New Orleans Baptist Theological Sem.

Univ. of New Orleans

Dillard Univ.

City Park

Art Mus.

Longue Vue Hse. & Gdns.

Metairie

Loyola Univ.

Tulane Univ.

Xavier Univ.

Audubon

Jefferson

Harvey

Marrero

Westwego

Estelle

Belle Promenade

JEAN LAFITTE N.H.P. AND PRES. (BARATARIA PRESERVE)

Lake Salvador

Couba Island

Timken Wildlife Management Area

Lakeside Shop. Ctr.

Clearview Shop. Ctr.

Treasure Chest Casino

Kenner

Louis Armstrong New Orleans Intl. Arpt.

The Esplanade

Zephyr Field

Harahan

River Ridge

Huey Long Bridge

Alario Ctr.

Audubon City

TPC of Louisiana

Bayou Segnette S.P.

Waggaman

Avondale

Salvador Wildlife Management Area

JEFFERSON PAR.
ST. CHARLES PAR.

Lake Cataouatche

TANGIPAHOA PARISH

ST. CHARLES PARISH

ST. JOHN THE BAPTIST PARISH

Frenier

St. Rose

Destrehan

Destrehan Plantation

New Sarpy

Luling

Boutte

Mimosa Park

Lone Star

Ama

Paradis

Des Allemands

LIVINGSTON PAR.
ST. JOHN THE BAPTIST PAR.

Manchac Wildlife Management Area

Lake Maurepas

Laplace

Norco

Montz

Taft

Hahnville

Killona

Lucy

Bayou des Allemands

Lac des Allemands

Pontchartrain Causeway

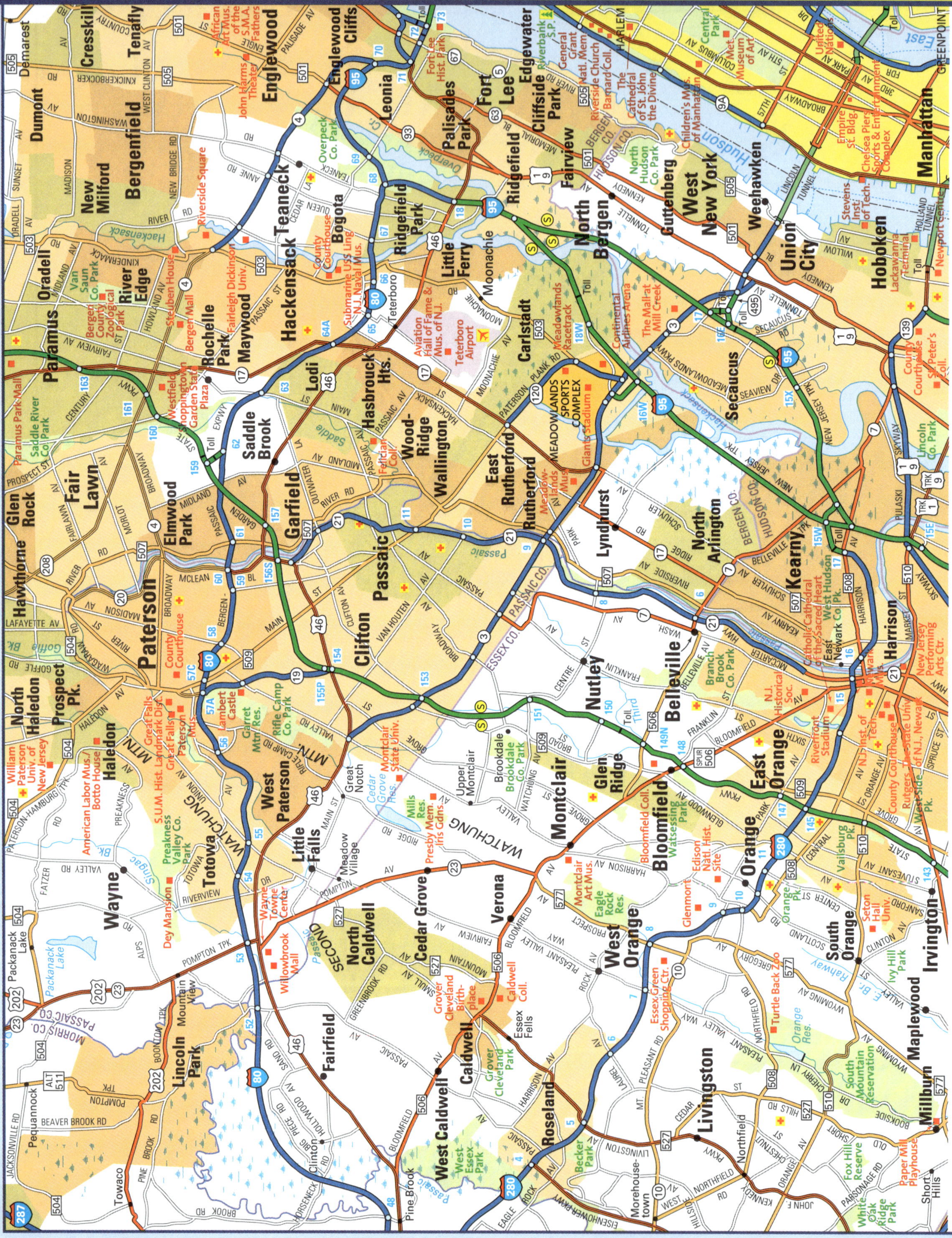

N

New York City

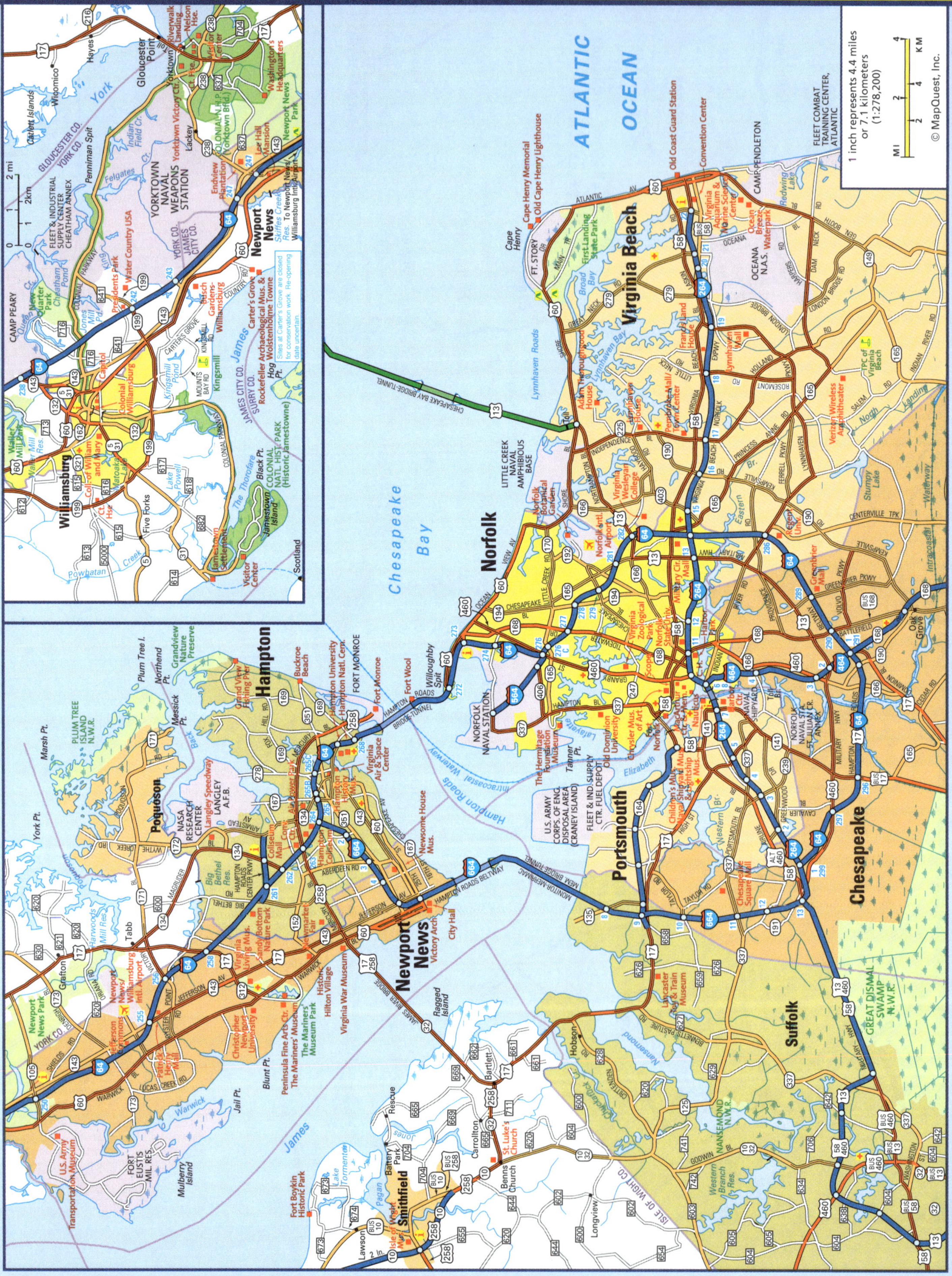

ATLANTIC OCEAN

CHESAPEAKE BAY BRIDGE-TUNNEL

Virginia Beach

Norfolk

Hampton

Newport News

Poquoson

Portsmouth

Chesapeake

Suffolk

Smithfield

Williamsburg

Newport News

Chesapeake Bay

Hampton Roads

James

1 inch represents 4.4 miles or 7.1 kilometers (1:278,200)

© MapQuest, Inc.

Ottawa
Omaha

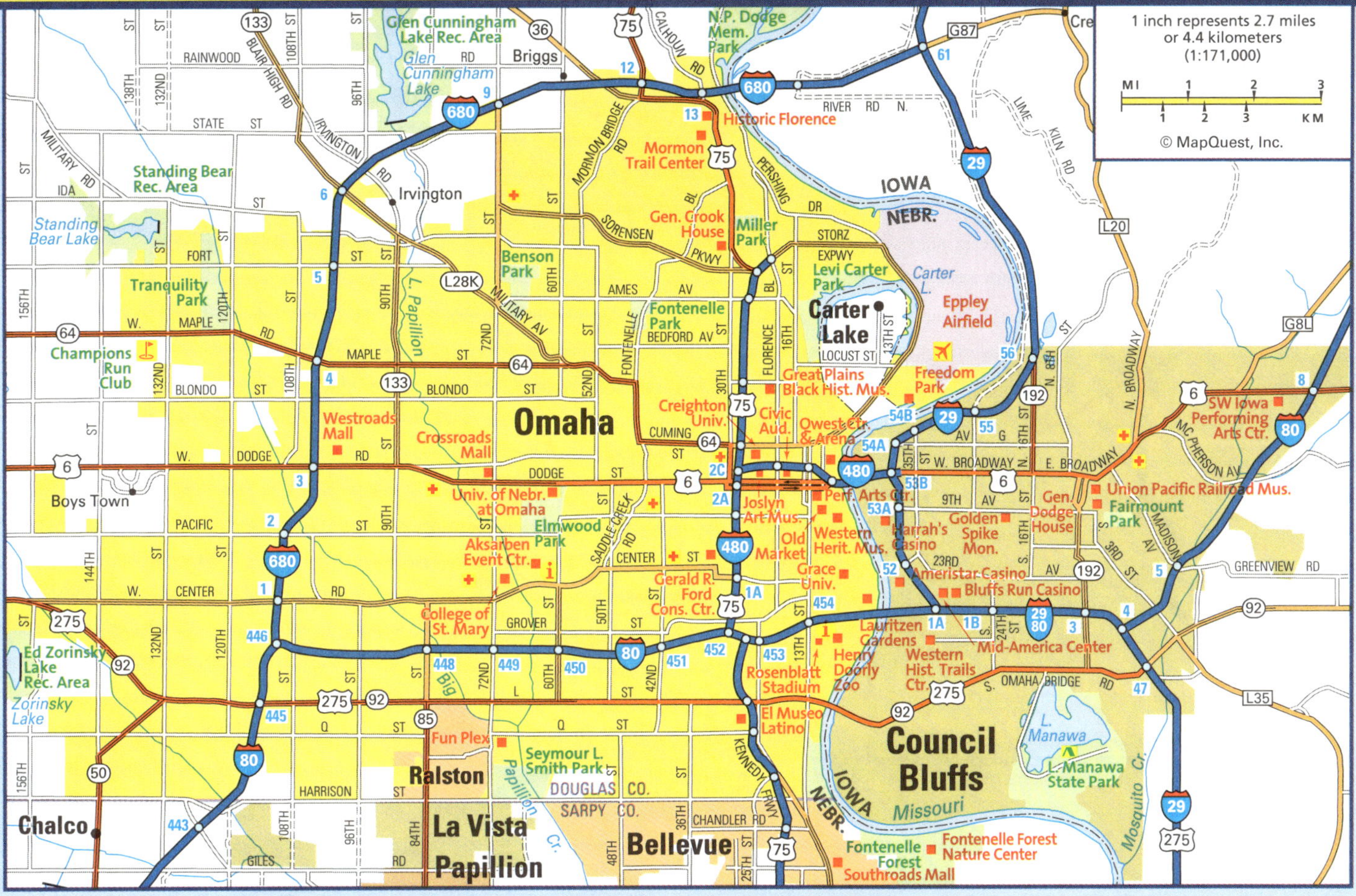

1 inch represents 2.7 miles
or 4.4 kilometers
(1:171,000)
© MapQuest, Inc.

MI 1 2 3
KM 1 2 3

P 33 Nebraska
P 21 Iowa

Omaha map

Glen Cunningham Lake Rec. Area
Glen Cunningham Lake
Briggs
Rainwood
State St
Standing Bear Rec. Area
Standing Bear Lake
Irvington
N.P. Dodge Mem. Park
Historic Florence
Mormon Trail Center
Mormon Bridge
Gen. Crook House
Miller Park
Tranquility Park
Champions Run Club
Benson Park
Fontenelle Park
Levi Carter Park
Carter Lake
Eppley Airfield
Westroads Mall
Crossroads Mall
Omaha
Creighton Univ.
Great Plains Black Hist. Mus.
Freedom Park
Qwest Ctr. & Arena
Civic Aud.
SW Iowa Performing Arts Ctr.
Union Pacific Railroad Mus.
Boys Town
Univ. of Nebr. at Omaha
Joslyn Art Mus.
Perf Arts Ctr.
Old Market
Western Herit. Mus.
Golden Spike Mon.
Gen. Dodge House
Fairmount Park
Aksarben Event Ctr.
Grace Univ.
Harrah's Casino
Ameristar Casino
Gerald R. Ford Cons. Ctr.
College of St. Mary
Lauritzen Gardens
Henry Doorly Zoo
Bluffs Run Casino
Western Hist. Trails Ctr.
Mid-America Center
Ed Zorinsky Lake Rec. Area
Zorinsky Lake
Rosenblatt Stadium
El Museo Latino
Council Bluffs
L. Manawa
Manawa State Park
Fun Plex
Seymour L. Smith Park
Ralston
Bellevue
Fontenelle Forest
Fontenelle Forest Nature Center
Southroads Mall
Chalco
La Vista
Papillion
Douglas Co.
Sarpy Co.
IOWA
NEBR.
Missouri

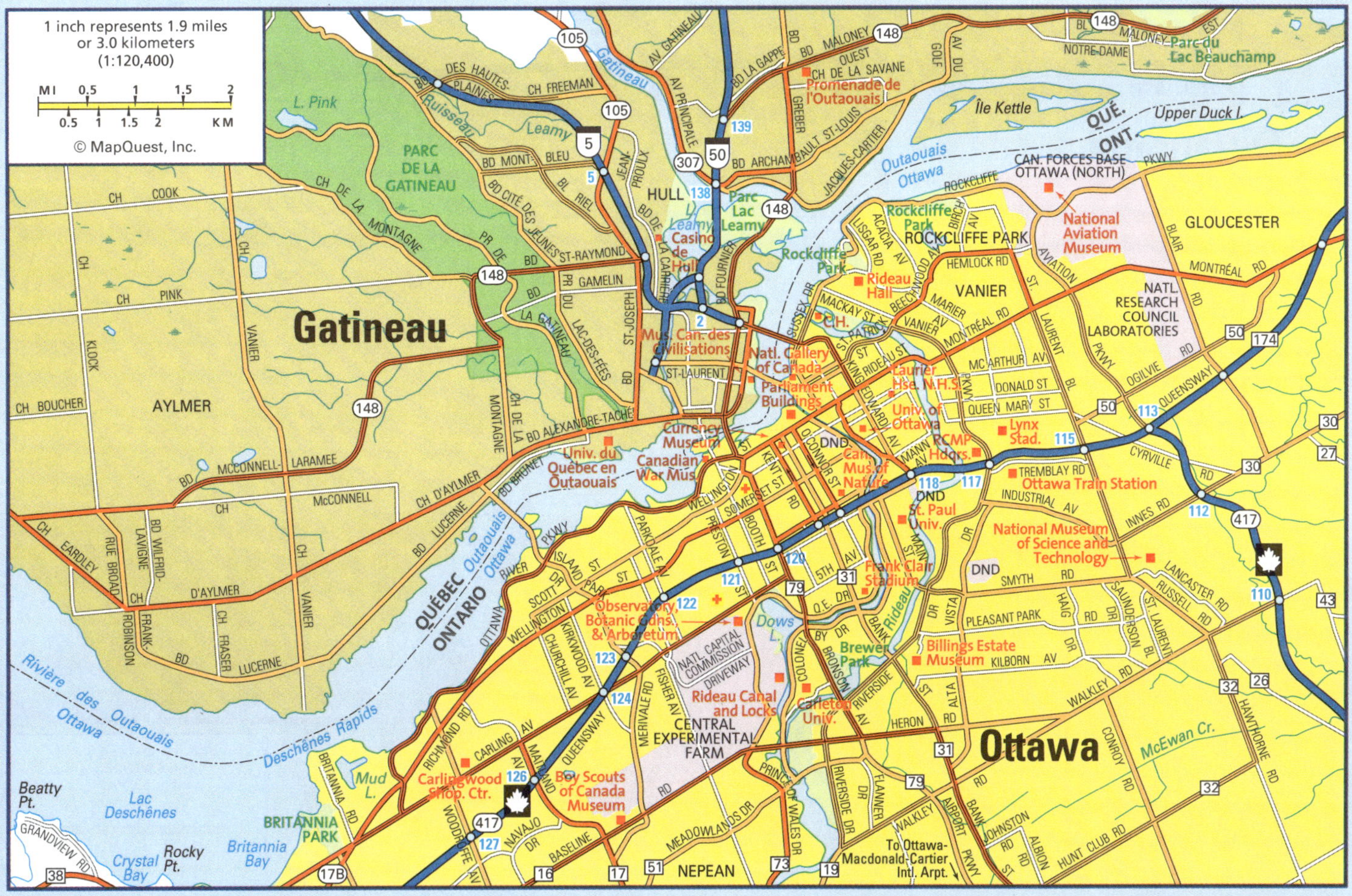

1 inch represents 1.9 miles
or 3.0 kilometers
(1:120,400)
© MapQuest, Inc.

MI 0.5 1 1.5 2
KM 0.5 1 1.5 2

P 64 Québec
P 62 Ontario

Ottawa map

Parc du Lac Beauchamp
Promenade de l'Outaouais
Île Kettle
Upper Duck I.
QUE.
ONT.
CAN. FORCES BASE OTTAWA (NORTH)
National Aviation Museum
L. Pink
PARC DE LA GATINEAU
Leamy
Casino de Hull
HULL
Parc Lac Leamy
Rockcliffe Park
Rideau Hall
GLOUCESTER
Gatineau
AYLMER
Mus. Can. des Civilisations
Natl. Gallery of Canada
Parliament Buildings
VANIER
NATL. RESEARCH COUNCIL LABORATORIES
Laurier Hse. N.H.S.
Univ. du Québec en Outaouais
Currency Museum
Canadian War Mus.
Univ. of Ottawa
Lynx Stad.
Ottawa Train Station
RCMP Hdqrs.
Canadian Mus. of Nature
Tremblay
DND
St. Paul Univ.
National Museum of Science and Technology
QUÉBEC
ONTARIO
Observatory
Botanic Gdns. & Arboretum
Frank Clair Stadium
DND
Natl. Capital Commission
Dows L.
Brewer Park
Billings Estate Museum
Rideau Canal and Locks
CENTRAL EXPERIMENTAL FARM
Carleton Univ.
Ottawa
McEwan Cr.
Beatty Pt.
Lac Deschenes
Mud L.
Britannia Bay
Deschenes Rapids
Rivière des Outaouais
Carlingwood Shop. Ctr.
Boy Scouts of Canada Museum
BRITANNIA PARK
Britannia Bay
Rocky Pt.
Crystal Bay
NEPEAN
To Ottawa-Macdonald-Cartier Int. Arpt.

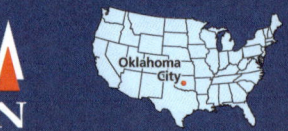

Oklahoma City
N

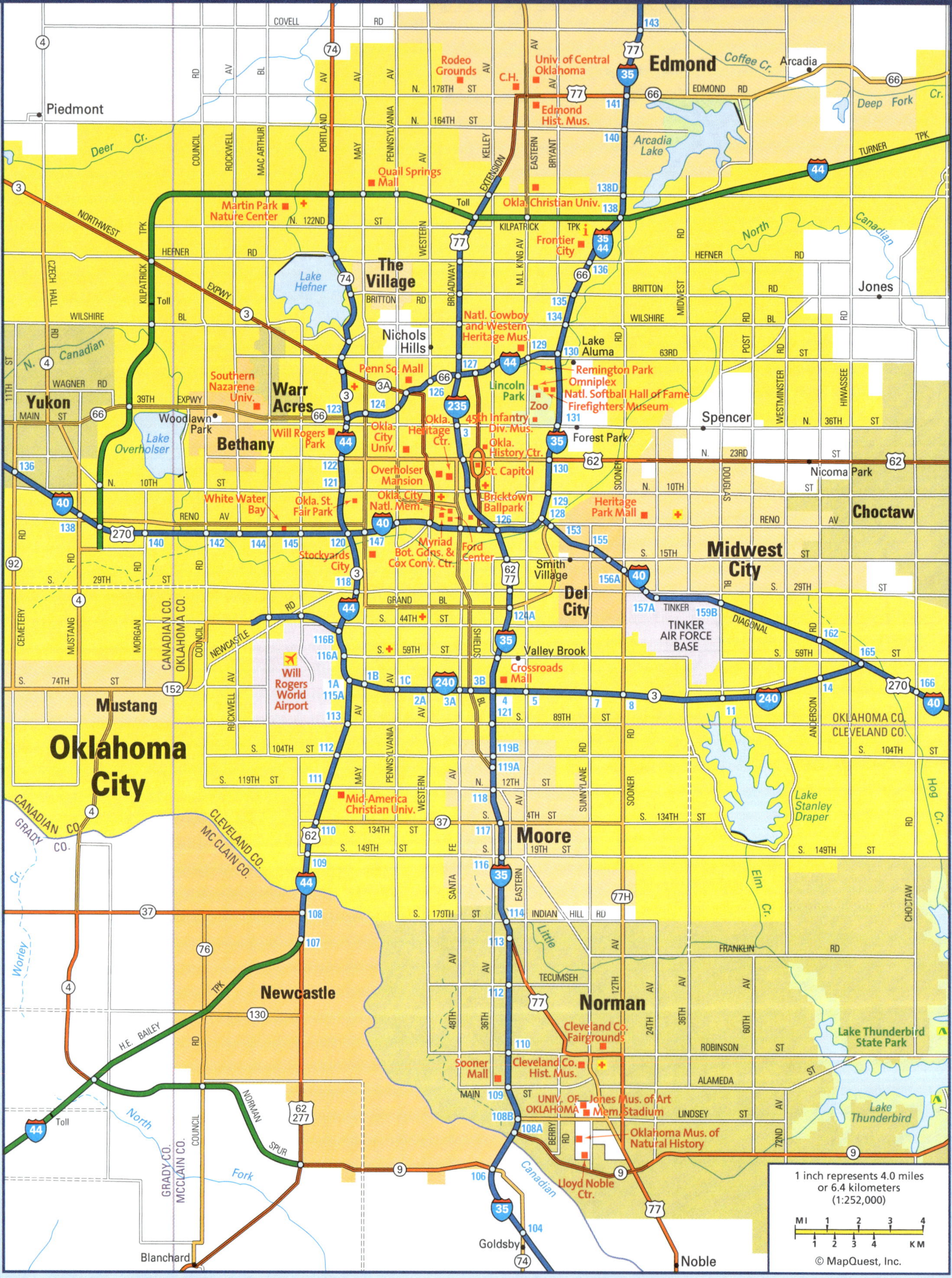
Edmond
Arcadia
Piedmont
Univ. of Central Oklahoma
Rodeo Grounds
C.H.
Edmond Hist. Mus.
Arcadia Lake
Deep Fork
Coffee Cr.
Deer Cr.
Quail Springs Mall
Martin Park Nature Center
Okla. Christian Univ.
Frontier City
Lake Hefner
The Village
Nichols Hills
Jones
Natl. Cowboy and Western Heritage Mus.
Lake Aluma
Remington Park
Omniplex
Natl. Softball Hall of Fame
Firefighters Museum
Lincoln Park
Zoo
Spencer
Forest Park
Nicoma Park
Choctaw
Penn Sq. Mall
Southern Nazarene Univ.
Warr Acres
Yukon
Woodlawn Park
Bethany
Lake Overholser
Will Rogers Park
Okla. City Univ.
Okla. Heritage Ctr.
45th Infantry Div. Mus.
Okla. History Ctr.
St. Capitol
Overholser Mansion
Okla. City Natl. Mem.
Bricktown Ballpark
White Water Bay
Okla. St. Fair Park
Heritage Park Mall
Myriad Bot. Gdns. & Cox Conv. Ctr.
Ford Center
Stockyards City
Smith Village
Del City
Midwest City
TINKER AIR FORCE BASE
Valley Brook
Crossroads Mall
Will Rogers World Airport
Mustang
Oklahoma City
Mid-America Christian Univ.
Moore
Lake Stanley Draper
OKLAHOMA CO.
CLEVELAND CO.
CANADIAN CO.
GRADY CO.
MC CLAIN CO.
Newcastle
Norman
Cleveland Co. Fairgrounds
Cleveland Co. Hist. Mus.
Sooner Mall
UNIV. OF OKLAHOMA
Jones Mus. of Art
Mem. Stadium
Oklahoma Mus. of Natural History
Lloyd Noble Ctr.
Lake Thunderbird State Park
Lake Thunderbird
Goldsby
Blanchard
Noble
Canadian
North Fork
Little
Elm Cr.
Hog Cr.
Worley Cr.
1 inch represents 4.0 miles or 6.4 kilometers (1:252,000)
MI
KM
© MapQuest, Inc.

P 44 Oklahoma

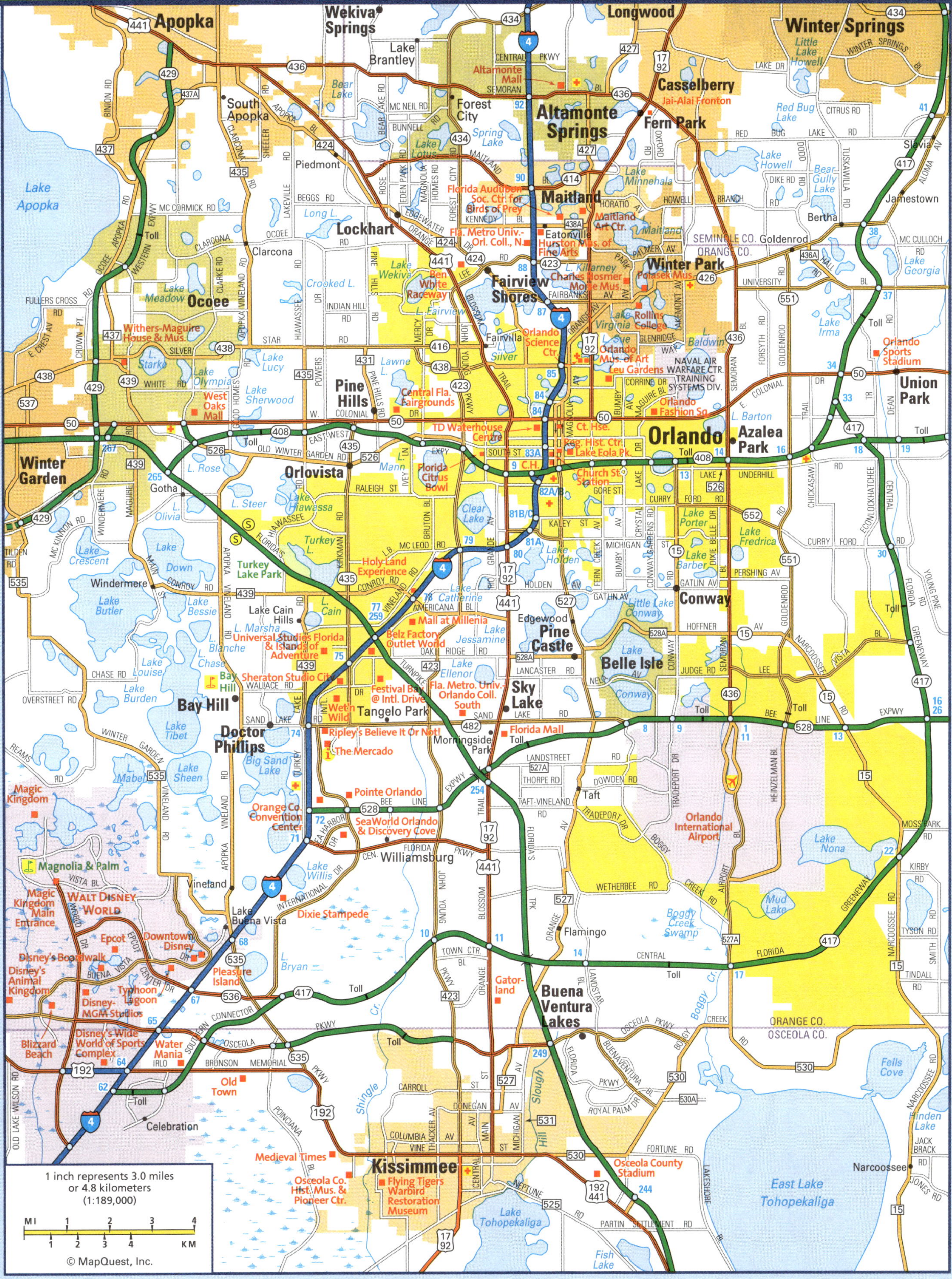

Orlando

Apopka
Wekiva Springs
Longwood
Winter Springs

Little Lake Howell
Lake Brantley
South Apopka
Bear Lake
Forest City
Altamonte Mall SEMORAN
Casselberry
Jai-Alai Fronton
Fern Park
Red Bug Lake

Piedmont
Altamonte Springs
Lake Howell
Bear Gully Lake
Slavia

Lockhart
Florida Audubon Soc. Ctr. for Birds of Prey
Maitland
Lake Minnehaha
Tuskawilla
Jamestown

Ocoee
Withers-Maguire House & Mus.
Fla. Metro Univ.- Orl. Coll., N.
Maitland Art Ctr.
Hurston Mus. of Fine Arts
Eatonville
Goldenrod
SEMINOLE CO.
ORANGE CO.
Bertha
MC CULLOCH

Clarcona
Charles Hosmer Morse Mus.
Winter Park
Potasek Mus.
Lake Georgia

Fairview Shores
Ben White Raceway
Rollins College
Lake Virginia
L. Killarney
Baldwin
Lake Irma

Pine Hills
Central Fla. Fairgrounds
Fairvilla
Orlando Science Ctr.
L. Sue
Orlando Mus. of Art
Leu Gardens
NAVAL AIR WARFARE CTR TRAINING SYSTEMS DIV.
Orlando Sports Stadium

Winter Garden
West Oaks Mall
Lawne
Orlando Fashion Sq.
Union Park

Orlovista
TD Waterhouse Centre
Reg. Hist. Ctr.
Ct. Hse.
Orlando
Azalea Park

Florida Citrus Bowl
Church St. Station
Lake Eola Pk.
UNDERHILL

Winter Garden
Gotha
Windermere
Lake Cain Hills
Holy-Land Experience
Mall at Millenia
Lake Holden
Lake Porter
Lake Fredrica
Conway

Turkey Lake Park
Belz Factory Outlet World
Lake Jessamine
Pine Castle
Little Lake Conway

Bay Hill
Universal Studios Florida & Island of Adventure
Sheraton Studio City
Festival Bay @ Intl. Drive
Fla. Metro. Univ. Orlando Coll. South
Sky Lake
Belle Isle

Doctor Phillips
Big Sand L.
Wet'n Wild
Ripley's Believe It Or Not!
The Mercado
Tangelo Park
Morningside Park
Florida Mall

Magic Kingdom
Pointe Orlando
Orange Co. Convention Center
SeaWorld Orlando & Discovery Cove
Taft
Orlando International Airport
Lake Nona

Magnolia & Palm
Williamsburg
Mud Lake

WALT DISNEY WORLD
Magic Kingdom Main Entrance
Epcot
Downtown Disney
Lake Buena Vista
Dixie Stampede
Boggy Creek Swamp

Disney's Boardwalk
Disney's Animal Kingdom
Disney-MGM Studios
Typhoon Lagoon
Pleasure Island
Gatorland
Buena Ventura Lakes

Blizzard Beach
Disney's Wide World of Sports Complex
Water Mania
Old Town
ORANGE CO.
OSCEOLA CO.
Fells Cove

Celebration
Medieval Times
Kissimmee
Flying Tigers Warbird Restoration Museum
Osceola Co. Hist. Mus. & Pioneer Ctr.
Osceola County Stadium
Narcoossee
Hinden Lake

East Lake Tohopekaliga
Lake Tohopekaliga
Fish Lake

1 inch represents 3.0 miles
or 4.8 kilometers
(1:189,000)

© MapQuest, Inc.

1 inch represents 3.3 miles
or 5.3 kilometers (1:208,193)

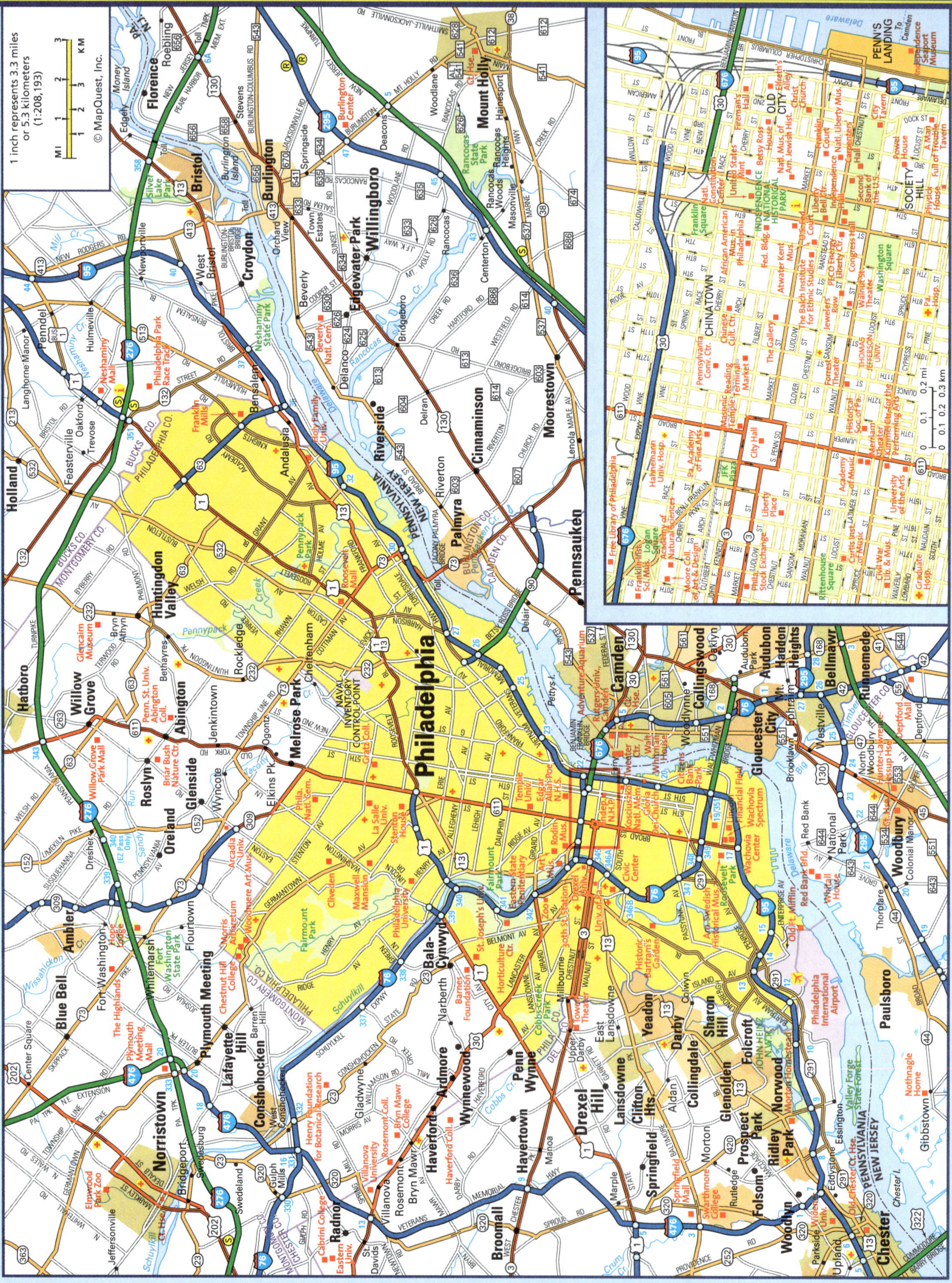

© MapQuest, Inc.

Map Labels

PENNSYLVANIA

NEW JERSEY

Florence
Roebling
Money Island
Bristol
Burlington
Burlington Columbus Rd
Mount Holly
Springside
Rancocas State Park
Rancocas Heights
Rancocas Woods
Masonville
Hainsport

Pennel
Langhorne Manor
Feasterville
Oakford
Trevose
Holland
West Bristol
Croydon
Hulmeville
Beverly
Willingboro
Edgewater Park
Centerton
Moorestown

Holland
Feasterville
Newportville
Andalusia
Bensalem
Delanco
Riverside
Delran
Cinnaminson

Huntingdon Valley
Glencairn Museum
Bryn Athyn
Rockledge
Cheltenham
Palmyra
Riverton
Pennsauken

Hatboro
Willow Grove
Abington
Jenkintown
Wyncote
Elkins Park
Melrose Park
Naval Inventory Control Point

Roslyn
Glenside
Oreland
Arcadia Univ.
Philadelphia
Camden
Audubon
Haddon Heights
Bellmawr

Blue Bell
Ambler
Fort Washington
Flourtown
Fairmount Park
Collingswood
Gloucester City
Woodbury

Plymouth Meeting
Lafayette Hill
Whitemarsh
Bala-Cynwyd
St. Joseph's Univ.
Philadelphia International Airport
Paulsboro

Norristown
Conshohocken
Gladwyne
Narberth
Ardmore
Penn Wynne
Yeadon
Darby
Folcroft
National Park

Bridgeport
Gulph Mills
Villanova
Bryn Mawr
Rosemont
Haverford
Wynnewood
Drexel Hill
Clifton Hts.
Sharon Hill
Glenolden
Prospect Park
Ridley Park
Woodlyn

Radnor
Cabrini College
Eastern Univ.
Broomall
Springfield
Lansdowne
Collingdale
Norwood
Folsom
Chester

Jeffersonville
Swedesburg
Bridgeport
Elmwood Park Zoo

Florida
Willow Grove
Park Mall

PHILADELPHIA CO.
BUCKS CO.
MONTGOMERY CO.
BURLINGTON CO.
CAMDEN CO.
GLOUCESTER CO.
DELAWARE CO.

Inset Map (Center City)

PENN'S LANDING

Independence Seaport Museum
OLD CITY
INDEPENDENCE NATIONAL HISTORICAL PARK
SOCIETY HILL
CHINATOWN

City Hall
JFK Plaza
Logan Square
Franklin Square
Washington Square
Rittenhouse Square

Free Library of Philadelphia
Pa. Academy of Fine Arts
Academy of Natural Sciences
Franklin Inst. Sci. Mus.
University of the Arts
Graduate Hosp.

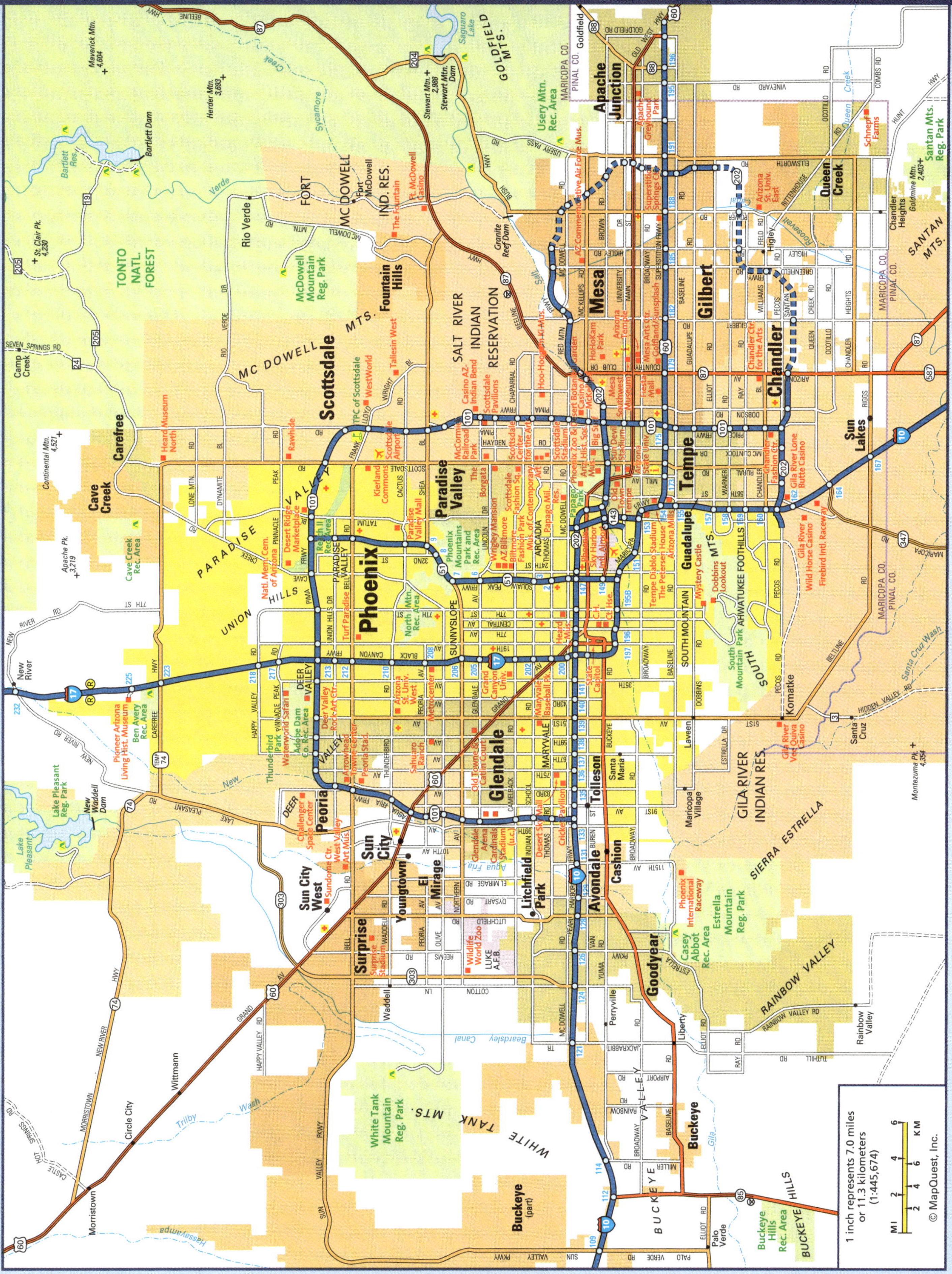

N

Pittsburgh

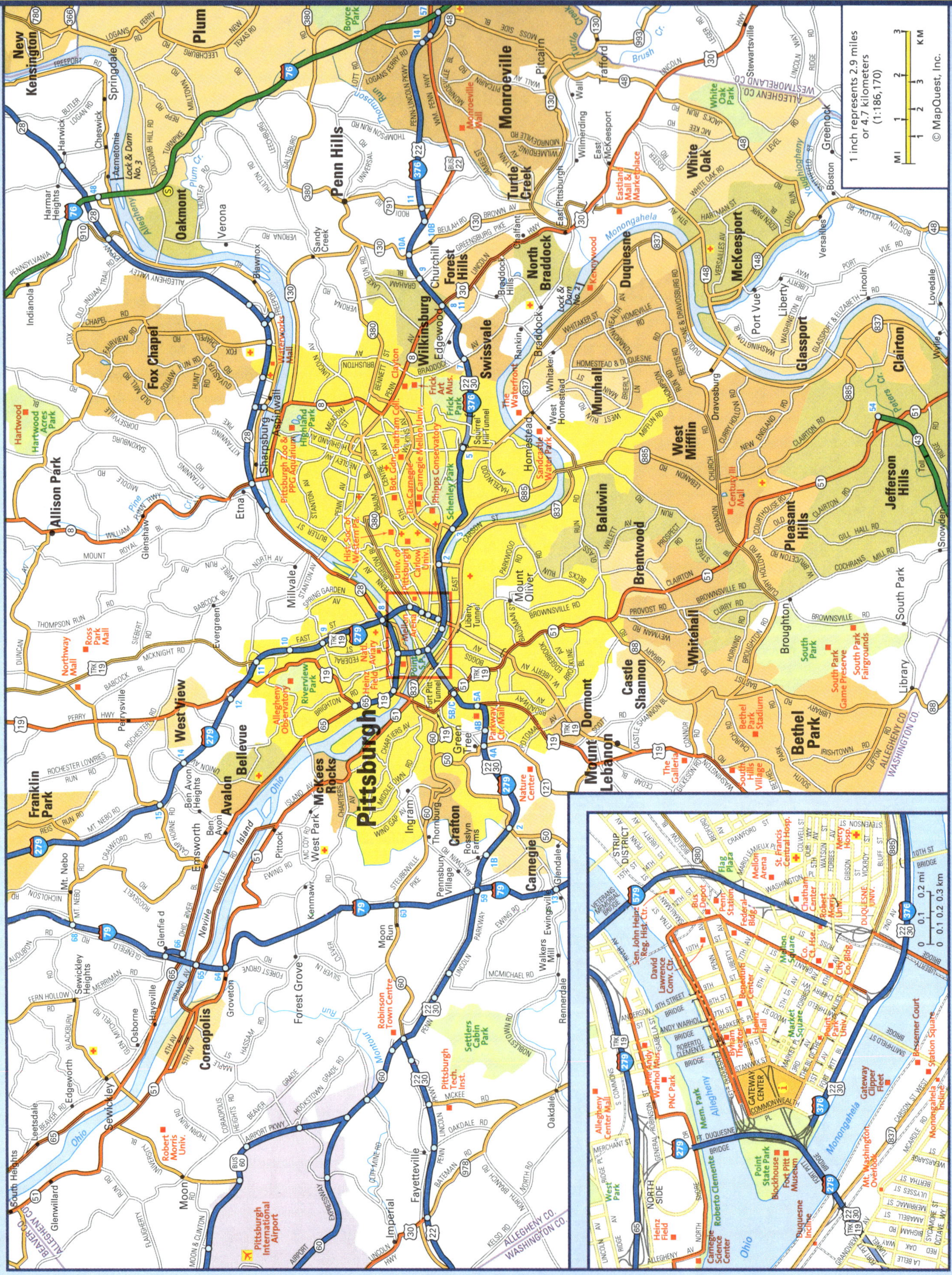

© MapQuest, Inc.

1 inch represents 2.9 miles or 4.7 kilometers (1:186,170)

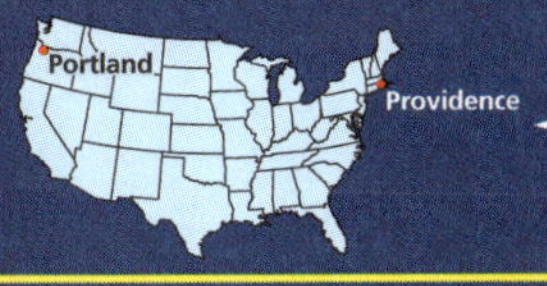
Portland
Providence
N

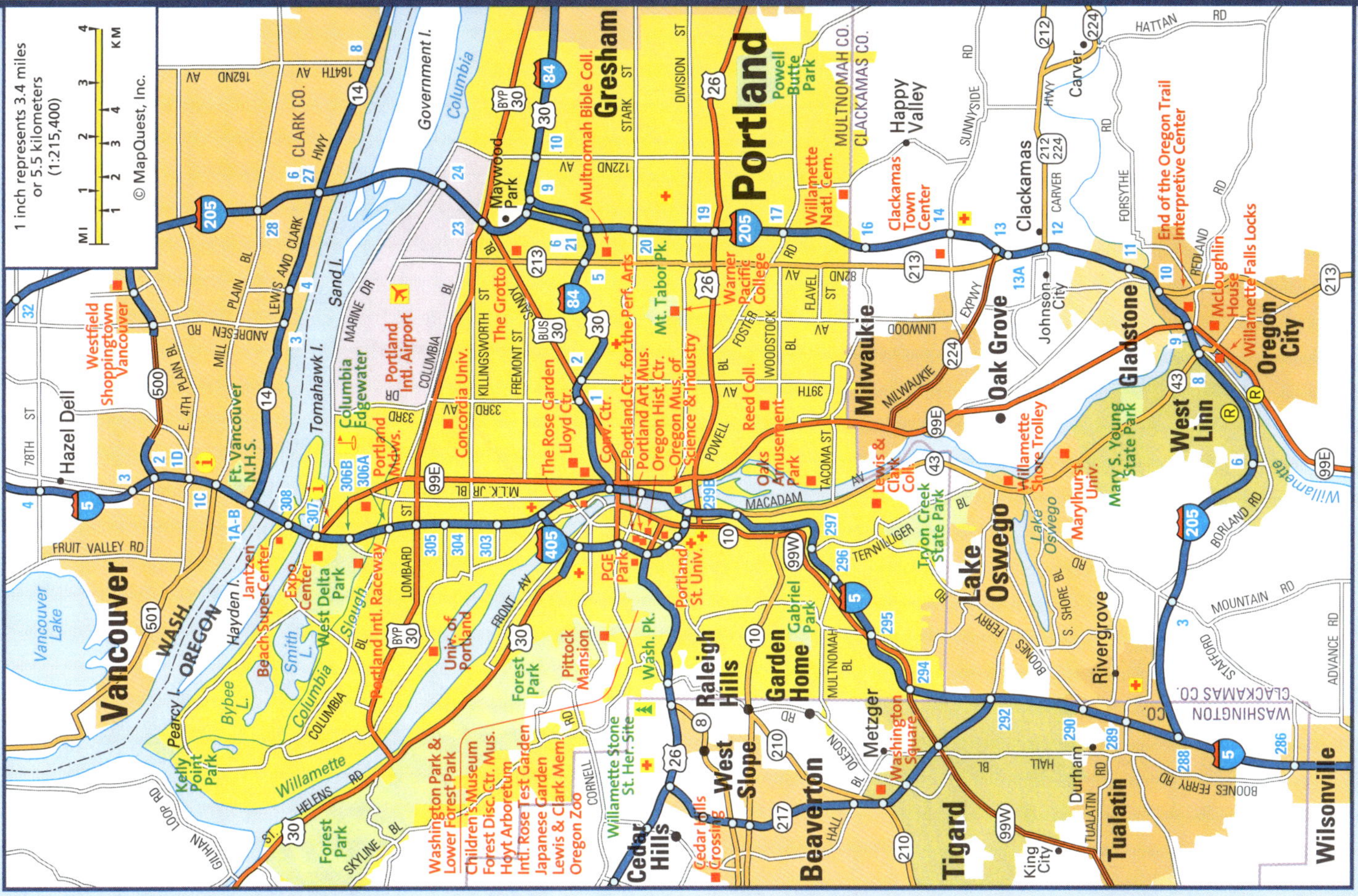
1 inch represents 3.4 miles or 5.5 kilometers (1:215,400)
MI
KM
© MapQuest, Inc.
Portland
Vancouver
Gresham
Milwaukie
Lake Oswego
Oak Grove
Gladstone
Oregon City
West Linn
Beaverton
Tigard
Tualatin
Wilsonville
Portland Intl. Airport

P 45 Oregon

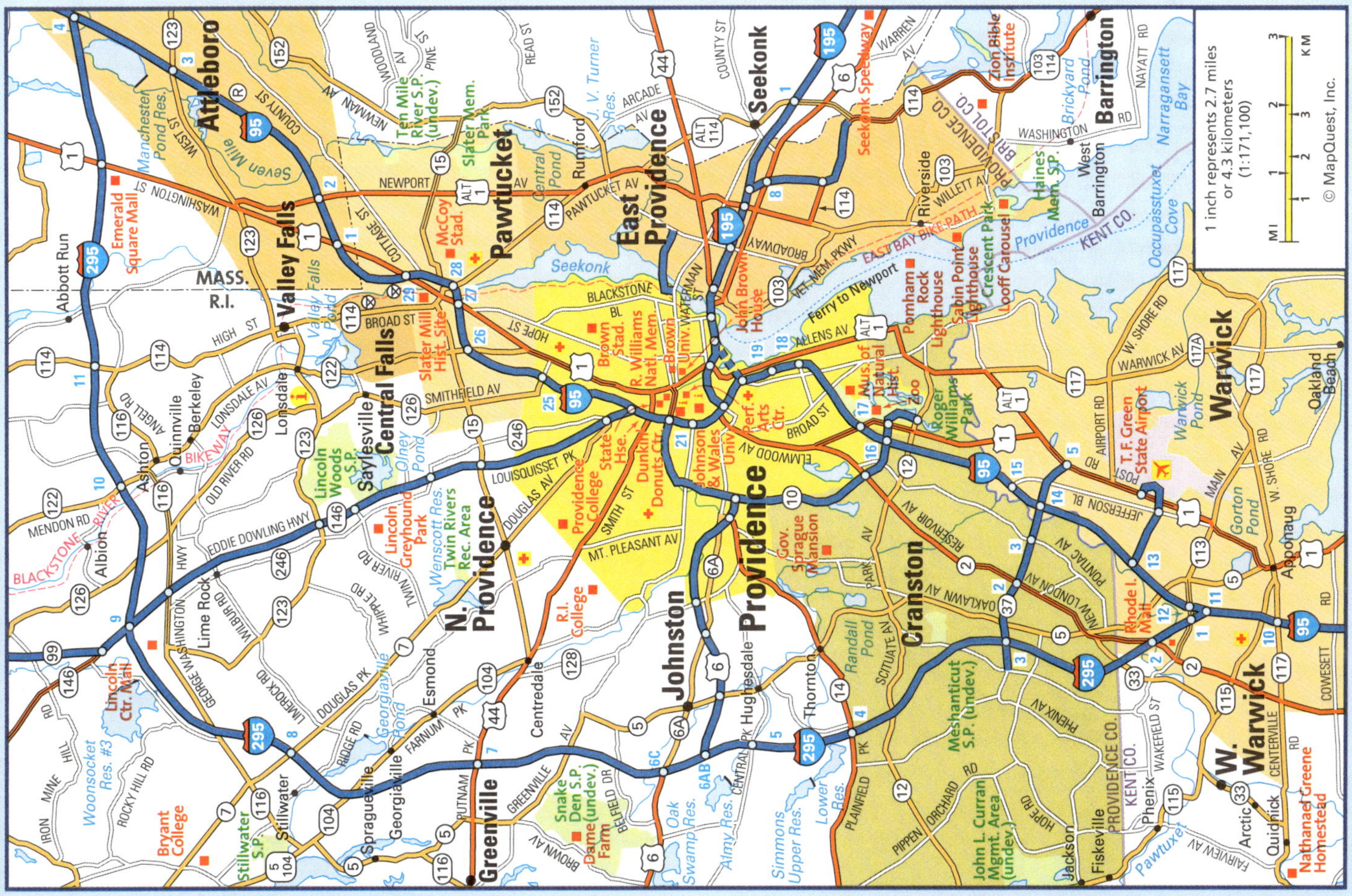
1 inch represents 2.7 miles or 4.3 kilometers (1:171,100)
MI
KM
© MapQuest, Inc.
Providence
East Providence
Pawtucket
Central Falls
Valley Falls
Attleboro
Seekonk
Barrington
Cranston
Warwick
W. Warwick
Johnston
N. Providence
Greenville
T.F. Green State Airport

P 14 Rhode Island

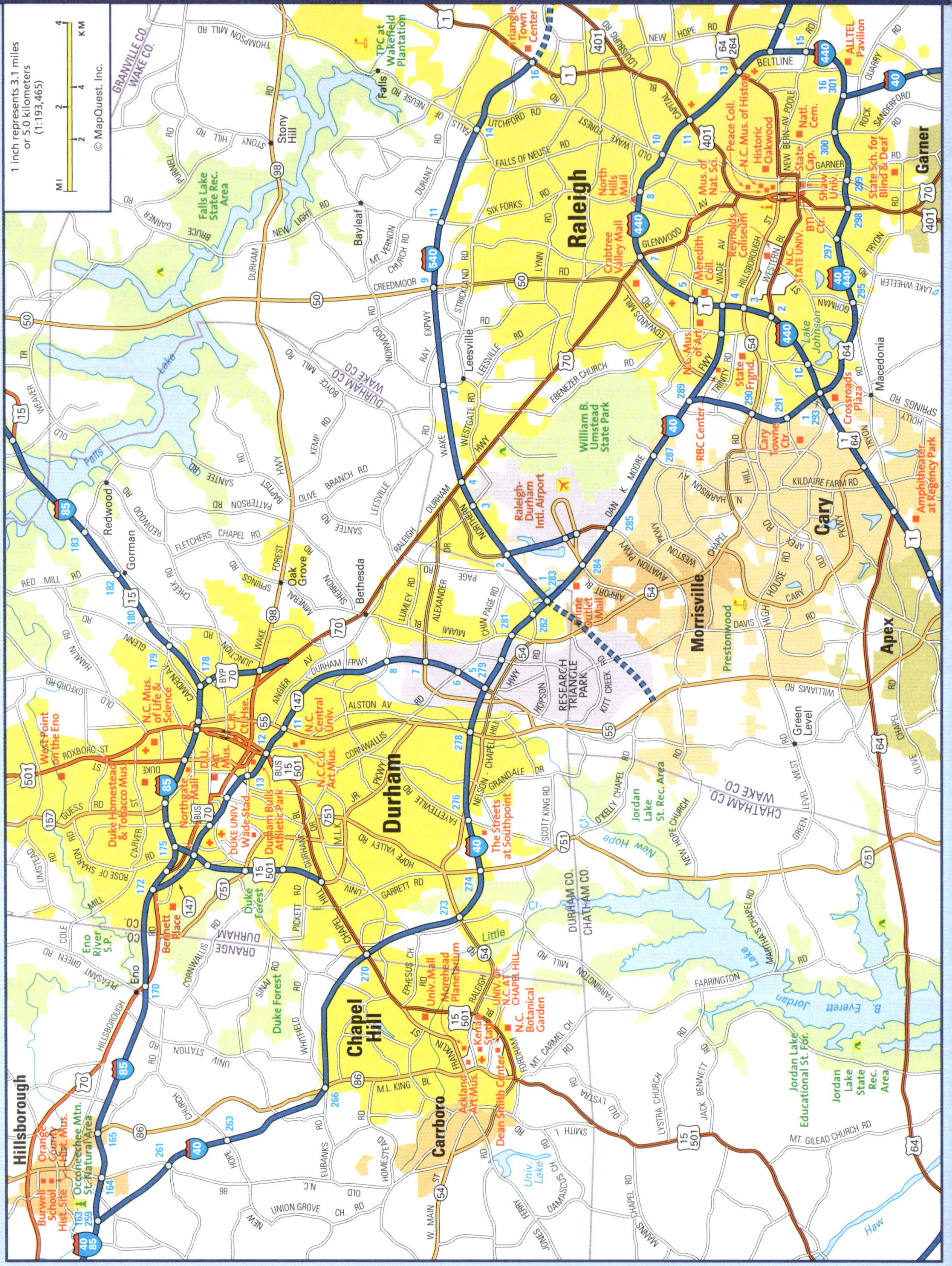

N

1 inch represents 3.1 miles
or 5.0 kilometers
(1:193,465)

© MapQuest, Inc.

KM
MI

Granville Co.
Wake Co.

THOMPSON MILL RD

Falls

Stony Hill

Falls Lake State Rec. Area

BRUCE

GARNER RD

PURNELL RD

NEW LIGHT

HILL

Bayleaf

MT. VERNON CHURCH RD

CREEDMOOR RD

STRICKLAND RD

Leesville

SIX FORKS RD

LYNN RD

RAY EXPWY

WESTGATE RD

50

70

EBENEZER CHURCH RD

William B. Umstead State Park

Raleigh-Durham Intl. Airport

DAN K. MOORE

AVIATION PKWY

WESTON PKWY

HARRISON AV

RBC Center

Cary Towne Ctr

Crossroads Plaza

Amphitheater at Regency Park

Cary

Apex

Morrisville

Research Triangle Park

KITT CREEK

HOPSON

Streets at Southpoint

NELSON

GRANDALE DR

SCOTT KING RD

Durham

Jordan Lake St. Rec. Area

Chatham Co.
Wake Co.

Green Level

NEW HOPE CHURCH RD

O'KELLY CHAPEL RD

FARRINGTON RD

Lake Jordan

B. Everett Jordan Lake

Jordan Lake Educational St. For.

Jordan Lake State Rec. Area

Chapel Hill

Carrboro

Univ. Mall
Morehead Planetarium

N.C. Botanical Garden

UNIV. OF N.C. AT CHAPEL HILL

Kenan Stad.

Ackland Art Mus.

Dean Smith Center

Univ. Lake

M.L. KING BL

MT. CARMEL CH. RD

MT. GILEAD CHURCH RD

Hillsborough

Burwell School Hist. Site

Occoneechee Mtn. St. Natural Area

Orange County Hist. Mus.

Eno River S.P.

West Point on the Eno

Duke Homestead & Tobacco Mus.

N.C. Mus. of Life & Science

Duke Forest

Bennett Place

Northgate Mall

D.U. Art Mus.

Duke Univ.
Wade Stad.

Durham Bulls Athletic Park

N.C. Central Univ.

N.C.C.U. Art Mus.

Raleigh

North Hills Mall

Crabtree Valley Mall

Meredith Coll.

Reynolds Coliseum

N.C. State Univ.

N.C. Mus. of Art

Peace Coll.

N.C. Mus. of History

Historic Oakwood

State Cap.

Shaw Univ.

Natl. Cem.

State Sch. for Blind & Deaf

State Frgnd.

ALLTEL Pavilion

Garner

TPC at Wakefield Plantation

Triangle Town Center

BELTLINE

Beltline

P 52
Virginia

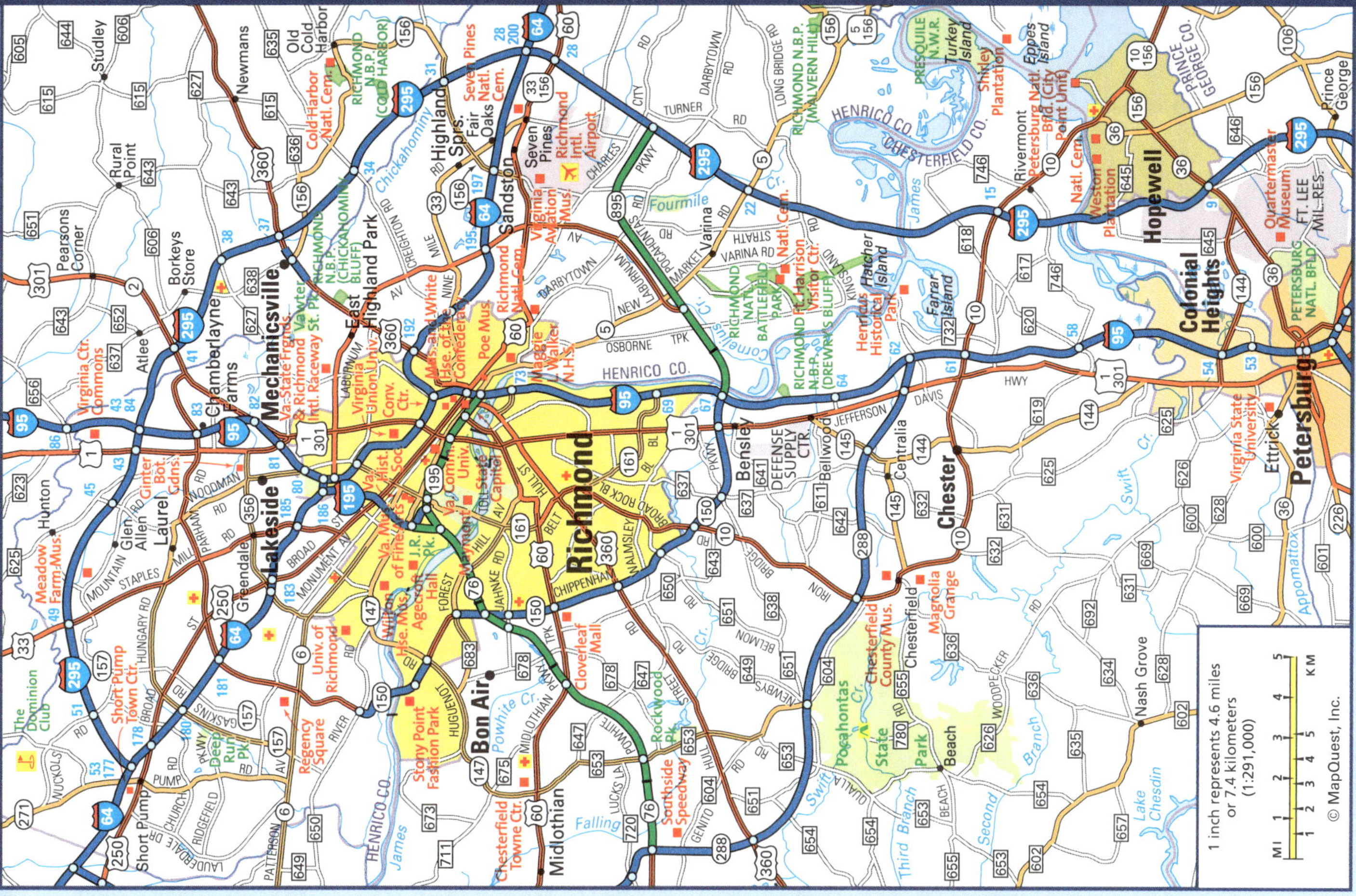

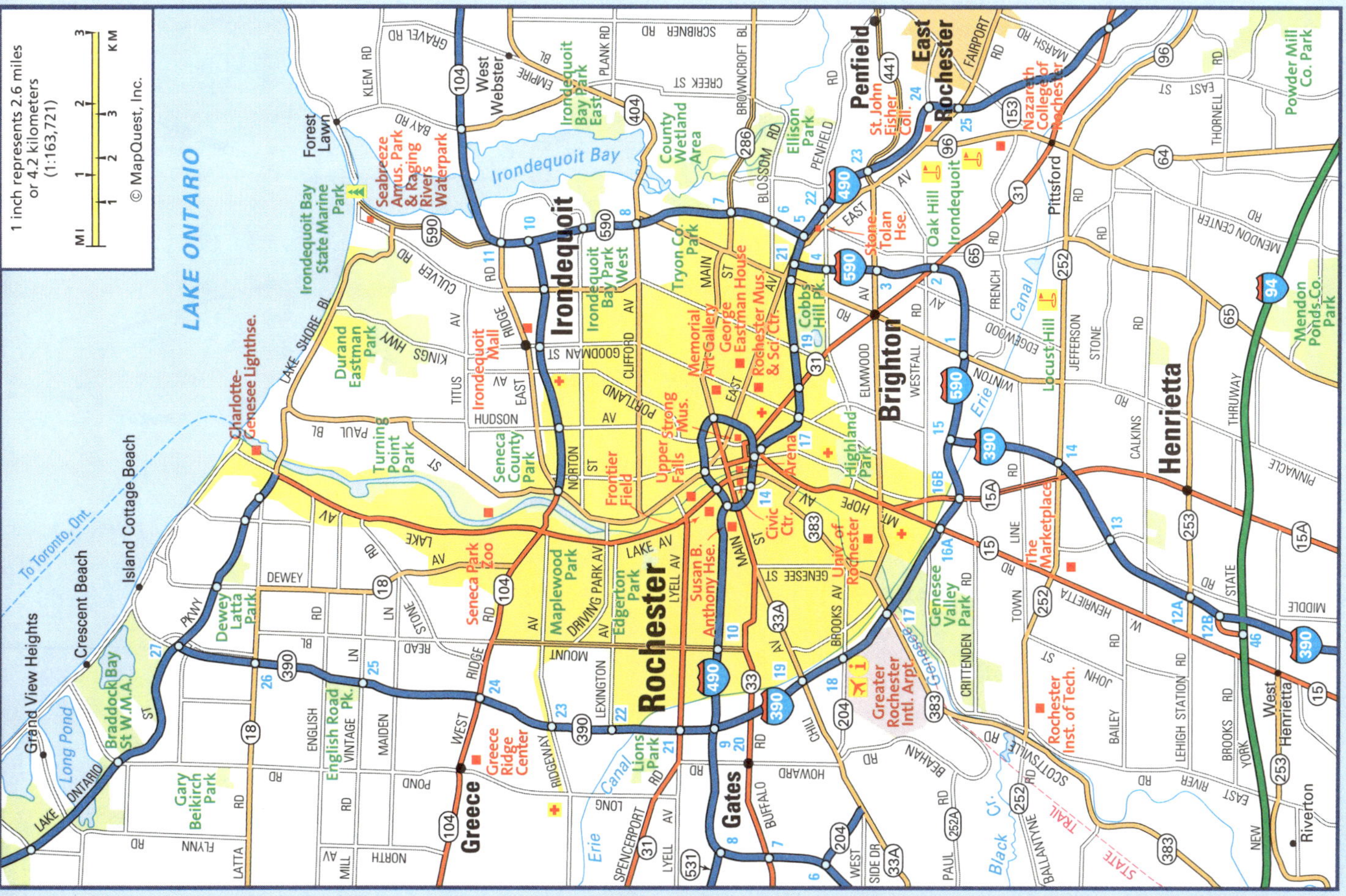

P 38
New York

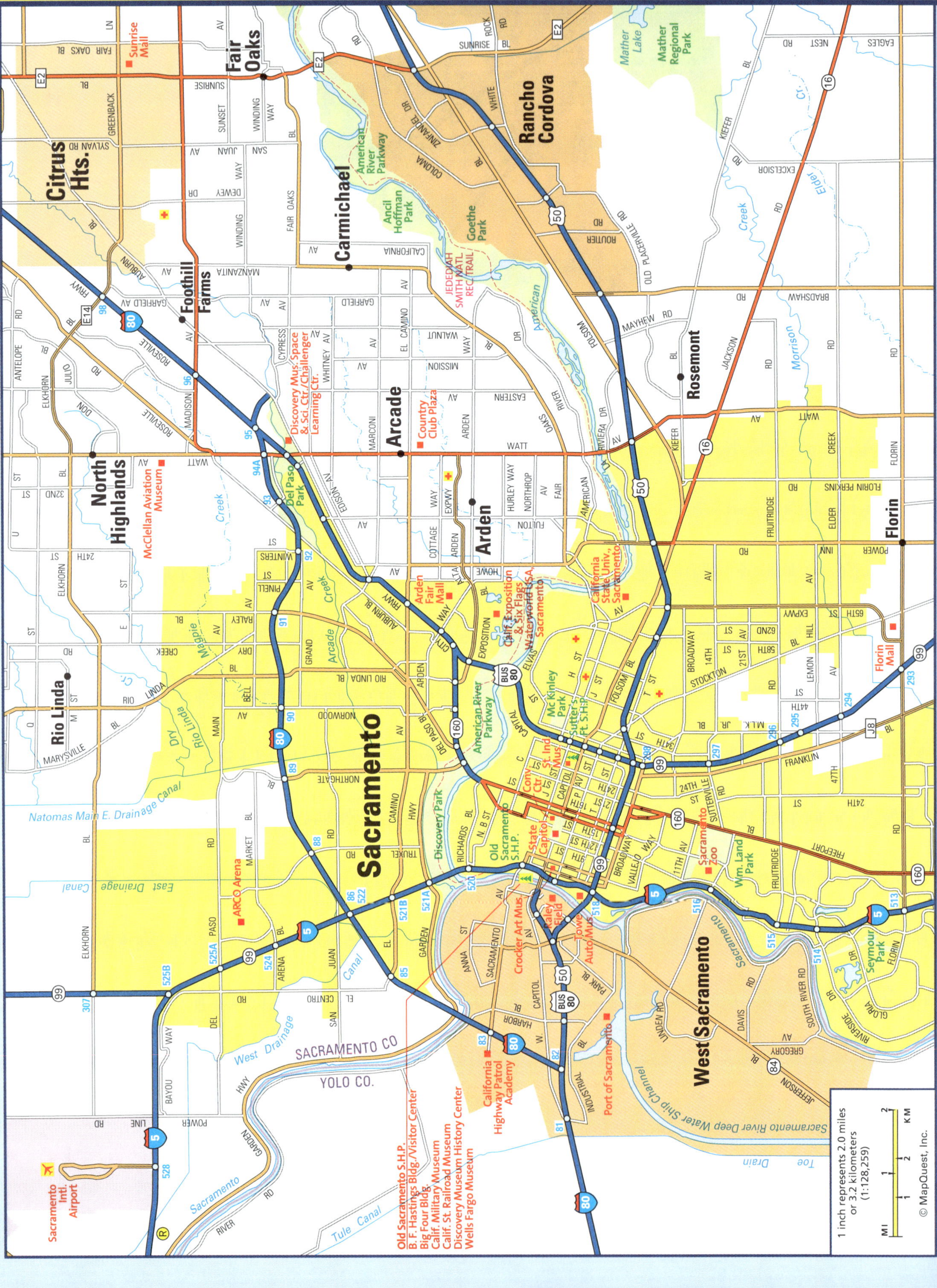

N

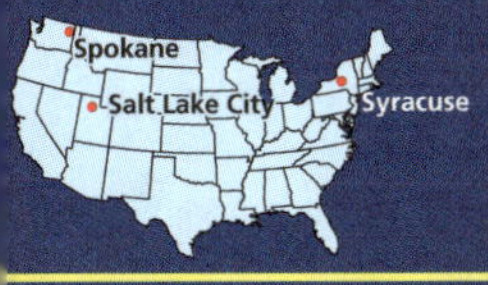

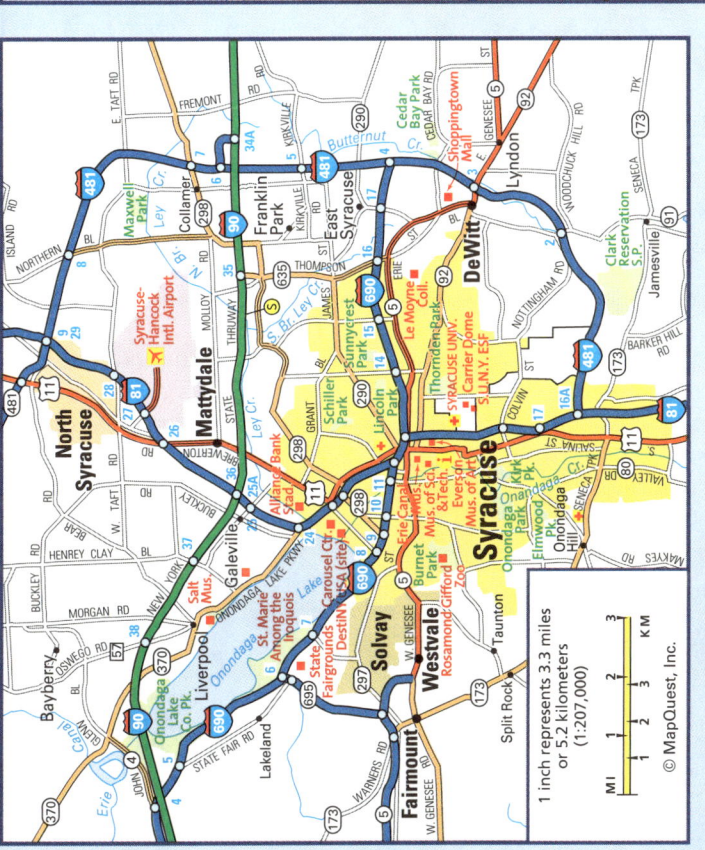

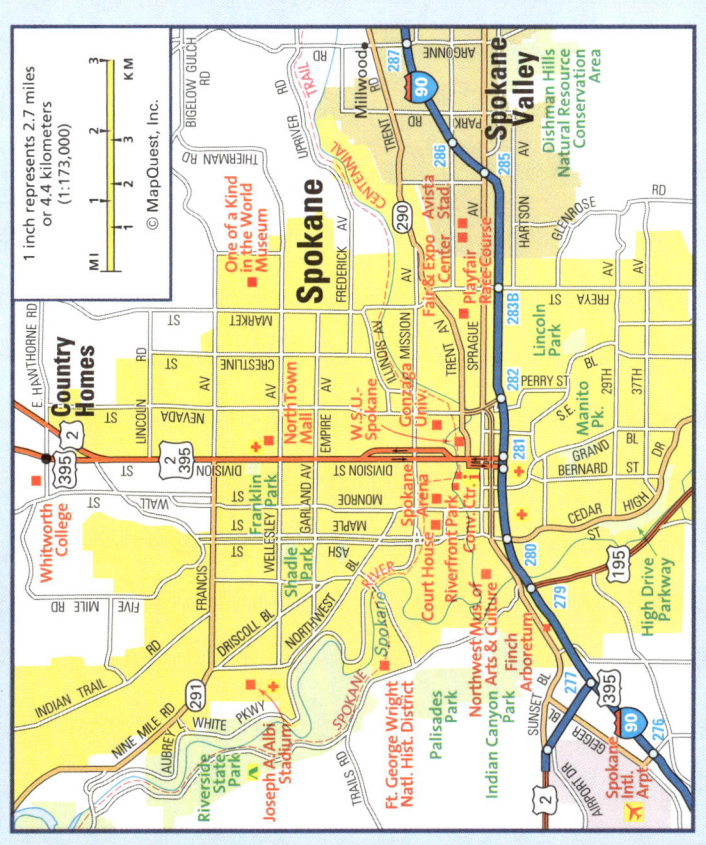

St. Louis

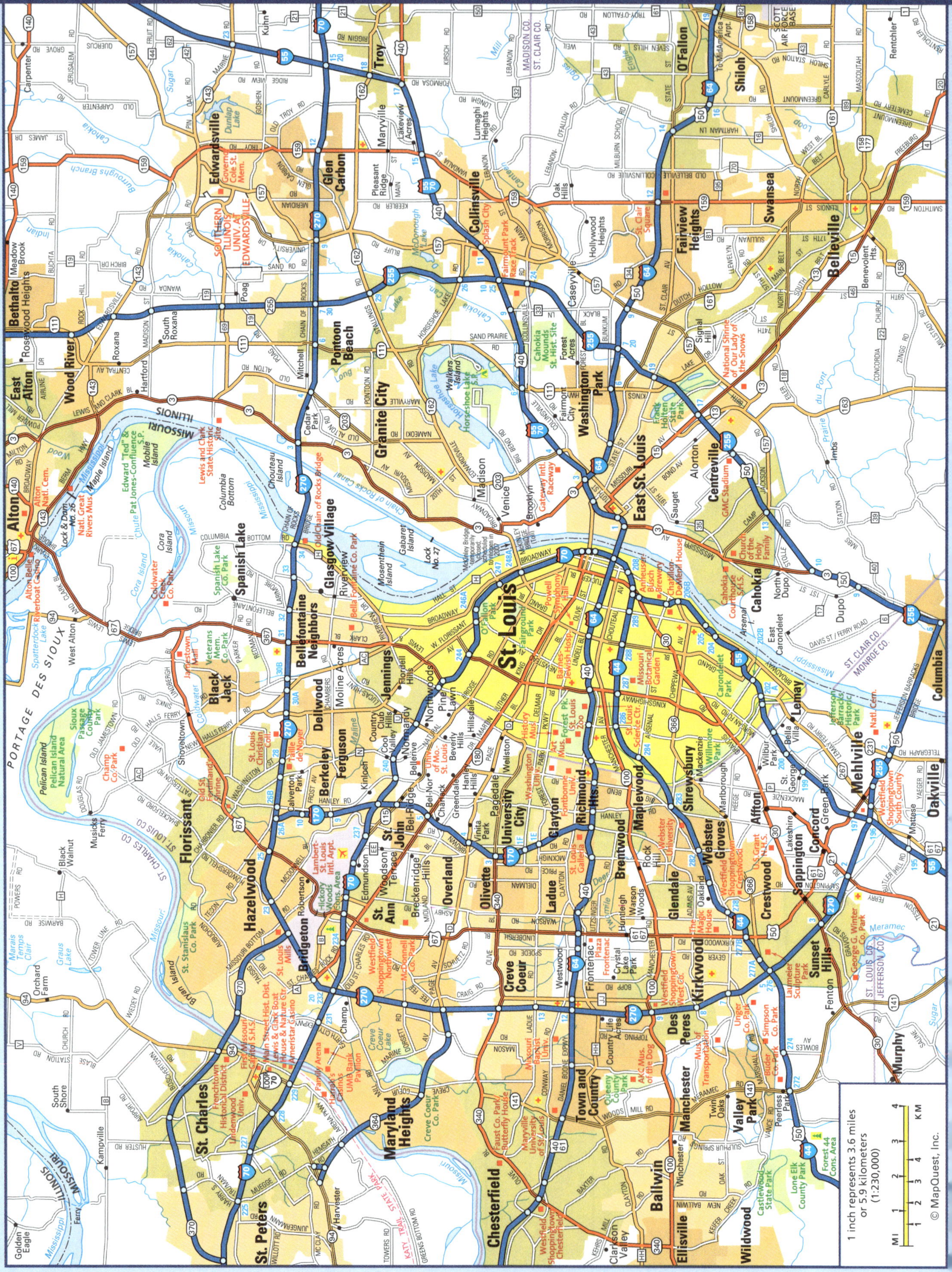

1 inch represents 3.6 miles
or 5.9 kilometers
(1:230,000)

© MapQuest, Inc.

1 inch represents 4.8 miles
or 7.8 kilometers (1:304,000)

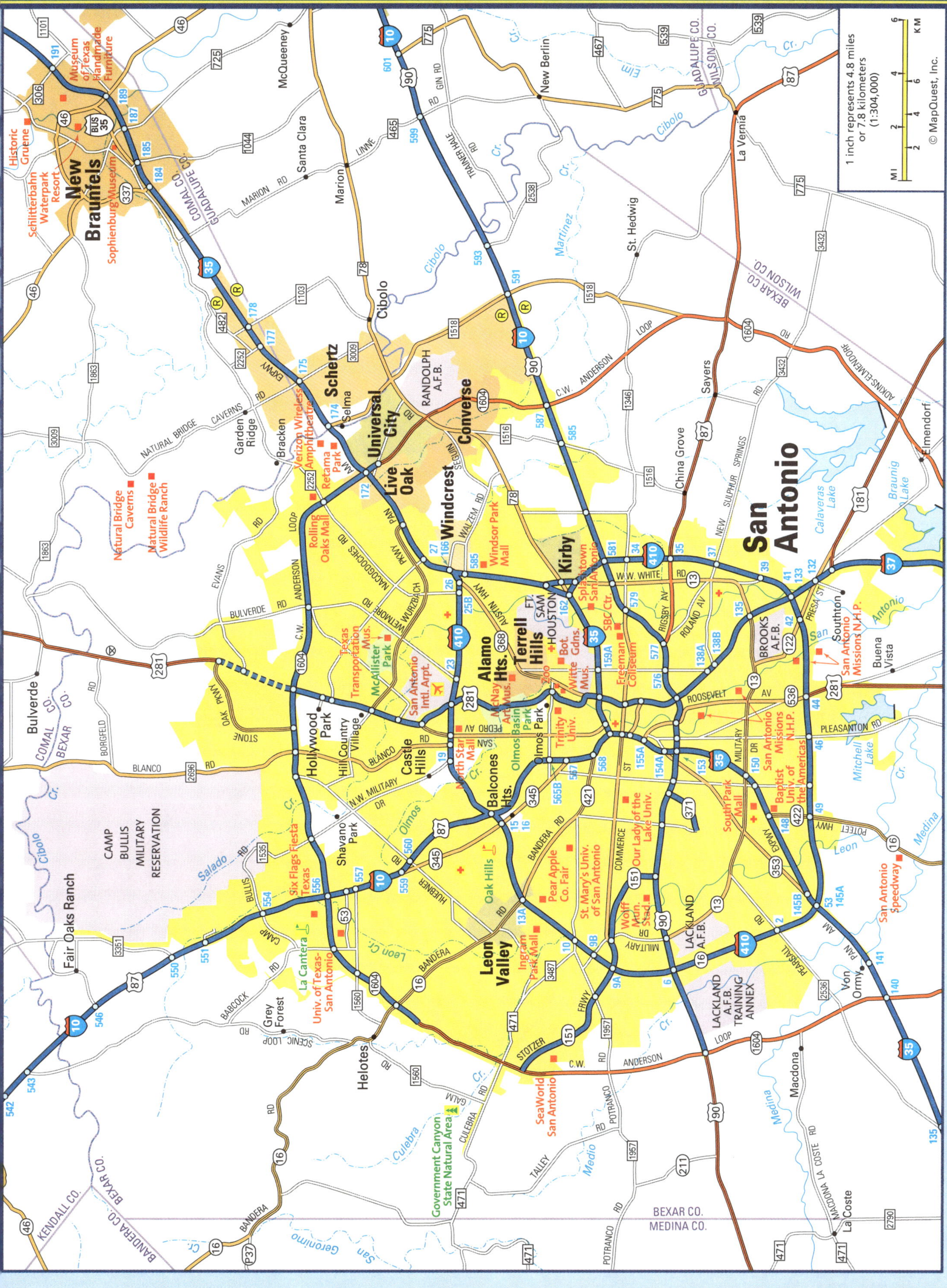

© MapQuest, Inc.

KM

MI

San Antonio

New Braunfels

Museum of Texas Handmade Furniture

Historic Gruene

Schlitterbahn Waterpark Resort

Sophienburg Museum

McQueeney

Santa Clara

New Berlin

La Vernia

St. Hedwig

Schertz

Natural Bridge Caverns

Natural Bridge Wildlife Ranch

Garden Ridge

Bracken

Verizon Wireless Amphitheatre

Retama Park

Selma

Universal City

Live Oak

RANDOLPH A.F.B.

Converse

Windcrest

Windsor Park Mall

China Grove

New Sulphur Springs

Calaveras Lake

Braunig Lake

Elmendorf

Rolling Oaks Mall

Kirby

Splashtown San Antonio

San Antonio

Texas Transportation Mus.

McAllister Park

FT. SAM HOUSTON

SBC Ctr.

San Antonio Intl. Airport

Bot. Gdns.

Zoo

Witte Mus.

Freeman Coliseum

BROOKS A.F.B.

San Antonio Missions N.H.P.

Buena Vista

Southton

Alamo Hts.

Terrell Hills

Hollywood Park

Hill Country Village

North Star Mall

Castle Hills

Trinity Univ.

Olmos Basin Park

Olmos Park

Southpark Mall

Pleasanton Rd

San Antonio Missions N.H.P.

Baptist Univ. of the Americas

Mitchell Lake

Balcones Hts.

Shavano Park

Six Flags Fiesta Texas

Oak Hills

CAMP BULLIS MILITARY RESERVATION

Fair Oaks Ranch

La Cantera

Univ. of Texas-San Antonio

Pear Apple Co. Fair

St. Mary's Univ. of San Antonio

Our Lady of the Lake Univ.

Wolff Mun. Stad.

COMMERCE

LACKLAND A.F.B.

San Antonio Speedway

Ingram Park Mall

Leon Valley

Grey Forest

Helotes

SeaWorld San Antonio

Government Canyon State Natural Area

LACKLAND A.F.B. TRAINING ANNEX

Von Ormy

La Coste

BEXAR CO.
MEDINA CO.

KENDALL CO.
BEXAR CO.

COMAL CO.
BEXAR CO.

GUADALUPE CO.
COMAL CO.

GUADALUPE CO.
WILSON CO.

BEXAR CO.
WILSON CO.

Macdona

N

PACIFIC OCEAN

San Diego

Del Mar

CARMEL VALLEY

SORENTO VALLEY

Los Peñasquitos Canyon Preserve

MIRA MESA

Poway

POWAY PKWY

SCRIPPS POWAY RD

SPRING CANYON RD

Miramar Res.

San Diego Aqueduct

San Vicente Reservoir

Sycamore Canyon County Open Space Preserve

Eucalyptus Hills

Lakeside

Santee

Santee Lakes

Torrey Pines State Reserve

Green Hosp.

Torrey Pines

UNIV. OF CALIF., SAN DIEGO

Scripps Inst. of Oceanography/ Birch Aquarium at Scripps

LA JOLLA

Mus. of Contemp. Art

Rose Canyon

Alliant Intl. University

MIRAMAR MARINE CORPS AIR STATION

Westfield Shoppingtown UTC

Shepherd Canyon

Oak Canyon

Mission Trails Regional Park

Cajon Speedway

Westfield Shoppingtown Parkway

El Cajon

WASHINGTON AV

Montgomery Field (Auxiliary City Arpt.)

Mission San Diego de Alcala

Lake Murray

San Diego Computer Mus.

La Mesa

Tecolote Canyon Natural Pk.

Qualcomm Stad.

Mission Bay

San Diego State Univ.

Spring Valley

Belmont Park

Mission Bay Park

SeaWorld San Diego

Univ. of San Diego

Fashion Valley

Old Town San Diego S.H.P.

San Diego Sports Arena

San Diego Zoo

Chollas Park

Lemon Grove

San Diego Intl. Arpt.

Balboa Park

San Diego

Sweetwater Reservoir

Point Loma Nazarene Univ.

U.S.M.C. RECRUIT DEPOT

Fleet Antisubmarine Warfare Training Ctr.

Fleet Combat Training Ctr.

U.S. NAVAL RESERVATION

Fort Rosecrans Natl. Cemetery

CABRILLO NATL. MON.

Pt. Loma Lighthouse

Pt. Loma

NORTH ISLAND N.A.S.

Mus. of Hist & Art

Hotel del Coronado

Coronado

SAN DIEGO NAVAL SUBMARINE BASE

SAN DIEGO NAVAL STATION

CORONADO NAVAL AMPHIBIOUS BASE

National City

Sunnyside

Westfield Shoppingtown Plaza Bonita

Bonita

Upper Otay Res.

Silver Strand State Beach

SWEETWATER MARSH N.W.R.

Chula Vista Nature Ctr.

Chula Vista

ARCO Olympic Training Center

Lower Otay Reservoir

NAVAL COMM. STATION

Poggi

Coors Amphitheater

Naval Space Surveillance Station

Imperial Beach

Tijuana Slough N.W.R.

Knott's Soak City U.S.A.

NAVAL AIR STATION

TIJUANA SLOUGH NATL. ESTUARINE RESERVE

San Ysidro

CALIF.
BAJA CALIF.

Border Field State Park

MONUMENT RD

U.S.
MEX.

Abelardo L Rodriguez Intl. Airport

Tijuana

1 inch represents 3.1 miles or 5.0 kilometers (1:195,000)

MI 1 2 3 4
KM 1 2 3 4

© MapQuest, Inc.

PASCO CO.
HILLSBOROUGH CO.

Crystal Springs

Sponge Docks
Tarpon Springs
Westin Innisbrook Resort
Innisbrook
Crystal Beach
East Lake
Ozona
Palm Harbor
Curlew
John Chestnut Sr. Park

Lutz
Northdale

Hillsborough River State Park

Dinosaur World

Dunedin
Westfield Shoppingtown Countryside
Knology Park
Oldsmar
Old Tampa Bay Park
Safety Harbor

Carrollwood
Lowry Park Zoo
Busch Gardens Tampa Bay

Temple Terrace

Thonotosassa

FLA. Strawberry Festival Frgnds.
Dover

Plant City

Clearwater Beach Island
Caladesi Island State Park
Clearwater Marine Aquarium
Sand Key Park
Clearwater
FLA. Metro Univ.-Tampa Coll., Pinellas
Ruth Eckerd Hall
Clearwater Mall

Town 'n Country
Raymond James Stadium
Univ. of Tampa
Ybar City
Fla Hard Rock Casino
State Frgnds.
Seffner
Mango
Sydney

Brandon
Valrico
Westfield Shoppingtown Brandon
Durant

Belleair Beach
Belleair Bluffs
Belleair Shore
Harbor Bluffs
Belleair
High Point
Bright House Networks Field
St. Petersburg-Clearwater Intl. Airport
Tampa Intl. Airport
Intl. Plaza
West Shore Plaza
Tampa
Palm River
Progress Village
Riverview
Bloomingdale
Lithia
Lithia Springs Park

Largo
Largo Mall
Pinewood Cultural Park
Lake Seminole Park

Indian Rocks Beach
Indian Shores
Seminole
Suncoast Seabird Sanctuary
Redington Shores
North Redington Beach
Redington Beach
Madeira Beach

Pinellas Park
Parkside Mall
Kenneth City
Lealman
Tyrone Sq. Mall
Natl. Cem.

Old Tampa Bay
Gandy Bridge
Hillsborough Bay
East Tampa
Gibsonton
Adamsville

St. Petersburg
Sunken Gardens
Florida Intl. Museum
Mus. of Fine Arts & St. Pete Mus. of History
Bayfront Center
Univ. of South Florida-St. Petersburg Campus
Salvador Dali Museum
Snug Harbor
Derby Lane (St. Petersburg Kennel Club)
Weedon Island Preserve
Port Tampa
MACDILL AIR FORCE BASE
Gadsden Point
E.G. Simmons Park

Tropicana Field
Tampa Mus. of Art
Henry B. Plant Mus.
Mem. Hosp.

Apollo Beach

Treasure Island
South Pasadena
Palms of Pasadena Hosp.
Gulfport
Boyd Hill Nature Park
Eckerd Coll.
Pinellas Point
St. Pete Beach
Maggiore

Tampa Bay

Ruskin
Sun City Center
Wimauma

Tierra Verde
PINELLAS N.W.R.
Gulf City
Sun City

Little Manatee River S.P.

GULF OF MEXICO

Fort De Soto Park
EGMONT KEY N.W.R.
Egmont Key S.P.

Willow

PASSAGE KEY N.W.R.

Rubonia
Terra Ceia
Madira Bickel Mound St. Arch. Site
Gillette
FLA. Gulf Coast Railroad Mus.
Parrish

Anna Maria
DeSoto Natl. Mem.
Portovant Indian Mound
Palmetto
South Florida Mus.
Memphis
Ellenton
Gamble Plantation Historic S.P.
Rye

Holmes Beach
Palma Sola
Anna Maria Key
Hist. Fishing Village
McKechnie Field
Bradenton
Manatee Village Hist. Park
Samoset
Lake Manatee S.P.
DeSoto Memorial Raceway

Bradenton Beach
Cortez
DeSoto Sq. Mall
Oneco
Whitfield Estates

Bayshore Gardens

Longboat Key
Sarasota/Bradenton Intl. Airport
John & Mable Ringling Mus. of Art
Sarasota Kennel Club
Kensington Park
Tallevast
Verna

Longboat Key
Sarasota Jungle Gardens
Van Wezel Performing Arts Hall
Mote Marine Lab/Aquarium
Marie Selby Botanical Gardens
Sarasota
Fruitville

MANATEE CO.
SARASOTA CO.

1 inch represents 6.6 miles
or 10.6 kilometers
(1:418,200)

© MapQuest, Inc.

P 16
Florida

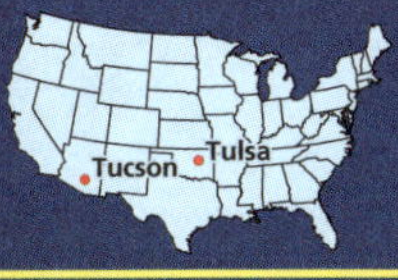

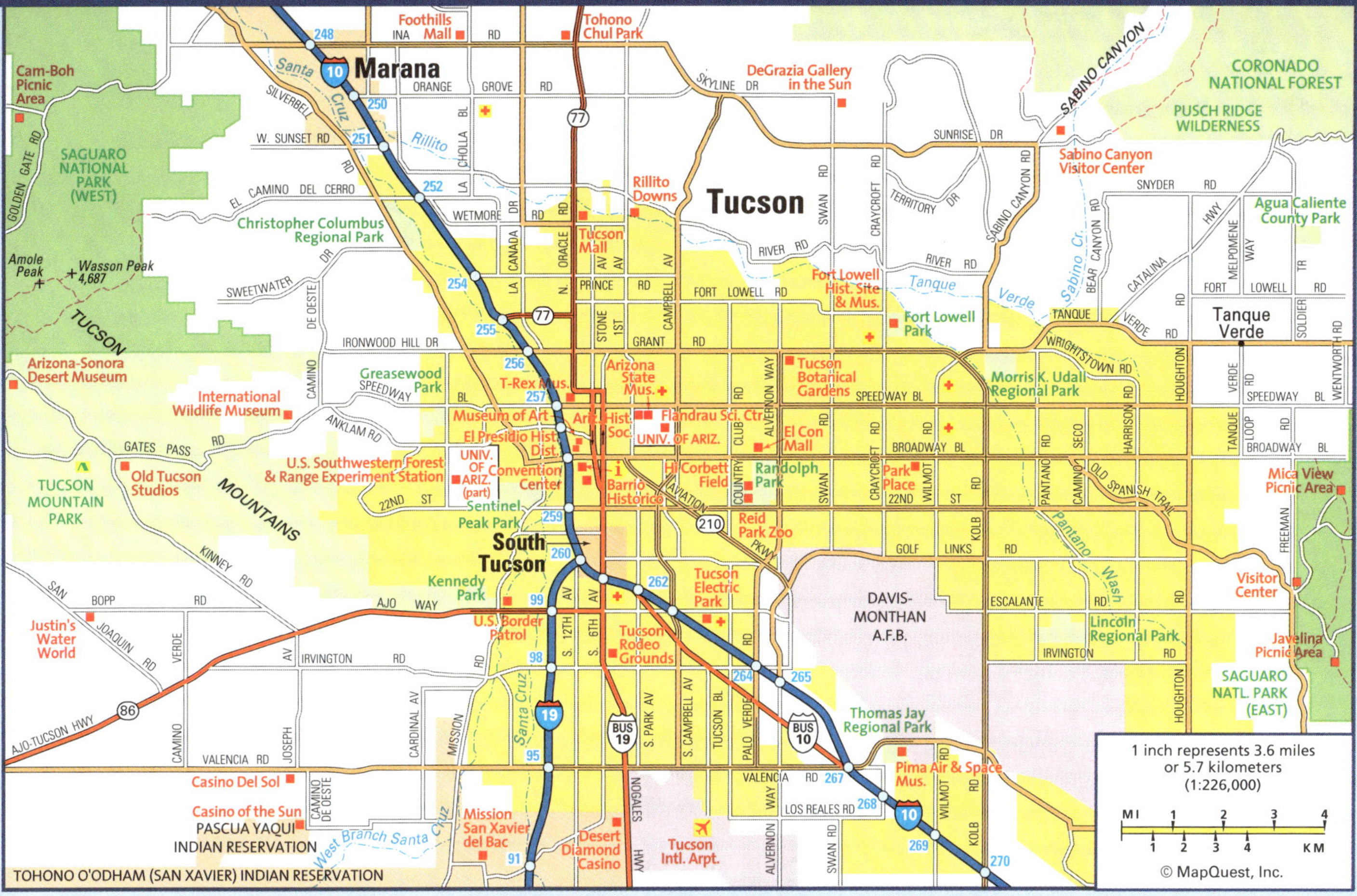

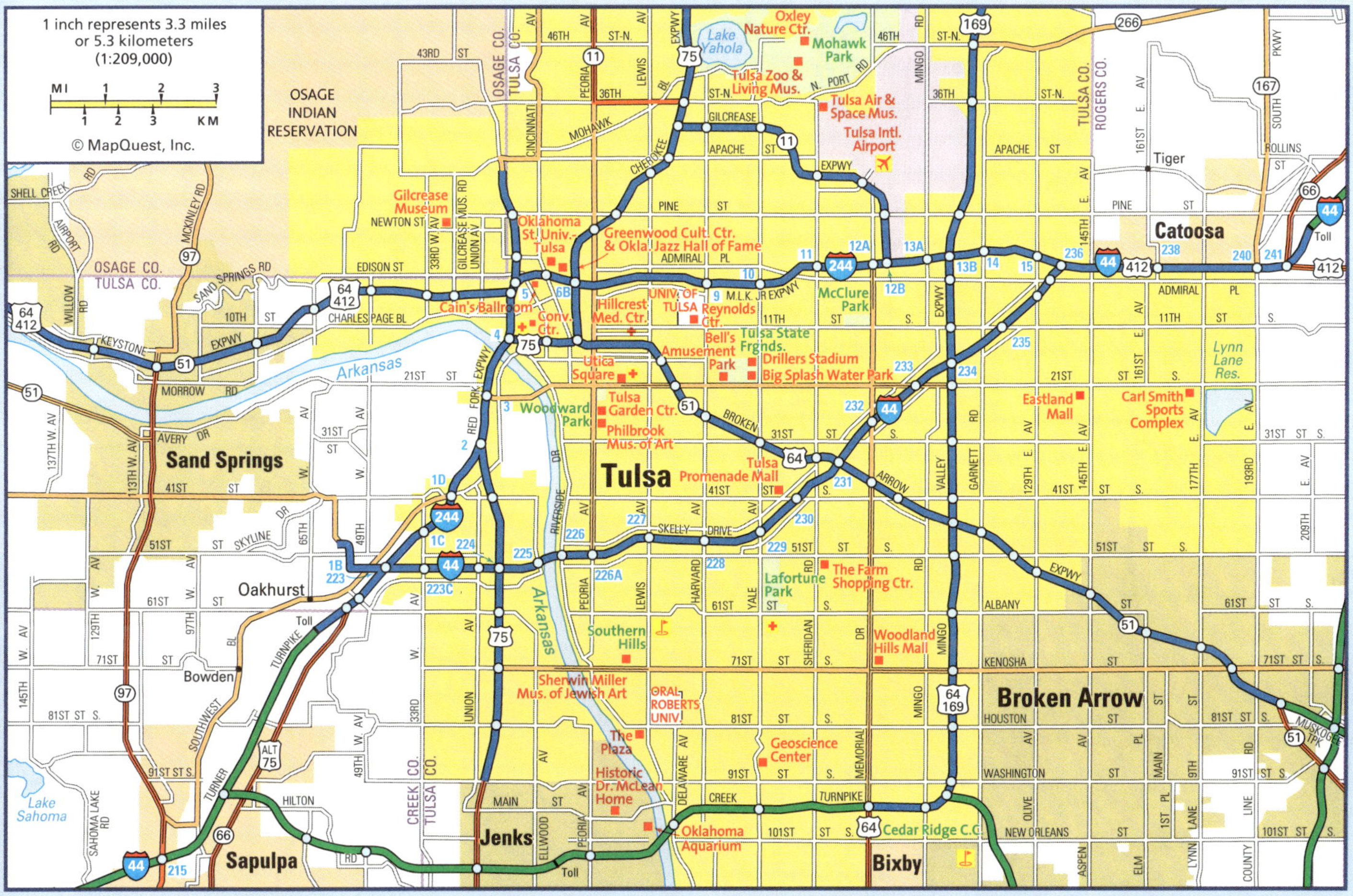

Vancouver map

West Vancouver, North Vancouver, Dist. Mun. of North Vancouver, Port Moody, Port Moody Cons. Area, Vancouver, Burnaby, Coquitlam, New Westminster, Surrey, Delta, Richmond, Lulu Island, Belcarra, Anmore

Lighthouse Park, Atkinson Lighthouse, Ambleside Park, Prospect Pt., Stanley Park, Ferguson Pt., Vancouver Aquarium & Zoo, Canada Place, Gastown, Chinatown, Science World, B.C. Place Stad., CNR/VIA Station, Granville I., John Hendrey Park, Queen Elizabeth Park, VanDusen Botanical Garden, Oakridge Shop. Ctr., Metrotown Centre, Central Pk., Burnaby Heritage Village, Robt. Burnaby Park, Simon Fraser Univ., Burnaby Mtn. Park, Burnaby Lake Reg. Park, Mundy Park, Irving House, Bear Creek Park

U.B.C. Mus. of Anthropology, Old Hastings Mill Store, Vancouver Maritime Museum, Vanier Park, West End, Vancouver Museum, Jericho Beach Park, Thunderbird Sports Centre, Univ. of British Columbia, Botanical Garden, Pacific Spirit Regional Park, Musqueam 2 I.R., Pt. Grey

Iona Beach Reg. Park, Iona I., Sea Island, Vancouver International Airport, Bridgeport, Middle Arm, Richmond Nature Park, Minoru Park, Mitchell I., Annacis, Capilano Suspension Bridge & Park, Lynn Canyon Park, Mt. Seymour Prov. Park, Racoon I., Buntzen Lake Rec. Area, Belcarra Regional Park, Bedwell Bay, Sasamat L., Deep Cove, Maplewood Farm, Cates Park, B.C. Rail Station, Capilano I.R. Welch, Seymour Cr. 2 I.R., Burrard Inlet 3 I.R., Lynn Valley

Burrard Inlet, English Bay, Burrard Inlet, Vancouver Harbour, Second Narrows, Strait of Georgia, North Arm, Fraser River, City Reach, Fraser

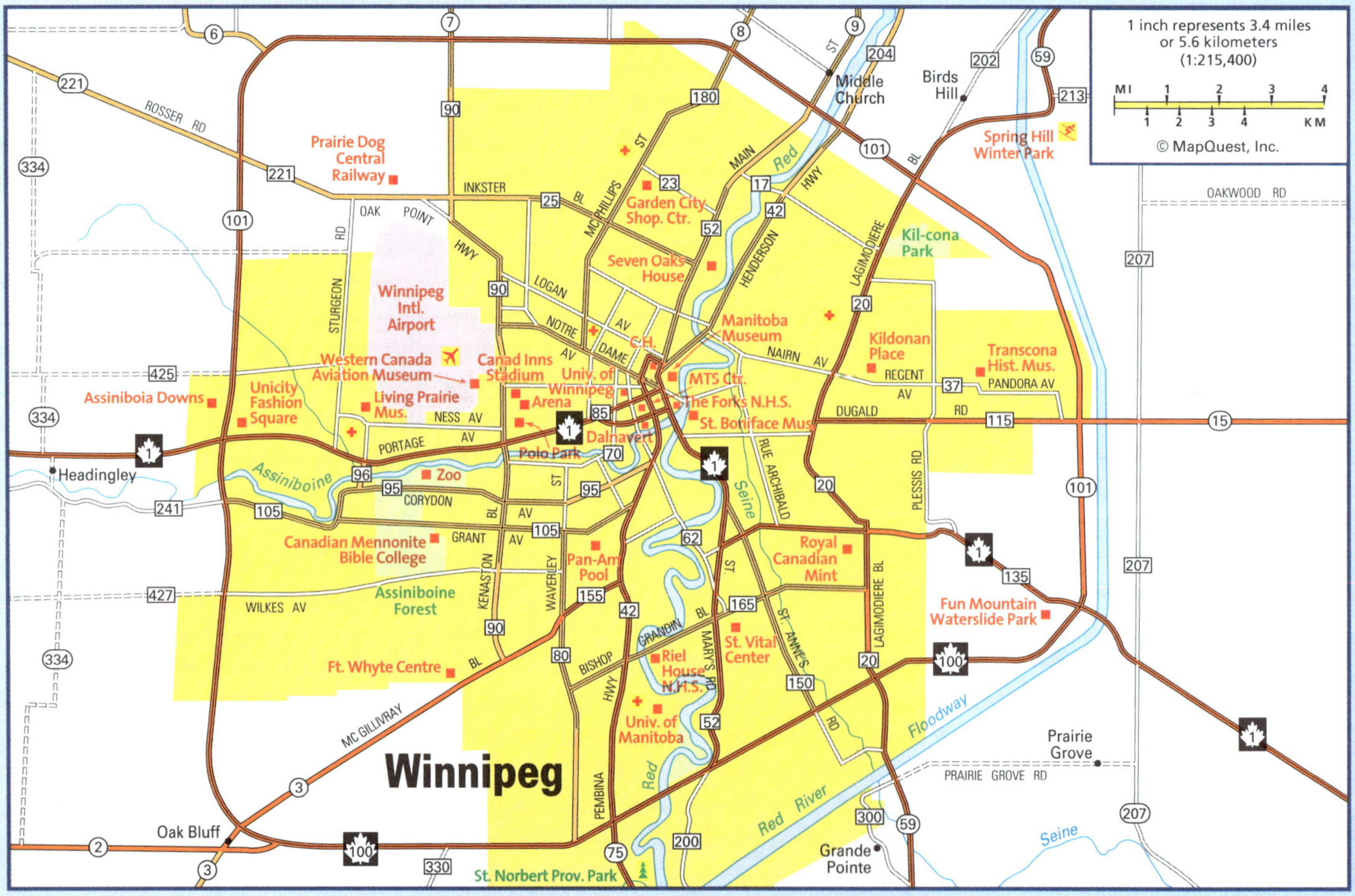

Scale bar: 1 inch represents 2.7 miles or 4.4 kilometers (1:173,000)
© MapQuest, Inc.

Winnipeg map

Winnipeg, Headingley, Oak Bluff, Grande Pointe, Prairie Grove, Middle Church, Birds Hill

Prairie Dog Central Railway, Garden City Shop. Ctr., Seven Oaks House, Manitoba Museum, Kil-cona Park, Kildonan Place, Transcona Hist. Mus., Spring Hill Winter Park, Winnipeg Intl. Airport, Western Canada Aviation Museum, Canad Inns Stadium, Univ. of Winnipeg, MTS Ctr., The Forks N.H.S., St. Boniface Mus., Living Prairie Mus., Assiniboia Downs, Unicity Fashion Square, Dalnavert, Polo Park, Zoo, Assiniboine Forest, Canadian Mennonite Bible College, Pan-Am Pool, Royal Canadian Mint, Fun Mountain Waterslide Park, Ft. Whyte Centre, Riel House N.H.S., St. Vital Center, Univ. of Manitoba, St. Norbert Prov. Park

Assiniboine River, Red River, Seine River, Floodway

Scale bar: 1 inch represents 3.4 miles or 5.6 kilometers (1:215,400)
© MapQuest, Inc.

N

Washington, D.C.

1 inch represents 2.6 miles or 4.1 kilometers (1:162,462)

© MapQuest, Inc.

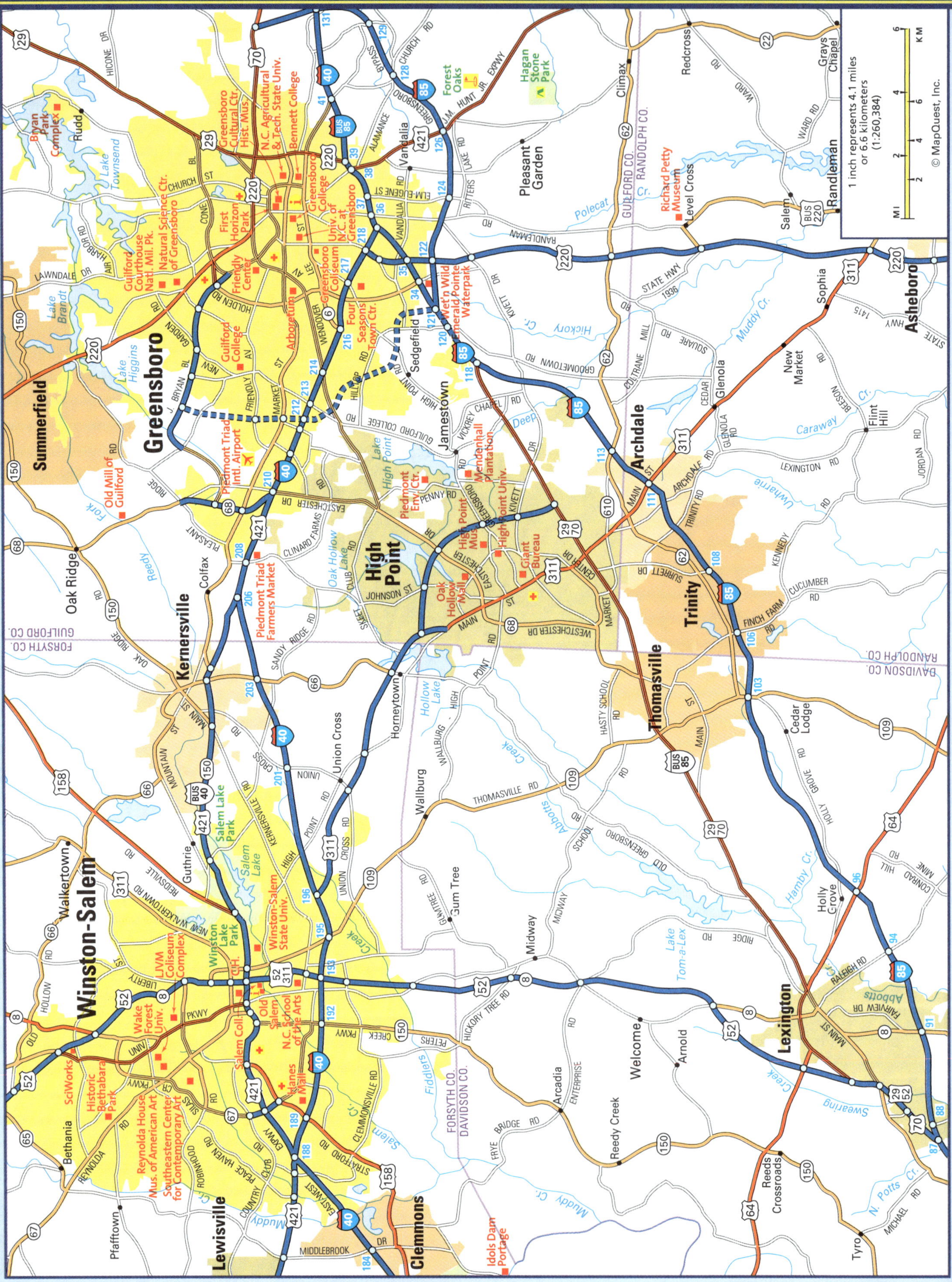

P 17
Georgia

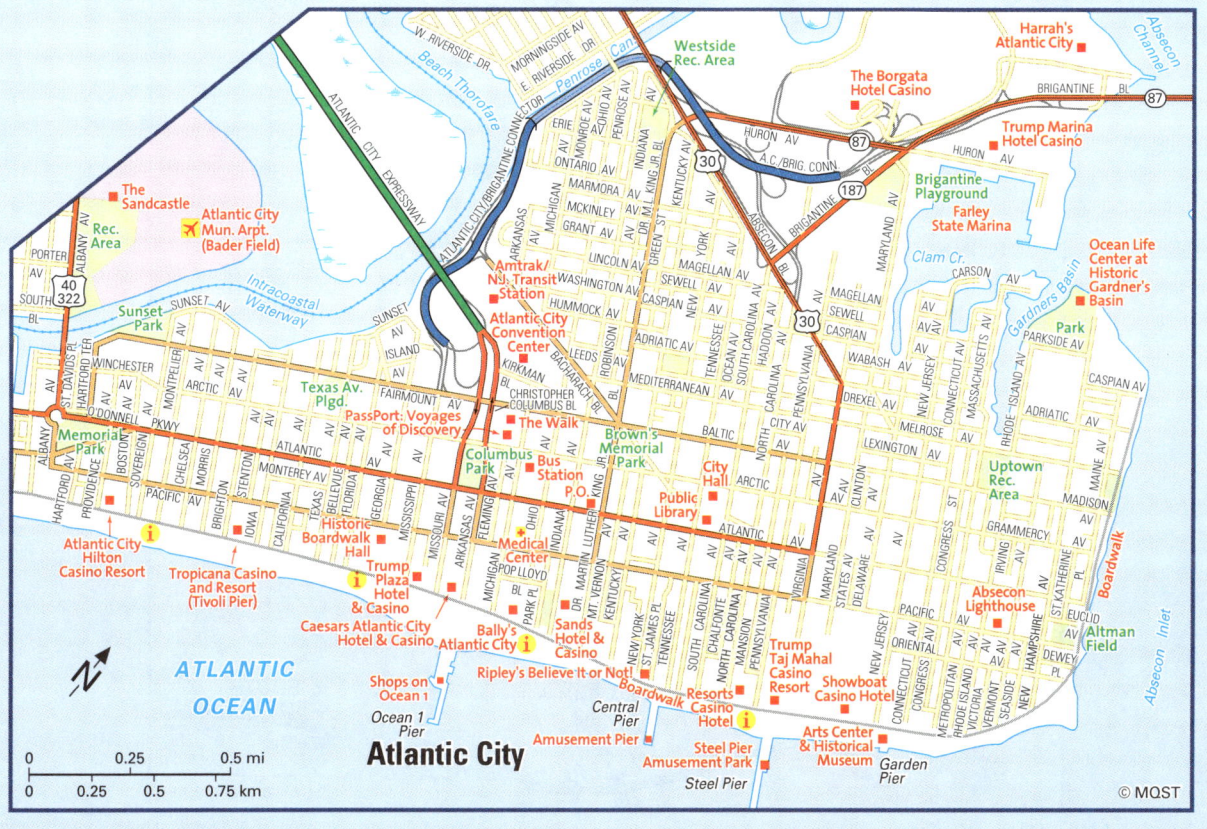

P 36
New Jersey

P 13
Maryland

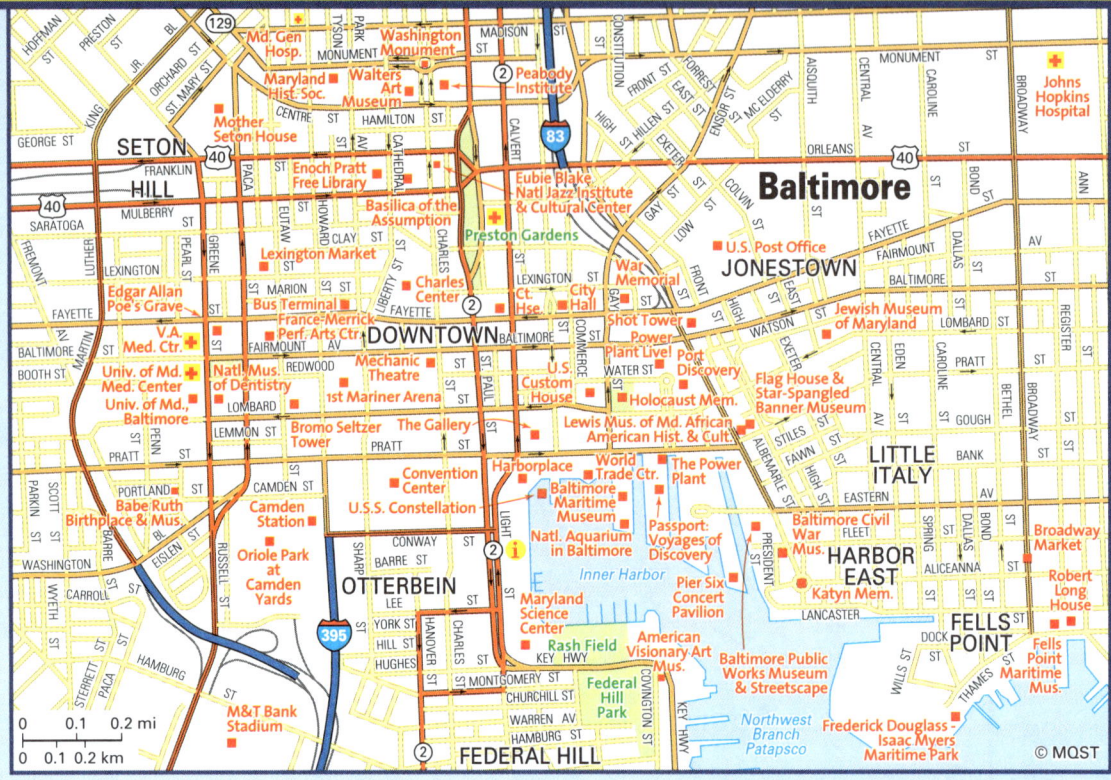

Baltimore

SETON HILL

JONESTOWN

DOWNTOWN

LITTLE ITALY

OTTERBEIN

HARBOR EAST

FELLS POINT

FEDERAL HILL

Johns Hopkins Hospital

Md. Gen. Hosp.
Washington Monument
Maryland Hist. Soc.
Walters Art Museum
Peabody Institute
Mother Seton House
Enoch Pratt Free Library
Eubie Blake Natl Jazz Institute & Cultural Center
Basilica of the Assumption
Preston Gardens
Lexington Market
Charles Center
War Memorial
City Hall
U.S. Post Office
Edgar Allan Poe's Grave
Bus Terminal
France-Merrick Perf. Arts Ctr.
Shot Tower
Power Plant Live!
Jewish Museum of Maryland
V.A. Med. Ctr.
Natl. Mus. of Dentistry
Mechanic Theatre
1st Mariner Arena
U.S. Custom House
Holocaust Mem.
Flag House & Star-Spangled Banner Museum
Univ. of Md. Med. Center
Univ. of Md. Baltimore
Bromo Seltzer Tower
The Gallery
Lewis Mus. of Md. African American Hist. & Cult.
The Power Plant
Babe Ruth Birthplace & Mus.
Convention Center
Harborplace
World Trade Ctr.
Baltimore Maritime Museum
Passport: Voyages of Discovery
Baltimore Civil War Mus.
Broadway Market
Camden Station
U.S.S. Constellation
Natl. Aquarium in Baltimore
Pier Six Concert Pavilion
Katyn Mem.
Robert Long House
Oriole Park at Camden Yards
Maryland Science Center
Rash Field
American Visionary Art Mus.
Baltimore Public Works Museum & Streetscape
Fells Point Maritime Mus.
M&T Bank Stadium
Federal Hill Park
Northwest Branch Patapsco
Frederick Douglass - Isaac Myers Maritime Park

0   0.1   0.2 mi
0   0.1   0.2 km

© MQST

Boston

CHARLESTOWN

NORTH END

WEST END

BEACON HILL

FINANCIAL DISTRICT

CHINATOWN

SOUTH BOSTON

Charlestown Navy Yard
Bunker Hill Pavilion
Hoosac Pier
U.S.S. Constitution
Boston Inner Harbor
North End Plgd.
U.S.C.G. Piers
Cambridgeside Galleria
Mus. of Science
Science Park
Hayden Planetarium
North Station
Copp's Hill Burying Ground
Old North Church
Paul Revere Mall
St. Stephens Church
Union Wharf
TD Banknorth Garden
Thomas P. O'Neill Federal Building
Paul Revere Hse.
Sargents Wharf
Lewis Wharf
Pierce Hichborn Hse.
Mass. Gen. Hosp.
State Service Ctr.
Charlesbank Playground
Old West Church
Harrison Gray Otis Hse.
Mus. of Afro-American Hist.
JFK Federal Bldg.
GOVERNMENT CENTER
Christopher Columbus Park
Commercial Wharf
Coburn's Gaming Hse.
Boston C.H.
Quincy Market
Long Wharf
Hayden Hse.
Middleton Hse.
Suffolk Univ.
Suffolk Co. State Ct. Hse.
Faneuil Hall
Central Wharf
New England Aquarium
Smith Hse.
Phillips School
King's Chapel
Old State Hse.
Boston Massacre Site
Custom Hse.
India Wharf
Rowe's Wharf
Ferry to Logan Intl. Airport
Hatch Memorial Shell
Charles St. Mtg. Hse.
Boston Athenaeum
Shaw Mem.
Old Corner Bookstore
Fosters Wharf
Emerson Coll.
Granary Burying Ground
Park Street Church
Dreams of Freedom
Old South Mtg. Hse.
Fan Pier
Moakley Federal Courthouse
Gibson House Mus.
Baylies Mansion
Public Garden
Boston Common
Boston Massacre Monument
The Opera House
Downtown Crossing
Federal Reserve Plaza
Children's Museum
Boston Fire Mus.
Arlington Street Church
Cen. Burying Ground
Boston Tea Party Ship & Mus.
South Station (Amtrak)
Trinity Church
Hancock Tower
Colonial Theatre
Wang Ctr. for the Perf. Arts
Tufts Med. Sch.
Harvard
Bus Terminal
New England Med. Ctr.
Boston Ctr. for the Arts

0   0.1   0.2 mi
0   0.1   0.2   0.3 km

© MQST

P 14
Massachusetts

P 43
Ohio

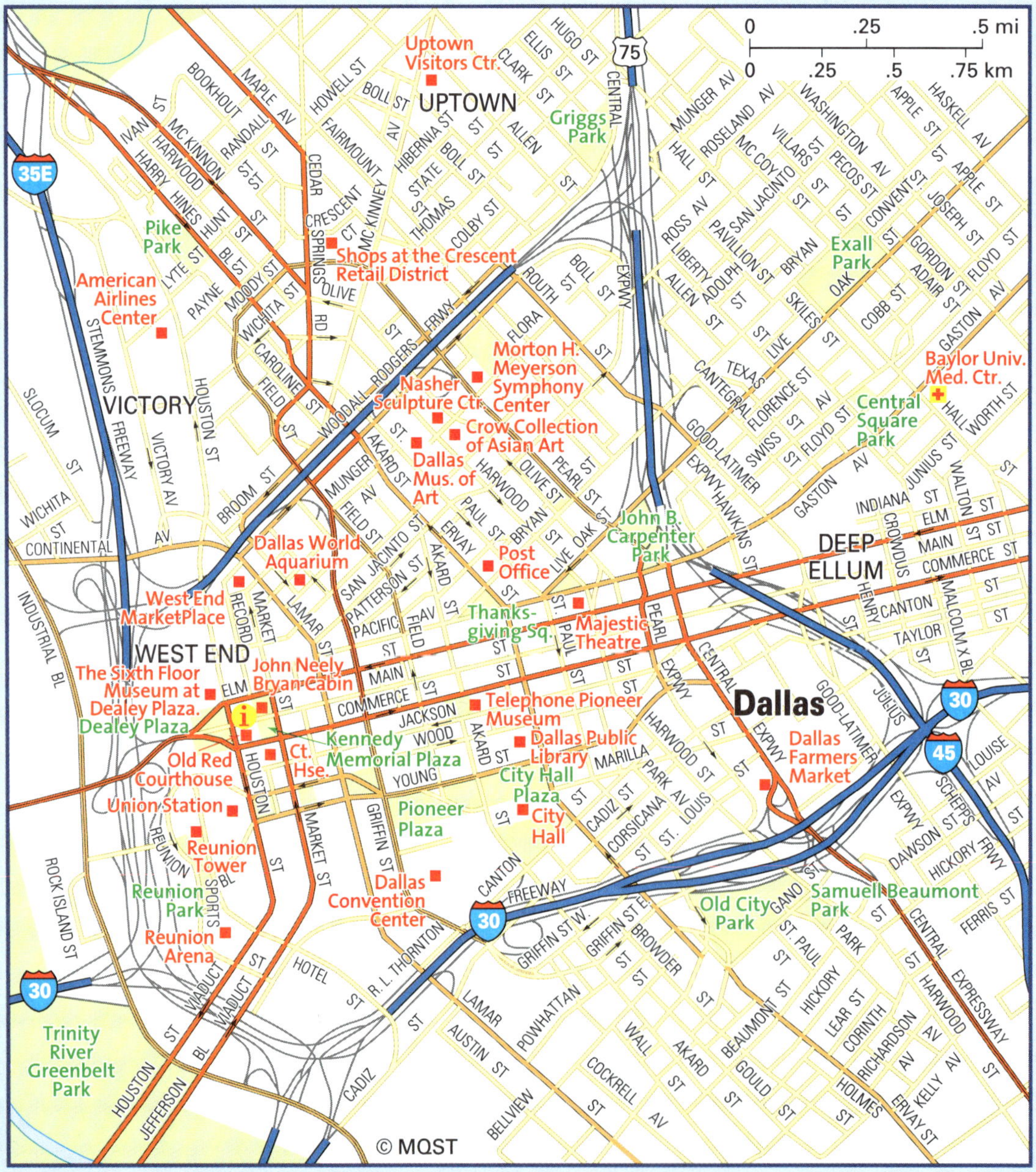

Cleveland

LAKE ERIE

N

0   0.25   0.5mi
0   0.25   0.5   0.75 km

William G. Mather Museum
Great Lakes Science Center
Rock and Roll Hall of Fame & Mus.
Intl. Women's Air & Space Mus.
Burke-Lakefront Airport
Cleveland Browns Stadium
USS Cod
NORTH MARGINAL
Cleveland Police Mus.
CLEVELAND MEMORIAL SHOREWAY
S. MARGINAL RD
KING AV
THE FLATS
Ct. Hse.
Amtrak Sta.
C.H. Convention Ctr.
LAKESIDE AV
LAKESIDE AV
HAMILTON AV
HAMILTON AV
ST. CLAIR AV
Galleria at Erieview
Scene Pavilion
The Mall
Federal Ct. Hse.
ST. CLAIR
ROCKWELL AV
RIVER RD
SPRUCE AV
DIVISION AV
Public Sq.
SUPERIOR
AV
DETROIT AV
Terminal Tower/ Tower City
Cleveland Arcade
PAYNE
Cuyahoga
CANAL RD
HURON RD
Lutheran Hosp.
Playhouse Square
CHESTER
OHIO CITY
Gund Arena
HURON RD
EUCLID
PROSPECT
Jacobs Field
CARNEGIE
CLEVELAND STATE UNIV.
West Side Mkt.
LORAIN
AV
SCRANTON
EAGLE AV
© MQST

---

0   .25   .5 mi
0   .25   .5   .75 km

Uptown Visitors Ctr.
UPTOWN
Griggs Park
Pike Park
Shops at the Crescent Retail District
American Airlines Center
Exall Park
Baylor Univ. Med. Ctr.
VICTORY
Morton H. Meyerson Symphony Center
Central Square Park
Nasher Sculpture Ctr.
Crow Collection of Asian Art
Dallas Mus. of Art
John B. Carpenter Park
DEEP ELLUM
Dallas World Aquarium
Post Office
West End MarketPlace
Thanks-giving Sq.
Majestic Theatre
Dallas
WEST END
The Sixth Floor Museum at Dealey Plaza.
John Neely Bryan Cabin
Telephone Pioneer Museum
Dallas Public Library
Dallas Farmers Market
Dealey Plaza
Kennedy Memorial Plaza
City Hall Plaza
Old Red Courthouse
Ct. Hse.
Pioneer Plaza
City Hall
Union Station
Dallas Convention Center
Reunion Tower
Reunion Park
Old City Park
Samuel Beaumont Park
Reunion Arena
Trinity River Greenbelt Park
© MQST

P 48
Texas

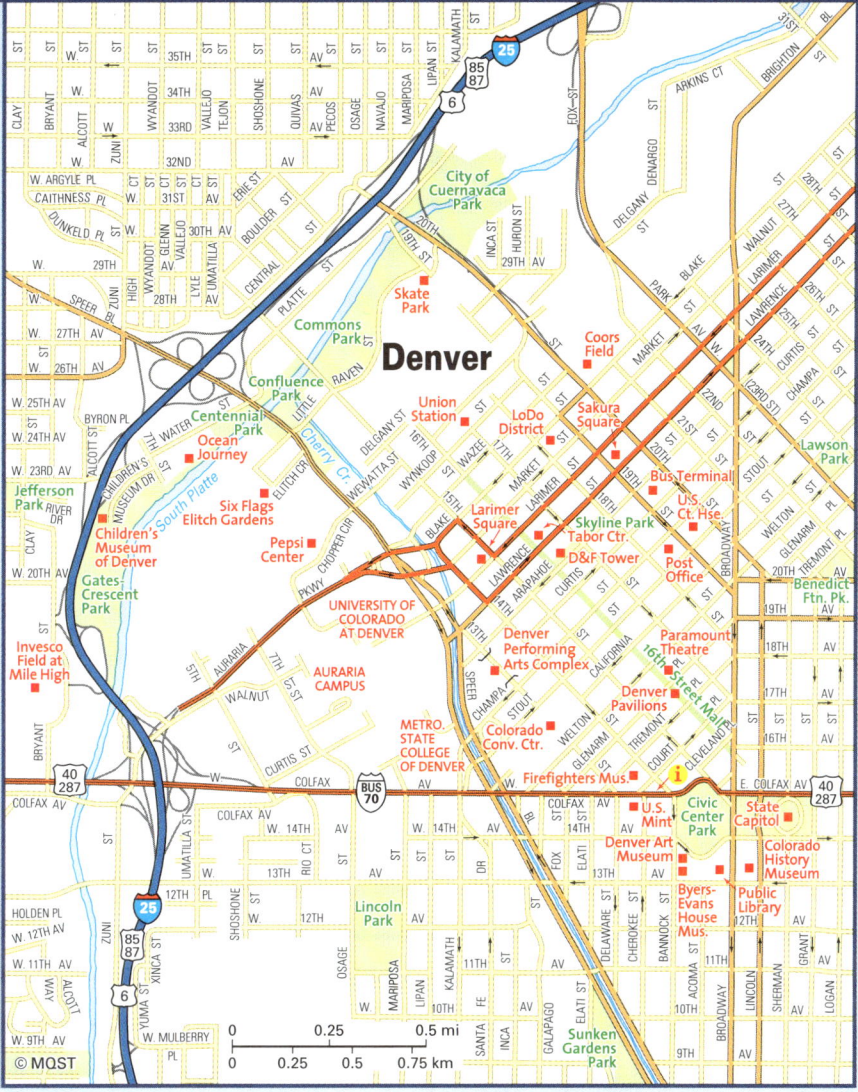

P 12
Colorado

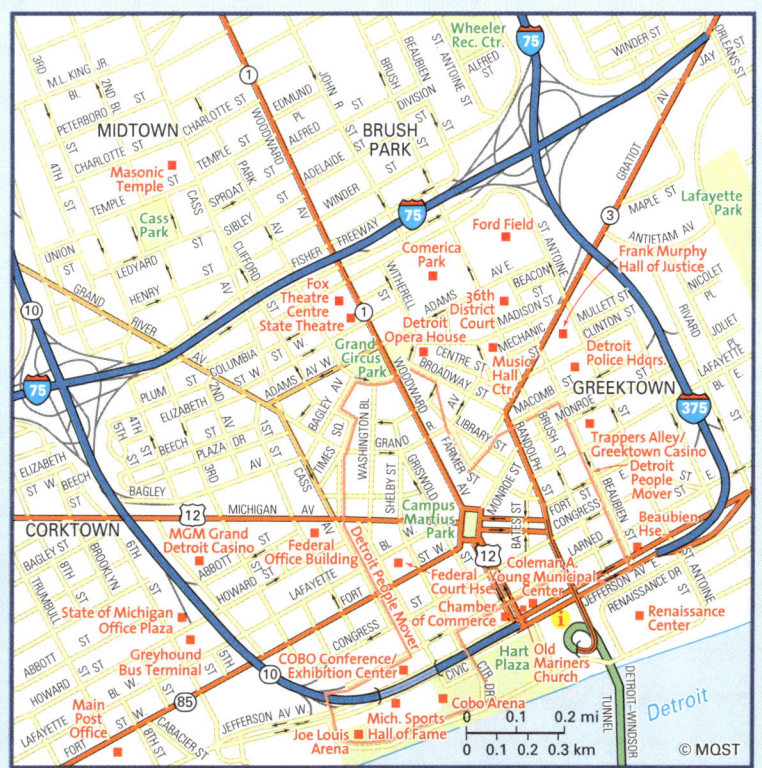

P 28
Michigan

P 48
Texas

Houston

Indianapolis

P 20
Indiana

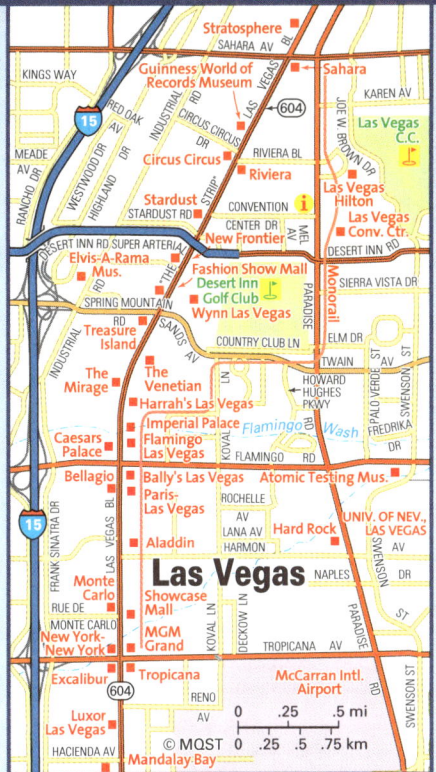

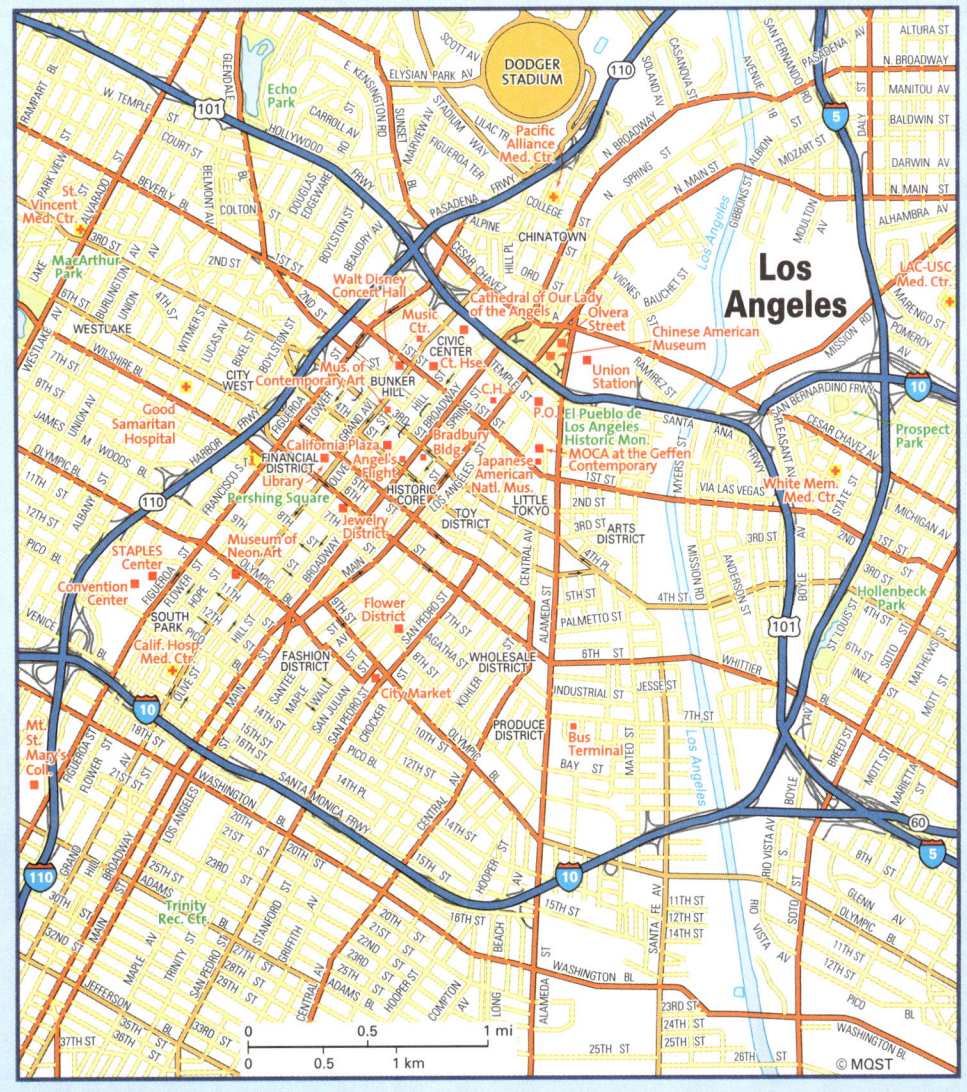

P 31
Missouri

P 34
Nevada

P 11
California

© MQST

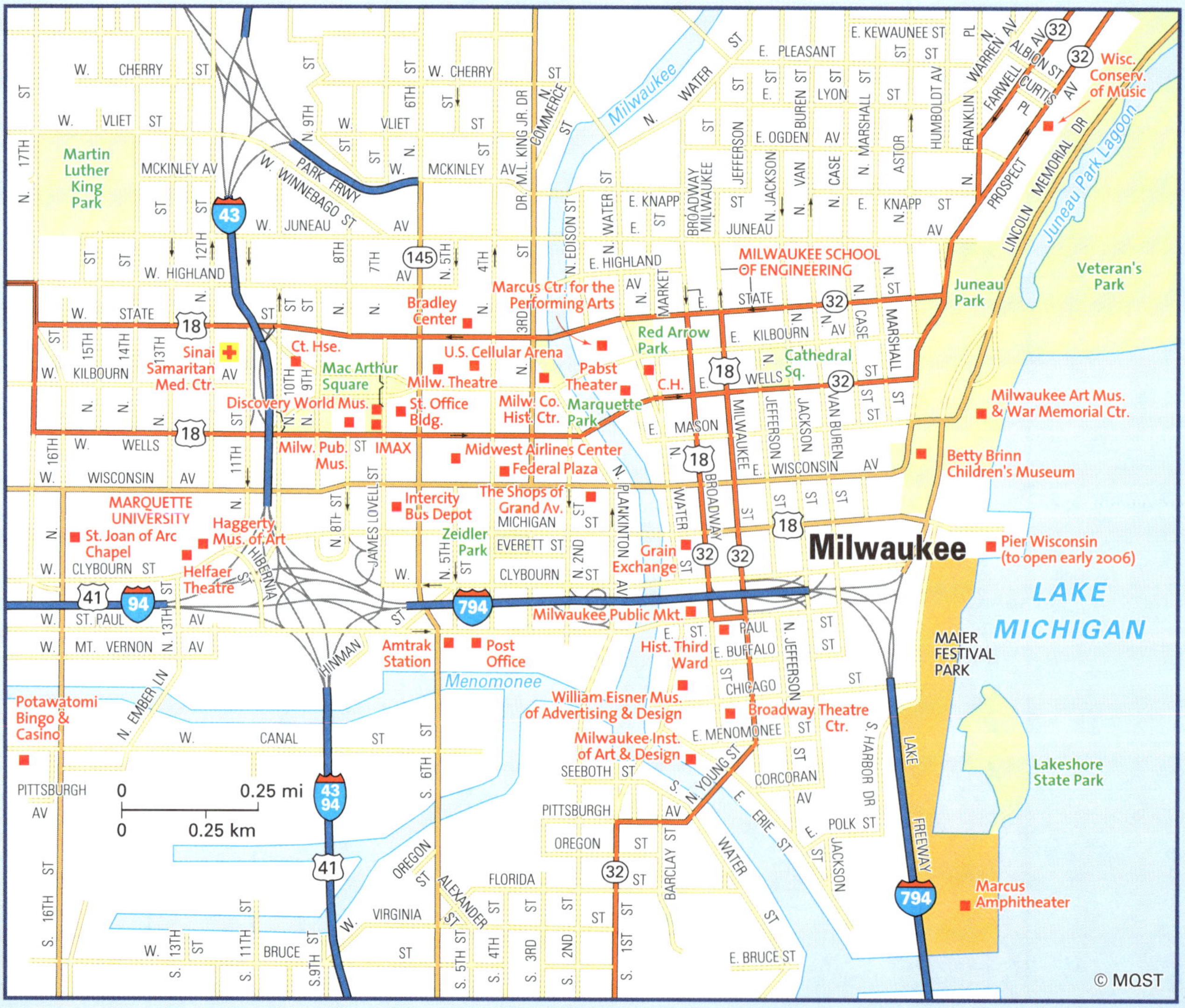

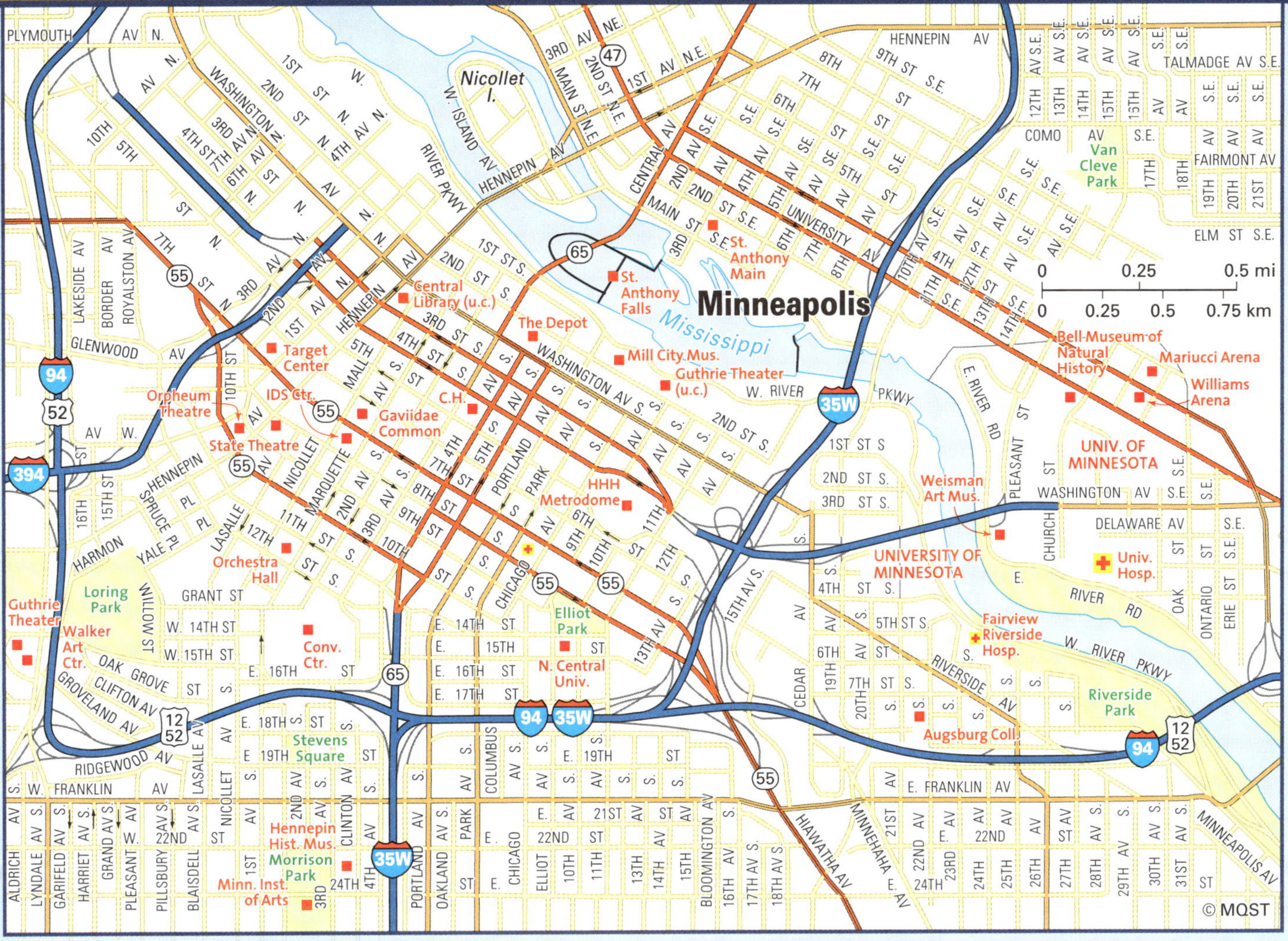

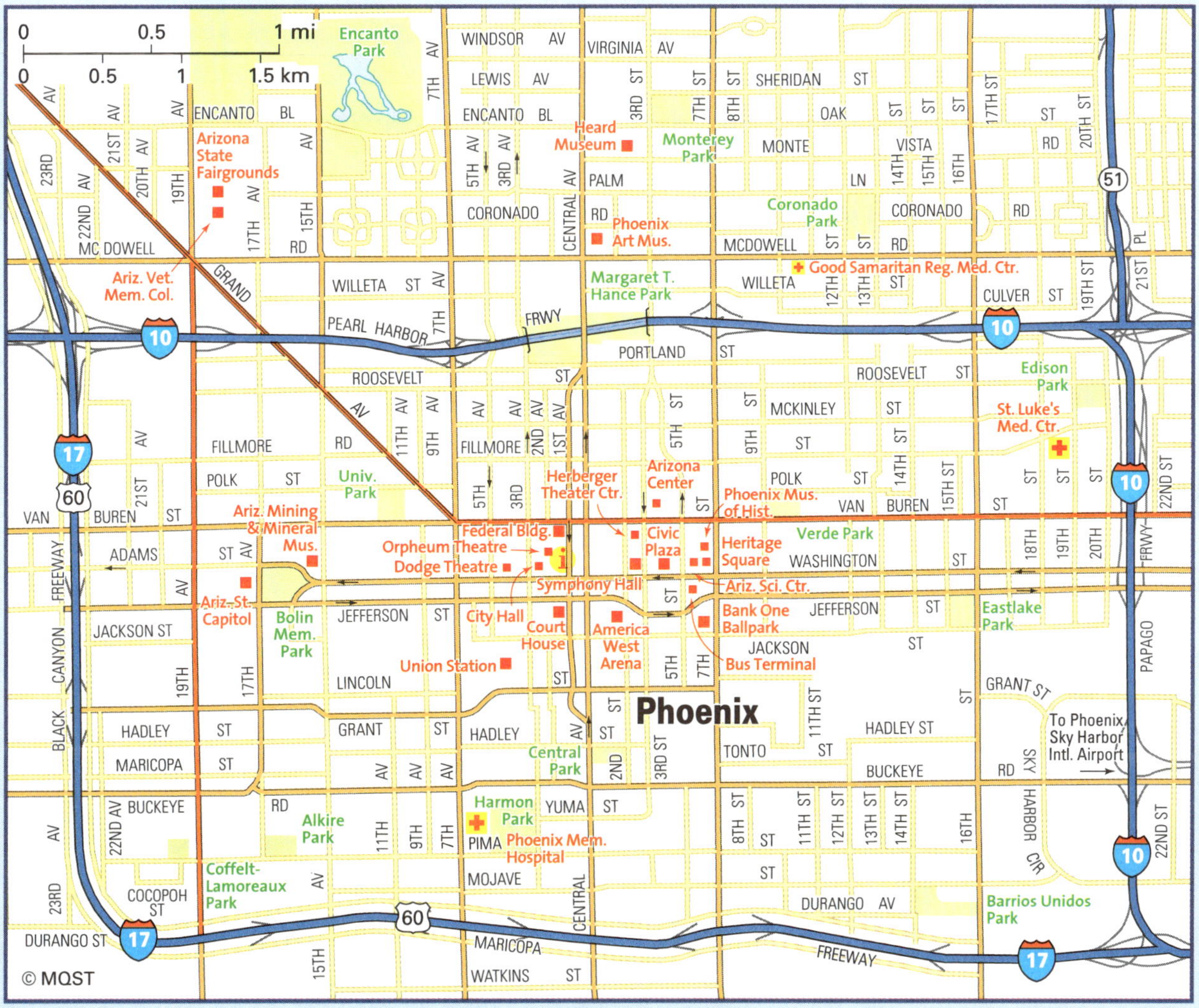

P 46
Pennsylvania

P 48
Texas

P 11
California

Pittsburgh

NORTH SIDE

West Park

Lincoln Av / Ridge Av / Ridge Pl / S. Commons / Merchant St / Anderson St / River Av

279 / TRK 19

Allegheny Center Mall

65

279 DR / General Robinson St

The Andy Warhol Mus.

PNC Park

Isabella St / Andy Warhol Bridge / 9th Street Bridge / 7th St Bridge / 6th St Bridge

Heinz Field

Veterans Memorial Bridge

© MQST

579

579 ST

Etna St / Smallman St / 12th St / 11th St / 10th St

Allegheny Av / North Shore Dr / Ft Duquesne Bridge

Mem. Park

Allegheny

Roberto Clemente Bridge

Ohio

David Lawrence Conv. Ctr.

Bus Depot

Penn Av / Liberty Av / 7th Av

Penn Station

Federal Bldg.

Carnegie Science Center

Byham Theater

Benedum Center

Heinz Hall

Mellon Arena

Washington Pl

GATEWAY CENTER

Market Pl / Market Square / 5th Av / 6th Av / 4th Av / Forbes Av

Mellon Square

Chatham Center

Commonwealth Pl

Point State Park / Blockhouse / Fort Pitt Museum

Fort Pitt Blvd / 3rd Av / 2nd Av / Smithfield St / Cherry Wy / Grant St / Ross St

Co. Ct. Hse.

Robert Morris Univ.

Duquesne Incline

376

Point Park Univ.

City Co. Bldg.

GIBSON ST

22 / 30

Fort Pitt Bridge

Monongahela

Grandview Av / Fort Pitt Tunnel

TRK 19 / 22 / 30

DUQUESNE UNIV.

2ND AV

885

Mt. Washington Overlook

837

Carson St West / McArdle Rd

Gateway Clipper Fleet

22 / 30 / 376

Red Oak Way / Bigham St / Amabell St / Merrimac St / Ulysses St / Bertha St / Wearsage / Smithfield St Bridge

Sycamore St / Octave Wy

Monongahela Incline

Bessemer Court

Station Square

Liberty Bridge

0   0.1   0.2 mi
0   0.1 0.2 0.3 km

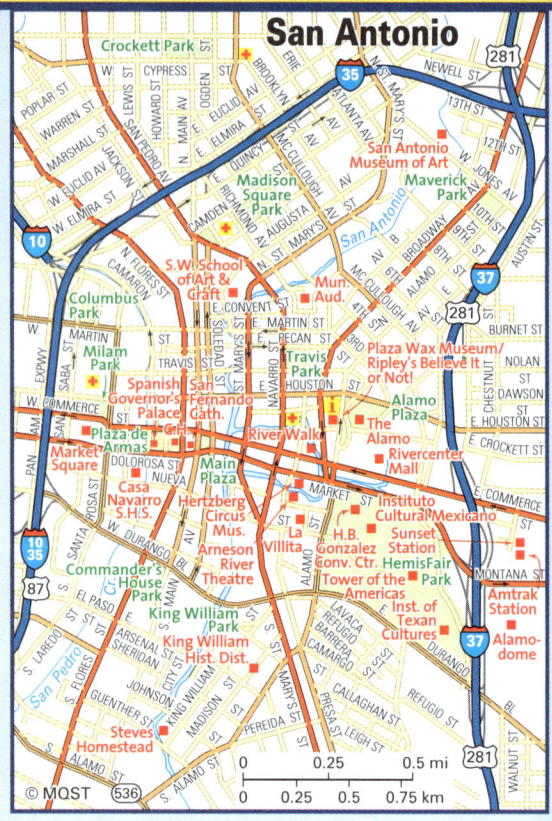

San Antonio

Crockett Park

281

35

10

Poplar St / Cypress St / Elmira St / Warren St / Euclid St / Main Av / Jones Av / 9th St / 10th St / 13th St

San Antonio Museum of Art

Maverick Park

Columbus Park

Madison Square Park

S.W. School of Art & Craft

Milam Park

San Antonio River

BROADWAY

37

281

Plaza Wax Museum/ Ripley's Believe It or Not!

Governor's Palace

Spanish Gath.

San Fernando

Travis Park

Mun. Aud.

Alamo Plaza

Plaza de Armas

Market Square

Main Plaza

River Walk

The Alamo

Rivercenter Mall

Casa Navarro S.H.S.

Hertzberg Circus Mus.

Instituto Cultural Mexicano

Commander's House Park

Arneson River Theatre

La Villita

H.B. Gonzalez Conv. Ctr.

Sunset Station

10 / 35

87

King William Park

Tower of the Americas

HemisFair Park

Inst. of Texan Cultures

King William Hist. Dist.

Amtrak Station

37

Alamodome

Steves Homestead

281

0   0.25   0.5 mi
0   0.25   0.5   0.75 km

© MQST   536

San Diego

163

San Diego Zoo

Balboa Park

Spanish Village Art Center

The Globe Theatres

S.D. Mus. of Man

Casa del Prado

S.D. Nat. Hist. Mus.

5

San Diego International Airport (Lindbergh Field)

PARK WEST

Timken Mus. of Art

House of Hospitality

Reuben H. Fleet Sci. Center

S.D. Mus. of Art

S.D. Hall of Champions Sports Mus.

Spreckels Organ Pavilion

Automotive Mus.

S.D. Aerospace Mus.

Starlight Bowl

NAVAL MEDICAL CENTER

HARBORVIEW

LITTLE ITALY

Veterans Mus. & Memorial Ctr.

5

Balboa Stadium

CORTEZ HILL

Maritime Museum

COLUMBIA

Copley Symphony Hall

Santa Fe Depot

Co. Ct. Hse.

Civic Center

Cruise Ship Terminal

Broadway Pier

Navy Pier

Mus. of Contemp. Art/San Diego

U.S. Court House

Spreckels Theatre

BROADWAY

S.D. Aircraft Carrier Mus.

Pantoja Park

GAS-LAMP

Fleet & Industrial Supply Center

MARINA

Horton Plaza

EAST VILLAGE

Seaport Village

Gaslamp Quarter & W.H. Davis House

PETCO Park

Villa Montezuma

Children's Mus./ Museo de los Niños

San Diego-Coronado Ferry

San Diego Bay

Embarcadero Marina Park

San Diego Convention Center

94

5

Convention Way

Waterfront Park

0   0.25   0.5 mi
0   0.25   0.5   0.75 km

© MQST

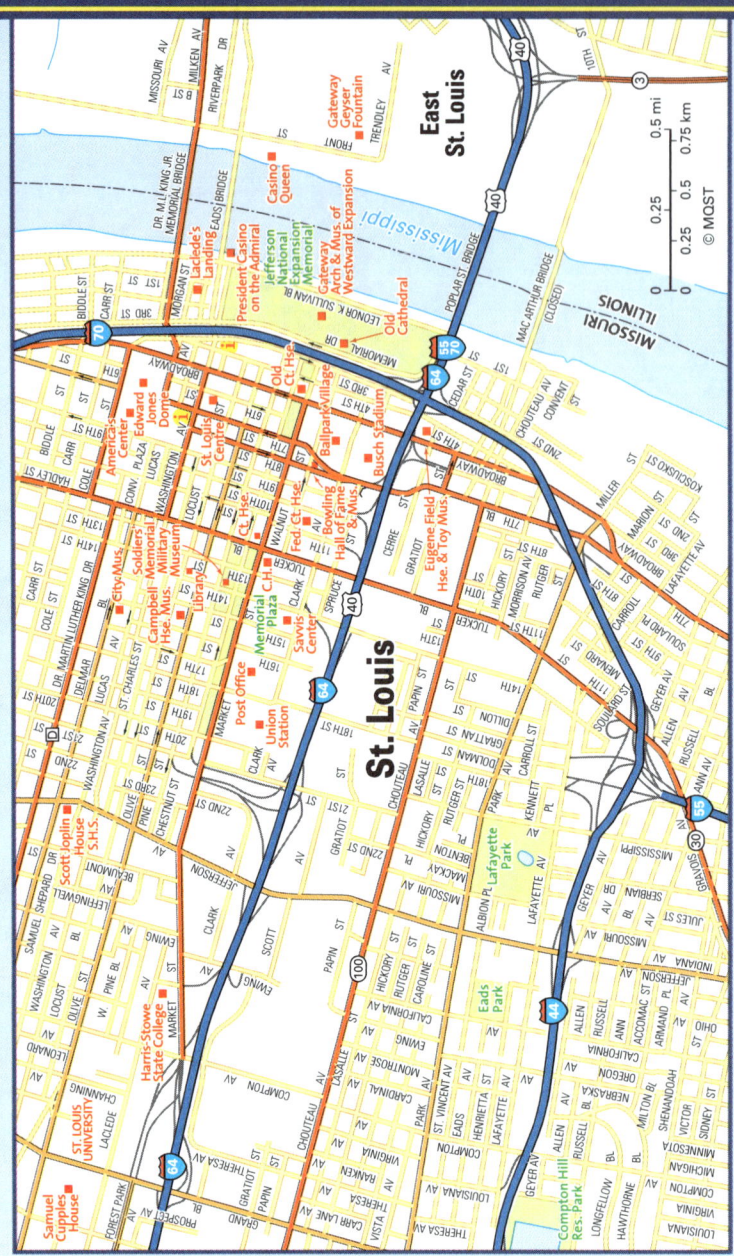

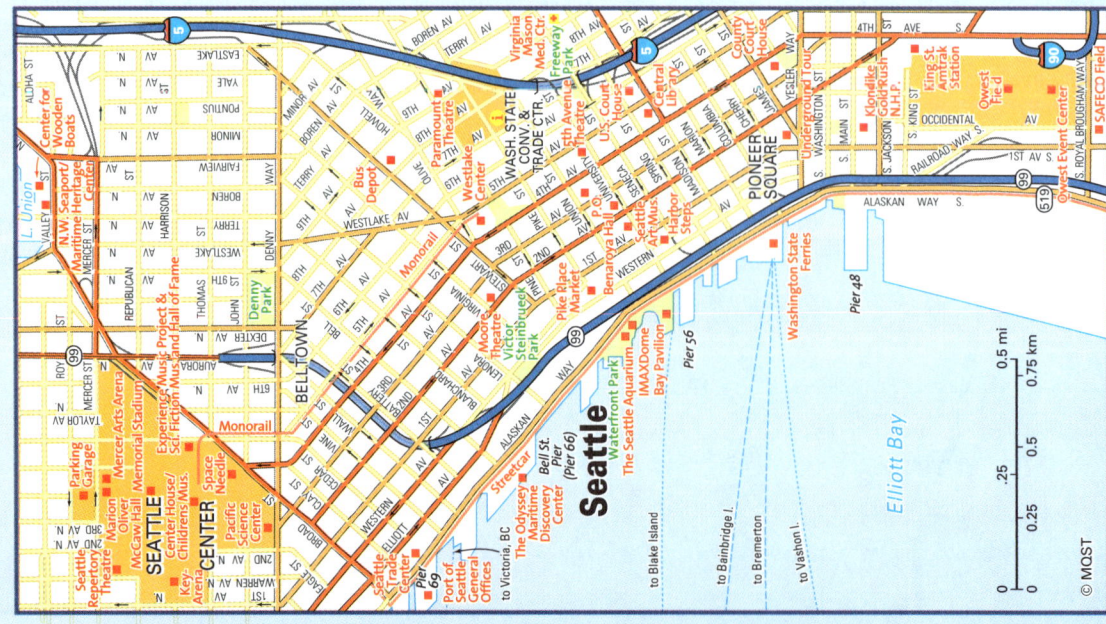

Washington, DC

American Map®

BusinessTravel
Reference Section

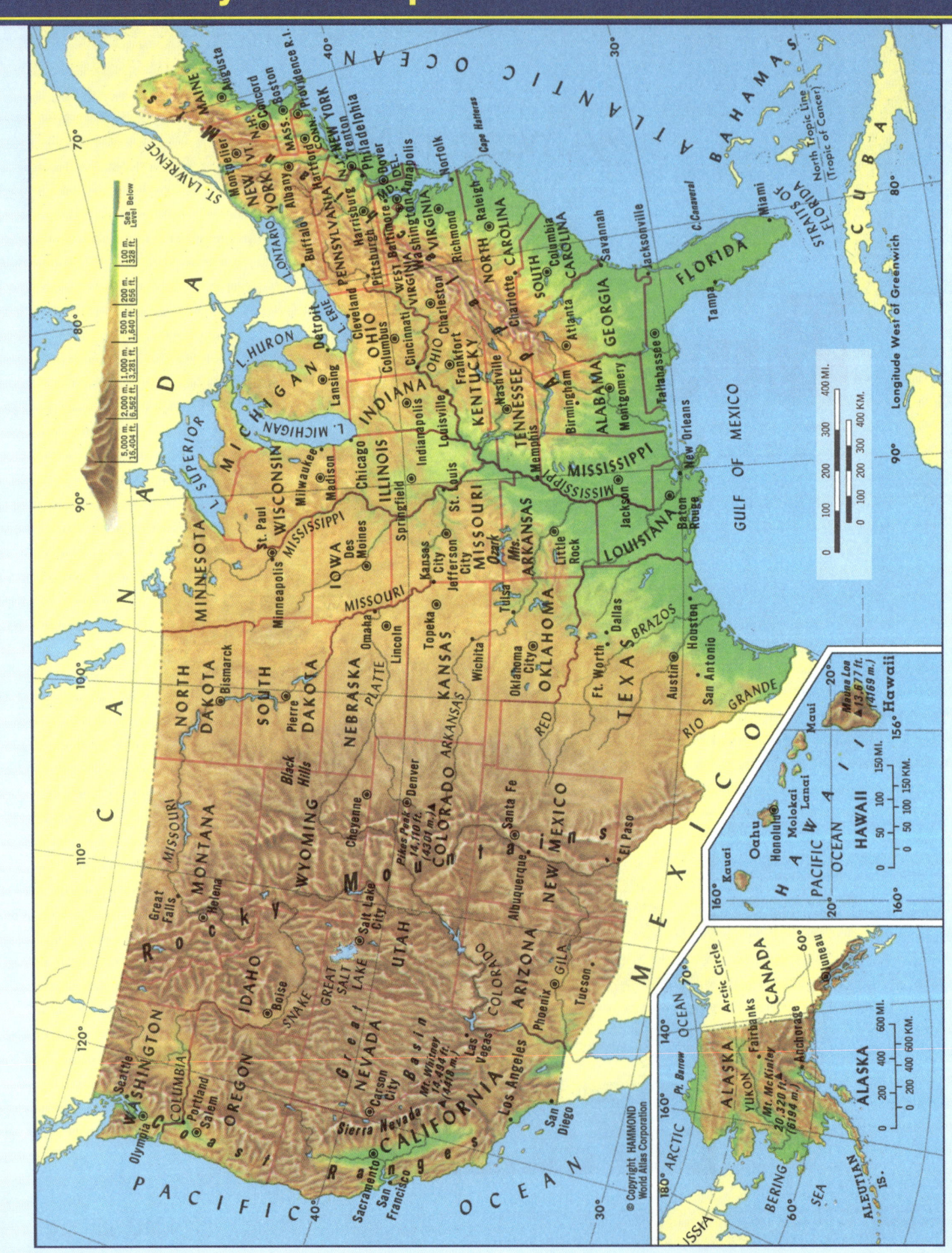

Features of this Section

These information-packed pages offer basic marketing data for all United States Core Based Statistical Areas (CBSAs), as defined by the U.S. Office of Management and Budget (OMB). Year 2004 statistical data, ranked by a variety of categories, are provided for all CBSAs. You will also find a number of convenient daily planning aids, such as area code listings, time zones, international dial codes, mileage charts, and more.

Contents

A note on CBSAs boundaries:

CBSAs are constituted of one or more entire counties. The two types of CBSAs are metropolitan statistical areas and micropolitan statistical areas, as defined by the OMB. Metropolitan statistical areas contain at least one "urbanized area" with a population of 50,000 or more. Micropolitian statistical areas contain at least "urban cluster" with a population of at least 10,000 but less than 50,000. For more information, see <www.census.gov/population/www/estimates/aboutmetro.html>.

Frequently Called Cities in the U.S., Canada, and the Caribbean

Alabama
Birmingham 205
Mobile 251
Montgomery 334

Alaska
all points 907

Arizona
Phoenix 602
Tucson 520

Arkansas
Little Rock 501
Pine Bluff 870

California
Anaheim 714
Bakersfield 661
Beverly Hills 818
Burbank 818
Fresno 559
Los Angeles
    Downtown 213
    Greater Metro Area 323
Oakland 510
Palo Alto 650
Palm Springs 760
Pasadena 626
Redding 530
Sacramento 916
San Bernardino 909
San Diego 619
San Francisco 415
San Jose 408
Santa Rosa 707

Colorado
Colorado Springs 719
Denver .... 303 & 720
Grand Junction 970

Connecticut
Hartford 860
New Haven 203
Stamford 203

Delaware
all points 302

District of Columbia
Washington, D.C. 202

Florida
Fort Lauderdale 954
Gainesville 352
Jacksonville 904
Miami .... 305 & 786
Orlando .... 321 & 407
Sarasota 941
Tallahassee 850
Tampa 813
West Palm Beach 561

Georgia
Albany 229
Atlanta
    Central 404
    Greater Metro Area ... 678 & 770
Augusta 706
Columbus 706
Macon 478
Savannah 912

Hawaii
all points 808

Idaho
all points 208

Illinois
Bloomington 309
Champaign 217

Chicago
    Inner 312
    Outer .... 224, 773 & 847
East St. Louis 618
Peoria 309
Rockford 815
Springfield 217

Indiana
Evansville 812
Fort Wayne 260
Gary 219
Indianapolis 317
Muncie 765
South Bend 574

Iowa
Cedar Rapids 319
Council Bluffs 712
Davenport 563
Des Moines 515
Sioux City 712

Kansas
Kansas City 913
Topeka 785
Wichita 316

Kentucky
Covington 859
Lexington-Fayette 859
Louisville 502
Owensboro 270

Louisiana
Baton Rouge 225
New Orleans 504
Shreveport 318

Maine
all points 207

Maryland
Annapolis .... 410 & 443
Baltimore .... 410 & 443
Bethesda .... 240 & 301

Massachusetts
Boston .... 617 & 857
Lawrence 978
Lowell 978
New Bedford .... 508 & 774
Springfield 413
Weymouth .... 339 & 781
Worcester .... 508 & 774

Michigan
Ann Arbor 734
Detroit 313
Grand Rapids 616
Lansing 517
Pontiac 248

Minnesota
Duluth 218
Minneapolis 612
Rochester 507
St. Cloud 320
St. Paul 651

Mississippi
Gulfport 228
Jackson 601

Missouri
Columbia 573
Kansas City 816
St. Louis 314
Springfield 417

Montana
all points 406

Nebraska
Lincoln 402

North Platte 308
Omaha 402

Nevada
Carson City 775
Las Vegas 702

New Hampshire
all points 603

New Jersey
Atlantic City 609
Camden 856
Elizabeth 908
Jersey City 201
Middletown 732
Newark 973
Paterson 973
Trenton 609

New Mexico
all points 505

New York
Albany 518
Binghamton 607
Buffalo 716
Long Island
    Nassau Co. 516
    Suffolk Co. 631
New York City
    Bronx .... 347, 718 & 917
    Brooklyn .... 347, 718 & 917
    Manhattan ... 212, 646 & 917
    Queens .... 347, 718 & 917
    Staten Island .... 347, 718 & 917
Plattsburgh 518
Poughkeepsie 845
Rochester 585
Syracuse 315
White Plains 914
Yonkers 914

North Carolina
Asheville 828
Charlotte 704
Durham 919
Greensboro 336
Raleigh 919
Rocky Mount 252
Wilmington 910
Winston-Salem 336

North Dakota
all points 701

Ohio
Akron .... 234 & 330
Cincinnati 513
Cleveland 216
Columbus 614
Dayton 937
Lorain 440
Toledo 419
Youngstown .... 234 & 330

Oklahoma
Enid 580
Oklahoma City 405
Tulsa 918

Oregon
Eugene 541
Portland .... 503 & 971
Salem .... 503 & 971

Pennsylvania
Allentown .... 484 & 610
Bethel Park 412
Erie 814
Harrisburg 717
Philadelphia .... 215 & 267
Pittsburgh 412

Rhode Island
all points 401

South Carolina
Charleston 843
Columbia 803
Greenville 864

South Dakota
all points 605

Tennessee
Chattanooga 423
Knoxville 865
Memphis 901
Nashville 615

Texas
Abilene 915
Amarillo 806
Austin 512
Corpus Christi 361
Dallas .... 214, 469 & 972
El Paso 915
Fort Worth .... 682 & 817
Galveston 409
Houston .... 281, 713 & 832
Lubbock 806
Odessa 915
San Antonio 210
Tyler 903
Waco 254

Utah
Cedar City 435
Salt Lake City 801

Vermont
all points 802

Virginia
Arlington .... 571 & 703
Norfolk 757
Richmond 804
Roanoke 540

Washington
Olympia 360
Seattle 206
Spokane 509
Tacoma 253

West Virginia
all points 304

Wisconsin
Eau Claire 715
Green Bay 920
Madison 608
Milwaukee 414

Wyoming
all points 307

Canada
Calgary 403
Edmonton 780
Hamilton .... 289 & 905
Halifax 902
Montreal 450
Ottawa 613
Quebec City 418
Regina 306
Sherbrooke 819
Thunder Bay 807
Toronto .... 416 & 647
Vancouver .... 604 & 778
Victoria 250
Windsor 519
Winnipeg 204

Caribbean
Anguilla 264
Antigua & Barbuda 268
Bahamas 242
Barbados 246
Bermuda 441
British Virgin Islands 284
Cayman Islands 345
Dominica 767
Dominican Republic 809
Grenada 473
Jamaica 876
Montserrat 664
Puerto Rico .... 787 & 939
St. Kitts & Nevis 869
St. Lucia 758
St. Vincent & Grenadines 784
Trinidad & Tobago 868
Turks & Caicos 649
U.S. Virgin Islands 340

Area Codes: Numerical Listing
for the U.S., Canada,
and the Caribbean

201	New Jersey - Northeastern (Shared with 551)
202	District of Columbia
203	Connecticut - Southwestern (Shared with 475)
204	Canada - Manitoba Province
205	Alabama - West Central
206	Washington - Seattle Metro Area
207	Maine
208	Idaho
209	California - Upper Central
210	Texas - San Antonio Metro Area
212	New York - New York City, Manhattan (Shared with 646 & 917)
213	California - Downtown Los Angeles
214	Texas - Dallas Metro & Outlying Area (Shared with 469 & 972)
215	Pennsylvania - Philadelphia Metro Area (Shared with 267 & 445)
216	Ohio - Cleveland Metro Area
217	Illinois - Central
218	Minnesota - Northern Third
219	Indiana - Northern
224	Illinois - Northwest (Outer) Chicago & Outlying Area (Shared with 847)
225	Louisiana - Baton Rouge General Area
228	Mississippi - Gulf Coast
229	Georgia - Southeastern (Shared with 912)
231	Michigan - Northw estern
234	Ohio - East Central (Shared with 330)
239	Florida - Southwestern
240	Maryland - Western Half (Shared with 301)
242	Caribbean - Bahamas
246	Caribbean - Barbados
248	Michigan - Detroit Metro Outlying Area
250	Canada - British Columbia Province (Excluding Vancouver Metro Area)
251	Alabama - Mobile Metro and Outlying Area
252	North Carolina - Northeastern
253	Washington - Tacoma Metro Area
254	Texas - Central
256	Alabama - North & East Central
260	Indiana - Northwestern
262	Wisconsin - Southeastern
264	Caribbean - Anguilla
267	Pennsylvania - Philadelphia Metro Area (Shared with 215 & 445)
268	Caribbean - Antigua & Barbuda
269	Michigan - Southwestern (Shared with 616)
270	Kentucky - Western Half
276	Virginia - Southwestern
281	Texas - Houston Metro & Outlying Area (Shared with 713 & 832)
284	Caribbean - British Virgin Islands
289	Canada - Lake Ontario Coastal Area (Excluding Toronto Metro area), Ontario Province (Shared with 905)
301	Maryland - Western Half (Shared with 240)
302	Delaware
303	Colorado - Denver Metro Area (Shared with 720)
304	West Virginia
305	Florida - Southern (Shared with 786)
306	Canada - Saskatchewan Province
307	Wyoming
308	Nebraska - Western Half
309	Illinois - West Central
310	California - Malibu/Santa Monica Area (Shared with 424)
312	Illinois - Inner Chicago
313	Michigan - Detroit Metro Area
314	Missouri - St. Louis Metro Area
315	New York - North Central
316	Kansas - Wichita Metro Area
317	Indiana - Central
318	Louisiana - Northern & Central
319	Iowa - Eastern
320	Minnesota - Central Third
321	Florida - East Central (Shared with 407)
323	California - Los Angeles Metro Area
330	Ohio - East Central (Shared with 234)
334	Alabama - South Central & Southeastern
336	North Carolina - Northwestern
337	Louisiana - Southwestern
339	Massachusetts - Boston Metro Outlying Area (Shared with 781)
340	Caribbean - United States Virgin Islands
345	Caribbean - Cayman Islands
347	New York - New York City, Outer Boroughs (Shared with 718 & 917)
351	Massachusetts - Northeastern (Shared with 978)
352	Florida - Upper West Central
360	Washington - Western Half (Excluding Seattle-Tacoma Metro Area)
361	Texas - Lower Gulf Coast
385	Utah (Excluding Salt Lake City Metro Area)
386	Florida - Northern
401	Rhode Island
402	Nebraska - Eastern Half
403	Canada - Southern Alberta Province
404	Georgia - Central Atlanta (Shared with 678 & 470)
405	Oklahoma - Oklahoma City Metro Area
406	Montana
407	Florida - East Central (Partially Shared with 321)
408	California - San Jose Area (Shared with 669)
409	Texas - Southeastern (Excluding General Houston Area)
410	Maryland - Eastern Half (Shared with 443)
412	Pennsylvania - Pittsburgh Metro Area (Shared with 878)
413	Massachusetts - Western
414	Wisconsin - Milwaukee Metro Area
415	California - San Francisco Metro Area
416	Canada - Toronto Metro Area, Ontario Province (Shared with 647)
417	Missouri - Southwestern
418	Canada - Eastern Quebec Province
419	Ohio - Northwestern (Shared with 567)
423	Tennessee - Northeastern & Southeastern
424	California - Malibu/Santa Monica Area (Shared with 310)
425	Washington - Seattle-Tacoma Metro Outlying Area
434	Virginia - South Central
435	Utah - (Excluding Salt Lake City Metro Area)
440	Ohio - Northeastern
441	Caribbean - Bermuda
443	Maryland - Eastern Half (Shared with 410)
445	Pennsylvania Metro Area (Shared with 215 & 267)
450	Canada - Montreal Metro Area, Quebec Province
469	Texas - Dallas Metro & Outlying Area (Shared with 214 & 972)
470	Georgia - Central Atlanta (Shared with 404, 678 & 770)
473	Caribbean - Grenada
475	Connecticut - Southwestern (Shared with 203)
478	Georgia - Central
479	Arkansas - Northwestern
480	Arizona - Phoenix Metro Outlying Area
484	Pennsylvania - Philadelphia Metro Outlying Area (Shared with 610 & 835)
501	Arkansas - Northwestern
502	Kentucky - North Central
503	Oregon - Portland-Salem Metro Area (Shared with 971)
504	Louisiana - New Orleans Metro Area
505	New Mexico
506	Canada - New Brunswick Province
507	Minnesota - Southern
508	Massachusetts - Southeastern (Shared with 774)
509	Washington - Eastern Half
510	California - Oakland-Berkeley Metro Area
512	Texas - Austin General Area
513	Ohio - Southwestern
514	Canada - Montreal Outlying Area
515	Iowa - Central
516	New York - Nassau County, Long Island
517	Michigan - South Central
518	New York - Upstate, Eastern Half
519	Canada - Southwestern Ontario Province
520	Arizona - Southeastern
530	California - Northeastern
540	Virginia - Western
541	Oregon - (Excluding Portland-Salem Metro Area)
551	New Jersey - Northeastern (Shared with 201)
559	California - Central
561	Florida - Lower East Central
562	California - Long Beach Area
563	Iowa - Eastern
567	Ohio - Northwestern (Shared with 419)
570	Pennsylvania - Northeastern
571	Virginia - Northeastern (Shared with 703)
573	Missouri - Eastern (Excluding Northeast and General St. Louis Area)
574	Indiana - North
580	Oklahoma - Western & Southeastern
585	New York - Southwestern (Shared with 716)
586	Michigan - East Central (Shared with 810)
601	Mississippi - Southern Half (Excluding Gulf Coast)
602	Arizona - Phoenix Metro Area
603	New Hampshire
604	Canada - Vancouver Metro Area, British Columbia Province (Shared with 778)
605	South Dakota
606	Kentucky - Eastern
607	New York - South Central
608	Wisconsin - Southwestern
609	New Jersey - Central & Southeastern

610	Pennsylvania - Philadelphia Metro Outlying Area (Shared with 484 & 835))	808	Hawaii
612	Minnesota - Western Minneapolis-St. Paul Metro Area	809	Caribbean - Dominican Republic
613	Canada - Southeastern Ontario Province (Excluding Toronto Metro Area)	810	Michigan - East Central
614	Ohio - Columbus Metro Area	812	Indiana - Southern
615	Tennessee - Nashville General Area	813	Florida - Tampa Area
616	Michigan - Southwestern (Shared with 269)	814	Pennsylvania - Central Western
617	Massachusetts - Boston Metro Area (Shared with 857)	815	Illinois - Northwestern
618	Illinois - Southern	816	Missouri - Kansas City Metro Area
619	California - San Diego Metro Area	817	Texas - Ft. Worth Metro Area (Shared with 682)
620	Kansas - Southern Half (Excluding Wichita Metro Area)	818	California - Burbank Area
623	Arizona - Phoenix Metro Outlying Area	819	Canada - Southern & Western Quebec Province
626	California - Pasadena Area	828	North Carolina - Southwestern
630	Illinois - West Side (Outer) Chicago & Outlying Area	830	Texas - Southwestern (Excluding San Antonio Metro Area)
631	New York - Suffolk County, Long Island	831	California - Monterey Area
636	Missouri - St. Louis Metro Outlying Area	832	Texas - Houston Metro & Outlying Area (shared with 281 & 713)
641	Iowa - Central	835	Pennsylvania - Philadelphia Metro Outlying Area (Shared with 484 & 610)
646	New York - New York City, Manhattan (Shared with 212 & 917)	843	South Carolina - Eastern
647	Canada - Toronto Metro Area, Ontario Province (Shared with 416)	845	New York- Southeastern (Excluding New York City, Long Island and Westchester County)
649	Caribbean - Turks & Caicos Islands	847	Illinois - Northwest (Outer) Chicago & Outlying Area (Shared with 224)
650	California - South Bay Area	848	New Jersey - East Central (Shared with 732)
651	Minnesota - Eastern Minneapolis-St. Paul Metro Area	850	Florida - Panhandle
660	Missouri - Northwestern	856	New Jersey - Southwestern
661	California - Bakersfield Area	857	Massachusetts - Boston Metro Area (Shared with 617)
662	Mississippi - Northern Half	858	California - Northwestern San Diego Metro Outlying Area
664	Caribbean - Montserrat	859	Kentucky - North Central
669	California - San Jose Area (Shared with 408)	860	Connecticut - (Excluding Southwestern Corridor) (Shared with 959)
671	Guam	862	New Jersey - North Central (Shared with 973)
678	Georgia - Atlanta Metro Outlying Area (Shared with 470 & 770)	863	Florida - Lower Central
682	Texas - Ft. Worth Metro Area (Shared with 817)	864	South Carolina - Northwestern
701	North Dakota	865	Tennessee - East Central
702	Nevada - Far Southeastern (Las Vegas General Area)	867	Canada - Northwest Territories, Nunavut & Yukon Province
703	Virginia - Northeastern (Shared with 571)	868	Caribbean - Trinidad & Tobago
704	North Carolina - South Central (Shared with 980)	869	Caribbean - St. Kitts & Nevis
705	Canada - Central Southeastern Ontario Province	870	Arkansas - (Excluding Northwestern)
706	Georgia - Northern Half (Excluding General Atlanta Area)	876	Caribbean - Jamaica
707	California - Northwestern	878	Pennsylvania - Southwestern (Shared with 724 & 412)
708	Illinois - South Side (Outer) Chicago & Outling Area	901	Tennessee - Memphis Metro Area
709	Canada - Newfoundland Province	902	Canada - Nova Scotia & Prince Edward Island Provinces
712	Iowa - Western	903	Texas - Northeastern
713	Texas - Houston Metro & Outlying Area (Shared with 281 & 832)	904	Florida - Northeastern
714	California - Anaheim & Santa Ana Area	905	Canada - Lake Ontario Coastal Area (Excluding Toronto Metro Area), Ontario Province (Shared with 289)
715	Wisconsin - Northern	906	Michigan - Upper Peninsula
716	New York - Western	907	Alaska
717	Pennsylvania - Southeastern (Excluding General Philadelphia Area)	908	New Jersey - Northwestern
718	New York - New York City, Outer Borough (Shared with 347 & 917)	909	California - San Bernardino Metro Area
719	Colorado - Southeastern	910	North Carolina - Southeastern
720	Colorado - Denver Metro Area (Shared with 303)	912	Georgia - Southeastern
724	Pennsylvania - Southwestern (Excluding Pittsburgh Metro Area) (Shared with 878)	913	Kansas - Kansas City Metro Area
727	Florida - West Central Coastal Area	914	New York - Southeastern (Excluding New York City and Long Island)
731	Tennessee - Eastern Third (Excluding Memphis Metro Area)	915	Texas - Central Western
732	New Jersey - East Central (Shared with 848)	916	California - Upper Central
734	Michigan - Southeastern	917	New York - New York City (Shared with 212, 347,646 & 718)
740	Ohio - Southeastern	918	Oklahoma - Northeastern
754	Florida - Ft. Lauderdale Area (Shared with 954)	919	North Carolina - North Central
757	Virginia - Southeastern	920	Wisconsin - Eastern
758	Caribbean - St. Lucia	925	California - Fairfield Area
760	California - Southern & Desert Area (Excluding San Diego Metro Area)	928	Arizona - Excluding Phoenix Metro Area and Southeast
763	Minnesota - Minneapolis - St. Paul Metro Outlying Area	931	Tennessee - Central (Excluding Nashville General Area)
765	Indiana - East Central	935	California - Southern San Diego Metro Outlying Area
767	Caribbean - Dominica	936	Texas - East Central
770	Georgia - Atlanta Metro Outlying Area (Shared with 470 & 678)	937	Ohio - South Central
772	Florida - Lower East Central (Shared with 561)	939	Caribbean - Puerto Rico (Shared with 787)
773	Illinois - Chicago Outer Metro Area	940	Texas - North Central
774	Massachusetts - Southeastern (Shared with 508)	941	Florida - Southwestern
775	Nevada - (Excluding Far Southeast, Las Vegas General Area)	949	California - Irvine Area, Southern Orange County
778	Canada - Vancouver Metro Area, British Columbia Province (Shared with 604)	952	Minnesota - Minneapolis - St. Paul Metro Outlying Area
780	Canada - Northern Alberta Provi nce	954	Florida - Ft. Lauderdale Area/Broward County
781	Massachusetts - Boston Metro Outlying Area (Shared with 339)	956	Texas - Lower Southwestern
784	Caribbean - St. Vincent & Grenadines	959	Connecticut (Excluding Southwestern Corridor) (Shared with 860)
785	Kansas - Northern Half	970	Colorado - Northern & Western
786	Florida - Southern (Shared with 305)	971	Oregon - Portland - Salem Metro Area (Shared with 503)
787	Caribbean - Puerto Rico (Shared with 939)	972	Texas - Dallas Metro and Outlying Area (Shared with 214 & 469)
801	Utah - Salt Lake City Metro Area	973	New Jersey - North Central (Shared with 862)
802	Vermont	978	Massachusetts - Northeastern (Shared with 351)
803	South Carolina - Central	979	Texas - Southeastern
804	Virginia - East Central	980	North Carolina - South Central (Shared with 704)
805	California - Santa Barbara Area	985	Louisiana - Southwestern
806	Texas - Panhandle	989	Michigan - Northeastern and Central
807	Canada - Western Ontario Province		

Dialing International Calls

FOR CODES OF PLACES NOT LISTED, DIAL "0" (OPERATOR)

For example, a call to Cape Town, South Africa, would be dialed:

011 + 27 + 21 + 123456

INTERNATIONAL ACCESS CODE	COUNTRY CODE	CITY ROUTING CODE	LOCAL NUMBER

Algeria	213
American Samoa ●	684
Argentina	54
Buenos Aires	11
Cordoba	351
La Plata	221
Rosario	341
Armenia	374
Aruba ●	297
All Points	8
Ascension Island ●	247
Australia	61
Adelaide	8
Brisbane	7
Canberra	2
Melbourne	3
Perth	8
Sydney	2
Austria	43
Graz	316
Innsbruck	512
Salzburg	662
Vienna	1
Azerbaijan	994
Baku	12
Bahrain ●	973
Bangladesh	880
Dhaka	2
Belarus	375
Minsk	17
Belgium	32
Antwerp	3
Brussels	2
Belize	501
Belize City	2
Belmopan	8
Bolivia	591
La Paz	2
Bosnia & Herzegovina	387
Sarajevo	33
Botswana ●	267
Brazil	55
Brasília	61
Rio de Janeiro	21
São Paulo	11
Brunei	673
Bandar Seri Begawan	2
Bulgaria	359
Sofia	2
Cameroon ●	237
Cape Verde Is. ●	238
Chile	56
Concepcion	41
Santiago	2
Valparaiso	32
China	86
Beijing	10
Fuzhou	591
Guangzhou	20
Hong Kong ★	852
Macau ★	853

Shanghai	21
Cote D'Ivoire ●	225
Colombia	57
Barranquilla	5
Bogota	1
Cali	2
Cartegena	5
Medellin	4
Costa Rica ●	506
Croatia	385
Zagreb	1
Cyprus	357
Nicosia	2
Czech Republic	420
Brno	5
Prague	2
Dem. Rep. of Congo	243
Kinshasa	12
Denmark ●	45
Djibouti ●	253
Ecuador	593
Cuenca	7
Guayaquil	4
Quito	2
Egypt	20
Alexandria	3
Cairo	2
Port Said	66
El Salvador ●	503
Estonia	372
Tallinn	2
Ethiopia	251
Addis Ababa	1
Faeroe Islands ●	298
Fiji ●	679
Finland	358
Helsinki	9
France ●	33
French Antilles ●	596
French Guiana ●	594
French Polynesia ●	689
Gabon ●	241
Georgia	995
Tblisi	32
Germany	49
Berlin	30
Bonn	228
Bremen	421
Cologne	221
Dresden	351
Dusseldorf	211
Frankfurt	69
Hamburg	40
Leipzig	341
Munich	89
Stuttgart	711
Ghana ●	233
Accra	21
Gibraltar ●	350

Greece	30
Athens	1
Greenland (Kalaallit Nunaat)	299
Godthab (Nuuk)	2
Guam ●	671
Guantanamo Bay ●	5399
Guatemala ●	502
Guinea	224
Conakry	4
Guyana	592
Georgetown	2
Haiti ●	509
Honduras ●	504
Hungary	36
Budapest	1
Iceland ●	354
India	91
Kolkata (Calcutta)	33
Mumbai (Bombay)	22
New Delhi	11
Indonesia	62
Jakarta	21
Iraq	964
Baghdad	1
Ireland	353
Cork	214
Dublin	1
Israel	972
Haifa	4
Jerusalem	2
Tel Aviv	3
Italy	39
Bologna	051
Florence	055
Genoa	010
Milan	02
Naples	081
Palermo	091
Rome	06
Venice	041
Japan	81
Hiroshima	82
Kobe	78
Kyoto	75
Osaka	6
Sapporo	11
Tokyo	3
Yokohama	45
Jordan	962
Amman	6
Kazakstan	7
Almaty	3273
Astana	3172
Kenya	254
Nairobi	2
Korea (Rep of)	82
Inchon	32
Pusan	51
Seoul	2
Kuwait ●	965

Kyrgyz Republic	996
Bishkek	312
Latvia ●	371
Lesotho ●	266
Liberia ●	231
Libya	218
Tripoli	21
Liechtenstein ●	423
Lithuania	370
Vilnius	2
Luxembourg ●	352
Macedonia	389
Skopje	2
Malaysia	60
Kuala Lumpur	3
Malta ●	356
Marshall Islands	692
Majuro	625
Mexico	52
Acapulco	744
Guadalajara	33
Mexico City	55
Monterrey	81
Micronesia	691
Ponape	320
Moldova	373
Kishinev	2
Monaco ●	377
Morocco	212
Marrakech	44
Tanger	399
Namibia	264
Windhoek	61
Nepal	977
Kathmandu	1
Netherlands	31
Amsterdam	20
Rotterdam	10
The Hague	70
Netherlands Antilles	599
Bonaire	717
Curacao	9
St. Maarten	5
New Caledonia ●	687
New Zealand	64
Auckland	9
Wellington	4
Nicaragua	505
Managua	2
Niger ●	227
Nigeria	234
Lagos	1
Norway ●	47
Oman ●	968

Pakistan	92
Islamabad	51
Karachi	21
Palau ●	680
Panama ●	507
Papua New Guinea ●	675
Paraguay	595
Asuncion	21
Peru	51
Lima	1
Philippines	63
Manila	2
Poland	48
Krakow	12
Warsaw	22
Portugal	351
Lisbon	21
Qatar ●	974
Romania ●	40
Russia	7
Moscow	095
St. Pierre & Miquelon ●	508
San Marino ●	378
Saudi Arabia	966
Jeddah	2
Mecca	2
Medina	4
Riyadh	1
Senegal ●	221
Sierra Leone	232
Freetown	22
Singapore ●	65
Slovakia	421
Bratislava	2
Presov	51
Slovenia	386
Ljubijana	1
South Africa	27
Cape Town	21
Johannesburg	11
Pretoria	12
Spain	34
Barcelona	93
Madrid	91
Valencia	96
Sri Lanka	94
Colombo	1
Suriname ●	597
Sweden	46
Stockholm	8
Switzerland	41
Berne	31
Geneva	22
Zurich	1

Taiwan	886
Taipei	2
Tajikistan	992
Dushanbe	372
Tanzania	255
Dar es Salaam	22
Thailand	66
Bangkok	2
Togo ●	228
Tunisia	216
Tunis	1
Turkey	90
Ankara	312
Istanbul	212,216
Izmir	232
Turkmenistan	993
Ashgabat	12
Uganda	256
Entebbe	42
Kampala	41
Ukraine	380
Kiev	44
United Arab Emirates	971
Abu Dhabi	2
Dubai	4
United Kingdom	44
Belfast	2890
Birmingham	121
Edinburgh	131
Glasgow	141
Liverpool	151
London	207, 208
Manchester	161
Sheffield	114
Southampton	2380
Uruguay	598
Montevideo	2
Uzbekistan	998
Tashkent	71
Vatican City	39
All places	6
Venezuela	58
Caracas	212
Maracaibo	261
Vietnam	84
Hanoi	4
Yemen	967
Sanaa	1
Yugoslavia	381
Belgrade	11
Zambia	260
Lusaka	1
Zimbabwe	263
Harare	4

★ = No country code required

● = No city routing code required

Note: City routing codes change frequently. The information above was current at the time of publication.

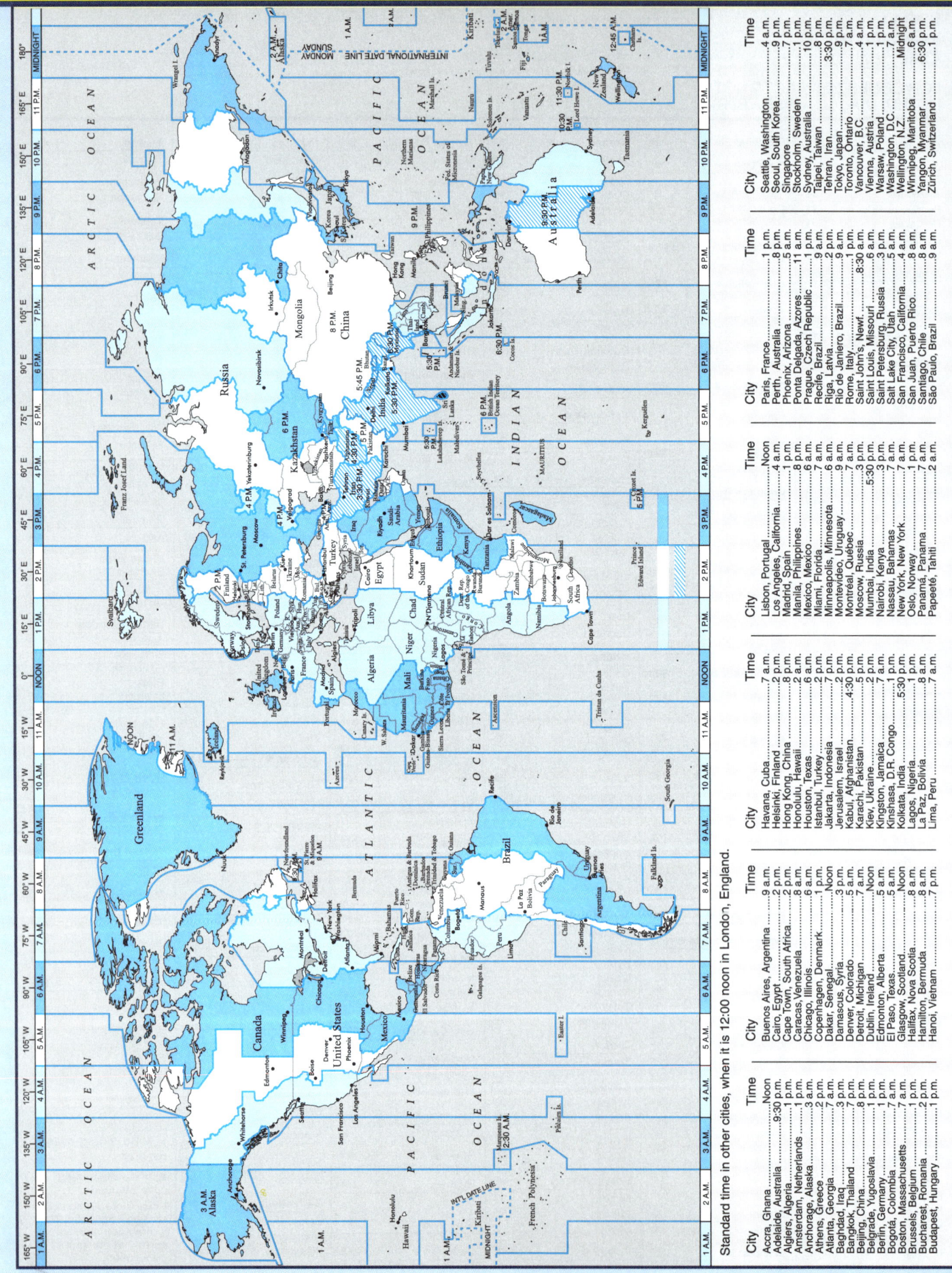

Standard time in other cities, when it is 12:00 noon in London, England.

City	Time
Accra, Ghana	Noon
Adelaide, Australia	9:30 p.m.
Algiers, Algeria	1 p.m.
Amsterdam, Netherlands	1 p.m.
Anchorage, Alaska	3 a.m.
Athens, Greece	2 p.m.
Atlanta, Georgia	7 a.m.
Baghdad, Iraq	3 p.m.
Bangkok, Thailand	7 p.m.
Beijing, China	8 p.m.
Belgrade, Yugoslavia	1 p.m.
Berlin, Germany	1 p.m.
Bogotá, Colombia	7 a.m.
Boston, Massachusetts	7 a.m.
Brussels, Belgium	1 p.m.
Budapest, Hungary	1 p.m.

City	Time
Buenos Aires, Argentina	9 a.m.
Cairo, Egypt	2 p.m.
Cape Town, South Africa	2 p.m.
Caracas, Venezuela	8 a.m.
Chicago, Illinois	6 a.m.
Copenhagen, Denmark	1 p.m.
Dakar, Senegal	Noon
Damascus, Syria	3 p.m.
Denver, Colorado	5 a.m.
Detroit, Michigan	7 a.m.
Dublin, Ireland	Noon
Edmonton, Alberta	5 a.m.
El Paso, Texas	5 a.m.
Glasgow, Scotland	Noon
Halifax, Nova Scotia	8 a.m.
Hamilton, Bermuda	8 a.m.
Hanoi, Vietnam	7 p.m.

City	Time
Havana, Cuba	7 a.m.
Helsinki, Finland	2 p.m.
Hong Kong, China	8 p.m.
Honolulu, Hawaii	2 a.m.
Houston, Texas	6 a.m.
Istanbul, Turkey	2 p.m.
Jakarta, Indonesia	7 p.m.
Jerusalem, Israel	Noon
Kabul, Afghanistan	3 p.m.
Karachi, Pakistan	4:30 p.m.
Kiev, Ukraine	2 p.m.
Kingston, Jamaica	7 a.m.
Kinshasa, D. R. Congo	1 p.m.
Kolkata, India	5:30 p.m.
Lagos, Nigeria	1 p.m.
La Paz, Bolivia	8 a.m.
Lima, Peru	7 a.m.

City	Time
Lisbon, Portugal	Noon
Los Angeles, California	4 a.m.
Madrid, Spain	1 p.m.
Manila, Philippines	8 p.m.
Mexico, Mexico	6 a.m.
Miami, Florida	7 a.m.
Minneapolis, Minnesota	6 a.m.
Montevideo, Uruguay	9 a.m.
Montréal, Québec	7 a.m.
Moscow, Russia	3 p.m.
Mumbai, India	5:30 p.m.
Nairobi, Kenya	3 p.m.
Nassau, Bahamas	7 a.m.
New York, New York	7 a.m.
Oslo, Norway	1 p.m.
Panamá, Panama	7 a.m.
Papeete, Tahiti	2 a.m.

City	Time
Paris, France	1 p.m.
Perth, Australia	8 p.m.
Phoenix, Arizona	5 a.m.
Ponta Delgada, Azores	11 a.m.
Prague, Czech Republic	1 p.m.
Recife, Brazil	9 a.m.
Riga, Latvia	2 p.m.
Rio de Janeiro, Brazil	9 a.m.
Rome, Italy	1 p.m.
Saint John's, Newf.	8:30 a.m.
Saint Louis, Missouri	6 a.m.
Saint Petersburg, Russia	3 p.m.
Salt Lake City, Utah	5 a.m.
San Francisco, California	4 a.m.
San Juan, Puerto Rico	8 a.m.
Santiago, Chile	8 a.m.
São Paulo, Brazil	9 a.m.

City	Time
Seattle, Washington	4 a.m.
Seoul, South Korea	9 p.m.
Singapore	7 p.m.
Stockholm, Sweden	1 p.m.
Sydney, Australia	10 p.m.
Taipei, Taiwan	8 p.m.
Tehran, Iran	3:30 p.m.
Tokyo, Japan	9 p.m.
Toronto, Ontario	7 a.m.
Vancouver, B.C.	4 a.m.
Vienna, Austria	1 p.m.
Warsaw, Poland	1 p.m.
Wellington, N.Z.	Midnight
Winnipeg, Manitoba	6 a.m.
Yangon, Myanmar	6:30 p.m.
Zürich, Switzerland	1 p.m.

Cities listed (reading down the right-hand axis, top to bottom):

WASHINGTON, DC
TORONTO, ON
SEATTLE, WA
SAN FRANCISCO, CA
SAN DIEGO, CA
SAN ANTONIO, TX
SALT LAKE CITY, UT
ST. LOUIS, MO
PORTLAND, OR
PITTSBURGH, PA
PHOENIX, AZ
PHILADELPHIA, PA
OKLAHOMA CITY, OK
NEW YORK, NY
NEW ORLEANS, LA
NASHVILLE, TN
MONTREAL, PQ
MINNEAPOLIS, MN
MILWAUKEE, WI
MIAMI, FL
MEMPHIS, TN
LOS ANGELES, CA
LAS VEGAS, NV
KANSAS CITY, MO
JACKSONVILLE, FL
INDIANAPOLIS, IN
HOUSTON, TX
DETROIT, MI
DENVER, CO
DALLAS, TX
COLUMBUS, OH
CLEVELAND, OH
CINCINNATI, OH
CHICAGO, IL
BUFFALO, NY
BOSTON, MA
BIRMINGHAM, AL
BALTIMORE, MD
ATLANTA, GA
ALBUQUERQUE, NM

Cities listed (reading across the bottom axis, left to right):

ALBUQUERQUE, NM
ATLANTA, GA
BALTIMORE, MD
BIRMINGHAM, AL
BOSTON, MA
BUFFALO, NY
CHICAGO, IL
CINCINNATI, OH
CLEVELAND, OH
COLUMBUS, OH
DALLAS, TX
DENVER, CO
DETROIT, MI
HOUSTON, TX
INDIANAPOLIS, IN
JACKSONVILLE, FL
KANSAS CITY, MO
LAS VEGAS, NV
LOS ANGELES, CA
MEMPHIS, TN
MIAMI, FL
MILWAUKEE, WI
MINNEAPOLIS, MN
MONTREAL, PQ
NASHVILLE, TN
NEW ORLEANS, LA
NEW YORK, NY
OKLAHOMA CITY, OK
PHILADELPHIA, PA
PHOENIX, AZ
PITTSBURGH, PA
PORTLAND, OR
ST. LOUIS, MO
SALT LAKE CITY, UT
SAN ANTONIO, TX
SAN DIEGO, CA
SAN FRANCISCO, CA
SEATTLE, WA
TORONTO, ON
WASHINGTON, DC

Legend (lower-left key box):

280
223

Top figure: Highway mileage
Bottom figure: Air mileage
Mileage figures are approx-
imate and are average taken
from various reliable sources.

Total Population

CBSA	POPULATION	RANK
New York-Newark-Edison, NY-NJ-PA Metro	18,736,586	1
Los Angeles-Long Beach-Santa Ana, CA Metro	13,006,527	2
Chicago-Naperville-Joliet, IL-IN-WI Metro	9,398,294	3
Philadelphia-Camden-Wilmington, PA-NJ-DE-MD Metro	5,800,413	4
Dallas-Fort Worth-Arlington, TX Metro	5,705,118	5
Miami-Fort Lauderdale-Miami Beach, FL Metro	5,346,010	6
Washington-Arlington-Alexandria, DC-VA-MD-WV Metro	5,189,088	7
Houston-Baytown-Sugar Land, TX Metro	5,130,511	8
Atlanta-Sandy Springs-Marietta, GA Metro	4,704,390	9
Detroit-Warren-Livonia, MI Metro	4,496,259	10
Boston-Cambridge-Quincy, MA-NH Metro	4,455,761	11
San Francisco-Oakland-Fremont, CA Metro	4,215,610	12
Phoenix-Mesa-Scottsdale, AZ Metro	3,654,002	13
Riverside-San Bernardino-Ontario, CA Metro	3,648,841	14
Seattle-Tacoma-Bellevue, WA Metro	3,183,926	15
Minneapolis-St. Paul-Bloomington, MN-WI Metro	3,115,214	16
San Diego-Carlsbad-San Marcos, CA Metro	2,972,165	17
St. Louis, MO-IL Metro	2,773,681	18
Baltimore-Towson, MD Metro	2,628,688	19
Tampa-St. Petersburg-Clearwater, FL Metro	2,563,390	20
Pittsburgh, PA Metro	2,412,526	21
Denver-Aurora, CO Metro	2,321,714	22
Cleveland-Elyria-Mentor, OH Metro	2,145,947	23
Portland-Vancouver-Beaverton, OR-WA Metro	2,062,457	24
Cincinnati-Middletown, OH-KY-IN Metro	2,060,020	25
Sacramento-Arden-Arcade-Roseville, CA Metro	1,990,366	26
Kansas City, MO-KS Metro	1,926,239	27
Orlando, FL Metro	1,851,675	28
San Antonio, TX Metro	1,832,456	29
San Jose-Sunnyvale-Santa Clara, CA Metro	1,756,162	30
Columbus, OH Metro	1,688,256	31
Providence-New Bedford-Fall River, RI-MA Metro	1,630,098	32
Virginia Beach-Norfolk-Newport News, VA-NC Metro	1,629,048	33
Las Vegas-Paradise, NV Metro	1,623,935	34
Indianapolis, IN Metro	1,611,194	35
Milwaukee-Waukesha-West Allis, WI Metro	1,517,694	36
Charlotte-Gastonia-Concord, NC-SC Metro	1,462,001	37
Austin-Round Rock, TX Metro	1,413,673	38
Nashville-Davidson-Murfreesboro, TN Metro	1,382,124	39
New Orleans-Metairie-Kenner, LA Metro	1,319,314	40
Memphis, TN-MS-AR Metro	1,250,399	41
Jacksonville, FL Metro	1,221,806	42
Louisville, KY-IN Metro	1,199,236	43
Hartford-West Hartford-East Hartford, CT Metro	1,182,417	44
Buffalo-Cheektowaga-Tonawanda, NY Metro	1,156,647	45
Richmond, VA Metro	1,145,408	46
Oklahoma City, OK Metro	1,140,319	47
Birmingham-Hoover, AL Metro	1,078,768	48
Rochester, NY Metro	1,044,679	49
Salt Lake City, UT Metro	1,017,152	50
Tucson, AZ Metro	913,496	51
Honolulu, HI Metro	911,333	52
Bridgeport-Stamford-Norwalk, CT Metro	905,906	53
Raleigh-Cary, NC Metro	898,752	54
Tulsa, OK Metro	890,907	55
Fresno, CA Metro	853,658	56
Dayton, OH Metro	845,398	57
New Haven-Milford, CT Metro	844,458	58
Albany-Schenectady-Troy, NY Metro	841,528	59
Oxnard-Thousand Oaks-Ventura, CA Metro	800,010	60
Omaha-Council Bluffs, NE-IA Metro	798,434	61
Worcester, MA Metro	779,512	62
Albuquerque, NM Metro	775,040	63
Allentown-Bethlehem-Easton, PA-NJ Metro	771,039	64
Grand Rapids-Wyoming, MI Metro	768,280	65
Baton Rouge, LA Metro	726,686	66
Bakersfield, CA Metro	713,645	67
El Paso, TX Metro	710,212	68
Akron, OH Metro	703,010	69
Springfield, MA Metro	685,943	70
Columbia, SC Metro	676,731	71
Greensboro-High Point, NC Metro	665,937	72
Poughkeepsie-Newburgh-Middletown, NY Metro	659,398	73
Toledo, OH Metro	658,597	74
Syracuse, NY Metro	654,615	75
McAllen-Edinburg-Pharr, TX Metro	642,074	76
Sarasota-Bradenton-Venice, FL Metro	641,420	77
Knoxville, TN Metro	640,696	78
Stockton, CA Metro	635,646	79
Little Rock-North Little Rock, AR Metro	632,290	80
Youngstown-Warren-Boardman, OH-PA Metro	591,161	81
Wichita, KS Metro	588,401	82
Greenville, SC Metro	585,298	83
Colorado Springs, CO Metro	575,170	84
Charleston-North Charleston, SC Metro	573,903	85
Scranton-Wilkes-Barre, PA Metro	548,725	86
Madison, WI Metro	529,311	87
Boise City-Nampa, ID Metro	523,298	88
Harrisburg-Carlisle, PA Metro	519,672	89
Lakeland-Winter Haven, FL Metro	513,989	90
Augusta-Richmond County, GA-SC Metro	512,617	91
Jackson, MS Metro	511,491	92
Portland-South Portland, ME Metro	511,203	93
Palm Bay-Melbourne-Titusville, FL Metro	509,694	94
Des Moines, IA Metro	509,346	95
Cape Coral-Fort Myers, FL Metro	503,053	96
Modesto, CA Metro	497,718	97
Chattanooga, TN-GA Metro	487,340	98
Lancaster, PA Metro	484,729	99
Deltona-Daytona Beach-Ormond Beach, FL Metro	472,690	100
Santa Rosa-Petaluma, CA Metro	472,358	101
Ogden-Clearfield, UT Metro	470,689	102
Lansing-East Lansing, MI Metro	457,201	103
Durham, NC Metro	456,102	104
Flint, MI Metro	444,695	105
Winston-Salem, NC Metro	441,047	106
Pensacola-Ferry Pass-Brent, FL Metro	434,400	107
Spokane, WA Metro	433,726	108
Lexington-Fayette, KY Metro	422,530	109
Salinas, CA Metro	418,102	110
Vallejo-Fairfield, CA Metro	416,654	111
Provo-Orem, UT Metro	415,207	112
Corpus Christi, TX Metro	409,361	113
Santa Barbara-Santa Maria-Goleta, CA Metro	407,310	114
Canton-Massillon, OH Metro	406,864	115
Fort Wayne, IN Metro	401,828	116
Mobile, AL Metro	399,912	117
Manchester-Nashua, NH Metro	398,500	118
York-Hanover, PA Metro	394,849	119
Visalia-Porterville, CA Metro	390,116	120
Reading, PA Metro	388,557	121
Springfield, MO Metro	386,298	122
Beaumont-Port Arthur, TX Metro	384,714	123
Asheville, NC Metro	384,686	124
Fayetteville-Springdale-Rogers, AR-MO Metro	382,973	125
Reno-Sparks, NV Metro	382,377	126
Shreveport-Bossier City, LA Metro	380,015	127
Davenport-Moline-Rock Island, IA-IL Metro	374,746	128
Brownsville-Harlingen, TX Metro	366,128	129
Peoria, IL Metro	365,345	130
Trenton-Ewing, NJ Metro	364,545	131
Salem, OR Metro	363,889	132
Huntsville, AL Metro	362,096	133
Montgomery, AL Metro	354,959	134
Hickory-Morganton-Lenoir, NC Metro	352,697	135
Port St. Lucie-Fort Pierce, FL Metro	349,682	136
Killeen-Temple-Fort Hood, TX Metro	347,446	137
Evansville, IN-KY Metro	345,888	138
Anchorage, AK Metro	343,612	139
Ann Arbor, MI Metro	341,745	140
Fayetteville, NC Metro	341,368	141
Tallahassee, FL Metro	337,061	142
Eugene-Springfield, OR Metro	331,900	143
Rockford, IL Metro	331,791	144
Kalamazoo-Portage, MI Metro	321,457	145
South Bend-Mishawaka, IN-MI Metro	319,986	146
Charleston, WV Metro	306,202	147
Savannah, GA Metro	304,469	148
Naples-Marco Island, FL Metro	297,619	149
Utica-Rome, NY Metro	297,598	150
Wilmington, NC Metro	295,406	151
Green Bay, WI Metro	294,254	152
Roanoke, VA Metro	292,819	153
Huntington-Ashland, WV-KY-OH Metro	285,666	154
Columbus, GA-AL Metro	283,657	155
Ocala, FL Metro	282,475	156
Fort Smith, AR-OK Metro	282,235	157
Boulder, CO Metro	280,996	158
Lincoln, NE Metro	280,381	159
Erie, PA Metro	280,152	160
Duluth, MN-WI Metro	275,129	161
Fort Collins-Loveland, CO Metro	269,231	162
Norwich-New London, CT Metro	265,569	163
Atlantic City, NJ Metro	264,055	164
Spartanburg, SC Metro	263,251	165
Lubbock, TX Metro	257,656	166
San Luis Obispo-Paso Robles, CA Metro	256,929	167
Santa Cruz-Watsonville, CA Metro	254,831	168
Gulfport-Biloxi, MS Metro	252,678	169
Binghamton, NY Metro	251,740	170
Holland-Grand Haven, MI Metro	249,988	171
Gainesville, FL Metro	246,884	172
Lafayette, LA Metro	246,050	173
Cedar Rapids, IA Metro	244,664	174
Bremerton-Silverdale, WA Metro	239,770	175
Hagerstown-Martinsburg, MD-WV Metro	237,013	176
Clarksville, TN-KY Metro	236,974	177
Amarillo, TX Metro	235,502	178
Kingsport-Bristol, TN-VA Metro	232,512	179
Barnstable Town, MA Metro	231,906	180
Merced, CA Metro	231,717	181
Lynchburg, VA Metro	231,010	182
Yakima, WA Metro	227,285	183
Macon, GA Metro	227,171	184
Topeka, KS Metro	226,163	185
Olympia, WA Metro	221,297	186
Waco, TX Metro	220,818	187
Laredo, TX Metro	217,923	188
Greeley, CO Metro	217,652	189
Champaign-Urbana, IL Metro	215,808	190
Appleton, WI Metro	213,079	191
Myrtle Beach-Conway-North Myrtle Beach, SC Metro	212,770	192
Chico, CA Metro	212,004	193
Kennewick-Richland-Pasco, WA Metro	210,844	194
Saginaw-Saginaw Township North, MI Metro	209,916	195
Burlington-South Burlington, VT Metro	205,324	196
Springfield, IL Metro	204,222	197
Longview, TX Metro	200,941	198
Sioux Falls, SD Metro	199,881	199
Houma-Bayou Cane-Thibodaux, LA Metro	199,245	200
Florence, SC Metro	196,985	201
Tuscaloosa, AL Metro	194,927	202
College Station-Bryan, TX Metro	194,037	203
Lake Charles, LA Metro	193,280	204
Medford, OR Metro	191,768	205
Racine, WI Metro	191,653	206
Torrington, CT Micro	189,803	207
Elkhart-Goshen, IN Metro	188,770	208
Prescott, AZ Metro	187,647	209
Tyler, TX Metro	186,264	210
Johnson City, TN Metro	185,518	211
Lafayette, IN Metro	183,783	212
Charlottesville, VA Metro	183,357	213
Las Cruces, NM Metro	182,035	214
Kingston, NY Metro	181,647	215
Fort Walton Beach-Crestview-Destin, FL Metro	181,471	216
Fargo, ND-MN Metro	179,489	217
Bellingham, WA Metro	178,551	218
Bloomington, IN Metro	178,253	219
St. Cloud, MN Metro	175,809	220
Redding, CA Metro	175,646	221
Athens-Clarke County, GA Metro	174,192	222
Rochester, MN Metro	174,190	223
Yuma, AZ Metro	174,159	224
Anderson, SC Metro	173,679	225
Lake Havasu City-Kingman, AZ Micro	173,567	226
Muskegon-Norton Shores, MI Metro	172,532	227
Lebanon, NH-VT Micro	171,437	228
Monroe, LA Metro	171,062	229
Terre Haute, IN Metro	169,499	230
Seaford, DE Micro	169,340	231
Parkersburg-Marietta, WV-OH Metro	163,138	232
Waterloo-Cedar Falls, IA Metro	162,804	233
Jackson, MI Metro	162,521	234
Joplin, MO Metro	162,424	235
Niles-Benton Harbor, MI Metro	162,229	236
Albany, GA Metro	160,614	237
Gainesville, GA Metro	160,370	238
Abilene, TX Metro	159,905	239
Oshkosh-Neenah, WI Metro	159,847	240
Greenville, NC Metro	159,353	241
Hilo, HI Micro	159,160	242
Bloomington-Normal, IL Metro	157,428	243
East Stroudsburg, PA Micro	156,276	244
Panama City-Lynn Haven, FL Metro	155,312	245
Janesville, WI Metro	154,741	246
Pascagoula, MS Metro	154,275	247
Punta Gorda, FL Metro	154,137	248
Hilton Head Island-Beaufort, SC Micro	154,110	249
Lexington-Thomasville, NC Micro	153,550	250
Blacksburg-Christiansburg-Radford, VA Metro	153,421	251
Ottawa-Streator, IL Micro	153,346	252
Daphne-Fairhope, AL Micro	152,986	253
Eau Claire, WI Metro	152,787	254
Columbia, MO Metro	152,440	255
Wichita Falls, TX Metro	151,616	256
Monroe, MI Metro	151,207	257
El Centro, CA Metro	150,768	258
Pueblo, CO Metro	149,472	259
Wheeling, WV-OH Metro	149,422	260
Johnstown, PA Metro	149,133	261
Jacksonville, NC Metro	148,621	262
Vineland-Millville-Bridgeton, NJ Metro	148,511	263
Yuba City-Marysville, CA Metro	148,101	264
Pottsville, PA Micro	147,359	265
Bangor, ME Metro	147,304	266
Decatur, AL Metro	146,537	267
Alexandria, LA Metro	146,386	268
Rocky Mount, NC Metro	145,019	269
Concord, NH Micro	144,687	270
Billings, MT Metro	144,236	271
Jefferson City, MO Metro	143,882	272
Sioux City, IA-NE-SD Metro	142,937	273
Springfield, OH Metro	142,396	274
Florence, AL Metro	141,259	275
State College, PA Metro	140,720	276
Traverse City, MI Micro	140,141	277
Burlington, NC Metro	138,987	278
Santa Fe, NM Metro	138,986	279
Battle Creek, MI Metro	138,480	280
Hanford-Corcoran, CA Metro	138,034	281
Iowa City, IA Metro	138,031	282
Kahului-Wailuku, HI Micro	137,520	283
Jamestown-Dunkirk-Fredonia, NY Micro	137,259	284
Salisbury, NC Micro	135,038	285
Statesville-Mooresville, NC Micro	134,830	286
Dover, DE Metro	134,615	287
Madera, CA Metro	134,194	288
Bend, OR Metro	133,644	289
Chambersburg, PA Micro	133,417	290
Texarkana, TX-Texarkana, AR Metro	132,584	291
Dothan, AL Metro	132,199	292
Napa, CA Metro	132,101	293
Pittsfield, MA Metro	131,892	294
Anderson, IN Metro	131,542	295
Hattiesburg, MS Metro	128,925	296
Dalton, GA Metro	128,843	297
La Crosse, WI-MN Metro	128,623	298
Weirton-Steubenville, WV-OH Metro	128,499	299
Tupelo, MS Micro	128,328	300
Wausau, WI Metro	128,152	301
Eureka-Arcata-Fortuna, CA Micro	127,570	302
Flagstaff, AZ Metro	127,438	303
Mansfield, OH Metro	127,432	304
Homosassa Springs, FL Micro	127,430	305
Morristown, TN Metro	127,072	306

CBSA	POPULATION	RANK
Altoona, PA Metro	126,915	307
Lumberton, NC Micro	126,599	308
Farmington, NM Metro	125,927	309
Glens Falls, NY Metro	125,441	310
Sierra Vista-Douglas, AZ Micro	125,157	311
Grand Junction, CO Metro	125,010	312
Odessa, TX Metro	122,701	313
Valdosta, GA Metro	122,590	314
Vero Beach, FL Metro	122,283	315
Lebanon, PA Metro	121,920	316
St. Joseph, MO-KS Metro	121,463	317
Warner Robins, GA Metro	121,393	318
Auburn-Opelika, AL Metro	120,228	319
Augusta-Waterville, ME Micro	119,426	320
Williamsport, PA Metro	118,535	321
Midland, TX Metro	118,434	322
Coeur d'Alene, ID Metro	118,402	323
Muncie, IN Metro	117,650	324
Rapid City, SD Metro	117,243	325
Sherman-Denison, TX Metro	116,045	326
Victoria, TX Metro	114,605	327
New Bern, NC Micro	114,482	328
Morgantown, WV Metro	113,860	329
Sheboygan, WI Metro	113,439	330
Wooster, OH Micro	113,407	331
Salisbury, MD Metro	113,323	332
Willimantic, CT Micro	113,250	333
Lawton, OK Metro	113,237	334
Goldsboro, NC Metro	112,487	335
Harrisonburg, VA Metro	112,290	336
Winchester, VA-WV Metro	112,008	337
Anniston-Oxford, AL Metro	111,715	338
East Liverpool-Salem, OH Micro	111,661	339
Allegan, MI Micro	111,572	340
Staunton-Waynesboro, VA Micro	111,277	341
Owensboro, KY Metro	110,872	342
Jonesboro, AR Metro	110,853	343
Michigan City-La Porte, IN Metro	110,712	344
Ogdensburg-Massena, NY Micro	110,514	345
Jackson, TN Metro	110,481	346
Elizabethtown, KY Metro	110,232	347
Decatur, IL Metro	109,831	348
Bay City, MI Metro	109,352	349
Danville, VA Metro	108,899	350
Mount Vernon-Anacortes, WA Metro	108,838	351
Bowling Green, KY Metro	108,545	352
Logan, UT-ID Metro	108,468	353
Idaho Falls, ID Metro	108,253	354
Lima, OH Metro	107,679	355
Cleveland, TN Metro	107,102	356
St. George, UT Metro	106,324	357
Sumter, SC Metro	106,232	358
Meridian, MS Micro	106,123	359
Lewiston-Auburn, ME Metro	106,087	360
Albany-Lebanon, OR Micro	105,925	361
Bluefield, WV-VA Micro	105,645	362
San Angelo, TX Metro	105,365	363
Pine Bluff, AR Metro	105,345	364
Kankakee-Bradley, IL Metro	105,097	365
Watertown-Fort Drum, NY Micro	105,082	366
Manhattan, KS Micro	104,432	367
Hammond, LA Micro	104,133	368
Lawrence, KS Metro	103,860	369
Gadsden, AL Metro	103,075	370
Ashtabula, OH Micro	102,352	371
Roseburg, OR Micro	102,107	372
Wenatchee, WA Metro	101,961	373
Ocean City, NJ Metro	101,481	374
Kokomo, IN Metro	101,371	375
Dunn, NC Micro	101,287	376
Adrian, MI Micro	100,933	377
Cumberland, MD-WV Metro	100,915	378
Ithaca, NY Metro	100,857	379
Missoula, MT Metro	100,706	380
Corning, NY Micro	99,381	381
Shelby, NC Micro	98,839	382
Whitewater, WI Micro	98,753	383
Fond du Lac, WI Metro	98,632	384
Bismarck, ND Metro	98,224	385
Cookeville, TN Micro	97,432	386
Tullahoma, TN Micro	97,093	387
Paducah, KY-IL Micro	96,978	388
Gettysburg, PA Micro	96,848	389
Brunswick, GA Metro	96,546	390
Truckee-Grass Valley, CA Micro	96,434	391
Longview-Kelso, WA Metro	95,725	392
Grand Forks, ND-MN Metro	95,531	393
Rome, GA Metro	94,242	394
New Castle, PA Micro	93,898	395
Enterprise-Ozark, AL Micro	93,559	396
Lexington Park, MD Micro	93,082	397
Sunbury, PA Micro	92,652	398
Richmond, KY Micro	92,112	399
New Philadelphia-Dover, OH Micro	91,853	400
Cape Girardeau-Jackson, MO-IL Micro	91,813	401
Hot Springs, AR Metro	91,562	402
Clarksburg, WV Micro	91,518	403
Sebring, FL Micro	91,200	404
Orangeburg, SC Micro	91,048	405
Elmira, NY Metro	90,197	406
Dubuque, IA Metro	89,898	407
Meadville, PA Micro	89,516	408
Opelousas-Eunice, LA Micro	88,639	409
Indiana, PA Micro	88,270	410
Mankato-North Mankato, MN Micro	88,122	411
Ukiah, CA Micro	87,696	412
Beaver Dam, WI Micro	87,528	413
Brainerd, MN Micro	86,569	414
Twin Falls, ID Micro	86,175	415
Fairbanks, AK Metro	86,098	416
Zanesville, OH Micro	85,840	417
Albertville, AL Micro	84,900	418
Midland, MI Micro	84,685	419
Pendleton-Hermiston, OR Micro	83,876	420
Cheyenne, WY Metro	83,743	421
Pocatello, ID Metro	83,718	422
Laurel, MS Micro	83,494	423
DuBois, PA Micro	83,240	424
Manitowoc, WI Micro	82,952	425
Olean, NY Micro	82,761	426
Danville, IL Metro	82,494	427
Lufkin, TX Micro	82,326	428
Bloomsburg-Berwick, PA Micro	82,315	429
Plattsburgh, NY Micro	81,857	430
Auburn, NY Micro	81,381	431
Ames, IA Metro	81,363	432
Talladega-Sylacauga, AL Micro	80,988	433
Key West-Marathon, FL Micro	80,915	434
Southern Pines, NC Micro	80,480	435
Corvallis, OR Metro	80,361	436
Kalispell, MT Micro	79,767	437
Beckley, WV Micro	79,711	438
Great Falls, MT Metro	79,462	439
Grants Pass, OR Micro	79,233	440
Somerset, PA Micro	79,217	441
Moses Lake, WA Micro	79,156	442
Sandusky, OH Metro	78,746	443
Cullman, AL Micro	78,353	444
Athens, TX Micro	77,836	445
Roanoke Rapids, NC Micro	77,641	446
Quincy, IL-MO Micro	77,524	447
Russellville, AR Micro	77,445	448
Portsmouth, OH Micro	77,230	449
Sevierville, TN Micro	76,676	450
Oak Harbor, WA Micro	76,268	451
Watertown-Fort Atkinson, WI Micro	76,161	452
Keene, NH Micro	76,132	453
Wilson, NC Micro	75,798	454
Warsaw, IN Micro	75,242	455
Wisconsin Rapids-Marshfield, WI Micro	75,197	456
Chillicothe, OH Micro	75,187	457
New Iberia, LA Micro	74,421	458
Bozeman, MT Micro	73,968	459
Columbia, TN Micro	73,440	460
Hinesville-Fort Stewart, GA Metro	73,242	461
Findlay, OH Micro	72,906	462
Mount Airy, NC Micro	72,805	463
Gallup, NM Micro	72,707	464
Galesburg, IL Micro	72,399	465
Owosso, MI Micro	72,221	466
Palatka, FL Micro	71,876	467
Martinsville, VA Micro	71,609	468
Columbus, IN Metro	71,588	469
Marion, IN Micro	71,447	470
Branson, MO Micro	71,383	471
Centralia, WA Micro	70,884	472
Searcy, AR Micro	70,781	473
Stillwater, OK Micro	70,592	474
Richmond, IN Micro	70,394	475
Muskogee, OK Micro	70,263	476
Aberdeen, WA Micro	69,290	477
Seneca, SC Micro	69,240	478
Marinette, WI-MI Micro	68,662	479
Bristol, VA Metro	68,596	480
Lincolnton, NC Micro	68,521	481
Greenwood, SC Micro	68,364	482
Grand Island, NE Micro	68,335	483
Frankfort, KY Micro	68,324	484
Helena, MT Micro	68,271	485
Stevens Point, WI Micro	68,120	486
Casper, WY Metro	67,821	487
Shawnee, OK Micro	67,467	488
North Wilkesboro, NC Micro	67,268	489
Port Angeles, WA Micro	66,960	490
Marion, OH Micro	65,891	491
Mount Pleasant, MI Micro	65,334	492
Klamath Falls, OR Micro	65,097	493
The Villages, FL Micro	64,844	494
Minot, ND Micro	64,465	495
Greeneville, TN Micro	64,434	496
Marquette, MI Micro	63,977	497
Athens, OH Micro	63,898	498
Hudson, NY Micro	63,894	499
Huntsville, TX Micro	63,455	500
Forest City, NC Micro	63,299	501
Rutland, VT Micro	63,118	502
Lancaster, SC Micro	63,001	503
Clearlake, CA Micro	62,990	504
Palm Coast, FL Micro	62,950	505
Charleston-Mattoon, IL Micro	62,945	506
Coos Bay, OR Micro	62,936	507
Sayre, PA Micro	62,904	508
Hutchinson, KS Micro	62,888	509
Marshall, TX Micro	62,672	510
Oneonta, NY Micro	62,334	511
Sturgis, MI Micro	62,141	512
Marion-Herrin, IL Micro	61,848	513
Fremont, OH Micro	61,571	514
Alamogordo, NM Micro	61,534	515
Kapaa, HI Micro	61,060	516
Laconia, NH Micro	60,904	517
Morehead City, NC Micro	60,739	518
Columbus, MS Micro	60,631	519
Norwalk, OH Micro	60,472	520
Salina, KS Micro	60,458	521
Nacogdoches, TX Micro	60,278	522
Greenville, MS Micro	60,195	523
Georgetown, SC Micro	60,170	524
LaGrange, GA Micro	60,165	525
Sterling, IL Micro	59,935	526
Faribault-Northfield, MN Micro	59,842	527
Carbondale, IL Micro	59,786	528
Roswell, NM Micro	59,597	529
Lake City, FL Micro	59,502	530
Batavia, NY Micro	59,348	531
Barre, VT Micro	59,305	532
Crowley, LA Micro	59,152	533
Kinston, NC Micro	58,643	534
Fergus Falls, MN Micro	58,521	535
Albemarle, NC Micro	58,476	536
Statesboro, GA Micro	58,027	537
Rio Grande City, TX Micro	58,014	538
Red Bluff, CA Micro	57,995	539
Somerset, KY Micro	57,945	540
Lewiston, ID-WA Metro	57,912	541
Ruston, LA Micro	57,801	542
Farmington, MO Micro	57,733	543
Point Pleasant, WV-OH Micro	57,580	544
Tiffin-Fostoria, OH Micro	57,538	545
Mount Vernon, OH Micro	57,055	546
Enid, OK Micro	56,971	547
Baraboo, WI Micro	56,960	548
Fairmont, WV Micro	56,794	549
Walla Walla, WA Micro	56,654	550
Phoenix Lake-Cedar Ridge, CA Micro	56,610	551
Oil City, PA Micro	56,378	552
Hobbs, NM Micro	56,320	553
Carson City, NV Metro	55,832	554
Ardmore, OK Micro	55,750	555
London, KY Micro	55,550	556
Elizabeth City, NC Micro	55,421	557
Edwards, CO Micro	55,398	558
Dublin, GA Micro	55,386	559
Palestine, TX Micro	55,064	560
Gloversville, NY Micro	55,049	561
Milledgeville, GA Micro	54,798	562
Muscatine, IA Micro	54,678	563
Abbeville, LA Micro	54,576	564
Gaffney, SC Micro	54,274	565
Scottsboro, AL Micro	54,006	566
Jasper, IN Micro	53,300	567
Ontario, OR-ID Micro	53,210	568
Granbury, TX Micro	53,173	569
Ashland, OH Micro	53,040	570
Natchez, MS-LA Micro	52,915	571
Payson, AZ Micro	52,882	572
Harriman, TN Micro	52,785	573
Rochelle, IL Micro	52,769	574
Greenville, OH Micro	52,725	575
Danville, KY Micro	52,685	576
McComb, MS Micro	52,463	577
Mason City, IA Micro	52,440	578
Morgan City, LA Micro	51,938	579
Waycross, GA Micro	51,814	580
Picayune, MS Micro	51,719	581
Shelton, WA Micro	51,394	582
Carlsbad-Artesia, NM Micro	51,228	583
Norfolk, NE Micro	51,228	584
Warrensburg, MO Micro	50,784	585
Athens, TN Micro	50,748	586
Malone, NY Micro	50,748	587
Eagle Pass, TX Micro	50,391	588
Kearney, NE Micro	50,187	589
Crossville, TN Micro	50,021	590
Ocean Pines, MD Micro	49,870	591
Platteville, WI Micro	49,577	592
Fort Polk South, LA Micro	49,495	593
Clinton, IA Micro	49,442	594
Paris, TX Micro	49,425	595
Bartlesville, OK Micro	49,390	596
Vicksburg, MS Micro	49,360	597
Sanford, NC Micro	49,320	598
Blytheville, AR Micro	49,273	599
Glasgow, KY Micro	49,247	600
Amsterdam, NY Micro	49,105	601
Cortland, NY Micro	48,922	602
Burlington, IA-IL Micro	48,887	603
Winona, MN Micro	48,856	604
Sidney, OH Micro	48,807	605
Mount Vernon, IL Micro	48,709	606
Jacksonville, TX Micro	48,351	607
Corsicana, TX Micro	48,087	608
Calhoun, GA Micro	47,930	609
Canon City, CO Micro	47,870	610
New Castle, IN Micro	47,682	611
Ponca City, OK Micro	47,663	612
Kendallville, IN Micro	47,621	613
Freeport, IL Micro	47,418	614
Oak Hill, WV Micro	47,206	615
Greenwood, MS Micro	47,079	616
Madisonville, KY Micro	46,981	617
Rockingham, NC Micro	46,961	618

CBSA	POPULATION	RANK	CBSA	POPULATION	RANK	CBSA	POPULATION	RANK
Del Rio, TX Micro	46,897	619	Scottsbluff, NE Micro	37,596	723	North Vernon, IN Micro	28,616	827
Durango, CO Micro	46,890	620	Hannibal, MO Micro	37,551	724	Forrest City, AR Micro	28,524	828
Douglas, GA Micro	46,673	621	Newton, IA Micro	37,505	725	Yazoo City, MS Micro	28,389	829
Coldwater, MI Micro	46,538	622	Lock Haven, PA Micro	37,498	726	Bainbridge, GA Micro	28,269	830
Bellefontaine, OH Micro	46,473	623	Durant, OK Micro	37,493	727	Washington, OH Micro	28,004	831
Lewistown, PA Micro	46,395	624	Mayfield, KY Micro	37,452	728	Fort Morgan, CO Micro	27,973	832
Bedford, IN Micro	46,302	625	West Plains, MO Micro	37,409	729	Mineral Wells, TX Micro	27,884	833
Wapakoneta, OH Micro	46,239	626	Okeechobee, FL Micro	37,397	730	Wauchula, FL Micro	27,853	834
Cadillac, MI Micro	46,199	627	Canton, IL Micro	37,340	731	Thomaston, GA Micro	27,767	835
Plymouth, IN Micro	46,162	628	Americus, GA Micro	37,310	732	Crescent City North, CA Micro	27,586	836
Bucyrus, OH Micro	46,009	629	Rock Springs, WY Micro	37,302	733	Great Bend, KS Micro	27,458	837
Washington, NC Micro	45,937	630	Bennington, VT Micro	37,264	734	Fitzgerald, GA Micro	27,377	838
Huntingdon, PA Micro	45,843	631	Corbin, KY Micro	37,167	735	Jesup, GA Micro	27,314	839
Kerrville, TX Micro	45,752	632	Coshocton, OH Micro	36,875	736	Sheridan, WY Micro	27,134	840
Elko, NV Micro	45,376	633	Dyersburg, TN Micro	36,850	737	Hays, KS Micro	27,064	841
Red Wing, MN Micro	45,345	634	Winfield, KS Micro	36,788	738	Silverthorne, CO Micro	27,030	842
El Dorado, AR Micro	45,320	635	Clewiston, FL Micro	36,679	739	Uvalde, TX Micro	26,953	843
Clovis, NM Micro	45,228	636	Montrose, CO Micro	36,474	740	Grants, NM Micro	26,815	844
St. Marys, GA Micro	45,164	637	Riverton, WY Micro	36,370	741	Lexington, NE Micro	26,734	845
Henderson, NC Micro	45,127	638	Astoria, OR Micro	36,328	742	Summerville, GA Micro	26,573	846
Selma, AL Micro	45,032	639	Peru, IN Micro	36,252	743	Vernal, UT Micro	26,484	847
Gardnerville Ranchos, NV Micro	44,695	640	Cedar City, UT Micro	36,232	744	New Ulm, MN Micro	26,435	848
Brigham City, UT Micro	44,484	641	Laurinburg, NC Micro	36,058	745	Altus, OK Micro	26,426	849
McAlester, OK Micro	44,326	642	Dixon, IL Micro	35,997	746	Jackson, WY-ID Micro	26,217	850
Bradford, PA Micro	44,250	643	Valley, AL Micro	35,973	747	Boone, IA Micro	26,111	851
Fort Leonard Wood, MO Micro	44,144	644	Plainview, TX Micro	35,965	748	Toccoa, GA Micro	25,901	852
Tahlequah, OK Micro	44,095	645	Pahrump, NV Micro	35,937	749	Harrisburg, IL Micro	25,647	853
Bogalusa, LA Micro	43,947	646	Fremont, NE Micro	35,905	750	Mexico, MO Micro	25,626	854
Harrison, AR Micro	43,738	647	Hutchinson, MN Micro	35,756	751	Deming, NM Micro	25,542	855
Keokuk-Fort Madison, IA-MO Micro	43,548	648	Moscow, ID Micro	35,619	752	Magnolia, AR Micro	25,289	856
Moultrie, GA Micro	43,296	649	Ottumwa, IA Micro	35,558	753	Connersville, IN Micro	25,113	857
Blackfoot, ID Micro	43,175	650	North Platte, NE Micro	35,538	754	Marshall, MN Micro	24,877	858
Thomasville, GA Micro	43,072	651	Seneca Falls, NY Micro	35,530	755	La Grande, OR Micro	24,685	859
Warren, PA Micro	42,810	652	Ellensburg, WA Micro	35,498	756	Moberly, MO Micro	24,679	860
Boone, NC Micro	42,790	653	Taylorville, IL Micro	35,098	757	Greensburg, IN Micro	24,622	861
Starkville, MS Micro	42,642	654	Corinth, MS Micro	34,825	758	Fort Valley, GA Micro	24,586	862
Alma, MI Micro	42,364	655	Owatonna, MN Micro	34,792	759	Wahpeton, ND-MN Micro	24,228	863
Duncan, OK Micro	42,283	656	Ada, OK Micro	34,750	760	West Helena, AR Micro	23,963	864
Mount Sterling, KY Micro	42,259	657	Newport, TN Micro	34,650	761	Fallon, NV Micro	23,837	865
Big Rapids, MI Micro	42,172	658	Monroe, WI Micro	34,590	762	City of The Dalles, OR Micro	23,713	866
Lewisburg, PA Micro	42,112	659	Batesville, AR Micro	34,587	763	Scottsburg, IN Micro	23,577	867
Rolla, MO Micro	41,948	660	Murray, KY Micro	34,578	764	Campbellsville, KY Micro	23,546	868
El Campo, TX Micro	41,908	661	Coffeyville, KS Micro	34,549	765	Liberal, KS Micro	23,545	869
Bemidji, MN Micro	41,851	662	Wabash, IN Micro	34,544	766	Tuskegee, AL Micro	23,451	870
Seymour, IN Micro	41,786	663	Easton, MD Micro	34,487	767	Arkadelphia, AR Micro	23,445	871
Minden, LA Micro	41,490	664	Chester, SC Micro	34,347	768	Beatrice, NE Micro	23,242	872
Safford, AZ Micro	41,410	665	Effingham, IL Micro	34,214	769	Pierre Part, LA Micro	23,194	873
Menomonie, WI Micro	41,383	666	Alexandria, MN Micro	34,196	770	Borger, TX Micro	23,086	874
Burley, ID Micro	41,373	667	Frankfort, IN Micro	34,020	771	Pampa, TX Micro	22,953	875
Wilmington, OH Micro	41,363	668	St. Marys, PA Micro	33,969	772	Dickinson, ND Micro	22,759	876
Jacksonville, IL Micro	41,267	669	Kill Devil Hills, NC Micro	33,644	773	Grenada, MS Micro	22,735	877
Rockland, ME Micro	41,261	670	Brookhaven, MS Micro	33,635	774	Levelland, TX Micro	22,487	878
Cambridge, OH Micro	41,118	671	De Ridder, LA Micro	33,586	775	Marshall, MO Micro	22,437	879
Lawrenceburg, TN Micro	41,045	672	Big Spring, TX Micro	33,585	776	Mitchell, SD Micro	22,352	880
Pullman, WA Micro	41,021	673	Decatur, IN Micro	33,479	777	Oskaloosa, IA Micro	22,116	881
Espanola, NM Micro	41,006	674	Angola, IN Micro	33,444	778	Parsons, KS Micro	21,927	882
Nogales, AZ Micro	40,937	675	Indianola, MS Micro	33,441	779	Cordele, GA Micro	21,895	883
Poplar Bluff, MO Micro	40,827	676	Stephenville, TX Micro	33,252	780	Sterling, CO Micro	21,889	884
Auburn, IN Micro	40,782	677	Arcadia, FL Micro	33,137	781	Spearfish, SD Micro	21,573	885
Willmar, MN Micro	40,756	678	Hope, AR Micro	33,116	782	Brookings, OR Micro	21,502	886
Celina, OH Micro	40,747	679	Camden, AR Micro	33,018	783	Maryville, MO Micro	21,479	887
Shelbyville, TN Micro	40,687	680	Butte-Silver Bow, MT Micro	32,969	784	Yankton, SD Micro	21,414	888
Alice, TX Micro	40,633	681	Lebanon, MO Micro	32,825	785	Jamestown, ND Micro	20,906	889
Logansport, IN Micro	40,495	682	Miami, OK Micro	32,774	786	Hood River, OR Micro	20,890	890
Centralia, IL Micro	40,466	683	Dodge City, KS Micro	32,760	787	Fairmont, MN Micro	20,875	891
Cedartown, GA Micro	40,292	684	Kennett, MO Micro	32,578	788	Prineville, OR Micro	20,716	892
La Follette, TN Micro	40,208	685	Macomb, IL Micro	32,469	789	Dumas, TX Micro	20,617	893
Rexburg, ID Micro	40,177	686	Beeville, TX Micro	32,399	790	Storm Lake, IA Micro	20,462	894
Sikeston, MO Micro	40,133	687	Iron Mountain, MI-WI Micro	32,365	791	Raymondville, TX Micro	20,292	895
Oxford, MS Micro	40,100	688	Madison, IN Micro	32,352	792	Guymon, OK Micro	20,193	896
Tifton, GA Micro	40,031	689	Sulphur Springs, TX Micro	32,316	793	Worthington, MN Micro	20,090	897
Union City, TN-KY Micro	39,749	690	Central City, KY Micro	31,663	794	Evanston, WY Micro	19,965	898
Berlin, NH-VT Micro	39,688	691	Kingsville, TX Micro	31,609	795	Pierre, SD Micro	19,823	899
Marshalltown, IA Micro	39,677	692	Albert Lea, MN Micro	31,606	796	Williston, ND Micro	19,637	900
Sedalia, MO Micro	39,580	693	Watertown, SD Micro	31,491	797	Price, UT Micro	19,501	901
Fort Dodge, IA Micro	39,522	694	Taos, NM Micro	31,483	798	Brownsville, TN Micro	19,449	902
Pontiac, IL Micro	39,476	695	Laramie, WY Micro	31,441	799	Los Alamos, NM Micro	18,796	903
Sault Ste. Marie, MI Micro	39,265	696	Paris, TN Micro	31,314	800	Woodward, OK Micro	18,472	904
Cornelia, GA Micro	39,258	697	Jennings, LA Micro	31,123	801	Bishop, CA Micro	18,287	905
Urbana, OH Micro	39,247	698	Brenham, TX Micro	31,043	802	Hereford, TX Micro	18,227	906
McMinnville, TN Micro	39,239	699	Dillon, SC Micro	31,009	803	Portales, NM Micro	18,191	907
Walterboro, SC Micro	39,197	700	Columbus, NE Micro	30,974	804	Spencer, IA Micro	16,839	908
Cleveland, MS Micro	39,154	701	Juneau, AK Micro	30,891	805	Spirit Lake, IA Micro	16,582	909
Defiance, OH Micro	39,140	702	Maysville, KY Micro	30,863	806	Atchison, KS Micro	16,551	910
Mountain Home, AR Micro	39,036	703	Alpena, MI Micro	30,711	807	Havre, MT Micro	16,248	911
Aberdeen, SD Micro	38,995	704	Middlesborough, KY Micro	30,447	808	Huron, SD Micro	16,240	912
Austin, MN Micro	38,876	705	Lincoln, IL Micro	30,268	809	Snyder, TX Micro	15,677	913
Garden City, KS Micro	38,868	706	Cambridge, MD Micro	30,238	810	Sweetwater, TX Micro	14,979	914
Gainesville, TX Micro	38,714	707	Bastrop, LA Micro	30,146	811	Lamesa, TX Micro	14,521	915
Huntington, IN Micro	38,592	708	Washington, IN Micro	30,020	812	Vernon, TX Micro	14,004	916
Emporia, KS Micro	38,581	709	Merrill, WI Micro	30,006	813	Kodiak, AK Micro	13,751	917
Paragould, AR Micro	38,537	710	Mountain Home, ID Micro	29,954	814	Ketchikan, AK Micro	13,346	918
Natchitoches, LA Micro	38,517	711	Clarksdale, MS Micro	29,871	815	Tallulah, AK Micro	13,089	919
Brownwood, TX Micro	38,511	712	Silver City, NM Micro	29,629	816	Andrews, TX Micro	13,026	920
Bay City, TX Micro	38,423	713	Brevard, NC Micro	29,587	817	Vermillion, SD Micro	12,893	921
Hastings, NE Micro	38,253	714	Troy, AL Micro	29,578	818	Pecos, TX Micro	12,169	922
Crawfordsville, IN Micro	38,216	715	Las Vegas, NM Micro	29,483	819			
Vincennes, IN Micro	38,204	716	Kirksville, MO Micro	29,266	820	CBSA Total	272,949,244	
Escanaba, MI Micro	38,158	717	Union, SC Micro	29,252	821	United States Total	292,936,668	
Selinsgrove, PA Micro	38,021	718	McPherson, KS Micro	29,221	822	CBSA (% of U. S. Total)	93.18	
Houghton, MI Micro	38,011	719	Van Wert, OH Micro	29,206	823			
Gillette, WY Micro	38,006	720	Mount Pleasant, TX Micro	28,982	824			
Pittsburg, KS Micro	37,774	721	Bennettsville, SC Micro	28,643	825			
Newberry, SC Micro	37,601	722	Brookings, SD Micro	28,625	826			

CBSA	POPULATION	RANK
New York-Newark-Edison, NY-NJ-PA Metro	2,385,135	1
Los Angeles-Long Beach-Santa Ana, CA Metro	1,297,685	2
Chicago-Naperville-Joliet, IL-IN-WI Metro	1,020,861	3
Miami-Fort Lauderdale-Miami Beach, FL Metro	859,686	4
Philadelphia-Camden-Wilmington, PA-NJ-DE-MD Metro	774,060	5
Boston-Cambridge-Quincy, MA-NH Metro	566,934	6
Detroit-Warren-Livonia, MI Metro	541,985	7
San Francisco-Oakland-Fremont, CA Metro	500,865	8
Washington-Arlington-Alexandria, DC-VA-MD-WV Metro	477,226	9
Tampa-St. Petersburg-Clearwater, FL Metro	468,201	10
Dallas-Fort Worth-Arlington, TX Metro	457,052	11
Phoenix-Mesa-Scottsdale, AZ Metro	428,944	12
Pittsburgh, PA Metro	424,992	13
Houston-Baytown-Sugar Land, TX Metro	414,592	14
Riverside-San Bernardino-Ontario, CA Metro	379,370	15
Atlanta-Sandy Springs-Marietta, GA Metro	371,595	16
St. Louis, MO-IL Metro	360,251	17
San Diego-Carlsbad-San Marcos, CA Metro	334,361	18
Seattle-Tacoma-Bellevue, WA Metro	325,927	19
Baltimore-Towson, MD Metro	318,255	20
Cleveland-Elyria-Mentor, OH Metro	313,227	21
Minneapolis-St. Paul-Bloomington, MN-WI Metro	303,887	22
Cincinnati-Middletown, OH-KY-IN Metro	242,262	23
Providence-New Bedford-Fall River, RI-MA Metro	231,968	24
Orlando, FL Metro	228,771	25
Sacramento-Arden-Arcade-Roseville, CA Metro	224,624	26
Kansas City, MO-KS Metro	221,360	27
Denver-Aurora, CO Metro	212,564	28
Portland-Vancouver-Beaverton, OR-WA Metro	210,782	29
San Antonio, TX Metro	200,352	30
Milwaukee-Waukesha-West Allis, WI Metro	190,773	31
Buffalo-Cheektowaga-Tonawanda, NY Metro	183,941	32
Las Vegas-Paradise, NV Metro	176,744	33
San Jose-Sunnyvale-Santa Clara, CA Metro	175,333	34
Sarasota-Bradenton-Venice, FL Metro	174,791	35
Virginia Beach-Norfolk-Newport News, VA-NC Metro	172,790	36
Columbus, OH Metro	170,970	37
Indianapolis, IN Metro	170,929	38
Hartford-West Hartford-East Hartford, CT Metro	164,983	39
New Orleans-Metairie-Kenner, LA Metro	152,337	40
Louisville, KY-IN Metro	148,489	41
Nashville-Davidson-Murfreesboro, TN Metro	143,305	42
Charlotte-Gastonia-Concord, NC-SC Metro	142,787	43
Birmingham-Hoover, AL Metro	138,594	44
Rochester, NY Metro	136,435	45
Jacksonville, FL Metro	135,337	46
Oklahoma City, OK Metro	131,915	47
Richmond, VA Metro	131,163	48
Tucson, AZ Metro	130,758	49
Honolulu, HI Metro	125,746	50
Memphis, TN-MS-AR Metro	125,545	51
Cape Coral-Fort Myers, FL Metro	121,746	52
New Haven-Milford, CT Metro	121,006	53
Bridgeport-Stamford-Norwalk, CT Metro	120,988	54
Allentown-Bethlehem-Easton, PA-NJ Metro	119,260	55
Albany-Schenectady-Troy, NY Metro	116,783	56
Dayton, OH Metro	115,892	57
Tulsa, OK Metro	108,627	58
Austin-Round Rock, TX Metro	105,831	59
Scranton-Wilkes-Barre, PA Metro	104,503	60
Palm Bay-Melbourne-Titusville, FL Metro	102,139	61
Deltona-Daytona Beach-Ormond Beach, FL Metro	101,898	62
Youngstown-Warren-Boardman, OH-PA Metro	101,769	63
Worcester, MA Metro	99,636	64
Akron, OH Metro	95,315	65
Springfield, MA Metro	94,468	66
Lakeland-Winter Haven, FL Metro	92,029	67
Albuquerque, NM Metro	89,851	68
Omaha-Council Bluffs, NE-IA Metro	88,542	69
Knoxville, TN Metro	87,888	70
Syracuse, NY Metro	87,087	71
Toledo, OH Metro	84,921	72
Port St. Lucie-Fort Pierce, FL Metro	84,741	73
Fresno, CA Metro	84,593	74
Oxnard-Thousand Oaks-Ventura, CA Metro	83,672	75
Salt Lake City, UT Metro	83,138	76
Greensboro-High Point, NC Metro	83,045	77
Grand Rapids-Wyoming, MI Metro	81,967	78
Harrisburg-Carlisle, PA Metro	75,508	79
Little Rock-North Little Rock, AR Metro	73,263	80
Columbia, SC Metro	73,131	81
Poughkeepsie-Newburgh-Middletown, NY Metro	73,109	82
El Paso, TX Metro	72,894	83
Raleigh-Cary, NC Metro	72,291	84
Baton Rouge, LA Metro	71,591	85
Naples-Marco Island, FL Metro	71,362	86
Wichita, KS Metro	71,080	87
Greenville, SC Metro	70,609	88
Lancaster, PA Metro	69,053	89
Ocala, FL Metro	68,917	90
Portland-South Portland, ME Metro	68,779	91
Asheville, NC Metro	67,813	92
Bakersfield, CA Metro	67,142	93
Chattanooga, TN-GA Metro	66,791	94
Stockton, CA Metro	64,635	95
McAllen-Edinburg-Pharr, TX Metro	62,169	96
Canton-Massillon, OH Metro	61,471	97
Charleston-North Charleston, SC Metro	61,333	98
Santa Rosa-Petaluma, CA Metro	60,413	99
Des Moines, IA Metro	58,455	100
Reading, PA Metro	57,994	101
Augusta-Richmond County, GA-SC Metro	57,792	102
Winston-Salem, NC Metro	57,180	103
Pensacola-Ferry Pass-Brent, FL Metro	56,415	104
Jackson, MS Metro	55,684	105
York-Hanover, PA Metro	54,279	106
Peoria, IL Metro	54,274	107
Barnstable Town, MA Metro	54,009	108
Spokane, WA Metro	53,878	109
Madison, WI Metro	53,555	110
Flint, MI Metro	53,403	111
Davenport-Moline-Rock Island, IA-IL Metro	52,422	112
Santa Barbara-Santa Maria-Goleta, CA Metro	52,405	113
Punta Gorda, FL Metro	52,138	114
Boise City-Nampa, ID Metro	51,849	115
Beaumont-Port Arthur, TX Metro	51,616	116
Springfield, MO Metro	51,313	117
Colorado Springs, CO Metro	51,043	118
Modesto, CA Metro	51,007	119
Shreveport-Bossier City, LA Metro	49,825	120
Corpus Christi, TX Metro	48,958	121
Evansville, IN-KY Metro	48,956	122
Mobile, AL Metro	48,806	123
Utica-Rome, NY Metro	48,698	124
Lansing-East Lansing, MI Metro	47,523	125
Fort Wayne, IN Metro	47,188	126
Charleston, WV Metro	47,100	127
Durham, NC Metro	46,948	128
Hickory-Morganton-Lenoir, NC Metro	46,063	129
Roanoke, VA Metro	45,972	130
Fayetteville-Springdale-Rogers, AR-MO Metro	45,917	131
Trenton-Ewing, NJ Metro	45,820	132
Salem, OR Metro	45,497	133
Eugene-Springfield, OR Metro	44,509	134
Huntington-Ashland, WV-KY-OH Metro	44,386	135
Lexington-Fayette, KY Metro	44,190	136
South Bend-Mishawaka, IN-MI Metro	43,369	137
Duluth, MN-WI Metro	42,987	138
Manchester-Nashua, NH Metro	42,733	139
Wilmington, NC Metro	42,493	140
Ogden-Clearfield, UT Metro	42,339	141
Salinas, CA Metro	42,203	142
Huntsville, AL Metro	41,781	143
Vallejo-Fairfield, CA Metro	41,423	144
Rockford, IL Metro	41,384	145
Montgomery, AL Metro	41,288	146
Prescott, AZ Metro	41,105	147
Brownsville-Harlingen, TX Metro	40,796	148
Reno-Sparks, NV Metro	40,659	149
Erie, PA Metro	40,424	150
Homosassa Springs, FL Micro	40,072	151
Binghamton, NY Metro	39,906	152
Kalamazoo-Portage, MI Metro	38,019	153
Visalia-Porterville, CA Metro	37,902	154
San Luis Obispo-Paso Robles, CA Metro	37,506	155
Kingsport-Bristol, TN-VA Metro	37,254	156
Fort Smith, AR-OK Metro	37,038	157
Atlantic City, NJ Metro	35,931	158
Lake Havasu City-Kingman, AZ Micro	35,821	159
Savannah, GA Metro	35,711	160
Norwich-New London, CT Metro	34,734	161
Vero Beach, FL Metro	34,571	162
Lynchburg, VA Metro	34,381	163
Green Bay, WI Metro	34,027	164
Spartanburg, SC Metro	33,488	165
Columbus, GA-AL Metro	33,084	166
Chico, CA Metro	32,724	167
Myrtle Beach-Conway-North Myrtle Beach, SC Metro	32,522	168
Seaford, DE Micro	32,198	169
Cedar Rapids, IA Metro	31,984	170
Topeka, KS Metro	31,888	171
Tallahassee, FL Metro	31,715	172
Hagerstown-Martinsburg, MD-WV Metro	31,370	173
Medford, OR Metro	30,663	174
Killeen-Temple-Fort Hood, TX Metro	30,596	175
Gulfport-Biloxi, MS Metro	30,314	176
Yuma, AZ Metro	30,148	177
Lincoln, NE Metro	29,937	178
Lubbock, TX Metro	29,378	179
Sebring, FL Micro	29,227	180
Johnstown, PA Metro	29,195	181
Saginaw-Saginaw Township North, MI Metro	29,157	182
Pottsville, PA Micro	29,047	183
Amarillo, TX Metro	28,960	184
Ann Arbor, MI Metro	28,824	185
Fayetteville, NC Metro	28,741	186
Longview, TX Metro	28,510	187
Waco, TX Metro	28,431	188
Johnson City, TN Metro	27,837	189
Springfield, IL Metro	27,640	190
Provo-Orem, UT Metro	27,397	191
Macon, GA Metro	27,220	192
Torrington, CT Micro	26,819	193
Tyler, TX Metro	26,756	194
Wheeling, WV-OH Metro	26,634	195
Redding, CA Metro	26,390	196
Bremerton-Silverdale, WA Metro	26,343	197
Fort Collins-Loveland, CO Metro	26,325	198
Holland-Grand Haven, MI Metro	26,017	199
Santa Cruz-Watsonville, CA Metro	25,831	200
Yakima, WA Metro	25,694	201
Ottawa-Streator, IL Micro	25,407	202
Olympia, WA Metro	25,382	203
Parkersburg-Marietta, WV-OH Metro	25,247	204
Gainesville, FL Metro	25,032	205
Lafayette, LA Metro	24,685	206
Lebanon, NH-VT Micro	24,618	207
Terre Haute, IN Metro	24,381	208
Daphne-Fairhope, AL Micro	24,295	209
Hilton Head Island-Beaufort, SC Micro	24,280	210
Anderson, SC Metro	24,083	211
Kingston, NY Metro	24,078	212
Florence, SC Metro	24,060	213
Waterloo-Cedar Falls, IA Metro	23,995	214
Weirton-Steubenville, WV-OH Metro	23,933	215
Champaign-Urbana, IL Metro	23,866	216
Racine, WI Metro	23,815	217
Pittsfield, MA Metro	23,803	218
Appleton, WI Metro	23,631	219
Niles-Benton Harbor, MI Metro	23,629	220
Lake Charles, LA Metro	23,617	221
Fort Walton Beach-Crestview-Destin, FL Metro	23,276	222
Sioux Falls, SD Metro	22,865	223
Tuscaloosa, AL Metro	22,840	224
Clarksville, TN-KY Metro	22,761	225
Boulder, CO Metro	22,740	226
Joplin, MO Metro	22,478	227
Altoona, PA Metro	22,391	228
Pueblo, CO Metro	22,370	229
Florence, AL Metro	22,292	230
Charlottesville, VA Metro	22,266	231
Muskegon-Norton Shores, MI Metro	22,062	232
Jamestown-Dunkirk-Fredonia, NY Micro	22,007	233
Chambersburg, PA Micro	21,875	234
Anchorage, AK Metro	21,859	235
Hilo, HI Micro	21,703	236
Houma-Bayou Cane-Thibodaux, LA Metro	21,651	237
Monroe, LA Metro	21,434	238
Merced, CA Metro	21,367	239
Abilene, TX Metro	21,297	240
Panama City-Lynn Haven, FL Metro	21,280	241
Burlington-South Burlington, VT Metro	21,069	242
Bellingham, WA Metro	21,055	243
Springfield, OH Metro	21,025	244
Jackson, MI Metro	20,955	245
Kennewick-Richland-Pasco, WA Metro	20,727	246
Elkhart-Goshen, IN Metro	20,719	247
Ocean City, NJ Metro	20,611	248
Traverse City, MI Micro	20,578	249
Las Cruces, NM Metro	20,412	250
Rochester, MN Metro	20,317	251
Lexington-Thomasville, NC Micro	20,276	252
Oshkosh-Neenah, WI Metro	20,268	253
Wichita Falls, TX Metro	20,259	254
Lebanon, PA Metro	20,135	255
Anderson, IN Metro	20,094	256
Eau Claire, WI Metro	20,065	257
Bloomington, IN Metro	19,919	258
Janesville, WI Metro	19,918	259
Billings, MT Metro	19,809	260
Napa, CA Metro	19,780	261
Bangor, ME Metro	19,615	262
Burlington, NC Metro	19,530	263
St. Cloud, MN Metro	19,505	264
Fargo, ND-MN Metro	19,436	265
Dothan, AL Metro	19,435	266
Grand Junction, CO Metro	19,226	267
Williamsport, PA Metro	19,212	268
Vineland-Millville-Bridgeton, NJ Metro	19,207	269
Hot Springs, AR Metro	19,163	270
Alexandria, LA Metro	19,156	271
Sierra Vista-Douglas, AZ Micro	19,118	272
Battle Creek, MI Metro	19,097	273
Salisbury, NC Micro	18,768	274
East Stroudsburg, PA Micro	18,744	275
Greeley, CO Metro	18,669	276
Roseburg, OR Micro	18,606	277
Mansfield, OH Metro	18,564	278
Decatur, AL Metro	18,540	279
Sioux City, IA-NE-SD Metro	18,533	280
Glens Falls, NY Metro	18,471	281
Rocky Mount, NC Metro	18,364	282
Lafayette, IN Metro	18,321	283
Danville, VA Metro	18,280	284
New Castle, PA Micro	18,166	285
St. Joseph, MO-KS Metro	18,099	286
St. George, UT Metro	18,071	287
Albany, GA Metro	18,007	288
Texarkana, TX-Texarkana, AR Metro	17,949	289
Bluefield, WV-VA Micro	17,820	290
Sunbury, PA Micro	17,786	291
Concord, NH Micro	17,641	292
Southern Pines, NC Micro	17,608	293
Bend, OR Metro	17,446	294
Sherman-Denison, TX Metro	17,405	295
Cumberland, MD-WV Metro	17,326	296
Yuba City-Marysville, CA Metro	17,290	297
Blacksburg-Christiansburg-Radford, VA Metro	17,236	298
Palm Coast, FL Micro	17,191	299
Monroe, MI Metro	17,187	300
Morristown, TN Metro	17,083	301
East Liverpool-Salem, OH Micro	17,081	302
Decatur, IL Metro	17,075	303
Laredo, TX Metro	17,058	304
Jefferson City, MO Metro	17,011	305
New Bern, NC Micro	16,995	306
La Crosse, WI-MN Metro	16,983	307
Augusta-Waterville, ME Micro	16,979	308

CBSA	POPULATION	RANK	CBSA	POPULATION	RANK	CBSA	POPULATION	RANK
Pascagoula, MS Metro	16,918	309	Beaver Dam, WI Micro	12,170	413	Harriman, TN Micro	8,781	517
Wausau, WI Metro	16,904	310	Marinette, WI-MI Micro	12,168	414	Batavia, NY Micro	8,767	518
College Station-Bryan, TX Metro	16,844	311	Bowling Green, KY Metro	12,013	415	Salina, KS Micro	8,723	519
Staunton-Waynesboro, VA Micro	16,789	312	Martinsville, VA Micro	11,959	416	Casper, WY Metro	8,720	520
Gadsden, AL Metro	16,683	313	Twin Falls, ID Micro	11,945	417	New Iberia, LA Micro	8,660	521
The Villages, FL Micro	16,640	314	Grand Forks, ND-MN Metro	11,923	418	Lawrence, KS Metro	8,649	522
Statesville-Mooresville, NC Micro	16,606	315	Wisconsin Rapids-Marshfield, WI Micro	11,908	419	Charleston-Mattoon, IL Micro	8,630	523
Bay City, MI Metro	16,428	316	Bristol, VA Metro	11,891	420	Logan, UT-ID Metro	8,582	524
Truckee-Grass Valley, CA Micro	16,357	317	Opelousas-Eunice, LA Micro	11,877	421	Lexington Park, MD Micro	8,561	525
Anniston-Oxford, AL Metro	16,183	318	Auburn, NY Micro	11,854	422	Lake City, FL Micro	8,560	526
Muncie, IN Metro	16,124	319	Ukiah, CA Micro	11,854	423	Corvallis, OR Metro	8,529	527
Eureka-Arcata-Fortuna, CA Micro	16,057	320	Elizabethtown, KY Metro	11,796	424	Albemarle, NC Micro	8,527	528
Athens-Clarke County, GA Metro	16,006	321	Warner Robins, GA Metro	11,787	425	Kapaa, HI Micro	8,500	529
Dover, DE Metro	16,000	322	Farmington, NM Metro	11,773	426	Farmington, MO Micro	8,497	530
Greenville, NC Metro	15,980	323	Laurel, MS Micro	11,759	427	Carson City, NV Metro	8,478	531
Sheboygan, WI Metro	15,866	324	Portsmouth, OH Micro	11,698	428	Baraboo, WI Micro	8,441	532
Grants Pass, OR Micro	15,858	325	Cullman, AL Micro	11,679	429	Shelton, WA Micro	8,429	533
Tupelo, MS Micro	15,853	326	Key West-Marathon, FL Micro	11,659	430	Walla Walla, WA Micro	8,417	534
Kahului-Wailuku, HI Micro	15,836	327	Lawton, OK Metro	11,652	431	Point Pleasant, WV-OH Micro	8,393	535
Mount Vernon-Anacortes, WA Metro	15,833	328	Great Falls, MT Metro	11,520	432	Natchez, MS-LA Micro	8,384	536
Santa Fe, NM Metro	15,731	329	Mount Airy, NC Micro	11,446	433	Burlington, IA-IL Micro	8,277	537
Paducah, KY-IL Micro	15,695	330	Kerrville, TX Micro	11,335	434	Elizabeth City, NC Micro	8,256	538
El Centro, CA Metro	15,525	331	Hammond, LA Metro	11,246	435	Tiffin-Fostoria, OH Micro	8,240	539
Albany-Lebanon, OR Micro	15,418	332	Seneca, SC Micro	11,237	436	Lincolnton, NC Micro	8,231	540
Meridian, MS Metro	15,392	333	Idaho Falls, ID Metro	11,189	437	Frankfort, KY Micro	8,212	541
Owensboro, KY Metro	15,378	334	Centralia, WA Micro	11,187	438	Greenville, OH Micro	8,175	542
Bloomington-Normal, IL Metro	15,292	335	Marion, IN Metro	11,136	439	Ames, IA Metro	8,165	543
Lima, OH Metro	15,244	336	Richmond, IN Micro	11,117	440	Marshall, TX Micro	8,162	544
Lewiston-Auburn, ME Metro	15,187	337	Fergus Falls, MN Micro	11,087	441	Sturgis, MI Micro	8,135	545
Coeur d'Alene, ID Metro	15,130	338	Clearlake, CA Micro	11,027	442	Lewistown, PA Micro	8,102	546
Michigan City-La Porte, IN Metro	15,057	339	Jacksonville, NC Metro	10,927	443	Helena, MT Micro	8,050	547
State College, PA Metro	15,036	340	Talladega-Sylacauga, AL Micro	10,867	444	Freeport, IL Micro	8,030	548
Victoria, TX Metro	14,951	341	Oak Harbor, WA Micro	10,849	445	Ponca City, OK Micro	8,003	549
Brainerd, MN Micro	14,932	342	Crossville, TN Micro	10,846	446	Alamogordo, NM Micro	7,858	550
Ashtabula, OH Micro	14,893	343	Payson, AZ Micro	10,745	447	Platteville, WI Micro	7,828	551
Gainesville, GA Metro	14,854	344	Muskogee, OK Micro	10,710	448	Lancaster, SC Micro	7,811	552
Corning, NY Micro	14,835	345	Morehead City, NC Micro	10,679	449	Clinton, IA Micro	7,793	553
Madera, CA Metro	14,808	346	Lufkin, TX Micro	10,672	450	Oak Hill, WV Micro	7,760	554
Clarksburg, WV Micro	14,805	347	Russellville, AR Micro	10,665	451	Paris, TX Micro	7,743	555
Salisbury, MD Metro	14,788	348	Keene, NH Micro	10,577	452	Mount Vernon, IL Micro	7,724	556
Ogdensburg-Massena, NY Micro	14,719	349	Hudson, NY Micro	10,576	453	Duncan, OK Micro	7,711	557
Tullahoma, TN Micro	14,659	350	Midland, MI Metro	10,543	454	Mount Vernon, OH Micro	7,702	558
Somerset, PA Micro	14,623	351	Kalispell, MT Micro	10,536	455	Barre, VT Micro	7,696	559
San Angelo, TX Metro	14,529	352	Aberdeen, WA Micro	10,440	456	McComb, MS Micro	7,683	560
DuBois, PA Micro	14,505	353	Hutchinson, KS Micro	10,431	457	Stevens Point, WI Micro	7,680	561
Port Angeles, WA Micro	14,451	354	Mountain Home, AR Micro	10,398	458	Scottsboro, AL Micro	7,670	562
Midland, TX Metro	14,442	355	Forest City, NC Micro	10,356	459	Dublin, GA Micro	7,593	563
Wooster, OH Metro	14,338	356	Missoula, MT Metro	10,304	460	Waycross, GA Micro	7,563	564
Fond du Lac, WI Metro	14,314	357	Marion-Herrin, IL Micro	10,286	461	McAlester, OK Micro	7,559	565
Athens, TX Metro	14,288	358	Dunn, NC Micro	10,280	462	Stillwater, OK Micro	7,559	566
Kokomo, IN Metro	14,225	359	Sevierville, TN Micro	10,243	463	New Castle, IN Micro	7,552	567
Columbia, MO Metro	14,192	360	Mankato-North Mankato, MN Micro	10,232	464	Carlsbad-Artesia, NM Micro	7,532	568
Meadville, PA Micro	14,046	361	Phoenix Lake-Cedar Ridge, CA Micro	10,223	465	Norwalk, OH Micro	7,496	569
Elmira, NY Metro	14,018	362	Hanford-Corcoran, CA Metro	10,191	466	Abbeville, LA Micro	7,494	570
Hattiesburg, MS Metro	13,999	363	Pendleton-Hermiston, OR Micro	10,141	467	Austin, MN Micro	7,468	571
Winchester, VA-WV Metro	13,999	364	Ocean Pines, MD Micro	10,136	468	LaGrange, GA Micro	7,443	572
Rapid City, SD Metro	13,912	365	Sayre, PA Micro	10,098	469	Glasgow, KY Micro	7,440	573
Wenatchee, WA Metro	13,909	366	Auburn-Opelika, AL Metro	10,083	470	Ashland, OH Micro	7,432	574
Willimantic, CT Micro	13,878	367	Fairmont, WV Micro	10,079	471	Ruston, LA Micro	7,421	575
Jonesboro, AR Metro	13,873	368	Grand Island, NE Micro	9,961	472	Norfolk, NE Micro	7,420	576
New Philadelphia-Dover, OH Micro	13,871	369	Plattsburgh, NY Micro	9,961	473	Bradford, PA Micro	7,418	577
Odessa, TX Metro	13,847	370	Cheyenne, WY Metro	9,941	474	Nacogdoches, TX Micro	7,410	578
Kankakee-Bradley, IL Metro	13,831	371	Greeneville, TN Micro	9,892	475	Washington, NC Micro	7,382	579
Jackson, TN Metro	13,817	372	Klamath Falls, OR Micro	9,888	476	Athens, TN Micro	7,371	580
Cookeville, TN Micro	13,662	373	Richmond, KY Micro	9,878	477	Crowley, LA Micro	7,344	581
Cleveland, TN Metro	13,610	374	Sterling, IL Micro	9,863	478	Harrison, AR Micro	7,326	582
Gettysburg, PA Micro	13,580	375	Wilson, NC Micro	9,849	479	Pahrump, NV Micro	7,270	583
Quincy, IL-MO Micro	13,575	376	Lewiston, ID-WA Metro	9,778	480	Jasper, IN Micro	7,259	584
Shelby, NC Micro	13,553	377	Searcy, AR Micro	9,776	481	Keokuk-Fort Madison, IA-MO Micro	7,259	585
Pine Bluff, AR Metro	13,539	378	Manhattan, KS Metro	9,761	482	Jacksonville, TX Micro	7,250	586
Harrisonburg, VA Metro	13,517	379	Ithaca, NY Metro	9,758	483	El Dorado, AR Micro	7,237	587
Goldsboro, NC Metro	13,488	380	North Wilkesboro, NC Micro	9,710	484	Warren, PA Micro	7,231	588
Morgantown, WV Metro	13,443	381	Findlay, OH Micro	9,678	485	Bucyrus, OH Micro	7,187	589
Dubuque, IA Metro	13,317	382	Oil City, PA Micro	9,567	486	Ontario, OR-ID Micro	7,179	590
Bloomsburg-Berwick, PA Micro	13,310	383	Watertown-Fort Atkinson, WI Micro	9,529	487	Easton, MD Micro	7,171	591
Danville, IL Metro	13,236	384	Rutland, VT Micro	9,504	488	Columbus, MS Micro	7,170	592
Bismarck, ND Metro	13,228	385	Flagstaff, AZ Metro	9,497	489	Gardnerville Ranchos, NV Micro	7,162	593
Indiana, PA Micro	13,133	386	Greenwood, SC Micro	9,493	490	Danville, KY Micro	7,150	594
Palatka, FL Micro	13,091	387	Georgetown, SC Micro	9,451	491	Berlin, NH-VT Micro	7,132	595
Cape Girardeau-Jackson, MO-IL Micro	13,038	388	Mason City, IA Micro	9,427	492	Muscatine, IA Micro	7,119	596
Rome, GA Metro	13,037	389	Granbury, TX Micro	9,394	493	Rockland, ME Micro	7,088	597
Brunswick, GA Metro	13,007	390	Shawnee, OK Micro	9,323	494	Madisonville, KY Micro	6,986	598
Adrian, MI Micro	12,912	391	Amsterdam, NY Micro	9,293	495	Greenville, MS Micro	6,984	599
Manitowoc, WI Micro	12,902	392	Laconia, NH Micro	9,271	496	Bedford, IN Micro	6,978	600
Sandusky, OH Metro	12,873	393	Minot, ND Micro	9,257	497	Rochelle, IL Micro	6,976	601
Lumberton, NC Micro	12,832	394	Enid, OK Micro	9,255	498	Hobbs, NM Micro	6,959	602
Longview-Kelso, WA Metro	12,784	395	Chillicothe, OH Micro	9,245	499	Huntingdon, PA Micro	6,904	603
Branson, MO Micro	12,723	396	Oneonta, NY Micro	9,223	500	Fort Dodge, IA Micro	6,876	604
Dalton, GA Metro	12,695	397	Warsaw, IN Micro	9,205	501	Faribault-Northfield, MN Micro	6,867	605
Iowa City, IA Metro	12,688	398	Moses Lake, WA Micro	9,128	502	Canton, IL Micro	6,864	606
Whitewater, WI Micro	12,591	399	Somerset, KY Micro	9,048	503	Gaffney, SC Micro	6,861	607
Galesburg, IL Micro	12,536	400	Red Bluff, CA Micro	9,035	504	Centralia, IL Micro	6,844	608
Allegan, MI Micro	12,469	401	Ardmore, OK Micro	9,022	505	Wapakoneta, OH Micro	6,844	609
Zanesville, OH Micro	12,464	402	Columbia, TN Micro	9,003	506	Poplar Bluff, MO Micro	6,843	610
Valdosta, GA Metro	12,411	403	Gloversville, NY Micro	8,983	507	Canon City, CO Micro	6,787	611
Roanoke Rapids, NC Micro	12,403	404	Columbus, IN Metro	8,948	508	Cadillac, MI Micro	6,776	612
Sumter, SC Metro	12,399	405	Owosso, MI Micro	8,915	509	Minden, LA Micro	6,752	613
Watertown-Fort Drum, NY Micro	12,396	406	Fremont, OH Micro	8,910	510	Picayune, MS Micro	6,717	614
Enterprise-Ozark, AL Micro	12,373	407	Marion, OH Micro	8,891	511	Aberdeen, SD Micro	6,685	615
Orangeburg, SC Micro	12,296	408	Kinston, NC Micro	8,888	512	Red Wing, MN Micro	6,661	616
Olean, NY Micro	12,240	409	Marquette, MI Micro	8,850	513	Escanaba, MI Micro	6,624	617
Beckley, WV Micro	12,223	410	Roswell, NM Micro	8,842	514	Corsicana, TX Micro	6,587	618
Albertville, AL Micro	12,191	411	Pocatello, ID Metro	8,808	515	Carbondale, IL Micro	6,572	619
Coos Bay, OR Micro	12,182	412	Bartlesville, OK Micro	8,796	516	London, KY Micro	6,571	620

CBSA	POPULATION	RANK
Scottsbluff, NE Micro	6,556	621
Jacksonville, IL Micro	6,539	622
Sanford, NC Micro	6,521	623
Rockingham, NC Micro	6,514	624
Bellefontaine, OH Micro	6,481	625
Brevard, NC Micro	6,476	626
Winona, MN Micro	6,437	627
Marshalltown, IA Micro	6,410	628
Lock Haven, PA Micro	6,402	629
West Plains, MO Micro	6,389	630
Malone, NY Micro	6,382	631
Bennington, VT Micro	6,366	632
Bozeman, MT Micro	6,340	633
La Follette, TN Micro	6,319	634
Union City, TN-KY Micro	6,315	635
Ottumwa, IA Micro	6,311	636
Fremont, NE Micro	6,294	637
Bogalusa, LA Micro	6,288	638
Coffeyville, KS Micro	6,285	639
Selma, AL Micro	6,279	640
Coldwater, MI Micro	6,237	641
Brownwood, TX Micro	6,224	642
Palestine, TX Micro	6,219	643
Blytheville, AR Micro	6,216	644
Kearney, NE Micro	6,208	645
Willmar, MN Micro	6,200	646
Sedalia, MO Micro	6,175	647
Plymouth, IN Micro	6,146	648
Hastings, NE Micro	6,116	649
Alexandria, MN Micro	6,112	650
Mount Pleasant, MI Micro	6,112	651
Cortland, NY Micro	6,074	652
Lawrenceburg, TN Micro	6,049	653
Morgan City, LA Micro	6,049	654
Taylorville, IL Micro	6,040	655
Milledgeville, GA Micro	6,038	656
Okeechobee, FL Micro	6,015	657
Albert Lea, MN Micro	6,012	658
Celina, OH Micro	6,005	659
Athens, OH Micro	6,004	660
St. Marys, PA Micro	5,992	661
Hannibal, MO Micro	5,965	662
Arcadia, FL Micro	5,962	663
Cambridge, OH Micro	5,955	664
Newton, IA Micro	5,947	665
Pontiac, IL Micro	5,947	666
Thomasville, GA Micro	5,943	667
Mayfield, KY Micro	5,933	668
Sidney, OH Micro	5,918	669
Huntsville, TX Micro	5,910	670
Logansport, IN Micro	5,909	671
El Campo, TX Micro	5,865	672
Alma, MI Micro	5,852	673
Valley, AL Micro	5,848	674
Iron Mountain, MI-WI Micro	5,837	675
Vicksburg, MS Micro	5,824	676
Vincennes, IN Micro	5,811	677
Winfield, KS Micro	5,801	678
Rolla, MO Micro	5,798	679
Astoria, OR Micro	5,726	680
Durant, OK Micro	5,724	681
Greenwood, MS Micro	5,722	682
Houghton, MI Micro	5,715	683
Lewisburg, PA Micro	5,702	684
Del Rio, TX Micro	5,699	685
Seymour, IN Micro	5,674	686
Brookings, OR Micro	5,667	687
Paris, TN Micro	5,661	688
Big Rapids, MI Micro	5,654	689
Gainesville, TX Micro	5,634	690
Statesboro, GA Micro	5,627	691
Pittsburg, KS Micro	5,617	692
Wabash, IN Micro	5,608	693
McMinnville, TN Micro	5,601	694
Henderson, NC Micro	5,599	695
North Platte, NE Micro	5,590	696
Mount Sterling, KY Micro	5,583	697
Miami, OK Micro	5,569	698
Burley, ID Micro	5,547	699
Montrose, CO Micro	5,547	700
Camden, AR Micro	5,545	701
Cornelia, GA Micro	5,545	702
Huntington, IN Micro	5,526	703
Sikeston, MO Micro	5,509	704
Newberry, SC Micro	5,503	705
Alpena, MI Micro	5,498	706
Gallup, NM Micro	5,471	707
Butte-Silver Bow, MT Micro	5,427	708
Selinsgrove, PA Micro	5,398	709
Kennett, MO Micro	5,393	710
Moultrie, GA Micro	5,392	711
Coshocton, OH Micro	5,385	712
Tahlequah, OK Micro	5,375	713
Paragould, AR Micro	5,359	714
Crawfordsville, IN Micro	5,352	715
Cambridge, MD Micro	5,331	716
Clovis, NM Micro	5,322	717
Dixon, IL Micro	5,306	718
Kendallville, IN Micro	5,284	719
Brenham, TX Micro	5,240	720
Cedartown, GA Micro	5,230	721
Defiance, OH Micro	5,218	722
Silver City, NM Micro	5,189	723
Corinth, MS Micro	5,184	724
Murray, KY Micro	5,181	725
Seneca Falls, NY Micro	5,143	726
Batesville, AR Micro	5,131	727
Ada, OK Micro	5,126	728
McPherson, KS Micro	5,118	729
Rio Grande City, TX Micro	5,105	730
Calhoun, GA Micro	5,103	731
Alice, TX Micro	5,097	732
Monroe, WI Micro	5,087	733
Walterboro, SC Micro	5,081	734
Shelbyville, TN Micro	5,078	735
Urbana, OH Micro	5,043	736
Wilmington, OH Micro	5,036	737
Eagle Pass, TX Micro	5,029	738
Riverton, WY Micro	5,023	739
Sault Ste. Marie, MI Micro	5,010	740
Dyersburg, TN Micro	4,999	741
Merrill, WI Micro	4,986	742
Hutchinson, MN Micro	4,981	743
Central City, KY Micro	4,966	744
Newport, TN Micro	4,941	745
Bay City, TX Micro	4,916	746
Great Bend, KS Micro	4,905	747
Frankfort, IN Micro	4,878	748
Harrisburg, IL Micro	4,872	749
Sulphur Springs, TX Micro	4,871	750
Bemidji, MN Micro	4,861	751
Brigham City, UT Micro	4,852	752
Union, SC Micro	4,838	753
Warrensburg, MO Micro	4,836	754
Plainview, TX Micro	4,833	755
Safford, AZ Micro	4,832	756
Hope, AR Micro	4,826	757
Deming, NM Micro	4,803	758
Big Spring, TX Micro	4,798	759
Effingham, IL Micro	4,783	760
Boone, NC Micro	4,780	761
Tifton, GA Micro	4,775	762
Lebanon, MO Micro	4,750	763
Espanola, NM Micro	4,733	764
Corbin, KY Micro	4,730	765
Auburn, IN Micro	4,727	766
Watertown, SD Micro	4,713	767
Emporia, KS Micro	4,695	768
Peru, IN Micro	4,683	769
Brookhaven, MS Micro	4,665	770
Owatonna, MN Micro	4,623	771
Bastrop, LA Micro	4,618	772
Kill Devil Hills, NC Micro	4,617	773
Blackfoot, ID Micro	4,615	774
New Ulm, MN Micro	4,611	775
Natchitoches, LA Micro	4,606	776
Americus, GA Micro	4,605	777
Douglas, GA Micro	4,597	778
Macomb, IL Micro	4,596	779
Durango, CO Micro	4,590	780
Stephenville, TX Micro	4,586	781
Menomonie, WI Micro	4,567	782
Fairbanks, AK Metro	4,556	783
Van Wert, OH Micro	4,554	784
Mineral Wells, TX Micro	4,552	785
Nogales, AZ Micro	4,544	786
Decatur, IN Micro	4,518	787
Lincoln, IL Micro	4,492	788
Chester, SC Micro	4,487	789
Maysville, KY Micro	4,383	790
Washington, IN Micro	4,370	791
Beatrice, NE Micro	4,330	792
Cleveland, MS Micro	4,295	793
Madison, IN Micro	4,246	794
Middlesborough, KY Micro	4,239	795
Fort Polk South, LA Micro	4,234	796
Ellensburg, WA Micro	4,222	797
Mexico, MO Micro	4,216	798
Sheridan, WY Micro	4,209	799
Jennings, LA Micro	4,206	800
Laurinburg, NC Micro	4,187	801
Boone, IA Micro	4,183	802
Fairmont, MN Micro	4,167	803
Taos, NM Micro	4,153	804
Pampa, TX Micro	4,123	805
Thomaston, GA Micro	4,115	806
Toccoa, GA Micro	4,094	807
De Ridder, LA Micro	4,091	808
Washington, OH Micro	4,086	809
Columbus, NE Micro	4,078	810
City of The Dalles, OR Micro	4,073	811
Oxford, MS Micro	4,070	812
Angola, IN Micro	4,019	813
Connersville, IN Micro	3,999	814
Magnolia, AR Micro	3,944	815
Hays, KS Micro	3,922	816
Lexington, NE Micro	3,899	817
Kirksville, MO Micro	3,872	818
Pullman, WA Micro	3,863	819
Wauchula, FL Micro	3,809	820
Parsons, KS Micro	3,805	821
Starkville, MS Micro	3,803	822
Bainbridge, GA Micro	3,798	823
Jamestown, ND Micro	3,797	824
Fitzgerald, GA Micro	3,795	825
Wahpeton, ND-MN Micro	3,795	826
Summerville, GA Micro	3,783	827
Troy, AL Micro	3,776	828
Clewiston, FL Micro	3,760	829
Uvalde, TX Micro	3,742	830
La Grande, OR Micro	3,734	831
Marshall, MO Micro	3,712	832
Fort Morgan, CO Micro	3,675	833
Las Vegas, NM Micro	3,657	834
Marshall, MN Micro	3,655	835
Dickinson, ND Micro	3,647	836
Borger, TX Micro	3,625	837
Campbellsville, KY Micro	3,624	838
Bennettsville, SC Micro	3,617	839
Moberly, MO Micro	3,609	840
Mitchell, SD Micro	3,599	841
Dillon, SC Micro	3,589	842
Fort Leonard Wood, MO Micro	3,568	843
Clarksdale, MS Micro	3,561	844
Mount Pleasant, TX Micro	3,553	845
Oskaloosa, IA Micro	3,529	846
Kingsville, TX Micro	3,508	847
Dodge City, KS Micro	3,484	848
Moscow, ID Micro	3,467	849
Worthington, MN Micro	3,461	850
Hinesville-Fort Stewart, GA Metro	3,426	851
Spirit Lake, IA Micro	3,411	852
Crescent City North, CA Micro	3,408	853
West Helena, AR Micro	3,404	854
Yazoo City, MS Micro	3,396	855
Arkadelphia, AR Micro	3,391	856
Storm Lake, IA Micro	3,359	857
Williston, ND Micro	3,350	858
Greensburg, IN Micro	3,336	859
Rexburg, ID Micro	3,332	860
Forrest City, AR Micro	3,324	861
Tuskegee, AL Micro	3,294	862
Bishop, CA Micro	3,272	863
Spearfish, SD Micro	3,269	864
Grenada, MS Micro	3,264	865
Elko, NV Micro	3,251	866
Cedar City, UT Micro	3,239	867
Altus, OK Micro	3,228	868
Rock Springs, WY Micro	3,210	869
Huron, SD Micro	3,197	870
Yankton, SD Micro	3,173	871
Jesup, GA Micro	3,162	872
Indianola, MS Micro	3,135	873
Brookings, SD Micro	3,132	874
Prineville, OR Micro	3,101	875
Grants, NM Micro	3,081	876
Sterling, CO Micro	3,071	877
North Vernon, IN Micro	3,064	878
Beeville, TX Micro	3,062	879
Spencer, IA Micro	3,035	880
Fallon, NV Micro	3,017	881
Garden City, KS Micro	2,947	882
Levelland, TX Micro	2,936	883
Maryville, MO Micro	2,929	884
Pierre, SD Micro	2,844	885
Cordele, GA Micro	2,805	886
Vernal, UT Micro	2,790	887
Laramie, WY Micro	2,739	888
Woodward, OK Micro	2,712	889
Hood River, OR Micro	2,711	890
St. Marys, GA Micro	2,689	891
Brownsville, TN Micro	2,657	892
Atchison, KS Micro	2,654	893
Price, UT Micro	2,626	894
Scottsburg, IN Micro	2,616	895
Pierre Part, LA Micro	2,565	896
Sweetwater, TX Micro	2,554	897
Fort Valley, GA Micro	2,521	898
Snyder, TX Micro	2,412	899
Los Alamos, NM Micro	2,329	900
Raymondville, TX Micro	2,328	901
Vernon, TX Micro	2,289	902
Hereford, TX Micro	2,277	903
Edwards, CO Micro	2,258	904
Portales, NM Micro	2,229	905
Dumas, TX Micro	2,220	906
Mountain Home, ID Micro	2,183	907
Gillette, WY Micro	2,156	908
Juneau, AK Micro	2,104	909
Havre, MT Micro	2,081	910
Liberal, KS Micro	2,029	911
Guymon, OK Micro	2,016	912
Lamesa, TX Micro	1,967	913
Jackson, WY-ID Micro	1,929	914
Andrews, TX Micro	1,642	915
Pecos, TX Micro	1,629	916
Tallulah, LA Micro	1,518	917
Evanston, WY Micro	1,496	918
Vermillion, SD Micro	1,322	919
Ketchikan, AK Micro	1,139	920
Silverthorne, CO Micro	1,091	921
Kodiak, AK Micro	775	922

CBSA Total		33,373,235
United States Total		36,555,990
CBSA (% of U.S. Total)		91.3

CBSA	POPULATION	RANK
New York-Newark-Edison, NY-NJ-PA Metro	3,395,678	1
Chicago-Naperville-Joliet, IL-IN-WI Metro	1,706,696	2
Atlanta-Sandy Springs-Marietta, GA Metro	1,355,188	3
Washington-Arlington-Alexandria, DC-VA-MD-WV Metro	1,323,322	4
Philadelphia-Camden-Wilmington, PA-NJ-DE-MD Metro	1,166,867	5
Miami-Fort Lauderdale-Miami Beach, FL Metro	1,061,817	6
Detroit-Warren-Livonia, MI Metro	1,029,919	7
Los Angeles-Long Beach-Santa Ana, CA Metro	988,141	8
Houston-Baytown-Sugar Land, TX Metro	838,124	9
Dallas-Fort Worth-Arlington, TX Metro	781,615	10
Baltimore-Towson, MD Metro	713,793	11
Memphis, TN-MS-AR Metro	561,394	12
Virginia Beach-Norfolk-Newport News, VA-NC Metro	519,730	13
New Orleans-Metairie-Kenner, LA Metro	497,992	14
St. Louis, MO-IL Metro	497,000	15
Cleveland-Elyria-Mentor, OH Metro	416,850	16
San Francisco-Oakland-Fremont, CA Metro	381,603	17
Richmond, VA Metro	351,415	18
Charlotte-Gastonia-Concord, NC-SC Metro	339,370	19
Birmingham-Hoover, AL Metro	304,006	20
Tampa-St. Petersburg-Clearwater, FL Metro	290,007	21
Riverside-San Bernardino-Ontario, CA Metro	284,036	22
Boston-Cambridge-Quincy, MA-NH Metro	283,482	23
Jacksonville, FL Metro	279,275	24
Orlando, FL Metro	279,015	25
Baton Rouge, LA Metro	249,377	26
Milwaukee-Waukesha-West Allis, WI Metro	246,216	27
Kansas City, MO-KS Metro	239,150	28
Jackson, MS Metro	236,613	29
Cincinnati-Middletown, OH-KY-IN Metro	235,469	30
Columbia, SC Metro	230,933	31
Indianapolis, IN Metro	229,998	32
Columbus, OH Metro	225,041	33
Nashville-Davidson-Murfreesboro, TN Metro	205,339	34
Pittsburgh, PA Metro	193,122	35
Charleston-North Charleston, SC Metro	181,236	36
Augusta-Richmond County, GA-SC Metro	178,610	37
Raleigh-Cary, NC Metro	178,177	38
Minneapolis-St. Paul-Bloomington, MN-WI Metro	173,204	39
Seattle-Tacoma-Bellevue, WA Metro	165,745	40
San Diego-Carlsbad-San Marcos, CA Metro	161,812	41
Greensboro-High Point, NC Metro	157,824	42
Louisville, KY-IN Metro	156,907	43
Shreveport-Bossier City, LA Metro	147,720	44
Montgomery, AL Metro	147,489	45
Sacramento-Arden-Arcade-Roseville, CA Metro	145,084	46
Buffalo-Cheektowaga-Tonawanda, NY Metro	144,347	47
Little Rock-North Little Rock, AR Metro	141,975	48
Las Vegas-Paradise, NV Metro	139,722	49
Mobile, AL Metro	138,232	50
Phoenix-Mesa-Scottsdale, AZ Metro	137,303	51
Durham, NC Metro	129,464	52
Denver-Aurora, CO Metro	128,670	53
Fayetteville, NC Metro	127,001	54
Oklahoma City, OK Metro	122,958	55
Dayton, OH Metro	121,933	56
Rochester, NY Metro	120,500	57
Hartford-West Hartford-East Hartford, CT Metro	117,460	58
Columbus, GA-AL Metro	113,179	59
Tallahassee, FL Metro	112,408	60
San Antonio, TX Metro	105,994	61
Austin-Round Rock, TX Metro	105,706	62
Savannah, GA Metro	103,687	63
Greenville, SC Metro	101,854	64
New Haven-Milford, CT Metro	101,700	65
Beaumont-Port Arthur, TX Metro	97,386	66
Macon, GA Metro	96,005	67
Bridgeport-Stamford-Norwalk, CT Metro	92,172	68
Flint, MI Metro	88,950	69
Winston-Salem, NC Metro	88,705	70
Florence, SC Metro	81,167	71
Tulsa, OK Metro	79,441	72
Toledo, OH Metro	79,004	73
Albany, GA Metro	78,940	74
Akron, OH Metro	78,211	75
Pensacola-Ferry Pass-Brent, FL Metro	77,071	76
Huntsville, AL Metro	77,052	77
Lakeland-Winter Haven, FL Metro	74,627	78
Trenton-Ewing, NJ Metro	73,230	79
Tuscaloosa, AL Metro	68,997	80
Chattanooga, TN-GA Metro	67,704	81
Providence-New Bedford-Fall River, RI-MA Metro	64,942	82
Lafayette, LA Metro	64,736	83
Poughkeepsie-Newburgh-Middletown, NY Metro	64,735	84
Rocky Mount, NC Metro	64,222	85
Vallejo-Fairfield, CA Metro	63,213	86
Killeen-Temple-Fort Hood, TX Metro	63,022	87
Youngstown-Warren-Boardman, OH-PA Metro	62,827	88
Omaha-Council Bluffs, NE-IA Metro	61,059	89
Albany-Schenectady-Troy, NY Metro	60,535	90
Grand Rapids-Wyoming, MI Metro	58,283	91
Monroe, LA Metro	56,790	92
Orangeburg, SC Micro	56,713	93
Portland-Vancouver-Beaverton, OR-WA Metro	56,422	94
Greenville, NC Metro	55,996	95
Spartanburg, SC Metro	55,589	96
Sumter, SC Metro	52,231	97
Gainesville, FL Metro	50,061	98
Syracuse, NY Metro	49,926	99
Gulfport-Biloxi, MS Metro	49,488	100
Harrisburg-Carlisle, PA Metro	49,054	101
Pine Bluff, AR Metro	48,951	102
Wilmington, NC Metro	48,347	103
Stockton, CA Metro	47,616	104
Deltona-Daytona Beach-Ormond Beach, FL Metro	46,769	105
Clarksville, TN-KY Metro	46,633	106
Lake Charles, LA Metro	46,308	107
Fresno, CA Metro	45,685	108
Palm Bay-Melbourne-Titusville, FL Metro	45,358	109
Atlantic City, NJ Metro	45,183	110
Wichita, KS Metro	45,084	111
Lexington-Fayette, KY Metro	43,939	112
Springfield, MA Metro	43,481	113
Meridian, MS Micro	43,388	114
Hilton Head Island-Beaufort, SC Micro	43,309	115
Lynchburg, VA Metro	43,218	116
Roanoke Rapids, NC Micro	42,780	117
San Jose-Sunnyvale-Santa Clara, CA Metro	42,647	118
Bakersfield, CA Metro	42,195	119
Sarasota-Bradenton-Venice, FL Metro	42,068	120
Port St. Lucie-Fort Pierce, FL Metro	41,913	121
Alexandria, LA Metro	41,825	122
Ann Arbor, MI Metro	40,798	123
Greenville, MS Micro	40,067	124
Saginaw-Saginaw Township North, MI Metro	40,045	125
Knoxville, TN Metro	39,789	126
Valdosta, GA Metro	39,304	127
Fort Wayne, IN Metro	38,544	128
Lansing-East Lansing, MI Metro	38,263	129
Goldsboro, NC Metro	37,934	130
Colorado Springs, CO Metro	37,680	131
Opelousas-Eunice, LA Micro	37,499	132
Cape Coral-Fort Myers, FL Metro	36,939	133
Roanoke, VA Metro	36,800	134
Danville, VA Metro	36,345	135
Longview, TX Metro	35,833	136
Tyler, TX Metro	34,534	137
Athens-Clarke County, GA Metro	34,517	138
Hattiesburg, MS Metro	34,367	139
Myrtle Beach-Conway-North Myrtle Beach, SC Metro	33,854	140
Ocala, FL Metro	33,659	141
South Bend-Mishawaka, IN-MI Metro	33,135	142
Jackson, TN Metro	32,881	143
Waco, TX Metro	32,737	144
Peoria, IL Metro	31,917	145
Texarkana, TX-Texarkana, AR Metro	31,845	146
Lumberton, NC Micro	31,704	147
Rockford, IL Metro	31,609	148
Pascagoula, MS Metro	31,427	149
Houma-Bayou Cane-Thibodaux, LA Metro	31,316	150
Dothan, AL Metro	31,023	151
Vineland-Millville-Bridgeton, NJ Metro	30,604	152
Salisbury, MD Metro	30,499	153
Wilson, NC Micro	30,142	154
Hammond, LA Micro	29,968	155
Warner Robins, GA Metro	29,809	156
Selma, AL Micro	29,624	157
Anderson, SC Metro	29,607	158
New Bern, NC Micro	29,562	159
Greenwood, MS Micro	29,310	160
Auburn-Opelika, AL Metro	28,001	161
Honolulu, HI Metro	27,572	162
Laurel, MS Micro	27,559	163
Milledgeville, GA Micro	27,392	164
Canton-Massillon, OH Metro	27,371	165
Kalamazoo-Portage, MI Metro	27,353	166
Dover, DE Metro	27,324	167
Jacksonville, NC Metro	26,593	168
Hinesville-Fort Stewart, GA Metro	26,385	169
Columbus, MS Micro	26,152	170
Tucson, AZ Metro	26,143	171
Tupelo, MS Micro	26,070	172
Cleveland, MS Micro	25,886	173
Talladega-Sylacauga, AL Micro	25,801	174
Burlington, NC Metro	25,762	175
Natchez, MS-LA Micro	25,740	176
Worcester, MA Metro	25,512	177
Charlottesville, VA Metro	25,102	178
McComb, MS Micro	25,066	179
Niles-Benton Harbor, MI Metro	24,788	180
Indianola, MS Micro	24,226	181
Kinston, NC Micro	24,104	182
Muskegon-Norton Shores, MI Metro	23,959	183
Allentown-Bethlehem-Easton, PA-NJ Metro	23,848	184
Hickory-Morganton-Lenoir, NC Metro	23,756	185
New Iberia, LA Micro	23,209	186
Dunn, NC Micro	23,193	187
College Station-Bryan, TX Metro	23,155	188
Seaford, DE Micro	23,066	189
Lawton, OK Metro	22,772	190
Henderson, NC Micro	22,585	191
Brunswick, GA Metro	22,492	192
Vicksburg, MS Micro	22,477	193
Davenport-Moline-Rock Island, IA-IL Metro	22,332	194
Georgetown, SC Micro	22,164	195
Clarksdale, MS Micro	21,895	196
Greenwood, SC Micro	21,876	197
Anniston-Oxford, AL Metro	21,626	198
Ruston, LA Micro	21,003	199
Salisbury, NC Micro	20,798	200
Shelby, NC Micro	20,752	201
Champaign-Urbana, IL Metro	20,573	202
Racine, WI Metro	20,319	203
Albuquerque, NM Metro	19,706	204
Springfield, IL Metro	19,600	205
Tuskegee, AL Micro	19,596	206
Martinsville, VA Micro	19,563	207
Asheville, NC Metro	19,368	208
Evansville, IN-KY Metro	19,219	209
Dublin, GA Micro	19,187	210
LaGrange, GA Micro	19,167	211
Lubbock, TX Metro	19,124	212
Des Moines, IA Metro	18,990	213
Elizabeth City, NC Micro	18,890	214
Madison, WI Metro	18,484	215
Enterprise-Ozark, AL Micro	18,427	216
Americus, GA Micro	17,807	217
Statesville-Mooresville, NC Micro	17,687	218
Florence, AL Metro	17,615	219
Decatur, AL Metro	17,427	220
Erie, PA Metro	17,335	221
Fort Walton Beach-Crestview-Destin, FL Metro	17,334	222
Lancaster, SC Micro	17,294	223
Blytheville, AR Micro	17,115	224
Panama City-Lynn Haven, FL Metro	16,988	225
El Paso, TX Metro	16,947	226
Morgan City, LA Micro	16,897	227
Anchorage, AK Metro	16,886	228
Thomasville, GA Micro	16,847	229
Statesboro, GA Micro	16,472	230
Kankakee-Bradley, IL Metro	16,323	231
Walterboro, SC Micro	16,275	232
Starkville, MS Micro	16,175	233
Decatur, IL Metro	15,881	234
Topeka, KS Metro	15,819	235
Yazoo City, MS Micro	15,598	236
Norwich-New London, CT Metro	15,392	237
Oxnard-Thousand Oaks-Ventura, CA Metro	15,346	238
El Dorado, AR Micro	15,223	239
Hagerstown-Martinsburg, MD-WV Metro	15,168	240
West Helena, AR Micro	15,149	241
Daphne-Fairhope, AL Micro	15,129	242
Gadsden, AL Metro	15,104	243
Natchitoches, LA Micro	15,076	244
Naples-Marco Island, FL Metro	14,965	245
Reading, PA Metro	14,951	246
Battle Creek, MI Metro	14,928	247
York-Hanover, PA Metro	14,906	248
Utica-Rome, NY Metro	14,861	249
Huntsville, TX Micro	14,812	250
Bennettsville, SC Micro	14,805	251
Salinas, CA Metro	14,710	252
Marshall, TX Micro	14,619	253
Charleston, WV Metro	14,483	254
Forrest City, AR Micro	14,402	255
Modesto, CA Metro	14,285	256
Rockingham, NC Micro	14,276	257
Dillon, SC Micro	14,211	258
Valley, AL Micro	14,074	259
Bogalusa, LA Micro	13,994	260
Lancaster, PA Metro	13,898	261
Minden, LA Micro	13,675	262
Laurinburg, NC Micro	13,636	263
East Stroudsburg, PA Micro	13,516	264
Chester, SC Micro	13,425	265
Lexington-Thomasville, NC Micro	13,396	266
Bastrop, LA Micro	13,362	267
Corpus Christi, TX Metro	13,307	268
Amarillo, TX Metro	13,225	269
Washington, NC Micro	13,043	270
Lima, OH Metro	12,968	271
Columbia, MO Metro	12,786	272
Palatka, FL Micro	12,729	273
Wichita Falls, TX Metro	12,500	274
Newberry, SC Micro	12,397	275
Rome, GA Metro	12,303	276
Jackson, MI Metro	12,279	277
Springfield, OH Metro	12,242	278
Camden, AR Micro	12,178	279
Southern Pines, NC Micro	12,160	280
Elizabethtown, KY Metro	12,090	281
Palestine, TX Micro	12,084	282
Lufkin, TX Micro	12,070	283
Lexington Park, MD Micro	12,037	284
Mansfield, OH Metro	11,962	285
Salt Lake City, UT Metro	11,644	286
Douglas, GA Micro	11,618	287
Hanford-Corcoran, CA Metro	11,561	288
Waycross, GA Micro	11,349	289
Gaffney, SC Micro	11,323	290
Bainbridge, GA Micro	11,237	291
Troy, AL Micro	11,187	292
Kingston, NY Metro	10,982	293
Tifton, GA Micro	10,876	294
Gainesville, GA Metro	10,861	295
Watertown-Fort Drum, NY Micro	10,846	296
Michigan City-La Porte, IN Metro	10,747	297
Crowley, LA Micro	10,729	298
Fort Valley, GA Micro	10,693	299
Waterloo-Cedar Falls, IA Metro	10,617	300
Lake City, FL Micro	10,528	301
Brookhaven, MS Micro	10,348	302
Anderson, IN Metro	10,331	303
Fort Smith, AR-OK Metro	10,331	304
Vero Beach, FL Metro	10,296	305
Hope, AR Micro	10,230	306
Bloomington-Normal, IL Metro	10,190	307
Oxford, MS Micro	10,185	308

CBSA	POPULATION	RANK
Jefferson City, MO Metro	10,155	309
Nacogdoches, TX Micro	10,129	310
Abilene, TX Metro	10,051	311
Jonesboro, AR Metro	9,934	312
Columbia, TN Micro	9,886	313
Moultrie, GA Micro	9,783	314
Brownsville, TN Micro	9,715	315
Grenada, MS Micro	9,624	316
Sanford, NC Micro	9,606	317
Magnolia, AR Micro	9,553	318
Union, SC Micro	9,541	319
Cordele, GA Micro	9,449	320
The Villages, FL Micro	9,286	321
Elkhart-Goshen, IN Metro	9,212	322
Sebring, FL Micro	9,093	323
Muskogee, OK Micro	9,011	324
Santa Barbara-Santa Maria-Goleta, CA Metro	8,995	325
Fort Polk South, LA Micro	8,951	326
Danville, IL Metro	8,939	327
Manhattan, KS Micro	8,887	328
Scranton-Wilkes-Barre, PA Metro	8,855	329
St. Marys, GA Micro	8,676	330
Bowling Green, KY Metro	8,507	331
Merced, CA Metro	8,449	332
Binghamton, NY Metro	8,398	333
Paducah, KY-IL Micro	8,304	334
Cambridge, MD Micro	8,237	335
Tallulah, LA Micro	8,092	336
Fitzgerald, GA Micro	8,016	337
Thomaston, GA Micro	7,937	338
Midland, TX Metro	7,852	339
Abbeville, LA Micro	7,805	340
Staunton-Waynesboro, VA Micro	7,794	341
Muncie, IN Metro	7,758	342
Carbondale, IL Micro	7,704	343
Corsicana, TX Micro	7,648	344
Lincoln, NE Metro	7,635	345
Punta Gorda, FL Metro	7,565	346
Jacksonville, TX Micro	7,441	347
Cape Girardeau-Jackson, MO-IL Micro	7,381	348
Hot Springs, AR Metro	7,380	349
Pierre Part, LA Micro	7,229	350
Janesville, WI Metro	7,086	351
Terre Haute, IN Metro	7,086	352
Spokane, WA Metro	7,048	353
Ocean Pines, MD Micro	7,022	354
Beckley, WV Micro	6,981	355
Forest City, NC Micro	6,935	356
Huntington-Ashland, WV-KY-OH Metro	6,837	357
Blacksburg-Christiansburg-Radford, VA Metro	6,725	358
Sandusky, OH Metro	6,689	359
Albemarle, NC Micro	6,684	360
Santa Rosa-Petaluma, CA Metro	6,621	361
Reno-Sparks, NV Metro	6,493	362
Paris, TX Micro	6,465	363
Springfield, MO Metro	6,450	364
Visalia-Porterville, CA Metro	6,374	365
Picayune, MS Micro	6,306	366
Victoria, TX Metro	6,244	367
Bremerton-Silverdale, WA Metro	6,232	368
Sherman-Denison, TX Metro	6,144	369
Manchester-Nashua, NH Metro	6,118	370
Ogden-Clearfield, UT Metro	5,984	371
Elmira, NY Metro	5,982	372
El Campo, TX Micro	5,967	373
Cedar Rapids, IA Metro	5,912	374
Seneca, SC Micro	5,876	375
Kokomo, IN Metro	5,735	376
Olympia, WA Metro	5,628	377
Fayetteville-Springdale-Rogers, AR-MO Metro	5,626	378
Palm Coast, FL Micro	5,561	379
El Centro, CA Metro	5,514	380
Brenham, TX Micro	5,511	381
Fairbanks, AK Metro	5,384	382
Odessa, TX Metro	5,343	383
Cedartown, GA Micro	5,312	384
Jennings, LA Micro	5,309	385
Arkadelphia, AR Micro	5,298	386
Clewiston, FL Micro	5,239	387
Jesup, GA Micro	5,189	388
Fort Leonard Wood, MO Micro	5,120	389
San Luis Obispo-Paso Robles, CA Metro	5,069	390
St. Joseph, MO-KS Metro	5,031	391
Weirton-Steubenville, WV-OH Metro	5,030	392
Marion, IN Micro	5,023	393
Bluefield, WV-VA Micro	5,009	394
Easton, MD Micro	4,953	395
Frankfort, KY Micro	4,927	396
Williamsport, PA Metro	4,908	397
Union City, TN-KY Micro	4,879	398
Johnson City, TN Metro	4,852	399
Athens, TX Micro	4,848	400
Madera, CA Metro	4,812	401
Dyersburg, TN Micro	4,806	402
Winchester, VA-WV Metro	4,775	403
Ocean City, NJ Metro	4,700	404
Sikeston, MO Micro	4,644	405
De Ridder, LA Micro	4,612	406
Bay City, TX Micro	4,607	407
Cumberland, MD-WV Metro	4,605	408
Johnstown, PA Metro	4,505	409
Portland-South Portland, ME Metro	4,487	410
Wheeling, WV-OH Metro	4,465	411
Chillicothe, OH Micro	4,455	412
Lincolnton, NC Micro	4,334	413
Sierra Vista-Douglas, AZ Micro	4,302	414
Owensboro, KY Metro	4,249	415
Barnstable Town, MA Metro	4,216	416
Morehead City, NC Micro	4,198	417
Tullahoma, TN Micro	4,192	418
Kingsport-Bristol, TN-VA Metro	4,095	419
Lawrence, KS Metro	4,042	420
Arcadia, FL Micro	3,944	421
Corinth, MS Micro	3,906	422
Ithaca, NY Metro	3,905	423
Galesburg, IL Micro	3,874	424
Marion, OH Micro	3,845	425
Key West-Marathon, FL Micro	3,827	426
Harrisonburg, VA Metro	3,815	427
Lafayette, IN Metro	3,750	428
Yuba City-Marysville, CA Metro	3,742	429
Cleveland, TN Metro	3,719	430
Malone, NY Micro	3,719	431
Ardmore, OK Micro	3,714	432
San Angelo, TX Metro	3,679	433
State College, PA Metro	3,655	434
Freeport, IL Micro	3,620	435
Iowa City, IA Metro	3,616	436
Pottsville, PA Micro	3,553	437
Morristown, TN Metro	3,536	438
Richmond, IN Micro	3,533	439
New Castle, PA Micro	3,510	440
Rochester, MN Metro	3,508	441
Zanesville, OH Micro	3,501	442
Dalton, GA Metro	3,429	443
Auburn, NY Micro	3,392	444
Green Bay, WI Metro	3,385	445
Bloomington, IN Metro	3,313	446
Jamestown-Dunkirk-Fredonia, NY Micro	3,286	447
Chambersburg, PA Micro	3,282	448
Homosassa Springs, FL Micro	3,268	449
Richmond, KY Micro	3,261	450
Mount Vernon, IL Micro	3,236	451
Ashtabula, OH Micro	3,223	452
Clovis, NM Micro	3,191	453
Lewisburg, PA Micro	3,167	454
Salem, OR Metro	3,164	455
Shelbyville, TN Micro	3,117	456
Danville, KY Micro	3,109	457
Beeville, TX Micro	3,095	458
Toccoa, GA Micro	3,073	459
Plattsburgh, NY Micro	3,065	460
Morgantown, WV Metro	3,051	461
Ogdensburg-Massena, NY Micro	3,043	462
Yuma, AZ Metro	3,041	463
Mount Pleasant, TX Micro	3,008	464
Kennett, MO Micro	3,007	465
Boise City-Nampa, ID Metro	3,003	466
Chico, CA Metro	2,986	467
Kennewick-Richland-Pasco, WA Metro	2,982	468
Madisonville, KY Micro	2,980	469
Sioux Falls, SD Metro	2,965	470
Hudson, NY Micro	2,963	471
Pueblo, CO Metro	2,947	472
Okeechobee, FL Micro	2,917	473
Mount Airy, NC Micro	2,899	474
Las Cruces, NM Metro	2,876	475
Pittsfield, MA Metro	2,865	476
Holland-Grand Haven, MI Metro	2,863	477
Monroe, MI Metro	2,804	478
Searcy, AR Micro	2,799	479
North Wilkesboro, NC Micro	2,754	480
McAllen-Edinburg-Pharr, TX Metro	2,719	481
Paris, TN Micro	2,653	482
Hobbs, NM Micro	2,646	483
Summerville, GA Micro	2,610	484
Eugene-Springfield, OR Metro	2,604	485
Boulder, CO Metro	2,507	486
Sulphur Springs, TX Micro	2,498	487
Quincy, IL-MO Micro	2,480	488
Cheyenne, WY Metro	2,455	489
Canon City, CO Micro	2,446	490
Oak Hill, WV Micro	2,434	491
Santa Cruz-Watsonville, CA Metro	2,398	492
Napa, CA Metro	2,397	493
Alamogordo, NM Micro	2,394	494
Duluth, MN-WI Metro	2,389	495
Glens Falls, NY Metro	2,370	496
Huntingdon, PA Micro	2,367	497
Stillwater, OK Micro	2,336	498
East Liverpool-Salem, OH Micro	2,323	499
Yakima, WA Metro	2,313	500
Altus, OK Micro	2,311	501
Athens, TN Micro	2,296	502
Joplin, MO Metro	2,287	503
Wauchula, FL Micro	2,279	504
Sioux City, IA-NE-SD Metro	2,264	505
St. Cloud, MN Metro	2,252	506
Poplar Bluff, MO Micro	2,205	507
Seneca Falls, NY Micro	2,161	508
Willimantic, CT Micro	2,139	509
Beaver Dam, WI Micro	2,138	510
Pontiac, IL Micro	2,138	511
Adrian, MI Micro	2,125	512
Fort Collins-Loveland, CO Metro	2,104	513
Torrington, CT Micro	2,095	514
Coffeyville, KS Micro	2,093	515
Ottawa-Streator, IL Micro	2,062	516
Warrensburg, MO Micro	2,058	517
Sault Ste. Marie, MI Micro	2,039	518
Portsmouth, OH Micro	2,025	519
Lincoln, IL Micro	2,005	520
Corning, NY Micro	1,973	521
Fairmont, WV Micro	1,934	522
Russellville, AR Micro	1,927	523
Scottsboro, AL Micro	1,924	524
Jacksonville, IL Micro	1,868	525
Mexico, MO Micro	1,840	526
Plainview, TX Micro	1,808	527
Sturgis, MI Micro	1,800	528
Shawnee, OK Micro	1,792	529
Bristol, VA Metro	1,763	530
Enid, OK Micro	1,746	531
Dixon, IL Micro	1,744	532
Salina, KS Micro	1,732	533
Oshkosh-Neenah, WI Metro	1,714	534
Oak Harbor, WA Micro	1,704	535
Fargo, ND-MN Metro	1,697	536
Fremont, OH Micro	1,695	537
Wooster, OH Micro	1,689	538
Burlington-South Burlington, VT Metro	1,682	539
Mayfield, KY Micro	1,678	540
Moberly, MO Micro	1,655	541
Minot, ND Micro	1,650	542
Parkersburg-Marietta, WV-OH Metro	1,650	543
Centralia, IL Micro	1,647	544
Alma, MI Micro	1,637	545
Allegan, MI Micro	1,628	546
Glasgow, KY Micro	1,626	547
Brownsville-Harlingen, TX Metro	1,607	548
Marion-Herrin, IL Micro	1,602	549
McAlester, OK Micro	1,572	550
Cornelia, GA Micro	1,569	551
Hannibal, MO Micro	1,553	552
Big Rapids, MI Micro	1,551	553
Clearlake, CA Micro	1,551	554
Lebanon, PA Metro	1,550	555
Calhoun, GA Micro	1,547	556
Rapid City, SD Metro	1,542	557
Sunbury, PA Micro	1,541	558
Ames, IA Metro	1,513	559
Hutchinson, KS Micro	1,512	560
Redding, CA Metro	1,510	561
Brownwood, TX Micro	1,490	562
Batavia, NY Micro	1,480	563
Provo-Orem, UT Metro	1,477	564
Burlington, IA-IL Micro	1,472	565
Altoona, PA Metro	1,463	566
Bay City, MI Metro	1,455	567
DuBois, PA Micro	1,444	568
Canton, IL Micro	1,437	569
Greeley, CO Metro	1,425	570
Somerset, PA Micro	1,421	571
Clarksburg, WV Micro	1,417	572
Coldwater, MI Micro	1,406	573
Meadville, PA Micro	1,383	574
Big Spring, TX Micro	1,374	575
Harriman, TN Micro	1,370	576
Albertville, AL Micro	1,358	577
Central City, KY Micro	1,352	578
Athens, OH Micro	1,349	579
Bellingham, WA Metro	1,342	580
McMinnville, TN Micro	1,340	581
Indiana, PA Micro	1,333	582
Cookeville, TN Micro	1,324	583
Murray, KY Micro	1,322	584
Pampa, TX Micro	1,301	585
Lamesa, TX Micro	1,296	586
Columbus, IN Metro	1,291	587
Fort Dodge, IA Micro	1,290	588
Charleston-Mattoon, IL Micro	1,287	589
Sedalia, MO Micro	1,277	590
Oneonta, NY Micro	1,275	591
Greeneville, TN Micro	1,266	592
Maysville, KY Micro	1,263	593
Bartlesville, OK Micro	1,262	594
Appleton, WI Metro	1,257	595
Mount Pleasant, MI Micro	1,252	596
Phoenix Lake-Cedar Ridge, CA Micro	1,212	597
Eureka-Arcata-Fortuna, CA Micro	1,206	598
Sheboygan, WI Metro	1,206	599
Grand Forks, ND-MN Metro	1,204	600
Campbellsville, KY Micro	1,191	601
Macomb, IL Micro	1,186	602
Gloversville, NY Micro	1,185	603
La Crosse, WI-MN Metro	1,179	604
Gettysburg, PA Micro	1,170	605
Brevard, NC Micro	1,168	606
Roswell, NM Micro	1,162	607
Mountain Home, ID Micro	1,161	608
Gainesville, TX Micro	1,152	609
Crescent City North, CA Micro	1,145	610
Flagstaff, AZ Metro	1,132	611
Great Falls, MT Metro	1,122	612
Farmington, MO Micro	1,116	613
Clinton, IA Micro	1,112	614
Vernon, TX Micro	1,095	615
Parsons, KS Micro	1,081	616
Olean, NY Micro	1,078	617
Mount Sterling, KY Micro	1,073	618
Kingsville, TX Micro	1,069	619
Harrisburg, IL Micro	1,057	620

CBSA	POPULATION	RANK	CBSA	POPULATION	RANK	CBSA	POPULATION	RANK
Midland, MI Micro	1,052	621	Logan, UT-ID Metro	439	725	Plymouth, IN Micro	189	829
Marshall, MO Micro	1,050	622	Selinsgrove, PA Micro	428	726	Roseburg, OR Micro	188	830
Winfield, KS Micro	1,044	623	Sevierville, TN Micro	426	727	Coos Bay, OR Micro	187	831
Santa Fe, NM Metro	1,021	624	Bend, OR Metro	424	728	Bemidji, MN Micro	184	832
Duncan, OK Micro	1,015	625	Marshalltown, IA Micro	411	729	Hays, KS Micro	183	833
Mankato-North Mankato, MN Micro	1,004	626	Mason City, IA Micro	410	730	Lewiston, ID-WA Metro	181	834
Fond du Lac, WI Micro	999	627	New Castle, IN Micro	409	731	Espanola, NM Micro	180	835
Tiffin-Fostoria, OH Micro	997	628	Platteville, WI Micro	405	732	Fremont, NE Micro	179	836
Traverse City, MI Micro	995	629	Muscatine, IA Micro	404	733	Eagle Pass, TX Micro	178	837
Dubuque, IA Metro	990	630	Owatonna, MN Micro	403	734	Menomonie, WI Micro	176	838
Walla Walla, WA Micro	990	631	Branson, MO Micro	401	735	Worthington, MN Micro	171	839
Snyder, TX Micro	974	632	Houghton, MI Micro	398	736	Willmar, MN Micro	164	840
Marquette, MI Micro	973	633	Wausau, WI Metro	397	737	Columbus, NE Micro	162	841
Point Pleasant, WV-OH Micro	962	634	Ottumwa, IA Micro	396	738	Merrill, WI Micro	162	842
Findlay, OH Micro	951	635	Connersville, IN Micro	393	739	Nogales, AZ Micro	155	843
Keokuk-Fort Madison, IA-MO Micro	949	636	Austin, MN Micro	384	740	Brookings, SD Micro	149	844
Atchison, KS Micro	933	637	Laramie, WY Micro	377	741	Vermillion, SD Micro	149	845
Lake Havasu City-Kingman, AZ Micro	924	638	Lewistown, PA Micro	356	742	Huron, SD Micro	148	846
Peru, IN Micro	906	639	Red Wing, MN Micro	355	743	Helena, MT Micro	147	847
Hilo, HI Micro	899	640	Winona, MN Micro	353	744	Baraboo, WI Micro	145	848
Lebanon, NH-VT Micro	889	641	Missoula, MT Metro	346	745	Kodiak, AK Micro	143	849
Urbana, OH Micro	889	642	Bismarck, ND Metro	343	746	Albert Lea, MN Micro	140	850
Carson City, NV Metro	885	643	Crawfordsville, IN Micro	343	747	Taos, NM Micro	140	851
Carlsbad-Artesia, NM Micro	872	644	London, KY Micro	339	748	La Follette, TN Micro	138	852
Ponca City, OK Micro	872	645	Manitowoc, WI Micro	337	749	Hood River, OR Micro	136	853
Lewiston-Auburn, ME Metro	864	646	Kirksville, MO Micro	334	750	Bedford, IN Micro	135	854
Medford, OR Metro	864	647	Keene, NH Micro	331	751	La Grande, OR Micro	135	855
Kill Devil Hills, NC Micro	853	648	Newton, IA Micro	326	752	Guymon, OK Micro	130	856
Concord, NH Micro	846	649	Wenatchee, WA Metro	326	753	Aberdeen, SD Micro	129	857
Levelland, TX Micro	840	650	Rock Springs, WY Micro	324	754	Auburn, IN Micro	128	858
Wilmington, OH Micro	835	651	Granbury, TX Micro	319	755	Crossville, TN Micro	128	859
Bloomsburg-Berwick, PA Micro	830	652	Barre, VT Micro	317	756	Uvalde, TX Micro	126	860
Moses Lake, WA Micro	830	653	Rochelle, IL Micro	317	757	Angola, IN Micro	124	861
Taylorville, IL Micro	804	654	Brainerd, MN Micro	315	758	Montrose, CO Micro	124	862
Amsterdam, NY Micro	788	655	Portales, NM Micro	315	759	Monroe, WI Micro	123	863
Batesville, AR Micro	776	656	St. George, UT Metro	314	760	Hutchinson, MN Micro	122	864
Emporia, KS Micro	774	657	Alice, TX Micro	309	761	Paragould, AR Micro	116	865
Bellefontaine, OH Micro	767	658	Red Bluff, CA Micro	308	762	Boone, IA Micro	112	866
Liberal, KS Micro	764	659	Gallup, NM Micro	304	763	Gardnerville Ranchos, NV Micro	112	867
Boone, NC Micro	760	660	Yankton, SD Micro	302	764	Mountain Home, AR Micro	112	868
Sterling, IL Micro	753	661	Grand Island, NE Micro	298	765	Wahpeton, ND-MN Micro	112	869
Eau Claire, WI Metro	750	662	Maryville, MO Micro	298	766	Brigham City, UT Micro	111	870
Kerrville, TX Micro	749	663	Sayre, PA Micro	298	767	Frankfort, IN Micro	111	871
Norfolk, NE Micro	747	664	Aberdeen, WA Micro	297	768	Gillette, WY Micro	111	872
Vincennes, IN Micro	746	665	Bozeman, MT Micro	296	769	Harrison, AR Micro	107	873
Sidney, OH Micro	743	666	Fallon, NV Micro	286	770	Wapakoneta, OH Micro	107	874
Bangor, ME Metro	733	667	Seymour, IN Micro	282	771	Los Alamos, NM Micro	106	875
Cullman, AL Micro	728	668	Centralia, WA Micro	280	772	Rexburg, ID Micro	105	876
Laredo, TX Metro	726	669	Marshall, MN Micro	280	773	Burley, ID Micro	104	877
Middlesborough, KY Micro	724	670	Albany-Lebanon, OR Micro	279	774	Fort Morgan, CO Micro	104	878
Newport, TN Micro	721	671	Bucyrus, OH Micro	278	775	Storm Lake, IA Micro	100	879
Whitewater, WI Micro	712	672	Stephenville, TX Micro	276	776	Riverton, WY Micro	99	880
Prescott, AZ Metro	708	673	Coeur d'Alene, ID Metro	275	777	Rockland, ME Micro	99	881
Oil City, PA Micro	699	674	Washington, IN Micro	274	778	Alpena, MI Micro	97	882
Faribault-Northfield, MN Micro	698	675	Van Wert, OH Micro	270	779	West Plains, MO Micro	97	883
Corvallis, OR Metro	696	676	Pecos, TX Micro	266	780	Alexandria, MN Micro	91	884
Rolla, MO Micro	693	677	Andrews, TX Micro	261	781	Jasper, TX Micro	90	885
Pittsburg, KS Micro	691	678	Grants, NM Micro	261	782	Ketchikan, AK Micro	89	886
Billings, MT Metro	690	679	Kendallville, IN Micro	261	783	Beatrice, NE Micro	87	887
Bradford, PA Micro	685	680	Grants Pass, OR Micro	258	784	Jamestown, ND Micro	87	888
Safford, AZ Micro	685	681	Kearney, NE Micro	258	785	Rio Grande City, TX Micro	86	889
Borger, TX Micro	674	682	Twin Falls, ID Micro	257	786	Blackfoot, ID Micro	84	890
Sweetwater, TX Micro	669	683	Lock Haven, PA Micro	256	787	Effingham, IL Micro	84	891
Pendleton-Hermiston, OR Micro	660	684	Hereford, TX Micro	255	788	Lexington, NE Micro	81	892
Kahului-Wailuku, HI Micro	658	685	Moscow, ID Micro	255	789	Sheridan, WY Micro	81	893
Lawrenceburg, TN Micro	658	686	Rutland, VT Micro	255	790	Huntington, IN Micro	77	894
New Philadelphia-Dover, OH Micro	658	687	Miami, FL Micro	253	791	Mitchell, SD Micro	77	895
Grand Junction, CO Metro	646	688	Silverthorne, CO Micro	252	792	City of The Dalles, OR Micro	76	896
Cambridge, OH Micro	640	689	Hastings, NE Micro	250	793	Fairmont, MN Micro	73	897
Defiance, OH Micro	640	690	Warren, PA Micro	246	794	Price, UT Micro	73	898
Ada, OK Micro	635	691	Deming, NM Micro	244	795	Butte-Silver Bow, MT Micro	72	899
Somerset, KY Micro	623	692	Kalispell, MT Micro	244	796	Spearfish, SD Micro	71	900
Durant, OK Micro	614	693	Truckee-Grass Valley, CA Micro	243	797	Decatur, IN Micro	69	901
Cortland, NY Micro	606	694	Juneau, AK Micro	242	798	Escanaba, MI Micro	67	902
Mineral Wells, TX Micro	605	695	Watertown-Fort Atkinson, WI Micro	242	799	St. Marys, PA Micro	67	903
Casper, WY Metro	601	606	Cadillac, MI Micro	241	800	Berlin, NH-VT Micro	62	904
Longview-Kelso, WA Metro	601	697	Marinette, WI-MI Micro	240	801	Celina, OH Micro	57	905
Ukiah, CA Micro	601	698	Kapaa, HI Micro	239	802	Dickinson, ND Micro	56	906
Farmington, NM Metro	599	699	North Platte, NE Micro	238	803	Brookings, OR Micro	53	907
Idaho Falls, ID Metro	597	700	Fergus Falls, MN Micro	234	804	Iron Mountain, MI-WI Micro	51	908
Port Angeles, WA Micro	586	701	Las Vegas, NM Micro	234	805	Jackson, WY-ID Micro	51	909
Shelton, WA Micro	585	702	McPherson, KS Micro	234	806	Watertown, SD Micro	51	910
Pullman, WA Micro	577	703	Oskaloosa, IA Micro	231	807	Pierre, SD Micro	50	911
Washington, OH Micro	577	704	Stevens Point, WI Micro	231	808	New Ulm, MN Micro	49	912
Del Rio, TX Micro	563	705	Ellensburg, WA Micro	228	809	Spirit Lake, IA Micro	47	913
Pahrump, NV Micro	550	706	Bennington, VT Micro	227	810	Spencer, IA Micro	46	914
Logansport, IN Micro	540	707	Astoria, OR Micro	223	811	Williston, ND Micro	46	915
Augusta-Waterville, ME Micro	538	708	Wisconsin Rapids-Marshfield, WI Micro	223	812	Vernal, UT Micro	45	916
Mount Vernon-Anacortes, WA Metro	518	709	Dumas, TX Micro	222	813	Greensburg, IN Micro	41	917
Norwalk, OH Micro	512	710	Wabash, IN Micro	219	814	Bishop, CA Micro	36	918
Warsaw, IN Micro	505	711	North Vernon, IN Micro	216	815	Evanston, WY Micro	35	919
Pocatello, ID Metro	501	712	Edwards, CO Micro	212	816	Havre, MT Micro	24	920
Sterling, CO Micro	489	713	Woodward, OK Micro	211	817	Scottsburg, IN Micro	16	921
Klamath Falls, OR Micro	472	714	Silver City, NM Micro	209	818	Prineville, OR Micro	10	922
Garden City, KS Micro	467	715	Payson, AZ Micro	207	819			
Tahlequah, OK Micro	467	716	Elko, NV Micro	205	820			
Great Bend, KS Micro	463	717	Lebanon, MO Micro	205	821	CBSA Total	34,584,936	
Raymondville, TX Micro	462	718	Corbin, KY Micro	204	822	United States Total	36,299,387	
Dodge City, KS Micro	457	719	Durango, CO Micro	202	823	CBSA (% of U.S. Total)	95.28	
Madison, IN Micro	457	720	Owosso, MI Micro	199	824			
Mount Vernon, OH Micro	455	721	Scottsbluff, NE Micro	196	825			
Ashland, OH Micro	453	722	Laconia, NH Micro	195	826			
Coshocton, OH Micro	447	723	Cedar City, UT Micro	191	827			
Ontario, OR-ID Micro	444	724	Greenville, OH Micro	189	828			

CBSA	POPULATION	RANK
Los Angeles-Long Beach-Santa Ana, CA Metro	5,745,884	1
New York-Newark-Edison, NY-NJ-PA Metro	3,975,570	2
Miami-Fort Lauderdale-Miami Beach, FL Metro	2,009,210	3
Chicago-Naperville-Joliet, IL-IN-WI Metro	1,730,299	4
Houston-Baytown-Sugar Land, TX Metro	1,625,781	5
Riverside-San Bernardino-Ontario, CA Metro	1,517,351	6
Dallas-Fort Worth-Arlington, TX Metro	1,415,900	7
Phoenix-Mesa-Scottsdale, AZ Metro	1,049,210	8
San Antonio, TX Metro	970,605	9
San Diego-Carlsbad-San Marcos, CA Metro	880,154	10
San Francisco-Oakland-Fremont, CA Metro	818,764	11
El Paso, TX Metro	583,708	12
McAllen-Edinburg-Pharr, TX Metro	576,227	13
Washington-Arlington-Alexandria, DC-VA-MD-WV Metro	555,330	14
Denver-Aurora, CO Metro	480,685	15
San Jose-Sunnyvale-Santa Clara, CA Metro	454,665	16
Austin-Round Rock, TX Metro	409,714	17
Las Vegas-Paradise, NV Metro	404,676	18
Fresno, CA Metro	400,140	19
Atlanta-Sandy Springs-Marietta, GA Metro	385,521	20
Orlando, FL Metro	361,521	21
Sacramento-Arden-Arcade-Roseville, CA Metro	347,929	22
Albuquerque, NM Metro	333,875	23
Boston-Cambridge-Quincy, MA-NH Metro	320,284	24
Philadelphia-Camden-Wilmington, PA-NJ-DE-MD Metro	315,485	25
Brownsville-Harlingen, TX Metro	313,895	26
Tampa-St. Petersburg-Clearwater, FL Metro	313,614	27
Bakersfield, CA Metro	301,126	28
Tucson, AZ Metro	297,778	29
Oxnard-Thousand Oaks-Ventura, CA Metro	287,341	30
Corpus Christi, TX Metro	228,160	31
Stockton, CA Metro	215,480	32
Visalia-Porterville, CA Metro	213,304	33
Salinas, CA Metro	211,902	34
Laredo, TX Metro	207,727	35
Seattle-Tacoma-Bellevue, WA Metro	204,658	36
Portland-Vancouver-Beaverton, OR-WA Metro	186,903	37
Modesto, CA Metro	184,384	38
Santa Barbara-Santa Maria-Goleta, CA Metro	149,858	39
Detroit-Warren-Livonia, MI Metro	146,058	40
Salt Lake City, UT Metro	136,846	41
Providence-New Bedford-Fall River, RI-MA Metro	128,006	42
Minneapolis-St. Paul-Bloomington, MN-WI Metro	122,484	43
Hartford-West Hartford-East Hartford, CT Metro	120,682	44
Las Cruces, NM Metro	119,011	45
Bridgeport-Stamford-Norwalk, CT Metro	118,687	46
Merced, CA Metro	116,819	47
El Centro, CA Metro	114,157	48
Kansas City, MO-KS Metro	112,202	49
Milwaukee-Waukesha-West Allis, WI Metro	107,283	50
Charlotte-Gastonia-Concord, NC-SC Metro	100,965	51
New Haven-Milford, CT Metro	95,897	52
Yuma, AZ Metro	95,565	53
Santa Rosa-Petaluma, CA Metro	94,305	54
Yakima, WA Metro	87,507	55
Oklahoma City, OK Metro	86,353	56
Springfield, MA Metro	86,320	57
Vallejo-Fairfield, CA Metro	84,526	58
Cleveland-Elyria-Mentor, OH Metro	79,208	59
Lubbock, TX Metro	78,185	60
Poughkeepsie-Newburgh-Middletown, NY Metro	77,640	61
Santa Cruz-Watsonville, CA Metro	72,160	62
Reno-Sparks, NV Metro	71,965	63
Naples-Marco Island, FL Metro	70,520	64
Santa Fe, NM Metro	69,690	65
Colorado Springs, CO Metro	67,475	66
Raleigh-Cary, NC Metro	67,242	67
Greeley, CO Metro	67,062	68
Salem, OR Metro	66,830	69
Madera, CA Metro	64,136	70
Allentown-Bethlehem-Easton, PA-NJ Metro	63,991	71
Hanford-Corcoran, CA Metro	63,934	72
New Orleans-Metairie-Kenner, LA Metro	63,611	73
Cape Coral-Fort Myers, FL Metro	62,024	74
Killeen-Temple-Fort Hood, TX Metro	61,126	75
Honolulu, HI Metro	59,591	76
Worcester, MA Metro	59,335	77
Pueblo, CO Metro	59,247	78
Lakeland-Winter Haven, FL Metro	58,123	79
Odessa, TX Metro	56,870	80
Rio Grande City, TX Micro	56,673	81
Baltimore-Towson, MD Metro	56,435	82
Rochester, NY Metro	54,975	83
Nashville-Davidson-Murfreesboro, TN Metro	54,883	84
Indianapolis, IN Metro	54,669	85
Grand Rapids-Wyoming, MI Metro	54,241	86
Boise City-Nampa, ID Metro	53,776	87
Virginia Beach-Norfolk-Newport News, VA-NC Metro	51,376	88
Sarasota-Bradenton-Venice, FL Metro	50,789	89
Jacksonville, FL Metro	50,710	90
Amarillo, TX Metro	50,363	91
Wichita, KS Metro	49,988	92
Kennewick-Richland-Pasco, WA Metro	49,546	93
Eagle Pass, TX Micro	48,267	94
Tulsa, OK Metro	47,567	95
Omaha-Council Bluffs, NE-IA Metro	47,551	96
St. Louis, MO-IL Metro	47,413	97
Victoria, TX Metro	47,357	98
San Luis Obispo-Paso Robles, CA Metro	44,984	99
Waco, TX Metro	44,549	100
Ogden-Clearfield, UT Metro	44,089	101
Reading, PA Metro	41,449	102
Sierra Vista-Douglas, AZ Micro	41,179	103
Trenton-Ewing, NJ Metro	40,265	104
Buffalo-Cheektowaga-Tonawanda, NY Metro	39,449	105
Durham, NC Metro	39,015	106
Fayetteville-Springdale-Rogers, AR-MO Metro	38,498	107
Midland, TX Metro	38,077	108
Greensboro-High Point, NC Metro	37,643	109
Deltona-Daytona Beach-Ormond Beach, FL Metro	37,613	110
College Station-Bryan, TX Metro	37,589	111
Gainesville, GA Metro	37,335	112
Del Rio, TX Micro	37,002	113
San Angelo, TX Metro	35,659	114
Napa, CA Metro	35,293	115
Atlantic City, NJ Metro	35,016	116
Columbus, OH Metro	34,811	117
Boulder, CO Metro	34,251	118
Beaumont-Port Arthur, TX Metro	33,969	119
Memphis, TN-MS-AR Metro	33,867	120
Yuba City-Marysville, CA Metro	33,764	121
Nogales, AZ Micro	33,552	122
Winston-Salem, NC Metro	33,437	123
Port St. Lucie-Fort Pierce, FL Metro	31,892	124
Rockford, IL Metro	31,783	125
Provo-Orem, UT Metro	31,484	126
Vineland-Millville-Bridgeton, NJ Metro	31,407	127
Alice, TX Micro	31,237	128
Toledo, OH Metro	30,756	129
Abilene, TX Metro	30,568	130
Richmond, VA Metro	30,419	131
Espanola, NM Micro	30,086	132
Lancaster, PA Metro	29,756	133
Roswell, NM Micro	28,085	134
Albany-Schenectady-Troy, NY Metro	27,478	135
Dalton, GA Metro	26,776	136
Palm Bay-Melbourne-Titusville, FL Metro	26,676	137
Moses Lake, WA Micro	26,460	138
Cincinnati-Middletown, OH-KY-IN Metro	25,732	139
Louisville, KY-IN Metro	25,197	140
Greenville, SC Metro	25,184	141
Chico, CA Metro	24,698	142
Fort Collins-Loveland, CO Metro	24,502	143
Hobbs, NM Micro	24,468	144
Birmingham-Hoover, AL Metro	24,193	145
Tyler, TX Metro	23,989	146
Des Moines, IA Metro	23,755	147
Las Vegas, NM Micro	23,033	148
Lansing-East Lansing, MI Metro	22,995	149
Davenport-Moline-Rock Island, IA-IL Metro	22,919	150
Kingsville, TX Micro	21,964	151
Alamogordo, NM Micro	21,106	152
Elkhart-Goshen, IN Metro	20,858	153
Carlsbad-Artesia, NM Micro	20,660	154
Wenatchee, WA Metro	20,631	155
Prescott, AZ Metro	19,791	156
Ocala, FL Metro	19,710	157
Farmington, NM Metro	19,556	158
Anchorage, AK Metro	19,468	159
Lake Havasu City-Kingman, AZ Micro	19,310	160
Wichita Falls, TX Metro	18,997	161
Fayetteville, NC Metro	18,895	162
Holland-Grand Haven, MI Metro	18,738	163
Columbia, SC Metro	18,589	164
Madison, WI Metro	18,447	165
Longview, TX Metro	18,444	166
Beeville, TX Micro	18,306	167
Hickory-Morganton-Lenoir, NC Metro	18,272	168
Uvalde, TX Micro	18,228	169
Hilo, HI Micro	18,219	170
Plainview, TX Micro	18,014	171
Taos, NM Micro	17,977	172
Syracuse, NY Metro	17,772	173
Fort Wayne, IN Metro	17,702	174
Raymondville, TX Micro	17,593	175
Pittsburgh, PA Metro	17,344	176
Eugene-Springfield, OR Metro	17,189	177
Garden City, KS Micro	16,767	178
Racine, WI Metro	16,671	179
Ukiah, CA Micro	16,594	180
Edwards, CO Micro	16,301	181
Pendleton-Hermiston, OR Micro	16,061	182
Clewiston, FL Micro	15,784	183
Sioux City, IA-NE-SD Metro	15,638	184
South Bend-Mishawaka, IN-MI Metro	15,432	185
Fort Smith, AR-OK Metro	15,323	186
Clovis, NM Micro	15,193	187
Asheville, NC Metro	15,155	188
Key West-Marathon, FL Micro	15,144	189
Deming, NM Micro	15,073	190
Lexington-Fayette, KY Metro	15,007	191
Topeka, KS Metro	14,921	192
Norwich-New London, CT Metro	14,779	193
Manchester-Nashua, NH Metro	14,654	194
Silver City, NM Micro	14,644	195
Saginaw-Saginaw Township North, MI Metro	14,496	196
Harrisburg-Carlisle, PA Metro	14,414	197
Charleston-North Charleston, SC Metro	14,413	198
Spokane, WA Metro	14,256	199
Medford, OR Metro	14,230	200
Flagstaff, AZ Metro	14,181	201
Baton Rouge, LA Metro	14,140	202
Little Rock-North Little Rock, AR Metro	14,042	203
El Campo, TX Micro	14,031	204
Dodge City, KS Micro	13,951	205
Mount Vernon-Anacortes, WA Metro	13,934	206
Gainesville, FL Metro	13,426	207
Kalamazoo-Portage, MI Metro	13,398	208
Bay City, TX Micro	13,380	209
Big Spring, TX Micro	13,377	210
Lufkin, TX Micro	13,084	211
Burlington, NC Metro	13,041	212
Grand Junction, CO Metro	12,960	213
Tallahassee, FL Metro	12,945	214
Safford, AZ Micro	12,926	215
Kingston, NY Metro	12,890	216
Sebring, FL Micro	12,708	217
East Stroudsburg, PA Micro	12,519	218
York-Hanover, PA Metro	12,443	219
Hilton Head Island-Beaufort, SC Micro	12,398	220
Redding, CA Metro	12,150	221
Liberal, KS Micro	12,102	222
Twin Falls, ID Micro	11,891	223
Ontario, OR-ID Micro	11,450	224
Bremerton-Silverdale, WA Metro	11,249	225
Hereford, TX Micro	11,198	226
Augusta-Richmond County, GA-SC Metro	11,106	227
Green Bay, WI Metro	10,940	228
Red Bluff, CA Micro	10,834	229
Flint, MI Metro	10,769	230
Olympia, WA Metro	10,764	231
Kahului-Wailuku, HI Micro	10,754	232
Lincoln, NE Metro	10,701	233
Wauchula, FL Micro	10,475	234
Utica-Rome, NY Metro	10,370	235
Youngstown-Warren-Boardman, OH-PA Metro	10,300	236
Lafayette, IN Metro	10,188	237
Bellingham, WA Metro	10,170	238
Athens-Clarke County, GA Metro	10,102	239
Dumas, TX Micro	9,948	240
Cheyenne, WY Metro	9,904	241
Columbus, GA-AL Metro	9,886	242
Dayton, OH Metro	9,873	243
Eureka-Arcata-Fortuna, CA Micro	9,802	244
Ann Arbor, MI Metro	9,792	245
Arcadia, FL Micro	9,718	246
Kerrville, TX Micro	9,662	247
Burley, ID Micro	9,661	248
Mount Pleasant, TX Micro	9,602	249
Knoxville, TN Metro	9,519	250
Spartanburg, SC Metro	9,491	251
Pensacola-Ferry Pass-Brent, FL Metro	9,378	252
Walla Walla, WA Micro	9,297	253
Gallup, NM Micro	9,268	254
Sherman-Denison, TX Metro	9,241	255
Vero Beach, FL Metro	9,196	256
Huntsville, TX Micro	9,133	257
Grants, NM Micro	9,107	258
Corsicana, TX Micro	9,082	259
Pecos, TX Micro	9,063	260
Clarksville, TN-KY Metro	9,026	261
Elko, NV Micro	9,012	262
Grand Island, NE Micro	8,999	263
Ottawa-Streator, IL Micro	8,993	264
Idaho Falls, ID Metro	8,961	265
Levelland, TX Micro	8,918	266
Carson City, NV Metro	8,836	267
Clearlake, CA Micro	8,760	268
Payson, AZ Micro	8,730	269
Huntsville, AL Metro	8,643	270
Willimantic, CT Micro	8,501	271
Fort Morgan, CO Micro	8,493	272
Wilmington, NC Metro	8,389	273
Seaford, DE Micro	8,345	274
Logan, UT-ID Metro	8,282	275
Shreveport-Bossier City, LA Metro	7,985	276
Lumberton, NC Micro	7,963	277
Jacksonville, NC Metro	7,956	278
Watertown-Fort Drum, NY Micro	7,948	279
Lawton, OK Metro	7,942	280
Scranton-Wilkes-Barre, PA Metro	7,892	281
Okeechobee, FL Micro	7,819	282
Nacogdoches, TX Micro	7,714	283
Chattanooga, TN-GA Metro	7,672	284
Fort Walton Beach-Crestview-Destin, FL Metro	7,662	285
Dunn, NC Micro	7,659	286
Whitewater, WI Micro	7,529	287
Jacksonville, TX Micro	7,407	288
Adrian, MI Micro	7,318	289
Harrisonburg, VA Metro	7,230	290
Lexington, NE Micro	7,227	291
Lamesa, TX Micro	7,226	292
Palestine, TX Micro	7,194	293
Champaign-Urbana, IL Metro	7,116	294
Greenville, NC Metro	7,114	295
Jamestown-Dunkirk-Fredonia, NY Micro	7,086	296
Myrtle Beach-Conway-North Myrtle Beach, SC Metro	7,042	297
Sanford, NC Micro	7,019	298
Salisbury, NC Micro	7,002	299
Janesville, WI Metro	6,977	300
Muscatine, IA Micro	6,812	301
Emporia, KS Micro	6,806	302
Peoria, IL Metro	6,665	303
Guymon, OK Micro	6,624	304
Brownwood, TX Micro	6,618	305
Albertville, AL Micro	6,518	306
Springfield, MO Metro	6,510	307
Allegan, MI Micro	6,491	308

CBSA	POPULATION	RANK	CBSA	POPULATION	RANK	CBSA	POPULATION	RANK
Lebanon, PA Metro	6,427	309	Rock Springs, WY Micro	3,749	413	Salisbury, MD Metro	2,183	517
Akron, OH Metro	6,404	310	Salina, KS Micro	3,722	414	Hudson, NY Micro	2,165	518
Lexington-Thomasville, NC Micro	6,391	311	Ocean City, NJ Metro	3,694	415	Kinston, NC Micro	2,151	519
Portales, NM Micro	6,375	312	Cedartown, GA Micro	3,692	416	Anderson, SC Metro	2,144	520
Muskegon-Norton Shores, MI Metro	6,344	313	Palm Coast, FL Micro	3,651	417	Duluth, MN-WI Metro	2,124	521
Rome, GA Metro	6,310	314	Cornelia, GA Micro	3,629	418	Cullman, AL Micro	2,122	522
Erie, PA Metro	6,306	315	Elizabethtown, KY Micro	3,627	419	Beaver Dam, WI Micro	2,116	523
Gulfport-Biloxi, MS Metro	6,237	316	Sulphur Springs, TX Micro	3,553	420	Muskogee, OK Micro	2,111	524
Goldsboro, NC Metro	6,212	317	Canton-Massillon, OH Metro	3,551	421	Malone, NY Micro	2,106	525
Scottsbluff, NE Micro	6,154	318	Watertown-Fort Atkinson, WI Micro	3,527	422	Blacksburg-Christiansburg-Radford, VA Metro	2,099	526
Truckee-Grass Valley, CA Micro	6,093	319	Tifton, GA Micro	3,517	423	Jackson, TN Metro	2,098	527
Blackfoot, ID Micro	6,065	320	Cedar Rapids, IA Metro	3,513	424	Newberry, SC Micro	2,082	528
Kankakee-Bradley, IL Metro	6,042	321	Fargo, ND-MN Metro	3,475	425	Burlington-South Burlington, VT Metro	2,065	529
St. George, UT Metro	5,993	322	Logansport, IN Micro	3,434	426	Huntington-Ashland, WV-KY-OH Metro	2,050	530
Athens, TX Micro	5,959	323	Hagerstown-Martinsburg, MD-WV Metro	3,424	427	Elmira, NY Metro	2,048	531
Binghamton, NY Metro	5,860	324	Roseburg, OR Micro	3,421	428	Anniston-Oxford, AL Metro	2,034	532
Joplin, MO Metro	5,787	325	Frankfort, IN Micro	3,413	429	Dothan, AL Metro	2,032	533
Savannah, GA Metro	5,753	326	Plymouth, IN Micro	3,406	430	Seneca, SC Micro	2,028	534
Klamath Falls, OR Micro	5,752	327	Casper, WY Metro	3,393	431	Auburn-Opelika, AL Metro	2,013	535
Morristown, TN Metro	5,748	328	Daphne-Fairhope, AL Micro	3,389	432	Fallon, NV Micro	2,011	536
Jackson, MS Metro	5,743	329	Oshkosh-Neenah, WI Metro	3,389	433	Laurel, MS Micro	2,005	537
Statesville-Mooresville, NC Micro	5,743	330	Pampa, TX Micro	3,387	434	Great Falls, MT Metro	1,989	538
Sterling, IL Micro	5,711	331	Houma-Bayou Cane-Thibodaux, LA Metro	3,374	435	Ellensburg, WA Micro	1,988	539
Montrose, CO Micro	5,701	332	Brenham, TX Micro	3,341	436	Albany, GA Metro	1,986	540
Bend, OR Metro	5,689	333	Pahrump, NV Micro	3,310	437	Tahlequah, OK Micro	1,986	541
Niles-Benton Harbor, MI Metro	5,678	334	Grants Pass, OR Micro	3,291	438	Gadsden, AL Metro	1,970	542
Punta Gorda, FL Metro	5,672	335	Warner Robins, GA Metro	3,287	439	Tiffin-Fostoria, OH Micro	1,967	543
Mount Airy, NC Micro	5,646	336	Willmar, MN Micro	3,285	440	Sedalia, MO Micro	1,965	544
Pocatello, ID Metro	5,582	337	Storm Lake, IA Micro	3,264	441	Fremont, NE Micro	1,964	545
Billings, MT Metro	5,519	338	Barnstable Town, MA Metro	3,256	442	Kingsport-Bristol, TN-VA Metro	1,946	546
Andrews, TX Micro	5,502	339	New Bern, NC Micro	3,231	443	Springfield, OH Metro	1,944	547
Moultrie, GA Micro	5,419	340	Monroe, MI Metro	3,200	444	Albert Lea, MN Micro	1,940	548
Mobile, AL Metro	5,381	341	North Wilkesboro, NC Micro	3,156	445	Ardmore, OK Micro	1,935	549
Wilson, NC Micro	5,353	342	Coeur d'Alene, ID Metro	3,147	446	Ottumwa, IA Micro	1,935	550
Decatur, AL Metro	5,290	343	Vernon, TX Micro	3,114	447	Florence, SC Metro	1,934	551
Hood River, OR Micro	5,280	344	Oak Harbor, WA Micro	3,054	448	Paris, TX Micro	1,932	552
Stephenville, TX Micro	5,277	345	Rapid City, SD Metro	3,037	449	Columbus, IN Metro	1,913	553
Bloomington-Normal, IL Metro	5,219	346	Panama City-Lynn Haven, FL Metro	3,008	450	Price, UT Micro	1,872	554
Portland-South Portland, ME Metro	5,208	347	Columbia, TN Micro	2,997	451	Jefferson City, MO Metro	1,870	555
Manhattan, KS Micro	5,184	348	Pascagoula, MS Metro	2,969	452	Hammond, LA Micro	1,866	556
Kapaa, HI Micro	5,102	349	Bloomington, IN Metro	2,949	453	Staunton-Waynesboro, VA Micro	1,865	557
Phoenix Lake-Cedar Ridge, CA Micro	5,057	350	Fort Polk South, LA Micro	2,938	454	Marion, IN Micro	1,855	558
Longview-Kelso, WA Metro	5,029	351	Waterloo-Cedar Falls, IA Metro	2,936	455	Hastings, NE Micro	1,843	559
Lincolnton, NC Micro	4,988	352	Columbia, MO Metro	2,916	456	Auburn, NY Micro	1,829	560
Albany-Lebanon, OR Micro	4,912	353	Bishop, CA Micro	2,915	457	Shawnee, OK Micro	1,829	561
Calhoun, GA Micro	4,900	354	Macon, GA Metro	2,912	458	Lexington Park, MD Micro	1,809	562
Texarkana, TX-Texarkana, AR Metro	4,891	355	Great Bend, KS Micro	2,902	459	Sandusky, OH Metro	1,801	563
Canon City, CO Micro	4,884	356	Gardnerville Ranchos, NV Micro	2,896	460	Kokomo, IN Metro	1,793	564
Snyder, TX Micro	4,789	357	Sturgis, MI Micro	2,895	461	Gillette, WY Micro	1,786	565
Montgomery, AL Metro	4,788	358	Brigham City, UT Micro	2,891	462	Pottsville, PA Micro	1,777	566
Charlottesville, VA Metro	4,755	359	Martinsville, VA Micro	2,856	463	Carbondale, IL Micro	1,775	567
Durango, CO Micro	4,750	360	St. Cloud, MN Metro	2,856	464	Tupelo, MS Micro	1,775	568
Russellville, AR Micro	4,750	361	Galesburg, IL Micro	2,834	465	Riverton, WY Micro	1,774	569
The Villages, FL Micro	4,731	362	Cookeville, TN Micro	2,832	466	Alma, MI Micro	1,758	570
Hinesville-Fort Stewart, GA Metro	4,712	363	Winfield, KS Micro	2,831	467	Missoula, MT Micro	1,743	571
Rocky Mount, NC Metro	4,689	364	Defiance, OH Micro	2,828	468	Hattiesburg, MS Metro	1,718	572
Norfolk, NE Micro	4,660	365	Jackson, WY-ID Micro	2,786	469	Lake City, FL Micro	1,708	573
Granbury, TX Micro	4,629	366	Lake Charles, LA Metro	2,757	470	Lewisburg, PA Micro	1,708	574
Sheboygan, WI Metro	4,622	367	Danville, IL Metro	2,752	471	Duncan, OK Micro	1,684	575
Dover, DE Metro	4,572	368	Enterprise-Ozark, AL Micro	2,718	472	Rockingham, NC Micro	1,673	576
Amsterdam, NY Micro	4,556	369	Tuscaloosa, AL Metro	2,716	473	Terre Haute, IN Metro	1,673	577
Gainesville, TX Micro	4,517	370	Pittsfield, MA Metro	2,702	474	Astoria, OR Micro	1,670	578
Palatka, FL Micro	4,511	371	Ashtabula, OH Micro	2,689	475	Mankato-North Mankato, MN Metro	1,651	579
Fremont, OH Micro	4,499	372	Fort Leonard Wood, MO Micro	2,687	476	Sumter, SC Metro	1,649	580
Battle Creek, MI Metro	4,491	373	Shelton, WA Micro	2,684	477	Charleston, WV Metro	1,640	581
Douglas, GA Micro	4,472	374	Columbus, NE Micro	2,677	478	Albemarle, NC Micro	1,625	582
Torrington, CT Micro	4,431	375	Ogdensburg-Massena, NY Micro	2,663	479	Mount Pleasant, MI Micro	1,621	583
Altus, OK Micro	4,418	376	Enid, OK Metro	2,661	480	North Platte, NE Micro	1,618	584
Appleton, WI Metro	4,405	377	Sterling, CO Micro	2,639	481	Florence, AL Metro	1,590	585
Rochester, MN Metro	4,404	378	Hot Springs, AR Metro	2,593	482	Lebanon, NH-VT Micro	1,570	586
Sweetwater, TX Micro	4,396	379	Greenwood, SC Micro	2,578	483	Stillwater, OK Micro	1,546	587
Bay City, MI Metro	4,384	380	Johnson City, TN Metro	2,565	484	Oneonta, NY Micro	1,531	588
Kendallville, IN Micro	4,254	381	Springfield, IL Metro	2,550	485	Concord, NH Micro	1,524	589
Shelbyville, TN Micro	4,216	382	Rexburg, ID Micro	2,529	486	Lima, OH Metro	1,514	590
Marshall, TX Micro	4,195	383	Grand Forks, ND-MN Metro	2,528	487	Cedar City, UT Micro	1,509	591
Warsaw, IN Micro	4,181	384	Glens Falls, NY Metro	2,497	488	Searcy, AR Micro	1,490	592
Marshalltown, IA Micro	4,159	385	Port Angeles, WA Micro	2,483	489	Coldwater, MI Micro	1,484	593
Corvallis, OR Metro	4,150	386	Norwalk, OH Micro	2,468	490	Branson, MO Micro	1,475	594
Lawrence, KS Metro	4,113	387	Brunswick, GA Metro	2,464	491	Owosso, MI Micro	1,474	595
Centralia, WA Micro	4,108	388	Monroe, LA Metro	2,452	492	Bartlesville, OK Micro	1,456	596
Crescent City North, CA Micro	4,105	389	Fond du Lac, WI Metro	2,451	493	Miami, OK Micro	1,446	597
Roanoke, VA Metro	4,104	390	Chambersburg, PA Micro	2,431	494	Danville, VA Metro	1,444	598
Michigan City-La Porte, IN Metro	4,044	391	Jonesboro, AR Metro	2,407	495	Jasper, IN Micro	1,432	599
Lafayette, LA Metro	4,025	392	Hope, AR Micro	2,402	496	Seymour, IN Micro	1,431	600
Mineral Wells, TX Micro	3,966	393	Los Alamos, NM Micro	2,402	497	Washington, NC Micro	1,429	601
Sioux Falls, SD Metro	3,958	394	Traverse City, MI Micro	2,402	498	East Liverpool-Salem, OH Micro	1,428	602
Borger, TX Micro	3,953	395	Laramie, WY Micro	2,389	499	Kalispell, MT Micro	1,415	603
Fairbanks, AK Metro	3,953	396	City of The Dalles, OR Micro	2,360	500	Ames, IA Metro	1,413	604
Iowa City, IA Metro	3,951	397	Cleveland, TN Metro	2,360	501	Muncie, IN Metro	1,400	605
Faribault-Northfield, MN Micro	3,940	398	Plattsburgh, NY Micro	2,359	502	Forrest City, AR Micro	1,397	606
Mountain Home, ID Micro	3,933	399	Alexandria, LA Metro	2,347	503	Gaffney, SC Micro	1,391	607
Gettysburg, PA Micro	3,932	400	St. Joseph, MO-KS Metro	2,347	504	Yazoo City, MS Micro	1,384	608
Jackson, MI Metro	3,925	401	Lynchburg, VA Metro	2,324	505	Pullman, WA Micro	1,382	609
Hutchinson, KS Micro	3,855	402	Worthington, MN Micro	2,322	506	Johnstown, PA Metro	1,377	610
Bowling Green, KY Metro	3,850	403	Kearney, NE Micro	2,279	507	Owatonna, MN Micro	1,370	611
Evansville, IN-KY Metro	3,836	404	Tullahoma, TN Micro	2,261	508	Hutchinson, MN Micro	1,362	612
Homosassa Springs, FL Micro	3,831	405	Findlay, OH Micro	2,248	509	Manitowoc, WI Micro	1,349	613
Silverthorne, CO Micro	3,815	406	Anderson, IN Metro	2,237	510	Corning, NY Micro	1,327	614
Southern Pines, NC Micro	3,798	407	Ponca City, OK Micro	2,231	511	Shelby, NC Micro	1,326	615
Valdosta, GA Metro	3,792	408	McMinnville, TN Micro	2,224	512	Mayfield, KY Micro	1,325	616
Aberdeen, WA Micro	3,787	409	Coos Bay, OR Micro	2,214	513	Mason City, IA Micro	1,322	617
Winchester, VA-WV Metro	3,781	410	Henderson, NC Micro	2,211	514	Midland, MI Micro	1,294	618
Ithaca, NY Metro	3,777	411	State College, PA Metro	2,195	515	Seneca Falls, NY Micro	1,287	619
Rochelle, IL Micro	3,753	412	Austin, MN Micro	2,189	516	Olean, NY Micro	1,269	620

CBSA	POPULATION	RANK
Meridian, MS Micro	1,259	621
Decatur, IL Metro	1,258	622
Prineville, OR Micro	1,252	623
Morgan City, LA Micro	1,247	624
Bozeman, MT Micro	1,242	625
Dixon, IL Micro	1,225	626
St. Marys, GA Micro	1,223	627
Warrensburg, MO Micro	1,223	628
Pine Bluff, AR Metro	1,201	629
Eau Claire, WI Metro	1,200	630
Waycross, GA Micro	1,184	631
Lancaster, SC Micro	1,173	632
Minot, ND Micro	1,171	633
LaGrange, GA Micro	1,166	634
Lewiston, ID-WA Metro	1,153	635
New Iberia, LA Micro	1,153	636
Forest City, NC Micro	1,149	637
Sevierville, TN Micro	1,143	638
Pittsburg, KS Micro	1,142	639
Wausau, WI Metro	1,134	640
Fitzgerald, GA Micro	1,124	641
Georgetown, SC Micro	1,120	642
La Crosse, WI-MN Metro	1,119	643
Mansfield, OH Metro	1,114	644
Batavia, NY Micro	1,089	645
Evanston, WY Micro	1,088	646
Decatur, IN Micro	1,086	647
Juneau, AK Micro	1,086	648
Gloversville, NY Micro	1,078	649
Americus, GA Micro	1,077	650
Owensboro, KY Metro	1,075	651
Lewiston-Auburn, ME Metro	1,068	652
Helena, MT Micro	1,054	653
Sunbury, PA Micro	1,052	654
Blytheville, AR Micro	1,044	655
Pontiac, IL Micro	1,038	656
Ada, OK Micro	1,036	657
Durant, OK Micro	1,033	658
Jesup, GA Micro	1,031	659
Paducah, KY-IL Micro	1,026	660
Charleston-Mattoon, IL Micro	1,025	661
Woodward, OK Micro	1,020	662
Baraboo, WI Micro	1,015	663
Augusta-Waterville, ME Micro	1,012	664
Orangeburg, SC Micro	1,011	665
Richmond, IN Micro	1,005	666
Talladega-Sylacauga, AL Micro	999	667
McAlester, OK Micro	998	668
Morehead City, NC Micro	998	669
Vernal, UT Micro	996	670
Dubuque, IA Metro	992	671
Freeport, IL Micro	989	672
Morgantown, WV Metro	986	673
Statesboro, GA Micro	986	674
Richmond, KY Micro	983	675
Fort Valley, GA Micro	982	676
Frankfort, KY Micro	975	677
Butte-Silver Bow, MT Micro	966	678
Abbeville, LA Micro	961	679
Kennett, MO Micro	958	680
Marion-Herrin, IL Micro	945	681
Bangor, ME Metro	941	682
Athens, TN Micro	939	683
Brookings, OR Micro	933	684
Fort Dodge, IA Micro	919	685
Opelousas-Eunice, LA Micro	918	686
Coffeyville, KS Micro	917	687
Wooster, OH Micro	912	688
Bloomsburg-Berwick, PA Micro	911	689
Stevens Point, WI Micro	901	690
Keokuk-Fort Madison, IA-MO Micro	884	691
Marshall, MN Micro	884	692
Bainbridge, GA Micro	870	693
Picayune, MS Micro	862	694
Greenwood, MS Micro	839	695
Scottsboro, AL Micro	838	696
Burlington, IA-IL Micro	833	697
Weirton-Steubenville, WV-OH Metro	830	698
Moscow, ID Micro	824	699
Parkersburg-Marietta, WV-OH Metro	824	700
Union City, TN-KY Micro	821	701
Clarksburg, WV Micro	817	702
Fergus Falls, MN Micro	817	703
Kill Devil Hills, NC Micro	816	704
Crawfordsville, IN Micro	804	705
Marion, OH Micro	800	706
Boone, NC Micro	786	707
Greeneville, TN Micro	786	708
Quincy, IL-MO Micro	784	709
Summerville, GA Micro	775	710
Hays, KS Micro	773	711
Washington, IN Micro	769	712
Ruston, LA Micro	768	713
Cape Girardeau-Jackson, MO-IL Micro	767	714
Thomasville, GA Micro	766	715
Beckley, WV Micro	753	716
Danville, KY Micro	749	717
Bismarck, ND Metro	747	718
Marshall, MO Micro	746	719
Roanoke Rapids, NC Micro	740	720
Williamsport, PA Metro	740	721
Sault Ste. Marie, MI Micro	739	722
Dublin, GA Micro	738	723
Barre, VT Micro	737	724
Cortland, NY Micro	737	725
Kodiak, AK Micro	737	726
Red Wing, MN Micro	735	727
La Grande, OR Micro	726	728
Arkadelphia, AR Micro	725	729
Auburn, IN Micro	714	730
New Philadelphia-Dover, OH Micro	706	731
Walterboro, SC Micro	705	732
Wheeling, WV-OH Metro	705	733
El Dorado, AR Micro	694	734
Columbus, MS Micro	692	735
Cumberland, MD-WV Metro	681	736
Parsons, KS Micro	679	737
Sheridan, WY Micro	679	738
Easton, MD Micro	678	739
Wisconsin Rapids-Marshfield, WI Micro	675	740
Brownsville, TN Micro	671	741
Clinton, IA Micro	658	742
Dillon, SC Micro	657	743
Milledgeville, GA Micro	655	744
Brainerd, MN Micro	652	745
Athens, OH Micro	650	746
Batesville, AR Micro	647	747
De Ridder, LA Micro	636	748
Keene, NH Micro	634	749
Angola, IN Micro	631	750
Winona, MN Micro	627	751
Murray, KY Micro	625	752
Mount Vernon, IL Micro	621	753
Ocean Pines, MD Micro	621	754
Somerset, PA Micro	602	755
New Castle, PA Micro	599	756
Huntingdon, PA Micro	585	757
McPherson, KS Micro	582	758
Natchez, MS-LA Micro	582	759
Natchitoches, LA Micro	581	760
Crossville, TN Micro	578	761
New Ulm, MN Micro	570	762
Corinth, MS Micro	565	763
Lincoln, IL Micro	565	764
Meadville, PA Micro	564	765
Big Rapids, MI Micro	554	766
Crowley, LA Micro	551	767
Marinette, WI-MI Micro	550	768
Van Wert, OH Micro	544	769
Somerset, KY Micro	536	770
Oxford, MS Micro	535	771
Elizabeth City, NC Micro	534	772
Bristol, VA Metro	532	773
Canton, IL Micro	531	774
Macomb, IL Micro	531	775
Bluefield, WV-VA Micro	528	776
Portsmouth, OH Micro	522	777
Starkville, MS Micro	522	778
Jacksonville, IL Micro	517	779
Bogalusa, LA Micro	510	780
Poplar Bluff, MO Micro	505	781
Vicksburg, MS Micro	504	782
Cadillac, MI Micro	498	783
Celina, OH Micro	495	784
Marquette, MI Micro	495	785
DuBois, PA Micro	493	786
Indianola, MS Micro	492	787
Minden, LA Micro	491	788
Altoona, PA Metro	489	789
Rutland, VT Micro	488	790
Greenville, MS Micro	486	791
Mount Vernon, OH Micro	486	792
Rolla, MO Micro	483	793
Greenville, OH Micro	476	794
Laconia, NH Micro	472	795
McComb, MS Micro	472	796
Mount Sterling, KY Micro	471	797
Glasgow, KY Micro	467	798
Madisonville, KY Micro	467	799
Cordele, GA Micro	460	800
Dyersburg, TN Micro	457	801
Sikeston, MO Micro	453	802
Wabash, IN Micro	450	803
Troy, AL Micro	448	804
West Plains, MO Micro	447	805
Bradford, PA Micro	445	806
Indiana, PA Micro	443	807
Peru, IN Micro	438	808
Cleveland, MS Micro	433	809
Taylorville, IL Micro	431	810
Zanesville, OH Micro	431	811
Farmington, MO Micro	430	812
Laurinburg, NC Micro	427	813
Chillicothe, OH Micro	425	814
Sidney, OH Micro	424	815
Tallulah, LA Micro	424	816
Cambridge, MD Micro	423	817
Centralia, IL Micro	417	818
Bedford, IN Micro	415	819
Yankton, SD Micro	413	820
Fairmont, WV Micro	409	821
Harrison, AR Micro	409	822
Lawrenceburg, TN Micro	409	823
Bennington, VT Micro	408	824
Bucyrus, OH Micro	405	825
Fairmont, MN Micro	395	826
Newton, IA Micro	392	827
Paragould, AR Micro	391	828
Sayre, PA Micro	383	829
Selinsgrove, PA Micro	383	830
Wapakoneta, OH Micro	381	831
Kirksville, MO Micro	380	832
New Castle, IN Micro	377	833
Harriman, TN Micro	369	834
Ketchikan, AK Micro	368	835
Spearfish, SD Micro	367	836
Mountain Home, AR Micro	359	837
Washington, OH Micro	353	838
Jennings, LA Micro	351	839
Lebanon, MO Micro	351	840
London, KY Micro	349	841
Ashland, OH Micro	347	842
Effingham, IL Micro	347	843
Thomaston, GA Micro	347	844
Magnolia, AR Micro	346	845
Newport, TN Micro	346	846
Menomonie, WI Micro	344	847
Paris, TN Micro	343	848
Watertown, SD Micro	342	849
Cambridge, OH Micro	341	850
Corbin, KY Micro	341	851
Huntington, IN Micro	341	852
Bellefontaine, OH Micro	337	853
Camden, AR Micro	336	854
Brevard, NC Micro	335	855
Madison, IN Micro	333	856
Bemidji, MN Micro	332	857
Urbana, OH Micro	330	858
Point Pleasant, WV-OH Micro	328	859
Oil City, PA Micro	320	860
Vincennes, IN Micro	320	861
Platteville, WI Micro	314	862
Atchison, KS Micro	309	863
Selma, AL Micro	309	864
Valley, AL Micro	308	865
Pierre Part, LA Micro	305	866
Oak Hill, WV Micro	301	867
West Helena, AR Micro	300	868
Alexandria, MN Micro	296	869
Houghton, MI Micro	291	870
Lewistown, PA Micro	290	871
Wahpeton, ND-MN Micro	290	872
Moberly, MO Micro	288	873
Clarksdale, MS Micro	286	874
Aberdeen, SD Micro	285	875
Harrisburg, IL Micro	285	876
La Follette, TN Micro	281	877
Toccoa, GA Micro	281	878
Middlesborough, KY Micro	279	879
Wilmington, OH Micro	273	880
Bastrop, LA Micro	263	881
Pierre, SD Micro	263	882
Mexico, MO Micro	258	883
Brookhaven, MS Micro	251	884
Monroe, WI Micro	251	885
Maysville, KY Micro	250	886
Coshocton, OH Micro	249	887
Hannibal, MO Micro	248	888
Rockland, ME Micro	245	889
Oskaloosa, IA Micro	241	890
Dickinson, ND Micro	239	891
Central City, KY Micro	238	892
Beatrice, NE Micro	235	893
Brookings, SD Micro	235	894
Scottsburg, IN Micro	234	895
Iron Mountain, MI-WI Micro	231	896
Williston, ND Micro	231	897
Jamestown, ND Micro	228	898
Lock Haven, PA Micro	228	899
Spencer, IA Micro	221	900
Campbellsville, KY Micro	220	901
Boone, IA Micro	217	902
Merrill, WI Micro	217	903
Berlin, NH-VT Micro	213	904
Chester, SC Micro	213	905
Havre, MT Micro	212	906
Bennettsville, SC Micro	204	907
Union, SC Micro	204	908
North Vernon, IN Micro	201	909
Alpena, MI Micro	192	910
Mitchell, SD Micro	192	911
Tuskegee, AL Micro	181	912
Escanaba, MI Micro	179	913
Huron, SD Micro	179	914
Greensburg, IN Micro	162	915
St. Marys, PA Micro	161	916
Maryville, MO Micro	159	917
Grenada, MS Micro	153	918
Warren, PA Micro	152	919
Vermillion, SD Micro	148	920
Connersville, IN Micro	141	921
Spirit Lake, IA Micro	134	922

CBSA Total		40,201,359
United States Total		41,143,351
CBSA (% of U.S. Total)		97.71

Total Households

CBSA	HOUSEHOLDS	RANK
New York-Newark-Edison, NY-NJ-PA Metro	6,818,599	1
Los Angeles-Long Beach-Santa Ana, CA Metro	4,257,854	2
Chicago-Naperville-Joliet, IL-IN-WI Metro	3,384,057	3
Philadelphia-Camden-Wilmington, PA-NJ-DE-MD Metro	2,185,750	4
Dallas-Fort Worth-Arlington, TX Metro	2,071,180	5
Miami-Fort Lauderdale-Miami Beach, FL Metro	2,023,093	6
Washington-Arlington-Alexandria, DC-VA-MD-WV Metro	1,949,290	7
Houston-Baytown-Sugar Land, TX Metro	1,794,422	8
Detroit-Warren-Livonia, MI Metro	1,723,533	9
Boston-Cambridge-Quincy, MA-NH Metro	1,712,655	10
Atlanta-Sandy Springs-Marietta, GA Metro	1,711,283	11
San Francisco-Oakland-Fremont, CA Metro	1,578,017	12
Phoenix-Mesa-Scottsdale, AZ Metro	1,334,212	13
Seattle-Tacoma-Bellevue, WA Metro	1,251,502	14
Minneapolis-St. Paul-Bloomington, MN-WI Metro	1,193,593	15
Riverside-San Bernardino-Ontario, CA Metro	1,150,039	16
St. Louis, MO-IL Metro	1,081,946	17
Tampa-St. Petersburg-Clearwater, FL Metro	1,079,049	18
San Diego-Carlsbad-San Marcos, CA Metro	1,051,344	19
Baltimore-Towson, MD Metro	1,008,010	20
Pittsburgh, PA Metro	993,772	21
Denver-Aurora, CO Metro	901,339	22
Cleveland-Elyria-Mentor, OH Metro	856,502	23
Cincinnati-Middletown, OH-KY-IN Metro	803,625	24
Portland-Vancouver-Beaverton, OR-WA Metro	796,287	25
Kansas City, MO-KS Metro	755,705	26
Sacramento-Arden-Arcade-Roseville, CA Metro	735,636	27
Orlando, FL Metro	705,005	28
Columbus, OH Metro	671,120	29
San Antonio, TX Metro	645,578	30
Providence-New Bedford-Fall River, RI-MA Metro	636,851	31
Indianapolis, IN Metro	629,264	32
Virginia Beach-Norfolk-Newport News, VA-NC Metro	604,810	33
Las Vegas-Paradise, NV Metro	600,039	34
Milwaukee-Waukesha-West Allis, WI Metro	599,727	35
San Jose-Sunnyvale-Santa Clara, CA Metro	584,841	36
Charlotte-Gastonia-Concord, NC-SC Metro	561,868	37
Nashville-Davidson-Murfreesboro, TN Metro	538,501	38
Austin-Round Rock, TX Metro	530,399	39
New Orleans-Metairie-Kenner, LA Metro	502,165	40
Louisville, KY-IN Metro	480,222	41
Jacksonville, FL Metro	473,296	42
Memphis, TN-MS-AR Metro	468,409	43
Buffalo-Cheektowaga-Tonawanda, NY Metro	465,606	44
Hartford-West Hartford-East Hartford, CT Metro	461,926	45
Oklahoma City, OK Metro	449,223	46
Richmond, VA Metro	444,509	47
Birmingham-Hoover, AL Metro	425,136	48
Rochester, NY Metro	401,432	49
Tucson, AZ Metro	359,967	50
Tulsa, OK Metro	349,541	51
Raleigh-Cary, NC Metro	344,684	52
Dayton, OH Metro	340,176	53
Albany-Schenectady-Troy, NY Metro	339,518	54
Salt Lake City, UT Metro	333,069	55
Bridgeport-Stamford-Norwalk, CT Metro	332,533	56
New Haven-Milford, CT Metro	328,465	57
Omaha-Council Bluffs, NE-IA Metro	307,833	58
Honolulu, HI Metro	300,269	59
Albuquerque, NM Metro	300,091	60
Allentown-Bethlehem-Easton, PA-NJ Metro	298,684	61
Worcester, MA Metro	296,987	62
Sarasota-Bradenton-Venice, FL Metro	285,475	63
Grand Rapids-Wyoming, MI Metro	283,695	64
Akron, OH Metro	279,711	65
Fresno, CA Metro	267,644	66
Greensboro-High Point, NC Metro	265,766	67
Baton Rouge, LA Metro	265,763	68
Springfield, MA Metro	265,464	69
Knoxville, TN Metro	265,037	70
Toledo, OH Metro	262,264	71
Columbia, SC Metro	259,429	72
Oxnard-Thousand Oaks-Ventura, CA Metro	258,235	73
Syracuse, NY Metro	256,686	74
Little Rock-North Little Rock, AR Metro	251,478	75
Youngstown-Warren-Boardman, OH-PA Metro	235,058	76
Poughkeepsie-Newburgh-Middletown, NY Metro	228,858	77
Greenville, SC Metro	228,501	78
Wichita, KS Metro	227,273	79
Scranton-Wilkes-Barre, PA Metro	224,599	80
Bakersfield, CA Metro	222,088	81
Charleston-North Charleston, SC Metro	221,207	82
El Paso, TX Metro	220,591	83
Cape Coral-Fort Myers, FL Metro	216,340	84
Madison, WI Metro	215,901	85
Colorado Springs, CO Metro	214,763	86
Palm Bay-Melbourne-Titusville, FL Metro	213,296	87
Portland-South Portland, ME Metro	208,429	88
Harrisburg-Carlisle, PA Metro	207,363	89
Stockton, CA Metro	204,446	90
Des Moines, IA Metro	200,761	91
Lakeland-Winter Haven, FL Metro	199,053	92
Deltona-Daytona Beach-Ormond Beach, FL Metro	197,286	93
Chattanooga, TN-GA Metro	195,114	94
Boise City-Nampa, ID Metro	191,380	95
Augusta-Richmond County, GA-SC Metro	190,452	96
Jackson, MS Metro	186,694	97
Durham, NC Metro	180,698	98
Lancaster, PA Metro	178,632	99
Lansing-East Lansing, MI Metro	178,559	100
Winston-Salem, NC Metro	177,559	101
McAllen-Edinburg-Pharr, TX Metro	177,551	102
Santa Rosa-Petaluma, CA Metro	176,599	103
Flint, MI Metro	174,489	104
Lexington-Fayette, KY Metro	170,741	105
Spokane, WA Metro	169,538	106
Pensacola-Ferry Pass-Brent, FL Metro	162,547	107
Asheville, NC Metro	161,504	108
Canton-Massillon, OH Metro	160,434	109
Modesto, CA Metro	160,415	110
Fort Wayne, IN Metro	156,340	111
York-Hanover, PA Metro	153,899	112
Springfield, MO Metro	152,912	113
Manchester-Nashua, NH Metro	151,862	114
Mobile, AL Metro	151,277	115
Davenport-Moline-Rock Island, IA-IL Metro	149,860	116
Ogden-Clearfield, UT Metro	148,272	117
Reno-Sparks, NV Metro	148,113	118
Reading, PA Metro	147,094	119
Shreveport-Bossier City, LA Metro	146,784	120
Port St. Lucie-Fort Pierce, FL Metro	145,448	121
Fayetteville-Springdale-Rogers, AR-MO Metro	145,320	122
Corpus Christi, TX Metro	144,438	123
Peoria, IL Metro	143,490	124
Huntsville, AL Metro	143,481	125
Beaumont-Port Arthur, TX Metro	141,112	126
Hickory-Morganton-Lenoir, NC Metro	138,637	127
Santa Barbara-Santa Maria-Goleta, CA Metro	138,606	128
Evansville, IN-KY Metro	138,434	129
Vallejo-Fairfield, CA Metro	137,495	130
Eugene-Springfield, OR Metro	134,908	131
Ann Arbor, MI Metro	134,260	132
Montgomery, AL Metro	133,444	133
Tallahassee, FL Metro	132,939	134
Trenton-Ewing, NJ Metro	130,580	135
Salem, OR Metro	130,238	136
Charleston, WV Metro	129,170	137
Rockford, IL Metro	127,111	138
Salinas, CA Metro	125,049	139
Kalamazoo-Portage, MI Metro	124,866	140
Wilmington, NC Metro	124,617	141
Anchorage, AK Metro	123,965	142
Roanoke, VA Metro	122,425	143
Naples-Marco Island, FL Metro	122,207	144
South Bend-Mishawaka, IN-MI Metro	122,015	145
Fayetteville, NC Metro	121,880	146
Killeen-Temple-Fort Hood, TX Metro	118,221	147
Huntington-Ashland, WV-KY-OH Metro	117,795	148
Ocala, FL Metro	117,038	149
Utica-Rome, NY Metro	116,332	150
Visalia-Porterville, CA Metro	116,039	151
Savannah, GA Metro	115,982	152
Green Bay, WI Metro	114,160	153
Provo-Orem, UT Metro	113,246	154
Duluth, MN-WI Metro	112,854	155
Lincoln, NE Metro	111,135	156
Boulder, CO Metro	110,947	157
Fort Smith, AR-OK Metro	108,185	158
Brownsville-Harlingen, TX Metro	106,936	159
Erie, PA Metro	106,539	160
Columbus, GA-AL Metro	105,262	161
Fort Collins-Loveland, CO Metro	104,401	162
Norwich-New London, CT Metro	103,670	163
Spartanburg, SC Metro	102,011	164
Binghamton, NY Metro	101,094	165
Barnstable Town, MA Metro	99,372	166
Atlantic City, NJ Metro	99,202	167
Lubbock, TX Metro	98,941	168
Gainesville, FL Metro	98,712	169
Cedar Rapids, IA Metro	97,562	170
Kingsport-Bristol, TN-VA Metro	97,347	171
San Luis Obispo-Paso Robles, CA Metro	96,888	172
Gulfport-Biloxi, MS Metro	96,531	173
Lafayette, LA Metro	92,820	174
Lynchburg, VA Metro	91,501	175
Hagerstown-Martinsburg, MD-WV Metro	91,441	176
Topeka, KS Metro	90,579	177
Santa Cruz-Watsonville, CA Metro	90,323	178
Myrtle Beach-Conway-North Myrtle Beach, SC Metro	89,887	179
Bremerton-Silverdale, WA Metro	89,605	180
Amarillo, TX Metro	88,096	181
Olympia, WA Metro	87,452	182
Macon, GA Metro	86,732	183
Clarksville, TN-KY Metro	86,444	184
Champaign-Urbana, IL Metro	86,265	185
Holland-Grand Haven, MI Metro	85,966	186
Springfield, IL Metro	85,236	187
Chico, CA Metro	82,914	188
Waco, TX Metro	81,398	189
Saginaw-Saginaw Township North, MI Metro	80,784	190
Appleton, WI Metro	80,527	191
Burlington-South Burlington, VT Metro	79,136	192
Prescott, AZ Metro	78,686	193
Johnson City, TN Metro	77,746	194
Sioux Falls, SD Metro	77,565	195
Tuscaloosa, AL Metro	77,070	196
Longview, TX Metro	75,892	197
Greeley, CO Metro	75,819	198
Medford, OR Metro	75,814	199
Florence, SC Metro	75,346	200
Torrington, CT Micro	75,019	201
Yakima, WA Metro	74,815	202
Kennewick-Richland-Pasco, WA Metro	73,975	203
Fargo, ND-MN Metro	72,974	204
Lake Charles, LA Metro	72,564	205
Racine, WI Metro	72,129	206
Charlottesville, VA Metro	71,517	207
Fort Walton Beach-Crestview-Destin, FL Metro	71,255	208
College Station-Bryan, TX Metro	71,208	209
Lake Havasu City-Kingman, AZ Micro	70,724	210
Houma-Bayou Cane-Thibodaux, LA Metro	70,460	211
Bloomington, IN Metro	70,435	212
Tyler, TX Metro	70,020	213
Punta Gorda, FL Metro	70,010	214
Merced, CA Metro	69,981	215
Lafayette, IN Metro	69,298	216
Kingston, NY Metro	69,261	217
Anderson, SC Metro	69,256	218
Bellingham, WA Metro	69,217	219
Lebanon, NH-VT Micro	69,077	220
Redding, CA Metro	68,553	221
Elkhart-Goshen, IN Metro	68,266	222
Seaford, DE Micro	68,079	223
Rochester, MN Metro	66,877	224
Athens-Clarke County, GA Metro	66,842	225
Parkersburg-Marietta, WV-OH Metro	66,555	226
Terre Haute, IN Metro	65,263	227
Monroe, LA Metro	65,175	228
St. Cloud, MN Metro	64,612	229
Muskegon-Norton Shores, MI Metro	64,424	230
Niles-Benton Harbor, MI Metro	63,799	231
Joplin, MO Metro	63,459	232
Waterloo-Cedar Falls, IA Metro	63,424	233
Panama City-Lynn Haven, FL Metro	62,985	234
Oshkosh-Neenah, WI Metro	62,567	235
Las Cruces, NM Metro	62,310	236
Greenville, NC Metro	62,219	237
Lexington-Thomasville, NC Micro	60,888	238
Wheeling, WV-OH Metro	60,823	239
Daphne-Fairhope, AL Micro	60,803	240
Columbia, MO Metro	60,272	241
Bangor, ME Metro	60,233	242
Ottawa-Streator, IL Micro	60,222	243
Jackson, MI Metro	59,967	244
Blacksburg-Christiansburg-Radford, VA Metro	59,933	245
Bloomington-Normal, IL Metro	59,927	246
Janesville, WI Metro	59,836	247
Eau Claire, WI Metro	59,522	248
Johnstown, PA Metro	59,445	249
Pottsville, PA Micro	58,987	250
Albany, GA Metro	58,700	251
Yuma, AZ Metro	58,575	252
Billings, MT Metro	58,533	253
Florence, AL Metro	58,428	254
Abilene, TX Metro	57,970	255
Decatur, AL Metro	57,939	256
Hilton Head Island-Beaufort, SC Micro	57,801	257
Pueblo, CO Metro	57,733	258
Laredo, TX Metro	57,447	259
Santa Fe, NM Metro	57,131	260
Homosassa Springs, FL Micro	57,090	261
Hilo, HI Micro	57,079	262
Monroe, MI Metro	56,366	263
Springfield, OH Metro	56,234	264
Pascagoula, MS Metro	56,028	265
Traverse City, MI Micro	55,781	266
East Stroudsburg, PA Micro	55,735	267
Wichita Falls, TX Metro	55,728	268
Alexandria, LA Metro	55,517	269
Pittsfield, MA Metro	55,410	270
Iowa City, IA Metro	55,380	271
Concord, NH Micro	55,291	272
Rocky Mount, NC Metro	54,927	273
Burlington, NC Metro	54,796	274
Battle Creek, MI Metro	54,614	275
Dothan, AL Metro	53,986	276
Gainesville, GA Metro	53,876	277
Jamestown-Dunkirk-Fredonia, NY Micro	53,751	278
Weirton-Steubenville, WV-OH Metro	53,697	279
Sioux City, IA-NE-SD Metro	53,554	280
Vero Beach, FL Metro	53,514	281
Jefferson City, MO Metro	53,131	282
Bend, OR Metro	52,975	283
Anderson, IN Metro	52,740	284
Chambersburg, PA Micro	52,633	285
Statesville-Mooresville, NC Micro	52,136	286
Eureka-Arcata-Fortuna, CA Micro	52,019	287
State College, PA Metro	51,791	288
Salisbury, NC Micro	51,633	289
Altoona, PA Metro	50,858	290
Dover, DE Metro	50,674	291
Morristown, TN Metro	50,609	292
Yuba City-Marysville, CA Metro	50,433	293
La Crosse, WI-MN Metro	50,257	294
Jacksonville, NC Metro	50,133	295
Texarkana, TX-Texarkana, AR Metro	49,479	296
Tupelo, MS Micro	49,466	297
Augusta-Waterville, ME Micro	49,429	298
Grand Junction, CO Metro	49,380	299
Glens Falls, NY Metro	49,304	300
Vineland-Millville-Bridgeton, NJ Metro	49,287	301
Wausau, WI Metro	49,066	302
Mansfield, OH Metro	48,915	303
Napa, CA Metro	48,166	304
Auburn-Opelika, AL Metro	48,130	305
Hattiesburg, MS Metro	48,046	306
Lebanon, PA Micro	47,396	307

CBSA	HOUSEHOLDS	RANK
Muncie, IN Metro	47,235	308
Sierra Vista-Douglas, AZ Micro	47,164	309
Kahului-Wailuku, HI Micro	46,981	310
Morgantown, WV Metro	46,683	311
Williamsport, PA Metro	46,544	312
Anniston-Oxford, AL Metro	46,110	313
St. Joseph, MO-KS Metro	45,910	314
Rapid City, SD Metro	45,683	315
Flagstaff, AZ Metro	45,615	316
Dalton, GA Metro	45,544	317
Danville, VA Metro	45,267	318
Lumberton, NC Micro	45,017	319
Warner Robins, GA Metro	44,966	320
Sherman-Denison, TX Metro	44,937	321
Coeur d'Alene, ID Metro	44,828	322
Decatur, IL Metro	44,768	323
Bluefield, WV-VA Micro	44,703	324
Odessa, TX Metro	44,520	325
Sheboygan, WI Metro	44,118	326
Staunton-Waynesboro, VA Micro	44,110	327
Bay City, MI Metro	44,046	328
Owensboro, KY Metro	43,947	329
New Bern, NC Micro	43,868	330
Winchester, VA-WV Metro	43,852	331
Jonesboro, AR Metro	43,792	332
Valdosta, GA Metro	43,784	333
Midland, TX Metro	43,670	334
Lewiston-Auburn, ME Metro	43,539	335
Goldsboro, NC Metro	42,985	336
Willimantic, CT Micro	42,964	337
East Liverpool-Salem, OH Micro	42,750	338
Jackson, TN Metro	42,499	339
Cleveland, TN Metro	42,279	340
Farmington, NM Metro	42,209	341
Salisbury, MD Metro	42,120	342
Ocean City, NJ Metro	42,066	343
Elizabethtown, KY Metro	41,834	344
Bowling Green, KY Metro	41,810	345
Gadsden, AL Metro	41,713	346
Kokomo, IN Metro	41,584	347
Michigan City-La Porte, IN Metro	41,550	348
Wooster, OH Micro	41,362	349
Victoria, TX Metro	41,299	350
Meridian, MS Micro	40,910	351
Mount Vernon-Anacortes, WA Metro	40,899	352
Roseburg, OR Micro	40,876	353
Paducah, KY-IL Micro	40,862	354
Albany-Lebanon, OR Micro	40,692	355
El Centro, CA Metro	40,674	356
Lima, OH Metro	40,608	357
Missoula, MT Metro	40,569	358
San Angelo, TX Metro	40,552	359
Allegan, MI Micro	40,536	360
Ogdensburg-Massena, NY Micro	40,438	361
Lawrence, KS Metro	40,320	362
Harrisonburg, VA Metro	39,925	363
Corning, NY Micro	39,775	364
Sumter, SC Metro	39,593	365
Ashtabula, OH Micro	39,583	366
Hot Springs, AR Metro	39,481	367
Cumberland, MD-WV Metro	39,447	368
Cookeville, TN Micro	39,404	369
Bismarck, ND Metro	39,394	370
Lawton, OK Metro	39,243	371
Sebring, FL Micro	39,042	372
Truckee-Grass Valley, CA Micro	38,868	373
Kankakee-Bradley, IL Metro	38,779	374
Ithaca, NY Metro	38,776	375
Brunswick, GA Metro	38,637	376
Manhattan, KS Metro	38,551	377
Madera, CA Metro	38,505	378
Hammond, LA Micro	38,213	379
Shelby, NC Micro	38,108	380
Sunbury, PA Micro	38,041	381
Tullahoma, TN Micro	37,910	382
Watertown-Fort Drum, NY Micro	37,806	383
Fond du Lac, WI Metro	37,698	384
Dunn, NC Micro	37,645	385
Pine Bluff, AR Metro	37,514	386
Wenatchee, WA Metro	37,414	387
Grand Forks, ND-MN Metro	37,295	388
Enterprise-Ozark, AL Micro	37,176	389
Idaho Falls, ID Metro	37,162	390
New Castle, PA Micro	37,053	391
Clarksburg, WV Micro	37,040	392
Adrian, MI Micro	36,976	393
Longview-Kelso, WA Metro	36,913	394
Whitewater, WI Micro	36,259	395
New Philadelphia-Dover, OH Micro	36,238	396
Richmond, KY Micro	36,216	397
Cape Girardeau-Jackson, MO-IL Metro	36,117	398
Key West-Marathon, FL Micro	35,974	399
Gettysburg, PA Micro	35,897	400
Hanford-Corcoran, CA Metro	35,867	401
St. George, UT Metro	35,617	402
Rome, GA Metro	35,407	403
Brainerd, MN Micro	35,191	404
Elmira, NY Metro	34,917	405
Orangeburg, SC Micro	34,527	406
Meadville, PA Micro	34,431	407
Dubuque, IA Metro	34,356	408
Indiana, PA Micro	34,183	409
Ukiah, CA Micro	33,943	410
Albertville, AL Micro	33,653	411
Lexington Park, MD Micro	33,524	412
Opelousas-Eunice, LA Micro	33,166	413
Southern Pines, NC Micro	33,153	414
Zanesville, OH Micro	33,138	415
Manitowoc, WI Micro	33,105	416
Danville, IL Metro	33,025	417
Mankato-North Mankato, MN Micro	33,023	418
Cheyenne, WY Metro	32,763	419
DuBois, PA Micro	32,746	420
Logan, UT-ID Metro	32,745	421
Midland, MI Micro	32,742	422
Grants Pass, OR Micro	32,582	423
Great Falls, MT Metro	32,471	424
Bloomsburg-Berwick, PA Micro	32,278	425
Beaver Dam, WI Micro	32,164	426
Beckley, WV Micro	32,081	427
Olean, NY Micro	31,913	428
Kalispell, MT Micro	31,878	429
Sandusky, OH Metro	31,715	430
Twin Falls, ID Micro	31,443	431
Corvallis, OR Metro	31,383	432
Laurel, MS Micro	31,342	433
Fairbanks, AK Metro	31,329	434
Cullman, AL Micro	31,328	435
Talladega-Sylacauga, AL Micro	31,265	436
Sevierville, TN Micro	30,951	437
Somerset, PA Micro	30,904	438
Plattsburgh, NY Micro	30,869	439
Auburn, NY Micro	30,635	440
Athens, TX Micro	30,609	441
Quincy, IL-MO Micro	30,407	442
Roanoke Rapids, NC Micro	30,402	443
Portsmouth, OH Micro	30,387	444
Wisconsin Rapids-Marshfield, WI Micro	30,378	445
Ames, IA Metro	30,283	446
Oak Harbor, WA Micro	30,149	447
Martinsville, VA Micro	30,009	448
Pocatello, ID Metro	29,971	449
Watertown-Fort Atkinson, WI Micro	29,577	450
Wilson, NC Micro	29,490	451
Pendleton-Hermiston, OR Micro	29,440	452
Keene, NH Micro	29,424	453
Lufkin, TX Micro	29,400	454
Russellville, AR Micro	29,395	455
Bristol, VA Metro	29,235	456
Branson, MO Micro	29,175	457
Mount Airy, NC Micro	29,089	458
Bozeman, MT Micro	28,882	459
Seneca, SC Micro	28,865	460
Findlay, OH Micro	28,731	461
Palatka, FL Micro	28,547	462
Richmond, IN Micro	28,454	463
Port Angeles, WA Micro	28,412	464
Marinette, WI-MI Micro	28,373	465
Galesburg, IL Micro	28,256	466
Chillicothe, OH Micro	28,167	467
Columbus, IN Metro	28,142	468
Frankfort, KY Micro	28,055	469
Columbia, TN Micro	27,986	470
Helena, MT Micro	27,844	471
Warsaw, IN Micro	27,842	472
Aberdeen, WA Micro	27,686	473
Stillwater, OK Micro	27,620	474
Marion, IN Micro	27,604	475
North Wilkesboro, NC Micro	27,558	476
Casper, WY Metro	27,477	477
Owosso, MI Micro	27,383	478
Centralia, WA Micro	27,245	479
Palm Coast, FL Micro	27,096	480
Muskogee, OK Micro	26,914	481
Greeneville, TN Micro	26,727	482
Searcy, AR Micro	26,656	483
Greenwood, SC Micro	26,596	484
Coos Bay, OR Micro	26,478	485
Moses Lake, WA Micro	26,345	486
Grand Island, NE Micro	26,122	487
Marquette, MI Micro	26,118	488
Morehead City, NC Micro	26,033	489
Clearlake, CA Micro	25,920	490
New Iberia, LA Micro	25,913	491
Rutland, VT Micro	25,906	492
Lincolnton, NC Micro	25,872	493
Klamath Falls, OR Micro	25,831	494
Minot, ND Micro	25,770	495
Stevens Point, WI Micro	25,765	496
Marion-Herrin, IL Micro	25,737	497
The Villages, FL Micro	25,497	498
Forest City, NC Micro	25,422	499
Hudson, NY Micro	25,302	500
Shawnee, OK Micro	25,264	501
Charleston-Mattoon, IL Micro	25,208	502
Sayre, PA Micro	24,774	503
Hutchinson, KS Micro	24,730	504
Carbondale, IL Micro	24,664	505
Barre, VT Micro	24,549	506
Laconia, NH Micro	24,484	507
Marion, OH Micro	24,359	508
Salina, KS Micro	24,058	509
Fairmont, WV Micro	23,998	510
Fremont, OH Micro	23,912	511
Lancaster, SC Micro	23,901	512
Hinesville-Fort Stewart, GA Metro	23,835	513
Georgetown, SC Micro	23,818	514
Oneonta, NY Micro	23,794	515
Somerset, KY Micro	23,695	516
Lewiston, ID-WA Metro	23,690	517
Kinston, NC Micro	23,640	518
Mount Pleasant, MI Micro	23,596	519
Sterling, IL Micro	23,536	520
Athens, OH Micro	23,519	521
Marshall, TX Micro	23,424	522
Sturgis, MI Micro	23,357	523
Fergus Falls, MN Micro	23,350	524
Point Pleasant, WV-OH Micro	23,168	525
Alamogordo, NM Micro	22,951	526
Enid, OK Micro	22,879	527
Norwalk, OH Micro	22,864	528
Batavia, NY Micro	22,574	529
Columbus, MS Micro	22,567	530
Baraboo, WI Micro	22,490	531
LaGrange, GA Micro	22,486	532
Nacogdoches, TX Micro	22,465	533
Oil City, PA Micro	22,460	534
Albemarle, NC Micro	22,314	535
Tiffin-Fostoria, OH Micro	22,165	536
Ardmore, OK Micro	22,066	537
Roswell, NM Micro	22,043	538
Phoenix Lake-Cedar Ridge, CA Micro	21,978	539
Lake City, FL Micro	21,971	540
Mason City, IA Micro	21,931	541
Gloversville, NY Micro	21,904	542
Scottsboro, AL Micro	21,902	543
London, KY Micro	21,774	544
Statesboro, GA Micro	21,750	545
Ruston, LA Micro	21,741	546
Harriman, TN Micro	21,738	547
Red Bluff, CA Micro	21,722	548
Farmington, MO Micro	21,686	549
Kapaa, HI Micro	21,445	550
Greenville, MS Micro	21,406	551
Crowley, LA Micro	21,405	552
Gaffney, SC Micro	21,393	553
Carson City, NV Metro	21,337	554
Ocean Pines, MD Micro	21,298	555
Crossville, TN Micro	21,179	556
Elizabeth City, NC Micro	21,158	557
Dublin, GA Micro	21,106	558
Gallup, NM Micro	21,064	559
Mount Vernon, OH Micro	20,953	560
Payson, AZ Micro	20,813	561
Granbury, TX Micro	20,747	562
Natchez, MS-LA Micro	20,739	563
Muscatine, IA Micro	20,737	564
Athens, TN Micro	20,593	565
Danville, KY Micro	20,567	566
Bartlesville, OK Micro	20,460	567
Greenville, OH Micro	20,418	568
Jasper, IN Micro	20,394	569
Abbeville, LA Micro	20,255	570
McComb, MS Micro	20,225	571
Edwards, CO Micro	20,089	572
Burlington, IA-IL Micro	20,035	573
Walla Walla, WA Micro	20,027	574
Glasgow, KY Micro	20,016	575
Hobbs, NM Micro	20,010	576
Rochelle, IL Micro	19,989	577
Faribault-Northfield, MN Micro	19,957	578
Clinton, IA Micro	19,955	579
Amsterdam, NY Micro	19,930	580
Ashland, OH Micro	19,816	581
Waycross, GA Micro	19,812	582
Shelton, WA Micro	19,651	583
Paris, TX Micro	19,544	584
Norfolk, NE Micro	19,406	585
Picayune, MS Micro	19,401	586
Carlsbad-Artesia, NM Micro	19,374	587
New Castle, IN Micro	19,292	588
Freeport, IL Micro	19,231	589
Madisonville, KY Micro	19,197	590
Kearney, NE Micro	19,051	591
Morgan City, LA Micro	19,050	592
Ponca City, OK Micro	18,989	593
Washington, NC Micro	18,972	594
Bedford, IN Micro	18,930	595
Oak Hill, WV Micro	18,900	596
Kerrville, TX Micro	18,801	597
Vicksburg, MS Micro	18,788	598
Bucyrus, OH Micro	18,752	599
Durango, CO Micro	18,727	600
Platteville, WI Micro	18,696	601
Warrensburg, MO Micro	18,614	602
Cortland, NY Micro	18,592	603
Mount Vernon, IL Micro	18,566	604
Blytheville, AR Micro	18,537	605
Huntsville, TX Micro	18,527	606
Sanford, NC Micro	18,524	607
Lewistown, PA Micro	18,489	608
Winona, MN Micro	18,484	609
Bellefontaine, OH Micro	18,262	610
Sidney, OH Micro	18,184	611
Rockingham, NC Micro	18,035	612
Harrison, AR Micro	18,000	613
El Dorado, AR Micro	17,976	614
Milledgeville, GA Micro	17,968	615
Fort Polk South, LA Micro	17,927	616
Gardnerville Ranchos, NV Micro	17,905	617
Cadillac, MI Micro	17,854	618
Selma, AL Micro	17,662	619

CBSA	HOUSEHOLDS	RANK
Calhoun, GA Micro	17,599	620
Red Wing, MN Micro	17,565	621
Corsicana, TX Micro	17,516	622
Rockland, ME Micro	17,515	623
Malone, NY Micro	17,503	624
Warren, PA Micro	17,465	625
Ontario, OR-ID Micro	17,456	626
Keokuk-Fort Madison, IA-MO Micro	17,447	627
Bradford, PA Micro	17,422	628
Mountain Home, AR Micro	17,408	629
Wapakoneta, OH Micro	17,331	630
Kendallville, IN Micro	17,239	631
McAlester, OK Micro	17,197	632
Duncan, OK Micro	17,160	633
Henderson, NC Micro	17,148	634
Jacksonville, TX Micro	17,136	635
Huntingdon, PA Micro	16,964	636
Plymouth, IN Micro	16,964	637
Clovis, NM Micro	16,954	638
Mount Sterling, KY Micro	16,894	639
Berlin, NH-VT Micro	16,827	640
Tahlequah, OK Micro	16,819	641
Poplar Bluff, MO Micro	16,799	642
Rolla, MO Micro	16,705	643
Douglas, GA Micro	16,611	644
Bogalusa, LA Micro	16,602	645
Boone, NC Micro	16,591	646
Thomasville, GA Micro	16,527	647
La Follette, TN Micro	16,514	648
Minden, LA Micro	16,500	649
Coldwater, MI Micro	16,488	650
Seymour, IN Micro	16,360	651
Cambridge, OH Micro	16,354	652
Union City, TN-KY Micro	16,308	653
Greenwood, MS Micro	16,306	654
Starkville, MS Micro	16,167	655
Centralia, IL Micro	16,156	656
Aberdeen, SD Micro	16,149	657
Moultrie, GA Micro	16,107	658
Lawrenceburg, TN Micro	15,994	659
Big Rapids, MI Micro	15,988	660
Jacksonville, IL Micro	15,927	661
Willmar, MN Micro	15,925	662
Escanaba, MI Micro	15,894	663
Wilmington, OH Micro	15,818	664
Rio Grande City, TX Micro	15,765	665
Austin, MN Micro	15,695	666
Elko, NV Micro	15,670	667
Pullman, WA Micro	15,648	668
McMinnville, TN Micro	15,640	669
Sikeston, MO Micro	15,602	670
Sedalia, MO Micro	15,597	671
Logansport, IN Micro	15,546	672
Marshalltown, IA Micro	15,505	673
Fort Dodge, IA Micro	15,477	674
Auburn, IN Micro	15,445	675
St. Marys, GA Micro	15,421	676
Bemidji, MN Micro	15,293	677
Paragould, AR Micro	15,277	678
Vincennes, IN Micro	15,267	679
Espanola, NM Micro	15,255	680
Scottsbluff, NE Micro	15,229	681
Defiance, OH Micro	15,226	682
Pittsburg, KS Micro	15,226	683
Urbana, OH Micro	15,218	684
Bennington, VT Micro	15,134	685
El Campo, TX Micro	15,083	686
Canon City, CO Micro	15,070	687
Menomonie, WI Micro	15,066	688
Walterboro, SC Micro	15,060	689
Astoria, OR Micro	15,054	690
Palestine, TX Micro	15,050	691
Oxford, MS Micro	15,022	692
Mayfield, KY Micro	15,006	693
Shelbyville, TN Micro	14,959	694
Hastings, NE Micro	14,924	695
Pahrump, NV Micro	14,919	696
Del Rio, TX Micro	14,887	697
Celina, OH Micro	14,872	698
Fort Leonard Wood, MO Micro	14,860	699
West Plains, MO Micro	14,852	700
Crawfordsville, IN Micro	14,848	701
Emporia, KS Micro	14,839	702
Durant, OK Micro	14,831	703
Cedartown, GA Micro	14,769	704
Newton, IA Micro	14,747	705
Newberry, SC Micro	14,735	706
Lock Haven, PA Micro	14,723	707
Houghton, MI Micro	14,719	708
Hannibal, MO Micro	14,652	709
Tifton, GA Micro	14,642	710
Easton, MD Micro	14,635	711
Dyersburg, TN Micro	14,605	712
Cornelia, GA Micro	14,583	713
Brownwood, TX Micro	14,565	714
Ottumwa, IA Micro	14,565	715
Coshocton, OH Micro	14,540	716
North Platte, NE Micro	14,535	717
Gainesville, TX Micro	14,527	718
Huntington, IN Micro	14,504	719
Corinth, MS Micro	14,459	720
Valley, AL Micro	14,444	721
Corbin, KY Micro	14,437	722
Pontiac, IL Micro	14,412	723

CBSA	HOUSEHOLDS	RANK
Newport, TN Micro	14,398	724
Fremont, NE Micro	14,392	725
Canton, IL Micro	14,391	726
Kill Devil Hills, NC Micro	14,338	727
Ellensburg, WA Micro	14,332	728
Winfield, KS Micro	14,292	729
Montrose, CO Micro	14,263	730
Murray, KY Micro	14,254	731
Coffeyville, KS Micro	14,238	732
Alma, MI Micro	14,235	733
Natchitoches, LA Micro	14,187	734
Rock Springs, WY Micro	14,159	735
Bay City, TX Micro	14,136	736
Eagle Pass, TX Micro	14,039	737
Burley, ID Micro	13,999	738
Alexandria, MN Micro	13,985	739
Gillette, WY Micro	13,966	740
Selinsgrove, PA Micro	13,950	741
Riverton, WY Micro	13,925	742
Hutchinson, MN Micro	13,903	743
Blackfoot, ID Micro	13,893	744
Ada, OK Micro	13,887	745
Peru, IN Micro	13,846	746
St. Marys, PA Micro	13,839	747
Sault Ste. Marie, MI Micro	13,786	748
Butte-Silver Bow, MT Micro	13,742	749
Brigham City, UT Micro	13,737	750
Taylorville, IL Micro	13,695	751
Americus, GA Micro	13,693	752
Batesville, AR Micro	13,680	753
Monroe, WI Micro	13,664	754
Laurinburg, NC Micro	13,590	755
Seneca Falls, NY Micro	13,579	756
Taos, NM Micro	13,579	757
Iron Mountain, MI-WI Micro	13,571	758
Alice, TX Micro	13,493	759
Camden, AR Micro	13,467	760
Cleveland, MS Micro	13,404	761
Owatonna, MN Micro	13,368	762
Moscow, ID Micro	13,298	763
Kennett, MO Micro	13,216	764
Laramie, WY Micro	13,201	765
Dixon, IL Micro	13,184	766
Wabash, IN Micro	13,178	767
Paris, TN Micro	13,163	768
Chester, SC Micro	13,136	769
Okeechobee, FL Micro	13,127	770
Effingham, IL Micro	13,107	771
Albert Lea, MN Micro	13,059	772
Lewisburg, PA Micro	12,976	773
Lebanon, MO Micro	12,945	774
Safford, AZ Micro	12,932	775
Angola, IN Micro	12,888	776
Miami, OK Micro	12,791	777
Brookhaven, MS Micro	12,786	778
Hope, AR Micro	12,714	779
Alpena, MI Micro	12,693	780
Nogales, AZ Micro	12,687	781
Brevard, NC Micro	12,629	782
Cambridge, MD Micro	12,590	783
Frankfort, IN Micro	12,589	784
Stephenville, TX Micro	12,570	785
Macomb, IL Micro	12,535	786
Madison, IN Micro	12,519	787
Watertown, SD Micro	12,499	788
De Ridder, LA Micro	12,486	789
Sulphur Springs, TX Micro	12,445	790
Middlesborough, KY Micro	12,372	791
Maysville, KY Micro	12,368	792
Garden City, KS Micro	12,335	793
Central City, KY Micro	12,318	794
Troy, AL Micro	12,144	795
Union, SC Micro	11,996	796
Merrill, WI Micro	11,968	797
Columbus, NE Micro	11,902	798
Decatur, IN Micro	11,070	799
Silver City, NM Micro	11,838	800
Juneau, AK Micro	11,624	801
Brenham, TX Micro	11,586	802
Kirksville, MO Micro	11,585	803
Plainview, TX Micro	11,554	804
Van Wert, OH Micro	11,537	805
Sheridan, WY Micro	11,518	806
Cedar City, UT Micro	11,483	807
Jennings, LA Micro	11,481	808
Dillon, SC Micro	11,463	809
Rexburg, ID Micro	11,365	810
Bastrop, LA Micro	11,190	811
Great Bend, KS Micro	11,143	812
Hays, KS Micro	11,094	813
McPherson, KS Micro	11,078	814
Las Vegas, NM Micro	11,066	815
Big Spring, TX Micro	11,045	816
Mineral Wells, TX Micro	11,016	817
Kingsville, TX Micro	10,985	818
Washington, IN Micro	10,975	819
Brookings, SD Micro	10,973	820
Washington, OH Micro	10,970	821
Arcadia, FL Micro	10,895	822
Thomaston, GA Micro	10,855	823
Dodge City, KS Micro	10,804	824
Clewiston, FL Micro	10,665	825
Lincoln, IL Micro	10,643	826
North Vernon, IN Micro	10,625	827

CBSA	HOUSEHOLDS	RANK
Jackson, WY-ID Micro	10,555	828
Harrisburg, IL Micro	10,517	829
Bainbridge, GA Micro	10,486	830
Bennettsville, SC Micro	10,447	831
New Ulm, MN Micro	10,432	832
Clarksdale, MS Micro	10,364	833
Boone, IA Micro	10,361	834
Fitzgerald, GA Micro	10,336	835
Silverthorne, CO Micro	10,335	836
Toccoa, GA Micro	10,141	837
Connersville, IN Micro	10,083	838
Magnolia, AR Micro	9,918	839
Altus, OK Micro	9,889	840
Summerville, GA Micro	9,877	841
La Grande, OR Micro	9,868	842
Brookings, OR Micro	9,798	843
Mount Pleasant, TX Micro	9,760	844
Fort Morgan, CO Micro	9,712	845
Lexington, NE Micro	9,612	846
Marshall, MN Micro	9,597	847
Deming, NM Micro	9,589	848
Mexico, MO Micro	9,585	849
Greensburg, IN Micro	9,556	850
Campbellsville, KY Micro	9,537	851
Forrest City, AR Micro	9,511	852
Beatrice, NE Micro	9,473	853
Jesup, GA Micro	9,466	854
Wahpeton, ND-MN Micro	9,390	855
City of The Dalles, OR Micro	9,341	856
Moberly, MO Micro	9,208	857
Scottsburg, IN Micro	9,189	858
Indianola, MS Micro	9,094	859
Dickinson, ND Micro	9,083	860
Borger, TX Micro	9,048	861
Crescent City North, CA Micro	9,019	862
Yazoo City, MS Micro	9,004	863
Mountain Home, ID Micro	9,003	864
Uvalde, TX Micro	8,926	865
Arkadelphia, AR Micro	8,894	866
Mitchell, SD Micro	8,890	867
Fort Valley, GA Micro	8,879	868
Spearfish, SD Micro	8,873	869
West Helena, AR Micro	8,866	870
Oskaloosa, IA Micro	8,852	871
Tuskegee, AL Micro	8,852	872
Fallon, NV Micro	8,850	873
Parsons, KS Micro	8,842	874
Grants, NM Micro	8,824	875
Fairmont, MN Micro	8,749	876
Vernal, UT Micro	8,732	877
Grenada, MS Micro	8,706	878
Pampa, TX Micro	8,697	879
Jamestown, ND Micro	8,566	880
Marshall, MO Micro	8,480	881
Cordele, GA Micro	8,359	882
Pierre Part, LA Micro	8,306	883
Wauchula, FL Micro	8,236	884
Williston, ND Micro	8,162	885
Beeville, TX Micro	8,125	886
Yankton, SD Micro	8,091	887
Maryville, MO Micro	8,035	888
Levelland, TX Micro	8,016	889
Bishop, CA Micro	7,938	890
Prineville, OR Micro	7,924	891
Sterling, CO Micro	7,861	892
Pierre, SD Micro	7,846	893
Los Alamos, NM Micro	7,722	894
Liberal, KS Micro	7,653	895
Worthington, MN Micro	7,652	896
Brownsville, TN Micro	7,506	897
Storm Lake, IA Micro	7,471	898
Hood River, OR Micro	7,279	899
Spirit Lake, IA Micro	7,251	900
Woodward, OK Micro	7,184	901
Price, UT Micro	7,141	902
Guymon, OK Micro	7,092	903
Spencer, IA Micro	7,085	904
Evanston, WY Micro	7,037	905
Huron, SD Micro	6,945	906
Dumas, TX Micro	6,920	907
Portales, NM Micro	6,769	908
Havre, MT Micro	6,401	909
Atchison, KS Micro	6,242	910
Hereford, TX Micro	6,105	911
Sweetwater, TX Micro	5,902	912
Raymondville, TX Micro	5,561	913
Snyder, TX Micro	5,500	914
Vernon, TX Micro	5,249	915
Ketchikan, AK Micro	5,174	916
Vermillion, SD Micro	4,688	917
Andrews, TX Micro	4,673	918
Kodiak, AK Micro	4,439	919
Lamesa, TX Micro	4,267	920
Tallulah, LA Micro	4,098	921
Pecos, TX Micro	3,748	922

CBSA Total	102,191,978	
United States Total	109,949,228	
CBSA (% of U.S. Total)	92.94	

CBSA	INCOME ($)	RANK
Los Alamos, NM Micro	87,091	1
San Jose-Sunnyvale-Santa Clara, CA Metro	84,410	2
Bridgeport-Stamford-Norwalk, CT Metro	72,694	3
Washington-Arlington-Alexandria, DC-VA-MD-WV Metro	70,274	4
San Francisco-Oakland-Fremont, CA Metro	70,241	5
Edwards, CO Micro	66,908	6
Oxnard-Thousand Oaks-Ventura, CA Metro	66,393	7
Juneau, AK Micro	65,908	8
Trenton-Ewing, NJ Metro	64,505	9
Boulder, CO Metro	63,564	10
Silverthorne, CO Micro	62,938	11
Boston-Cambridge-Quincy, MA-NH Metro	62,499	12
Santa Cruz-Watsonville, CA Metro	62,070	13
Lexington Park, MD Micro	61,912	14
Vallejo-Fairfield, CA Metro	61,825	15
Minneapolis-St. Paul-Bloomington, MN-WI Metro	61,567	16
Torrington, CT Micro	61,086	17
Santa Rosa-Petaluma, CA Metro	60,993	18
Manchester-Nashua, NH Metro	60,207	19
Anchorage, AK Metro	59,559	20
Denver-Aurora, CO Metro	59,519	21
Napa, CA Metro	59,311	22
Poughkeepsie-Newburgh-Middletown, NY Metro	59,157	23
Raleigh-Cary, NC Metro	58,064	24
Hartford-West Hartford-East Hartford, CT Metro	57,991	25
Atlanta-Sandy Springs-Marietta, GA Metro	57,620	26
Gardnerville Ranchos, NV Micro	57,535	27
Jackson, WY-ID Micro	57,485	28
Kodiak, AK Micro	57,352	29
Ann Arbor, MI Metro	57,216	30
Gillette, WY Micro	57,012	31
Chicago-Naperville-Joliet, IL-IN-WI Metro	56,906	32
Holland-Grand Haven, MI Metro	56,732	33
Appleton, WI Metro	56,482	34
Honolulu, HI Metro	56,161	35
Fort Collins-Loveland, CO Metro	56,018	36
Monroe, MI Metro	55,864	37
Rochester, MN Metro	55,832	38
Norwich-New London, CT Metro	55,734	39
Ogden-Clearfield, UT Metro	55,473	40
New York-Newark-Edison, NY-NJ-PA Metro	55,471	41
Baltimore-Towson, MD Metro	55,412	42
Seattle-Tacoma-Bellevue, WA Metro	55,379	43
Salt Lake City, UT Metro	55,244	44
Concord, NH Micro	54,622	45
Salinas, CA Metro	54,609	46
Madison, WI Metro	54,499	47
Austin-Round Rock, TX Metro	54,475	48
Ketchikan, AK Micro	54,385	49
Detroit-Warren-Livonia, MI Metro	53,992	50
Worcester, MA Metro	53,813	51
Fairbanks, AK Metro	53,775	52
Faribault-Northfield, MN Micro	53,637	53
Kahului-Wailuku, HI Micro	53,606	54
Philadelphia-Camden-Wilmington, PA-NJ-DE-MD Metro	53,444	55
San Diego-Carlsbad-San Marcos, CA Metro	53,333	56
Colorado Springs, CO Metro	53,147	57
Naples-Marco Island, FL Metro	53,126	58
Dallas-Fort Worth-Arlington, TX Metro	53,099	59
Red Wing, MN Micro	52,879	60
New Haven-Milford, CT Metro	52,707	61
Truckee-Grass Valley, CA Micro	52,588	62
Racine, WI Metro	52,474	63
Olympia, WA Metro	52,393	64
Portland-Vancouver-Beaverton, OR-WA Metro	52,291	65
Santa Barbara-Santa Maria-Goleta, CA Metro	52,194	66
East Stroudsburg, PA Micro	52,192	67
Charlotte-Gastonia-Concord, NC-SC Metro	52,186	68
Watertown-Fort Atkinson, WI Micro	52,072	69
Bremerton-Silverdale, WA Metro	52,070	70
Bloomington-Normal, IL Metro	51,857	71
Burlington-South Burlington, VT Metro	51,855	72
Sacramento-Arden-Arcade-Roseville, CA Metro	51,447	73
Reno-Sparks, NV Metro	51,374	74
Provo-Orem, UT Metro	51,203	75
Whitewater, WI Micro	51,145	76
Elko, NV Micro	51,058	77
Des Moines, IA Metro	50,872	78
Rock Springs, WY Micro	50,832	79
Sheboygan, WI Metro	50,687	80
Indianapolis, IN Metro	50,664	81
Kansas City, MO-KS Metro	50,485	82
Richmond, VA Metro	50,427	83
Barnstable Town, MA Metro	50,419	84
Allegan, MI Micro	50,340	85
Milwaukee-Waukesha-West Allis, WI Metro	50,049	86
Hilton Head Island-Beaufort, SC Micro	49,999	87
Owatonna, MN Micro	49,924	88
Kennewick-Richland-Pasco, WA Metro	49,857	89
Green Bay, WI Metro	49,856	90
Fond du Lac, WI Metro	49,771	91
Los Angeles-Long Beach-Santa Ana, CA Metro	49,766	92
Wausau, WI Metro	49,728	93
Houston-Baytown-Sugar Land, TX Metro	49,691	94
Hutchinson, MN Micro	49,595	95
Phoenix-Mesa-Scottsdale, AZ Metro	49,524	96
Laconia, NH Micro	49,436	97
Lancaster, PA Metro	49,430	98
Cincinnati-Middletown, OH-KY-IN Metro	49,414	99
Beaver Dam, WI Micro	49,404	100
Omaha-Council Bluffs, NE-IA Metro	49,358	101
Cedar Rapids, IA Metro	49,289	102
Oak Harbor, WA Micro	49,244	103
Willimantic, CT Micro	49,197	104
Allentown-Bethlehem-Easton, PA-NJ Metro	49,182	105
Columbus, OH Metro	49,175	106
Evanston, WY Micro	49,139	107
Adrian, MI Micro	49,050	108
Kill Devil Hills, NC Micro	48,980	109
York-Hanover, PA Metro	48,956	110
Rochelle, IL Micro	48,932	111
Grand Rapids-Wyoming, MI Metro	48,907	112
Albany-Schenectady-Troy, NY Metro	48,872	113
Gainesville, GA Metro	48,752	114
Stevens Point, WI Micro	48,752	115
Oshkosh-Neenah, WI Metro	48,661	116
Easton, MD Micro	48,608	117
Midland, MI Micro	48,504	118
Janesville, WI Metro	48,489	119
Reading, PA Metro	48,434	120
Las Vegas-Paradise, NV Metro	48,431	121
Portland-South Portland, ME Metro	48,431	122
St. Louis, MO-IL Metro	48,421	123
Brigham City, UT Micro	48,355	124
Charlottesville, VA Metro	48,276	125
Kapaa, HI Micro	48,088	126
Granbury, TX Micro	48,012	127
Springfield, IL Metro	47,974	128
Lansing-East Lansing, MI Metro	47,920	129
Harrisburg-Carlisle, PA Metro	47,877	130
Gettysburg, PA Micro	47,866	131
Nashville-Davidson-Murfreesboro, TN Metro	47,767	132
Auburn, IN Micro	47,684	133
Warner Robins, GA Metro	47,678	134
San Luis Obispo-Paso Robles, CA Metro	47,615	135
Rochester, NY Metro	47,537	136
Greeley, CO Metro	47,520	137
Monroe, WI Micro	47,505	138
Sidney, OH Micro	47,471	139
Rockford, IL Metro	47,416	140
Defiance, OH Micro	47,401	141
Huntsville, AL Metro	47,396	142
Manitowoc, WI Micro	47,347	143
Findlay, OH Micro	47,316	144
Sioux Falls, SD Metro	47,287	145
Wapakoneta, OH Micro	47,130	146
Keene, NH Micro	47,120	147
Santa Fe, NM Metro	47,120	148
Baraboo, WI Micro	47,101	149
Durham, NC Metro	47,091	150
Providence-New Bedford-Fall River, RI-MA Metro	47,051	151
Virginia Beach-Norfolk-Newport News, VA-NC Metro	47,002	152
St. Cloud, MN Metro	46,993	153
Warsaw, IN Micro	46,957	154
Atlantic City, NJ Metro	46,951	155
Hudson, NY Micro	46,867	156
Mount Vernon-Anacortes, WA Metro	46,851	157
Jacksonville, FL Metro	46,841	158
Corvallis, OR Metro	46,835	159
Elkhart-Goshen, IN Metro	46,769	160
Urbana, OH Micro	46,756	161
Akron, OH Metro	46,746	162
Key West-Marathon, FL Micro	46,741	163
Pierre, SD Micro	46,676	164
Bend, OR Metro	46,674	165
Peoria, IL Metro	46,641	166
Jackson, MI Metro	46,582	167
Lincoln, NE Metro	46,508	168
Angola, IN Micro	46,507	169
Kokomo, IN Metro	46,488	170
Kingston, NY Metro	46,468	171
Barre, VT Micro	46,440	172
Columbus, IN Metro	46,419	173
Riverside-San Bernardino-Ontario, CA Metro	46,419	174
Wichita, KS Metro	46,286	175
Cleveland-Elyria-Mentor, OH Metro	46,266	176
Celina, OH Micro	46,233	177
Ocean City, NJ Metro	46,225	178
Boise City-Nampa, ID Metro	46,200	179
Traverse City, MI Micro	46,191	180
Carson City, NV Metro	46,163	181
Cape Coral-Fort Myers, FL Metro	46,069	182
Fort Wayne, IN Metro	46,063	183
Fort Walton Beach-Crestview-Destin, FL Metro	46,040	184
Boone, IA Micro	45,983	185
Sandusky, OH Metro	45,979	186
Kankakee-Bradley, IL Metro	45,965	187
Jasper, IN Micro	45,811	188
Durango, CO Micro	45,738	189
Orlando, FL Metro	45,698	190
Lebanon, NH-VT Micro	45,684	191
Statesville-Mooresville, NC Micro	45,649	192
Mankato-North Mankato, MN Micro	45,643	193
Kendallville, IN Micro	45,528	194
Frankfort, KY Micro	45,520	195
Stockton, CA Metro	45,427	196
Newton, IA Micro	45,401	197
Southern Pines, NC Micro	45,379	198
Winchester, VA-WV Metro	45,360	199
Plymouth, IN Micro	45,343	200
Dayton, OH Metro	45,312	201
Sarasota-Bradenton-Venice, FL Metro	45,298	202
Idaho Falls, ID Metro	45,126	203
Owosso, MI Micro	45,124	204
Fallon, NV Micro	45,088	205
Ames, IA Metro	45,069	206
Bellefontaine, OH Micro	45,028	207
Topeka, KS Metro	45,022	208
Lebanon, PA Metro	45,018	209
Wisconsin Rapids-Marshfield, WI Micro	44,958	210
McPherson, KS Micro	44,950	211
Louisville, KY-IN Metro	44,943	212
Daphne-Fairhope, AL Micro	44,932	213
Bismarck, ND Metro	44,931	214
Springfield, MA Metro	44,910	215
Huntington, IN Micro	44,892	216
Columbia, TN Micro	44,888	217
Muscatine, IA Micro	44,868	218
New Ulm, MN Micro	44,856	219
Dixon, IL Micro	44,804	220
Crawfordsville, IN Micro	44,802	221
Pontiac, IL Micro	44,783	222
Ottawa-Streator, IL Micro	44,637	223
Columbia, SC Metro	44,607	224
Jefferson City, MO Metro	44,568	225
Michigan City-La Porte, IN Metro	44,563	226
Winston-Salem, NC Metro	44,550	227
Wooster, OH Micro	44,494	228
St. Marys, GA Micro	44,465	229
Ocean Pines, MD Micro	44,421	230
Davenport-Moline-Rock Island, IA-IL Metro	44,415	231
Kalamazoo-Portage, MI Metro	44,404	232
Iowa City, IA Metro	44,366	233
Palm Coast, FL Micro	44,299	234
Lincolnton, NC Micro	44,277	235
Bennington, VT Micro	44,271	236
Salem, OR Metro	44,197	237
Dover, DE Metro	44,155	238
Frankfort, IN Micro	44,142	239
Flint, MI Metro	44,141	240
Fremont, OH Micro	44,046	241
Cheyenne, WY Metro	44,045	242
Lexington-Fayette, KY Metro	44,010	243
Palm Bay-Melbourne-Titusville, FL Metro	43,979	244
Batavia, NY Micro	43,929	245
La Crosse, WI-MN Metro	43,911	246
Miami-Fort Lauderdale-Miami Beach, FL Metro	43,901	247
Modesto, CA Metro	43,894	248
Chambersburg, PA Micro	43,863	249
Wilmington, OH Micro	43,850	250
Hagerstown-Martinsburg, MD-WV Metro	43,834	251
Dubuque, IA Metro	43,825	252
Charleston-North Charleston, SC Metro	43,792	253
South Bend-Mishawaka, IN-MI Metro	43,755	254
Willmar, MN Micro	43,732	255
Lewisburg, PA Micro	43,695	256
Greensburg, IN Micro	43,694	257
Phoenix Lake-Cedar Ridge, CA Micro	43,628	258
Seaford, DE Micro	43,596	259
Bozeman, MT Micro	43,591	260
Greensboro-High Point, NC Metro	43,587	261
Norwalk, OH Micro	43,460	262
Vero Beach, FL Metro	43,418	263
San Antonio, TX Metro	43,387	264
Memphis, TN-MS-AR Metro	43,381	265
Hilo, HI Micro	43,355	266
Savannah, GA Metro	43,336	267
Albuquerque, NM Metro	43,313	268
Syracuse, NY Metro	43,296	269
Eau Claire, WI Metro	43,274	270
Sterling, IL Micro	43,257	271
Mount Vernon, OH Micro	43,252	272
Bellingham, WA Metro	43,156	273
Lincoln, IL Micro	43,150	274
Wabash, IN Micro	43,149	275
Logan, UT-ID Metro	43,137	276
Springfield, OH Metro	43,050	277
Hood River, OR Micro	43,044	278
Little Rock-North Little Rock, AR Metro	43,025	279
Columbus, NE Micro	42,963	280
Effingham, IL Micro	42,923	281
Canton-Massillon, OH Metro	42,914	282
Longview-Kelso, WA Metro	42,908	283
Greenville, OH Micro	42,860	284
Wilmington, NC Metro	42,782	285
Greenville, SC Metro	42,778	286
Midland, TX Metro	42,770	287
Marshall, MN Micro	42,769	288
Freeport, IL Micro	42,718	289
Spirit Lake, IA Micro	42,718	290
Lafayette, IN Metro	42,701	291
Flagstaff, AZ Metro	42,687	292
Pittsfield, MA Metro	42,652	293
Toledo, OH Metro	42,651	294
Seymour, IN Micro	42,640	295
Evansville, IN-KY Metro	42,607	296
Port St. Lucie-Fort Pierce, FL Metro	42,598	297
Menomonie, WI Micro	42,562	298
Champaign-Urbana, IL Metro	42,538	299
Sioux City, IA-NE-SD Metro	42,510	300
Morehead City, NC Micro	42,492	301
Lawrence, KS Metro	42,456	302
Merrill, WI Micro	42,409	303
Staunton-Waynesboro, VA Micro	42,408	304
Shelton, WA Micro	42,386	305
Peru, IN Micro	42,347	306
Birmingham-Hoover, AL Metro	42,332	307
Waterloo-Cedar Falls, IA Metro	42,254	308
Logansport, IN Micro	42,239	309

Median Household Income

CBSA	INCOME ($)	RANK
Sanford, NC Micro	42,230	310
Anderson, IN Metro	42,221	311
Marion, OH Metro	42,212	312
Madison, IN Micro	42,183	313
North Vernon, IN Micro	42,172	314
Coldwater, MI Micro	42,124	315
Fargo, ND-MN Metro	42,123	316
Washington, OH Micro	42,118	317
Sturgis, MI Micro	42,091	318
Glens Falls, NY Metro	42,071	319
Roanoke, VA Metro	42,065	320
Vernal, UT Micro	42,028	321
Alexandria, MN Micro	41,997	322
Winona, MN Micro	41,988	323
Rockland, ME Micro	41,980	324
Tampa-St. Petersburg-Clearwater, FL Metro	41,979	325
Decatur, IN Micro	41,970	326
St. George, UT Metro	41,935	327
Vineland-Millville-Bridgeton, NJ Metro	41,927	328
Coeur d'Alene, ID Metro	41,911	329
Wenatchee, WA Metro	41,884	330
Buffalo-Cheektowaga-Tonawanda, NY Metro	41,879	331
Helena, MT Micro	41,869	332
Tulsa, OK Metro	41,859	333
Pascagoula, MS Metro	41,749	334
Burlington, NC Metro	41,744	335
Casper, WY Metro	41,711	336
Marshalltown, IA Micro	41,711	337
New Castle, IN Micro	41,685	338
Van Wert, OH Micro	41,670	339
Auburn, NY Micro	41,621	340
Bay City, MI Metro	41,620	341
Ashland, OH Micro	41,600	342
Battle Creek, MI Metro	41,579	343
Gainesville, TX Micro	41,547	344
Elizabethtown, KY Metro	41,466	345
Brainerd, MN Micro	41,426	346
Muskegon-Norton Shores, MI Metro	41,423	347
Lexington-Thomasville, NC Micro	41,408	348
Oskaloosa, IA Micro	41,356	349
Tyler, TX Metro	41,310	350
Dalton, GA Metro	41,292	351
Niles-Benton Harbor, MI Metro	41,275	352
Rapid City, SD Metro	41,184	353
Killeen-Temple-Fort Hood, TX Metro	41,182	354
Pittsburgh, PA Metro	41,145	355
Calhoun, GA Micro	41,107	356
Kearney, NE Micro	41,091	357
Victoria, TX Metro	41,079	358
Pensacola-Ferry Pass-Brent, FL Metro	41,059	359
Spokane, WA Metro	41,033	360
Connersville, IN Micro	41,020	361
Fayetteville, NC Metro	40,975	362
Albany-Lebanon, OR Micro	40,965	363
Billings, MT Metro	40,962	364
Montgomery, AL Metro	40,931	365
Austin, MN Micro	40,912	366
Sherman-Denison, TX Metro	40,874	367
Burlington, IA-IL Micro	40,857	368
Plattsburgh, NY Micro	40,848	369
Augusta-Richmond County, GA-SC Metro	40,837	370
St. Marys, PA Micro	40,823	371
Clinton, IA Micro	40,816	372
Salina, KS Micro	40,816	373
Oklahoma City, OK Metro	40,795	374
Jackson, MS Metro	40,729	375
Saginaw-Saginaw Township North, MI Metro	40,727	376
Ithaca, NY Metro	40,690	377
Knoxville, TN Metro	40,678	378
Spartanburg, SC Metro	40,662	379
Baton Rouge, LA Metro	40,661	380
Tiffin-Fostoria, OH Micro	40,657	381
Fayetteville-Springdale-Rogers, AR-MO Metro	40,626	382
Albert Lea, MN Micro	40,620	383
Hickory-Morganton-Lenoir, NC Metro	40,598	384
Salisbury, NC Micro	40,591	385
Rutland, VT Micro	40,583	386
Columbia, MO Metro	40,531	387
Tucson, AZ Metro	40,520	388
Mansfield, OH Metro	40,505	389
Harrisonburg, VA Metro	40,491	390
Ukiah, CA Micro	40,489	391
Brevard, NC Micro	40,451	392
Chattanooga, TN-GA Metro	40,433	393
Medford, OR Metro	40,433	394
Punta Gorda, FL Metro	40,395	395
Corning, NY Micro	40,393	396
Salisbury, MD Metro	40,379	397
Fremont, NE Micro	40,348	398
Dodge City, KS Micro	40,306	399
Decatur, IL Metro	40,304	400
Eugene-Springfield, OR Metro	40,290	401
Seneca, SC Micro	40,241	402
Fairmont, MN Micro	40,226	403
Pendleton-Hermiston, OR Micro	40,169	404
Myrtle Beach-Conway-North Myrtle Beach, SC Metro	40,166	405
Anderson, SC Metro	40,083	406
Grand Junction, CO Metro	40,073	407
Jackson, TN Metro	40,062	408
Jacksonville, IL Micro	40,057	409
Borger, TX Micro	40,032	410
Garden City, KS Micro	40,018	411
Chillicothe, OH Micro	40,013	412
Blackfoot, ID Micro	40,006	413
Brenham, TX Micro	39,986	414
Houma-Bayou Cane-Thibodaux, LA Metro	39,938	415
Duluth, MN-WI Metro	39,911	416
Lynchburg, VA Metro	39,911	417
Georgetown, SC Micro	39,876	418
Port Angeles, WA Micro	39,869	419
Elmira, NY Metro	39,851	420
Pocatello, ID Metro	39,841	421
Owensboro, KY Metro	39,835	422
Shelbyville, TN Micro	39,815	423
Seneca Falls, NY Micro	39,800	424
Grand Island, NE Micro	39,793	425
Watertown, SD Micro	39,791	426
Hanford-Corcoran, CA Metro	39,780	427
State College, PA Metro	39,751	428
Montrose, CO Micro	39,687	429
Taylorville, IL Micro	39,687	430
Selinsgrove, PA Micro	39,686	431
Madera, CA Metro	39,664	432
Albemarle, NC Micro	39,660	433
Lafayette, LA Metro	39,655	434
Beatrice, NE Micro	39,599	435
Panama City-Lynn Haven, FL Metro	39,591	436
Astoria, OR Micro	39,585	437
Grand Forks, ND-MN Metro	39,566	438
Fergus Falls, MN Micro	39,564	439
Clarksville, TN-KY Metro	39,528	440
Asheville, NC Metro	39,490	441
Lakeland-Winter Haven, FL Metro	39,451	442
Alma, MI Micro	39,447	443
Augusta-Waterville, ME Micro	39,407	444
Binghamton, NY Metro	39,403	445
Hastings, NE Micro	39,357	446
Mason City, IA Micro	39,334	447
Lima, OH Metro	39,274	448
Worthington, MN Micro	39,266	449
Liberal, KS Micro	39,236	450
Tallahassee, FL Metro	39,209	451
Wahpeton, ND-MN Micro	39,203	452
Brookings, SD Micro	39,190	453
Spencer, IA Micro	39,174	454
Zanesville, OH Micro	39,151	455
Macon, GA Metro	39,140	456
Lewiston-Auburn, ME Metro	39,136	457
North Platte, NE Micro	39,077	458
Platteville, WI Micro	39,069	459
Galesburg, IL Micro	39,052	460
Yankton, SD Micro	39,045	461
Erie, PA Metro	39,023	462
Escanaba, MI Micro	39,022	463
New Orleans-Metairie-Kenner, LA Metro	38,983	464
Decatur, AL Metro	38,969	465
Corpus Christi, TX Metro	38,957	466
Andrews, TX Micro	38,950	467
Woodward, OK Micro	38,949	468
New Bern, NC Micro	38,943	469
Sheridan, WY Micro	38,889	470
Brunswick, GA Metro	38,861	471
Bedford, IN Micro	38,859	472
Deltona-Daytona Beach-Ormond Beach, FL Metro	38,855	473
Warrensburg, MO Micro	38,849	474
Fort Dodge, IA Micro	38,842	475
Lexington, NE Micro	38,817	476
Gulfport-Biloxi, MS Metro	38,736	477
Hutchinson, KS Micro	38,735	478
Walla Walla, WA Micro	38,734	479
Centralia, WA Micro	38,691	480
Bucyrus, OH Micro	38,690	481
Youngstown-Warren-Boardman, OH-PA Metro	38,661	482
Amarillo, TX Metro	38,644	483
St. Joseph, MO-KS Metro	38,644	484
Bishop, CA Micro	38,621	485
Norfolk, NE Micro	38,614	486
Mountain Home, ID Micro	38,608	487
Cornelia, GA Micro	38,602	488
Guymon, OK Micro	38,593	489
Bakersfield, CA Metro	38,566	490
Prescott, AZ Metro	38,559	491
Aberdeen, SD Micro	38,536	492
Merced, CA Metro	38,534	493
Marquette, MI Micro	38,497	494
Lewiston, ID-WA Metro	38,493	495
Sayre, PA Micro	38,487	496
Warren, PA Micro	38,453	497
Lake Charles, LA Metro	38,440	498
LaGrange, GA Micro	38,433	499
Storm Lake, IA Micro	38,415	500
Tullahoma, TN Micro	38,376	501
Marion, IN Micro	38,332	502
Utica-Rome, NY Metro	38,308	503
Rocky Mount, NC Metro	38,303	504
Bloomsburg-Berwick, PA Micro	38,293	505
New Philadelphia-Dover, OH Micro	38,291	506
Prineville, OR Micro	38,270	507
Beaumont-Port Arthur, TX Metro	38,258	508
Longview, TX Metro	38,234	509
Ashtabula, OH Micro	38,228	510
Keokuk-Fort Madison, IA-MO Micro	38,226	511
Canton, IL Micro	38,213	512
Missoula, MT Metro	38,199	513
Moses Lake, WA Micro	38,185	514
Winfield, KS Micro	38,171	515
Pahrump, NV Micro	38,164	516
Goldsboro, NC Metro	38,137	517
Dunn, NC Micro	38,131	518
Fort Leonard Wood, MO Micro	38,115	519
Kalispell, MT Micro	38,084	520
Washington, NC Micro	38,025	521
City of The Dalles, OR Micro	38,017	522
Fresno, CA Metro	37,960	523
Twin Falls, ID Micro	37,936	524
Manhattan, KS Micro	37,925	525
Rome, GA Metro	37,870	526
Lancaster, SC Micro	37,854	527
Yakima, WA Metro	37,840	528
Vicksburg, MS Micro	37,834	529
Canon City, CO Micro	37,772	530
Fort Morgan, CO Micro	37,747	531
Atchison, KS Micro	37,724	532
North Wilkesboro, NC Micro	37,693	533
Redding, CA Metro	37,643	534
Cadillac, MI Micro	37,612	535
Bartlesville, OK Micro	37,587	536
Lawton, OK Metro	37,577	537
Quincy, IL-MO Micro	37,569	538
Sevierville, TN Micro	37,559	539
Jamestown, ND Micro	37,534	540
Jacksonville, NC Metro	37,525	541
Minot, ND Micro	37,512	542
Yuba City-Marysville, CA Metro	37,482	543
Muncie, IN Metro	37,476	544
Farmington, NM Metro	37,435	545
Bangor, ME Metro	37,423	546
Columbus, GA-AL Metro	37,423	547
Cortland, NY Micro	37,398	548
Cape Girardeau-Jackson, MO-IL Micro	37,382	549
Iron Mountain, MI-WI Micro	37,373	550
Marinette, WI-MI Micro	37,350	551
Cambridge, MD Micro	37,333	552
Scranton-Wilkes-Barre, PA Metro	37,315	553
Bemidji, MN Micro	37,307	554
Visalia-Porterville, CA Metro	37,305	555
Scottsburg, IN Micro	37,286	556
Williamsport, PA Metro	37,275	557
Bowling Green, KY Metro	37,235	558
Tupelo, MS Micro	37,202	559
Mount Pleasant, MI Micro	37,187	560
Richmond, IN Micro	37,166	561
Greenwood, SC Micro	37,165	562
Sault Ste. Marie, MI Micro	37,154	563
Springfield, MO Metro	37,129	564
Coshocton, OH Micro	37,112	565
Wichita Falls, TX Metro	37,052	566
Centralia, IL Micro	37,047	567
Mitchell, SD Micro	36,994	568
Bloomington, IN Metro	36,945	569
La Grande, OR Micro	36,934	570
Watertown-Fort Drum, NY Micro	36,922	571
Dickinson, ND Micro	36,830	572
Shelby, NC Micro	36,827	573
Terre Haute, IN Metro	36,803	574
Kerrville, TX Micro	36,773	575
Dumas, TX Micro	36,769	576
Gloversville, NY Micro	36,760	577
East Liverpool-Salem, OH Micro	36,744	578
Pueblo, CO Metro	36,731	579
Lufkin, TX Micro	36,701	580
Hays, KS Micro	36,692	581
Hannibal, MO Micro	36,681	582
Boone, NC Micro	36,640	583
Cleveland, TN Metro	36,640	584
Riverton, WY Micro	36,632	585
Florence, SC Metro	36,596	586
Alpena, MI Micro	36,573	587
Price, UT Micro	36,529	588
Big Rapids, MI Micro	36,512	589
Aberdeen, WA Micro	36,506	590
Cedar City, UT Micro	36,484	591
Mount Vernon, IL Micro	36,399	592
Marshall, TX Micro	36,373	593
Charleston, WV Metro	36,357	594
Parkersburg-Marietta, WV-OH Metro	36,240	595
Enid, OK Micro	36,234	596
Paducah, KY-IL Micro	36,213	597
Sumter, SC Metro	36,213	598
Mobile, AL Metro	36,153	599
Danville, IL Metro	36,126	600
Greenville, NC Metro	36,118	601
Olean, NY Micro	36,115	602
Oneonta, NY Micro	36,086	603
Sierra Vista-Douglas, AZ Micro	36,084	604
Ellensburg, WA Micro	36,077	605
San Angelo, TX Metro	36,050	606
Athens, TX Micro	36,045	607
Gaffney, SC Micro	35,998	608
New Castle, PA Micro	35,947	609
Williston, ND Micro	35,945	610
Waco, TX Metro	35,933	611
Roseburg, OR Micro	35,926	612
Jamestown-Dunkirk-Fredonia, NY Micro	35,884	613
Bradford, PA Micro	35,832	614
Rexburg, ID Micro	35,829	615
Harriman, TN Micro	35,826	616
Wilson, NC Micro	35,814	617
Athens-Clarke County, GA Metro	35,784	618
Hinesville-Fort Stewart, GA Metro	35,745	619
Meadville, PA Micro	35,743	620
Huntingdon, PA Micro	35,739	621

CBSA	INCOME ($)	RANK
Albany, GA Metro	35,713	622
Great Falls, MT Metro	35,676	623
Shreveport-Bossier City, LA Metro	35,612	624
Moscow, ID Micro	35,534	625
Pottsville, PA Micro	35,528	626
Abilene, TX Metro	35,462	627
Tuscaloosa, AL Metro	35,435	628
Tifton, GA Micro	35,397	629
Mount Airy, NC Micro	35,367	630
Marshall, MO Micro	35,363	631
Fort Valley, GA Micro	35,341	632
Snyder, TX Micro	35,328	633
Mount Pleasant, TX Micro	35,295	634
Newberry, SC Micro	35,288	635
Searcy, AR Micro	35,278	636
Palestine, TX Micro	35,259	637
Sterling, CO Micro	35,255	638
Enterprise-Ozark, AL Micro	35,235	639
Jesup, GA Micro	35,224	640
Great Bend, KS Micro	35,208	641
Amsterdam, NY Micro	35,189	642
Altoona, PA Metro	35,140	643
Carlsbad-Artesia, NM Micro	35,123	644
Pierre Part, LA Micro	35,025	645
Fort Polk South, LA Micro	35,020	646
Joplin, MO Metro	35,017	647
Marion-Herrin, IL Micro	34,996	648
Berlin, NH-VT Micro	34,978	649
Albertville, AL Micro	34,977	650
Ottumwa, IA Micro	34,977	651
Branson, MO Micro	34,966	652
Charleston-Mattoon, IL Micro	34,951	653
Odessa, TX Metro	34,950	654
Chico, CA Metro	34,936	655
Florence, AL Metro	34,914	656
Cullman, AL Micro	34,913	657
Bristol, VA Metro	34,870	658
Emporia, KS Micro	34,864	659
De Ridder, LA Micro	34,794	660
Cedartown, GA Micro	34,789	661
Yuma, AZ Metro	34,782	662
Texarkana, TX-Texarkana, AR Metro	34,779	663
Hot Springs, AR Micro	34,777	664
Milledgeville, GA Micro	34,775	665
Sulphur Springs, TX Micro	34,771	666
Malone, NY Micro	34,769	667
Kingsport-Bristol, TN-VA Metro	34,719	668
The Villages, FL Micro	34,694	669
Duncan, OK Micro	34,691	670
Shawnee, OK Micro	34,687	671
Maryville, MO Micro	34,682	672
Lewistown, PA Micro	34,670	673
Oil City, PA Micro	34,664	674
Pampa, TX Micro	34,659	675
Spearfish, SD Micro	34,652	676
Ocala, FL Metro	34,641	677
Ogdensburg-Massena, NY Micro	34,636	678
Chester, SC Micro	34,634	679
Clewiston, FL Micro	34,627	680
Scottsbluff, NE Micro	34,604	681
Mexico, MO Micro	34,603	682
Red Bluff, CA Micro	34,581	683
Weirton-Steubenville, WV-OH Metro	34,557	684
Blacksburg-Christiansburg-Radford, VA Metro	34,514	685
Morristown, TN Metro	34,509	686
Talladega-Sylacauga, AL Micro	34,433	687
Burley, ID Micro	34,417	688
Dothan, AL Metro	34,417	689
El Campo, TX Micro	34,403	690
El Centro, CA Metro	34,362	691
Macomb, IL Micro	34,353	692
Safford, AZ Micro	34,339	693
Fort Smith, AR-OK Metro	34,309	694
Elizabeth City, NC Micro	34,285	695
Dyersburg, TN Micro	34,262	696
Kinston, NC Micro	34,238	697
Batesville, AR Micro	34,219	698
Ontario, OR-ID Micro	34,202	699
Union, SC Micro	34,191	700
Anniston-Oxford, AL Metro	34,188	701
Hobbs, NM Micro	34,178	702
Scottsboro, AL Micro	34,151	703
Ponca City, OK Micro	34,145	704
Lubbock, TX Metro	34,127	705
Coos Bay, OR Micro	34,095	706
Columbus, MS Micro	34,087	707
Thomasville, GA Micro	34,056	708
Sedalia, MO Micro	34,032	709
Lake Havasu City-Kingman, AZ Micro	34,029	710
Huntsville, TX Micro	34,017	711
Homosassa Springs, FL Micro	33,977	712
Grants Pass, OR Micro	33,968	713
Mineral Wells, TX Micro	33,920	714
Monroe, LA Metro	33,917	715
Vincennes, IN Micro	33,884	716
Klamath Falls, OR Micro	33,840	717
Gainesville, FL Metro	33,826	718
New Iberia, LA Micro	33,824	719
Eureka-Arcata-Fortuna, CA Micro	33,818	720
Athens, TN Micro	33,738	721
Sikeston, MO Micro	33,730	722
Altus, OK Micro	33,713	723
Russellville, AR Micro	33,707	724
DuBois, PA Micro	33,695	725
Sunbury, PA Micro	33,693	726
Payson, AZ Micro	33,660	727
Richmond, KY Micro	33,627	728
Lock Haven, PA Micro	33,621	729
Paragould, AR Micro	33,611	730
Mayfield, KY Micro	33,591	731
Moberly, MO Micro	33,591	732
Pine Bluff, AR Metro	33,571	733
Brownwood, TX Micro	33,554	734
Stephenville, TX Micro	33,543	735
Levelland, TX Micro	33,532	736
Bay City, TX Micro	33,514	737
Madisonville, KY Micro	33,509	738
Huron, SD Micro	33,505	739
Picayune, MS Micro	33,501	740
Johnson City, TN Metro	33,500	741
Coffeyville, KS Micro	33,480	742
El Paso, TX Metro	33,474	743
Union City, TN-KY Micro	33,465	744
Farmington, MO Micro	33,448	745
Paris, TX Micro	33,410	746
Hattiesburg, MS Metro	33,399	747
Washington, NC Micro	33,362	748
Cumberland, MD-WV Metro	33,275	749
Gadsden, AL Metro	33,272	750
Crossville, TN Micro	33,261	751
Valdosta, GA Metro	33,255	752
Big Spring, TX Micro	33,247	753
Corsicana, TX Micro	33,246	754
Danville, KY Micro	33,246	755
Espanola, NM Micro	33,233	756
Plainview, TX Micro	33,189	757
Alamogordo, NM Micro	33,176	758
Somerset, KY Micro	33,153	759
Henderson, NC Micro	33,094	760
Clearlake, CA Micro	33,072	761
Dublin, GA Micro	33,055	762
Forest City, NC Micro	33,048	763
Cambridge, OH Micro	32,958	764
Greeneville, TN Micro	32,920	765
Danville, VA Metro	32,912	766
Okeechobee, FL Micro	32,903	767
Lawrenceburg, TN Micro	32,850	768
Butte-Silver Bow, MT Micro	32,843	769
Brookings, OR Micro	32,821	770
Jonesboro, AR Metro	32,779	771
Wheeling, WV-OH Metro	32,779	772
Laurinburg, NC Micro	32,734	773
Johnstown, PA Metro	32,732	774
Alexandria, LA Metro	32,720	775
El Dorado, AR Micro	32,696	776
Summerville, GA Micro	32,673	777
Parsons, KS Micro	32,594	778
Vernon, TX Micro	32,583	779
Alice, TX Micro	32,546	780
Lebanon, MO Micro	32,545	781
Auburn-Opelika, AL Metro	32,520	782
Abbeville, LA Micro	32,515	783
Sebring, FL Micro	32,500	784
Paris, TN Micro	32,499	785
Thomaston, GA Micro	32,491	786
Murray, KY Micro	32,489	787
Lake City, FL Micro	32,485	788
Arcadia, FL Micro	32,476	789
Clarksburg, WV Micro	32,462	790
Americus, GA Micro	32,413	791
Mountain Home, AR Micro	32,354	792
McMinnville, TN Micro	32,344	793
Martinsville, VA Micro	32,249	794
Nogales, AZ Micro	32,222	795
Orangeburg, SC Micro	32,216	796
Havre, MT Micro	32,175	797
Pittsburg, KS Micro	32,174	798
Ardmore, OK Micro	32,173	799
Indiana, PA Micro	32,156	800
Rolla, MO Micro	32,090	801
Glasgow, KY Micro	32,078	802
Walterboro, SC Micro	32,077	803
College Station-Bryan, TX Metro	32,041	804
Las Cruces, NM Metro	32,024	805
Fairmont, WV Micro	32,018	806
Clovis, NM Micro	31,976	807
Hammond, LA Micro	31,963	808
Wauchula, FL Micro	31,963	809
Toccoa, GA Micro	31,880	810
Harrisburg, IL Micro	31,833	811
Statesboro, GA Micro	31,815	812
Huntington-Ashland, WV-KY-OH Metro	31,805	813
Cookeville, TN Micro	31,787	814
Douglas, GA Micro	31,787	815
Jacksonville, TX Micro	31,763	816
McAlester, OK Micro	31,730	817
Oxford, MS Micro	31,727	818
Houghton, MI Micro	31,669	819
Grants, NM Micro	31,657	820
Beckley, WV Micro	31,616	821
Lamesa, TX Micro	31,591	822
Meridian, MS Micro	31,524	823
Silver City, NM Micro	31,504	824
Valley, AL Micro	31,491	825
Harrison, AR Micro	31,462	826
Arkadelphia, AR Micro	31,457	827
Point Pleasant, WV-OH Micro	31,455	828
Laramie, WY Micro	31,441	829
Mount Sterling, KY Micro	31,407	830
Camden, AR Micro	31,406	831
Campbellsville, KY Micro	31,396	832
Corinth, MS Micro	31,377	833
Crescent City North, CA Micro	31,327	834
Del Rio, TX Micro	31,305	835
Minden, LA Micro	31,265	836
Morgan City, LA Micro	31,233	837
Morgantown, WV Metro	31,211	838
Laredo, TX Metro	31,160	839
Palatka, FL Micro	31,044	840
Beeville, TX Micro	31,019	841
Rockingham, NC Micro	31,006	842
Muskogee, OK Micro	30,999	843
Roswell, NM Micro	30,904	844
Portsmouth, OH Micro	30,842	845
Stillwater, OK Micro	30,832	846
Durant, OK Micro	30,810	847
Magnolia, AR Micro	30,797	848
Kingsville, TX Micro	30,743	849
Laurel, MS Micro	30,706	850
Pullman, WA Micro	30,698	851
Hereford, TX Micro	30,644	852
Bainbridge, GA Micro	30,601	853
Jennings, LA Micro	30,586	854
Hope, AR Micro	30,562	855
Brookhaven, MS Micro	30,527	856
Crowley, LA Micro	30,517	857
Central City, KY Micro	30,493	858
Nacogdoches, TX Micro	30,464	859
Ada, OK Micro	30,437	860
Waycross, GA Micro	30,383	861
Taos, NM Micro	30,370	862
Somerset, KY Micro	30,175	863
Miami, OK Micro	30,040	864
Poplar Bluff, MO Micro	30,025	865
London, KY Micro	29,972	866
Moultrie, GA Micro	29,846	867
Grenada, MS Micro	29,814	868
Vermillion, SD Micro	29,791	869
Las Vegas, NM Micro	29,724	870
Brownsville, TN Micro	29,698	871
Lumberton, NC Micro	29,657	872
Kirksville, MO Micro	29,574	873
Fitzgerald, GA Micro	29,510	874
Blytheville, AR Micro	29,492	875
Uvalde, TX Micro	29,461	876
Bluefield, WV-VA Micro	29,439	877
Athens, OH Micro	29,428	878
Tahlequah, OK Micro	29,416	879
Bennettsville, SC Micro	29,410	880
Ruston, LA Micro	29,263	881
Dillon, SC Micro	29,200	882
Brownsville-Harlingen, TX Metro	28,974	883
Portales, NM Micro	28,937	884
Maysville, KY Micro	28,900	885
Roanoke Rapids, NC Micro	28,777	886
West Plains, MO Micro	28,643	887
Natchitoches, LA Micro	28,504	888
Forrest City, AR Micro	28,057	889
Sweetwater, TX Micro	27,991	890
Carbondale, IL Micro	27,839	891
Oak Hill, WV Micro	27,825	892
Cordele, GA Micro	27,796	893
McComb, MS Micro	27,498	894
Troy, AL Micro	27,478	895
McAllen-Edinburg-Pharr, TX Metro	27,453	896
Bastrop, LA Micro	27,213	897
Greenville, MS Micro	27,178	898
La Follette, TN Micro	27,170	899
Starkville, MS Micro	27,095	900
Newport, TN Micro	27,059	901
Gallup, NM Micro	26,941	902
Yazoo City, MS Micro	26,716	903
Kennett, MO Micro	26,654	904
Indianola, MS Micro	26,511	905
Bogalusa, LA Micro	26,220	906
Natchez, MS-LA Micro	26,087	907
Pecos, TX Micro	25,773	908
Cleveland, MS Micro	25,404	909
Opelousas-Eunice, LA Micro	25,061	910
Clarksdale, MS Micro	24,880	911
Greenwood, MS Micro	24,847	912
Selma, AL Micro	24,823	913
West Helena, AR Micro	24,650	914
Corbin, KY Micro	24,314	915
Tuskegee, AL Micro	23,970	916
Eagle Pass, TX Micro	23,955	917
Raymondville, TX Micro	23,497	918
Deming, NM Micro	23,189	919
Tallulah, LA Micro	23,154	920
Middlesborough, KY Micro	21,122	921
Rio Grande City, TX Micro	18,866	922
CBSA Median	39,034	
United States Median	46,475	

Average Household Income

CBSA	INCOME ($)	RANK
Bridgeport-Stamford-Norwalk, CT Metro	112,345	1
San Jose-Sunnyvale-Santa Clara, CA Metro	111,425	2
Los Alamos, NM Micro	98,853	3
San Francisco-Oakland-Fremont, CA Metro	96,646	4
Washington-Arlington-Alexandria, DC-VA-MD-WV Metro	91,250	5
Edwards, CO Micro	90,722	6
Trenton-Ewing, NJ Metro	87,701	7
Oxnard-Thousand Oaks-Ventura, CA Metro	85,139	8
Boulder, CO Metro	84,363	9
Jackson, WY-ID Micro	83,947	10
Santa Cruz-Watsonville, CA Metro	83,726	11
Boston-Cambridge-Quincy, MA-NH Metro	83,355	12
Naples-Marco Island, FL Metro	80,522	13
Napa, CA Metro	80,490	14
Silverthorne, CO Micro	80,257	15
New York-Newark-Edison, NY-NJ-PA Metro	79,327	16
Santa Rosa-Petaluma, CA Metro	77,976	17
Minneapolis-St. Paul-Bloomington, MN-WI Metro	77,413	18
Torrington, CT Micro	77,259	19
Juneau, AK Micro	77,236	20
Denver-Aurora, CO Metro	77,118	21
Ann Arbor, MI Metro	76,302	22
Chicago-Naperville-Joliet, IL-IN-WI Metro	75,420	23
Atlanta-Sandy Springs-Marietta, GA Metro	75,313	24
Manchester-Nashua, NH Metro	74,597	25
Hartford-West Hartford-East Hartford, CT Metro	74,377	26
Easton, MD Micro	74,194	27
Vallejo-Fairfield, CA Metro	73,984	28
Raleigh-Cary, NC Metro	73,812	29
Santa Barbara-Santa Maria-Goleta, CA Metro	73,600	30
Anchorage, AK Metro	73,599	31
Gardnerville Ranchos, NV Micro	73,249	32
Salinas, CA Metro	72,295	33
San Diego-Carlsbad-San Marcos, CA Metro	72,196	34
Poughkeepsie-Newburgh-Middletown, NY Metro	72,170	35
Dallas-Fort Worth-Arlington, TX Metro	72,036	36
Los Angeles-Long Beach-Santa Ana, CA Metro	71,787	37
Austin-Round Rock, TX Metro	71,667	38
Honolulu, HI Metro	71,560	39
Baltimore-Towson, MD Metro	71,493	40
Lexington Park, MD Micro	71,286	41
Seattle-Tacoma-Bellevue, WA Metro	71,206	42
Philadelphia-Camden-Wilmington, PA-NJ-DE-MD Metro	71,099	43
Hilton Head Island-Beaufort, SC Micro	70,748	44
Fort Collins-Loveland, CO Metro	70,466	45
Detroit-Warren-Livonia, MI Metro	70,323	46
Rochester, MN Metro	70,294	47
Salt Lake City, UT Metro	69,992	48
Kahului-Wailuku, HI Micro	69,417	49
Charlotte-Gastonia-Concord, NC-SC Metro	69,377	50
Truckee-Grass Valley, CA Micro	69,241	51
Houston-Baytown-Sugar Land, TX Metro	69,234	52
Norwich-New London, CT Metro	69,176	53
New Haven-Milford, CT Metro	68,740	54
Worcester, MA Metro	68,588	55
Kodiak, AK Micro	68,509	56
Reno-Sparks, NV Metro	68,130	57
Holland-Grand Haven, MI Metro	67,671	58
Madison, WI Metro	67,669	59
Ogden-Clearfield, UT Metro	67,411	60
Sacramento-Arden-Arcade-Roseville, CA Metro	67,173	61
Concord, NH Micro	67,151	62
Portland-Vancouver-Beaverton, OR-WA Metro	67,071	63
Vero Beach, FL Metro	66,887	64
Colorado Springs, CO Metro	66,680	65
Appleton, WI Metro	66,482	66
Phoenix-Mesa-Scottsdale, AZ Metro	66,404	67
Indianapolis, IN Metro	66,290	68
Midland, MI Micro	66,038	69
Monroe, MI Metro	65,882	70
Barnstable Town, MA Metro	65,816	71
Bloomington-Normal, IL Metro	65,720	72
Richmond, VA Metro	65,649	73
Fairbanks, AK Metro	65,623	74
Bremerton-Silverdale, WA Metro	65,384	75
Kansas City, MO-KS Metro	65,373	76
Ketchikan, AK Micro	65,296	77
Cincinnati-Middletown, OH-KY-IN Metro	65,200	78
Burlington-South Burlington, VT Metro	65,142	79
Santa Fe, NM Metro	65,076	80
Milwaukee-Waukesha-West Allis, WI Metro	65,031	81
Key West-Marathon, FL Micro	65,010	82
Des Moines, IA Metro	64,944	83
Ocean City, NJ Metro	64,763	84
Charlottesville, VA Metro	64,747	85
Durham, NC Metro	64,450	86
Red Wing, MN Micro	64,414	87
Gillette, WY Micro	64,362	88
Cape Coral-Fort Myers, FL Metro	64,142	89
Kill Devil Hills, NC Micro	64,111	90
Columbus, OH Metro	64,065	91
Provo-Orem, UT Metro	64,065	92
Miami-Fort Lauderdale-Miami Beach, FL Metro	63,828	93
Olympia, WA Metro	63,726	94
St. Louis, MO-IL Metro	63,646	95
Sarasota-Bradenton-Venice, FL Metro	63,619	96
Laconia, NH Micro	63,498	97
Nashville-Davidson-Murfreesboro, TN Metro	63,409	98
Faribault-Northfield, MN Micro	63,341	99
San Luis Obispo-Paso Robles, CA Metro	63,332	100
Omaha-Council Bluffs, NE-IA Metro	63,154	101
Racine, WI Metro	63,141	102
Granbury, TX Micro	63,067	103
Las Vegas-Paradise, NV Metro	62,939	104
East Stroudsburg, PA Micro	62,859	105
Kapaa, HI Micro	62,855	106
Gainesville, GA Metro	62,823	107
Albany-Schenectady-Troy, NY Metro	62,673	108
Kennewick-Richland-Pasco, WA Metro	62,548	109
Allentown-Bethlehem-Easton, PA-NJ Metro	62,524	110
Corvallis, OR Metro	62,501	111
Portland-South Portland, ME Metro	62,357	112
Durango, CO Micro	62,307	113
Whitewater, WI Micro	62,110	114
Bend, OR Metro	61,982	115
Jacksonville, FL Metro	61,957	116
Hudson, NY Micro	61,877	117
Springfield, IL Metro	61,839	118
Grand Rapids-Wyoming, MI Metro	61,812	119
Huntsville, AL Metro	61,807	120
Cleveland-Elyria-Mentor, OH Metro	61,522	121
Watertown-Fort Atkinson, WI Micro	61,229	122
Akron, OH Metro	61,145	123
Providence-New Bedford-Fall River, RI-MA Metro	61,102	124
Orlando, FL Metro	60,961	125
Harrisburg-Carlisle, PA Metro	60,903	126
Rochester, NY Metro	60,897	127
Lansing-East Lansing, MI Metro	60,799	128
Lancaster, PA Metro	60,731	129
Mount Vernon-Anacortes, WA Metro	60,619	130
Greeley, CO Metro	60,584	131
Southern Pines, NC Micro	60,513	132
Oak Harbor, WA Micro	60,445	133
Cedar Rapids, IA Metro	60,439	134
Allegan, MI Micro	60,426	135
Green Bay, WI Metro	60,323	136
Wausau, WI Metro	60,254	137
Reading, PA Metro	60,225	138
Savannah, GA Metro	60,200	139
Riverside-San Bernardino-Ontario, CA Metro	60,159	140
Sheboygan, WI Metro	60,124	141
Midland, TX Metro	60,114	142
Iowa City, IA Metro	60,073	143
Stevens Point, WI Micro	60,004	144
Port St. Lucie-Fort Pierce, FL Metro	59,769	145
Atlantic City, NJ Metro	59,669	146
Virginia Beach-Norfolk-Newport News, VA-NC Metro	59,634	147
Boise City-Nampa, ID Metro	59,508	148
Rochelle, IL Micro	59,481	149
Lexington-Fayette, KY Metro	59,447	150
Willimantic, CT Micro	59,436	151
Traverse City, MI Micro	59,418	152
Oshkosh-Neenah, WI Metro	59,381	153
Statesville-Mooresville, NC Micro	59,280	154
Louisville, KY-IN Metro	59,272	155
Rockford, IL Metro	59,191	156
Daphne-Fairhope, AL Micro	59,172	157
Kingston, NY Metro	59,136	158
York-Hanover, PA Metro	59,083	159
Lebanon, NH-VT Micro	58,995	160
Winston-Salem, NC Metro	58,993	161
Adrian, MI Micro	58,945	162
Lincoln, NE Metro	58,945	163
Bennington, VT Micro	58,912	164
Keene, NH Micro	58,904	165
Memphis, TN-MS-AR Metro	58,869	166
Stockton, CA Metro	58,854	167
Fort Walton Beach-Crestview-Destin, FL Metro	58,522	168
Peoria, IL Metro	58,483	169
Ames, IA Metro	58,393	170
Findlay, OH Micro	58,367	171
Rock Springs, WY Micro	58,365	172
Sioux Falls, SD Metro	58,348	173
Birmingham-Hoover, AL Metro	58,281	174
Carson City, NV Metro	58,193	175
Dayton, OH Metro	58,188	176
Columbia, SC Metro	58,109	177
Janesville, WI Metro	58,095	178
St. Cloud, MN Metro	58,062	179
Owatonna, MN Micro	58,033	180
Fort Wayne, IN Metro	58,004	181
Greensboro-High Point, NC Metro	57,988	182
Ocean Pines, MD Micro	57,959	183
Barre, VT Micro	57,940	184
Elkhart-Goshen, IN Metro	57,933	185
Charleston-North Charleston, SC Metro	57,928	186
Wichita, KS Metro	57,743	187
San Antonio, TX Metro	57,677	188
Sandusky, OH Metro	57,668	189
Jackson, MI Metro	57,616	190
Hilo, HI Micro	57,585	191
Pierre, SD Micro	57,561	192
Fond du Lac, WI Metro	57,559	193
Albuquerque, NM Metro	57,552	194
Monroe, WI Micro	57,467	195
Columbus, IN Metro	57,443	196
Kalamazoo-Portage, MI Metro	57,331	197
Lawrence, KS Metro	57,330	198
Tampa-St. Petersburg-Clearwater, FL Metro	57,307	199
Wapakoneta, OH Micro	57,201	200
Warsaw, IN Micro	57,126	201
Beaver Dam, WI Micro	57,105	202
Springfield, MA Metro	57,081	203
Hutchinson, MN Micro	56,955	204
Sidney, OH Micro	56,954	205
Warner Robins, GA Metro	56,954	206
Kankakee-Bradley, IL Metro	56,928	207
Wilmington, NC Metro	56,922	208
Baraboo, WI Micro	56,912	209
Palm Coast, FL Micro	56,900	210
Pittsfield, MA Metro	56,885	211
Greenville, SC Metro	56,868	212
Palm Bay-Melbourne-Titusville, FL Metro	56,811	213
Elko, NV Micro	56,801	214
Modesto, CA Metro	56,737	215
Winchester, VA-WV Metro	56,713	216
Idaho Falls, ID Metro	56,685	217
Fallon, NV Micro	56,574	218
Little Rock-North Little Rock, AR Metro	56,549	219
Ithaca, NY Metro	56,484	220
Mankato-North Mankato, MN Micro	56,452	221
Syracuse, NY Metro	56,432	222
Phoenix Lake-Cedar Ridge, CA Micro	56,378	223
Flint, MI Metro	56,377	224
Kokomo, IN Metro	56,299	225
Seaford, DE Micro	56,163	226
Lewisburg, PA Micro	56,157	227
Tyler, TX Metro	56,115	228
Bellingham, WA Metro	56,096	229
Georgetown, SC Micro	56,064	230
Dubuque, IA Metro	56,007	231
Gettysburg, PA Micro	55,952	232
Tulsa, OK Metro	55,912	233
Angola, IN Micro	55,904	234
Wenatchee, WA Metro	55,857	235
Bozeman, MT Micro	55,845	236
Pittsburgh, PA Metro	55,790	237
Davenport-Moline-Rock Island, IA-IL Metro	55,765	238
Manitowoc, WI Micro	55,765	239
Columbia, TN Micro	55,737	240
La Crosse, WI-MN Metro	55,732	241
South Bend-Mishawaka, IN-MI Metro	55,692	242
Auburn, IN Micro	55,677	243
Bismarck, ND Metro	55,676	244
Champaign-Urbana, IL Metro	55,613	245
Jackson, MS Metro	55,563	246
Toledo, OH Metro	55,476	247
Lebanon, PA Metro	55,456	248
Jasper, IN Micro	55,404	249
Lafayette, IN Metro	55,396	250
Brigham City, UT Micro	55,388	251
Flagstaff, AZ Metro	55,379	252
Topeka, KS Metro	55,356	253
Wisconsin Rapids-Marshfield, WI Micro	55,283	254
Knoxville, TN Metro	55,268	255
Salem, OR Metro	55,255	256
Canton-Massillon, OH Metro	55,214	257
Frankfort, KY Micro	55,178	258
New Orleans-Metairie-Kenner, LA Metro	55,169	259
Tucson, AZ Metro	55,114	260
Morehead City, NC Micro	55,113	261
Owosso, MI Micro	55,094	262
Evanston, WY Micro	55,073	263
Muscatine, IA Micro	55,071	264
New Ulm, MN Micro	55,051	265
Boone, IA Micro	55,029	266
Jefferson City, MO Metro	55,017	267
Defiance, OH Micro	55,006	268
Willmar, MN Micro	54,989	269
Roanoke, VA Metro	54,851	270
Sanford, NC Micro	54,844	271
Spirit Lake, IA Micro	54,802	272
Celina, OH Micro	54,797	273
Cheyenne, WY Metro	54,791	274
Evansville, IN-KY Metro	54,765	275
Buffalo-Cheektowaga-Tonawanda, NY Metro	54,667	276
Ukiah, CA Micro	54,664	277
Fargo, ND-MN Metro	54,644	278
Columbia, MO Metro	54,628	279
Sioux City, IA-NE-SD Metro	54,493	280
Baton Rouge, LA Metro	54,399	281
Niles-Benton Harbor, MI Metro	54,389	282
Urbana, OH Micro	54,383	283
Lafayette, LA Metro	54,372	284
Logan, UT-ID Metro	54,340	285
Medford, OR Metro	54,324	286
Ottawa-Streator, IL Micro	54,318	287
Montgomery, AL Metro	54,287	288
Plymouth, IN Micro	54,272	289
Dixon, IL Micro	54,233	290
Wooster, OH Micro	54,181	291
Huntington, IN Micro	54,117	292
Pensacola-Ferry Pass-Brent, FL Metro	54,110	293
Oklahoma City, OK Metro	54,101	294
Rockland, ME Micro	53,979	295
Victoria, TX Metro	53,924	296
Augusta-Richmond County, GA-SC Metro	53,901	297
Dover, DE Metro	53,900	298
Newton, IA Micro	53,819	299
Waterloo-Cedar Falls, IA Metro	53,819	300
Michigan City-La Porte, IN Metro	53,806	301
Pontiac, IL Micro	53,775	302
Tallahassee, FL Metro	53,767	303
McPherson, KS Micro	53,758	304
Eau Claire, WI Metro	53,746	305
Fremont, OH Micro	53,711	306
Hood River, OR Micro	53,695	307
Lincolnton, NC Micro	53,695	308
Chattanooga, TN-GA Metro	53,652	309

CBSA	INCOME ($)	RANK
Dalton, GA Metro	53,596	310
Bellefontaine, OH Micro	53,524	311
Gainesville, TX Micro	53,513	312
Crawfordsville, IN Micro	53,500	313
Hagerstown-Martinsburg, MD-WV Metro	53,472	314
Spokane, WA Metro	53,439	315
Billings, MT Metro	53,346	316
Vineland-Millville-Bridgeton, NJ Metro	53,338	317
Brunswick, GA Metro	53,325	318
Mount Vernon, OH Micro	53,279	319
Jackson, TN Metro	53,272	320
St. George, UT Metro	53,263	321
Saginaw-Saginaw Township North, MI Metro	53,255	322
Glens Falls, NY Metro	53,250	323
Macon, GA Metro	53,233	324
Springfield, OH Metro	53,199	325
Bay City, MI Metro	53,190	326
Rapid City, SD Metro	53,188	327
Anderson, IN Metro	53,171	328
Casper, WY Metro	53,151	329
Punta Gorda, FL Metro	53,105	330
Fayetteville-Springdale-Rogers, AR-MO Metro	53,097	331
Chambersburg, PA Micro	53,075	332
Sherman-Denison, TX Metro	53,071	333
Effingham, IL Micro	53,035	334
Kendallville, IN Micro	52,913	335
Sheridan, WY Micro	52,864	336
Eugene-Springfield, OR Metro	52,824	337
Hanford-Corcoran, CA Metro	52,754	338
Burlington, NC Metro	52,739	339
Greenville, OH Micro	52,654	340
Prescott, AZ Metro	52,654	341
Spartanburg, SC Metro	52,628	342
State College, PA Metro	52,609	343
Corpus Christi, TX Metro	52,601	344
Austin, MN Micro	52,594	345
Staunton-Waynesboro, VA Micro	52,582	346
Greensburg, IN Micro	52,559	347
Grand Junction, CO Metro	52,541	348
Sterling, IL Micro	52,541	349
Bartlesville, OK Micro	52,475	350
Batavia, NY Micro	52,467	351
Alexandria, MN Micro	52,466	352
Corning, NY Micro	52,465	353
Fresno, CA Metro	52,445	354
Salisbury, MD Metro	52,425	355
Winona, MN Micro	52,417	356
Longview-Kelso, WA Metro	52,336	357
St. Marys, GA Micro	52,329	358
Killeen-Temple-Fort Hood, TX Metro	52,287	359
Wilmington, OH Micro	52,285	360
Brenham, TX Micro	52,228	361
Decatur, IL Metro	52,228	362
Menomonie, WI Micro	52,190	363
Coeur d'Alene, ID Metro	52,152	364
Madera, CA Metro	52,131	365
Myrtle Beach-Conway-North Myrtle Beach, SC Metro	52,067	366
Columbus, NE Micro	52,009	367
Brainerd, MN Micro	51,941	368
Bakersfield, CA Metro	51,806	369
Washington, OH Micro	51,790	370
Freeport, IL Micro	51,787	371
Battle Creek, MI Metro	51,776	372
Harrisonburg, VA Metro	51,749	373
New Castle, IN Micro	51,700	374
Asheville, NC Metro	51,675	375
Kerrville, TX Micro	51,596	376
Frankfort, IN Micro	51,592	377
Deltona-Daytona Beach-Ormond Beach, FL Metro	51,554	378
Amarillo, TX Metro	51,541	379
Houma-Bayou Cane-Thibodaux, LA Metro	51,535	380
Logansport, IN Micro	51,515	381
Lakeland-Winter Haven, FL Metro	51,512	382
Lincoln, IL Micro	51,507	383
Binghamton, NY Metro	51,503	384
LaGrange, GA Micro	51,482	385
Seymour, IN Micro	51,444	386
Rutland, VT Micro	51,426	387
Marion, OH Micro	51,387	388
Helena, MT Micro	51,358	389
Norwalk, OH Micro	51,348	390
Muskegon-Norton Shores, MI Metro	51,342	391
Lake Charles, LA Metro	51,325	392
Pocatello, ID Metro	51,272	393
Pascagoula, MS Metro	51,248	394
Longview, TX Metro	51,244	395
Marshall, MN Micro	51,243	396
Athens-Clarke County, GA Metro	51,185	397
Shelton, WA Micro	51,171	398
Owensboro, KY Metro	51,168	399
Elizabethtown, KY Metro	51,143	400
Calhoun, GA Micro	51,135	401
Burlington, IA-IL Micro	51,039	402
Mansfield, OH Metro	51,032	403
Lynchburg, VA Metro	51,029	404
Seneca, SC Micro	51,029	405
Panama City-Lynn Haven, FL Metro	51,025	406
Bowling Green, KY Metro	51,006	407
Bishop, CA Micro	50,941	408
Wabash, IN Micro	50,937	409
Auburn, NY Micro	50,920	410
Fayetteville, NC Metro	50,911	411
Vernal, UT Micro	50,891	412
Plattsburgh, NY Micro	50,858	413
Elmira, NY Metro	50,853	414
Beaumont-Port Arthur, TX Metro	50,851	415
Sturgis, MI Micro	50,817	416
Coldwater, MI Micro	50,758	417
Muncie, IN Metro	50,748	418
Hickory-Morganton-Lenoir, NC Metro	50,735	419
Charleston, WV Metro	50,725	420
Visalia-Porterville, CA Metro	50,723	421
Astoria, OR Micro	50,697	422
Decatur, AL Metro	50,695	423
Vicksburg, MS Micro	50,676	424
Anderson, SC Metro	50,656	425
Dodge City, KS Micro	50,593	426
Lexington-Thomasville, NC Micro	50,570	427
Columbus, GA-AL Metro	50,540	428
Kalispell, MT Micro	50,529	429
Kearney, NE Micro	50,527	430
Redding, CA Metro	50,497	431
Peru, IN Micro	50,469	432
Gulfport-Biloxi, MS Metro	50,388	433
Albany-Lebanon, OR Micro	50,386	434
Decatur, IN Micro	50,379	435
Ellensburg, WA Micro	50,357	436
Merced, CA Metro	50,289	437
Gainesville, FL Metro	50,279	438
Yakima, WA Metro	50,256	439
Brevard, NC Micro	50,239	440
Marshalltown, IA Micro	50,210	441
Salisbury, NC Micro	50,210	442
Grand Forks, ND-MN Metro	50,197	443
Port Angeles, WA Micro	50,193	444
Salina, KS Micro	50,187	445
Rome, GA Metro	50,183	446
Garden City, KS Micro	50,173	447
Brookings, SD Micro	50,140	448
Pendleton-Hermiston, OR Micro	50,125	449
Madison, IN Micro	50,110	450
New Bern, NC Micro	50,088	451
Erie, PA Metro	50,081	452
Selinsgrove, PA Micro	50,052	453
Fergus Falls, MN Micro	50,044	454
Zanesville, OH Micro	50,033	455
Ashland, OH Micro	50,012	456
Greenville, NC Metro	50,011	457
Rocky Mount, NC Metro	49,992	458
Hays, KS Micro	49,966	459
Jacksonville, IL Micro	49,934	460
Connersville, IN Micro	49,915	461
Watertown, SD Micro	49,900	462
Yankton, SD Micro	49,881	463
Cornelia, GA Micro	49,862	464
Worthington, MN Micro	49,849	465
Fairmont, MN Micro	49,845	466
Shreveport-Bossier City, LA Metro	49,842	467
Spencer, IA Micro	49,834	468
Yuba City-Marysville, CA Metro	49,829	469
Chillicothe, OH Micro	49,826	470
Waco, TX Metro	49,815	471
Mason City, IA Micro	49,812	472
Duluth, MN-WI Metro	49,796	473
Florence, SC Metro	49,766	474
Lima, OH Metro	49,754	475
Bloomington, IN Metro	49,745	476
Merrill, WI Micro	49,729	477
Missoula, MT Metro	49,712	478
Borger, TX Micro	49,655	479
Walla Walla, WA Micro	49,654	480
Springfield, MO Metro	49,643	481
Liberal, KS Micro	49,623	482
Manhattan, KS Micro	49,592	483
Cambridge, MD Micro	49,587	484
North Vernon, IN Micro	49,574	485
Youngstown-Warren-Boardman, OH-PA Metro	49,531	486
Lewiston-Auburn, ME Metro	49,525	487
Grand Island, NE Micro	49,523	488
Albemarle, NC Micro	49,515	489
Tifton, GA Micro	49,495	490
Albert Lea, MN Micro	49,470	491
Scranton-Wilkes-Barre, PA Metro	49,461	492
Tullahoma, TN Micro	49,455	493
Albany, GA Metro	49,321	494
Bloomsburg-Berwick, PA Micro	49,319	495
Van Wert, OH Micro	49,309	496
Taylorville, IL Micro	49,272	497
St. Joseph, MO-KS Metro	49,256	498
Clarksville, TN-KY Metro	49,237	499
Boone, NC Micro	49,219	500
Hutchinson, KS Micro	49,209	501
Tuscaloosa, AL Metro	49,152	502
Lewiston, ID-WA Metro	49,109	503
Tupelo, MS Micro	49,109	504
Mitchell, SD Micro	49,098	505
Augusta-Waterville, ME Micro	49,083	506
Goldsboro, NC Metro	49,065	507
Utica-Rome, NY Metro	49,060	508
Mobile, AL Metro	49,049	509
Hastings, NE Micro	49,045	510
Twin Falls, ID Micro	49,028	511
Mount Pleasant, MI Micro	49,026	512
Fort Dodge, IA Micro	49,007	513
North Platte, NE Micro	48,987	514
Oskaloosa, IA Micro	48,986	515
Blackfoot, ID Micro	48,941	516
San Angelo, TX Metro	48,939	517
Fremont, NE Micro	48,920	518
Chico, CA Metro	48,903	519
Athens, TX Micro	48,891	520
Cape Girardeau-Jackson, MO-IL Micro	48,872	521
Seneca Falls, NY Micro	48,844	522
Montrose, CO Micro	48,805	523
Pueblo, CO Metro	48,736	524
Woodward, OK Micro	48,710	525
Marquette, MI Micro	48,663	526
Paducah, KY-IL Micro	48,663	527
Marion, IN Micro	48,659	528
Snyder, TX Micro	48,635	529
Aberdeen, SD Micro	48,633	530
Shelbyville, TN Micro	48,626	531
Escanaba, MI Micro	48,589	532
Sayre, PA Micro	48,542	533
Centralia, WA Micro	48,540	534
Cleveland, TN Metro	48,518	535
Moses Lake, WA Micro	48,496	536
Greenwood, SC Micro	48,476	537
Wichita Falls, TX Metro	48,425	538
Warrensburg, MO Micro	48,403	539
Quincy, IL-MO Micro	48,402	540
Harriman, TN Micro	48,337	541
Wilson, NC Micro	48,332	542
Winfield, KS Micro	48,310	543
Bangor, ME Metro	48,237	544
Storm Lake, IA Micro	48,201	545
Bemidji, MN Micro	48,200	546
Clinton, IA Micro	48,199	547
Keokuk-Fort Madison, IA-MO Micro	48,164	548
Lubbock, TX Metro	48,160	549
Williston, ND Micro	48,154	550
Milledgeville, GA Micro	48,108	551
St. Marys, PA Micro	48,099	552
College Station-Bryan, TX Metro	48,093	553
Alma, MI Micro	48,082	554
Mount Pleasant, TX Micro	48,039	555
Monroe, LA Metro	48,027	556
Cortland, NY Micro	48,026	557
North Wilkesboro, NC Micro	48,023	558
Guymon, OK Micro	48,022	559
Williamsport, PA Metro	48,019	560
Tiffin-Fostoria, OH Micro	48,012	561
Dunn, NC Micro	48,007	562
Lexington, NE Micro	48,004	563
Galesburg, IL Micro	48,003	564
Farmington, NM Metro	47,999	565
Platteville, WI Micro	47,920	566
Sulphur Springs, TX Micro	47,888	567
Canton, IL Micro	47,855	568
Texarkana, TX-Texarkana, AR Metro	47,830	569
Andrews, TX Micro	47,819	570
Minot, ND Micro	47,802	571
Lufkin, TX Micro	47,745	572
Washington, IN Micro	47,740	573
Marshall, TX Micro	47,670	574
Riverton, WY Micro	47,617	575
Oneonta, NY Micro	47,603	576
Beatrice, NE Micro	47,591	577
Big Rapids, MI Micro	47,581	578
Sevierville, TN Micro	47,558	579
Canon City, CO Micro	47,534	580
Iron Mountain, MI-WI Micro	47,520	581
Parkersburg-Marietta, WV-OH Metro	47,466	582
Terre Haute, IN Metro	47,459	583
Ashtabula, OH Micro	47,405	584
Hot Springs, AR Metro	47,392	585
Fort Morgan, CO Micro	47,388	586
Jamestown, ND Micro	47,376	587
Warren, PA Micro	47,376	588
Norfolk, NE Micro	47,353	589
Moscow, ID Micro	47,340	590
Shelby, NC Micro	47,323	591
El Centro, CA Metro	47,319	592
Dothan, AL Metro	47,314	593
Pahrump, NV Micro	47,257	594
Cadillac, MI Micro	47,229	595
Sierra Vista-Douglas, AZ Micro	47,166	596
New Philadelphia-Dover, OH Micro	47,152	597
Hattiesburg, MS Metro	47,141	598
Fort Valley, GA Micro	47,124	599
Bristol, VA Metro	47,121	600
Florence, AL Metro	47,112	601
Blacksburg-Christiansburg-Radford, VA Metro	47,063	602
City of The Dalles, OR Micro	47,043	603
Sumter, SC Metro	47,021	604
Enid, OK Micro	46,960	605
Lawton, OK Metro	46,958	606
Ponca City, OK Micro	46,939	607
Yuma, AZ Metro	46,905	608
Vernon, TX Micro	46,859	609
Dumas, TX Micro	46,854	610
Odessa, TX Metro	46,844	611
Oxford, MS Micro	46,839	612
Bedford, IN Micro	46,805	613
Stephenville, TX Micro	46,803	614
Mount Vernon, IL Micro	46,796	615
Richmond, IN Micro	46,790	616
Marion-Herrin, IL Micro	46,743	617
Abilene, TX Metro	46,729	618
Jesup, GA Micro	46,723	619
La Grande, OR Micro	46,689	620
Red Bluff, CA Micro	46,679	621

CBSA	INCOME ($)	RANK	CBSA	INCOME ($)	RANK	CBSA	INCOME ($)	RANK
Prineville, OR Micro	46,664	622	Picayune, MS Micro	44,527	726	Campbellsville, KY Micro	41,921	830
Great Falls, MT Metro	46,651	623	Newberry, SC Micro	44,521	727	Portsmouth, OH Micro	41,808	831
Sterling, CO Micro	46,651	624	Clewiston, FL Micro	44,473	728	Lake City, FL Micro	41,784	832
Albertville, AL Micro	46,628	625	Laurinburg, NC Micro	44,449	729	Del Rio, TX Micro	41,781	833
Nogales, AZ Micro	46,606	626	Huntingdon, PA Micro	44,424	730	Kirksville, MO Micro	41,762	834
Bucyrus, OH Micro	46,576	627	Big Spring, TX Micro	44,415	731	Jacksonville, IL Micro	41,736	835
New Castle, PA Micro	46,571	628	Nacogdoches, TX Micro	44,377	732	Kingsville, TX Micro	41,721	836
Lancaster, SC Micro	46,568	629	Huron, SD Micro	44,365	733	Arkadelphia, AR Micro	41,714	837
El Campo, TX Micro	46,563	630	Morgantown, WV Metro	44,362	734	Walterboro, SC Micro	41,714	838
El Paso, TX Metro	46,522	631	Jonesboro, AR Micro	44,357	735	Poplar Bluff, MO Micro	41,711	839
Searcy, AR Micro	46,510	632	Weirton-Steubenville, WV-OH Metro	44,347	736	Laurel, MS Micro	41,620	840
Huntsville, TX Micro	46,491	633	Atchison, KS Micro	44,331	737	Corinth, MS Micro	41,616	841
Eureka-Arcata-Fortuna, CA Micro	46,476	634	Laredo, TX Metro	44,299	738	Harrison, AR Micro	41,553	842
Jamestown-Dunkirk-Fredonia, NY Micro	46,448	635	Beckley, WV Metro	44,257	739	Harrisburg, IL Micro	41,510	843
Watertown-Fort Drum, NY Micro	46,428	636	Ogdensburg-Massena, NY Micro	44,251	740	Houghton, MI Micro	41,501	844
Spearfish, SD Micro	46,403	637	Elizabeth City, NC Micro	44,235	741	Carbondale, IL Micro	41,468	845
Wahpeton, ND-MN Micro	46,385	638	Henderson, NC Micro	44,232	742	McMinnville, TN Micro	41,468	846
Carlsbad-Artesia, NM Micro	46,377	639	Union City, TN-KY Micro	44,227	743	Point Pleasant, WV-OH Micro	41,353	847
Cedar City, UT Micro	46,366	640	Maryville, MO Micro	44,226	744	Somerset, PA Micro	41,321	848
Pampa, TX Micro	46,361	641	Ottumwa, IA Micro	44,219	745	Morgan City, LA Micro	41,174	849
Kingsport-Bristol, TN-VA Metro	46,351	642	Brownwood, TX Micro	44,165	746	Ruston, LA Micro	41,047	850
Palestine, TX Micro	46,348	643	Wheeling, WV-OH Metro	44,104	747	Brookhaven, MS Micro	41,045	851
Columbus, MS Micro	46,274	644	Butte-Silver Bow, MT Micro	44,098	748	Uvalde, TX Micro	41,020	852
Meadville, PA Micro	46,263	645	Dyersburg, TN Micro	44,003	749	Natchitoches, LA Micro	40,928	853
Centralia, IL Micro	46,206	646	Espanola, NM Micro	44,003	750	Alamogordo, NM Micro	40,912	854
Scottsbluff, NE Micro	46,196	647	Magnolia, AR Micro	43,939	751	Brownsville-Harlingen, TX Metro	40,885	855
Mount Airy, NC Micro	46,193	648	Oil City, PA Micro	43,897	752	Rockingham, NC Micro	40,837	856
Thomasville, GA Micro	46,169	649	Brookings, OR Micro	43,866	753	Havre, MT Micro	40,798	857
Ocala, FL Metro	46,153	650	Scottsboro, AL Micro	43,807	754	Ada, OK Micro	40,769	858
Amsterdam, NY Micro	46,103	651	Pullman, WA Micro	43,759	755	Camden, AR Micro	40,749	859
Jacksonville, NC Metro	46,089	652	Macomb, IL Micro	43,746	756	Jennings, LA Micro	40,746	860
Gloversville, NY Micro	46,086	653	Laramie, WY Micro	43,735	757	Brownsville, TN Micro	40,714	861
Price, UT Micro	46,083	654	Burley, ID Micro	43,716	758	Silver City, NM Micro	40,701	862
Alexandria, LA Metro	46,078	655	Okeechobee, FL Micro	43,710	759	Paris, TN Micro	40,691	863
Branson, MO Micro	46,047	656	Plainview, TX Micro	43,710	760	Somerset, KY Micro	40,647	864
Aberdeen, WA Micro	45,988	657	Wauchula, FL Micro	43,701	761	Cordele, GA Micro	40,459	865
Anniston-Oxford, AL Metro	45,988	658	Emporia, KS Micro	43,680	762	Moultrie, GA Micro	40,459	866
Duncan, OK Micro	45,987	659	Lebanon, MO Micro	43,673	763	London, KY Micro	40,396	867
Joplin, MO Metro	45,964	660	Orangeburg, SC Micro	43,665	764	Parsons, KS Micro	40,389	868
Mountain Home, ID Micro	45,935	661	Vincennes, IN Micro	43,657	765	Valley, AL Micro	40,370	869
Fort Leonard Wood, MO Micro	45,880	662	Fort Polk South, LA Micro	43,625	766	Central City, KY Micro	40,302	870
Charleston-Mattoon, IL Micro	45,866	663	Crossville, TN Micro	43,623	767	Summerville, GA Micro	40,275	871
Marinette, WI-MI Micro	45,846	664	Athens, TN Micro	43,620	768	Grants, NM Micro	40,240	872
Shawnee, OK Micro	45,829	665	Paragould, AR Micro	43,602	769	Hereford, TX Micro	40,227	873
Payson, AZ Micro	45,823	666	Murray, KY Micro	43,586	770	Blytheville, AR Micro	40,061	874
Pierre Part, LA Micro	45,817	667	Las Cruces, NM Metro	43,534	771	Maysville, KY Micro	40,057	875
Lamesa, TX Micro	45,782	668	Thomaston, GA Micro	43,447	772	McComb, MS Micro	40,003	876
Alpena, MI Micro	45,779	669	Mineral Wells, TX Micro	43,440	773	Fitzgerald, GA Micro	39,997	877
Fort Smith, AR-OK Metro	45,742	670	Lock Haven, PA Micro	43,418	774	Portales, NM Micro	39,968	878
Cullman, AL Micro	45,735	671	Hinesville-Fort Stewart, GA Metro	43,355	775	Bluefield, WV-VA Micro	39,896	879
Auburn-Opelika, AL Metro	45,669	672	Danville, VA Metro	43,341	776	Greenville, MS Micro	39,847	880
Coshocton, OH Micro	45,657	673	Hammond, LA Micro	43,339	777	Durant, OK Micro	39,729	881
East Liverpool-Salem, OH Micro	45,628	674	Stillwater, OK Micro	43,308	778	Waycross, GA Micro	39,682	882
Hannibal, MO Micro	45,622	675	Sikeston, MO Micro	43,299	779	Las Vegas, NM Micro	39,612	883
Scottsburg, IN Micro	45,622	676	Sedalia, MO Micro	43,261	780	McAllen-Edinburg-Pharr, TX Metro	39,441	884
Pottsville, PA Micro	45,610	677	Abbeville, LA Micro	43,235	781	Beeville, TX Micro	39,417	885
Clearlake, CA Micro	45,605	678	Clarksburg, WV Micro	43,227	782	Hope, AR Micro	39,318	886
Enterprise-Ozark, AL Micro	45,563	679	Americus, GA Micro	43,199	783	Roanoke Rapids, NC Micro	39,303	887
Kinston, NC Micro	45,546	680	Sebring, FL Micro	43,160	784	Troy, AL Micro	39,034	888
Rexburg, ID Micro	45,513	681	Meridian, MS Micro	43,148	785	Clarksdale, MS Micro	38,999	889
Roseburg, OR Micro	45,499	682	Johnstown, PA Metro	43,140	786	Grenada, MS Micro	38,998	890
Dublin, GA Micro	45,474	683	Huntington-Ashland, WV-KY-OH Metro	43,131	787	Lumberton, NC Micro	38,887	891
New Iberia, LA Micro	45,458	684	Douglas, GA Micro	43,100	788	Yazoo City, MS Micro	38,881	892
Homosassa Springs, FL Micro	45,439	685	Glasgow, KY Micro	43,100	789	Dillon, SC Micro	38,726	893
Valdosta, GA Metro	45,435	686	Pittsburg, KS Micro	43,005	790	Tahlequah, OK Micro	38,566	894
Gaffney, SC Micro	45,428	687	Clovis, NM Micro	43,000	791	West Plains, MO Micro	38,552	895
Dickinson, ND Micro	45,422	688	Ardmore, OK Micro	42,965	792	Bastrop, LA Micro	38,521	896
De Ridder, LA Micro	45,414	689	Fairmont, WV Micro	42,950	793	Natchez, MS-LA Micro	38,433	897
Morristown, TN Metro	45,389	690	Alice, TX Micro	42,945	794	Indianola, MS Micro	38,428	898
Olean, NY Micro	45,341	691	DuBois, PA Micro	42,885	795	Greenwood, MS Micro	38,385	899
Statesboro, GA Micro	45,320	692	Taos, NM Micro	42,882	796	Bennettsville, SC Micro	38,375	900
Johnson City, TN Metro	45,289	693	Coffeyville, KS Micro	42,879	797	Miami, OK Micro	38,294	901
Grants Pass, OR Micro	45,239	694	Rolla, MO Micro	42,867	798	Forrest City, AR Micro	38,135	902
Cedartown, GA Micro	45,209	695	Cumberland, MD-WV Metro	42,841	799	Sweetwater, TX Micro	38,071	903
Klamath Falls, OR Micro	45,202	696	Berlin, NH-VT Micro	42,798	800	Selma, Al. Micro	37,821	904
Danville, KY Micro	45,192	697	Forest City, NC Micro	42,759	801	Cleveland, MS Micro	37,729	905
Great Bend, KS Micro	45,189	698	Toccoa, GA Micro	42,651	802	Oak Hill, WV Micro	37,711	906
El Dorado, AR Micro	45,165	699	Palatka, FL Micro	42,650	803	Gallup, NM Micro	37,570	907
Hobbs, NM Micro	45,157	700	Crescent City North, CA Micro	42,646	804	Tuskegee, AL Micro	36,857	908
Mayfield, KY Micro	45,146	701	Chester, SC Micro	42,585	805	West Helena, AR Micro	36,390	909
Paris, TX Micro	45,097	702	Sunbury, PA Micro	42,553	806	Bogalusa, LA Micro	36,138	910
Washington, NC Micro	45,023	703	Lawrenceburg, TN Micro	42,515	807	Opelousas-Eunice, LA Micro	36,038	911
Corsicana, TX Micro	44,999	704	Roswell, NM Micro	42,515	808	Kennett, MO Micro	35,869	912
Madisonville, KY Micro	44,899	705	Crowley, LA Micro	42,470	809	Corbin, KY Micro	35,540	913
Lake Havasu City-Kingman, AZ Micro	44,890	706	Mountain Home, AR Micro	42,436	810	Newport, TN Micro	35,382	914
Marshall, MO Micro	44,884	707	Farmington, MO Micro	42,401	811	La Follette, TN Micro	35,360	915
Levelland, TX Micro	44,855	708	Greeneville, TN Micro	42,323	812	Pecos, TX Micro	34,348	916
Sault Ste. Marie, MI Micro	44,844	709	Union, SC Micro	42,318	813	Eagle Pass, TX Micro	34,061	917
Ontario, OR-ID Micro	44,833	710	Minden, LA Micro	42,283	814	Deming, NM Micro	32,831	918
Altus, OK Micro	44,804	711	Cambridge, OH Micro	42,275	815	Tallulah, LA Micro	32,074	919
Batesville, AR Micro	44,802	712	Lewistown, PA Micro	42,240	816	Raymondville, TX Micro	31,893	920
Danville, IL Metro	44,783	713	Moberly, MO Micro	42,175	817	Middlesborough, KY Micro	30,734	921
Malone, NY Micro	44,773	714	McAlester, OK Micro	42,169	818	Rio Grande City, TX Micro	27,764	922
Talladega-Sylacauga, AL Micro	44,736	715	Muskogee, OK Micro	42,152	819			
Mexico, MO Micro	44,715	716	Arcadia, FL Micro	42,151	820	CBSA Average	51,715	
Bay City, TX Micro	44,681	717	Starkville, MS Micro	42,142	821	United States Average	63,301	
Coos Bay, OR Micro	44,675	718	Bainbridge, GA Micro	42,137	822			
Russellville, AR Micro	44,667	719	Safford, AZ Micro	42,103	823			
Altoona, PA Metro	44,649	720	Martinsville, VA Micro	42,097	824			
Bradford, PA Micro	44,636	721	Indiana, PA Micro	42,072	825			
Pine Bluff, AR Metro	44,636	722	Mount Sterling, KY Micro	42,006	826			
Gadsden, AL Metro	44,589	723	Vermillion, SD Micro	41,997	827			
Richmond, KY Micro	44,584	724	Cookeville, TN Micro	41,995	828			
The Villages, FL Micro	44,529	725	Athens, OH Micro	41,982	829			

CBSA	SALES ($ MIL)	RANK
New York-Newark-Edison, NY-NJ-PA Metro	196,075	1
Los Angeles-Long Beach-Santa Ana, CA Metro	149,468	2
Chicago-Naperville-Joliet, IL-IN-WI Metro	114,708	3
Dallas-Fort Worth-Arlington, TX Metro	80,861	4
Miami-Fort Lauderdale-Miami Beach, FL Metro	76,054	5
Philadelphia-Camden-Wilmington, PA-NJ-DE-MD Metro	71,318	6
Washington-Arlington-Alexandria, DC-VA-MD-WV Metro	69,616	7
Atlanta-Sandy Springs-Marietta, GA Metro	66,855	8
Houston-Baytown-Sugar Land, TX Metro	64,859	9
Boston-Cambridge-Quincy, MA-NH Metro	62,501	10
San Francisco-Oakland-Fremont, CA Metro	54,895	11
Detroit-Warren-Livonia, MI Metro	54,196	12
Phoenix-Mesa-Scottsdale, AZ Metro	46,740	13
Seattle-Tacoma-Bellevue, WA Metro	45,819	14
Minneapolis-St. Paul-Bloomington, MN-WI Metro	45,156	15
San Diego-Carlsbad-San Marcos, CA Metro	38,485	16
St. Louis, MO-IL Metro	36,545	17
Tampa-St. Petersburg-Clearwater, FL Metro	36,175	18
Riverside-San Bernardino-Ontario, CA Metro	35,322	19
Baltimore-Towson, MD Metro	34,414	20
Denver-Aurora, CO Metro	32,188	21
Pittsburgh, PA Metro	30,742	22
Cleveland-Elyria-Mentor, OH Metro	29,515	23
Orlando, FL Metro	28,082	24
Cincinnati-Middletown, OH-KY-IN Metro	26,911	25
Kansas City, MO-KS Metro	26,672	26
Portland-Vancouver-Beaverton, OR-WA Metro	26,075	27
San Jose-Sunnyvale-Santa Clara, CA Metro	25,478	28
Columbus, OH Metro	25,389	29
Sacramento-Arden-Arcade-Roseville, CA Metro	25,199	30
San Antonio, TX Metro	23,941	31
Indianapolis, IN Metro	22,370	32
Las Vegas-Paradise, NV Metro	22,362	33
Milwaukee-Waukesha-West Allis, WI Metro	21,749	34
Austin-Round Rock, TX Metro	20,713	35
Charlotte-Gastonia-Concord, NC-SC Metro	20,133	36
Nashville-Davidson-Murfreesboro, TN Metro	18,084	37
Virginia Beach-Norfolk-Newport News, VA-NC Metro	17,841	38
Providence-New Bedford-Fall River, RI-MA Metro	17,387	39
Jacksonville, FL Metro	17,115	40
Richmond, VA Metro	16,122	41
New Orleans-Metairie-Kenner, LA Metro	15,868	42
Memphis, TN-MS-AR Metro	15,760	43
Oklahoma City, OK Metro	15,504	44
Louisville, KY-IN Metro	15,276	45
Hartford-West Hartford-East Hartford, CT Metro	15,177	46
Salt Lake City, UT Metro	14,940	47
Birmingham-Hoover, AL Metro	14,223	48
Rochester, NY Metro	14,125	49
Raleigh-Cary, NC Metro	12,963	50
Grand Rapids-Wyoming, MI Metro	12,806	51
Dayton, OH Metro	12,509	52
Buffalo-Cheektowaga-Tonawanda, NY Metro	12,405	53
Bridgeport-Stamford-Norwalk, CT Metro	12,319	54
Omaha-Council Bluffs, NE-IA Metro	11,209	55
Knoxville, TN Metro	10,896	56
Tucson, AZ Metro	10,749	57
Albany-Schenectady-Troy, NY Metro	10,659	58
Tulsa, OK Metro	10,404	59
Albuquerque, NM Metro	10,203	60
Greensboro-High Point, NC Metro	10,072	61
Honolulu, HI Metro	9,933	62
Oxnard-Thousand Oaks-Ventura, CA Metro	9,910	63
New Haven-Milford, CT Metro	9,648	64
Wichita, KS Metro	9,574	65
Sarasota-Bradenton-Venice, FL Metro	9,501	66
Toledo, OH Metro	9,366	67
Little Rock-North Little Rock, AR Metro	9,072	68
Baton Rouge, LA Metro	9,068	69
Worcester, MA Metro	9,044	70
Akron, OH Metro	8,964	71
Syracuse, NY Metro	8,818	72
Allentown-Bethlehem-Easton, PA-NJ Metro	8,767	73
Fresno, CA Metro	8,766	74
Columbia, SC Metro	8,655	75
Madison, WI Metro	8,342	76
Des Moines, IA Metro	8,204	77
Greenville, SC Metro	8,003	78
Scranton-Wilkes-Barre, PA Metro	7,865	79
Cape Coral-Fort Myers, FL Metro	7,816	80
El Paso, TX Metro	7,808	81
Charleston-North Charleston, SC Metro	7,641	82
Colorado Springs, CO Metro	7,584	83
Portland-South Portland, ME Metro	7,555	84
Poughkeepsie-Newburgh-Middletown, NY Metro	7,436	85
Springfield, MA Metro	7,362	86
Palm Bay-Melbourne-Titusville, FL Metro	7,213	87
Harrisburg-Carlisle, PA Metro	7,196	88
Youngstown-Warren-Boardman, OH-PA Metro	7,156	89
Boise City-Nampa, ID Metro	7,044	90
Lancaster, PA Metro	6,917	91
Bakersfield, CA Metro	6,895	92
Manchester-Nashua, NH Metro	6,872	93
Jackson, MS Metro	6,662	94
Lexington-Fayette, KY Metro	6,542	95
McAllen-Edinburg-Pharr, TX Metro	6,528	96
Stockton, CA Metro	6,209	97
Fayetteville-Springdale-Rogers, AR-MO Metro	6,182	98
Mobile, AL Metro	6,156	99
Deltona-Daytona Beach-Ormond Beach, FL Metro	6,118	100
Santa Rosa-Petaluma, CA Metro	6,018	101
Augusta-Richmond County, GA-SC Metro	5,967	102
Lakeland-Winter Haven, FL Metro	5,934	103
Spokane, WA Metro	5,914	104
Chattanooga, TN-GA Metro	5,837	105
Winston-Salem, NC Metro	5,821	106
Springfield, MO Metro	5,675	107
Canton-Massillon, OH Metro	5,657	108
Lansing-East Lansing, MI Metro	5,512	109
Boulder, CO Metro	5,392	110
Ogden-Clearfield, UT Metro	5,360	111
Pensacola-Ferry Pass-Brent, FL Metro	5,313	112
Flint, MI Metro	5,301	113
Santa Barbara-Santa Maria-Goleta, CA Metro	5,273	114
Roanoke, VA Metro	5,249	115
Provo-Orem, UT Metro	5,241	116
Davenport-Moline-Rock Island, IA-IL Metro	5,236	117
Asheville, NC Metro	5,231	118
Reno-Sparks, NV Metro	5,173	119
York-Hanover, PA Metro	5,107	120
Huntsville, AL Metro	5,011	121
Fort Wayne, IN Metro	4,972	122
Durham, NC Metro	4,970	123
Beaumont-Port Arthur, TX Metro	4,861	124
Modesto, CA Metro	4,842	125
Salinas, CA Metro	4,811	126
Peoria, IL Metro	4,783	127
Anchorage, AK Metro	4,763	128
Ann Arbor, MI Metro	4,736	129
Evansville, IN-KY Metro	4,707	130
Naples-Marco Island, FL Metro	4,694	131
Wilmington, NC Metro	4,692	132
Shreveport-Bossier City, LA Metro	4,636	133
Tallahassee, FL Metro	4,632	134
Savannah, GA Metro	4,521	135
Eugene-Springfield, OR Metro	4,478	136
Corpus Christi, TX Metro	4,461	137
Trenton-Ewing, NJ Metro	4,348	138
Rockford, IL Metro	4,327	139
Hickory-Morganton-Lenoir, NC Metro	4,302	140
Salem, OR Metro	4,273	141
Port St. Lucie-Fort Pierce, FL Metro	4,256	142
Vallejo-Fairfield, CA Metro	4,227	143
Green Bay, WI Metro	4,220	144
Montgomery, AL Metro	4,210	145
Myrtle Beach-Conway-North Myrtle Beach, SC Metro	4,194	146
Kalamazoo-Portage, MI Metro	4,112	147
Lincoln, NE Metro	4,091	148
Reading, PA Metro	4,078	149
South Bend-Mishawaka, IN-MI Metro	4,031	150
Charleston, WV Metro	4,002	151
Fayetteville, NC Metro	3,973	152
Barnstable Town, MA Metro	3,949	153
Fort Collins-Loveland, CO Metro	3,831	154
Lubbock, TX Metro	3,766	155
Erie, PA Metro	3,731	156
Hagerstown-Martinsburg, MD-WV Metro	3,725	157
Huntington-Ashland, WV-KY-OH Metro	3,714	158
Duluth, MN-WI Metro	3,657	159
Atlantic City, NJ Metro	3,641	160
Gulfport-Biloxi, MS Metro	3,608	161
Ocala, FL Metro	3,594	162
Brownsville-Harlingen, TX Metro	3,592	163
Lafayette, LA Metro	3,554	164
Amarillo, TX Metro	3,503	165
Sioux Falls, SD Metro	3,483	166
Eau Claire, WI Metro	3,481	167
Cedar Rapids, IA Metro	3,382	168
Killeen-Temple-Fort Hood, TX Metro	3,361	169
Visalia-Porterville, CA Metro	3,354	170
Utica-Rome, NY Metro	3,336	171
Spartanburg, SC Metro	3,296	172
San Luis Obispo-Paso Robles, CA Metro	3,281	173
Columbus, GA-AL Metro	3,242	174
Elkhart-Goshen, IN Metro	3,238	175
Norwich-New London, CT Metro	3,206	176
Appleton, WI Metro	3,201	177
Saginaw-Saginaw Township North, MI Metro	3,194	178
Gainesville, FL Metro	3,188	179
Tyler, TX Metro	3,169	180
Fargo, ND-MN Metro	3,127	181
Santa Cruz-Watsonville, CA Metro	3,055	182
Champaign-Urbana, IL Metro	2,997	183
Fort Walton Beach-Crestview-Destin, FL Metro	2,966	184
Waco, TX Metro	2,945	185
Burlington-South Burlington, VT Metro	2,936	186
St. Cloud, MN Metro	2,918	187
Springfield, IL Metro	2,894	188
Topeka, KS Metro	2,871	189
Medford, OR Metro	2,845	190
Fort Smith, AR-OK Metro	2,843	191
Holland-Grand Haven, MI Metro	2,796	192
Macon, GA Metro	2,723	193
Lebanon, NH-VT Micro	2,665	194
Billings, MT Metro	2,658	195
Seaford, DE Micro	2,654	196
Concord, NH Micro	2,652	197
Longview, TX Metro	2,647	198
Lynchburg, VA Metro	2,636	199
Hilton Head Island-Beaufort, SC Micro	2,624	200
Kingsport-Bristol, TN-VA Metro	2,596	201
Joplin, MO Metro	2,594	202
Olympia, WA Metro	2,548	203
Houma-Bayou Cane-Thibodaux, LA Metro	2,531	204
Binghamton, NY Metro	2,523	205
Torrington, CT Micro	2,518	206
Greeley, CO Metro	2,502	207
Florence, SC Metro	2,500	208
Johnson City, TN Metro	2,489	209
Lake Charles, LA Metro	2,488	210
Tuscaloosa, AL Metro	2,479	211
Traverse City, MI Micro	2,469	212
Racine, WI Metro	2,458	213
Panama City-Lynn Haven, FL Metro	2,449	214
Rochester, MN Metro	2,447	215
Lake Havasu City-Kingman, AZ Micro	2,437	216
Bremerton-Silverdale, WA Metro	2,428	217
Chico, CA Metro	2,421	218
Lafayette, IN Metro	2,407	219
Prescott, AZ Metro	2,404	220
Terre Haute, IN Metro	2,403	221
Bangor, ME Metro	2,356	222
Santa Fe, NM Metro	2,352	223
Charlottesville, VA Metro	2,350	224
Laredo, TX Metro	2,348	225
Yakima, WA Metro	2,345	226
Bellingham, WA Metro	2,344	227
Kennewick-Richland-Pasco, WA Metro	2,340	228
Daphne-Fairhope, AL Micro	2,336	229
Clarksville, TN-KY Metro	2,279	230
College Station-Bryan, TX Metro	2,265	231
La Crosse, WI-MN Metro	2,226	232
Ottawa-Streator, IL Micro	2,207	233
Statesville-Mooresville, NC Micro	2,204	234
Monroe, LA Metro	2,180	235
Dothan, AL Metro	2,147	236
Bloomington-Normal, IL Metro	2,140	237
Bend, OR Metro	2,125	238
Wheeling, WV-OH Metro	2,124	239
Columbia, MO Metro	2,122	240
Kahului-Wailuku, HI Micro	2,098	241
Anderson, SC Metro	2,098	242
Ocean City, NJ Metro	2,089	243
Albany, GA Metro	2,069	244
Bloomington, IN Metro	2,052	245
Wausau, WI Metro	2,040	246
Waterloo-Cedar Falls, IA Metro	2,027	247
Dalton, GA Metro	2,023	248
Oshkosh-Neenah, WI Metro	2,019	249
Dover, DE Metro	2,016	250
Pittsfield, MA Metro	2,015	251
Hilo, HI Micro	1,998	252
Sioux City, IA-NE-SD Metro	1,996	253
Greenville, NC Metro	1,980	254
Athens-Clarke County, GA Metro	1,974	255
Kingston, NY Metro	1,965	256
Muskegon-Norton Shores, MI Metro	1,958	257
Abilene, TX Metro	1,931	258
Altoona, PA Metro	1,923	259
Missoula, MT Metro	1,920	260
Battle Creek, MI Metro	1,919	261
Punta Gorda, FL Metro	1,918	262
Flagstaff, AZ Metro	1,902	263
Lima, OH Metro	1,882	264
Gainesville, GA Metro	1,880	265
Blacksburg-Christiansburg-Radford, VA Metro	1,875	266
Valdosta, GA Metro	1,867	267
Wichita Falls, TX Metro	1,861	268
Key West-Marathon, FL Micro	1,839	269
Vineland-Millville-Bridgeton, NJ Metro	1,839	270
Janesville, WI Metro	1,831	271
East Stroudsburg, PA Micro	1,827	272
Yuma, AZ Metro	1,821	273
Iowa City, IA Metro	1,817	274
Niles-Benton Harbor, MI Metro	1,817	275
Grand Junction, CO Metro	1,810	276
Augusta-Waterville, ME Micro	1,800	277
Rapid City, SD Metro	1,797	278
Parkersburg-Marietta, WV-OH Metro	1,787	279
Springfield, OH Metro	1,786	280
Merced, CA Metro	1,780	281
Mount Vernon-Anacortes, WA Metro	1,759	282
Texarkana, TX-Texarkana, AR Metro	1,758	283
Pueblo, CO Metro	1,756	284
Rocky Mount, NC Metro	1,749	285
Burlington, NC Metro	1,745	286
Hattiesburg, MS Metro	1,741	287
Tupelo, MS Micro	1,737	288
Harrisonburg, VA Metro	1,730	289
Mansfield, OH Metro	1,730	290
Jackson, TN Metro	1,721	291
Jefferson City, MO Metro	1,710	292
Vero Beach, FL Metro	1,706	293
Redding, CA Metro	1,698	294
Alexandria, LA Metro	1,690	295
Elizabethtown, KY Metro	1,674	296
Salisbury, MD Metro	1,664	297
Lewiston-Auburn, ME Metro	1,645	298
Florence, AL Metro	1,636	299
Sumter, SC Metro	1,633	300
Lexington-Thomasville, NC Micro	1,624	301
Kankakee-Bradley, IL Metro	1,618	302
Fond du Lac, WI Metro	1,612	303
Sheboygan, WI Metro	1,605	304
Dubuque, IA Metro	1,594	305
Jamestown-Dunkirk-Fredonia, NY Micro	1,590	306
St. George, UT Metro	1,588	307
Bowling Green, KY Metro	1,588	308

CBSA	SALES ($ MIL)	RANK
Idaho Falls, ID Metro	1,586	309
Muncie, IN Metro	1,580	310
Jackson, MI Metro	1,580	311
Watertown-Fort Drum, NY Micro	1,572	312
Bismarck, ND Metro	1,569	313
Williamsport, PA Metro	1,562	314
Chambersburg, PA Micro	1,559	315
Johnstown, PA Metro	1,553	316
Eureka-Arcata-Fortuna, CA Micro	1,551	317
Lawrence, KS Metro	1,546	318
Las Cruces, NM Metro	1,545	319
Morgantown, WV Metro	1,534	320
Decatur, IL Metro	1,532	321
Lawton, OK Metro	1,531	322
Midland, TX Metro	1,530	323
Sevierville, TN Micro	1,523	324
State College, PA Metro	1,519	325
Mankato-North Mankato, MN Micro	1,513	326
Monroe, MI Metro	1,512	327
Napa, CA Metro	1,511	328
Findlay, OH Micro	1,510	329
Cookeville, TN Micro	1,505	330
Sierra Vista-Douglas, AZ Micro	1,498	331
Winchester, VA-WV Metro	1,485	332
Odessa, TX Metro	1,484	333
Decatur, AL Metro	1,482	334
Anniston-Oxford, AL Metro	1,480	335
Staunton-Waynesboro, VA Micro	1,464	336
Homosassa Springs, FL Micro	1,463	337
St. Joseph, MO-KS Metro	1,457	338
Victoria, TX Metro	1,457	339
Yuba City-Marysville, CA Metro	1,452	340
New Bern, NC Micro	1,452	341
Lebanon, PA Metro	1,451	342
Sherman-Denison, TX Metro	1,445	343
Paducah, KY-IL Micro	1,434	344
Brainerd, MN Micro	1,433	345
Bay City, MI Metro	1,430	346
Bozeman, MT Micro	1,427	347
Grand Forks, ND-MN Metro	1,419	348
Warner Robins, GA Metro	1,415	349
Jacksonville, NC Metro	1,397	350
Jonesboro, AR Metro	1,389	351
Farmington, NM Metro	1,383	352
Hot Springs, AR Metro	1,375	353
Owensboro, KY Metro	1,374	354
Anderson, IN Metro	1,364	355
Roseburg, OR Micro	1,356	356
Coeur d'Alene, ID Metro	1,354	357
Cheyenne, WY Metro	1,350	358
Kokomo, IN Metro	1,344	359
Manhattan, KS Micro	1,341	360
Brunswick, GA Metro	1,338	361
Keene, NH Micro	1,334	362
San Angelo, TX Metro	1,325	363
Pascagoula, MS Metro	1,323	364
Cape Girardeau-Jackson, MO-IL Micro	1,313	365
Wooster, OH Micro	1,312	366
Shelby, NC Micro	1,309	367
Meridian, MS Micro	1,303	368
Wenatchee, WA Metro	1,302	369
Auburn-Opelika, AL Metro	1,292	370
Hammond, LA Micro	1,282	371
Chillicothe, OH Micro	1,275	372
Morristown, TN Metro	1,274	373
Ocean Pines, MD Micro	1,267	374
Danville, VA Metro	1,262	375
Bluefield, WV-VA Micro	1,260	376
Wisconsin Rapids-Marshfield, WI Micro	1,259	377
Kalispell, MT Micro	1,257	378
Michigan City-La Porte, IN Metro	1,236	379
DuBois, PA Micro	1,228	380
Richmond, KY Micro	1,228	381
Pottsville, PA Micro	1,228	382
Willimantic, CT Micro	1,223	383
Goldsboro, NC Metro	1,220	384
Ogdensburg-Massena, NY Micro	1,215	385
Baraboo, WI Micro	1,207	386
Cumberland, MD-WV Metro	1,206	387
Lumberton, NC Micro	1,203	388
Ames, IA Metro	1,198	389
East Liverpool-Salem, OH Micro	1,196	390
Ukiah, CA Micro	1,191	391
Rome, GA Metro	1,189	392
Cleveland, TN Metro	1,181	393
Whitewater, WI Micro	1,177	394
New Philadelphia-Dover, OH Micro	1,176	395
Grand Island, NE Micro	1,165	396
Longview-Kelso, WA Metro	1,160	397
Fairbanks, AK Metro	1,157	398
Gadsden, AL Metro	1,154	399
North Wilkesboro, NC Micro	1,151	400
Sebring, FL Micro	1,149	401
Ithaca, NY Metro	1,144	402
Laconia, NH Micro	1,143	403
Albany-Lebanon, OR Micro	1,142	404
Allegan, MI Micro	1,138	405
Glens Falls, NY Metro	1,138	406
Twin Falls, ID Micro	1,134	407
Ashtabula, OH Micro	1,126	408
Salisbury, NC Micro	1,124	409
Truckee-Grass Valley, CA Micro	1,122	410
Quincy, IL-MO Micro	1,122	411
Beckley, WV Micro	1,115	412
Logan, UT-ID Metro	1,107	413
Sandusky, OH Metro	1,103	414
Orangeburg, SC Micro	1,103	415
Casper, WY Metro	1,099	416
Lufkin, TX Micro	1,096	417
Zanesville, OH Micro	1,093	418
Bristol, VA Micro	1,093	419
Albertville, AL Micro	1,089	420
Branson, MO Micro	1,089	421
Tullahoma, TN Micro	1,087	422
Weirton-Steubenville, WV-OH Metro	1,084	423
Elmira, NY Metro	1,075	424
Grants Pass, OR Micro	1,075	425
Martinsville, VA Micro	1,074	426
Southern Pines, NC Micro	1,074	427
El Centro, CA Metro	1,067	428
Adrian, MI Micro	1,057	429
Indiana, PA Micro	1,055	430
Midland, MI Micro	1,053	431
Stevens Point, WI Micro	1,049	432
Plattsburgh, NY Micro	1,042	433
Mount Airy, NC Micro	1,017	434
Mason City, IA Micro	1,016	435
Madera, CA Micro	1,015	436
Opelousas-Eunice, LA Micro	1,012	437
Great Falls, MT Metro	985	438
Edwards, CO Micro	984	439
Kill Devil Hills, NC Micro	984	440
Russellville, AR Micro	978	441
Clarksburg, WV Micro	975	442
Watertown-Fort Atkinson, WI Micro	969	443
Lexington Park, MD Micro	967	444
Cullman, AL Micro	965	445
London, KY Micro	956	446
New Castle, PA Micro	954	447
Pocatello, ID Metro	945	448
Somerset, KY Micro	944	449
Sunbury, PA Micro	941	450
Gettysburg, PA Micro	938	451
Wilson, NC Micro	938	452
Corning, NY Micro	937	453
Danville, KY Micro	934	454
Kapaa, HI Micro	932	455
Minot, ND Micro	929	456
Columbus, IN Metro	925	457
Rutland, VT Micro	925	458
Pine Bluff, AR Metro	923	459
Warsaw, IN Micro	921	460
Olean, NY Micro	920	461
Hanford-Corcoran, CA Metro	918	462
Bloomsburg-Berwick, PA Micro	917	463
Somerset, NJ Micro	914	464
Barre, VT Micro	907	465
Morehead City, NC Micro	907	466
Salina, KS Micro	900	467
Ardmore, OK Micro	898	468
Centralia, WA Micro	897	469
Columbus, MS Micro	894	470
Mount Pleasant, MI Micro	892	471
Durango, CO Micro	890	472
Enterprise-Ozark, AL Micro	886	473
New Iberia, LA Micro	883	474
Beaver Dam, WI Micro	883	475
Marquette, MI Micro	881	476
Hutchinson, KS Micro	880	477
Greenwood, SC Micro	871	478
Richmond, IN Micro	870	479
Meadville, PA Micro	867	480
Carson City, NV Metro	864	481
Dunn, NC Micro	863	482
Stillwater, OK Micro	857	483
Nacogdoches, TX Micro	855	484
Marion-Herrin, IL Micro	852	485
Frankfort, KY Micro	851	486
Palatka, FL Micro	850	487
Helena, MT Micro	849	488
Gallup, NM Micro	847	489
Manitowoc, WI Micro	846	490
Muskogee, OK Micro	845	491
Pendleton-Hermiston, OR Micro	845	492
Poplar Bluff, MO Micro	842	493
Galesburg, IL Micro	841	494
McComb, MS Micro	839	495
Boone, NC Micro	833	496
Jasper, IN Micro	832	497
Kearney, NE Micro	827	498
LaGrange, GA Micro	823	499
Port Angeles, WA Micro	819	500
Nogales, AZ Micro	818	501
Sayre, PA Micro	799	502
Lewiston, ID-WA Metro	796	503
Monroe, WI Micro	794	504
Corvallis, OR Metro	782	505
Searcy, AR Micro	779	506
Laurel, MS Micro	778	507
Sanford, NC Micro	777	508
Effingham, IL Micro	771	509
Carbondale, IL Micro	768	510
Kinston, NC Micro	767	511
Forest City, NC Micro	766	512
Coos Bay, OR Micro	765	513
Marinette, WI-MI Micro	763	514
Columbia, TN Micro	761	515
Georgetown, SC Micro	757	516
Bemidji, MN Micro	750	517
Easton, MD Micro	748	518
Talladega-Sylacauga, AL Micro	742	519
Seymour, IN Micro	741	520
Enid, OK Micro	740	521
Red Bluff, CA Micro	739	522
Tifton, GA Micro	732	523
Lake City, FL Micro	730	524
Burlington, IA-IL Micro	728	525
Bennington, VT Micro	727	526
Aberdeen, SD Micro	725	527
Batavia, NY Micro	724	528
Faribault-Northfield, MN Micro	719	529
Oneonta, NY Micro	718	530
Seneca, SC Micro	716	531
Charleston-Mattoon, IL Micro	713	532
Roanoke Rapids, NC Micro	712	533
Oil City, PA Micro	706	534
Palm Coast, FL Micro	703	535
Aberdeen, WA Micro	699	536
Gardnerville Ranchos, NV Micro	698	537
Douglas, GA Micro	697	538
Rockland, ME Micro	694	539
Klamath Falls, OR Micro	692	540
Ponca City, OK Micro	692	541
Freeport, IL Micro	688	542
Athens, TX Micro	687	543
Owosso, MI Micro	687	544
Roswell, NM Micro	687	545
Albemarle, NC Micro	686	546
Vicksburg, MS Micro	685	547
Sidney, OH Micro	685	548
Urbana, OH Micro	683	549
Sterling, IL Micro	682	550
Marion, IN Micro	680	551
Farmington, MO Micro	679	552
Norfolk, NE Micro	676	553
Thomasville, GA Micro	671	554
Greeneville, TN Micro	670	555
Dublin, GA Micro	669	556
El Dorado, AR Micro	668	557
Danville, KY Micro	663	558
Gloversville, NY Micro	660	559
Crossville, TN Micro	659	560
Winona, MN Micro	656	561
Red Wing, MN Micro	656	562
Greenville, MS Micro	654	563
Statesboro, GA Micro	653	564
Jackson, WY-ID Micro	650	565
Cadillac, MI Micro	650	566
Auburn, NY Micro	650	567
Granbury, TX Micro	648	568
Huntsville, TX Micro	647	569
Willmar, MN Micro	644	570
Elizabeth City, NC Micro	644	571
Ruston, LA Micro	641	572
Hudson, NY Micro	639	573
Astoria, OR Micro	639	574
Hobbs, NM Micro	639	575
Phoenix Lake-Cedar Ridge, CA Micro	638	576
Paragould, AR Micro	637	577
Clinton, IA Micro	637	578
Palestine, TX Micro	636	579
Henderson, NC Micro	636	580
Natchez, MS-LA Micro	631	581
Portsmouth, OH Micro	631	582
Fergus Falls, MN Micro	631	583
Moses Lake, WA Micro	631	584
Silverthorne, CO Micro	626	585
Milledgeville, GA Micro	624	586
McMinnville, TN Micro	622	587
Selinsgrove, PA Micro	621	588
Washington, NC Micro	621	589
Platteville, WI Micro	620	590
Muscatine, IA Micro	619	591
McAlester, OK Micro	618	592
Lancaster, SC Micro	618	593
Rochelle, IL Micro	618	594
Marshall, TX Micro	614	595
Norwalk, OH Micro	613	596
Paris, TX Micro	612	597
Marion, OH Micro	610	598
Oak Harbor, WA Micro	609	599
Scottsboro, AL Micro	609	600
Walla Walla, WA Micro	609	601
Ontario, OR-ID Micro	608	602
Lincolnton, NC Micro	607	603
Clovis, NM Micro	604	604
Rock Springs, WY Micro	603	605
Brigham City, UT Micro	603	606
Kerrville, TX Micro	597	607
Menomonie, WI Micro	594	608
Payson, AZ Micro	594	609
Berlin, NH-VT Micro	591	610
Watertown, SD Micro	588	611
Iron Mountain, MI-WI Micro	587	612
Fremont, OH Micro	585	613
Defiance, OH Micro	583	614
Waycross, GA Micro	583	615
Shawnee, OK Micro	583	616
Duncan, OK Micro	582	617
Harrison, AR Micro	580	618
Murray, KY Micro	579	619
Fremont, NE Micro	578	620

CBSA	SALES ($ MIL)	RANK
Mount Vernon, IL Micro	577	621
Montrose, CO Micro	573	622
Calhoun, GA Micro	572	623
Columbus, NE Micro	568	624
Carlsbad-Artesia, NM Micro	563	625
Durant, OK Micro	561	626
Clearlake, CA Micro	559	627
St. Marys, GA Micro	559	628
Madisonville, KY Micro	558	629
Rockingham, NC Micro	552	630
Morgan City, LA Micro	552	631
Alexandria, MN Micro	545	632
Gillette, WY Micro	545	633
El Campo, TX Micro	544	634
Scottsbluff, NE Micro	543	635
Athens, TN Micro	541	636
Gaffney, SC Micro	540	637
Cortland, NY Micro	539	638
West Plains, MO Micro	537	639
Big Rapids, MI Micro	536	640
Burley, ID Micro	535	641
Jacksonville, TX Micro	535	642
Keokuk-Fort Madison, IA-MO Micro	534	643
Greenville, OH Micro	534	644
Bradford, PA Micro	531	645
Lock Haven, PA Micro	531	646
Mount Vernon, OH Micro	529	647
Athens, OH Micro	529	648
Escanaba, MI Micro	527	649
Bartlesville, OK Micro	527	650
Garden City, KS Micro	527	651
Corsicana, TX Micro	526	652
Plymouth, IN Micro	526	653
Austin, MN Micro	524	654
Union City, TN-KY Micro	523	655
Bedford, IN Micro	520	656
Owatonna, MN Micro	517	657
Tahlequah, OK Micro	515	658
Riverton, WY Micro	513	659
Ottumwa, IA Micro	512	660
Fort Dodge, IA Micro	508	661
Del Rio, TX Micro	507	662
Fort Leonard Wood, MO Micro	507	663
Ada, OK Micro	503	664
Alamogordo, NM Micro	503	665
Hastings, NE Micro	503	666
Marshalltown, IA Micro	502	667
Sedalia, MO Micro	499	668
Warren, PA Micro	499	669
Vincennes, IN Micro	498	670
Moultrie, GA Micro	497	671
Mountain Home, AR Micro	497	672
Cedar City, UT Micro	497	673
Glasgow, KY Micro	496	674
Crawfordsville, IN Micro	496	675
Elko, NV Micro	492	676
Point Pleasant, WV-OH Micro	492	677
Albert Lea, MN Micro	491	678
Auburn, IN Micro	491	679
North Platte, NE Micro	488	680
Rolla, MO Micro	486	681
Oxford, MS Micro	484	682
Houghton, MI Micro	484	683
Dodge City, KS Micro	482	684
Mount Pleasant, TX Micro	480	685
Sturgis, MI Micro	479	686
Taylorville, IL Micro	478	687
Abbeville, LA Micro	475	688
Lewistown, PA Micro	475	689
Cornelia, GA Micro	474	690
Hutchinson, MN Micro	471	691
Dyersburg, TN Micro	470	692
Gainesville, TX Micro	468	693
Wilmington, OH Micro	467	694
Walterboro, SC Micro	466	695
Malone, NY Micro	464	696
Eagle Pass, TX Micro	462	697
Blytheville, AR Micro	462	698
Dixon, IL Micro	460	699
Fairmont, WV Micro	460	700
Butte-Silver Bow, MT Micro	460	701
Marshall, MN Micro	459	702
Sault Ste. Marie, MI Micro	456	703
Newport, TN Micro	455	704
Crowley, LA Micro	454	705
Rexburg, ID Micro	452	706
Juneau, AK Micro	449	707
Alma, MI Micro	448	708
Tiffin-Fostoria, OH Micro	445	709
Picayune, MS Micro	443	710
Jacksonville, IL Micro	443	711
Wapakoneta, OH Micro	443	712
Pontiac, IL Micro	443	713
Sikeston, MO Micro	442	714
Batesville, AR Micro	441	715
Okeechobee, FL Micro	440	716
Corinth, MS Micro	438	717
Taos, NM Micro	438	718
Hinesville-Fort Stewart, GA Metro	437	719
Hays, KS Micro	435	720
New Ulm, MN Micro	434	721
Brownwood, TX Micro	433	722
Ellensburg, WA Micro	431	723
Lewisburg, PA Micro	430	724
Yankton, SD Micro	430	725
Harriman, TN Micro	429	726
Coffeyville, KS Micro	428	727
Amsterdam, NY Micro	427	728
Oak Hill, WV Micro	426	729
Sulphur Springs, TX Micro	424	730
Safford, AZ Micro	423	731
Brookhaven, MS Micro	423	732
Selma, AL Micro	422	733
Angola, IN Micro	420	734
Alpena, MI Micro	419	735
Kendallville, IN Micro	418	736
Pittsburg, KS Micro	417	737
Logansport, IN Micro	416	738
Kennett, MO Micro	416	739
Hannibal, MO Micro	415	740
New Castle, IN Micro	415	741
Minden, LA Micro	414	742
Ashland, OH Micro	413	743
Harrisburg, IL Micro	412	744
The Villages, FL Micro	410	745
Great Bend, KS Micro	408	746
Winfield, KS Micro	407	747
Bellefontaine, OH Micro	406	748
Fort Polk South, LA Micro	405	749
Altus, OK Micro	403	750
Washington, OH Micro	403	751
Greenwood, MS Micro	400	752
Lawrenceburg, TN Micro	400	753
Brenham, TX Micro	399	754
Moscow, ID Micro	398	755
Campbellsville, KY Micro	398	756
La Follette, TN Micro	398	757
Huntington, IN Micro	394	758
Maysville, KY Micro	394	759
Americus, GA Micro	393	760
Stephenville, TX Micro	393	761
Canon City, CO Micro	392	762
McPherson, KS Micro	390	763
Mount Sterling, KY Micro	390	764
Bogalusa, LA Micro	390	765
Plainview, TX Micro	389	766
Warrensburg, MO Micro	387	767
Lebanon, MO Micro	386	768
Alice, TX Micro	386	769
Sheridan, WY Micro	385	770
Middlesborough, KY Micro	383	771
Madison, IN Micro	382	772
Bay City, TX Micro	381	773
Merrill, WI Micro	379	774
Natchitoches, LA Micro	378	775
Laramie, WY Micro	376	776
Grenada, MS Micro	375	777
Paris, TN Micro	375	778
Mayfield, KY Micro	374	779
Kingsville, TX Micro	373	780
Troy, AL Micro	371	781
Macomb, IL Micro	371	782
Pierre, SD Micro	370	783
Shelton, WA Micro	369	784
Emporia, KS Micro	367	785
Mitchell, SD Micro	366	786
Cambridge, OH Micro	366	787
Cambridge, MD Micro	365	788
Fitzgerald, GA Micro	365	789
Coshocton, OH Micro	365	790
Starkville, MS Micro	364	791
Celina, OH Micro	361	792
Brevard, NC Micro	359	793
City of The Dalles, OR Micro	357	794
St. Marys, PA Micro	357	795
Rio Grande City, TX Micro	357	796
Brookings, SD Micro	356	797
Hood River, OR Micro	354	798
Worthington, MN Micro	352	799
Decatur, IN Micro	351	800
Bucyrus, OH Micro	351	801
Newton, IA Micro	350	802
Seneca Falls, NY Micro	350	803
Jesup, GA Micro	348	804
Fairmont, MN Micro	347	805
Centralia, IL Micro	346	806
Huntingdon, PA Micro	346	807
Greensburg, IN Micro	346	808
Shelbyville, TN Micro	344	809
Hope, AR Micro	343	810
Kirksville, MO Micro	341	811
Bainbridge, GA Micro	340	812
Valley, AL Micro	340	813
Canton, IL Micro	339	814
Dickinson, ND Micro	337	815
Thomaston, GA Micro	333	816
Clewiston, FL Micro	329	817
Peru, IN Micro	323	818
Toccoa, GA Micro	322	819
Newberry, SC Micro	321	820
Pecos, TX Micro	321	821
Brookings, OR Micro	321	822
La Grande, OR Micro	320	823
Coldwater, MI Micro	317	824
Pahrump, NV Micro	315	825
Indianola, MS Micro	315	826
Jennings, LA Micro	315	827
Liberal, KS Micro	314	828
Spencer, IA Micro	314	829
Williston, ND Micro	313	830
Camden, AR Micro	311	831
Washington, IN Micro	310	832
Deming, NM Micro	310	833
Cordele, GA Micro	307	834
Silver City, NM Micro	305	835
Boone, IA Micro	303	836
Fort Morgan, CO Micro	303	837
Wabash, IN Micro	302	838
Spirit Lake, IA Micro	298	839
Big Spring, TX Micro	297	840
Vernal, UT Micro	297	841
Price, UT Micro	296	842
Corbin, KY Micro	295	843
Laurinburg, NC Micro	293	844
Lexington, NE Micro	293	845
Miami, OK Micro	291	846
Bishop, CA Micro	291	847
Borger, TX Micro	289	848
Van Wert, OH Micro	285	849
Jamestown, ND Micro	284	850
Evanston, WY Micro	283	851
Lincoln, IL Micro	282	852
Prineville, OR Micro	277	853
Spearfish, SD Micro	277	854
Blackfoot, ID Micro	277	855
Cedartown, GA Micro	276	856
Magnolia, AR Micro	274	857
Guymon, OK Micro	272	858
Moberly, MO Micro	272	859
Chester, SC Micro	268	860
North Vernon, IN Micro	267	861
Mineral Wells, TX Micro	266	862
Storm Lake, IA Micro	266	863
De Ridder, LA Micro	264	864
Beatrice, NE Micro	263	865
Forrest City, AR Micro	262	866
Frankfort, IN Micro	262	867
Cleveland, MS Micro	261	868
Dillon, SC Micro	261	869
Las Vegas, NM Micro	259	870
Mountain Home, ID Micro	258	871
Fallon, NV Micro	258	872
Clarksdale, MS Micro	257	873
Maryville, MO Micro	255	874
Fort Valley, GA Micro	252	875
Espanola, NM Micro	252	876
Central City, KY Micro	252	877
Woodward, OK Micro	251	878
Uvalde, TX Micro	249	879
Parsons, KS Micro	249	880
Ketchikan, AK Micro	248	881
Pampa, TX Micro	247	882
Connersville, IN Micro	247	883
Mexico, MO Micro	246	884
Oskaloosa, IA Micro	243	885
Pullman, WA Micro	241	886
Summerville, GA Micro	241	887
Arcadia, FL Micro	240	888
Crescent City North, CA Micro	240	889
Bastrop, LA Micro	239	890
Arkadelphia, AR Micro	239	891
Sterling, CO Micro	235	892
Huron, SD Micro	229	893
Scottsburg, IN Micro	227	894
Wahpeton, ND-MN Micro	226	895
Bennettsville, SC Micro	221	896
Hereford, TX Micro	218	897
Grants, NM Micro	210	898
Havre, MT Micro	209	899
Union, SC Micro	194	900
Kodiak, AK Micro	192	901
Brownsville, TN Micro	190	902
Yazoo City, MS Micro	187	903
Dumas, TX Micro	185	904
Marshall, MO Micro	177	905
Portales, NM Micro	176	906
West Helena, AR Micro	175	907
Wauchula, FL Micro	173	908
Beeville, TX Micro	170	909
Lamesa, TX Micro	170	910
Levelland, TX Micro	148	911
Vernon, TX Micro	145	912
Atchison, KS Micro	137	913
Los Alamos, NM Micro	137	914
Sweetwater, TX Micro	132	915
Snyder, TX Micro	129	916
Pierre Part, LA Micro	118	917
Raymondville, TX Micro	117	918
Vermillion, SD Micro	113	919
Andrews, TX Micro	103	920
Tallulah, LA Micro	98	921
Tuskegee, AL Micro	86	922

CBSA Total	3,483,342	
United States Total	3,682,710	
CBSA (% of U.S. Total)	94.59	

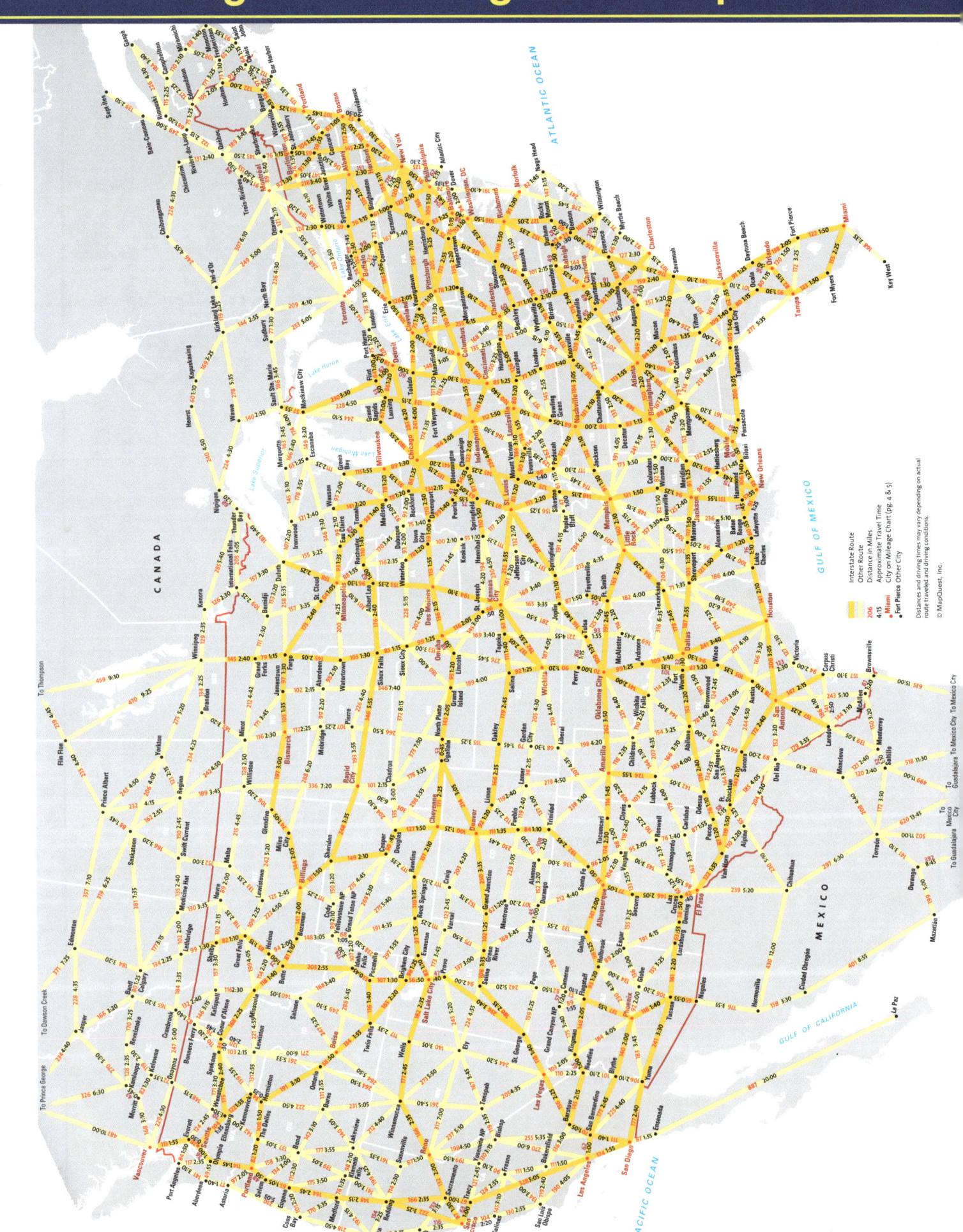